The Green Thumb
Garden Handbook

Completely Revised and Expanded

Books by George (Doc) and Katy Abraham

The Green Thumb Book of Fruits and Vegetables

The Green Thumb Book of Greenhouses

The Green Thumb Book of Indoor Gardening

The Green Thumb Garden Handbook

Green Thumb Tricks for the Classroom

Green Thumb Wisdom

Growing Plants from Seed

Houseplant R_x

Organic Gardening Under Glass

Our Land and Its Care

Raise Vegetables, Fruits, and Herbs Without a Garden

GEORGE (DOC) AND KATY ABRAHAM

The Green Thumb
Garden Handbook

**Completely Revised
and Expanded**

THE LYONS PRESS

Author's Note:

The pesticide picture changes almost daily. Since this book went to press, some chemicals once considered relatively safe have been reevaluated. Any inadvertent mention of Diazinon, Kelthane, or Benlate (Benomyl) should be disregarded. See alternatives in Chapters 14 and 17. We've tried to maintain a balance on pesticides and urge you to consider IPM (integrated pest managment).

For more alternatives to chemical controls, write to your State College of Agriculture, or contact us at: P.O. Box 579, Naples, NY 14512.

Copyright © 1992, 1999 by George (Doc) and Katy Abraham

Printed in the United States of America

10 9 8 7 6 5 4 3 2 1

The Library of Congress has cataloged the original paperback edition of this book as follows:

Abraham, George, 1915–
        The green thumb garden handbook / George (Doc) and
    Katy Abraham. — Completely rev. and expanded.
        p.   cm.
        Originally published: Completely rev. and expanded.
    Englewood Cliffs, N.J.: Prentice-Hall, c1977.
        Includes bibliographical references and index.
        1. Gardening.   I. Abraham, Katy.   II. Title.
        [SB453.A25 1992]
        635—dc20   92-2552
                                                            CIP

ISBN 1-55821-905-6

Contents

•

Introduction

•

Our first *Green Thumb Garden Handbook* was written to enable gardeners to find helpful information on most garden topics without thumbing through countless volumes. The book went through 14 printings. Gardening had just become America's number one hobby. Today it is even more popular, among all age groups. Our own children have grown and married, and they, their spouses, and our grandchildren are now finding their own gardening pleasure in and around their homes.

In the past twelve years new and better varieties of plants have been developed. The terrarium craze has crested and leveled off, and hanging baskets have been even more popular than in the days of Nebuchadnezzar's hanging gardens of Babylon. Gardening in small spaces has increased with the number of urban and suburban gardeners. The green plant boom is evidence of mankind's hunger for green living things in his environment. Most importantly, there is an increased awareness that man must live in harmony with nature as well as with his fellow man if life as we know it is to survive on this planet. This awareness brought on the ban of hard pesticides, and encouraged research for and development of natural controls of harmful insects and breeding of resistant varieties to thwart both insects and diseases.

All of these are reasons for this new, completely revised and expanded handbook for plant lovers. No one book can answer all questions in the various fields of horticulture; but in an effort to make this book the best of its kind, we sifted through twelve years of our newspaper and magazine articles, and took into account the hundreds of thousands of letters received through the *Green Thumb* columns and our weekly radio and television programs. We took advantage of valuable information compiled by researchers at state colleges and the USDA, as well as plantsmen at seed houses and nurseries. We owe special thanks to dozens of these individuals and institutions who have been so helpful.

America has some of the best seedsmen in the world and without their help this book would not be possible. They spend millions of dollars in research and catalogs which are a valuable storehouse of information. Although space does not permit us to mention them all, we do appreciate all of the help given us with the book and with our own research.

A special debt of gratitude is due Bob and Mary Jane Mann for endless hours which they spent clipping and indexing material from our columns. Without their help we never could have met the publication dateline. We are grateful to Betty Noon and Ina Jaeger for special assistance in proofreading when fresh eyes were needed. Charles Wilson of Joseph Harris Seed Co., Roger Way of the New York State Experiment

Station, and Robert Schery of the Lawn Institute have given many helpful suggestions for the vegetable, fruit, and lawn sections respectively. Bill Dress of the Bailey Hortorium at Cornell University has been ever ready to help us with the most up-to-date scientific names for plants. No credits would be complete without mention of editor Carol Cartaino's meticulous scrutiny.

George (Doc) and Katy Abraham
Naples, New York 14512

CHAPTER I

How to Grow a Lawn ...
or a Lawn Substitute

•

In the late 1800s, Senator John J. Ingalls wrote: "Next in importance to the divine profusion of water, light and air—may be reckoned the universal beneficence of grass. Grass is the forgiveness of nature—her constant benediction."

Grass planted on the good earth has a wholesome influence on our health and climate. One acre of grass near your home has the cooling effect of a 140,000-pound air conditioner (that's 70 tons!). That same grass gives off 2,400 gallons of water (48 barrels) each single summer day to be recycled in our atmosphere, keeping our earth from becoming a desert. Also grass acts as a blotter, soaking up noise, water, and smog. And grass plants are among the best dust mops on earth, catching much of the falling particles found in millions of tons of pollutants released into the atmosphere each year.

Grass Lawns Are Healthy

Next time you get disgusted with your lawn and threaten to replace it with black top or synthetic turf, better think twice: Studies show that schools using synthetic turfs are plagued with a growing number of injuries to athletes. Injuries on artificial turf are more severe than those incurred on ordinary grass. Researchers suspect the higher rate of injury on synthetic turf is because it affords better traction—which leads to harder hitting in aggressive games.

Artificial grass warms up quickly under a hot sun, sending midday air temperatures up, for instance, as high as 150 degrees in Alabama. Tests at Michigan State showed that live grass reduced September temperatures 15 degrees.

Nor is an artificial lawn cheap to maintain. In fact, natural grass maintenance costs are less than artificial turf. At Purdue University's football field, yearly resodding costs $2,600, including labor and materials. Artificial turf manufacturers claim the same area would cost from $25,000 to $30,000. Cost of maintenance (including resodding) for live grass for a year was $4,475 with artificial turf producers claiming a cost almost five times as much.

Besides, look what grass does: 1) Freshens air. 2) Filters out dust and dirt. 3) Controls erosion. 4) Reduces glare. 5) Cools your home. Of the total amount of sun heat striking the surface of a lawn, 5 percent is reflected, 5 percent is absorbed, and 50 percent is eliminated by the lawn's cooling process. 6) Grass helps deaden sound. 7) Grass is essential to song and game birds and small animals.

1

Preparing Soil for a Lawn

Grass seed is not hard to please. It will grow in almost any soil. But growing grass and having an attractive lawn are not necessarily the same thing. To grow a good lawn, meaning one with dense, healthy, turf, you need reasonably good soil. Grass will grow at its best in soil which is neither too loose nor too tight, just porous enough to absorb water readily.

In most cases you can improve the existing soil a lot cheaper than you can import costly topsoil. In fact, tests show that the cost of building up the present soil is usually only one-third that of buying topsoil. Fertilizer, good seed, and ample organic matter help a lawn to help itself. Grass started from an enriched subsoil will at the end of two or three years have enough humus from its own root growth and clippings to nurse itself along, with the help of annual feedings, for you and succeeding generations to enjoy. The only time you have to buy extra soil is when you want to raise the level of the lawn or when the existing soil is nothing but pure gumbo, too poor quality to serve as a good seed bed. (See SOILS AND FERTILIZERS, Chapter XIII, for detailed information.)

Spread 50 to 60 pounds of a balanced fertilizer evenly over each 1,000 square feet of lawn area or, if you use manure or compost, spread 2 or 3 cubic feet over each 1,000 square feet of lawn and mix it with the soil. If you prefer, you can use peat moss (about 3 bales for each 1,000 square feet of lawn).

This mixing will strengthen the sand or loosen the clay, whichever is necessary. You need make no soil analysis because you can hardly overdo this procedure. (Never add sand to clay because this will pack the clay even tighter.)

If you use peat moss, or if you already have suitable soil, be sure to add plant food or a complete fertilizer. Every soil should be fed before planting. "Complete" fertilizer or plant food means it contains all three of the chemical substances your lawn will need:

Nitrogen, which gives your lawn its rich dark-green color and promotes leaf and stem growth.

Phosphorus, which stimulates root growth and helps plants make a fast start.

Potassium, which helps plants resist diseases and encourages a luxuriant condition.

Now you have soil geared to play host to a fine, healthy turf. It's neither heavy nor sandy, nor so hard that it will crack when it dries and leave open spaces. If you have special problems, such as planting a lawn on a slope or in shady, virtually sunless areas, you will find answers later in this chapter. Otherwise, you are ready to rake the soil evenly and loosely.

In raking, don't attempt to remove every little stone. A light rolling will take care of them. Grass roots grow under them and find protection there from the sun. However, if you have purchased topsoil, it should be free of stones because you paid for soil, not stones.

You are now ready to begin seeding, but remember: it takes a well planned lawn to reach its peak the second and third years after planting. Don't expect a perfect carpet of grass the first year. After the first year, you'll still have some bad spots. These can be corrected simply by loosening the soil and scattering on some grass seed.

Selecting Grass Seed

What kind of grass seed will give you the kind of lawn you like best? By and large, a mixture of a few different types of grass seeds makes a better lawn than does seed of a single variety. All varieties have advantages and disadvantages. Some are more drought-resistant and remain green long after other varieties have dried and turned brown in summer. Others are likely to die if mowed too short and therefore should never be used by those who like a "crew-cut" lawn. Still other varieties are very susceptible to plant diseases. One variety must be planted either alone or only with members of its own family or grasses or it gets crowded out.

Read the label on the package before you buy any grass seed mixture. And don't let the names of grasses on the label confuse you.

Most grass seed mixtures are classified as having seeds of:

1. persistent, fine-textured grasses
2. coarse or temporary grasses
3. white clover

The coarse or temporary or "hay" grasses will not give the kind of lawn most people want. As the word "temporary" indicates, these seeds serve best when a lawn is wanted quickly to cover the soil for one season until proper preparations can be made for seeding a permanent lawn. These coarse and temporary grasses include tall fescue, meadow fescue, timothy, and redtop, and the ryegrasses, including Italian rye, perennial rye, domestic rye, and common rye.

Persistent, fine-textured grasses will, as their name implies, give the kind of permanent, fine-textured lawn home gardeners like to have. The main varieties are Kentucky bluegrass, red fescue (including Chewings and other varieties), colonial bentgrass, and rough bluegrass (also known as *Poa trivialis*).

The labels on the grass seed mixture package sometimes list these varieties under their particular names. For example: "Common Kentucky Bluegrass" and "Merion Kentucky Bluegrass." Or, in the case of the fescues, "Creeping Red Fescue," "Illahee Red Fescue" and "Pennlawn Red Fescue." Or, in the case of bentgrasses, "Highland Bentgrass" and "Astoria Bentgrass."

Any mixture for seeding a permanent lawn should be made up of at least 80 percent of these persistent, fine-textured grass seeds.

The most rugged of them is Kentucky bluegrass, which needs the least care and is probably the best suited for most amateur gardeners who want a good lawn without spending too much effort and money. But Kentucky bluegrass has two disadvantages: It can be permanently injured if it is clipped or mowed very short; and, like most grasses, it turns brown in dry weather, but it recovers its rich green color quickly when the dry season is over. A seed mixture containing at least 40 percent Kentucky bluegrass (plus another 40 percent of other persistent, fine-textured grasses) will usually produce a good lawn under average conditions. Lawns which are exposed to more than an average amount of sun should preferably be seeded with mixtures containing at least 55 percent Kentucky bluegrass.

The list of new bluegrass varieties increases almost daily, so you may have to rely on the judgment of the seed producers (and your local nurseryman) as to which is best for your locality. Some of the newer selections, such as Fylking and Pennstar, can be mowed as low as an inch high (regular varieties are best mowed $1^1/_2$ to 2 inches high). Let's hope the hybridizers can combine the good features of all the varieties into one good all-purpose variety. It would help us a lot—especially when someone asks us, "What's the best bluegrass?"

A little bluegrass goes a long way. Each pound contains 2 million seeds, and if applied at the rate of 3 pounds per 1,000 square feet should end up with anything from twenty to thirty seeds of bluegrass per square inch, considering there are other seeds in the mixture.

The important thing is to include Kentucky bluegrass in a mixture. Many people like a single grass on the lawn, but our experience has shown it's more sensible to blend bluegrass varieties with fine fescues to avoid serious lawn problems. Don't be impatient with seed germination. It can take up to twenty-six days for some seed to start.

If you live in the northern part of the United States and want a lawn with little care or expenditure of money, put in red fescue. Red fescue establishes more rapidly from seed than do the bluegrasses, although they do not establish rapidly by vegetative means, that is, by underground stems. It won't make a perfect green carpet, but it's a good low-maintenance grass. Red fescue requires the smallest amount of fertilizers, pesticides, and water of any lawn grass variety used in the northern United States. It has a special mechanism for conserving water. During long dry periods, the grass stops growing, thus coping with moisture stress. When it is in this "summer dormancy," it is not advisable to water it, even though the grass turns brown. In fact, irregular or improper watering could "confuse" the natural mechanism of dormancy, causing complete kill of the grass. The brown turf will recover when cooler, damper weather arrives. No mowing is necessary during the dormant stage.

For very dry soils, red fescue is the best suited variety. Rainier, creeping red fescue, Pennlawn, Illahee fescue, and Chewings fescue are popular because they are more drought-resistant as well as shade-tolerant than most other varieties and can withstand considerable neglect. They usually take longer to attain their healthy green in early spring, but retain their color longer into the summer than other grasses, which by that time have usually become brown.

A moderate amount of fescue is desirable in a mixture for a home lawn. Its rather quick sprouting makes it useful as a nurse grass. Disadvantages of the fescues are that they die easily if clipped or mowed very short or if they are overwatered. If they are used alone, it takes more power to mow them than it does most other varieties. This toughness has earned the fescues the nickname "wire grasses." Fescues do better when used with bluegrass in the mixture.

Those who want to build a low-maintenance lawn using red fescues are advised to follow these steps.

1. Choose a seed mixture containing 70 percent red fescues, either a creeping type or Chewings type—preferably both. The remainder should consist of 20 percent perennial rye grass and 10 percent common Kentucky bluegrasses. The recom-

mended amount of the mixture for an area of 1,000 square feet (20 feet × 50 feet) is 5 pounds.

2. If soil test indicates the pH level is above 5.0, no lime is needed; if below this, spread 50 pounds of lime per 1,000 square feet. Then work in 10 pounds of 10-10-10 fertilizer per 1,000 square feet.

3. The seeded area should be covered with a layer of loose straw (1 bale per 1,000 square feet). If possible, roll lightly to firm the straw and seed against the soil. Water for fifteen minutes every day (if there is no rain) for three weeks. After three weeks, remove the straw and put it in a compost pile.

Red fescues do not like wet spots, so careful soil preparation is important.

Bentgrasses are not popular with experts, even though this variety may produce good lawns which withstand close clipping exceptionally well. Some colonial bentgrass in the mixture with Kentucky bluegrass thickens the turf in midsummer when the bluegrass is semi-dormant. This thickening, aside from its improved appearance of the lawn, also helps keep weeds out. But bentgrasses are very susceptible to diseases, require intensive care, more feeding, regular watering and mowing to look well.

Redtop and annual ryegrasses are of the temporary varieties. Any mixture containing more than 10 percent of them is likely to produce an inferior lawn. Their use is practical, however, on slopes. The fast sprouting of the seed helps prevent the washing away of the soil by rains as well as the washing away of the seeds of slower-growing grasses in the mixture. (See *Lawns on Slopes* section later in this chapter.)

HOW GOOD IS RYEGRASS? Something new is going on in the grass seed world. Perennial ryegrasses are on the market which resemble bluegrass. These ryegrasses are easy to start and do look much of the time about the same as would a bluegrass turf. However, none of the ryegrasses mow quite as cleanly as does bluegrass (the leaf tips tend to fray, and get "gray hair"—like you see when a turf is mowed with dull blades). There is some difference in appearance seasonally, too; many ryegrasses do not hold up in midwinter and early spring as well as does bluegrass. However, Norlea is a Canadian selection showing excellent winter hardiness.

There's some question as to how hardy ryegrasses are in cold regions or in areas with little snow cover and lots of drying wind. Perennial ryegrasses blend much better with bluegrass-fescue turf than does annual rye. Annual ryegrass does not completely die out in winter, and during the second year some of the plants turn into coarse clumps almost as unsightly as tall fescue. Perennial ryegrass (a different species from the annual) does not behave this way and the modern, selected varieties remain fine-textured and much of the time indistinguishable from bluegrass in the sod. Annual ryegrass is more aggressive and prevents bluegrass from becoming established when used in a mixture. There is no objection to 10 to 20 percent (even up to 50 percent) perennial ryegrass in a seeding mixture to provide the quick cover that bluegrass will not.

Perennial ryegrasses do tend to grow a bit faster than bluegrasses and fine fescues, and make for a little more frequent mowing, which might be objectionable.

Manhattan ryegrass is a distinctive variety, hardy, low-growing, and dark green. Others are on the market, and one company claims that its perennial ryegrass lawns on sandy soils do better and outlast ones that are exclusively bluegrass-fescue.

A pound of the seed of the fine-textured grasses costs about three times as much as a pound of seed of coarse grasses, but this doesn't mean it is more expensive to plant a lawn with the fine-textured seeds. Seeds of fine-textured grasses are much smaller and lighter so that a pound of them contains about eight times as many seeds as a pound of the coarse seeds.

For example, a pound of Kentucky bluegrass contains about 2 million seeds, but a pound of rye grass only about 250,000. A pound of coarse seeds makes a cheaper and bigger package, but contains fewer seeds than a pound of fine textured seeds.

Some grass seed mixtures contain white clover seed, which many gardeners consider to be a weed. It is a broad-leaved plant which draws nitrogen from the air and nourishes the soil with it, thus supplying that important substance to the grass. Clover is deep-rooted and drought-resistant, adding a green touch to the lawn in summer when the grass has turned brown. Mowing clover will not harm it. Its disadvantages are that it becomes slippery when the lawn is wet and it stains badly. Also bees may be attracted to it. To many folks it is objectionable because it has white flower heads and grows in patches.

Some seed mixtures include the intermediate or giant forage varieties of clover rather than the dwarf type (labeled "Wild White Clover" or "Kentish Wild White Clover") preferable for lawns.

Warm-Season Grasses

Zoysias: The overly publicized zoysias (Zoysia japonica and Z. matrella) form a good sod in midsummer, being tolerant of summer traffic, low fertility, heat, and drought. They also require less mowing. Disadvantages of zoysias are that they turn an unsightly brown from autumn until midspring, are not resistant to traffic and weed invasion when dormant, and they must for all practical purposes be started from plugs or sprigs of sod. Zoysia has survived all the way up to Minnesota, but not all zoysias are consistently hardy in northern winters. The Meyer strain of zoysia is pretty tough to kill, even by cold winters.

In the heat of summer, the zoysia is great, but its growing season in the north is just too short. It starts to go off color no later than October, and it won't begin to green up until sometime in May. Some people get around this problem by spraying the browned grass with a dye and it works fairly well. Kentucky bluegrass, if you can pull it through the summer in good shape, is usually green until after Christmas, and picks up again in March.

Zoysia spreads by runners that grow both above and below ground. These runners can dip a foot or so down in good soil to get under obstructions, and spring up on the other side. Because of this, it is difficult to get rid of once it is established so don't plant it unless you want to tolerate its disadvantages.

U-3 Bemuda grass, a southern grass, has the same advantages and disadvantages of zoysia, with lack of winter hardiness a special hazard.

Korean Lespedeza is a fine-leaved legume used as a temporary cover. Used with bluegrass and others as a "nurse" crop, it shades the seedlings of a mixture until they can become established. It will not stand frost.

Bahia is a southern grass of coarse appearance. It roots deeply and takes foot traffic well. Forms tough seedheads which are hard to mow.

Centipede has a fine texture but is coarser than Bermuda and most zoysias. It has trailing stolons and is good for poor soils, requiring minimum maintenance where it grows. Not hardy.

Buffalo grass produces a grayish-green turf, shows up as straw color in drought or cold weather. It is used where rainfall is insufficient, especially in arid areas such as western Texas.

Carpet grass produces a coarse-leaved, loose sod, and is used chiefly on acid, sandy, boggy soils where better species have a tough time. Not hardy.

SEEDING RATES FOR LAWNGRASS

Seed Mixtures Predominantly:	Lbs. per 1,000 Square Feet	Millions of Seeds per Lb.
I. "Northerners," normally planted autumn or early spring:		
Kentucky Bluegrass	2-4	2
Fescues	5-7	$1/3$
Bentgrass	1-2	7
Poa trivialis ("Rough Bluegrass")	2-3	$2 1/2$
New Rye Grass (Perennial)	2-3	$1/4$
Redtop	1-2	5
Clover (5-10% in mixtures)	$1/10$-1	$3/4$
II. "Southerners," normally planted spring or summer:		
Bermuda (hulls removed 50% lighter rate than unhulled)	1-4	2
Bahia	2-5	$1/5$
Carpet	2-4	$1 1/4$
Centipede	$1/4$-1	$1/2$
Zoysia (mostly vegetative, untreated seed slow)	1-2	5
Buffalo ("burs")	1-2	$1/15$
Lespedeza, Korean	1-3	$1/4$

*Accurate, uniform distribution is seldom possible at rates less than 2 lbs. per 1,000 sq. ft. unless the seed is "extended" or mixed with cornmeal, sand, sifted soil, fertilizer or vermiculite. (Courtesy American Potash Institute and The Lawn Institute)

When to Sow Grass Seed:

The soil is loose and mellow, the seed bed is well prepared. The seed has been carefully chosen. The next step is to scatter the seed evenly. But what time of year should this be done for best results?

Fall is by far the best time to seed a lawn, though probably four of every five home gardeners do the job in spring. In most climates the ideal time for sowing seed and for the early growth of the seedling grass is between the last part of August and the early part of October. This is the time nature itself selects for seeding. Wild grasses bloom in summer, but nature delays dropping of seeds and their after-ripening until August or September. At that time, the seed falls on soil which is still warm, but the season of drought is over, the hot days are getting shorter and the cool nights are getting longer. Dews are heavier. Soil moisture conditions are more favorable. Unlike spring thundershowers, fall rains tend to be gentle, soaking into the soil for the benefit of the grass. Fall grass seedlings will be vigorous yearlings the following spring, better able to withstand the heat and weeds which come in summer.

There are yet other advantages to fall seeding:

The great hordes of weeds and insects which flourish during hot weather die with the first frost, making available more space, nutrients, sunlight, and freedom for the grass. There is less exposure to plant diseases in fall. And there is economy in fall seeding too. Fewer seeds will produce equal or even better turf. Tests have shown that four pounds of seed scattered evenly over 1,000 square feet of soil in fall will produce grass of equal or better quality than an abnormally high seeding rate of six to eight pounds of the same seed mixture sown in the spring!

If seeding can't be done earlier, it is probably better to do it even as late as December than to wait until spring because December seedlings will still have more months of good growing weather before summer than spring seedlings.

Finally, fall is preferred by gardeners for grass seeding because garden chores are less demanding than in spring, thus giving more time for devotion to lawn work.

But if you can't do the job sooner, it can be done in spring, too. Owners of new homes, for example, may not want to leave the soil bare from spring to fall. The first rule for spring sowing is: The earlier, the better. The earlier the seed is in the soil, the greater the opportunity for the grass to grow strong enough to withstand summer heat.

FROST SEEDING Some gardeners wait until the "last snow" and scatter seed on it. If there is not a mat of old vegetation which will keep the seed from sinking all the way to the soil as it melts, the snow might have some value. Snow and cold won't harm the life of the seed, and chances are as the snow, ice, or slush melts it will settle the seed gently onto soil that is probably pitted by frost, which makes tiny niches for the seed to start sprouting. There may even be some "preconditioning" of the seed for germination through absorption of moisture, although sprouting will not start until the temperature warms up.

You can wait to sow until after the snow has melted, but the lawn may be mushy by then. Seldom can the soil be cultivated or even scratched so early as seed can be planted by frost action.

Even if you have no snow, you can go ahead and sow. Tiny frost cracks will catch some seed. Will seed on top of snow make good bird feed? Yes, birds will eat some of it and you may have to add more in spots. Frankly, we are not crazy about "Frost Seeding."

If at all possible, seeding should be done before May 15 or after August 15. If you must do it during the three intervening months, it will be to your advantage to protect the seed by covering the soil with straw or some other material. This will protect the seed from the summer sun as well as conserve moisture in the soil from evaporation. Instructions on how to cover lawns (a technique known as "mulching") are in the section *Lawns on Slopes* later in this chapter. Or, you might prefer to plant a temporary lawn with any of the fast-growing temporary coarse grasses to be replaced during the more favorable planting season.

SOWING THE SEED A cyclone seeder (found in any farm store) is still the best way to apply grass seed evenly. You fill it with grass seed, then walk into the wind, slowly turning the crank which in turn paddles the seed out uniformly. Some lawn makers walk back and forth, until all of the area is covered. Others cut the specified amount of seed in half. Then they seed the entire area, walking north and south. When finished, they proceed to sow the entire area again (with the other half of the seed) walking cross-wise, or east and west.

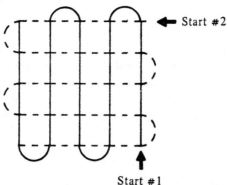

Start #2

Start #1

The most efficient way to get good coverage with grass seed is to follow this pattern.

THE SEED GOES INTO THE SOIL Saying the seed goes "into" the soil means exactly that; grass seed usually needs to be pushed down a bit into the soil, unless the surface is loose and lumpy.

If this is done, the seed will not be blown away by winds, the roots can obtain a stronger hold on the soil faster, and the warm earth enveloping the seed will hasten its germination.

To push the seed firmly into the soil you can use a light roller or you can pull the backside of a broom-type rake over the seeded soil. If you use a roller of the water-ballast type, don't fill it to more than about one-fourth. More about this is in the section *Rolling Your Lawn*.

A common error in seeding is to use far more seed than is necessary. This is not only wasteful—often it is harmful. Some gardeners throw twice or three times as much seed as is necessary for a good lawn. The grass then comes up too thick and the result is about the same as if you were crowding one hundred persons into a house built for ten. Life would be uncomfortable and unhealthy for all, and possibly none would thrive for long.

Some gardeners say the reason they oversow is to make up for poor soil. But poor soil cannot support large numbers of plants as well as it can a few. If the soil is poor it can be helped by building it up as explained earlier in this chapter, not by extra-heavy seeding. For the proper quantity of seed, consult the chart "Seeding Rates for Lawngrass" earlier in this chapter, or check the label on your seed package.

Lawn seed normally germinates in seven days to two weeks or longer. But germination and the rate of growth of your lawn may be quite uneven. That's nothing to worry about. Seeds are bound to rest in the soil at different depths and some varieties in the seed mixture grow faster than the rest. Cheap mixtures start out fast, but peter out within a year or two. After grass has come up, avoid walking on it until after it has been mowed 3 or 4 times.

THICKEN UP A THIN LAWN If your lawn has thin, bald spots, does it pay to scatter grass seed to "thicken" your lawn? A lot of money and time is wasted by merely scattering grass seed over a hard crust of earth or even over existing grass. Along the side of a road many grass and weed seeds fall on hard, unbroken ground and still grow. Some of the grass seed that falls on hard, "skinny lawns" will also grow, but here's what you can do to help increase your "take" when seeding into a thin lawn: 1) Take an iron-tooth rake, or one of the many hand tools designed especially to scratch, slice, or scarify the soil surface. 2) Rake up as much of the loose "thatch" (built up vegetative debris—leaves, stems, clippings) as you can. 3) Discard the thatch (put it on compost pile), and then sow the seed so it falls on bare ground. 4) Scatter a light coating of fine peat moss over the seed. 5) Water daily til young plants are well established.

ROLLING YOUR LAWN It has been said with much truth that a roller is the most misunderstood, overused lawn tool. There are only four important uses for a roller:

1) To press grass seed into the soil. Use a light roller for this purpose, one weighing 75 to 100 pounds. Go over the newly seeded soil just once, because if you push the seed too deep it may never come up. And if you press the soil too firmly, it will not remain porous enough for best growth. 2) To press the young grass seedlings back into the soil in early spring following a fall seeding, after they have been heaved up by the action of winter frosts. Use a light roller for this. 3) To press small stones back into the soil so that they will not be hit by the lawn mower blades. 4) If the soil has become unusually loose, light rolling will make it firm again and also push back the roots of possibly loosened grass. But don't overdo it. Grass thrives best in porous soil.

Wrong use or overuse of a roller can do much damage. An overly heavy roller will compact the soil, especially if the soil is wet. Compacted soils prevent penetration of water, air, and nutrients. Grass roots need all of these. Lack of them will cause roots to grow thin and shallow. Wet soil will stick to the roller. Delay rolling until the soil is dry and, of course, if you plan to roll newly seeded soil, don't water it until the rolling is done.

Finally, a roller is not the proper tool to smooth uneven lawns. It can't be expected to do that job even if it weighs 40 tons. To straighten bumps and depressed areas in your lawn, spread topsoil atop existing lawn in depressed areas, and smooth the surface. Or, you can lift the present sod off with a spade, fill in the depressed areas with soil, then replace the sod. If the bumps are not serious enough to interfere with mowing, we suggest you leave it alone.

Weeds frequently take over where grass growth has been impeded by the use of a very heavy roller.

AERATING LAWNS If your soil is a heavy clay type, and if you've got time on your hands, you may want to rent an aerator to run over the grass. This machine punches holes into the soil, allowing air and water to enter. Few home owners take the trouble to aerate their lawns. It's good for golf course maintenance but for the home gardener it's a chore that can be eliminated.

SHOULD YOU SEED OR SOD? We're often asked this question. If you have to haul in expensive topsoil, it's just as cheap to sod a lawn, and if you want an instant lawn, sod is the answer. Whether you seed or sod, make sure you select good grass varieties. Sod about 3/4 inch thick is fine. Thicker sod usually doesn't knit to the soil bed as quickly. Lay the sod immediately upon its arrival. To let it lie around and dry out is an invitation for trouble. A common mistake is to lay sod on a dry, rock-hard base. The soil bed should be equally well prepared for either sod or seed planting. It should be worked up loosely just as any seedbed so that roots will penetrate the soil. It can be fertilized before laying sod, or the sodded area can be fed a liquid fertilizer after the sod is placed. If you fertilize the sod with dry fertilizer, be sure to water it immediately so it won't burn the grass. Be sure to "break the joints" or lay the strips in a staggered fashion, close together, as floor tile is laid. Any spaces caused by irregular cutting should be filled with soil. Sod should be rolled lightly or tamped to firm it in place; then it should be watered thoroughly. If sod is placed on a moist soil bed you get knitting within a few days. The old roots of transplanted sod cease to function, but new rootlets will penetrate the soil bed. After sod has been laid, you'll want to water once or twice a week (watering hastens knitting).

When grass is 3 inches high, set your mower to that height and mow. If you set blades lower, the mower may suck up the sod and get caught. After sod has "knitted" into the soil, you can set blades to mow a little closer, perhaps 2 to 2 1/2 inches.

Watering

Few gardening topics are as controversial as how to water a lawn. And all the prevailing opinions on the subject "hold a lot of water"—even the extreme school of thought which says that you can have a healthy lawn without watering it at all.

The major opinions about watering a lawn fall into three general approaches:

1. Don't.
2. Do it lightly, but often.
3. Do it rarely, but plentifully each time.

The one thing on which there is general agreement is that a newly planted lawn should be watered generously and often from the time of seeding through the sprouting and growing of the new grass. Frequent watering of newly seeded grass will encourage fast growth. The faster and the more densely the grass grows, the less opportunity will there be for weeds to get started.

Watering the soil generously once a week after the seedlings are up will encourage them to grow deep roots which, in turn, will enable them to better withstand later droughts. Deep roots also help prevent heaving of the soil by winter freezes and thaws.

But now let us turn to these three differing opinions about watering established lawns:

THE "DON'T" THEORY Those who say not to water your lawn at all point out quite accurately that most "perennial" (persistent, fine-textured) grasses normally enter a semi-dormant state during the hot summer season. You need not worry if these grasses turn brown and at times seem to be dead during prolonged dry periods. They bounce back from their straw-like appearance to rich greenness after the first good rain. What's more, tests have shown that grass which has been allowed to remain dormant in summer will be more vigorous in autumn than grass which has been kept green by watering during the summer. And unwatered lawns frequently have fewer weeds than watered lawns.

Choice of the "don't" theory becomes easy to make if your community enforces a ban on lawn sprinkling, if you are forced to declare your own ban because of the expense of sprinkling, if your own spring or well water supply is running low, or if you lack the time for lawn chores. If any of these fit your situation, you're likely to be a "don't" exponent by necessity and convenience.

But many a gardener wonders, with obvious justification, why, after spending the effort to beautify his home with a lawn, he should allow it to turn brown at the one time of the year when he can appreciate it most, which may lead him to examine with care the two theories which follow.

THE "LIGHTLY-AND-OFTEN" THEORY Watering lightly and often can keep your lawn cool, lush, and sparkling with greenness even at the height of a severe drought. Golf-course keepers prove that the theory works. But, remember, they water their turf with unfailing regularity, usually daily, and never allow the soil to dry. That's the crux of the "lightly-and-often" theory. It works well as long as you keep the soil uniformly moist all the time (easier said than done). Built-in sprinklers with automatic timers are the ideal solution, but the average home lawn grower isn't likely to install such complicated apparatus.

Once the soil has been allowed to dry to a depth of much more than an inch, the "lightly-and-often" theory runs into serious trouble. A hot sun and brisk wind dry soil quickly. Then, watering merely the surface, when the soil has been allowed to dry to a considerable depth, will only "tease" the grass. It will be encouraged to develop shallow roots which weaken it and make it less resistant to drought. Besides, this kind of "surface watering" is more encouraging to weeds than grass. That's why many turn to the less burdensome theory which follows.

THE "RARELY-AND-PLENTIFULLY" THEORY Because surface watering of a very dry soil encourages shallow grass roots and weeds, many gardeners make it their rule to water deeply or not at all. Once the soil has been allowed to dry to a depth of 2 or 3 inches, a lot of water is needed to bring the moisture level up again. Average soil under drought conditions loses about 50 gallons of water daily for each 1,000 square feet, or 350 gallons a week. Under average conditions, about three hours of steady sprinkling are required once a week to replace that amount. Once that has been accomplished, no watering will be needed according to this theory for about a week. Then, the complete job needs to be done again. If you want to measure how many inches of water your sprinkling is depositing, place several tin cans on your lawn under the arc of the sprinklers, then after noting the amount of water empty it on the spot where the cans were sitting.

One way to cut down on watering time is to use a larger hose. With 50 pounds of pressure, a 50 foot hose of $1/2$-inch diameter takes about two hours to put $1/2$ inch of water on 1,500 square feet of lawn. The same job can be done in half the time with a $5/8$-inch hose or in one third the time, with a $3/4$-inch hose.

How to Mow a Lawn

Delilah sheared off Samson's locks, the Bible tells us, and he lost his strength. The opposite is likely to be true for grass. Clipping, if done the right way, will strengthen and help make your lawn handsome, healthy and, if such is possible for a lawn, happy. The key phrase is "the right way." Doing it wrong can damage your lawn.

MOW HIGH AND OFTEN Remember these four words? They're the best answer to most lawn mowing. Mowing "high" means never cut your grass shorter than an inch (except in late fall, as explained below, when $3/4$ to 1 inch is ideal).

In hot weather, especially when droughts are possible, grass should never be cut shorter than $1 1/2$ to $2 1/2$ inches. "Scalping" or shaving your lawn closer than that invites troubles. Many fine lawns have been ruined by cutting so close that the soil showed. Such close mowing exposes the bottoms of the plants to the hot sun, weakens the roots, and encourages the growth of crabgrass. Moreover, during the warm season, short grass allows the sun and wind to dry the soil more quickly, and the sun may heat the soil so much as to possibly injure the grass roots.

In contrast, high, thick grass protects soil from the sun and wind and discourages the growth of weeds. But don't carry this idea too far. There is no advantage in allowing grass to reach a height of much more than 3 inches, if that much. Grass taller than that may be injured by "shock" from the sudden loss of leaf surface if you shorten it drastically from that height in a single cutting. Tall grass is easily matted, causing it to be more susceptible to diseases. That's why you should mow often, cutting a little each time before the grass grows too tall.

A closely clipped lawn needs more water than one cut higher. In spite of the greater leaf surface, the high-cut lawn needs less water because it has a larger and deeper root system and can thus draw upon a greater reserve of moisture in the soil. Shading leaf blades help restrict soil exposure and evaporation. If you've been cutting your lawn at less than 2 inches, improve drought tolerance of your lawn by raising the height of cut to 2 inches. A high-cut lawn will be generally healthier.

If yours is a newly planted lawn, begin mowing as soon as the grass has grown to about 2 inches. Keep it well mowed because this will encourage "stooling," or filling in at the base.

An average lawn needs about 20 to 23 cuttings each year and each of these cuttings should ideally remove 1 to 2 inches of grass leaves. Mowing with such regularity will also result in cutting away the seed heads of weeds, and thereby keep them from multiplying. An often-used lawn mower is the strongest weapon against weeds at a lawn grower's command.

In fall, once the hot days of drought are past, it becomes advisable to cut your grass progressively shorter until it stops its annual growth and becomes dormant in late autumn. At that time, grass preferably should measure about 1 inch. Tests have shown that grass at that length survives winter with far less susceptibility to diseases, winter killing, and smothering than grass which enters and passes the winter season at 3 inches or taller. Tall grass is likely to become matted from being pressed down either by its own weight or by the pressure of rain or snow. And matting leaves grass susceptible to diseases and other harm.

A WORD ABOUT MOWERS: The kind of mower you use—reel or the newer rotary type—is a matter of personal preference. The important thing for the sake of your lawn is that the machine is in good condition. Follow the manufacturer's instructions carefully as to oiling and other care. With most mowers, oil should be added every five operating hours and replaced every 25 hours. Crankcase oil should be changed every year at the start of the mowing season in early spring.

Rotary mowers cut by impact, the whirling blade hitting the grass. Good reel mowers are often preferred by those who want to do an especially exacting job, but rotary mowers have an incomparable ability to cut tall and wiry weeds.

KEEP YOUR LAWN MOWER SHARP: If your lawn is nice and green but takes on a grayish, brownish, or yellowish cast after moving, then your blade is either too dull or set too close. Dull blades can bruise the tips of the grass, resulting in a yellowish or brownish appearance of the lawn. This shows up more often with rotary mowers. If you mow too close, you expose the inside portion of each clump of grass, and as a result the lawn has that burned or faded look.

When you mow, don't follow the same route every time. Mow grass in a different direction, especially if you use a reel mower. We like to mow so that the mower will throw clippings where they'll be worked over again in a subsequent pass. In other words, mow so that the clippings are thrown into the path of the next swath. This cuts them twice and they, ll disappear more readily into the soil surface.

LAWN MOWER DANGER: Many people are unaware of the dangers of mowers. Here are a few "don'ts" to keep in mind: 1) Don't mow when grass is wet, especially banks or slopes. 2) Don't mow areas where loose stones or gravel has been scattered. 3) Don't mow banks in evening or early morning as dew makes grass slippery. 4) Don't rev the motor full-blast while mowing. Grass doesn't need it. 5) If you mow on a slope, use cleats to prevent slipping. The majority of mower accidents occur on slopes. 6) Don't fuel a mower while it's hot or running, 7) Don't let mower run while you do an errand. Shut it off. 8) If riding a mower, always keep feet well away from the openings where blades are. Same goes for push mowers, which are run by motors. 9) When cleaning underneath, always unhook the spark plug wire, since it's possible to start the motor by turning the blade. 10) Never reach for anything in the path of a mower unless you have turned it off. All mowers can become dangerous machines in careless hands—and in the vicinity of careless toes.

CLIPPINGS—LEAVE 'EM WHERE THEY FALL? In the course of an average year, the home lawn grower will mow a total growth of about 36 inches of grass and all of this clipped grass contains valuable soil nutrients. These clippings contain nitrogen, phosphorus, and potassium, the same three important substances mentioned earlier as requirements for building up the soil to make it an ideal host for a lawn. If these clippings are raked and removed, the soil must eventually be "fed" or fertilized to replace the loss of these vital substances. A more practical way is simply to leave the clippings as they fall. They will decompose and turn into a perfect soil conditioner. Gradually these decayed clippings, together with decomposing root growth will in a few years convert themselves into a topsoil which is nothing less than "tailored to your own grass."

But one word of warning. If you have allowed your grass to grow to a height where clippings measure more than 4 inches, it is better to rake them and remove them from the lawn. Clippings of that length might bunch together and cover the lawn like a mat. Plant diseases germinate easily and quickly under matted clippings.

(These clippings need not be wasted. Add them to the compost pile, and the nutrients they contain will be saved for repeated use.)

Just as grass clippings are valuable food for your lawn, so are all kinds of leaves which fall from trees and shrubbery onto your lawn each fall. Like grass clippings, leaves contain soil nutrients and they can reduce the amount of fertilizer you use. It is wasteful to rake and discard leaves when they can be of such good use right on the lawn where they fall. But leaves, because of their size, are even more apt to become matted than long grass clippings. To avoid that danger,

MOW THE LEAVES Many gardeners mow the leaves right into the lawn to improve the turf. Most rotary mowers have a leaf-mulching attachment that catches and grinds the leaves for composting. You might also rent or share a compost shredder-grinder which makes quick work of leaves, tall weeds, and other materials, returning the pulverized residue to the soil where it acts as a soil conditioner.

Feeding Your Lawn

Grass is the most thankful plant around your house. It comes up year after year and chances are you don't feed it regularly, unless you're a lawn "nut." However, when you see a nice green lawn in hot summer, chances are it's well watered, and fed annually. All lawns respond to feeding because nutrients are lost from the lawn's soil and must be replaced if the grass is to thrive year after year.

Heavy showers leach nutrients from the soil. Also, various natural soil processes tie up nutrients so that grass roots cannot utilize them. If you remove grass clippings and throw them away after mowing your lawn, you are taking away the nutrients contained in these clippings. That's why we recommend leaving clippings on. Clover in a mixture hauls nitrogen from the air and places it in the soil for plants to feed on—one reason we like clover in our lawn.

Watering a lawn is not a substitute for furnishing it with food or fertilizer. Grass growing on an impoverished soil needs longer to retrieve its greenness after a drought than grass on a well fed soil. Starved soils also pose an open invitation for weeds, which can thrive on fewer nutrients than grass. Starved grass tends to grow in bunches or in "tufts" rather than forming a tight, carpet-like soil cover. This tufting opens space for invasion by weeds. And feeding makes other chores less necessary. By encouraging the grass it keeps down weeds and protects the soil. A turf encouraged by regular feeding wears better, looks better, and refreshes the air better.

A few years ago we could afford to squander fertilizer, but today the watchword is efficiency. Few lawns actually need all the plant food that experts have been recommending to get the ultimate in color and density. Most lawns can get by with only one feeding every year. Areas bearing heavy traffic can use more. If you've been feeding heavily, you can reduce your accustomed fertilization routine without serious disadvantage to your lawn.

Whatever you do, don't think heavy fertilization is a cure-all for lawn problems. Lawn grasses are quite adaptable. Ever notice how the grass grows along a roadside or bank, and no one pampers it one bit?

WHAT TO FEED? The kind of plant food you give your lawn isn't as important as the fact that you do apply it. All lawns respond favorably to plant food which contains the three chemical substances discussed earlier, nitrogen, phosphorus, and potassium. These are found in many kinds of "organic" as well as "inorganic" plant foods in varying quantities. Organic foods are those made up of once-living matter, such as rotting lawn clippings, leaf mold, or rotting manure. Inorganic foods are those produced through chemical processes in a laboratory. One such plant food is "5-10-5," which contains 5 percent nitrogen, 10 percent phosphorus, and 5 percent potassium in a 100 pound bag. "10-20-10" contains the same proportion of each of these ingredients, but is twice as concentrated and should, therefore, be used at half the rate. Or you can use a liquid plant food such as "23-19-17," applied at time of watering.

The chart below shows the correct amounts to use for various types of plant foods, powders, and liquids, or granules.

HOW TO FEED The amounts shown need not be followed exactly, but using much more than suggested can result in "burning" of the grass.

It is important that plant food be spread evenly. Otherwise, as the food affects the color of the grass, there will be light and dark streaks on the lawn. A mechanical

	Amount to Be Used Per 1, 000 Square Feet	
Plant Food	Established Lawns	New Lawns
4-6-0 (treated sewage sludge)	25 lbs.	50 lbs.
5-10-5	25-40 lbs.	40-50 lbs.
10-6-4	10-15 lbs.	20 lbs.
10-10-10 or 10-20-10	10 lbs.	20 lbs.
Liquid plant food (23-19-17)	$1/2$ lb. to 11 gals. of water	

spreader will do the job as perfectly as possible. If you apply inorganic plant food, be sure the grass is dry when applying to avoid burning. Then, immediately after the application, water the lawn to wash the plant food from the grass blades into the ground. An advantage of liquid foods is that they do not cause burning. If slight burning occurs, the grass will usually recover quickly without any treatment by you. If you have clover on your lawn, you may want to nourish that plant by spreading 35 to 50 pounds of ground limestone on each 1,000 square feet every three or four years. This lime can be mixed with the plant food. But lime should not be applied more often than suggested, especially if the soil is alkaline. (See Chapter XIII for more information on lime.)

WHEN TO FEED The ideal times for feeding your lawn are fall and early spring—or both? The chances of leaf-burning are slimmest then. Rains (and after fall, the melting snows) take the food down into the soil next to the root system. A lawn fed in fall will resist next summer's drought more ably. A lawn fed in early spring is encouraged to grow new shoots for a tighter, better turf. Fescue or perennial ryegrass lawns profit most from feeding in cool weather, southern grasses in warm seasons. After a good meal, grasses will begin growing beneath the surface as well as above. You'll notice the increase in beauty, and to your delight, the improvement in your lawn's quality.

Lawn Troubles

SHADY LAWNS The sun, which causes many lawns to become dry and brown, is nevertheless a friend of grass. And too much shade, meaning lack of sun exposure, is an enemy of grass. Shaded lawns need more plant food than lawns blessed with adequate exposure to the sun's rays because they are not able to manufacture food as readily.

If the shaded part of your lawn happens to be under a shallow-rooted tree, such as Norway, Sugar or Red maples, your problem may be doubled by the fact that the tree's shallow roots rob the soil of nutrients needed by the grass. Additional plant food is even more needed for grass growing in shaded areas under shallow-rooted trees.

Aside from giving added feedings, you can improve growth of grass in shaded areas by selecting those varieties of grasses best suited to shade.

Red fescue can flourish in shaded areas where other grasses fail. A seed mixture containing about 70 percent red fescue is likely to do well in shaded areas. If the soil is moist, rough-stalked meadow grass (*Poa trivialis*) will be ideal for planting in a shady spot. After you have seeded your entire lawn with your selected seed mixture you can re-seed the shady spots, where the general mixture has failed to sprout, with red fescue or meadow grass.

There's one great compensation once you have managed to produce a lawn on shady spots: because of its protected position from the sun, the grass is likely to stay green longer during droughts unless tree roots compete. But in some shady areas almost any grass will refuse to grow, and you'll probably save time and effort by constructing a flagstone or concrete terrace or a rock garden. Or you can plant one of the many grass "substitutes" discussed later in this chapter.

LAWNS ON SLOPES Mowing on steep slopes is difficult, and what may prove even more difficult is to get grass growing on steeply sloping terrain in the first place. Rains tend to wash seed and even topsoil away before growth can get underway. Sometimes it is possible to start a lawn on slopes by using a seed mixture containing some of the fast-growing temporary grasses such as redtop and the new ryegrasses. Their fast growth helps prevent the washing away of topsoil and of the seed of the slower-growing permanent grasses.

If this is unsuccessful, the best method for growing a lawn on a slope is to mulch the seed, which means to protect it from washout with a temporary cover. Mulching also helps prevent quick drying of the soil and in that way hastens germination. Materials used for mulching are straw, hay, burlap, cloth netting, and plastic mesh.

Straw is the cheapest and probably the most satisfactory mulching material. It is clean and it is easy to put on and take off. Its disadvantage is that it is easily blown off by the wind and, therefore, should be wetted down. A 2- or 3-inch layer of straw, just enough so that the ground can barely be seen, is sufficient. Oat straw is most suitable for the purpose, but hay and wheat straw can also be used. Bear in mind that too thick a mulch might smother the seedlings.

Hay as mulch is more difficult to spread, and also, it contains weed seed which may get hold in the soil. Mushroom manure has been used as a mulch, but is difficult to remove. Cotton netting (or burlap, if you can get it) tacked down to the soil with pegs has the advantage that it need not be removed because it gradually rots. This is called erosion net. It is available in garden centers and is ideal for holding seed on slopes. Plastic "polyethylene" netting which can be fastened with wooden stakes, wirestaples, spikes, or clothespins driven into the ground should be removed once the grass has reached a height of about 1 inch. These plastic nettings are called *geotextiles* and are available in garden stores.

If the slope is unusually steep so that the growing and mowing problem is severe, you might consider the same advice given for lawns so shady that grass is difficult to grow, namely, you may prefer to plant a grass substitute.

BURNED LAWNS Unsightly, brown "burned" spots on grass can result from an overdose of chemical fertilizers, insect infestation, spilled gasoline, and several other causes.

To avoid spilling of gasoline or oil on grass, don't tip your power lawn mower and don't fill your car's gasoline tank to the top, so as to avoid possible spilling as you enter or leave the driveway.

Fertilizer burns when applying chemical fertilizer can be prevented by using them in moderate amounts at each feeding. But don't use them during very hot weather or when the grass is moist from rains, dew, or watering. Instead, water the grass thoroughly after applying the fertilizer so as to wash it off the grass blades into the soil where it can do no harm. If you use a fertilizer spreader, be sure to shut the machine off when you stop it on the lawn.

Even the sun can "scald" the lawn if a rubber mat, piece of metal, or even an item of clothing is left on the lawn while the sun is at its height on a hot day. Sometimes, insects are the cause of the brown "burned" spots as is explained later in this chapter. Still another frequent cause of brownish spots on grass is female dogs voiding on the lawn. Take an iron-tooth rake and loosen up the brown spots, then take a garden hose and drench the areas to leach out the urine, then sprinkle on a little lime, sow grass seed, scatter a little peat moss on and let the seed send up new plants. Most people don't bother touching the burned spots and let rain neutralize them. Grass eventually comes up, green and healthy. Actually, the grass becomes stimulated and is greener than spots not voided upon by dogs.

Another source of brownish lawn spots is shallow soil above cesspools, septic tanks, or just above a large hidden stone. An easy remedy for these spots is frequent watering to replace the evaporated moisture.

None of these "burned" discolorations is to be confused with the overall browning of lawns during drought, or the browning effect caused by dull blades on a mower. Grass recovers from these dry periods without damage as was explained in the section *Watering Your Lawn*.

BARE SPOTS When your lawn, or any part of it, has less than one-third good, healthy grass, it's probably best to plow the area, turn the topsoil over, and start a new lawn as explained at the start of this chapter. But if there exists at least one-third good grass, the simpler and less expensive way probably is to repair the poor portions.

Bare spots in lawns can come about for several reasons: Perhaps the seed was planted too deeply or not deep enough. Or, it was washed or blown away. Young seedlings may have died from the lack of water or drowned from too much of it. Diseases may have killed the sprouts. Or, the soil is starved and needs plant food. The best time for re-seeding bare spots is early fall, but it can be done successfully at any time of the year if the lawn is kept properly watered. With proper care (as described for new lawns earlier in this chapter) new grass will grow within a month after seeding.

THATCH Thatch is a term used to describe the residues that accumulate at the base of sod, mostly ligneous sheaths, stems, and roots. This layer supposedly acts like a thatched roof—shedding water away from the roots. *Clippings do not form thatch*. Thatch is mostly wiry, ligneous stems.

De-thatching is a tough job and we doubt if that is as serious a problem as many claim. The recommendation that a lawn be de-thatched every spring and fall is ridiculous. If yours is an ordinary lawn you shouldn't worry about thatch. Tests have shown that earthworms, if allowed to live, will largely take care of the thatch problem. Researchers in some states are putting fungi on turf in hope of breaking down hard-to-digest materials in dead grass and stems. Within a few years we should have a number of alternatives to the time-consuming process of mechanical de-thatching.

HOLES IN GRASS Chances are the critter that's digging up the grass is the skunk, a highly beneficial animal. Skunks are fond of grubs, worms, insects, and almost anything that lives under sod or in the soil. In the process of searching for these they dig up the grass. Moles also make holes in search for grubs. Birds will also make tiny holes in search of the same type of food. We've also seen certain types of wasps or bees make holes in the ground.

We hesitate to recommend a chemical control for this, but if you feel you must do something add Sevin or Diazinon to the grass. This will kill the insects, and the skunks and moles will go elsewhere for their share of grubs and bugs. I think I'd merely rake the loose grass back and scatter a little grass seed in the area. In a short while you won't be able to see where the skunk scratched up the grass.

MOLES Moles do not eat roots of plants or grasses; 95 percent of their diet consists of grubs and other insect forms. Their only damage is the raised tunnels they make, looking for insects. Mice use the tunnels and mice are the villains which eat the roots. You can fight moles with traps and baits, besides using pesticides to kill off the grubs in the soil. Red pepper, moth balls, fiberglass insulation, castor beans and garlic inserted in the runways all have been used by home gardeners. If you feel you must be rid of a mole, see Chapter XVII.

MOSS Moss in your lawn is a signal the soil is undernourished and the grass is starving. That's why moss often develops under shallow-rooted trees. There, the tree's roots invade the top foot of soil, the same layer from which grass must draw its nourishment.

Our information about moss in lawns isn't much different from what it was 25 years ago. Everyone knows that mosses produce a spongy, green, felt-like mat over the soil surface. Wind and rain spread the spores of mosses, and with a little moisture growth starts. People think that mosses crowd out grass. Not so. Mosses simply fill in the spaces where there's no grass. Mosses are associated with neglected lawns.

Here are some reasons moss occurs in lawns: 1) poor drainage, but not always; 2) high soil acidity, yet you often see moss in highly alkaline soils; 3) poor soil aeration; 4) wet conditions (we've seen moss in droughty soils); 5) too much shade, yet moss often grows in full sun; 6) high humidity; and 7) low fertility. Closely mowed lawns are prone to moss attack, especially if the lawn lacks aggressive grasses. Boosting the soil fertility does a lot to discourage mosses. Loosening up the soil by raking or cultivation enhances drainage and aeration. Sometimes you can increase drainage by installing tiles. If moss is growing near trees, cutting out some tree limbs may eliminate it. Then rebuild the depleted soil with a good serving of lawn food; and re-seed the area.

Some turf specialists use iron sulfate or ferrous ammonium sulfate, at a rate of 1 to 3 ounces to a gallon of water per 1,000 square feet. Others use copper sulfate, applied in a diluted solution of 2 to 3 ounces to a gallon per 1,000 square feet of lawn. These materials kill the moss, and then you should take an iron-tooth rake and rake it out to prevent the formation of a tight layer of dead moss over the soil surface. Loosen up the soil, scatter in some grass seed, add a thin layer of peat moss and put the lawn sprinkler on.

If you want to eliminate moss growing between stones, or in cracks on your driveway, "paint" it with gasoline (dangerous), kerosene, or used motor oil, or even sprinkle with salt. These materials may sterilize the soil temporarily, so don't use where you want to sow grass seed.

A greenish scum on lawns and gardens indicates algae growth. As with mosses, spores are spread by wind and splashing raindrops. Upon drying algae can form a tough, black crust. Algae like a wet, waterlogged soil, a high soil fertility, and a high amount of sunlight. Use copper sulfate at rate of 1 to 2 ounces per 12 quarts as a drench for 1,000 square feet of area. After the algae is killed and the dead scum raked, you can put on hydrated lime at rate of 2 to 3 pounds per 1,000 square feet.

Actually, neither algae nor mosses are harmful to existing grasses, but most people consider it unsightly. We have places on the north side of our home where moss is an attractive ground cover.

FAIRY RINGS Mushrooms and toadstools sometimes grow in a circular arrangement called "fairy rings" on lawns. Rings can be anywhere from 3 to 9 inches wide and can encircle an area from a few inches to 30 feet in diameter. For centuries people believed these "fairy rings" were due to night dancing of elves, leprechauns, and fairies. These rings reappear in the same spot year after year, but each summer the diameter will be larger than it was the year before.

Many of the mushrooms are white to light beige and are large enough to be spotted from a passing car; these may last for several weeks. Others are small, brown and so short-lived that they go unnoticed. If you observe the rings for a few weeks, here's what you'd notice: 1) a dark green ring in the grass; 2) a week or two later, the fungal fruiting bodies (mushrooms) appear, and 3) the grass in the ring stops growing and turns yellow.

What causes the grass to be lush and green in the ring at first? The microorganisms secrete enzymes which release nitrogen from organic compounds. This is like feeding the grass a nitrogen fertilizer.

Shortly after the mushrooms fade and die, the grass in the ring turns yellow-green due to a shortage of nutrients. Thus, the grass in the ring has gone from feast to famine. *Control*: None that is very effective.

Toadstools are nature's way of breaking down organic matter. Some folks rake them off with a steel-tooth rake. Surface-applied fungicides will do no good with fairy rings. Even soaking a chemical as caustic as fumigants into the soil seldom assures elimination. The best advice is to live with fairy rings and look at them as one of nature's interesting works of art.

Some claim that a solution of epsom salts will control fairy rings. Others go to the trouble of digging up the soil in the ring and replacing it with fresh soil. This might sound reasonable (and like a lot of work) but will not necessarily prevent subsequent infestation. Remember, there are billions of fungi spores everywhere in the air (and soil). Our advice is to feed heavily over the affected area and the blemish will not be too noticeable.

Weeds—and How to Cope with Them

Weeds are the killjoy of many lawn growers. It's nice to have a weedless green carpet of grass, but it's not easy to obtain. People with manicured lawns are constantly bucking Mother Nature because in a community like a lawn, Nature continually tries to establish diversity in the form of weeds. Thus you must labor at maintaining what is essentially an artificial ecosystem. You can have a picture-book lawn, but be prepared to fight weeds. Weeds don't make a poor lawn. Poor lawns make weeds.

A well nourished soil thickly covered with healthy, vigorous, frequently mowed grass offers little hospitality to weed seeds. They cannot thrive in the shade of flourishing grass. What's more, growing weeds find it repugnant to have a lawn mower clip them and snip off their seed heads with annoying regularity. A lawn mower is a formidable enemy of weeds.

Weeds flourish: in soil which has become too impoverished to play host to healthy grass; in lawns which have bare spots;

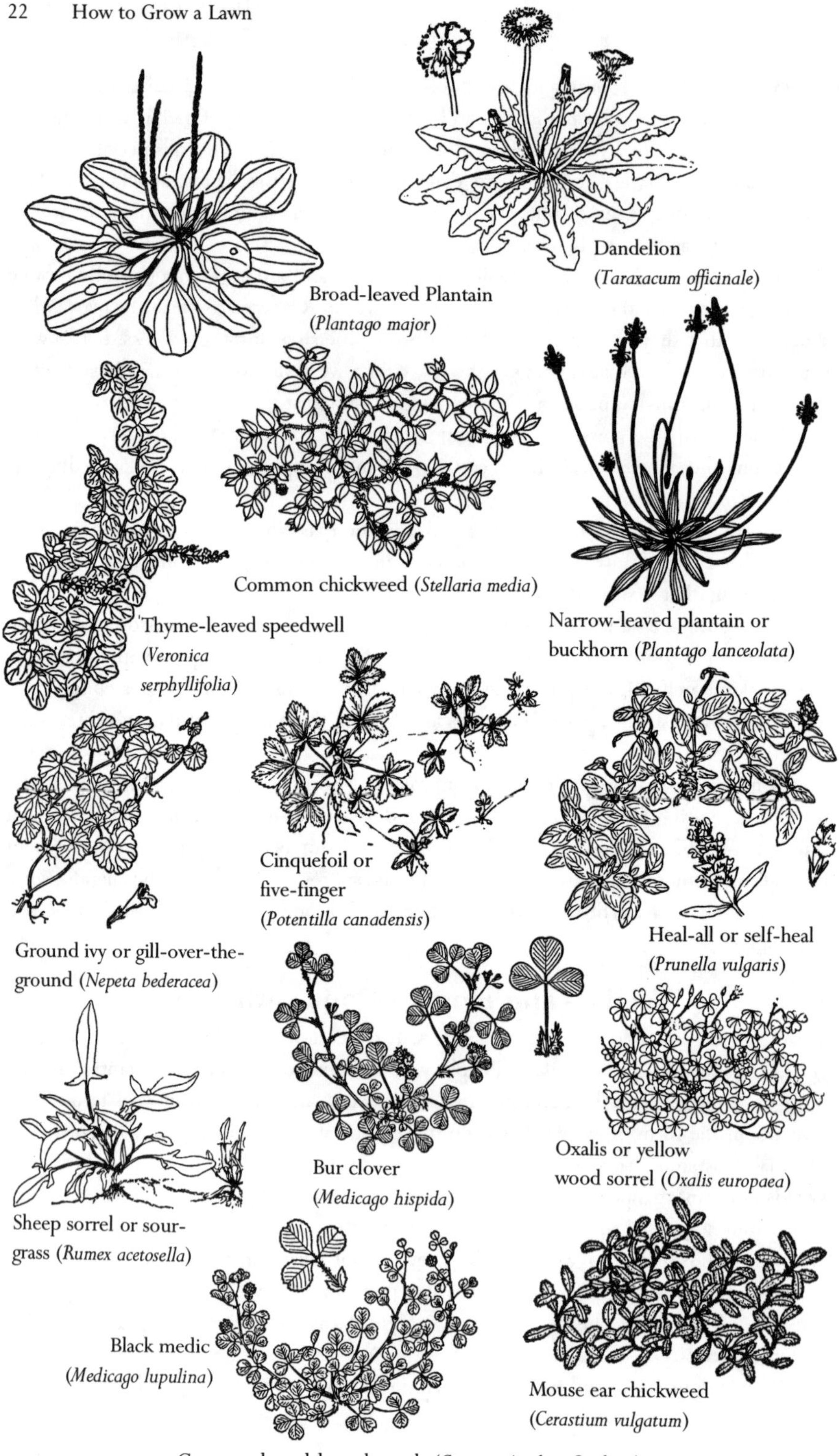

Broad-leaved Plantain
(*Plantago major*)

Dandelion
(*Taraxacum officinale*)

Common chickweed (*Stellaria media*)

Thyme-leaved speedwell
(*Veronica
serphyllifolia*)

Narrow-leaved plantain or
buckhorn (*Plantago lanceolata*)

Cinquefoil or
five-finger
(*Potentilla canadensis*)

Heal-all or self-heal
(*Prunella vulgaris*)

Ground ivy or gill-over-the-
ground (*Nepeta bederacea*)

Bur clover
(*Medicago hispida*)

Oxalis or yellow
wood sorrel (*Oxalis europaea*)

Sheep sorrel or sour-
grass (*Rumex acetosella*)

Black medic
(*Medicago lupulina*)

Mouse ear chickweed
(*Cerastium vulgatum*)

Common broad-leaved weeds (*Courtesy Amchem Products*)

when grass has become sparse enough for weed seeds to gain a foothold without competition from grass.

The strongest defense against weeds is, simply, to practice the principles of good lawn-keeping as explained in detail earlier in this chapter:

Feed the soil properly.

Mow your lawn frequently, but never cut the grass too short.

Promptly re-seed bare spots.

Preventing weeds is easier than getting rid of them once they are entrenched. Bear in mind that most of the weeds in your lawn are down below. One researcher recovered from 10,000 to 30,000 viable weed seeds in a square yard of soil, 10 inches deep. And weed seeds are hardy. For example, plantain and purslane can survive burial for 40 years. Dock can sprout after 70 years in the soil.

HAND WEEDING Except where weeds are just getting a start, or occur in isolated patches, hand weeding isn't too practical. And with a big lawn, even a hoe or weed-remover isn't anything near a match for the task. If you're hard up for exercise or like taking out your day's frustrations on a patch of plantain, hand weeding can't do any harm.

CHEMICAL WEED KILLERS Chemical weed killers can be a pain in the grass. These products are changed so fast, garden center clerks can hardly keep up with them; they are often misused. As a result many innocent plants are killed off. If you're a true lawn crank and cannot stand weeds of any kind, then resort to weed killers. Follow instructions on the label to the letter. Don't hesitate to contact your state college for the latest information on weed killers.

Remember that chemical weed killers are no substitute for sound lawn-culture methods. Rather, they should be looked upon as devices to help you clear weeds from your lawn so that you can renew the principles of lawn care. In using these weed-killers, remember these important points:

1. Chemical weed killer, like chemical fertilizer, can "burn" your grass, and therefore, it is important that you water the lawn thoroughly after each application to wash the chemicals off the grass into the soil.

2. Because of the danger of such burns, do not apply these chemicals while the grass is wet from rain, dew, or prior watering. Watering your lawn immediately after application of weed-killing chemicals is also important for another reason: these chemicals cannot work in soil without moisture. In fact, weeds on hot, dry soil are practically resistant to these chemicals.

3. If your lawn is newly planted, delay use of chemicals until after the grass has been mowed several times. Chemicals can harm very young grass.

Also keep in mind there are different types of weed killers for different types of weeds. Whichever you use, use with caution?

COPING WITH NARROW-LEAVED WEEDS Generally speaking, narrow-leaved weeds are tougher to control than broad-leafed types. What will work on one will often be ineffective on the other. To be on the safe side, take a sample of your weed to your garden-store clerk so he can be sure to provide you with the right herbicide, if you're bent on using chemical controls.

Dipping tip end of posion ivy or other weed in a jar of weedkiller sometimes works well. Plants absorb the weedkiller through the leaves, causing plant to commit suicide. This is especially useful when weeds are near trees or other plants where spraying would injure other vegetation. (*Courtesy DuPont Co.*)

When buying a chemical weed killer for narrow-leaved weeds keep in mind there are two kinds:

1. "Pre-Emergence" types, applied early in spring before the weed seed germinates. These work on the seed; but don't expect miracles, because any soil that's had crabgrass for years has tons of weed seeds that are tough to kill.
2. "Post-Emergence" weed killers. These work on the weeds themselves, so don't be alarmed if you see browned areas in your lawn after applying. Once you've killed off the plants, rake up the debris, scatter on plant food, then sow grass seed. Water daily to get the grass up so it can crowd out the crabgrass which comes in late summer.

CRABGRASS: The most serious narrow-leaved weed in lawns, crabgrass is such a regular, and unwelcome, visitor on home lawns that many a suburban dweller braces himself each spring for this annual "Battle of the Crabgrass." Part of the key to the problem is in the word "annual." Crabgrass is an annual plant, meaning it lives for only one season. The first frost each fall usually kills all crabgrass plants. But before the plants die, they spread seed which brings forth a new crop in spring.

A single crabgrass plant can produce as many as 300,000 seeds; any neighbor's crabgrass plant can supply your whole neighborhood with seed. These seeds need no more for their growth than some rain, temperatures about 65 degrees, and a bare spot on the soil.

Pulling crabgrass out of the soil by hand or with a small dandelion rake is one tedious way of getting rid of the plants as well as their seed heads. Do this before seeds ripen and scatter. Since the plants die each fall anyway, all you really need to accomplish is to keep the seed from spreading. Earlier in this chapter, you were advised to leave your mowed grass clippings on the lawn to replenish soil nourishment. Here is an exception to that rule: if your lawn has crabgrass, use a grass catcher on your mower in July and August when the crabgrass forms its seed heads. Then, throw away all clippings with the crabgrass seed heads among them (do not put on compost pile).

BROAD-LEAVED WEEDS Broad-leaved plants such as dandelion, plantain, buckhorn, chickweed, and buttercup are a lot easier to kill off than crabgrass. These and other broadleaf weeds can easily be destroyed by using 2-4-D, or prepared weed killers ready to apply, either as granules or in liquid form. 2-4-D will not touch narrow-leaved grasses such as crabgrass, quackgrass, and others. Weed killers containing 2-4-D or 2-4-5-T will kill clover in your grass, so be prepared to knock out this plant when applying the

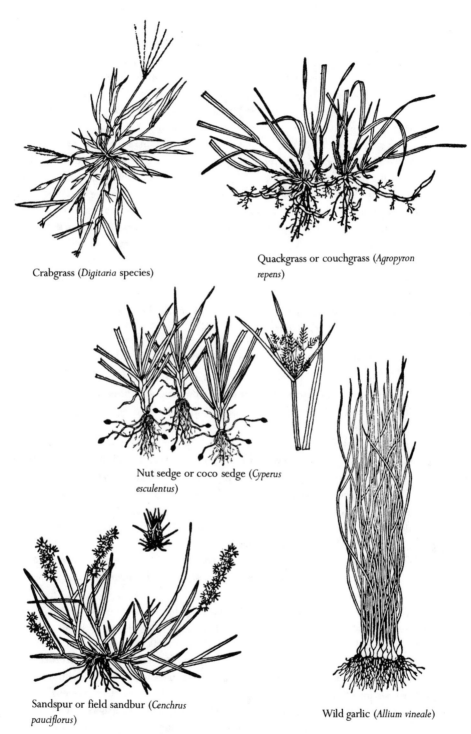

Crabgrass (*Digitaria* species)

Quackgrass or couchgrass (*Agropyron repens*)

Nut sedge or coco sedge (*Cyperus esculentus*)

Sandspur or field sandbur (*Cenchrus pauciflorus*)

Wild garlic (*Allium vineale*)

Common narrow-leaved weeds (*Courtesy Amchem Products*)

chemicals. These weed killers will also kill shrubs and nearby vegetation, and for that reason should be applied only on days when there is little wind so that it will not drift to nearby plants. Because of these disadvantages some home gardeners will not use these chemicals, or will only "spot apply" them by dipping a sponge tied to a stick into the solution and then rubbing the sponge against the weeds. If you do apply any weed killer with a sprinkling can, mark that can so that you or someone else will not mistakenly use the same can to sprinkle flowers and vegetables. *It takes only a tiny amount of weed killer residue to ruin some plants. Note:* You can mix a quart of ammonia with a pint of water and rinse out the sprinkling can or sprayer, this helps to neutralize weed-killer residue.

Two of the most common broad-leaved weeds are veronica and ground ivy.

VERONICA: Also called "Creeping Speedwell," Veronica is a creeping perennial with dime-size, scalloped leaves. It produces tiny, pale-blue flowers each April on slender, thread-like stalks. It's a stubborn, fast-spreading weed which remains unharmed by most chemicals. But it can be destroyed by applying a solution of 4 ounces of Endothal in 12 $^1/_2$ gallons of water. Most garden centers or farm supply stores handle this chemical.

GROUND IVY (NEPETA): This is a flat-growing vine known also as "Gill-Over-the-Ground" and "Creeping Charlie." It has leaves the size of a quarter and forms mats on the ground as it spreads roots wherever the stems touch the ground (it was originally imported as a ground cover). Control it with 2-4-D.

Insects—and How to Get Rid of Them

When a well fed, properly watered lawn turns brown despite the care you give it, chances are underground insects are active. A wide variety of insects living below the surface of the soil are liable to attack grass, chewing its roots or sucking juices from the leaves.

Many people ask the question: Why do some of our nicest lawns have the heaviest infestations of white grubs, especially in dry summers? Turf specialists feel that it has a lot to do with soil moisture. The nicest lawns are those that are irrigated regularly; eggs of turf-damaging beetles—be they Japanese beetles or chafers—need at least 10 to 11% soil moisture to survive.

According to entomologists, beetles can delay their egg-laying flights through early summer droughts until a heavy rain comes. Then, the beetles take to the air in search of suitable locations to lay their eggs. Within 16 days the eggs, with sufficient moisture in the soil, swell to four times their original size. That's why manicured, *filet mignon*-type lawns seem to have so many grub problems.

The term "grub" can refer to many species of insects. A white grub can be the immature or larval state of any number of beetles, including Japanese beetle, May or June bug, masked chafer, European chafer, Oriental beetle, Asiatic garden beetle, or others. They are "U"- or "C"-shaped and found in the soil just below the turf surface.

All these grubs feed on grass roots during late summer and fall. In late autumn, they tunnel deeper into the soil, especially in regions where the soil surface freezes. Then in spring they return to the grass root zone and start feeding. Telltale signs that such pests may have invaded your lawn are dug-up turfs, mole tunnels and runways, and visits by skunks who feed on these insects. You can check for the presence of insects or their

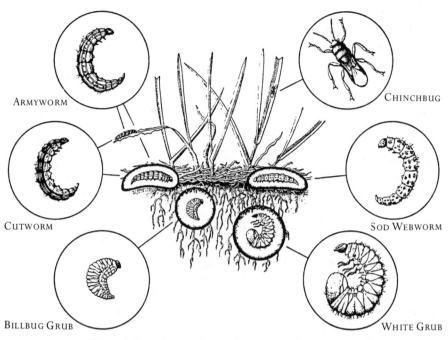

ARMYWORM

CHINCHBUG

CUTWORM

SOD WEBWORM

BILLBUG GRUB

WHITE GRUB

Common Lawn Insects (*Courtesy O. M. Scott and Sons Company*)

grubs by rolling back some loose sod in suspected areas and seeing whether pests are there. Chinch bug damage is caused by nymph stages of the insect, of which there are five, ranging in size from tiny specks to $1/8$ inch long, which suck juice from glass blades.

LAWN INSECTICIDES Many insecticides are available at your garden store, as sprays, in granular form, or as powders for "dusting" the lawn. Check labels carefully for the names of insects which each one controls, and check with your state agricultural college or garden center for latest chemical recommendations. Experience has shown sprays to be somewhat more effective. Chemical control of grubs is difficult for the home gardener for several reasons. First, the grubs live in soil that is protected by a sod layer. You don't notice grubs until you see large, brown, dead spots in the lawn. If a pesticide is applied the material must be soaked into the grass-root zone where the grubs are located.

In the past, insecticides with a long residual life, such as Chlordane, had been used to prevent grub damage. However, at this writing these can no longer be used because of their damage to the environment as a whole. Sevin is presently a recommended pesticide but it is very toxic to bees.

If you want to use chemical means to fight grubs anyway, early spring, about April, is about the best time to de-grub your lawn. At that time the grubs are still dormant and it is far easier to fight them than when they have become active. Most insecticides are poisonous and you should avoid inhaling dusts or sprays. Clean your hands and face and other exposed parts of your body after applying any insecticide. Water your lawn thoroughly after application to drench the pesticide into the grass-root zone and eliminate any surface residue.

NATURAL CONTROLS Only time will tell what damage has been done to natural predators such as birds, animals, and beneficial insects by the use of now-banned pesticides such as DDT, Chlordane, and Dieldrin. We feel that birds are the best insect control you can have around your yard. In spring we watch grackles and starlings, as well as robins and other song birds gleaning the lawn of insects. All through the summer, song birds continue "de-bugging" the property as they raise from one to four broods of fledglings with insatiable appetites.

We provide feeders for birds from late fall until early spring, as well as natural food shrubs and nesting sites (see Chapter II). We have been repaid a thousand times over. Toads, frogs, and dragonflies, as well as wasps and hornets, help to keep our lawn and garden clean of insect pests. (For more on natural controls, see Chapter XIV.)

Lawn Diseases—and How to Cure Them

Lawns are prey to no less than one hundred different diseases, although they are not likely to be serious except on bentgrass and highly managed lawns. No single chemical can cure all of them, and recommendations change rapidly, so consult your local garden center or state agricultural college for the latest recommended remedy. But prevention is preferred over treatment. Most lawns are not so readily damaged by diseases if not overstimulated by high feeding.

Fortunately, newer turfgrass varieties have been bred with at least a measure of resistance to diseases. A generation ago almost every bluegrass lawn was victim of excessive leaf spot in spring. Now almost all of the new varieties resist this disease. A mixture of several varieties should give you a reasonable disease-proof turf WITHOUT fungicidal sprayings.

One of the latest innovations in lawncare is the use of endophytes—"infected" turf grasses that survive extreme drought conditions better than other grasses and also kill insects. An endophyte can be either bacteria or fungi that live within another plant without causing disease. These endophytes are found in broadleaf plants and grasses throughout the world. How endophytes work is a mystery, but they are believed to be fungi that produce toxins which disrupt the biology of insects. Plant breeders hope to harness these endophytes ("End-o-fights") as important tools in reducing insect population.

NON-CHEMICAL LAWNS The trend toward non-chemical lawns is spreading all over America. In the past, the suburban picture perfect lawn soaked in toxic herbicides and pesticides did more than kill bugs—it made many people sick, mainly because of careless application. Environmentalists, dedicated gardeners, pest control people, and manu-facturers of alternative lawn-care products have shown that organic ideas spread faster than crabgrass. News wire services, such as Associated Press, have carried stories about non-chemical lawns and many writers tell horror stories experienced by some homeowners. Because of these problems, there has been a boom in sales for oldline organic gardening products.

A Louis Harris poll conducted for *Organic Gardening* magazine found that 60% of fruit and vegetable gardeners use no chemical pesticides or synthetic fertilizers—up 52% from 2 years before. Mike McGrath, editor of *Organic Gardening*, said chemical use in a lawn or garden has become like smoking—people are more aware of its hazards to the environment; people are taking it personally.

In one village, an organizer of what is called a Great American Dandelion Dig persuaded authorities to stop spraying 113 acres of parklands with herbicides. The villagers now go after them the old fashioned way—on their knees.

At present, about 15% of U.S. households use commercial lawn services that apply pesticides, says the Environmental Protection Agency. It estimates that another 20 to 25% of households are do-it-yourselfers, also using pesticides on their lawns.

Sheila Daar, executive director of the Biointegral Resource Center in San Francisco, says that most spraying is absolutely unnecessary and that "these sprays knock off the natural enemies of pests of all sorts." She also says there are now about 60 beneficial insects that can be purchased through the mail for lawns and gardens to control pests without the toxic dangers of pesticides. (Source sheet at end of chapter).

The Ringer Corporation, based in Minneapolis, sells an array of non-toxic products for lawns and gardens. For years retailers treated Ringer representatives as if they were peddling snake oil, Associated Press reported. Sales went nowhere. But the public mood has changed. Bob Ringer, the company's public affairs coordinator, says the company recorded $14 million in sales in one year and is marketing its products through 12,000 retailers—up from 1000 five years ago. Ringer says this is not a fad. He believes non-chemical lawns are here to stay.

CHEMICAL LAWNS Now for the other side of the coin. Although we have advocated organic methods for over 40 years, we present information for the "chemical side" with the proviso that it be used only in extreme cases. Homeowners are partially to blame for the overuse of pesticides—they want picture perfect lawns.

While lawns have many turf diseases, there's a ray of hope that many of these diseases can be checked with systemic fungicides. These are applied to the grass and are absorbed through the root system. At the present time, the composition of fungicides changes frequently. Hence it is best to consult with your state college of agriculture. The systemics give excellent control of Sclerotinia dollar spot, fusarium, smut, pink patch, snow mold, and others. Some golf course diseases are controlled marginally, if at all, by the systemic fungicides.

Here are some of the most frequently occurring lawn diseases and some recommended remedies:

SNOW MOLD: This is also known as "winter scald" or fusarium patch; it spreads while snow is covering the lawn. When the snow melts, patches of dense, cotton-like growth show the presence of the disease. It is usually more severe on lawns in low-lying areas, especially when large piles of snow have covered the grass for long periods. Most lawns will recover from snow mold without treatment when the grass dries and the ground warms; however, severe cases may kill grass. You can decrease the susceptibility of your lawn to this disease by fertilizing the grass no later than September (late fertilizing leaves lawns more susceptible), by keeping the lawn well mowed, and by keeping leaves and other ground coverings off the lawn before snow covers it. Also refrain from piling heavy accumulations of snow on the lawn. If the grass does not recover by early summer, dig up the surface with an iron-tooth rake and reseed.

"GOING OUT" DISEASE: This mostly hits bluegrass, shows itself through the yellowing and thinning of grass in April and May. Actidione, plus sunny weather, checks it.

FADING OUT DISEASE: This is also known as black mold, produces off-color, yellow-green patches on the grass. A white cloth rubbed over the grass will show sooty black smudges. Actidione or Captan applied according to manufacturer's directions will cure it.

BROWN PATCH: This is also called summer blight, occurs when night temperatures remain above 70 degrees F. and when the relative humidity reaches 100 percent and shows itself with circular rings on the lawn resembling smoke rings. The remedy is the same as for fading out disease.

DOLLAR SPOT: Brown circular patches, about the size of a silver dollar, appear on the lawn during cool, wet periods in spring, summer, or fall. Cobwebby growths appear whenever there is dew. Tiny yellow spots on the grass blades turn bleached or off-white soon after. Cadmium preparations help.

TURF BLIGHT: The disease kills grass by attacking the roots and crowns, is known as *helminthosporium and curvularia*, and causes brown discoloration of grass which is often mistakenly blamed on drought or improper nutrition. Loosen surface, remove debris. Dust with Captan and reseed.

MILDEW: White "powder" on grass means mildew, and in some cases it's so bad you can actually see it fly in the air when you touch the grass. Merion bluegrass is highly susceptible to mildew, as are Windsor, Fylking, and Pennstar. Resistant types include Nugget, Delta, Park, and Newport. In shaded areas, plant fescue (creeping red) and rough bluegrass (*Poa trivialis*). Both grasses are not only highly resistant to mildew, but much more shade-tolerant than Kentucky bluegrass. Chemical control is hardly effective unless you use frequent applications. The best solution is to use resistant varieties of bluegrass.

RUST: Red coloring on grass indicates rust. Since it takes the rust several days to infect and form reddish pustules on the grass foliage, it is most predominant on the older leaves—the very ones which would be exposed after mowing. Don't worry about it, as the disease usually disappears as the season wanes. Certain fungicides such as Actidione or Zineb will check it, but we don't think they are worth the effort.

Ground Covers ... Living Carpets for Beauty

Ordinarily, grass is the best "ground cover" you can have, but if you have a situation where grass isn't practical, you must resort to something that takes its place. Steep slopes that can't be mowed, spots too shady for grass, or places where tree roots are too competitive require a ground cover of some sort. Here are some ground covers you might consider for a problem situation.

Latin Name	Common Name	Light Requirements	Comments
Achillea tomentosa	Woolly yarrow	Sun or shade	6"-12". Rock gardens and between flagstone walks.
Aegopodium podograria	Goutweed	Sun or shade	8"-12". Dry soils. Fine along house walls.
Ajuga reptans	Bugleweed	Sun or shade	12". Fast spreader.
Akebia quinata	Fiveleaf Akebia	Sun, semi-shade	14"-18". May need trimming to keep it confined.
Arabis alpina	Alpine Rockcress	Sun	8". Good for rockeries.
Arctostaphylos uva ursi	Bearberry	Sun, semi-shade	6"-8". Forms thick mats.
Arenaria caespitosa	Moss Sandwort	Shade	2"-3". Good between bricks or flagstone.
Armeria maritima	Common Thrift	Full sun	6"-8". Same as above.
Asperula odorata	Sweet Woodruff	Shade	8"-10". Fine under shrubs.
Calluna vulgaris	Scotch Heather	Sun	24". Good in mass plantings.
Cerastium tomentosum	Snow in Summer	Sun	3"-4". Very aggressive.
Convallaria majalis	Lily-of-the-Valley	Sun or shade	12". Leaves die down in winter.
Coronilla varia	Crown Vetch	Full sun, semi-shade	12"-18". Steep banks.
Cotoneaster adpressa (several good varieties)	Creeping Cotoneaster	Sun	12". Banks, rock gardens.
Cytisus albus	Broom	Sun	12"-18". Edging.
Dianthus arenarius	Sand Pink	Sun or shade	4-8". Borders. Remove seed pods regularly for continuous bloom.
Diervilla lonicera	Dwarf honeysuckle	Sun or shade	3". Dry banks. Spreads by underground stems.
Epimedium alpinum (several types)	Epimedium	Semi-shade	6"-10". Grows well in shade, among rocks.
Erica carnea	Heath	Sun	6"-12". Around rhododendrons, azaleas.

Latin Name	Common Name	Light Requirements	Comments
Euonymus obovatus	Euonymus	Shade	12"-14". Slopes.
Euonymus radicans (several good types available)	Wintercreeper	Sun	4"-12". Good under trees.
Genista pilosa	Silky Broom	Sun	8"-12". Among rocks.
Gypsophila repens	Creeping Gypsophila	Sun	6"-10". Rockery and walls.
Hedera Helix baltica	Baltic English Ivy	Shade	6"-10". Under trees, along walls.
Hedera Helix bulgaria	Bulgarian English Ivy	same	same
Hemerocallis fulva	Tawny Daylily	Sun or shade	24"-36". Slopes, any bare soil.
Hosta decorata	Broad-leaved Plantain Lily	Sun or shade	12"-15". Slopes, along walls on north side.
H. lancifolia	Narrow-leaved plantain Lily	Sun or shade	18". Same as above
Hydrangea petiolaris	Climbing Hydrangea	Sun, semi-shade	24"-36". Climbs over rock piles.
Hypericum calycinum	St. Johnswort	Shade	12". Along walls.
Iberis sempervirens	Evergreen Candytuft	Shade	12". Rockeries.
Juniperus horizontalis (several good types)	Creeping juniper Andorra juniper etc.	Sun	12"-14". Banks and level ground.
Liriope spicata	Lily Turf, Liriope	Sun or shade	8"-12". Under trees, level ground.
Lonicera japonica halliana	Hall's Honeysuckle	Sun or shade	Creeper, good on banks.
Mahonia repens	Dwarf Holly Grape	Sun or shade	12"-18". Rockeries.
Nepeta hederacea	Gill-Over-the-Ground	Sun or shade	1" creeper. Lawn weed that's aggressive in problem areas.
Ophiopogon japonicus	Mondo Grass	Sun or shade	8"-10". Shady spots. Ideal where nothing else will grow.
Pachistima canbyi	Pachistima	Sun or shade	8"-10". Edging plant, rocky areas, under taller shade-loving shrubs.
Pachysandra terminalis	Japanese Spurge or Pachysandra	Shade; yellows in full sun	12"-14". Good for under trees. Shady slopes.

Latin Name	Common Name	Light Requirements	Comments
Parthenocissus quinquefolia (also Ampelopsis quinquefolia)	Woodbine or Virginia Creeper	Sun or shade	Vine grows anywhere, climbs on anything.
Phlox subulata	Moss Pink	Full sun	2"-3". Slopes, dry walls.
Polygonum	Mexican Bamboo	Sun or shade	6"-8". Steep slopes, poor soil. Very aggressive.
Pueraria thunbergiana	Kudzu Vine	Sun or shade	1"-2". Soil binder, bank cover. Very aggressive. Use caution — must be kept confined by clipping.
Rhus aromatica	Fragrant Sumac	Full sun	3"-4". Good for steep banks.
Rosa rugosa	Rugosa Rose	Sun	24"-36". Steep banks.
Rosa wichuraiana	Memorial Rose	Sun, semi-shade	12"-24". Steep slopes.
Sedum acre	Stone Crop	Sun	2"-3". Rock gardens, walls, between flatstones.
Symphoricarpos orbiculatus	Coral Berry or Indian Currant	Sun, semi-shade	36". Steep slopes.
Teucrium chamaedrys	Germander	Sun	10"-12". Edging.
Thymus serphyllum	Creeping Thyme	Full sun	2". Between stones, terraces.
Veronica (several types)	Speedwell	Sun	2"- 12". Under trees.
Vinca minor	Myrtle or Periwinkle or Vinca	Sun	12". Around evergreens, slopes.
Viola cultivars	Violets	Sun or shade	6". Grows anywhere, especially under trees.

Our thanks to the University of Missouri for help on this selection.

33

Green Thumb Tips on Lawns

*Temporary lawns cost money. Invest in good grass seed for a permanent lawn and have green grass as long as your house lasts.

*There is no perfect grass. Watch out for "wonder" grasses. You buy them, plant them, and "wonder" why they don't grow.

*Grass seed sowed on snow is for the birds? Best to wait and sow the seed on a good, well prepared seed bed.

*After grading your lawn, give it time to settle before sowing. Loam soils often settle 20 percent, or one-fifth of their original depth.

*Mow grass as soon as you have something to mow. Mowing encourages filling out at the base.

*Don't lime your lawn every year! It does more harm than good. Once every four years is safer, but feed once a year.

*Don't panic if grass starts to burn in hot weather. If the grass is a permanent type, it'll bounce back after the first rain.

*Sprinkling during a hot sun is harmless but wasteful.

*Don't be a lawn crank!

CHAPTER II

Landscaping Your
Home Grounds

•

Trees, shrubs, and other greenery help make a house a home. They are also good air conditioners. A mature, well watered tree can produce a cooling effect equal to ten room air conditioners running twenty hours a day.

If you removed all the leaves from a mature tree and placed them flat on the ground so they touched one another, the leaves would cover a space of four acres. On the tree each of these leaves acts as a miniature air conditioner. A well placed shade tree can lower the temperature in your home by 20 degrees.

Similarly, good landscaping cuts down on your fuel bills in winter. A properly located shade tree lowers your fuel bill by as much as 30 percent by acting as a windbreak. To heat an ordinary house, it takes twice as much fuel at a temperature of 32 degrees and a wind of 12 miles per hour as it does for the same temperature and a wind of 3 miles per hour.

Trees, shrubs, and grass filter out odors and dust particles and cut down on noise pollution. These green servants also help to purify the air by taking in carbon dioxide and giving off oxygen. One authority suggests America plant one tree for every ten automobiles and one hundred trees for every truck on the road. It would be a great investment. Trees, unlike most things you buy, increase in value with time.

Simply stated, landscaping is nothing more than dressing up your outdoor living area. Americans take great pride in beautifying their homes. At least $9 billion is spent each year in this country on yards, lawns, and gardens. Experts suggest that 10 to 30 percent of the cost of a new home should be spent for landscaping. With that much money and comfort, utility, and liveability at stake, it would be well worth the effort to plan landscaping work with care. Your home is one of your best hedges against inflation or recession. Anything you do to enhance it is like putting money in the bank.

Spending money to keep your property looking neat and attractive outdoors is just as important as spending money on carpeting, draperies, and other fixtures indoors. Not everyone who owns property is an expert in landscaping, but this doesn't mean you can't do a good job. Don't hesitate to consult a good local nurseryman for advice. There are trees, shrubs, and other plants to meet every need. This chapter covers pitfalls amateurs often encounter, and stresses lasting beauty with a minimum of care.

Foundation Planting

Aside from the lawn (see Chapter I) your foundation planting—the plants around the base of your house—is your most important landscaping. You can spruce up your home front by selecting shrubs listed in our charts later. Before attempting to landscape, take photos, or on a piece of drawing paper draw your home front and sketch in plants which you might like to have. You want an irregular skyline silhouette, with tallest plants on the corners for softening effect. Under windows, place the spreading types so they won't obstruct the view. Stick to no more than three different types of shrubs. Your local nurseryman will be glad to help you make intelligent choices even if you are struggling with a low budget.

Here are a few dozen quick Do's and Don'ts for a budgeting home landscaper to consider for that "million-dollar look."

DON'TS

1. Don't overlook the shrub's mature size.
2. Don't plant all one variety in a straight row.
3. Don't have too great a variety of plants.
4. Don't be afraid to start with small plants.
5. Don't overcrowd. Shrubs and trees need room to grow.
6. Don't be impatient if newly set shrubs don't start fast. It takes some weeks for buds to break.

Avoid planting tall-growing shrubs too near entrance and under windows. Keep shrubs pruned regularly so they don't grow out of bounds.

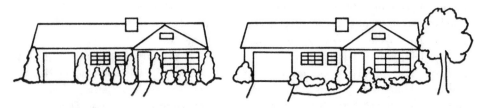

Don't plant all one type of shrub in your foundation planting. It's too monotonous.

7. Don't be afraid to combine evergreens with non-evergreens. (See Chapter III.) Avoid planting tall-growing shrubs too near entrance and under windows. Keep shrubs pruned regularly so they don't grow out of bounds. Don't plant all one type of shrub in your foundation planting. It's too monotonous.
8. Don't plant tall shrubs under a window.
9. Don't plant sun-loving plants in shady places.
10. Don't try to rejuvenate relic evergreens.
11. Don't plant trees near utility lines or too near property lines.
12. Don't plant trees and large shrubs where they will later obstruct a view.

DO'S

1. Do study nursery catalogues carefully.
2. Do plant shrubs at least 3 feet from the house wall and about 3 feet apart.
3. Do let part of your foundation show.
4. Do make holes large enough (don't cram a ten-dollar shrub in a two-dollar hole).
5. Do "heel" your plants in ground if you cannot set them out immediately.
6. Do mix humus and plant foods in soil for growth.
7. Do water all shrubs copiously, at least once a week.
8. Do prune tips of roots back at planting time and practice moderate annual pruning.
9. Do keep your shrubs sprayed and feed at least once yearly.
10. Do have neat, sharp borders in front of your planting.
11. Do use annuals and perennials among your foundation plantings.
12. Do use shrubs to screen off undesirable views.

SHRUBS FOR YOUR HOME'S ENTRANCE

These shrubs with colorful foliage, flowers, or fruits will help make the entrance to your home more inviting.

Plant Name	Height at Maturity (Ft.)	Color of Bloom	Time of Bloom	Comments
Lily-of-the-Valley Flowering Shrub (Andromeda)	6	Waxy white	April-May	Compact, glossy leaves, bell-shaped flowers
Beauty Bush (Kolkwitzia)	6-8	Shell pink	June-July	Upright growing, useful for tall houses, tolerates dry, sandy soils
Buddleias Charming Dubonnet, Ile-de-France	4-5	Pink, lilac, wine, white	July-Aug.	Fragrant long flower sprays
Burning Bush (Euonymus)	5-7	Yellow	May	Red autumn fruits and foliage

Plant Name	Height at Maturity (Ft.)	Color of Bloom	Time of Bloom	Comments
Golden Privet (Ligustrum) or Chartreuse Bush	4-6	White	June	Bright variegated yellow-green foliage
Golden Syringa (Philadelphus)	4-5	White	May-June	Golden-yellow foliage
Philadelphus, Belle Etoile	5	White	May-June	Star-like flowers
Philadelphus, Minnesota Snowflake	6-8	White	May-June	Large double flowers
Philadelphus virginalis	6	White	June-Aug.	Fragrant double flowers
Rosa Hugonis (see Chapter VII, ROSES FOR THE HOME GARDEN)	4-6	Yellow	May	Fine shrub rose
Rosa Rugosa	4-6	Pink	May through summer	Rich green foliage, large red fruit
Scarlet Quince	4-5	Red	April-May	Early spring blooms
Spiraea vanhouttei	6	White	May	A national favorite called "Bridal Wreath"
Sweet Shrub (Calycanthus)	6	Reddish-brown	June-July	Spicy flowers
Viburnum carlesii	5-6	White	April-May	Fragrant flowers. Never spray with sulfur
Viburnum carlcephalum	5-6	White	April-May	Hybrid more showy than carlesii
Weigela, Eva Rathke	4-5	Red	May-June	Trumpet-shaped flowers
Weigela, Variegated	4-5	Pale pink	June	Green and white foliage
Winterberry (Euonymus radicans erecta)	4-5	Red berries	Fall and winter	Evergreen foliage

SHRUBS FOR UNDER WINDOWS

Reaching heights of no more than 5 feet, these shrubs are suitable for planting in front of the house under windows where taller plants would obstruct the view as well as light and air.

Plant Name	Height at Maturity (Ft.)	Color of Bloom	Time of Bloom	Comments
Abelia grandiflora, Glossy Abelia	3	White, pink	June-frost	Good for sun or partial shade
Barberry (*Barberis*) Green Leaf Barberry Red Leaf Barberry	3-5	Yellow	April	Thorny red fall and winter berries
Calacanthus, Spicebush	4	Chocolate brown	June	Exotic pods filled with aromatic seeds
Caryopteris, Hardy Blue Spirea	2	Blue	Late summer	Tolerates warm, dry, sunny spots
Coralberry or Indian Currant, *Symphoricarpos orbiculatus*	5	White	May-June	Coral-colored berries in fall
Cotoneaster divaricata, Spreading Cotoneaster	4-6	Pink	June	Graceful plant with tiny, round, glossy leaves, red autumn berries
Currant, Flowering *Ribes*	4-5	Yellow or red	May	Flowers useful in arrangements. Tolerates light shade
Deutzia gracilis	2-3	White, pink	May	Fine twiggy growth, handsome low-growing shrub
Honeysuckle (*Lonicera*), L. Compacta nana	4-5	Yellow	May	Red fall and winter berries
L. Zabelii	4-5	Pink	May-June	Blue-green leaves
Hydrangea, blue *Hydrangea macrophylla*	3	Blue to pinkish	June-Sept.	Low-growing shrubby plant, large round bloom clusters
Hydrangea, Snowball	3-5	White	July to frost	Good for shade

Plant Name	Height at Maturity (Ft.)	Color of Bloom	Time of Bloom	Comments
Hypericum (Hidcote)	4-5	Yellow	May-July	Freezes back in winter, restarts from base in spring
Kerria, Golden Glow	4-5	Golden-yellow	June-frost	Light green branches give winter interest
Mahonia aquifolium, Oregon Grape Holly	3-4	Yellow	May	Grape-like blue berries in large clusters, summer to frost
Pieris Japonica, Lily-of-the-Valley Shrub	4	Creamy white	April-May	Likes acid soil and semi-shade
Potentilla, Gold Drop	3-4	Yellow	June to frost.	Mound of green and gold
Snowberry, *Symphoricarpos albus*	4-5	Pink	June	Waxy white autumn berries
Spirea Anthony Waterer, Pink Spirea	2-3	Pinkish-red	June-Sept.	Fine dwarf shrub Delicate flower sprays ideal for bouquets.
Spirea macrothyrsa	4	Pink	June-frost	Full sun; will stand semi-shade. Flowers suitable for cutting.
Vitex macrophylla, Chaste Tree	4-5	Lavender	July-Sept.	Graceful shrub; dainty flower spikes
Weigela, Eva Rathke	4-5	Red	May-June	Trumpet-shaped flowers
Weigela, Variegated	4-5	Pale pink	June	Green and white foliage

SHRUBS FOR CORNERS

These taller-growing shrubs are suitable for planting at the corners of a house, garage, or porch yard. For ranch houses, a single plant may be sufficient for the desired effect, but in houses more than one story high, several plants in each corner may be desirable for the "framing" effect given by these plants to the landscape.

Plant Name	Height at Maturity (Ft.)	Color of Bloom	Time of Bloom	Comments
Althaea (Rose of Sharon)	8-10	White, pink purple, red, blue	August	Columnar growing
Beauty Bush (*Kolkwitzia*)	6-8	Shell pink	June-July	Tolerates poor, sandy soils. Dry corners near buildings.
Crape Myrtle (*Lagerstroemia*)	4-6	Red, pink	July	Dies back each winter, comes back every spring.
Daphne mezereum	5	Pink	May-June	Beautiful aroma, berries toxic
Euonymus Sarcoxie (Emerald Pillar Shrub)	6-8			Shiny green leaves
Forsythia, Spring Glory	6-8	Yellow	April-May	Spectacular bloomer
Forsythia, Lynwood Gold	6-8	Yellow	April-May	Deep-yellow blossoms
High Bush Cranberry	8	White	May-June	Scarlet fall and winter fruits
Lilac, French Hybrids	8-12	Assorted colors	May	Double flowering
Lilac, common	15	Deep purple, white, red, pink, lavender	May	Fragrant flowers
Philadelphus, Minnesota Snowflake	6-8	White	May-June	Large double flowers
Prunus Tomentosa, Nanking Cherry	4-5	White	April-May	Cherry-red fruit
Pyracantha, Firethorn	4-6	Creamy White	May	Orange-red berries

Plant Name	Height at Maturity (Ft.)	Color of Bloom	Time of Bloom	Comments
Smoke Tree (*Rhus cotinus*)	12	Cream, pink-purple	May	Feathery blooms; cloud-like blooms. Good accent plant. Only female trees bloom.
Sweet Honeysuckle (*Lonicera*)	8-12	Pink, cream, red	May	Profuse bloomers. Red berries
Spiraea van Houttei	6	White	May	Covered with blooms, graceful branching
Tamarix (Tamarisk)	8	Rosy-pink	May-June	Lacy effect
Variegated Leaf Dogwood	6-8	White	June	Silver and green foliage
Viburnum (Japanese Snowball) *opulus compacta*	5	White	May-July	Pure white snow-balls. Never spray with sulfur.
Weigela vanicekii, Cardinal shrub	6	Red	Spring, summer, fall	Large, trumpet-shaped flowers

SHRUBS WITH AROMATIC FOLIAGE OR FLOWERS

Most people think of lilac and mock orange when fragrant shrubs are mentioned. However, these are a number of others that can make your yard a delight many more months of the year. Some that are hardy in northern areas include:

Aralia spinosa (Hercules club)
Buddleia alternifolia (Butterfly Bush)
Calycanthus floridus (Sweet-Scented Shrub or Strawberry Shrub)
Caryopteris incana (Blue Spirea)
Clethra alnifolia (Pink Pepper Bush)
Clethra paniculata (White Pepper Bush)
Cotinus coggygyria, Rhus cotinus (Smoke Bush)
Daphne mezereum (Daphne)
Lindera benzoin (Spicebush)
Myrica caroliniensis and M. pennsylvanica (Bayberry)
Philadelphus coronarius (Mock Orange)
Rhus aromatica (Fragrant sumac)
Syringa species (True Lilac)
Syringa species (True Lilac)

Viburnum carlesii and V. carlcephalum (Fragrant Snowball)

Vitex macrophylla (Chaste Tree)

There are others which are less hardy, so consult your nurseryman for those adaptable to your area.

SHRUBS WITH COLORED STEMS

Planted among evergreens, these shrubs with colorful stems will add variety to the landscape. Usually the color is most pronounced in young stems. It is therefore desirable to prune the stems sharply each year to encourage new growth. Shrubs in this category include Tatarian dogwood (*Cornus alba*) with blood-red stems; Siberian dogwood (*C. alba sibirica*) with red stems; red osier dogwood (*C. stolonifera*) with red stems, though not as beautifully colored as the two mentioned first; golden twig dogwood (*C. stolonifera flaviramea*) with yellow stems, and *Kerria Japonica* with bright green stems.

SHRUBS FOR THE SEASHORE

Because the salty air near the seashore can damage new leaves of shrubs, the following varieties are recommended for cottages and homes in such locations:

Autumn Elaeagnus (*E. umbellata*)

Pfitzer's Juniper (*P. chinensis pfitzeriana*)

California Privet (*Ligustrum ovalifolium*)

Bayberry (*Myrica pennsylvanica*)

Beach Plum (*Prunus maritima*)

Rugosa Rose (*Rosa rugosa*)

Serviceberry, Shadbush (*Amelanchier*)

Chokecherry (*Aronia arbutifolia*)

Wintergreen Barberry (*Berberis thunbergii*)

Summersweet (*Clethra alnifolia*)

Spreading Cotoneaster (*Cotoneaster divaricata*)

Tatarian Honeysuckle (*Lonicera tatarica*)

Swiss Mountain Pine (*Pinus mugo*)

Firethorn (*Pyracantha coccinea lalandii*)

Meadow Rose (*Rosa blanda*)

Multiflora Rose (*Rosa multiflora*)

Prairie Rose (*Rosa setigera*)

Scotch Broom (*Cytisus scoparius*)

Tamarisk (*Tamarix*)

Russian Olive (*Elaeagnus angustifolia*)

Inkberry (*Ilex glabra*)

Regel Privet (*Ligustrum obtusifolium regelianum*)

Japanese Yew (*Taxus cuspidata*)

Withe-Rod (*Viburnum cassinoides*)

European Cranberry bush (*Viburnum opulus*)

Planting Shrubs

Fall and spring are the best times for planting trees and shrubs. If you are moving the shrubs from another location, be sure to dig up all the roots possible. You can do this by digging a circular trench around the plant, thrusting your spade as deep as necessary. Roots usually extend as far out from the plant under the soil as the spread of branches above the soil, and just as moving into another home is a somewhat unsettling experience for you, so is the experience of being moved disturbing for a plant. Roots are especially affected by the change but you can make their job easier after the replanting by cutting back the branches of moved shrubs by about one-third. If you are planting in heavy soil, you can aid drainage by dumping a pail of perlite in the bottom of the hole. Or you can mix the perlite with some of the soil in the hole before setting the tree or shrub.

Trees or shrubs from the nursery come "bare root," "balled and burlape" (B & B), or in paper, metal, or plastic containers. Bare root stock has been in cold storage during the winter months and should be planted as soon as possible, but if you cannot plant the trees or shrubs within two days, then "heeling in" is in order. This simply means digging a trench in a shady spot and setting the roots in, pouring on some water, and covering the roots with soil. Keep all bare rooted nursery stock out of direct sun till planting time.

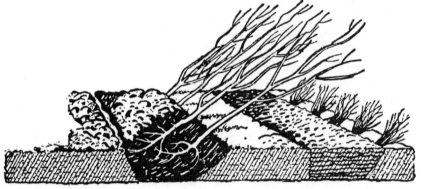

If bare-rooted nursery stock arrives before you get a chance to plant it, heel the plants in the ground as shown. Water well and cover roots with soil.

If you don't want to dig a trench, place the plants flat on the ground (in the shade), hose down the tops and bottoms thoroughly, and cover with a piece of black plastic. When you're ready to plant, remove the plastic, snip off the tip ends of the roots, and prune off one-third of the top. We don't like to place bare rooted stock in a bucket of water where it'll remain several days. The roots turn black and slimy, and plants suffocate from a lack of oxygen. Balled and burlaped nursery stock can be kept alive until you're ready to plant simply by covering the soil ball with leaves, peat moss, or compost.

If stock is wrapped in burlap, plant entire ball, wrap and all. If in plastic, *remove the wrap* before planting. Some plastic wraps look like burlap, so don't let them fool you! Loosen the plastic and use the wrap for a "sling": grab the four corners and set the entire ball into the hole, then gently pun the plastic out from underneath. Proceed to fill in the hole with soil.

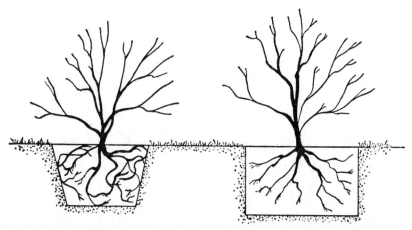

In planting any shrub or tree, make hole large enough to accommodate roots without crowding. Never twist or wrap roots in hole before covering, as shown at left. (*Courtesy University of Maine*)

FEEDING AND WATERING Give plant food to your shrubs at least once a year and water them at least once a week in dry weather. One reason trees, shrubs, and evergreens die in winter is a lack of water in the soil. Never let your plants go into the winter dry. It's seldom that winter cold kills these plants, but drying of the tissues due to wind and sun is detrimental. So keep your plants watered. If you live in an area where there's a shortage of water, use laundry water for your plants. Of course, we don't want dishwater or laundry water to run off into a stream or well, but we feel they can be used on compost piles, in flower beds, around trees and ornamentals, and in the vegetable garden. Alternate it with clean water and the soaps, ammonia, and detergents will be diluted and harmless.

PRUNING FLOWERING SHRUBS Most flowering shrubs look their best if allowed to grow in their natural shape. However, pruning is usually necessary to control size and density so a plant will flower and look better, and to put new life into a declining plant. Pruning is a stimulating process but try to follow the natural contour of the plant.

If shrubs are pruned at the wrong time of year, flower buds may be cut off. There are two groups of flowering shrubs. Those that flower in the spring bear flowers on wood produced the year before. So, if these shrubs are pruned right after blossoming, more flowering wood will be produced for the next year.

Shrubs that flower in summer bear flowers on wood produced the same year. Thus, if they are pruned late fall or in early spring, more flowering wood will be produced.

Examples of spring-flowering shrubs include dogwood, viburnum, mock orange, lilac, azalea, allspice bush (*Calycanthus*), beauty bush, flowering quince, daphne, deutzia, forsythia, mountain laurel, honeysuckle, and flowering almond.

Summer blooming shrubs that can be pruned in late summer, fall, or winter include Abelia, Buddleia (butterfly bush or summer lilac), sweet pepperbush, Kerria, rose of Sharon, spirea Anthony Waterer, tamarix, and vitex (chaste tree). (See shrub charts for more information on individual shrub blooming dates.)

Any time shrubs have broken limbs, or are too thick, get out the clippers and start pruning, regardless of season. The only thing you might lose is some flowers for this or next year's show.

BEFORE   **AFTER**

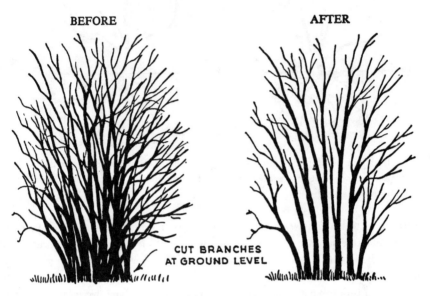

CUT BRANCHES
AT GROUND LEVEL

Right way of pruning flowering shrubs. Prune by thinning out some of the older branches each year, and remove any branches that criss cross or rub against each other. (*Courtesy University of Maine*)

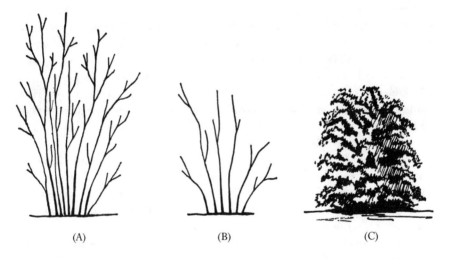

(A)   (B)   (C)

(A) Unpruned shrub. (B) Shrub pruned properly. (C) New growth comes from bottom, resulting in graceful, compact form with foliage all over. (*Courtesy University of Maine*)

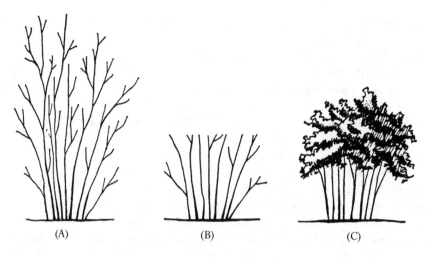

(A)   (B)   (C)

Wrong way to head back a flowering shrub: (A) Unpruned shrub. (B) "Beheaded" shrub sheared across the top forces shoots from the top of the plant. (C) New growth will be made only at top, with no leaves or flowers at base (a bare-branched, bushy-topped shrub). (*Courtesy University of Maine*)

Upper inset shows where old blossom head should be pruned to avoid losing next year's lilac crop. Lower circle shows where to cut broken branches. (*Courtesy Rochester Parks Department*)

If your shrubs are an overgrown jungle of stems through neglect, there are two ways to handle them: 1) cut the entire bush back to the ground and let all new growth come up, or 2) prune the oldest and poorest branches right back to the ground. There's more to pruning than we've mentioned but don't be bogged down by a lot of rules. It's better to prune than not to prune, and remember, "When pruning, be a barber, not a butcher." (For pruning of evergreens see Chapter III.)

EDGING YOUR BORDERS A foundation planting or flower bed won't look its best unless you put a good edge around it. Some gardeners like a straight edge, but we prefer one with slight curves. A good edge is to your planting what a neat hem is to a garment. One way to tell what an edged border will look like is to lay your garden hose along the planting, in the shape you think it should be. There is no need for an edge that cuts halfway into your lawn and it doesn't have to be too deep.

Once you've laid out the pattern for the edge you want, take a spade or axe and mark the line. Then you can use a dull axe or spade to remove the sod from the bedding area (the bedding side of your defined line). An edge 2 inches deep is sufficient; if deeper, you'll have trouble running the lawn mower parallel to it. A good edge neatly defines your flower bed, evergreen plantings, or individual plant, and after entire border is edged, fill in the area with your favorite mulch material. A thin layer of mulch in an edged border sets your whole house off and does a lot to keep weeds down and moisture in the ground.

CUT OFF SEED PODS? Is it necessary to cut off seed pods of flowering shrubs or trees? If you can easily reach the pods and have the time, cut them off, mainly for show. There are variances among shrubs. If the pods are left on lilacs, for example, they will still produce a crop of blossoms the following year, in spite of the drain from seed development. With lilacs, ash, birch, and catalpa it makes no difference, but with shrubs like magnolias, rhododendrons, and mountain laurel removing the seed pods is a great benefit. If your seed pods are not removed with care you may remove next year's flowers.

Shrubs Make Your House a Home

If your yard is sizeable, don't be afraid to spend as much money on the outside of your home as you would to decorate the interior. Remember, more people see the outside than the inside, and the shrubs may outlast the furniture.

Shrub	Features	Pruning	Troubles	Control
Abelia grandiflora (Abelia)	Glossy-leaved 3' shrub with pink and white arbutus-like blooms from early summer till frost. Will tolerate semi-shade.	Prune lightly in early spring or late fall	None	
Althaea (Rose of Sharon) (*Hibiscus syriacus*)	White, purple, pink, red, and blue flowers, some doubles; late summer until frost. Grows in most well drained soils. 6'-12'.	Cut out winter-killed wood in Spring. Annual trimming to two dormant buds keep shrubs low and very floriferous.	Bud drop. May be due to hot, dry weather, lack of soil nutrients.	Water and feed plants well.
Buddleia (Butterfly Bush) (Summer Lilac)	Long spikes of white, purple, lavender flowers throughout late summer. 3'.	Cut back to ground in spring.	Winterkills.	Heavy pruning in spring.
Calycanthus (Allspice Bush)	Red-brown flowers in early spring. Glossy foliage. Flowers and bark fragrant. 4'-5'.	Neat growing needs hardly any pruning.	None	
Caryopteris (Blue Mist)	Silvery green foliage, light blue flowers in autumn. 3'.	Cut back to ground in spring.	Winterkills.	Heavy pruning in spring.
Chaenomeles (Flowering Quince) (*Cydonia* is the quince grown for fruit: see Chapter XII)	Called "japonica." White, scarlet, salmon pink blooms in early spring. Produces flowers and fruit year after year. 6'-8'.	Cut out dead twigs, those growing tall and leggy. Remove 1/3 growth each year. Early spring is best time.	Fireblight	Remove dead wood.

Shrub	Features	Pruning	Troubles	Control
Clethra (Pepper Bush)	Compact, neat plant with finger-like clusters of small scented white or pink flowers in late August. 4'-5'.	In spring cut out excess branches.	None	
Cornus (Shrubby Dogwoods)	Colorful foliage, blossoms and neat habit of growth. Spring bloomer. 4'-6'.	Needs little pruning. Cut out dead wood.	Scale. Leaf curl, due to dry weather.	Malathion, water during dry spells.
Cotoneaster divaricata (Pronounced "Ko-to-nee-aster")	Shiny dark green leaves. Red berries and foliage in fall. Tolerates drought, full sun. Up to 4'.	Trim new growth back to desired height in spring.	None serious	
Deutzia gracilis (Dwarf Deutzia)	Charming low growing foundation shrub, white and pink flowers in late spring. Likes full sun. 3'. Deutzia Pride of Rochester, 5'.	Trim little, if any, just after blooming.	None	
Daphne mezereum (Daphne)	Fragrant pink lilac-like blooms in early spring. 4'. Self-sows madly. Give plants to your friends.	Needs no pruning except for dead wood.	Tips may winter-kill.	Trim off dead tips in spring.
Euonymus (*Winged Euonymus* or *Firebush*)	Has corky ridges on branches. Fall foliage a deep red. Bright orange fruits. 3'-5'.	None except to trim out winterkilled wood.	None	
		Seldom needed. Snip out extra long shoots as necessary.		

Shrub	Features	Pruning	Troubles	Control
Forsythias (Golden Bells)	Handsome early-blooming shrub for boundary lines, banks, and hedges. 5'-7'.	Trim after blooming. Do not shear into ball shape, as this is one shrub that likes to weep or grow gracefully.	Failure to bloom due to cold weather.	Do not prune heavily. Plant in protected spot if winters are severe.
A. G. hydrangea (Hills of Snow)	Snowy balls of white flowers in June and July. 4'.	Best to cut plants back to ground each spring or fall to prevent sprawl.	Powdery mildew, rust and Botrytis blight.	Dust with sulfur.
Hydrangea (Peegee Hydrangea)	Coarse shrub with white flowers in August. Overused yet handsome. 10'.	Cut plant back each spring for shrub-like growth. If you want it treelike, prune very little.	None	
Hydrangea macrophylla (Florist's Hydrangea)	Snowy blue, pink, or white blooms in summer. 3'-4'.	Scatter a handful of aluminum sulfate at base of plant for blue blooms, lime for pink. (White varieties cannot be changed)	Flower buds winterkill in cold areas.	Protect by covering with leaves and baskets.
Kalmia (Mountain Laurel)	Evergreen foliage, grows in sun or shade. Early spring bloomer. 4'-8'.	Needs very little. (For more detail see Chapter III).	Leaf spot disease.	Dust with Captan.
Kerria japonica (Golden Glow)	Golden-yellow double or single flowers in summer and fall. 4'-5'. Tolerates semi-shade.	Prune late fall or early spring.	None	

Shrub	Features	Pruning	Troubles	Control
Hibiscus moscheutos (Hibiscus)	Large (6"-8" across) saucer-shaped flowers, pink, white, lavender, red. In North plant dies back each winter, starts all new growth in spring. 4'-5'.	Cut stems back to ground in spring.	None	
Ilex verticillata (Swamp Holly, Winterberry)	Hardy deciduous holly, to 10'. Handsome red berries remain on bush. Tolerates moist places.	Trim out center of bush for fatter berries.	None	
Kolkwitzia (Beauty Bush)	Masses of dainty pink flowers in June and July. 5'-10'. Needs full sun.	Cut out long shoots after blooming. Do not shear.	None	
Lagerstroemia (Crepe Myrtle)	Fine lilac-like plant blooming in late summer and early fall. 12'-15'.	Prune back in fall.	Winterkills in cold areas.	Give winter mulch and winter protection.
Lonicera tatarica (Honeysuckle)	Small light or dark pink or yellow flowers late May, early June. Red berries summer and fall. 8'-12', dwarf varieties also available.	Cut out long shoots in fall.	None	
Philadelphus (Mock Orange)	Creamy flowers, highly fragrant, singles and doubles. Growth is coarse. Up to 10'. Spring bloomer.	Prune after blossoming in spring. Overgrown plants should be shortened drastically in early spring. Thin out branches as they become crowded. Never shear.	Lack of blossoms due to cold; also improper pruning removes buds.	Do not prune tips.

Shrub	Features	Pruning	Troubles	Control
Prunus (Flowering almonds)	Group includes shrubs 3'-6'. Double pink early blooms in spring, usually before leaves come out.	Little pruning needed. Cut out sprouts from below point of graft, as wild stock may take over.	None serious	
Pyracantha (Firethorn)	Keeps shiny green foliage nearly all winter. Orange-scarlet berries, thorny twigs. 4'-6'.	Let grow to natural shape except for such pruning as may be necessary for fireblight.	Often bears every other year. Susceptible to fireblight. Berries turn black and fall.	Cut out wilted branches and burn or seal in plastic bag and discard. Spray or dust with Captan.
Physocarpus (Golden Ninebark)	White or pinkish flowers early summer; bright yellow leaves in fall, grows to 10'.	Prune out dead wood anytime.	None serious	
Rhododendron (Azaleas, Rhododendrons)	Large family of spring flowering beauties, many colors. Vary in height from 18" to 10'. Most are evergreen. Prefer semi-shade and acid soil	None	Borer

Lacewing fly

Mealybugs, scale (for more details see Chapter III). | Trim shoots early spring. Spray Malathion in May. (See section on Insect and Disease Control) |
| *Rhus cotinus, cotinus coggygria* (Smoke Bush, Smoke Tree) | A garden favorite for 2,000 years. Small cream or purple-pink flowers, plume-like threads, June to fall, produce interesting effect, can be used in bouquets. Center of attraction in lawn. 15' high. Royal Purple favored for its purple foliage. | Prune out dead wood anytime. | Wilt disease

Sections of the plant may winterkill. | Prune and burn.

Prune out in spring. |

Shrub	Features	Pruning	Troubles	Control
Ribes aureum Yellow Flowering Currant	Tiny yellow fragrant flowers in June. Hardy everywhere. 3'-6'.	None ordinarily. Prune dead wood anytime.	None	
Ribes sanguineum Red Flowering Currant	Clusters of tiny red flowers in early spring. 4'-6'. Hardy, does well in semi-shade.	Same as above.	None	
Salix caprea (French Pussy Willow)	Beautiful pink catkins twice the size of regular pussy willow 8'-10'.	Cut out winterkilled shoots in spring.	None	
Salix purpurea nana (Dwarf Arctic Willow)	Feathery plant ideal in wet or heavy soils. Foliage is neat blue-gray-green and can be clipped for formal effect or left natural. 4'.	Thin out old wood in spring.	None	
Spiraea (Spireas)	An important group of landscape plants. *S. vanhouteii* (Bridal Wreath) grows 6', dainty white blooms in spring. *S. anthony waterer* (Dwarf Red Spirea) and *S. bumalda* grow 4', make good foundation plants. Summer bloomer.	If neglected cut back to ground in fall for new growth in spring. Otherwise thin out scraggy canes. Prune back to 6" of ground in spring before growth starts. If blooms are cut as soon as they start to fade, they'll continue until late fall.	Aphids	Nicotine sulfate or garlic-red pepper spray as soon as noticed.
			None	
Sweetscented Viburnum (*V. carlesii*) (*V. carlcephalum*)	White fragrant flowers in spring, foliage bronzy in fall. 6'.	Need little pruning. Thin out shoots after flowering.	None serious	Never spray with sulfur after leaves have come out.

Shrub	Features	Pruning	Troubles	Control
Syringa (Lilac)	Bush or small tree up to 20'. Flowers in June, fragrant and profuse, great nostalgic appeal. American, French, Persian, Japanese varieties. Japanese tree lilac has showy white blooms in late June. Considered a coarse shrub by some.	Cut out dead wood, most suckers in early spring. You may or may not cut faded blooms. If you do prune, do so directly after blooming period. To rejuvenate old bush, cut ½ to ⅓ of old wood out in a 3-yr. period.	Leaf miner. Scale. Borers. Failure to bloom due to improper planting, too much shade, close planting, too many suckers at base, dry summers. Powdery mildew (not serious). Bacterial blight: plants turn black and die.	Lindane. Lime sulfur in early spring. Borer paste. Karathane. None
Tamarix (Tamarisk)	Handsome shrub with lacy pink flowers, feathery foliage. 10'. Do not confuse tamarix with tamarack (*larix*) or larch.	Prune lightly after blooming period in spring.	Parts may winter-kill.	Prune out dead limbs in spring.
Viburnums	Large and important group with showy spring flowers, green foliage in summer, and vivid autumn coloration.			

Shrub	Features	Pruning	Troubles	Control
Viburnum opulus European "Snowball" or Cranberry Bush	Used for hiding unsightly spots. Red berries in summer and fall, leaves red in autumn. 10'-12'.	Thin out weak stems in spring.	Aphids cause leaves to curl.	Nicotine sulfate (or garlic-red pepper spray) or Malathion in early spring. Never spray any viburnum with sulfur.
Vitex (Chaste Tree)	Showy spikes of lavender-blue flowers July to fall. 8'-10' unless pruned back.	Trim to desired height in early spring.	None	
Weigela (Weigela)	Trumpet-shaped flowers. Variegated type has pale pink blooms and cream and green foliage. 5'.	Thin out badly neglected plants and cut back to proper size in fall or winter.	None	
Wisteria (Tree form) (Wisteria)	Drooping clusters of lavender, white pea-like flowers in spring. Grows to 10'. Tree needs support.	Thin out dead wood only, in spring.	Non-blooming.	Age (tree will not bloom til it is old enough) or too rich soil: dig trench around base of plant, remove soil, replace with poor soil (or soil mixed with coal ashes).

Good Hedges Make Good Neighbors

Robert Frost said that good fences make good neighbors, and so do good hedges, since a hedge is a living fence. Today, backyard space is at a premium, and we all crave privacy.

You can have privacy and beauty with a living fence that will grow to any height you want with little care. Hedges filter out noise, dust, and pollutants, an extra bonus for planting them. Best of all this is one fence that needs no painting, will not rust, and needs no replacement.

Many shrubs today are tailored for your backyard. They grow tall and narrow, taking up little space. Some of the new varieties of plants are so upright and neat that they need very little care in the way of pruning or trimming—a boon in these days of high cost of labor and crowded weekends.

Before you set out any screen plants, first consider the effect you want. You can have tall hedges—reaching 20 feet or so, medium hedges that are 6 feet or so, dwarf or miniature hedges only 12 to 24 inches high. If you have a postage stamp-size backyard, stay away from rampant growers such as multiflora roses (see Chapter VII) unless space is no problem and you want an impenetrable barrier. Another point to keep in mind is that you can manipulate hedges so they'll grow to any desired height simply by trimming. The cordless hedge trimmers can save you time, money, and achy arms and should be on your list of desirable garden equipment.

In planting a hedge, be sure to dig a trench deep enough to hold the roots without crowding. After setting the plants into the trench, add soil and firm around the base of the plants. Water well, feed the soil once a year with a balanced plant food, and pack sawdust or peat moss around the bottoms of the plants to keep weeds down. To achieve tighter-growing plants at the bottom of the hedge—and thus add to your privacy—prune the plants severely to about 4 inches above the ground at planting time. Trim hedges as often as you like, but not later in the year than early September.

The following list of shrubby plant materials is not complete. If you live in tropical areas of the country, you'll want to use plant materials indigenous to your area. These may include many of the green, broad-leaved plants which do well in warm areas.

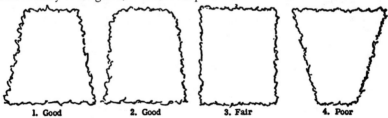

| 1. Good | 2. Good | 3. Fair | 4. Poor |

Hedges are trimmed in various shapes and sizes; some are good, some are bad. Numbers 1 and 2 are best for trimming most hedges.

Hedge	Effect	Height and Growth Habit
Althaea (Rose of Sharon)	Pink, purple, red, white, blue blossoms, double and single varieties.	Let grow to 10'. Trimming cuts off buds and loses flower show.
Amur River privet (Ligustrum amurense)	Green foliage, blue-black winter berries.	Untrimmed, reaches 15'-20'. Very hardy in cold regions. Stop trimming after September.
Barberry (Berberis)	Many forms. Green or maroon leaves, red berries.	Varieties 18" to 6', attractive trimmed or untrimmed. Can be trimmed to any desired height. Thorns make it a good barrier plant.
Canadian Hemlock (Tsuga Canadensis)	Fine, dark green foliage.	Grows to height of 60' if unpruned. Excellent hedge plant when sheared. Ideal for borders.
Cotoneaster	Pink flowers in June, glossy leaves, fiery red berries.	Graceful spreading plant, best to let grow with little trimming. Varieties 8" to 4'.
Cydonia Chaenomeles Flowering Quince	Red or pink flowers early in spring; yellow fruits for quince jelly.	Grows 4'-6'. Best if left untrimmed. However, may be kept down to 4' by topping (shearing top). Side pruning not needed.
Elaeagnus angustifolia Russian Olive	Narrow, silvery-gray foliage all summer. White flowers in June. Yellow nut-like fruits in fall (see Bird Plantings chart).	Grows 15'. Tends to branch rather low but can be trimmed to suit your needs. Good screen and windbreak, tolerates soot, salt, wind, and dust. Ideal for city backyards.
E. umbellata	Broad, silvery foliage	
Elm, Chinese (Ulmus Parvi)	Green foliage	Can be trained or trimmed to any size you wish (will grow to 40' untrimmed). Fast grower, becomes bushier from ground up with every trimming. Good windbreak, tight compact hedge for borders.

Hedge	Effect	Height and Growth Habit
Euonymus sarcoxie Emerald Pillar Shrub	Dark, shiny, green leaves.	Grows 6'-8' in compact columns, can also be used for entrances, corners. Makes solid green wall, evergreen the year round except in very cold regions.
Euonymus radicans erecta Winterberry Beauty	Shiny green foliage, red berries.	Evergreen wall 4'-5', depending how much you wish to trim. Sun or semi-shade.
Forsythia (Golden Bells)	Showy yellow flowers in spring, before leaves appear. Leaves green in summer, bronzy in fall.	Some varieties weep, others grow upright. Don't shear too heavily as you'll remove floral effect. Weeping types spread to 10', and are 8'-10' high. Upright types are 10'-12' high and about 10' wide. Neither type suitable for sheared hedge effect. Both ideal for screen effect.
Honeysuckle (*Lonicera* spps.)	Fragrant white or pink flowers; red berries are food for birds.	Best effect if allowed to grow to full height 10'-12'. Can be kept lower if desired. Ideal as fence, hedge, or border.
Hypericum (*Hidcote*)	Fragrant yellow, cup-like flowers June to mid-October.	In cold winters freezes back, but comes back in spring. Cut old growth to ground in spring. Forms a dainty little hedge (18" high) but not one that will give you privacy.
Korean Box (*Buxus koreana*)	Glossy foliage. Small-leaved.	3', clip into formal hedge or let it grow natural. Thrives in cold where other boxwoods will not.
Poplar, Lombardy	Fast-growing, high columnar hedge screen. Shiny foliage.	For best effect should be allowed to grow full height (50'), but can be trimmed any size. Hybrids are popular. All poplars susceptible to Cytospora canker. Prune out dead limbs, or cut back dead trees. New shoots come up from base. Tolerates wet soil.
Potentilla (Buttercup Flower)	Yellow flowers summer and late autumn. Creamy yellow foliage.	2'-3', tends to be sprawling. Ideal for low carefree hedges and needs only occasional trimming.

Hedge	Effect	Height and Growth Habit
Privets (*Ligustrum*) Several kinds: *L. regelianum* *L. ovalifolium* etc. *L. vicaria* (Chartreuse Shrub)	Glossy green foliage, berries all year long. Creamy yellow foliage.	Can be trimmed any height. For screen effect, allow to grow untrimmed to maximum height of 15'. California Privet freezes back at zero degrees. In spring, cut back to ground and new growth will appear.
Rhamnus frangula columnaris Upright Glossy Buckthorn	Glossy dark green foliage. White flowers, pink and red berries in fall.	Grows to 15', ideal for hedges, windbreaks, and background plant. Trim tops to desired height. Sides need no trimming. Ideal plant for along the sidewalk. Tolerates smog and polluted air. Good screen around swimming pools, patio, and property lines.
Rosa floribunda*	Flowers all season in a wide range of colors.	2'-3' high, ideal for hedges but for full effect do not shear tops or you'll remove buds.
Rose multiflora*	Robin Hood has small, white blooms, hybrid musk rose, small red flowers; thorny, glossy, dense foliage.	Normally grows 5'-6' but can be cut to any height. Needs room (grows up to 10' wide) and is not suitable for small properties.
Rosa rugosa*	Red blooms from June to October. Heavy crinkled green foliage. Large red fruits.	For flowers do not trim tops and avoid heavy shearing. 4'-6'. Especially valuable in seashore gardens and where winters are rough.
Spiraea vanhouttei "Bridal Wreath"	Graceful, arching branches of snow-white flowers in May.	5'-6'. Since flowers are formed on current year's growth, you can trim plant in early spring to any height.
Teucrium (Germander)	Fine-leaved, gray-green foliage.	1' high, sheared for border plantings. Effective with Santolina (ground cypress) in formal gardens.
Willow, Arctic *Salix Purpurea nana*; "Blue-Leaf Arctic Willow"	Narrow, gray-blue-green leaves.	3'-4', ideal for low-growing hedges. Can be clipped for formal effects, or left natural.

* See Chapter VII, ROSES FOR THE HOME GARDEN.

VINES FOR SECLUSION AND CHARM

As living spaces become smaller, there is a craving to enclose outdoor living areas. Vines are perfect for this purpose, giving a feeling of grace and airiness as well as cozy seclusion. Here is a list of good vines and their special interest features:

Vine	Description	Comments
Akebia (*Akebia trifoliata*)	Numerous small purple flowers in April, among dark green trifoliate leaves.	Grows very fast; not fussy as to soil. Will grow in sun or shade. No troubles.
Baltica Ivy (*Hedera helix* and other species)	New varieties come in green, gold, and purple, attractively-veined foliage. *H. cavendishii* is variegated. A crinkled variety also available.	Excellent evergreen cover when given something to climb on. Can be used as ground cover as well as for screening. All grow rapidly and do well in sun or shade. Red spider mites and scale sometimes bother. For control, see section on diseases and insects.
Bittersweet (*Celastrus loeseneri*)	Orange-scarlet berries cover the vines and last all winter. Good for dried arrangements. Green (sometimes greenish-white) leaves stay on the vine until late fall.	Can be trained on a trellis. Very vigorous: don't let it climb an apple tree or it will choke the tree.
Boston Ivy (*Ampelopsis veitchi*)	Maple-leaved foliage which turns a rich reddish-purple in autumn.	Tolerates any kind of soil as long as it is well drained. Likes full sun, preferring an eastern or southern exposure. Runners attach themselves readily to walls.
Clematis species	Beautiful star-shaped flowers in a wide range of colors; red, white, purple, pink, orchid, blue, and bicolors, in both single and double varieties. Both large-flowered varieties produce an abundance of bloom throughout the summer by careful selection of varieties. Long-lasting as cut flowers.	Does not give the screening effect other vines do but lends charm and distinction to any outdoor living area. Should be cut back each year for best growth, likes a loose, rich soil, kept moist by a good mulch. Crown should be covered with 2″ or 3″. Will grow in sun or semi-shade.

Vine	Description	Comments
Climbing Hydrangea (*Hydrangea petiolaris*)	Hydrangea-like white fragrant blossoms on short spurs among rich dark green shrub-like foliage.	Sturdy vine does well in sun or shade. Attains a height of 20' if left to grow but can be trained at a lower height. Not a fast grower but when established, forms a dense cover.
Dutchman's Pipe (*Aristolochia durior*)	Handsome heart-shaped leaves. Flowers bronzy, resembling a miniature dutch pipe—but not too showy.	Forms a perfect screen with its beautiful overlapping foliage. Adapts well in sun or shade. Vigorous, fast grower with no troubles.
Evergreen Bittersweet (*Euonymus kewensis* and *E. radicans vegetus*)	Handsome glossy foliage, female plants produce colorful berries. Variegated varieties as well as small-leaved ones available.	Grows well in sun or shade. Stems are woody and can be trained in shrub form. Clings well to any surface when allowed to grow as vine. May have same troubles as ivy but more resistant to them.
Firethorn (*Pyracantha*)	Showy trusses of creamy white flowers in late spring followed by orange-scarlet berries. Small-leaved evergreen foliage.	Can be trained in many shapes, as a shrub, a vine or a hard-to-penetrate hedge plant. Does well in dry soil.
Gold Hops (*Humulus lupulus*)	Golden form of the green variety which is used to make beer. Chartreuse fruit panicles hang gracefully among golden leaves.	Fast, easy grower. Hardy in any kind of soil. No troubles.
Honeysuckle (*Lonicera*)	Dainty pink or yellow blooms and combinations of the two on this old-fashioned, clean, strong vine.	No vine gives such nostalgic fragrance on a summer evening. Excellent on banks and can either be trained as a climbing vine or a ground cover.
Silver Lace Vine (*Polygonum*)	Foamy sprays of white flowers in summer. Small leaves. Rampant grower, profuse bloomer.	Grows very fast—15'-20' the first year. No insects bother it. Likes well drained soil and sunny exposure. Clings to any support.

Vine	Description	Comments
Trumpet Vine *Bignonia (Campsis)*	Comes in yellow and red varieties which bloom throughout summer into fall. Graceful compound leaf.	Flowers very showy. Hummingbirds love them. Completely hardy, with no particular soil needs. Clings tenaciously to whatever support is available. No insects bother it.
Wisteria	Magnificent clusters of pink, violet or white pea-like flowers on long panicles—some as much as 4'.	A tricky vine to grow. Advisable to grow the grafted varieties as they bloom earlier. Flower buds can be killed by extremely low temperature. Not recommended for Idaho, Me., Iowa, No. Michigan, Minn., Montana, Neb., N.H., Vermont, N.D., S.D., Wisc., Wyoming.

Hardy Ferns

Ferns are attractive and easy to grow; ideal for shady spots, though there are many that tolerate sun. They are excellent in a foundation planting, as a background for annuals or perennials, around birdbaths and pools, and in woodland settings, adding an air of grace and coolness.

Ferns are an ancient type of vegetation which occupied the world millions of years before seed-producing plants existed. They are strictly foliage plants and do not produce flowers. Ferns like a soil high in humus content, but will tolerate a variety of soils. Almost pure leaf mold is ideal. They also like an abundant supply of water.

The best time to transplant ferns is in the spring or in fall, a couple weeks after a frost. Keep the roots moist after transplanting. Plant most ferns about 10 inches apart.

Here are ferns for sunny or shady places:

Onoclea sensibilis (Sensitive Fern)	18″
Dennstaedtia punctiloba (Hayscented Fern)	24″
Pteretis nodulosa (Ostrich Fern)	30″
Woodwardia virginica (Virginia Chain Fern)	36″
Thelypteris palustris (Marsh Fern)	24″

Here are outdoor ferns only for shady situations

Adiantum pedatum (Maidenhair Fern)	18″-24″
Aspidium acrostichoides (Wood Fern or Polystichum)	12″
Aspidium spinulosum (Evergreen Wood Fern)	30″
Asplenium filix-foemina (Lady Fern)	24″-30″
Osmunda cinnamonea (Cinnamon Fern)	6″
Osmunda claytoniana (Clayton Fern)	24″-30″

TROUBLES: Outdoor ferns have few if any insect or disease pests. Burning of leaf tip and leaf edges is due to hot sun or dry soils. When shade-loving types get too much sun, the leaves turn yellow and the edges take on a scorched appearance.

Wildflower Gardening

A wildflower garden is not for everyone but can add something unique to your landscape. Most wildflowers are not difficult to grow once you understand their nature. You can start a wildflower bed two different ways: 1) buying plants or seeds from commercial growers; 2) gathering them from their native sites. Keep in mind that many are protected by law and cannot be gathered from native sites unless construction projects are going to uproot them.

Great care must be taken when digging wildflowers or they'll not survive. Many wildflower species have been depleted because of careless uprooting. Your best bet is to buy hardy wildflowers from a nursery. Nursery-grown plants are usually better suited to your garden than those dug up in the wild.

Success depends on planting wildflowers in the same conditions under which they grow naturally. For example, marsh marigolds, swamp iris, and cattails like boggy conditions. Arbutus, goldenrod, most asters, and daisies, and black-eyed Susans like poor, dry soil. Do not plant sun lovers in the shade and do not try to grow woodsy shade lovers in the sun. Take note of the conditions around your home before you attempt to start a wildflower garden.

Many of our favorite wildflowers like shade and humusy soil. The north side of the house where few tame flowers will grow can be made into a wildflower bed if the soil is prepared to resemble conditions where shade-loving plants are growing naturally.

Study wildflower catalogs and reference books before you plant. Flowers which grow naturally in wooded areas like generous amounts of humus in the soil, and moisture during hot weather.

Spring is probably the best time to start a wildflower garden, although some plants can be moved in fall. We've had good luck moving early-flowering species such as Dutchman's Breeches in fall. The secret is to keep the soil moist after transplanting, especially during a dry fall.

Warning! Be careful about adding wildflowers to your front lawn. Some neighbors may object to the *no one lives here* look of a wildflower front yard, and city officials sometimes frown upon wildflower yards and have passed ordinances prohibiting them.

Ornamental Grasses

Just as there is renewed interest in ferns and hanging baskets, there's a revival in the use of ornamental grass in home landscaping. See Chapter V for more information.

Landscaping Steep Slopes

Slopes present a problem to many home owners. If you don't keep them mowed or plant an aggressive ground cover, they grow into a jungle of weeds and detract from the beauty of your home. If grass is out of the question because of steepness, shade, or stoniness, then consider ground covers (see Chapter I). Crown Vetch is okay on steep rocky slopes, but don't expect it to compete with all weeds. Once it gets established it'll do a good job of covering a slope. It needs full sun and should be started by seed treated with a bacteria inoculum or by plants. Other suggestions include evergreen bittersweet (Euonymus), Hall's honeysuckle, pachysandra, and vinca. Pachysandra, or Japanese spurge, tends to develop yellowish foliage in full sun and dark green leaves in semi-shade. If you have the space, few things beat shrubs with attractive fruits and berries for winter effect and food for birds. Some include Indian currant (*Symphoricarpos orbiculatus*), red- and greenleaf barberry (*Barberis*), snowberry (*Symphoricarpos albus*), and honeysuckle (*Lonicera*), to name a few (see chart of *Plantings to Make Your Home More Attractive to Birds*). Shrubs for shady banks include Indian currant (*Coralberry*), snowberry, and sweet honeysuckle. Vinca (Periwinkle) and Vinca (Myrtle) also do well in a shady situation.

DRY STONE WALLS You don't need a cement wall to retain a slope. A dry stone wall (a wall made without mortar) is a handy device for holding a bank in place and is cheaper to build because it needs neither solid footing dug down below the frost line, nor forms to hold poured concrete. Usually, suitable stones can be found along the countryside. If you don't want to take the time to gather them or if none are available in your area, they can be found at lumber yards.

You can use flat field stones or rounded hardheads. Flat stones are easier to build with. They need a slight pitch of 1 or 2 inches for each foot of height. Fit the stones snugly together and don't forget to have them tilt or slope slightly into the bank so they won't buckle outward. An important fact to keep in mind: as each tier of stones is laid, tamp wet soil firmly in place behind them. If you do not do this the wall may collapse during or soon after a heavy rainstorm.

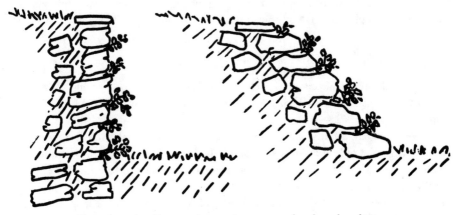

Two ways to handle steep slopes using stones and rock garden plants.

DOUBLE DRY STONE WALLS For high banks you can use two dry stone walls, separated by a level portion or terrace, 3 or more feet wide. This area can be mowed or used for a flower bed, low shrubs, or evergreens. If the bank is sloping it might be easier to have just one wall and plant the remaining slope with weeping shrubs, vines, or dwarf shrubs such as English ivy (*Hedera helix*), *Euonymus*, Hall's honeysuckle (*Lonicera*), or you can use forsythia, a fine weeping shrub for banks. Plant any of these in a staggered fashion across the face of the bank. With new plantings it's a good idea to place a mulch of peat, sawdust, lawn clippings, or straw on the ground around each shrub or vine to check erosion, keep weeds out, and retain moisture.

ROCK GARDENS Another way to handle a slope is to make a rock garden. This is done by setting rocks into the soil so that they protrude enough to make an attractive setting. Space is left between each rock, and soil added if needed. Small plants are set in these spaces so that they will fill the areas between the rocks. A good rule to follow is to select rocks which are similar in color and texture. They can be colorful, but not so varied that they are disquieting. Flowers should be selected in the same manner and put in groups. With a large enough area you may want to have plants for continual bloom. Whatever you do, don't make your rock garden look like a heavy pile of rocks. Plenty of space between each rock with carefully selected plants can make a pleasing scene in your landscape picture.

We do not wish to discourage anyone who is a rock garden lover, but the novice should bear in mind that rock gardens take much effort to keep them weeded and maintained. Eventually plants become established so that maintenance is less, but we never saw a rock garden that did not require care.

Some of the best plants for rock gardens are hardy varieties of sedum, echeveria, and sempervivens (hen-and-chickens). All include interesting shapes and sizes and are adaptable for planting between rocks. Foliage effect is their strong point but some have pretty blossoms as well.

For a list of some good bulbs, annuals, and perennials for the home rock garden, see the chapters on annuals, perennials, and bulbs. There are also a few low-growing evergreens such as Andorra and Bar Harbor Juniper, and others, which are suitable for rock garden plantings if kept pruned. Consult your nurseryman for those suitable in your area.

Trees

Today's landscape architects say a well placed shade tree in good health adds up to $1,000 to the value of your home. A tree that costs $30 today may be worth $250 or more in five to ten years.

When we talk about planting a tree we aren't necessarily referring to a giant oak, nor is a large plot of land needed. You can put in dwarf-size fruit trees that grow to be 6 to 10 feet tall. These trees are not only ornamental, but produce shade and fruit for the family.

PLAN BEFORE YOU PLANT Planning before planting a tree is even more important than when planting shrubs, because trees, once grown to a height, stand at their location virtually as a lifetime proposition. Moving them is difficult and often impossible, and they may inhibit growth of trees and shrubs nearby. Cutting a tree down later involves considerable work or expense, so selecting the right kind of tree and planting it in the right way in the right location on your first attempt is very important.

First, decide why you want to plant a tree. Is it for shade? For decoration? To obtain the tree's fruits? Or maybe for all of these reasons. Perhaps you want a tree which gives shade but doesn't clutter up the grounds below with falling fruits and flowers. If this last idea appeals to you, you need not give up planting trees such as maple, horse chestnut, and crabapple whose fruit production can be controlled and prevented by applying hormone sprays or chemical preparations available at your garden store (see *Preventing Unwanted Fruit*). Hormone sprays contain naphthalene-acetic acid, which, if applied at blooming time, according to manufacturers' directions, retards the tree's fruit-producing capability.

Keep sufficient space between trees. Consider the size of their roots and branches when fully grown. Crowded trees are likely to grow misshapen as their roots compete for food and moisture. Trees should never be less than 15 feet from any building and should be kept a safe distance from sewer pipes, cesspools, sidewalks, driveways, and curbs where their roots may cause damage or be injured or retarded. Note: Keep trees at least 50 feet away from septic tank or leach bed, as roots willl raise havoc. If you do use trees, insist on the small types such as mountain ash, flowering crab, red bud, etc. Maples and the larger trees will plug the lines.

If possible, avoid planting weak-wooded trees which break easily in storms and whose branches are brittle. These include catalpa, box elder, white and Carolina poplar, Chinese elm, silver maple, horse chestnut, tree of heaven, European white birch (susceptible to borers), and willow. However, since most of these are fast-growing and extremely tolerant of adverse conditions, there are times when they serve a useful purpose (a tree—Ailanthus—still grows in Brooklyn).

PLANTING Most trees prosper best in well drained soil containing humus, which is decomposed organic matter. Many gardeners fill the planting holes with rotted compost, peat, rotted manure, even dead fish. These materials not only provide the desired humus, but also help dry soil to hold moisture. On the other hand, good drainage is vital to a tree's quick recovery from the shock of being transplanted. Several inches of crushed stone or gravel in the bottom of the planting hole is often helpful in heavy soils.

All evergreen trees should be planted with their roots surrounded by a ball of soil (see Chapter III). Non-evergreen trees whose trunks about a foot above ground level measure less than 2 inches in diameter can be planted "bare root," without soil attached to their roots. But in that case the roots should be covered with moist burlap and never allowed to become dry. Cut frayed roots off bare-root trees before planting and, to compensate for this loss of nourishment-supplying roots, also remove one-third to one-half of the branches on the side and top, especially those branches which rub or criss-cross each other and those with weak crotches.

The planting hole must be large enough so the roots can be spread out. Otherwise, they might become tangled or intercrossed and eventually strangle the tree. If the leaves on one side of an established tree in late fall have a lighter color and fall earlier than normal, chances are the roots are strangling it due to improper planting.

Trees up to three inches in diameter should be supported by stakes or iron piping. Small trees moved with a ball of earth at the roots normally need no stake support.

While trees may be planted in spring or fall, fall planting is occasionally unsuccessful because of dryness rather than cold. Prolonged cold weather in winter can kill newly planted trees, but more often, trees planted in fall are killed by lack of moisture. Make

When selecting a tree for your home grounds, keep its future size in mind. This chart shows how large some common landscape trees will grow in ten years.

(Courtesy Morton Arboretum)

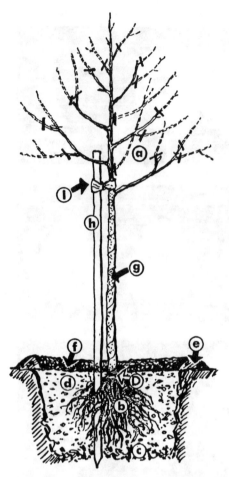

Planting a tree:
(a) Thin and shorten branches in a manner to preserve the natural form of the tree. In shortening branches, cut $1/4''$ above branch or bud. Entire lower branches may often be removed (cut close to trunk. (b) Cut cleanly all dried or broken roots. (c) Loosen bottom of hole; several inches of crushed stone or gravel may be added for drainage. (d) Plant in topsoil mixed with one-quarter peat moss or woods loam.

(e) Leave circular depression to catch water. (f) Mulch with peat moss or strawy manure. (g) Wrap with kraft tree tape or burlap to the lowest remaining branch. (h, 1) Stake, using proper means to protect tree from guy wire. (*Courtesy Kelly Bros. Nurseries*)

planted trees, but more often, trees planted in fall are killed by lack of moisture. Make sure newly planted trees go into the winter with plenty of moisture in the soil; water right up to hard freezing. Other helpful measures include applying an anti-dessicant (see *Winter Protection* in Chapter III) and wrapping the trunk.

WRAPPING THE TRUNK Wrapping of newly planted trees tends to prevent the bark from drying out; it also prevents sun scald (in winter, sun's rays hit the frozen trunk and cause alternate thawing and freezing, which splits the bark). You can use sisal wrap, burlap, aluminum foil, or waterproof paper in strips 4 inches wide (if they are short strips fasten them together at the ends). Start at the ground, wrapping spirally with about a 2-inch overlap, then wrap and tie with twine (never use wire) to hold in place. For a small tree you can also use various "tree guards" on the market.

WHEN WILL PLANTS BUD OUT? Many gardeners who plant dormant nursery stock such as roses, ornamental trees and shrubs wonder when their plants will start to bud out. Some of these items will fool you. For example, a locust can take as much as six months before buds start to break. Many newly planted fruit trees do the same, while

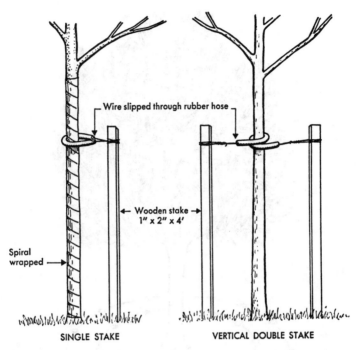

Wire slipped through rubber hose

Wooden stake
1" x 2" x 4'

Spiral
wrapped

SINGLE STAKE   **VERTICAL DOUBLE STAKE**

Newly planted trees should be staked until they become established. Never run a wire around the trunk, use a section of garden hose. (*Courtesy University of Maine*)

others will start to send out new shoots within a couple of weeks. One way to break the dormancy of nursery stock is to prune the tops back one-third at planting time. You can tell if your plants are alive or not by using the fingernail test. Gently skin back a portion of the bark; if it looks green and moist underneath, the plant is alive and should grow for you. Or test by breaking off a small piece of a shoot. If it snaps with a dry crackle, try a few more shoots. If these snap off as well, chances are the plant is dead.

FEEDING TREES Fall is the best time for feeding because it stimulates soil bacteria which break down minerals into a form a tree can absorb. There are three common ways to feed trees: 1) broadcasting, or scattering plant food on the ground; 2) punching holes in the ground and filling with either liquid or dry plant food; 3) root feeding with water pressure. Any one of the three is suitable, although many tree men prefer to punch holes in the soil. We have also seen orchardists all over the country apply dry fertilizer on top of the ground, without drilling holes, and they get results.

A crowbar makes a fine tool for making holes. Punch a series of openings 18 inches deep in concentric circles around the base of the tree. The first ring should be about 2-3 feet from the trunk, with holes spaced about 18 to 24 inches apart in the circle. Other circles should be placed three feet from each other until you reach the outside of the longest branch. Use about one pound of a balanced plant food for each inch of trunk circumference, or you can use a gallon of liquid solution for each hole.

To feed a tree punch holes around the tree in this pattern. Make holes 18 inches deep and 18 to 24 inches apart (a crowbar is a handy tool) at outer edge of the branches, or a foot or two beyond the dripline. (*Courtesy Michigan State University*)

The water pressure method consists of hooking a garden hose to a unit containing plant food cartridges (available in garden stores) fastened to a sharp metal rod. When water is turned on, the rod works its way to the root zone, where fertilizer is released.

PREVENTING UNWANTED FRUIT Often home owners have flowering or shade trees which produce unwanted fruit and seeds which interfere with the lawn mowing, clog gutter pipes, and make a mess around the place. To prevent this fruiting many have had good luck using synthetic hormone sprays containing napthalene-acetic acid (sold under various trade names such as Amid-Thin, App-L-Set, Parmone, etc.) which eliminate or greatly reduce fruit setting, retard fruit development, or cause dropping of young fruits without causing any apparent damage to the health of the tree. (See "Thinning Fruits" under *Apples* in Chapter XII.) These materials can be used to prevent fruit from setting on western catalpa, horse chestnut, Carolina poplar, Norway maple, tree of heaven, maidenhair-tree (Ginkgo), Kentucky coffee tree, crabapples, as well as many kinds of regular apple trees. The insecticide Sevin, also used for thinning fruit, is death on bees, especially when applied during the blooming period. We do not recommend it for fruit thinning for that reason.

Usually, the time to apply hormone fruit preventers is when the trees are in full bloom, or on tiny developing fruits. It only takes a small amount of spray to do the job.

PRUNING TREES This is best done in fall or winter when trees are leafless and you can see weak crotches, crossing or rubbing limbs, and poorly grown limbs. If your trees are large and you have had no experience along these lines, it is better to call a reputable professional arborist. If you need to thin limbs that are making your grounds too shady, the same applies. The cuts caused by pruning will heal fast in the early spring following winter pruning. Also, in winter the chances of tree diseases and insects are less because these enemies of trees are fewest then. Don't worry if a tree bleeds sap in winter. Summer pruning is necessary only when limbs begin scraping buildings or have grown so

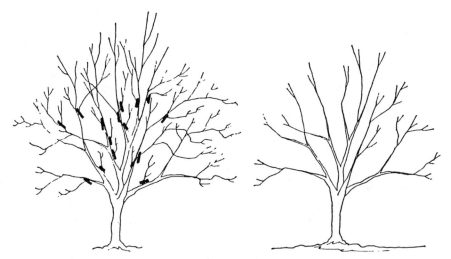

Pruning a flowering tree such as crabapple or hawthorn: Unpruned tree is shown at left, with marks indicating points where inner branches should be removed and length of remaining branches reduced. Make cuts as close as possible to the remaining branches. At right, pruning is complete.

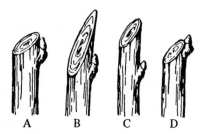

Right and wrong way of cutting off shoots when pruning:
(*Courtesy University of Maine*)

(A) Just right   (C) Too far from bud
(B) Too sloping and too far from bud   (D) Too close to bud

low as to pose danger or inconvenience. Prune limbs leaving a narrow collar. Pruning wounds need no wound dressing.

TREATING TREE WOUNDS If a tree wound does not heal properly, infection may set in and spread to the "heartwood" of the tree, weakening it and making it likely to collapse in storms or high winds. After a tree is wounded, its own defense system goes into action. It first forms a chemical barrier in the wood behind the wound to prevent infection. These barriers are effective in stopping wood-inhabiting bacteria and fungi. The wound often heals itself. But in some instances the bacteria may get through the

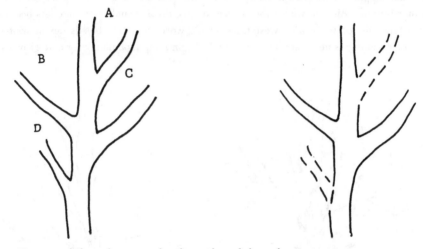

Narrow-angled crotches are weaker than wide-angled crotches. In pruning a young tree cut out the limbs making the narrowest angle with the trunk. A and D are too weak. B and C are just right. Drawing at right shows A and D removed, leaving the two wide-angled branches (B and C).

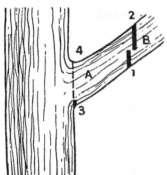

Removal of a large limb. Cut upward at (1) halfway through branch. Cut downward at (2) to finish removing bulk of branch B. Undercut branch at (3) to prevent bark tearing. Make final cut (4) leaving a narrow collar so bark can grow over the wound (A).

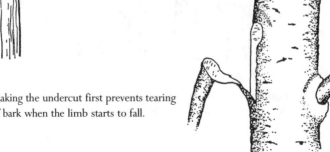

Making the undercut first prevents tearing of bark when the limb starts to fall.

protective chemical barrier. Then the tree has another line of defense: the injured cambium produces special cells that seal off or "compartmentalize" the wood that's infected. The microorganisms may spread up and down within this compartment, causing the wood to discolor and decay, but the decay does not spread sideways into new wood. It's like a tree within a tree. The old infected tree inside is sealed off from new wood. Not all the microorganisms are bad. One kind may block another and keep it from infecting the tree.

What can you do when a tree is gashed by a lawn mower or garbage truck, or damaged by fire, ice or a skidding car? If the damage is extensive call a good "tree man." If you can't afford his services and want to tackle the job yourself, do this: 1) Make all limb cuts at collar. Leave no stubs. 2) Take a good sharp knife and remove the injured bark and wood so that healthy bark is in contact with sound wood at the margins. This helps a tree help itself and brings about faster "compartmentalization" of the wound.

Right and wrong way of cutting off branches. (A) Wrong way, leaves stub which invites decay. (B) Right way: cut is made so a narrow collar remains on the trunk, and bark can grow over the wound.

 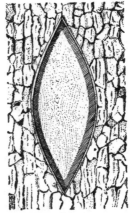

To repair an irregular-shaped wound, take a sharp knife and cut back as shown. Bark is trimmed in elliptical shape to allow rainwater to run off at bottom. (*Courtesy USDA*)

The best way to prevent decay on tree trunks is to avoid making a wound. Put a gravel mulch or a barrier around your trees so you don't crack into the bark with a mower. Anyone who cuts a tree limb off and leaves a 6-inch stub on the trunk ought to spend a night in jail. Tree stubs do NOT heal over. They rot out, forming a funnel that catches water, which favors more and more rot in the trunk.

(Left) You can save a tree which has been girdled by rabbits, mice, or deer by "bridge grafting" early in the spring (see instructions in propagation Chapter XV).
(Right) If only partially damaged, cover the injured area with moist sphagnum moss. Keep moist by wrapping securely with a sheet of plastic to keep tissue from drying out.

CALCULATING THE VALUE OF SHADE TREES Shade trees enhance the value of your home, as well as improve the environment. It's a good idea to take pictures of your shade trees NOW in case they are destroyed by a storm so you can claim income tax deduction for their loss. "Before" and "after" photos can help to substantiate your claim.

Just how valuable shade trees are in terms of dollars and cents is always debatable. The Internal Revenue Service contends that the value of a shade tree is the amount by which the value of the property as a whole is decreased as a result of loss of the tree. By this method of calculation, you can deduct only the loss in market value of your property. Many people think you can collect the replacement value of the tree that was destroyed. Not true.

We hope the time soon comes when the professional arborist's estimate will be the accepted authority for any property losses involving trees and other specimen plants.

TREE STUMPS Often home owners need to have a tree cut down, leaving a stump to look at for years. Before you cut down any tree, make sure it is absolutely necessary. Don't remove a tree (especially a large one) until you've considered all alternative solutions. Ask a reliable tree man to determine if a tree should be treated or saved.

If it must be cut down, and if you can afford to pay a little more to have the stump removed by a de-stumper, do so. If a stump is to remain you can use it to grow flowers such as petunias, morning glories, or nasturtiums. Place a window box, tub, or pan on top of the stump and fill it with flowers; or if there is a cavity, add soil and plant directly inside it.

If you live in an area where there is no regulation against burning, you can burn the stump out by soaking it with kerosene, saltpeter, used motor oil, etc. Drill holes into the stump about a foot deep and fill with these materials. A draft can be created by placing an old oil drum over it, with holes in each side. This acts as a chimney.

There's no magic material you can add to a stump to make it decay fast. The greatest wonder material you can use for reducing a stump is free, and is found in any woods. Look for a rotted log or stump and scoop up some of the woods earth and scatter it on the surface of the stump you want to remove. It takes about three years or so to rot it down.

If you want to get rid of a stump in a hurry, rent a de-stumping machine, a marvelous gadget which grinds the stump down in a jiffy. You'll get a bonus: wood chips, ideal for a mulch around trees, shrubs, and evergreens (see Mulches in Chapter XIII).

Insect and Disease Control for Trees and Shrubs

Ornamental plants fall heir to hundreds of insects and diseases not listed in this or any other book. By using an all-purpose pesticide you can avoid having to diagnose the trouble. We've had wonderful success with the all-purpose sprays suitable for trees, shrubs, and evergreens.

If you don't want to use an all-purpose spray, here are recommended treatments for the more common insects and diseases on an individual basis:

Pest or Disease	Pesticide to Use	Amount Per Gallon of Spray
Spider Mites	Detergent or buttermilk spray; (see Chapter XIV)	4 tbs.
Aphids	Malathion (25% wettable powder) or Nicotine sulfate	4 tbs. 1 tsp. to 2 qts. soapy water
Thrips, beetles chewing insects	Malathion (25% wettable powder)	4 tbs.
Leaf spots, rusts	Zineb (65% powder)	1 tbs.
Mildew	Karathane, 25% powder, or sulfur	$1/2$ tsp. Kar. 1 tbs. Sul.

Use slightly rounded tablespoons for the wettable powders. These are available at your garden store, mixed or separately. It's best to apply a pesticide before trouble begins. That means keeping a residue of spray on the foliage at all times by renewal doses every ten days. Applications are more effective when applied to dry foliage and allowed to dry on leaves in a short time. Do not spray flowers when in full bloom. If you use a dust, apply in the morning when dew is still on the foliage.

Some plants have a waxy leaf covering which causes sprays to run off or collect in droplets. Liquid household detergents make a fine "wetting," "spreading," or "sticking" agent if used with the pesticide at a rate of $1/3$ teaspoon per gallon of water. See Chapter XII (*Fighting Bugs Without Chemicals*) and Chapter XIV for a number of nonchemical controls to try on your ornamental plants.

SYSTEMICS: Systemic insecticides and fungicides are a hopeful tool in the gardening world for fighting pests. Once the systemic gets into the sap, it goes into all parts of the plant. When an insect bites a leaf, it gets some of the chemical in the sap and dies. Advantages to this type of bug-killer is that there is no residue on the outside, it can be applied to a tall tree without using a sprayer or special equipment, and it does not affect wildlife if properly applied.

You can apply systemic insecticides in three different ways: through the soil, through the foliage, or by direct application into the stem. For example, if you want to check the dreaded birch leaf miner, you can apply a granule systemic to the base of the plant. We prefer to punch holes around the tree or shrub, as described under feeding, and then put the systemic insecticide in the holes proportioned according to directions. Caution: Do not use on edible crops.

Other Troubles of Trees, Shrubs, and Evergreens

WHY TREES AND SHRUBS FAIL TO FRUIT OR FLOWER There are many reasons why trees and shrubs fail to flower and we'll mention a few:

1. Too rich a soil. Excess nitrogen gives lots of leaves and discourages flower bud formation. Stop feeding. You can cut down on the amount of nitrogen plants take up by root pruning. Insert a spade vertically into the soil at various places around the plant, going out as far as the spread of the branches. Severing roots stops the uptake of some of the nitrogen.
2. Too much shade. Heavy branches overhead will shut out light, as will a garage or other building. Plants that need sun just won't bloom in shade. Even some shade-tolerant plants bloom better in a well lighted spot.
3. Competition with nearby tree and shrub roots robs moisture and nutrients.
4. Age of the tree or shrub. Some plants, especially fruit trees (including ornamental crabapples) will not bloom or bear much before five years of age. Sooner or later they'll all bear.
5. Weather conditions. Frost during or just before blossoming period kills buds; severe winter cold will also often kill buds. Those closest to the ground may survive.
6. Pruning at the wrong time of year that removes flower buds. Try pruning your shrubs right after the blooming period is over and you won't remove next year's flower buds (see *Pruning Flowering Shrubs*).
7. Deep planting. Sometimes plants are set in too deeply, causing a lack of nitrogen around the roots. Poor drainage or too much water will cause the same problem.

GIRDLED TREES If trees could talk, they'd moan, "My girdle is killing me!" And they can be right, because many trees are slowly choking to death because of girdling roots. How do roots grow crooked enough to choke off nutrients and cause a tree to commit suicide? Two ways: 1) Improper planting. Some planters, eager to get rid of the roots of bare-root stock, wind them up like a ball of string before covering with soil. This happens especially when you have a small hole for a large plant. The roots grow and expand and gradually strangle the base of the tree. 2) Obstructions: Sometimes trees planted along a paved street suffer from girdling. Let's say that a gardener did spread the

girdling root

When planting a tree, make hole large enough. Never wad roots into a ball or allow them to criss-cross each other. Such roots strangle a tree as it grows.

roots out in all directions at planting time. The roots then grow out in all directions, but when a large root finds a barrier under a pavement, it tends to turn around and grow away from the street, heading toward the open areas between curb and sidewalk. This "bending" or changing direction may cause younger roots to cross over older roots, and tangling follows. Large rocks, wire fences that extend into the ground, cement sidewalks—any substantial barrier to tree roots—can also cause girdling. We often see the girdled mass on the soil surface. There may be a pronounced swelling at the base of the trunk, and some branches may show a dieback due to starvation.

Suggestion: Have an arborist look your tree over. He can take a mallet and a chisel and in a few minutes sever the root that's choking the tree. It's a good idea to take a 2-inch section out of the root to prevent the cut ends from reuniting. The cut surfaces are then coated with a tree paint or wound dressing.

Home owners should check their trees from time to time. Many don't and when they finally notice something is wrong, it is too late to help.

DON'T KILL YOUR TREES WITH SOIL A person who is having a home built should inform the builder he wants to save as many sound, well placed trees as possible. It takes anywhere from 20 to 50 years or longer to grow a good healthy full-size tree.

Many trees are needlessly killed by piling up soil around the base of the trunk during the grading process. While trees vary in their ability to take soil around their trunks, generally speaking, if the soil is sandy and well drained, the grade can be raised about six to eight inches without appreciable damage. However, if the soil is heavy and poorly drained, raising the grade 4 inches or so around a tree can shut off air to the roots and cause suffocation.

If getting a good slope on your lawn necessitates adding fill dirt, consider building a dry well of stones around the trunk to allow air and moisture to get to the trunk and roots. Lay the stones loose without cement between them. The size of a tree well depends on the size of the tree. Landscapers figure that the diameter of the well should be at least four times the diameter of a mature tree. If the tree is not fully grown, try to estimate the diameter it will be when it is mature. Tile drains running out laterally from the bottom aid drainage.

WINTER INJURY When a tree splits up and down the trunk, the trouble is very likely winter injury, known as "southwest injury." It gets its name from the fact that the southwest side of the tree is more often exposed to the sun and there's more freezing and thawing on that side, especially in soils that are poorly drained. Sometimes cracks develop in the bark on northern and eastern exposures, but more often the trouble is on the southwest side. *Control*: Take a sharp knife and trim off the loose bark back to live tissue, and the bark will heal over the wound.

White exterior latex paint or whitewash can be painted on a tree trunk to combat southwest injury. Either material can be painted completely around the trunk without injuring the tree, but has little if any effect on insects and diseases.

SALT DAMAGE Ten million tons of salt are used on American roads in one winter. A thousand pounds of salt per mile of roadway in a state such as Connecticut is not uncommon in single doses. When the snow melts, where does all this salt go? Sodium chloride and calcium chloride are the two salts commonly used as road de-icers. They dissolve and move freely with melted snow and ice. Waterways next to salted roads contain high concentrations of salt. Salt building up near highways can be toxic to plants; salt concentrations in the soil are high within 20 feet of the road. Salt has a harmful effect on soil structure. When salt dissolves, sodium is released and breaks down the particles, tightening up a soil. This reduces aeration and plants are often strangled. Tests in New Hampshire show that early fall leaf coloration and the decline of sugar maples along roads is associated with increased sodium in the wood and chloride in the leaves.

Damage from salt spray carried to the aerial parts of plants is noticeable especially on the side facing the wind. Evergreen needles turn brown. Fortunately, most grasses tolerate salt better than trees or shrubs.

Plants with resinous or scale-covered buds show little bud damage, as do evergreens with a wax or bloom on the needles. The bluer the spruce, the less it is harmed by salt spray. The most resistant trees are horse chestnut, Ailanthus, Norway maple, cottonwood, black locust, honeylocust, red oak, and sugar maple, as well as English and black walnuts, shagbark hickory, and chokecherry.

Least resistant to salt include bur oak, apple, hawthorn, box elder, amelanchier, white mulberry, and American beech. While the blue spruce and jack and mugo pine show little damage, white, red, and Scotch pines, yew, white spruce, and hemlock are very susceptible. In deciduous shrubs, the most resistant are caragana, staghorn sumac, common and Japanese lilacs, and honeysuckle. Least resistant are flowering quince, Bumaldi spirea, kolkwitzia, and gray and red osier dogwoods. Applying an anti-dessicant spray to the foliage will help protect trees and shrubs near a road. (See Chapter III.)

CARS CAUSE POOR PLANT GROWTH Automobiles affect trees and shrubs along roads and parking areas, as well as plants in your flower boxes and gardens, by sending out ozone, a toxic pollutant formed by the reaction of automobile exhaust and sunlight.

Internal combustion engines give off nitrogen oxides and unburned hydrocarbons. Sunlight causes a splitting of the nitrogen oxides to form atomic oxygen, which combines with nitrogen to form poisonous ozone (O_3), which not only causes damage to trees and shrubs but also to man and animals.

This pollutant is not restricted to main traffic areas, but is distributed into your home and greenhouse and gardens by air movement (wind). Depending on air speed, ozone concentration may spread 8 miles or so from the highway. Ozone causes more injury to plants than any other aerial toxicant. However, the automobile also produces others, such as carbon monoxide, fluorides, chlorides, sulfur dioxide, peroxyacetyl nitrate (PAN), and oxides of nitrogen, which plants and humans must cope with.

Ozone causes "flecking" on the leaves of plants. The flecks are dead spots in which chlorophyll has been destroyed. Ozone enters the plant's leaves through gates called stomata. When these gates are closed (night time, dry conditions) no fleck injury can occur because the ozone can't get into the leaf.

Ozone can also cause smaller flower size, change in flower color, reduced crops, and altered maturity dates. One researcher found that blossom size on petunia plants was reduced by 40 percent, with no visible injury to the plants' leaves. Other types of injury include bronzing, stippling, and bleaching of leaf surfaces. The injury may look like mite, red spider, aphid, or leafhopper injury, but when close examination does not reveal the presence of these pests, there's a good chance that injury may be due to ozone exposure. Maple, dogwood, various evergreens, redbud, oak, petunia, geraniums, morning glory, tomato, bean, squash, cucumber, and pumpkin are some of the more sensitive plants. Some plants are more resistant to ozone injury. Let's hope we will soon have cars which produce fewer nitrogen oxides and hydrocarbons from the tail pipes.

WEED KILLER DAMAGE If leaves of deciduous trees or needles of evergreens take on a twisted, distorted look, suspect damage from weed killers. "Weed and feed" preparations can drift from lawns onto trees and other plants. Never use weed killers on a windy day. Trees along the roadside are sometimes hit by weed killers sprayed by highway crews.

MOSS ON TREES HARMFUL? Is that green moss on the trunk of trees harmful? Moss rots shingles, but it does no harm to trees. The common sight of trees covered with algae and moss is nothing to worry about. In fact, such trees are nature's compasses. The moss is usually more abundant on the north side of the tree because the heat of the sun in that direction is not strong enough to dry out the bark. Moss and algae like damp areas where little sunlight penetrates. If you don't like the looks of the moss or algae you can eliminate it by spraying with the fungicide Maneb, 2 tablespoons to a gallon of water. Maneb is sold in garden stores under brand names such as Dithane M-22 and Manzate.

WALNUT POISONING Walnut trees secrete a toxic substance through the roots called juglone. This often kills ornamental plants as well as vegetables. Dead walnut trees do not exude the substance, nor is it found in walnut sawdust or wood chips. The following plants will tolerate walnut poisoning: beauty bush, tatarian honeysuckle, Norway spruce, common juniper, lliac, mock orange, hawthorn, variegated euonymus (vine), violet, bleeding heart, Jacob's ladder, phlox divaricata, blue hydrangea, hosta, tiger lily, daylily hybrids, bee balm, foxglove, white mulberry, black cherry, black locust, multiflora rose, blackberry, wild raspberry, bittersweet, purple nightshade, sweet rocket, goldenrod, violet, buttercup, and grasses of many varieties.

There are probably many more plants which can grow near a walnut tree. If you can grow fruit or vegetables near a walnut tree and they are not affected, it's perfectly safe to go ahead and eat the produce. Walnut poisoning does not affect the fruit and is harmless to humans.

GREEN THUMB FACTS ABOUT SOME FAVORITE LANDSCAPE TREES

Tree	Uses, Habits, and Features	Troubles	Control
Aesculus Horse Chestnut	Showy, white candle-like flowers and large leaves. Grows 60'. Messy habit of littering lawn with nuts and scorched leaves. Red-flowered variety sterile, avoids this problem.	Leaf scorch or drying of foliage. Due to dry weather or, sometimes, Anthracnose.	Captan (spraying not usually practical for small property).
Acer palmatum Japanese Maple	Fine specimen tree with bright red foliage. 15'.	Winterkills. Leaves turn olive green. Scorched leaves in summer.	None. Species are variable. Needs lots of water on hot days.
Acer platanoides Norway Maple	Used for lawn plantings, street trees. 70'.	*All maples are subject to the following problems to some degree:* Wilt disease may be caused by fungus or leaking gas. Maple gall mite, causes tiny galls which disfigure leaves. Galls many shapes. Leaf-chewing pests. Midsummer leaf fall due to wet spring, verticillium wilt, salt or road heat.	Have gas company check. Cut out dead limbs.
Schwedler's Norway Maple	Bright red spring foliage turning to bronze green. A slow grower, reaches 70'.		Lime-sulfur before leaves open.
Acer saccharum Sugar Maple	Grows 90', nearly maintenance-free. Striking fall coloration. Can be tapped for maple syrup.		Malathion. None for verticillium. Feed, water regularly to build up vigor.

Tree	Uses, Habits, and Features	Troubles	Control
Acer saccharinum Silver Maple	Weak-wooded, fast growing, 70′. Undersides of leaves and bark of trunk silvery. Can be tapped for maple syrup, as can sugar maple.	Frost crack or winter injury (southwest injury). Causes long fissures on south or south-west side of tree, sometimes full length of tree. Bleeding of broken or pruned branches. Wetwood (sap oozing down trunk). Woolly Maple Scale. Woolly aphids on underside of leaves.	Scrape loose bark back. Trees on poorly drained soil are more subject. Not serious. Insert drain tube. Malathion in early summer.
Ailanthus Tree of Heaven	A tough tree, grows in worst soils, all kinds of unfavorable conditions.	Weak-wooded. Odor of male flowers obnoxious.	Avoid it unless nothing else will grow.
Albizzia Mimosa	A fast grower, 20′ high. Foliage fern-like and attractive.	Winterkills. Hardy as far north as Washington, DC. Weak-wooded.	Prune out dead wood each year to strengthen it.
Betula Birch, Gray and Paper	Fine specimen trees. 50′. Canoe or paper birch is best.	Prone to borers, leafminer and die-back disease.	Start spraying with Lindane in May. Cut out dead branches. Use systemic insecticide for miners when trees are under 15′.
Cercis Redbud or Judas Tree	Fine specimen trees for small lawns. 15′-20′. Pink, white blooms and heart-shaped leaves.	None serious	
Cladrastis Yellow Wood	Clusters of pea-like yellow flowers in early summer, leaves arranged in feather fashion, 30′-40′.	Not absolutely hardy in North.	

Tree	Uses, Habits, and Features	Troubles	Control
Cornus Dogwood Tree	Fine selection of blossoms (white, pink, deep pink) and foliage effects (some varie-gated leaf types are striking). Ideal for small yard. To 20'. Resents deep planting; prefers moving in spring.	Crown rot, anthracnose, and leaf spot. Curling leaves (due to dry weather).	None. Spray with Cap-tan during bloom period and during summer. Keep watered and mulched.
Crataegus Hawthorn	Handsome small trees; 20'. Pink flowers bloom in clusters. Wood is spiny.	Leaf spot disease.	Captan spray weekly.
Fagus (Beech)			
F. sylvatica European Beech	Leaves turn bronzy late fall. 50'-60'.	All beeches are threatened by a new beech disease— to prevent it be sure to avoid hitting the trunk with lawn mower, etc., to avoid a wound that will give the fungus a point of entry (beeches are thin-skinned). All beeches occa-sionally troubled by aphids.	
F. s. atropunicacea Purple-leaf Beech	To 50'.		
F. s. pendula Weeping European Beech	To 50'.		
F. s. riversi River's European Beech			
F. sylvanica *asplenifolia* Fern-leaf Beech	A beautiful tree, 50'-60'.		
F. grandifolia Common American Beech	Can't be bought in nurseries but you can start one from a beech nut; to 60'. Smooth silvery-gray bark, edible nuts.		
Gleditsia *triacanthos inermis* (also see Locusts under *Robinia*)	Thornless honey locusts, many varieties also seedless, com-pound leaves, clusters of pink or white flowers, 35'-50', in-cludes Shademaster, Sunburst, Moraine, Imperial honey locusts.	Spider mites, leaf-hoppers, mimosa webworm in some areas.	Spray with Malathion in summer.

Tree	Uses, Habits, and Features	Troubles	Control
Hamamelis Witch Hazel	Interesting "off season" trees. 20′-30′, blooming in fall or winter when snow is on ground.	None	
Koelreuteria Golden Rain Tree	Attractive small tree to 15′, ideal for small properties, Yellow flowers in clusters 12″ long in summer, bladder-shaped seed pods in summer and fall. Leaves arranged in feather fashion.	None	
Larix Tamarack, Larch or Hachmatack	Valuable timber tree and ornamental conifer: a semi-evergreen losing its needes. 70′.	Larch sawfly which strips foliage.	Malathion in late May.
Magnolia Magnolia	Spectacular trees, ideal for specimen plantings. Not all hardy. 20′-30′. White, pink blossoms early spring.	Scale and mealybugs cause black mold, suck sap.	Malathion, 2 $\frac{1}{2}$ pints of 50% per 100 gals. of water in August.
Malus Crabapple	Smart colorful lawn trees, 10′-20′. Fruit used for jelly. Hopa, Almey, dolgo, and hyslop produce clouds of pink and white blooms in spring, red fruit in fall. Betchel's Crab has double flowers, soft pink blossoms, no fruit.	Susceptible to borers and other troubles of apples (see Apple).	Keep sprayed with Malathion and Captan.
Platanus Sycamore, London Plane, Buttonball	Hardy tree; ideal for landscaping under adverse conditions of soil, smoke, soot or smog. 70′. Some feel tree is messy.	Leaf scorch, which is not serious. Anthracnose causes brown foliage to shed.	None that's practical. Rake fallen leaves and burn. Tree usually recovers.

Tree	Uses, Habits, and Features	Troubles	Control
Populus Poplar	While a poor land-scape tree, useful for preventing soil erosion, windbreaks, and along highways. 70'.	Female trees shed messy "cotton" flowers. Trees are weak-wooded and susceptible to cyostospora or wilt.	No control.
Prunus Flowering Plums, Cherries, Almonds, Peaches	Few ornamentals are more breathtaking than the Prunus group. Varieties with single and double flowers. All excellent for small yard, up to 30'. One of showiest is *Prunus subhirtella pendula*, Weeping Japanese Cherry. Many flowering plum varieties have purple foliage as striking as the blossoms.	Same trouble fruit cherries have (see Cherries). Borers in trunk.	Keep trees sprayed with Captan and Malathion when not in bloom. Fill holes with borer paste.
Quercus White, Red, Pin Oaks	Among finest of trees, withstand storms, have fewer insects and diseases. Wonderful lawn trees. 70'. Oaks put on our most colorful show in fall. They need good drainage for best growth.	Oak galls. Oak wilt fungus, a new threat to every species.	Lime sulfur dormant spray. Avoid injuring tree. Prune in late summer.
Q. coccinea Scarlet Oak	To 70'. Scarlet in autumn.	None	
Q. imbricaria Shingle Oak	Pyramidal when young, rounded top at maturity, fast-growing, 50'-60'. Bronzy leaves in fall. Ideal for lawns, street plantings, specimen trees.	None	
Q. palustris Pin Oak	Pyramidal shape, finely "cut" leaves, orange-red in fall. Fastest growing of the oaks.	Gets iron chlorosis (leaves turn yellow) in wet, alkaline soils.	Give good drainage. Apply iron chelates to soil

Tree	Uses, Habits, and Features	Troubles	Control
Q. rubra maxima Eastern Red Oak	50'-60', large leaves, dull red in fall, kept on the tree late.	Will not tolerate pollution.	
Robinia hispida Locusts Do not confuse with Honeylocusts which are gleditsia (see Landscape chart)	Trees grow 40'-50', some have clusters of pink or white flowers in early summer. Trees leaf out late in spring.	Borers, but not fatal. Leaf miner.	None Spray with Malathion in summer.
Salix Willows	Picturesque trees with graceful drooping branches, considered a "weed" by many. Tree is messy and sheds twigs, a nattural habit, 70'.	Short-lived; has heavy root systems, often troublesome. Tar spot and black scab. Willow beetles.	Plant at least 40' from sewer lines. Wettable sulfur in spring. Malathion in June.
Sophora Japonica Japanese Pagoda Tree, Chinese Scholar Tree	Lone grape-like yellow-white blooms July to September. Grows 40'-50'. A wonderful tree for streets and small space.	None	
Sorbus Mountain Ash	Highly desirable lawn tree, 30'. Upright and globular forms. Showy orange berries, ideal for jelly, bird food.	Lack of flowers or berries. Borers. Fireblight.	Age. Trees bear 5 to 7 years. May be due to poor weather at pollination time. Fill holes with borer paste. Prune out dead limbs.
Ulmus Elms	Stately trees, 70'. Graceful, clean habits of growth. New hybrids resistant to Dutch Elm disease.	Dutch Elm disease. Wetwood disease, sap flows down trunk. Elm leaf drop due to fungus. Elm leaf beetle causes leaves to be riddled with holes.	None. Use resistant elm strains. Insert drain tube to carry off fermented sap. Don't worry about it. Rake leaves in fall. Spray with Malathion about June 1.

Green thumb note: Trees have many problems not listed in this chart: Leaf-chewing insects and diseases such as leafspot and twig blight, to name a few. (See all-purpose spray formula under *Shrubs*). Usually Malathion, Captan, or Ferbam will check most insect and disease pests. Dogs can burn a tree. In a city such as New York, about 60,000 trees are lost yearly, and the greatest part of this loss is blamed on dogs. A screen protects against this type of injury (see Chapter XVII). Man, too, brings about many tree troubles, by burning leaves under a tree or by hitting it with a lawn mower. Feed your trees regularly to build up vigor, and usually they'll live as long as you do, with proper selection of species.

"TAILORED" SHADE TREES

You no longer have to worry about planting a tree too large for your property. There are trees "tailored" to fit any situation. Though nurserymen have been slow to accept the "tailored" tree concept, more and more are handling smaller trees. One who has done a lot to develop the idea is Edward H. Scanlon of Olmstead Falls, Ohio. Mr. Scanlon has traveled all over the world in search of compact trees for street plantings and gardeners who are looking for "something different" to fit today's crowded spaces.

Here are a few trees to consider where space is more or less limited:

Latin Name	Common Name	Height in Feet
Acer platanoides Cleveland	Cleveland Norway Maple	30
Acer rubrum conica Scanlon	Scanlon Red Maple	30 to 50
Acer buergerianum	Trident Maple	25
Aesculus castanea brioti	Ruby Red Horse Chestnut	30
Betula pendula gracilis	Cutleaf weeping birch	35
Carpinus betulus pyramidalis	Pyramidal European Hornbeam	35
Carpinus betulus quercifolia	Oakleaf European Hornbeam	25
Crataegus oxycantha Paulii	Paul's Scarlet Hawthorn	25
Crataegus lavallei	Lavalle Hawthorn	25
Fraxinus excelsior umbraculifera	Globeheaded European Ash	27
Ginkgo biloba var. Palo Alto	Palo Alto Ginkgo	35
Koelreuteria paniculata	Golden Rain tree	25
Laburnum vossii	Golden Chain tree	15
Malus sp.	Flowering Crabapples	15
Phellodendron amurense	Chinese Cork tree	39
Prunus sp. (a large family)	Flowering plums, cherries	20
Pyrus calleryana	Callery Pear	30
Quercus sp.	Various oaks including Sawtooth, shingle, red, white	40
Robinia hispida macrophylla	Flowering Globe Locust (pink)	40
Sophora japonica	Chinese Scholar tree	30
Sorbus aucuparia	European Mountain Ash	30
Tilia cordata	Little-leaf Linden	30
Ulmus Carpinifolia	Buisman elm	35
Zelkova serrata	Japanese Keaki Tree or Zelkova "Elm"	40

TREES LISTED ACCORDING TO SIZE

Here are a few ornamental trees to consider for your property. See your nurseryman about them. If he doesn't have them, he may be able to suggest substitutes.

TREES 20 TO 35 FEET IN HEIGHT

Latin Name	Common Name
Acer ginnala	Amur Maple
Acer palmatum	Japanese Maple
Amelanchier laevis	Shadblow
Aralia spinosa	Hercules Club
Asimina triloba	Pawpaw
Caragana arborescens	Siberian Pea Tree
Carpinus caroliniana	American Hornbean ("Musclewood")
Catalpa bungei	Catalpa
Cercidiphyllum japonicum	Katsura tree
Cercis canadensis	American Redbud
Chionanthus virginicus	White fringe tree
Cladrastis lutea	Yellow Wood
Cornus florida and *C. mas*	Dogwood, Cornelian Cherry
Crataegus oxycantha (and other varieties)	Hawthorn
Eleagnus angustifolia	Russian Olive
Halesia	Silver Bells or Snowdrop Tree
Hamamelis virginiana	Witch Hazel
Hydrangea paniculata grandiflora	Pee Gee Hydrangea
Koelreuteria paniculata	Golden Rain Tree
Laburnum vossi	Golden Chain Tree
Magnolia soulangeana	Saucer Magnolia
Magnolia stellata	Star Magnolia
Malus arnoldiana, *M. atrosanguinea* *M. floribunda* *M. ioensis* (double) *M. purpurea*	Crabapple, all ideal for the small property owner.
Malus sylvestris	Common Dwarf Apple
Ostrya virginiana	Hophornbeam
Prunus cerasifera and variants	Purple Leaf Plum
Pyrus calleryana	Bradford Pear
Rhus aromatica *R. copallina* *R. typhina*	Fragrant Sumac Shiny Sumac Staghorn Sumac
Sophora japonica	Japanese Pagoda or Chinese Scholar Tree
Sorbus aucuparia	European Mountain Ash
Syringa amurensis japonica	Japanese Tree Lilac
Syringa vulgaris	Common Lilac trained to "tree"

TREES 40 TO 50 FEET OR MORE IN HEIGHT

Latin Name	Common Name
Acer platanoides	Norway Maple, includes red-leaved sports such as Schwedler's, Crimson King, etc.
Acer rubrum	Red Maple
Acer saccharum	Sugar Maple
Acer saccharinum	Silver Maple
Betula lutea	Yellow Birch
B. papyrifera	Paper Birch
B. pendula	European White Birch
B. populifolia	Gray Birch
Carya ovata *	Shagbark Hickory
Castanea mollissima *	Chinese Chestnut—two trees needed for nut production
Fagus grandifolia	American Beech
F. sylvatica	European Beech, has many shapes; Pyramidal, Weeping, Purple-leaved, Tricolored copper, and Golden Yellow, and also a fern-leaved variety.
Fraxinus americana	American or White Ash
Ginkgo biloba	Maiden-Hair tree
Gleditsia triancanthos	Honeylocust—includes "Sunburst" and "Moraine" Locusts
Juglans nigra *	Black walnut
J. cinerea *	Butternut
J. sieboldiana *	Heartnut
J. regia *	Persian or English Walnut
Liquidambar styraciflua	Sweetgum
Liriodendron tulipifera	Tulip Tree
Magnolia acuminata	Cucumber Tree
Platanus acerifolia	London Plane Tree, Sycamore
Populus tremuloides	Quaking Aspen
Prunus serotina	Black Cherry
Quercus borealis	Red Oak
Quercus imbricaria	Shingle Oak
Quercus palustris	Pin Oak—fastest grower in Oak family
Quercus coccinea	Scarlet Oak
Robinia pseudoacacia	Black Locust
Salix alba var. tristis	Weeping Willow
Salix alba var. vitellina	Golden Willow
Salix babylonica	Babylon Weeping Willow
Tilia americana	Basswood, or American Linden
Tilia cordata	Little-leaf European Linden or European Basswood
Ulmus pumila	Chinese Elm

*If you're not prepared to gather nuts in fall, do not plant nut species because they interfere with mowing.
Note: Nuts of Juglans species listed here are edible.

TREES AND SHRUBS FOR WINDBREAKS AND PRIVACY

Almost any tree can be used as a windbreak. The size you use depends upon the size of your property.

Common Name	Latin Name	Screen or Windbreak
Arborvitae (pyramidal)	*Thuja occidentalis*	Screen and Windbreak
Ash	*Fraxinus*	Windbreak
Austrian Pine	*Pinus nigra*	Windbreak
Colorado Spruce	*Picea pungens*	Screen and Windbreak
Eastern Red Cedar	*Juniperus virginia*	Screen and Windbreak
Fir	*Abies*	Windbreak
Hawthorn	*Crataegus*	Screen
Hemlock (Canadian)	*Tsuga canadensis*	Screen and Windbreak
Holly (American)	*Ilex opaca*	Screen
Hornbeam	*Carpinus*	Windbreak
Lilac	*Syringa*	Screen
Lombardy Poplar	*Populus*	Screen and Windbreak
Norway Maple	*Acer platanoides*	Windbreak
Oaks	various *Quercus*	Windbreak
Osage Orange	*Maclura*	Windbreak
Russian Olive	*Eleagnus*	Screen
Siberian Spruce	*Picea omorika*	Windbreak
Siberian Pea Tree	*Caragana*	Screen and Windbreak
Sugar Maple	*Acer saccharum*	Windbreak
Upright Japanese Yew	*Taxus*	Screen
White Spruce	*Picea glauca*	Windbreak
White Pine	*Pinus strobus*	Screen and Windbreak

TREES THAT TOLERATE CITY CONDITIONS

City trees take a beating from smoke, poor light, dust, and dozens of other pollutants. Still, there are some that do well in spite of these adverse conditions.

Latin Name	Common Name
Acer campestre	Hedge Maple
Acer platanoides	Norway Maple
Ailanthus altissima	Tree of Heaven
Crataegus phaenopyrum	Washington Hawthorn
Fraxinus americana	White Ash
Fraxinus excelsior	European Ash
Fraxinus pennsylvanica	Green Ash
Gymnocladus dioicus	Kentucky Coffee Tree
Gleditsia triancanthos cultivars	Honey Locust

Latin Name	Common Name
Koelreuteria paniculata	Golden Rain Tree
Malus species	Flowering Crabapples
Phellodendron amurense	Amur Corktree
Picea pungens	Colorado Spruce
Platanus species	Plane Tree, Sycamore
Quercus rubra maxima	Eastern Red Oak
Quercus imbricaria	Shingle Oak
Sophora japonica	Japanese Pagoda Tree
Tilia species	Linden

SOME TREES THAT TOLERATE PARTIAL SHADE

Not many trees take a heavily shaded situation, but some take that shade better than others. Here are a few recommended by Ohio State University.

Latin Name	Common Name
Amelanchier species	Serviceberry, Shadbush
Carpinus species	Hornbeam
Cercis canadensis	Eastern Redbud
Cornus alternifolia	Pagoda Dogwood
Cornus florida	Flowering Dogwood
Halesia species	Silverbell
Ilex species	Holly
Magnolia virginiana	Sweetbay Magnolia
Styrax japonicum	Japanese Snowball
Thuja occidentalis	American Arborvitae
Tsuga canadensis	Canadian Hemlock
Viburnum lentago	Nannyberry Viburnum

SOME SHRUBS THAT TOLERATE SHADE

Latin Name	Common Name
Hydrangea	Hydrangea, Hills of Snow
Kalmia	Mountain Laurel
Lonicera tatarica	Sweet Honeysuckle, Tatarian Honeysuckle
Rhododendron	Azalea & Rhododendron
Symphorocarpos albus	Snowberry
Symphorocarpos orbiculatus	Coralberry, Indian Currant
Taxus	Taxus, upright and spreading Japanese Yew

TREES AND SHRUBS THAT TOLERATE MOIST SPOTS

Latin Name	Common Name
Arborvitae	Thuja or Arborvitae
Acer rubrum	Red or Swamp Maple
Acer platanoides	Norway Maple
Acer saccharinum	Silver Maple
Acer negundo	Box Elder
Alnus glutinosa	European Alder
Amelanchier species	Sarvis, June Berry, Service Berry
Betula nigra	River Birch
Betula pendula	European White Birch
Calycanthus	Sweet Shrub
Carpinus caroliniana	American Hornbeam
Carya species	Bitternut Hickory
Cercidiphyllum japonicum	Katsura Tree
Cercis canadensis	Redbud, Judas Tree
Clethra	Pepper Bush (shrub)
Cornus alternifolia	Pagoda Dogwood
Cornus species	Red-Stemmed Dogwood, Osier, etc. (shrub)
Cornus mas	Cornelian Cherry, Dogwood
Fraxinus species	Ash
Gladitsia triacanthos	Thornless locusts such as Moraine, Shademaster, Sunburst, etc.
Latex species	Larch
Liquidambar stryraciflua	American Sweetgum
Magnolia virginia	Sweet Bay Magnolia
Metasequoia glyptostroboides	Dawn Redwood
Populus species	Lombardy and other poplars
Sambucus	Elderberry (shrub)
Spirea macrothrysa	Everblooming Pink Spirea (shrub)
Salix species	Pussy Willow (shrub) & Weeping Willow
Taxodium distichum	Bald Cypress
Tilia americana	American Basswood
Tsuga canadensis	Canadian Hemlock
Viburnum opulus	High-Bush Cranberry (shrub)

TREES THAT TOLERATE DRY SOILS

Whenever you plant a tree in sandy soil, always add some rotted compost or other form of organic matter to prevent rapid drainage. Here are a few trees that will take dry soils (recommended by Ohio State University).

Latin Name	Common Name
Acer buergerianum	Trident Maple
Acer campestre	Hedge Maple
Acer ginnala	Amur Maple
Acer platanoides	Norway Maple
Acer tataricum	Tatarian Maple
Ailanthus altissima	Tree of Heaven
Betula populifolia	Gray Birch
Corylus colurna	Turkish Hazel
Elaeagnus angustifolia	Russian Olive
Fraxinus pennsylvanica	Green Ash
Gymnocladus dioicus	Kentucky Coffee Tree
Gleditsia cultivars	Honey Locust
Juniperus species	Juniper
Koelreuteria paniculata	Golden Rain Tree
Pinus sylvestris	Scotch Pine
Sassafras albidum	Sassafras
Sophora japonica	Japanese Pagoda Tree

SHRUBS FOR DRY PLACES

Latin Name	Common Name
Barberis	Barberry, Green leaf, Red leaf
Forsythia species	Forsythia
Hibiscus moscheutos	Hibiscus
Ligustrum amurense	Amur River Privet
Lonicera tatarica	Tatarian Honeysuckle
S. albus	Snowberry
Symphoricarpos orbiculatus	Coralberry or Indian Currant

TREES AND SHRUBS FOR FALL COLOR

Common Name	Latin Name	Shade
PREDOMINANTLY RED		
Dogwood	*Cornus* species	Bright Red
Franklinia	*Gordonia*	Crimson
Katsura Tree	*Cercidiphyllum schwedleri*	Bronze, scarlet, and gold
Red Maple	*Acer platinoides*	Purplish-red summer and fall
Red Maple	*Acer rubrum*	Brilliant red in fall
Oak	*Quercus* (species)	
(Note: All oaks are	*Q. coccinea* (Scarlet Oak)	Red
showy in fall)	*Q. imbricaria* (Shingle Oak)	Reddish-pink
	Q. palustris (Pin Oak)	Red

Common Name	Latin Name	Shade
Shadblow	*Amelanchier*	Red, yellow tints
Sourwood	*Oxydendrum*	Scarlet red
American Sweetgum	*Liquidambar*	Red with gold and bronze

PREDOMINANTLY ORANGE

Common Name	Latin Name	Shade
Hawthorns	*Crataegus*	Yellow-orange
American Hornbeam	*Ostrya*	Reddish-orange with yellow tints
Sugar Maple	*Acer saccharum*	Brilliant reddish-orange

PREDOMINANTLY YELLOW

Common Name	Latin Name	Shade
Mountain Ash	*Sorbus*	Bronzy yellow
White Ash	*Fraxinus*	Yellow and other tints
Beech	*Fagus* species	Yellow, deep brown in winter
Cherry (Flowering)	*Prunus*	Deep yellow
Kentucky Coffee Tree	*Gymnocladus*	Brown pods showier than yellow foliage
Ginkgo	*Ginkgo*	Gold
Hickories	*Carya* species	Yellow
European Larch	*Larix*	Yellow, then brown
Linden	*Tilia*	Yellow, then brownish
Locust	*Gleditsia*	Yellow, muddy brown later

YELLOW

Common Name	Latin Name	Shade
Poplar	*Populus* species	Long-lasting bright yellow leaves
Norway Maple	*Acer Platinoides*	Gold
American Redbud	*Cercis*	Light yellow
Tulip Tree	*Liriodendron*	Orange-yellow
Black Walnut	*Juglans*	Yellow
(note: All walnut species turn yellow in fall)		
Willow	*Salix* species	Last to lose their yellow leaves in fall

TREES AND SHRUBS THAT PROVIDE FOOD FOR BIRDS Birds are the best pesticide you can get: a pair of flickers can eat 5,000 ants in one meal, a brown thrasher can eat 6,180 insects in less than twenty-four hours, a pair of warblers can rid your plants of 12,000 aphids in one day. Birds are thankful friends and you can keep them around your home just by seeing that they have a place to nest and food to eat.

All coniferous evergreens provide food for various species of birds when cones open and discharge the seeds. However, their chief value in attracting birds is that most of them provide ideal nesting places, especially the spruces and firs. The dense foliage hides nests, and the needles discourage predators. The best plantings for birds are provided by using berried shrubs and trees plus some spruce trees for nesting.

Some trees and shrubs especially attract birds, and while our list is by no means complete, the plants listed are generous with their berries and seeds, and can be found in most nursery catalogs.

FRUIT-PRODUCING TREES AND SHRUBS
ATTRACTIVE TO BIRDS

Tree or Shrub	Features	Comments
Birch (all species) *Betula*	Flowers green and brown catkins. Fruit flaky seeds.	All birch have seeds attractive to birds from early fall to late winter.
Blueberry, High-Bush Blueberry *Vaccinium corymbosum*	Flowers white to pinkish; late May. Fruit blue-black; fall.	One of the *most* sought after berries. Buy recommended variety in your area.
Cherry, Fire or Pin *Prunus pennsylvanica*	Flowers white; early May. Fruit small, red; late August.	Beautiful in flower, this great favorite of 80 species keeps birds away from cultivated fruit.
Cornelian Cherry *Cornus mas*	Flowers mass of tiny yellow blooms in March. Fruit scarlet; August.	Attractive ornamental, food, and nesting tree. Proper pruning can make it into a 12′ to 15′ tree. Free from pests.
Crabapple, Japanese Flowering *Malus floribunda*	Flowers pink to white; early May. Fruit yellow and red; late August to mid-October.	Hardy, dependable for food and nesting. Small apple-like fruits remain for winter birds. For other outstanding varieties try *M. zumi calocarpa* and *M. Red Jade.*
Sargent Crabapple, *M. sargentii*	Flowers white, mid-May. Fruit deep red; fall.	
Cotoneaster, Early *C. adpressa praecox*	Flowers white; June. Fruit scarlet; September.	Spectacular, low semi-evergreen, with masses of bite-size berries. Also good are Mayflower, *C. multiflora calocarpa* and *C. horizantalis*, both higher branching, with profuse berries.
Dogwood, White Flowering *Cornus florida* Dogwood, Japanese *C. kousa*	Flowers white; mid-May. Fruit bright red; fall. Flowers white; mid-June. Fruit bright scarlet.	Loveliest small ornamental tree native to the east. At least one hundred birds eagerly feed on these bright berries. Fine for migrating as well as winter birds. Japanese Dogwood equally popular.

Tree or Shrub	Features	Comments

Shrub Dogwood
  Cornus alba siberica,
  C. racemosa
  C. stolonifera
	Flowers yellowish-white, late May. Fruit white to blue, July.	*C. racemosa* is thicket forming, with fruits on red stems. Red-Osier, *C. stolonifera*, has brilliant red branches, spreads easily. All make striking winter display and pruning keeps them so. Coral Beauty superior.

Elderberry *Sambucus canadensis*	Flowers cream, June. Fruit purple; August to October.	Seven leaflets on a stem set off flat wheel-like clusters of blooms. An attractive fruiting shrub. (See Chapter XII.)

Firethorn
  Pyracantha, coccinea
  laandii
	Flowers June. Fruit orange-red; October.	Masses of brilliant berries in fall and winter make good emergency food. Heavy evergreen foliage provides cover. Try *P. wateri*, compact, hardy; also *P. rogersiana* (dwarf red).

Hemlock *Tsuga canadensis*	Flowers May Fruit cones all year.	Particularly good for nesting and shelter. Seeds in small cones are fine fall and winter food.
Hawthorn, Paul's Scarlet *Crataegus oxyacantha*	Flowers deep pink; June. Fruit red berries; late summer to fall.	Compact, 20'-30'. Small-leaved tree laden with double-pink flowers followed by red berries.
Hawthorn, Washington *Crataegus phaenopyrum*	Flowers white, mid-June. Fruit bright red.	Fine nesting tree. Its clusters of profuse berries are unsurpassed for lasting into winter.
Honeysuckle, Tatarian *Lonicera tatarica*	Flowers deep pink, light pink or yellow; May, June. Fruit red berries; July through early fall.	Tall, dense shrub. Will grow to 10' to 15'.
Holly, American *Ilex opaca*	Flowers inconspicuous, white. Fruit scarlet; all winter.	Our best holly native to the Eastern Seaboard and one of the most attractive trees to birds. Desirable to one hundred varieties. Special favorites are St. Mary's, shrubby, and Croonenburg. Both sexes needed for fruit. (See Chapter III.)

Tree or Shrub	Features	Comments
Holly, Japanese *Ilex crenata*	Flowers white. Fruit black.	Seventy-five hardy attractive varieties, small and tall. All liked by countless species of birds. Try *I. pernyi, I. convexa;*
Holly, English *Ilex aquifolium*	Flowers white, berries red; leaves lustrous green. 40' tall.	*I. pendunculosa* is shrubby, hardy, with spineless leaves, brilliant fruit on drooping stems. Hardiest of deciduous hollies are Winterberry, *I. verticillata* and *I. serrata*, hardy to -15 degrees F.
Magnolia, Star *M. stellata*	Flowers white, star- shaped; March to April. Fruit red- seeded cones, September.	Red seeds emerge from soft green cones hanging on semi- elastic threads. Try M. *soul- angeana* (Saucer) and for the South. *M. grandiflora* is spectacular.
Mountain Ash *Sorbus aucuparia*	Flowers cream, June. Fruit gold or red.	Graceful fine-leaved tree. Grows to 20' to 30'. Especially attrac- tive to cedar waxwings early fall to mid-winter.
Mulberry *Morus alba tatarica*	Flowers April-June. Fruit white, pinkish to purple.	Marvelous early summer fruit for birds. They bypass cherries for mulberries. Messy—don't plant near walks. *M. pendula* is weeping form. Plant both male and female. Hardy.
Pine, White *Pinus strobus*	Flowers early spring. Fruit cone seeds all year.	Pine family *the* most important food source for birds. Two other fine choices are Swiss Stone Pine, *P. cembra*, slow- growing, compact, lush green foliage; and Japanese White Pine, *P. parviflora*, slow grower, outstanding.
Regel Privet *Ligustrum obtusifolium regelianum*	Flowers white, June- July. Fruit blue-black; early fall through winter.	Moderate size shrub with grace- ful branches.
Red Chokeberry *Aronia arbutifolia*	Flowers white; late May. Fruit bright red; fall.	Common shrub in eastern woods, 15'-20'. Fruit abundant, dependable, a great favorite. Try *A. brilliantissima*.

Tree or Shrub	Features	Comments
Russian Olive *Elaeagnus angustifolia,* and *E. umbellata*	Flowers silvery out- side, yellow within in spring. Fruit yellow coated berries, silver scales; early fall.	Both species highly recom- mended; clusters of berries which birds, including game birds, devour. Fine for nests and shelter. Both hardy coun- try wide and near sea shore.
Serviceberry of Shadbush *Amelanchier canadensis*	Flowers white; late April. Fruit dark red; July.	Midsummer fruit especially ap- pealing for fledglings. Early white blossoms a delightful display.
Sumac *Rhus glabra* (smooth)	Flowers cream; June, July. Fruit cluster of red fuzzy berries.	Birds love the seeds of the "red candles," especially in midwin- ter and early spring when food is scarce.
Viburnum, European Cranberry *V. opulus*	Flowers white; late May. Fruit red to black on red stalks.	Scarlet fruits last well into win- ter. Not eaten until frozen repeatedly. The many varieties of viburnum make this family *first* choice of deciduous shrubs for birds. *V. maries* double file not as susceptible to aphids, has good branching habit. Try *V. wrighti*, *V. sieboldi* and *V. opulus compactum* (dwarf).
Skimmia, Reeves *S. reevesiana*	Flowers pure white; April and May. Fruit dark crimson.	Low evergreen compact plant 1′ to 1 1/2′, good for ground feeders. Not hardy in northern areas.

Our thanks to the Garden Club of America for information from their publication *Berried Treasures for the Birds*.

Green Thumb Tips

*Good landscape planning pays! Ninety percent of the home owners who do it themselves do it improperly.

*Don't follow a hit-and-miss system of planting. Draw a plan first! Invest in nursery-grown stock, at least for the foundation planting.

*Poor soils mean poor growth. Use plenty of compost or peat moss if you are planting trees or shrubs, especially in foundation plantings.

*Don't be afraid to use trellises, fences, and gates to soften areas around your home. White is the best color to paint lattice or trellises.

*Don't overlook the use of vines to enhance your home.

*Keep hedges trimmed regularly. Rounded tops shed snow better than flat tops. The base should be wider than the tops.

*Your shrubs or lawn won't look neat unless you keep the edges trimmed and the plants weeded or mulched.

*Make your plantings simple. A few well-spaced trees and shrubs are more effective than a "jungle" planting.

CHAPTER III

Narrow and
Broad-leaved Evergreens

•

Evergreens give year-round beauty and present no serious "leaf-drop" problem in the fall. Nine out of ten home owners wish to include at least some evergreens in their landscape, and there's no reason why you can't use them with non-evergreens to avoid monotony. You have a choice between two types of evergreen; the narrow-leaved or coniferous (cone-bearing) and the broad-leaved or flowering types. Both are useful for home plantings, although they require care of a different sort from that of the non-evergreen plants commonly used. They represent a greater initial investment, but over the years evergreens cost you no more for enhancing your home than does your lawn.

Narrow-Leaved Evergreens (Coniferous)

The point to remember about coniferous evergreens is that they have definite shapes. Evergreens are very good against a light background, but they don't soften stark lines as well as the loose-growing deciduous shrubs, and they won't grow where floods of water and snow fall from the roof.

Evergreens vary in different parts of the country. The South and West have types different from the ones found in the East. Check your local nurserymen for varieties suited to your area. Evergreens mentioned in this book are found mostly in the East and Midwest. The following listing will help you select narrow-leaved evergreens for your home plantings.

EVERGREEN SHAPES AND SIZES *Group 1: Large upright trees*: Hard to keep trimmed to a desired height; should not be used in the foundation planting. They are better used as a showy specimen in the lawn, as a boundary, or a windbreak away from the house. *Examples*: Douglas fir, Scotch pine, Colorado blue spruce, Canadian hemlock.

Group 2: Medium upright trees: Those which can be used either as a specimen or as accent evergreens in the foundation planting. For example the *Taxus cuspidata capitata* might reach heights of over 25 feet if left untrimmed, but it is easily pruned and kept within bounds when used as an accent around doorways or on corners. The Canadian hemlock is usually used as a specimen, since in its natural state it can grow to 50 or 60 feet. Yet it is often used in foundation plantings because of its compactness and grace, and it can be kept to 5 or 6 feet if pruned 3 or 4 times a summer season. Unfortunately, most home owners neglect to prune regularly so they soon have overgrown trees around the foundations. *Examples*: *Taxus cuspidata capitata*, American arborvitae, spiny Greek juniper, Canadian hemlock (if kept trimmed).

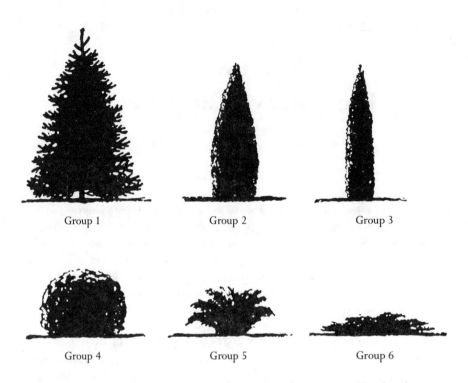

Group 1   Group 2   Group 3

Group 4   Group 5   Group 6

Group 3: Columnar trees: More slender upright types, reach a maximum height of 30 to 40 feet if left untrimmed. They can be used either as specimens or as accent trees in the foundation planting if pruned regularly. Several upright junipers and arborvitaes meet this description. *Examples*: Pyramidal arborvitae, red cedar (juniper), Irish juniper, columnar Chinese juniper.

Group 4: Globular: Low-growing types can be used under windows, or as "framing" for the tall types or "softeners" on the corners and at entrances. *Examples*: globe arborvitae, mugo pine.

Group 5: Spreaders: Used in the same manner as the globular types, but they do not give as formal an appearance. They lend a more graceful effect to the lines of the house. *Examples*: Pfitzer's juniper, *Taxus cuspidata* (spreading), Hetzi juniper, Savin's juniper, Andorra juniper.

Group 6: Low prostrate types: Used for "softening" steps, covering slopes, or giving year-round interest to rock gardens. Useful for banks adjacent to split level homes. *Examples*: Andorra juniper, Sargent juniper, Japanese juniper.

LANDSCAPING WITH EVERGREENS One of the most common mistakes is to plant the wrong evergreen in the wrong place. Putting one that grows one hundred feet tall next to the house is not sensible. Keep in mind that most smaller evergreens used in foundation plantings will grow twenty to thirty feet tall if left untended. Yearly pruning will keep shrubs neat, compact, and the right height. There are evergreens available to fit any space.

EVERGREENS THAT CAN BE USED
IN FOUNDATION PLANTINGS IF KEPT PRUNED

Latin Name	Common Name	Comments
Chamaecyparis pisifera filifera	False Cypress	Upright, grows to 15'. May wind burn.
Ilex opaca	American Holly	Grows in full sun or light shade. To insure fruit, set plant one male tree or graft one or more male branches onto a female tree. Ideal as specimen, grows up to 25'.
Ilex verticillata	English Holly	Not hardy in all areas. Up to 30'.
Juniperus chinensis columnaris	Chinese Juniper	Useful for screen. Up to 30'.
Juniperus chinensis pfitzeriana	Pfitzer's or Spreading Juniper	Foundation planting. Up to 6'.
Juniperus virginiana	Eastern Red Cedar. Has many cultivars.	Tolerates dry soil. Female plant has bluish berries. Up to 30'.

Juniper: The "Red Cedar" or Juniper family is one of the most important. There is a fine variegated golden-leaved type. See the selection at your nursery. Do not grow any juniper in shade. All prefer full sun.

Pinus mugo mughus	Mugo Pine ("Swiss Mountain Pine")	Useful in foundation planting but must be trimmed each spring. Spreading; up to 12'.
Taxus cuspidata	Japanese or Spreading Yew	Ideal for foundation planting, hedges, tubs, and other containers. Up to 8'.
	There are numerous forms of spreading yews, of different color and branching habit, such as	
	T. intermedia, T. brownii, T. densiformis	Clipped to any size. 4' to 16'.
Taxus cuspidata capitata	Upright yew. Includes Hatfield and Hicks types.	Ideal as specimen plants, or in foundation planting. Can be sheared or left informal. Up to 20'.

Latin Name	Common Name	Comments
Thuja occidentalis	American Arborvitae or upright arborvitae.	Mother tree from which came 50 types of other arborvitae. Ideal for hedge, foundation planting, tubs and other containers. Up to 40'.
Thuja occidentalis woodwardii	Globe Arborvitae	Globe form used in foundation planting, tubs and boxes. 2' tall.

MEDIUM-LARGE TREES USEFUL AS SPECIMEN TREES

Latin Name	Common Name	Comments
Abies concolor	White Fir	Beautiful specimen tree. Needles, blue-green, give soft
Abies concolor (cont.)		appearance. Ideal in open areas. Tolerates heat, drought and city conditions. Up to 50'.
Abies balsamea	Balsam Fir	Popular Christmas tree tolerates wet spots. Up to 50'.
Larix decidua *L. laricina*	European Larch American Larch or "Tamarack"	Sheds foliage in fall, grows new foliage each spring. Does well on dry soil, but American Larch takes wet ground. Use as specimen trees only. Up to 50'.
Tsuga canadensis	Canadian Hemlock	Fast grower. Can reach 50'; can be kept trimmed to 5'. Lives in sun or shade, moist or even dry soils. Can be sheared to any height. Ideal for hedge, specimen, windbreak, screen.

LARGER TREES, 50 FEET OR MORE, FOR LARGE PROPERTIES

Latin Name	Common Name	Comments
Chamaecyparis obtusa	Hinoki or False Cypress	Up to 75'. Pest-free, has many cultivars. Useful in the landscape as specimen.

Latin Name	Common Name	Comments
Picea abies	Norway Spruce	Has 6″ cones, largest of all spruce. Good for screen, windbreak, and specimen. Tolerates wide range of soils. Up to 60′.
Picea engelmannii	Englemann Spruce	A narrow, pyramidal tree, dark green foliage. Branches stiff, needles sharply pointed. Specimen tree. Up to 75′.
Picea glauca	White Spruce	Blue-green needles are heat- and drought-resistant. Good for windbreaks and specimen trees. 60′ or more.
Picea glauca densa	Black Hills Spruce	Bluish foliage, slow growing. Ideal for lawn. Up to 60′.
Picea omorika	Serbian Spruce	Glossy green needles with whitish undersides. Ideal in parks, lawns, or as background plant. One of the best spruces. Up to 60′.
Picea pungens (and variants)	Colorado Spruce	Likes full sun. Ideal specimen tree if blue foliage cultivars are selected. Up to 60′.
Pinus nigra var. *austriaca*	Austrian Pine	Handsome, fast grower. Needles 5″-7″ long; two to a bundle. Grows in acid or alkaline soil. Bark has gray lines. Ideal as specimen, screen, windbreak. Bark reddish brown. Up to 60′.
Pinus resinosa	Red Pine	Needles 3″-6″ long, two per bundle, brighter green than needles of Austrian pine. Grows in poor soils and is used same as Austrian pine. Up to 60′.
Pseudotsuga menziesii (Also listed as *P. douglasii*)	Douglas Fir	Fast grower, graceful. Soft blue foliage. One of the best for specimen, hedge. Pest-free. Likes well drained soil. Up to 70′.

PLANTING AND TRANSPLANTING EVERGREENS Spring and fall are ideal times for setting out new evergreens. Always plant them as soon as you get them if they are sold balled and burlapped ("B&B"). Never carry them by the tops, but rather by the entire ball of earth. If you cannot plant them immediately, keep the shrubs out of hot sun and drying winds. Wet sawdust around the roots keeps the plants happy until you're ready to plant. Container-grown stock, if kept watered, will stand for some time if you are unable to plant them immediately. Papier mâché tubs make it possible to plant evergreens, trees, and shrubs at any time of the year. If the root ball is wrapped with plastic and you are not able to plant the evergreen within a day or two, punch a hole near the top (for watering) and near the bottom (for drainage) so they can be kept moist. Remember to remove this plastic when planting the shrub, since it will not rot away as does burlap. Just loosen the plastic and slide it out from under the ball after you have set it in the hole. Containers such as metal and papier mâché should also be cut away or shrubs gently lifted out of them. If they are wrapped in burlap, no need to remove it at all. It doesn't even have to be untied if the string is of natural fiber. If it is synthetic, then it should be cut in several places.

When planting, there are several things to keep in mind. First, dig a hole larger and deeper than the ball of earth. Maintain a good loamy topsoil with plenty of peat or compost mixed in to fill around the ball. Fill halfway with good soil and pack firmly with feet. Settle by filling the hole with water. After that, put in some soil, leaving a 2- or 3-inch depression around the plant to catch the rainwater or hose water. Never mound soil up around the base of the tree, as this sheds water. Never cover the hole completely, as you lose water that way.

Keep evergreens at least 3 feet from the foundation wall because the wall acts like a blotter and draws moisture from the roots and soil. Be sure your evergreens get a good watering twice a week while they are getting established. On especially hot days you can mist the foliage. After they have been in the ground a month or so, see that they have a good watering at weekly intervals and be sure to water during hot, dry summers. By "a good watering" we do not mean a sodden condition. Too much water is just as detrimental as too little. A good pailful each time is normal for the size evergreens that would be used in a foundation planting. Of course, regular good soaking rains will help alleviate the chore.

Some evergreens (and non-evergreens) are so dense it's almost impossible to grow grass underneath. Allow the needles to build up under the tree and crowd out the weeds; it will look nice and neat. Or you can remove the needles and keep the area under the tree bare. If grass won't grow naturally beneath the tree, it's a waste of time and money trying to get a seeding started. It may be possible to cut out some branches to let sunlight in, but we wouldn't risk ruining the looks of a tree just for the sake of getting grass to grow.

LIVING CHRISTMAS TREES If you have the space, a good way to add evergreens to your yard is to use "living Christmas trees," and plant them outdoors afterwards. Here are a few tips for success: Keep the tree watered daily indoors (a potted tree with a cubic foot of soil in its container takes up a quart or two of water daily) and plant it within a

Whether planting a tree from your nursery or transplanting one from your own property, have a hole dug first. Hole should be 6 to 9 inches wider and 4 to 6 inches deeper than the ball on the plant being planted. Mix soil from the hole with ⅓ peat moss or leaf mold.

Add mixed soil to the hole until the soil ball sets about 1 inch below the soil grade.

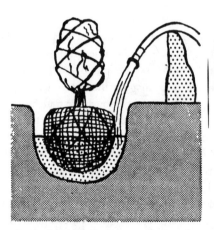

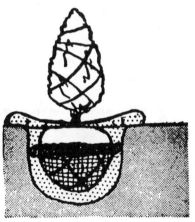

Untie twine and roll burlap back slightly (if wrapped with plastic, be sure to remove or slash all around). Continue filling with soil, tamp some more and add extra water. Leave a saucer-like depression around base of plant.

Gradually add soil and water. Tamp soil with feet to shut out air pockets.

(*Courtesy University of Rhode Island*)

day or two after Christmas. Have a hole already dug outdoors, and water the tree well after you set it out. Then put a mulch of sawdust, wood chips, etc. around it. Indoors, a living tree often starts to break dormancy and buds start to swell. Putting such a tree

  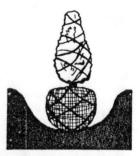

In digging out any shrub, be sure to get as large a soil ball as possible. Slip a piece of burlap (or other mesh material) underneath; wrap and tie the ball with it. Lift the soil ball with your hands. Never lift an evergreen or shrub by the top.

Right: Evergreen wrapped and ready to plant. Use a few nails to pin the burlap or mesh tightly around the ball to hold the soil in place. Then tie securely with twine before lifting soil ball. (*Courtesy University of Rhode Island*)

outdoors in very cold weather can deform it, unless you water it well with warm water and give it some form of winter protection. *Note*: Christmas tree lights (outdoor or indoor) can scorch leaves and brown foliage. Try to hang bulbs clear of the foliage as much as possible.

SUMMER MULCHING A mulch of crushed stone, shredded bark, or peat moss in a circular area beneath a tree gives a well-kept look and helps conserve moisture during dry spells.

Evergreens, whether in borders or as specimen plants, look neat and sharp when mulched and edged. Any mulch (see Chapter XIII) is good because it keeps weeds out and moisture in. Edging can be done with a spade (see Chapter II). The only care thereafter is the removal of a weed or two and freshening up the edge once or twice yearly. If you like annuals among evergreens, plant them right through the mulch.

FEEDING Newly planted evergreens need a mulch and watering more than they need doses of plant food. Liquid feeding supplies both water and extra nutrients, but be careful about using chemical fertilizers. Once evergreens have become established, they will respond to occasional feedings. Water is more important for survival, and you must not count on rain or snow to fulfill this need.

PRUNING Newly planted evergreens seldom need pruning. After your tree is well established you can do a little trimming each year, beginning before the plants have reached the full size desired. You can trim an evergreen just about any time "the shears are sharp." In some nurseries, pruning or shearing is a year-round job, which indicates that the time you trim evergreens isn't too important. You have the choice of trimming them into formal shapes, or allowing them to grow naturally. We prefer to "pluck" our evergreens in the foundation planting. This consists of reaching in and snipping out a branch here, and one there, so that from a bird's eye view, the bush is star-shaped. Specimen trees in lawns need little or no trimming.

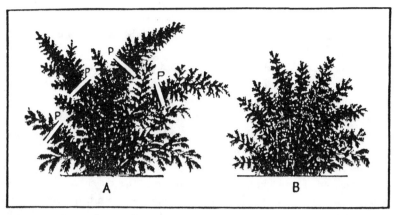

When pruning evergreens, prune out longest shoots and try to leave a natural informal effect. Shearing into a "ball" takes away natural beauty. Trim your evergreens instead of "shaving" them. (*Courtesy University of Maine*)

If spreading and upright types are not kept in bounds you're apt to have a jungle forest effect around your home, so be prepared to spend some time each year trimming your evergreens.

WINTER PRECAUTIONS One reason evergreens winterburn or winterkill is strong, drying winds in winter or early spring. All evergreens lose water from the leaves from winter winds. If the ground is lacking in moisture, water lost from the leaves cannot be immediately replaced and drying out, browning of leaves, or "windburning" takes place. Even though water is present in the soil, it may be frozen solid and therefore unavailable to plant roots. The secret is to keep evergreens well watered right up until the snow flies.

WINTER MULCHING: A winter mulch helps retain moisture in the soil and prevents rapid temperature changes at the soil line. In late fall put 2 or 3 inches of straw, peat, cocoa-bean shell, buckwheat hulls, or sawdust around the base. Anything you have available for a mulch will work, but you should never let evergreens go into the winter with a dry soil.

WILT-PROOF SPRAYS: Spraying evergreens with latex wilt-proofing material available in garden centers seals the pores and stops water loss. Try spraying them with a material known as antidessicant or anti-transpirants, available under several trade names. Spray top and bottom sides of leaves in early December and again in February.

PROTECTION: Protect your investment: You've handled your balled or tubbed evergreens with care, placed them in the hole, watered well, and mulched them. Now, if your evergreens are in a windy spot, your best bet is to build a screen of some sort to keep wind off for the first winter.

Don't winterize evergreens with plastic sheets. On sunny days the heat is trapped inside and evergreens are cooked to death. Even holes in the plastic are not enough to let the heat escape. Burlap (if you can get it) makes a good screen, although somewhat unsightly. Burlap wrapped around four posts driven into the ground does a fine job of protecting the plants from drying winds.

Some gardeners wrap each evergreen individually, a good trick for new transplants. For wrapping, it's hard to find a substitute for burlap, since it is porous enough for light and air to pass through but it doesn't trap heat inside. (Other loose-weave fabrics may be used as long as they are able to withstand the rigors of stormy weather.)

If evergreens are under a dripping eave, try to divert the water so it won't splash on the foliage and freeze. The ice crystals magnify the sun's rays, heat the foliage, and cause brown spots which show up the following spring.

PROPAGATING EVERGREENS If you are in no hurry, you can start your own evergreens from cuttings. However, it takes three to five years to get a respectable size evergreen, so be prepared to wait. The yew (or *taxus*), arborvitae, juniper, and others can be rooted by taking cuttings about 8 inches long and inserting them in cold frames containing a mixture of sand and perlite or vermiculite. Place the cuttings in the mixture close together (about $1\,1/2$ inches between the stems). You can help rooting along by dipping the cuttings in a hormone powder which stimulates the formation of a callus at the base.

Leave the cuttings in the cold frame all winter, and keep them covered with evergreen boughs or straw to protect against direct sunlight. In spring, once the weather begins to warm up, the covering can be removed and cuttings should be watered and misted. By early June of the following year, you should have a good patch of cuttings rooted.

How about evergreens started from seed? Gather cones in fall or winter, and remove seeds by placing cones near a radiator or in an oven, with just the pilot on. Enough heat is generated to open the cones so you can shake the seed out. Sow seed in a mixture of sand and peat moss in a cold frame. Cover with wire screen to keep out rodents and by the time spring rolls around, seed will be ready to sprout. Seedlings can be kept in the cold frame for about a year, after which they can be planted in rows in the garden (about a foot apart), and later on moved to a permanent spot.

COMMON EVERGREEN TROUBLES *Black or brown areas, especially around the base.* Usually due to dog-burn (i.e. urine burn) and it's worst on arborvitae. *Control*: Snip off discolored areas. Put up wire fence, or use nicotine sulfate spray on the foliage once a week. Another trick is to apply rope repellent around evergreens. (See Chapter XVII.) Foul odor keeps dogs away.

Brownish or yellowish areas high up in an area out of dog reach. This can be due to last winter's ice. Water from leaking eaves causes ice to form on evergreens, and the ice acts like a magnifying glass when the sun hits, scorching the foliage even in cold weather. Damage shows up as bleached or strawlike color. *Suggestion*: Fix eaves. Cut off off-color parts and new growth will come in.

Browning on one side. Salt damage causes browning, especially on the windward side or highway side of tree. (See Chapter II for more information on salt damage.)

Overall browning can mean tree is dead or dying. This may be due to winterkilling if you live in a northern area. If browning is on inside only, it's nothing to worry about. Evergreens shed innermost needles and these are brown.

Overall yellowing of foliage. Caused by red spider mites. These suck sap and cause mottling or yellowing of foliage. *Control*: Spray with miticide once weekly for three weeks. See section on Insect and Disease Control.

Browning of new tip growth. Caused by frost injury. Will slow growth but not serious.

White specks on needles and stems followed by yellowing. May be scale or mealybugs. Spray with Malathion once a week.

Holes chewed in the leaves of yew and rhododendron. Work of the black vineweevil. *Control*: Spray the foliage and the area underneath and around the plants with Lindane. Diazinon (Spectracide) might be helpful.

Ragged needles in localized areas. Due to wasp-like insect called the sawfly. Adults feed on needles day and night. *Control*: Spray with Malathion.

Chewed needles, buds, and new shoots tied in a loose mass of silk. Spruce bud worm. *Control*: Apply Malathion just as young buds are opening. This pest has many enemies, notably purple martins, which eat the adults, and spiders, which destroy the eggs.

Tips of spruce branches affected by pineapple-shaped galls due to spruce gall aphid injury. These turn brown and unsightly in late summer.

Greenish (turning to brown), pineapple-shaped growths on tips of branches. Due to spruce gall aphid. Galls are most visible (tan or brownish) in August. *Control*: Handpicking and burning (or sealing in plastic and discarding) is somewhat helpful if you can reach them. Spray in spring, just as growth begins, using Malathion. Spray again in August, since the pest spends the winter as a tiny, greenish, immature aphid in crevices around the bud scales.

Dead needles at tips of branches and pitch dripping from buds. Work of pine shoot moth. *Control*: Difficult. Cut off infested shoots and burn or seal in plastic bag and discard. Injury more apparent in spring. Spray tree at weekly intervals, starting in early May.

Tiny white specks or scales on needles. Pine leaf scale. Found on various evergreens, including pines, spruces, hemlocks, and firs. Heavy infestations weaken trees. *Control*: In June eggs hatch into crawling young which move about for a short time; spray with Malathion to kill this vulnerable stage. Summer spraying is useless, except in mid-August when a second generation is produced from eggs. Spray again then to kill the crawlers.

Bagworm injury on Juniper. One-inch male moth, female remains in bag. Larvae feed in spindle-shaped bag on evergreen and deciduous foliage.

Bags or sac-like growths on red cedars, arborvitae, pines, spruce, or hemlocks. Due to bagworms, a leaf-chewing pest. Bags can be of various sizes and are unsightly. *Control:* As soon as seen pick bags off and burn (or seal in plastic bag) before eggs hatch. Spray with Malathion in May.

Brownish-orange galls on cedars. Cedar-apple rust. (See *Junipers*.)

Brown tips on pines and spruces. Diplodia tip blight, a fungus disease. *Control:* Difficult. Spray with Captan in spring.

Resinous pitch running down trunk, accompanied by dieback of branches. Due to cytospora canker, a disease more prevalent on spruces. *Control:* None. Cut off dead branches and burn or seal in plastic bag and discard.

Twisted Leaves. Due to weed killer injury. (See Chapter II.)

EVERGREENS IN YOUR LANDSCAPE

•**Arborvitae** (*Thuja Occidentalis*) Arborvitaes ("tree of life") have foliage that is flat, lacy, and soft to the touch. It's a joy to shear arborvitae because of its "softness" and the pleasant aroma given off as it is cut. Keep dogs away from your arborvitaes; it is very sensitive to dogburn.

GREEN THUMB CARE: Arborvitae makes a fine windbreak, hedge, or border planting. The globe arborvitae and the upright types are commonly used in landscape planning. The pyramidal arborvitae makes an ideal boundary line hedge. All arbor vitaes need full sun and lots of moisture in the soil. The golden arborvitae needs full sun to bring out its peculiar golden coloring. Both types stand shearing well and can be trained to almost any shape. They do best in a moist soil, but thrive on any moderately fertile, well drained soil. They do not like the dry, dusty, and smoky atmosphere that generally prevails in cities.

PRUNING: You can prune the upright or globe arborvitae any time of the year. An annual shearing of the ends of the twigs stimulates new side growth on the branches and makes the foliage thicker. Too frequent shearing may give the tree a shaved, unnatural look.

Neglecting pruning means you'll have to be drastic and remove a lot of growth, either all at once or over a period of three years. Heavy pruning may also give that butchered look and it will be quite a while before the tree can fill in again.

Old plants that have been neglected can be "topped" (that is, the top cut back) any time to induce bushiness. If your pyramidal arborvitae is not already bushy, prune the top back and scatter plant food around the base.

TROUBLES: Arborvitae dogburns badly and should be screened or fenced to keep these animals away. Various repellents are on the market. One of them is repellent rope, which can be cut in pieces and placed around evergreens or in flower beds frequented by dogs. Or it can be left intact and strung as a barrier. (See Chapter XVII.)

Don't become alarmed if you see brown foliage on the inside of the tree in late summer and fall. It's just natural shedding.

Windburn is another problem of arborvitae and other evergreens, due to dry winds and sunny days in late winter and early spring. Windburn is aggravated by dry soil—a good reason for soaking the soil in the fall.

●**Canadian Hemlock** (*Tsuga canadensis*) For an unusually good evergreen which will grow in sun or shade, consider the graceful hemlock. Hemlocks are less formal in outline than the firs and spruces: their limbs spread horizontally and branch into many small branchlets which droop gracefully. With their fine, feathery foliage they are attractive in youth and attain great dignity in old age.

Hemlocks will stand severe pruning, growing dense and velvety; thus they make excellent hedges. They grow best in an acid soil and like plenty of moisture.

PRUNING: Although the Canadian Hemlock will grow to 60 feet tall, it still makes a good item in foundation planting. The best way to keep it down is to cut the top out each spring or fall and to shear the tips or end growth to keep the plant compact. A hemlock looks best if allowed to "weep" a little, and you get this effect from a plant growing in a limited area by shearing, then allowing new growth to come out from the sheared branches.

Once you get it to the height you want, it should be trimmed to that height each year. Constant trimming is the best way to keep evergreens the desired size. It's much easier to do this than to let them grow tall and reduce them later. Most evergreens do not bounce back or fill in after drastic pruning as do non-evergreens.

TROUBLES: *Hemlock Scale.* If the tops of your hemlock plantings look denuded, blame it on the hemlock scale. *Control:* Injured hemlocks can be brought back to health by feeding a complete plant food such as 5-10-5 in the fall and spraying with a dormant lime-sulfur solution in early March. Avoid getting lime sulfur on buildings, as it stains paint.

●**Junipers** (*Juniperus*) Junipers are one of the most important groups of evergreens used in home landscaping. The most popular juniper is Pfitzer's (pronounced "fits-her"), a fast grower which must be pruned regularly to keep it in bounds. Pfitzer's juniper is probably one of the best for foundation plantings. If trimmed properly it is graceful and lacy looking. Savin's is another spreader growing to the same height (4 feet to 5 feet). Many low-growing types take on a handsome purple cast with the advent of cold weather. For upright specimens we prefer *taxus* to junipers, because the columnar forms often windburn and spread apart.

PRUNING: Young junipers, two or three years in the foundation planting, need little or no pruning. Limit it to cutting back the ends of branches. Let the shrubs grow star-shaped, or zig-zag fashion. Allow the end of one branch to stick out a bit farther than another. Never prune them into a round shape, because spreading junipers do not grow that way naturally. Some pruning can be done every year or so. Carefully selected long branches can be removed at the base of the plant. If these branches are beneath others, the upper branches will usually droop down to cover the pruning scar and fill in the spot.

Where spreading junipers have been neglected for some years, there's not much you can do to rejuvenate without creating a "plucked chicken" look. Always cut long branches off flush, to avoid stubs. Upright or columnar types are pruned by shearing in spring, summer, or fall.

TROUBLES: *Scale insect.* Look closely at the foliage for tiny grayish-white objects. These almost escape notice, yet they multiply in great numbers and suck the juice from the tissue, eventually causing the plants to brown and die. The pine needle scale is found on pines, spruce, hemlock, firs, and junipers. These insects pass winter in the egg stage beneath the scale covering. *Control:* Use Malathion 50 percent emulsifiable grade, at the rate of 1 1/2 quarts in 100 gallons of water, applied in late May. Or in April, use lime sulfur at rate of 1 quart to 9 quarts of water, applied any time before new growth starts. Lime sulfur should be used according to directions on the container. It does a fine job as a clean-up spray to control wintering forms of mites, scale, aphids, mealybugs, and lace bugs.

Never use any dormant spray when the temperature is below 40 degrees F. or above 70 degrees F. Above or below those temperatures, the oil may become separated and cause burning. Never use any of the so-called miscible ("mixable") oils on evergreens unless you follow instructions on the container. Evergreens are very sensitive to oil, and more tolerant to lime-sulfur sprays.

Red spider mite. If your junipers have a yellowish color on the foliage even though you fed and watered the plants, be on the lookout for spider mites. They cause the foliage to grow twisted and droopy, with a sickly, yellowish cast. Too small to be seen with the naked eye, they often fool gardeners into thinking something is wrong with the soil. To detect, hold a white paper under the branches and tap them; if mites are present they will fall onto the paper and will appear as moving specks. Another cause of yellowed foliage on Pfitzer, Savin, Irish, and similar junipers is the juniper scale. Organic gardeners can use buttermilk solution: 1/2 cup buttermilk and 4 cups wheat flour to 5 gallons of water. See also: section on Control of Insects and Diseases.

Cedar-apple rust. Where apples and cedars grow together the cedars often become infested with numerous galls an inch or more in diameter. These galls form long, yellow, tongue- or sputnik-like outgrowths (which some folks think are blossoms). Harmful spores are spread from these projections by the wind. These spores infect the leaves of apples, which often become so seriously infected that they drop prematurely. Damage to cedars is not too serious, although the ends of the branches bearing the galls usually die. *Control*: Spraying cedars with Captan or Ferbam when the "horns" begin to appear is helpful.

●**Pines** (*Pinus*) Pines are increasing in popularity as specimen trees and they have the advantage of holding their needles well. Some may object to the red pine's tendency to be top-open. Austrian pine has a more stately appearance. Perhaps the Scotch pine is preferable to either because it is more compact. Its needles are shorter and stiffer. Most pines should be used as specimen trees because of their large growth habit. Mugo Pine is an exception. It is a shrubby form that will grow open and sparse unless trimmed. It is good in foundation plantings if the new growth or "candles" are pruned back each summer. Otherwise it will crowd other plants.

Identifying principal tall pines is easy: simply count the number of needles in each cluster. For example, the white pine has five needles in a cluster, each cluster being 5 or 6 inches long, bluish green, and soft to the touch. Austrian pine has two needles, 4 to 7 inches long, in a cluster; Scotch Pine has two needles per cluster which are 2 inches long and twisted, as well as sharp at the tips. Red pine has two needles in a cluster which is 4 to 6 inches long and rather glossy.

PRUNING: With pines, firs, and spruces, pruning should be confined to correcting defects and cutting back tips to make the tree more compact and dense. To achieve the effect of bushiness of firs and spruces, shear off the soft new growth in spring and if necessary give them another pruning later on in the season. Try to cut at a point where there is a dormant bud, so that the little branch will be able to grow the following year from a new bud.

Most pines should be sheared or pruned between mid-June and mid-July, and all you do is trim back the leader (top) and laterals (side branches). The growth is soft, then, and limber, and there's enough of the growing season left for the tree to form a cluster of new buds at the end of the shortened leader and laterals.

TROUBLES: *Pine Needle Scale.* Troublesome on pines and related conifers. It does its damage by sucking juice from the needles, causing them to turn brown and die. *Control*: The whitish pine leaf scale yields readily to sprays of miscible oils. It's a good idea to give the trees a summer spray, and one again the following May. To mix a gallon of spray, add 5 1/4 tablespoonfuls of miscible oil. Or you can use Malathion: four teaspoonfuls to a gallon of water.

European pine shoot moth. The moth lays eggs which hatch into larvae that attack the ends of side shoots of most of our common varieties of pine. The infected shoot will bend out of shape and usually continue to grow. Buds and shoots are often killed outright by the feeding of the tiny worm. When this happens the secondary buds develop, resulting in bushy or broom-like tips. This type of injury slows down growth and causes the pines to lose their value as ornamentals or as Christmas trees. The European pine shoot moth has caused considerable damage to red pine, mugo pine, Scotch pine, and Austrian pine. *Control*: Cut out all infested branches, usually found at the tops of trees. Then burn them, or seal in plastic bags and discard. Do this before May, because then the moths come out as dark brown worms, 3/4 inch long. Spraying early kills newly hatched worms as they feed on the needle bases before entering the buds. Use Malathion as a dust or spray.

●**Spruce** (*Picea*) The spruces have long been favorite Christmas trees because of their compact, bushy growth and conical shape. The Norway spruce, with its long, dark, lustrous green needles, has the disadvantage of losing its foliage quickly, especially if the tree is jarred or brushed against. If the butt is immersed in water, the needles stay on longer. The white spruce (often called "cat spruce" due to an alleged unpleasant odor given off by the needles when brought indoors) seems to lose its needles less quickly as a Christmas tree.

Few evergreens have had the popularity of the Colorado blue spruce (*Picea pungens*). It is a magnificent tree, with its narrow pyramidal crown, the "shingled" or layered effect of the branches, and deep bluish cast. Usually the bluest trees are found in deep gorges of high altitudes. When grown from seed, only a small portion of them develop a bright blue color; the majority are of greenish cast with a slightly bluish tendency. The bluish color is due to a powdery substance on the outside of the needles known as "bloom" or sheen. (You see the same thing on a plum or grape.) The color is more pronounced in late spring and summer but later, with rains and snows, most of the blue disappears. Thus you cannot judge the color of a blue spruce except in the spring and summer. This popular evergreen has been widely adapted for ornamental planting because it grows well under a wide range of conditions. It makes a fine specimen tree for the lawn and can be used as a lighted Christmas tree. The Colorado blue spruce likes lots of sunlight and is sensitive to crowding from other trees. On sandy soils newly planted trees can be injured by dry weather, so they should be well watered during the first season, and it won't do a bit of harm to also water them profusely the second year after planting.

Because blue spruce is so striking, it has been indiscriminately used in foundation plantings. Some argue that a stiff blue spruce planted in front of the house is so conspicuous that it conflicts with the house as the center of interest. Also, unless pruned regularly, it grows too large for close planting.

IMPROVING THE COLOR: We are often asked if there's any way to enhance the color of these trees. For an answer, we wrote one of the largest growers of evergreens in America. This specialist told us that blue spruces improve their color to a pronounced blue sheen where an acid condition prevails in the soil. Iron sulfate sprinkled around the drip of the branches and watered in should result in color improvement.

PRUNING SPRUCES: Spruces can be pruned any time of the year. When pruning spruces (also pines and firs), keep in mind that the trees grow in whorls or layers. The pruning of this group of evergreens is confined to correcting defects and cutting back part of the new growth to make the tree more compact and dense. Make the cuts near a spot where there is a dormant bud, so that the little branch will be able to grow the following year. It should have an area of 20 feet or more in diameter to grow, but sometimes it becomes necessary to trim the sides or restrict the top growth. You can keep the spruce down artificially by shearing the tips of the soft new growth in spring. Done annually, this will give your compact plants a formal, rather than natural, look. Do not attempt to bring a big spruce down to size by cutting into old wood. You can't be drastic with evergreens.

If the top is taller than you like, it can be cut out and a new leader (top) will form to take its place. Sometimes the lower branches of a spruce die out; this is due to lack of sun or overcrowding. Cut the dead branches flush to the trunk. No new growth will come to replace the dead limbs. You can prevent further loss of low branches by cutting out all nearby limbs that shut out light.

If your evergreen has the top broken, don't worry because usually one of the branches will bend up and form a new top. To hurry matters along, you can select one of the side branches nearest the top of the tree, bend it vertically, and tie it to a stake; it will train itself to start a new top. After a year or two the tree will have a brand new top and you can remove the stake.

TROUBLES: *Spruce Gall Aphids.* Cause small pineapple-like growths on the branches. Aphids remain in the cone-shaped galls until August, when the unsightly growth cracks open and allows the winged aphids to escape. *Control*: Ordinarily, you can spray in early spring while the trees are dormant, using lime sulfur or miscible oil. Spray trees with Malathion in mid-April or sooner; also concentrate on killing the adults in August, using Malathion, 1 teaspoon to 4 quarts of water. This will kill the aphids as they are released from the cones. On trees 15 feet or shorter, a systemic pesticide applied from March to June will do a good job.

Spruce mite. May be troublesome on spruce, arborvitae, hemlock, and many other evergreens. *Control*: It can be checked by spraying or dusting with a rotenone-sulfur combination, 4 tablespoons of wettable sulfur plus 4 tablespoons of 4 percent rotenone in each gallon of water; or use Malathion, 1 teaspoon to 2 quarts of water. Also try buttermilk, $1/2$ cup plus 4 cups wheat flour to 5 gallons of water.

It will take two to three treatments at seven- to ten-day intervals with any treatment to do the job. Even a stiff syringing with plain water from the garden hose, if repeated every few days for a month, will greatly reduce mite infestation.

Cytospora Twig Canker. When bottom limbs die off and you see pitch oozing near the affected parts, look for twig canker, a fungus disease of spruces. Usually the branches near the ground become infected and die first. Dead needles persist for a while, then shed in early summer. *Control*: Cut out and burn, or seal in a plastic bag and discard, dead and dying branches. Spraying the trees with Ferbam at 4 ounces in 12 gallons of water will help prevent the spread of the trouble—if two doses are made fourteen days apart. Put the first dose on when new growth starts to appear in spring.

•**Japanese yew** (Taxus) One of the most outstanding evergreens on the landscape today (and about the best for shady spots) is without doubt yews properly called the Japanese *Taxus*. People like the yew for its dark evergreen needles, attractive red fruit, its freedom from many insects and diseases, and its adaptability to soils—as well as its high degree of tolerance for shade.

When the Japanese yew is grown from seed it is an upright tree, 30 feet or more in height; if it is reproduced by cuttings, it forms the wide-spreading, slow-growing shrub found in nurseries. This shrub may be more expensive to buy than common evergreens;

the reason is that it takes years of annual pruning for them to be sheared and grown into the shapely plants that are for sale in the nursery.

The female bushes produce attractive, bright-scarlet berries, whose seed may contain dangerous amounts of an alkaloid called taxine. Caution your children against eating these or any other unusual berry. The foliage and bark are toxic to animals, although rabbits and deer do eat them in winter.

The University of Michigan has been studying yews for years and has selected what it feels are the most oustanding:

Taxus media hicksii, known as Hicks Yew, is upright, compact, and has ascending branches that are ideal for accent plants on corners, in sun or in shade.

Taxus media hatfieldii is somewhat more vase-shaped and maintains its foliage better than *hicksii.* It may winterburn in windy spots.

Taxus media hicksii columnaris is a very compact, columnar plant, free of objectionable horizontal side branches.

Taxus cuspidata capitata (upright Japanese yew) is the only true upright or pyramidal yew, growing naturally with a two-to-one height-spread ratio. (Unfortunately, this variety is losing favor in some areas due to center die-out disease [cause unknown].) This pyramidal form can be used to soften corners. Nursery men sometimes grow this yew from cuttings, selecting the tips of the upper branches for growing into upright trees, and using the tips of the side branches for growing the spreading types. In fact, the term *capitata* is not a valid name, and all *capitatas* are the wild-tree types of Japanese yew.

Taxus baccata repandens, a good, dark green, low-spreading shrub, has drooping branches.

Taxus cuspidata nana is a slow-growing, irregular shrub that's spreading and dwarf.

Taxus media densiformis, a low, compact type that grows twice as wide as it is high, is a dwarf spreader.

Taxus cuspidata thayeri is the outstanding large spreading type of yew: vase-shaped, flat-topped, compact, and with a good dark green color.

Both *Taxus cuspidata nigra* and *Taxus media brownii* are also good; they are moderately compact shrubs that spread as far as they are tall. No doubt there are other yews that are just as good.

Ground "hemlock" is not a hemlock but *Taxus canadensis,* a native American sprawling evergreen often found in woods. It grows 1 to 2 feet tall and has scarlet berries. We've used the greens in our greenhouse work, but doubt if you can move it from the shade of forest trees, since it is not well suited to open, windswept spots.

FEEDING: All yews are moderate feeders and respond to feedings of manure or fertilizers.

MULCHING: Since the plant is relatively shallow-rooted, it should never be cultivated. Yews like a cool, moist soil for best development, so give them a mulch of peat moss or sawdust.

TROUBLES: *The taxus weevil.* If your Japanese yew is wilting, or the foliage is turning yellowish and the plant is dying, look to the soil for the trouble. The taxus weevil is becoming so serious a pest that nurserymen are searching for suitable substitutes for this wonderful evergreen. *Control:* Look under the soil around your plants for black adult beetles. If they're present, apply Diazinon, being sure to coat the branches close to the ground heavily. Also, treat the soil surface. By doing this, you give a soil deposit protection against newly emerging adult beetles the following season. Early summer is a good time to fight this pest. The taxus weevil, or black vine weevil, is troublesome on many other evergreens, particularly on hemlocks.

Mealybugs. Mealybugs appear as white masses on the tips of the branches and along the trunk. *Control:* Spray with Malathion, 1 tablespoon to 2 quarts of water. *Lecanium scale* also may infect the yew. Malathion sprayed early in summer checks this. A systemic pesticide applied from early spring to late summer is effective on both these pests.

JAPANESE YEWS ARE VERY SENSITIVE TO WET FEET. Do not let a downspout throw water directly at the base of the roots of Japanese yews. If water remains around a Japanese yew for even a couple of days, they take on a rusty brown color and eventually die.

BROAD-LEAVED EVERGREENS

Broad-leaved evergreens are valuable in landscape planting because they have both foliage and flowers. (Narrow-leaved evergreens have only foliage effect).

●**Andromeda** (*Pieris floribunda*) A good evergreen shrub with clusters of lily-of-the-valley-like flowers that bloom in March, April, or May. The native mountain andromeda (*Pieris floribunda*), hardy in the northeast, grows to 6 feet. The Japanese andromeda (*Pieris japonica*) is perhaps a handsomer shrub, but is not as hardy. In our region, the mountain andromeda bears clusters of tiny, cream-colored, waxy bells in May. Andromedas like a moist, peaty soil, and partial shade.

●**Azaleas** The terms "azalea" and "rhododendron" are confusing. Until recently, the term "azalea" referred to the deciduous (i.e., those that shed leaves) or partly evergreen plants with small, thin leaves, as opposed to those with large, thick, leathery evergreen leaves considered to be a feature of rhododendrons. But in fact, all azaleas are of the genus Rhododendron. However, nurserymen, garden centers, and the general public continue to make a distinction between azaleas and rhododendrons on the basis of leaf size and texture—deciduous vs. evergreen. While this method of classification may be incorrect botanically, it serves a useful purpose.

In a nutshell, azaleas are divided into four groups: 1) native species such as *R. nudiflorum* ("Pinxterbloom"); 2) oriental species such as *R. Japonicum* (e.g., Japanese azalea) 3) hybrids such as *R. mollis*, (Knaphill and Exbury); 4) evergreen types such as Kurume, Glenn Dale, etc.

A lot of attention has been focused on the colorful hybrids known as Exbury and Knaphill. While these and other deciduous hybrid azaleas are spectacular, we shouldn't lose sight of the fact that many of our native azaleas are extremely hardy, attractive, and nearly disease- and insect-free.

If you're fond of azaleas, forget plant classification and concentrate on lengthening the blooming period. Exbury and Knaphill hybrids are hardy even as far north as central Maine and upstate New York. You should get at least two months of continuous bloom from early July to late August by using the Korean, Pinkshell, Pinxterbloom, Flame, Sweet, and Swamp varieties. *Azalea mollis* and the Exbury, Knaphill, and Ghent hybrids will bloom even when winter temperatures go to 20 degrees F. below zero. If you live in cold regions, steer clear of evergreen types of azaleas such as the Kurume and the Indian varieties.

Azaleas take the same care and have the same troubles as rhododendrons, and they are more adaptable than rhododendrons for foundation planting because they are shorter and more compact.

•**Rhododendrons**   Rhododendrons are useful for specimen plants and accent plantings, and they harmonize well with nonevergreens. Why aren't many good rhododendrons used for landscape effect? Perhaps the reason is that while some species are hardy, others are finicky. That's why it is so important to check with your local nurseryman on the hardiness of various species before planting them.

Our advice to gardeners who want extremely hardy rhododendrons is to stick to three native flowering types: 1) *R. maximum* (Rosebay), a broad-leaved, high-growing (6 feet) type familiar to visitors in the Alleghenies. It blooms in June with clouds of light pink, deep pink, lavender, and white blossoms. 2) *R. catawbiense*, which blooms in May, is orchid to rose-pink in color and grows 3 to 5 feet tall. Its leaves are smaller than *R. maximum*. 3) The small-leaved *Rhododendron carolinianum* is inclined to bear heavily and is also very hardy.

The *Rhododenron maximum* is hardiest of all, while *R. catawbiense* is one of the showiest. The chief drawback of *catawbiense* is that people tire of its monotonous magenta color. We've been observing the varieties that are hardy in Highland Park in Rochester, New York and we would like to mention a few hybrids that you might try: Album elegans, Boule de Neige, Caractacus, Charles Dickens, Lee's Dark Purple, Mrs. Charles Sargent, and Roseum elegans.

LOCATION: Most rhododendrons prefer partial shade, although a number of varieties will grow in full sun. A general rule to follow is the larger the leaf surface, the more shade is required. This doesn't always hold true, since we have seen large-leaved rhododendrons growing in full sun. Very large-leaved varieties should be planted in shade or their leaves will assume a wilted appearance and the entire plant will suffer. Hot sun and dry winds will cause leaves to scorch in summer or winter.

We prefer planting and transplanting all azaleas and rhododendrons in spring because they get a chance to become established.

SOIL: Azaleas, rhododendrons, and heaths actually like acid soil. A simple soil test with litmus paper (see Chapter XIII) will tell you if you have an acid soil. In limestone regions it is imperative to make the soil acid before planting these ornamentals. This may be done by digging a pit about 2 feet deep and filling it with soil to which large quantities of organic matter have been added—as much as one-fourth to one-half by volume. The remainder can be ordinary garden soil. Peat moss, rotted manure, pine needles—any rotted vegetable matter—is useful for this purpose. Now add finely powdered sulfur at the rate of 1 pound per 100 square feet and work it into the soil. Never add lime to acid-loving plants.

An ideal soil for rhododendrons should contain humus to keep roots cool in hot weather. They do not like a heavy soil that's poorly drained. When oak-leafmold or peat moss comprises about 50 percent of the soil, it takes care of acidity, aeration, and drainage.

MULCHING: Keep in mind that rhododendrons are shallow-rooted, and therefore should never be cultivated but rather mulched and left undisturbed. Both rhododendrons and azaleas like a mulch of sawdust, peat moss, wood chips, bark, or oak leaves. A mulch of peat moss alone is ideal. It should be kept moist, as dry peat can become impervious to water.

FEEDING: Go easy on feeding rhododendrons and azaleas. If anything, feed an acid fertilizer or iron sulfate. Scatter a tablespoon around the base of each plant any time leaves start to yellow.

PRUNING: Go easy on pruning rhododendrons and azaleas because the buds for next year's bloom are already on this year's plant. Prune rhododendrons after blooming; don't cut too deeply, just remove the spent blossoms before they form seed pods (on azaleas you don't even have to remove the spent blooms). You are mainly pruning for shape (or symmetry), and to remove dead wood and extra-long shoots.

TROUBLES: *Wind and sunburn*. Cause the leaves to turn brown in summer or winter. The so-called "anti-wilt" sprays of plastic or wax emulsions slow down the rate of water loss from leaves and can protect both narrow- and broad-leaved evergreens from heat and drought. In addition, you should water your plants regularly. Poor drainage due to clay soils is often responsible for mottled gray coloring of foliage (see Chapter XIII).

Leaf spot and die-back. Rhododendrons get leaf spot (fungus) disease, which can usually be checked by dusting with Captan. Also, these broad-leaved plants are attacked by a die-back blight caused by the same fungus which is responsible for lilac blight. If you see a brownish, shrunken appearance advancing rapidly down the twigs, followed by wilting or death of parts above, that's die-back. *Control*: Prune diseased areas below the brown parts.

Lace Bug. Punctures the leaf tissue, sucks out sap, causes light spotting, and eventually dries the leaves. *Control*: Spray with Malathion, or any of the newer insecticides.

Stem borer. Drills down center of stem, causing wilting. Keeping your plants sprayed with Malathion will protect them against this pest.

Midge: Works on buds. Use Malathion.

Scale and Mealybug are sap-sucking pests. Use Malathion.

White Fly. Use liquid detergent, 1 tablespoon per gallon of water.

Bud and twig blight, another fungus disease, has been rampant; it causes flowers to blast or to rot on rhododendrons and azaleas. *Control*: Prune all blasted buds and dead twigs. Spraying with bordeaux mixture or Captan after the flowering period is over protects new buds and kills the fungus, plus spores.

Red Spider Mite. Another sap-sucking pest, causes mottling and browning. See section on Control of Insects and Diseases.

•Heaths and Heathers Heaths (*Erica*) and heathers (*Calluna*) are usually listed together in nursery catalogues because they have much the same habit of growth and take the same care. They are shrubby, small-needled plants with an abundance of pink or white flowers. They like a well drained soil and a sunny spot. They are tricky to grow in clay soils and in cold regions. We cannot get them to winter over in our area, but in nearby Rochester, New York, where temperatures near the lake are a bit milder, we have seen them survive if mulched heavily with evergreen boughs.

If your soil is heavy you should add lots of peat moss or rotted compost. They need an acid soil the same as rhododendrons and azaleas. In cold regions they can be wintered over in pots and brought inside if there is ample humidity, such as a greenhouse or conservatory would provide. Outside, they must be watered during dry weather. They have very few troubles if soil and climate are right.

Calluna vulgaris, wild Scottish heather, is probably the most hardy variety to try. It has tiny rose-colored, bell-shaped flowers in great profusion. Your nurseryman can tell you which varieties of heaths and heathers are suitable for your area.

●**Holly** Interest in hollies is zooming, especially the hardy, native American Holly (*Ilex opaca*). Many gardeners have shied away from this tough plant because it was believed that it wasn't hardy enough for rugged northeastern winters. We know of an American holly plantation near us which has survived weather of 30 degrees F. below zero, proof these plants can take it. But all hollies are extremely sensitive to early freezing of poorly ripened wood.

Some selections (*Ilex opaca*) that have withstood our winters are: old heavy berry, cardinal, Stann, bountiful, Merry Christmas, old leatherleaf (male), Christmas hedge, Freeman, Arden, Delia Bradley, and son of Delia Bradley (male).

The English hollies set their flower buds in the autumn. Although the wood and foliage are winter hardy, the flower buds survive only the mildest of winters. Japanese hollies that are protected with mulch or snow each winter may survive. The Japanese red berry holly (*Ilex cornuta burfordii*) makes a nice pot plant indoors in a basement for winter. It blooms in March with a sweet fragrance and will set fruit without pollination. However, it cannot stand cold winter temperatures.

GREEN THUMB CARE: Holly does well only in a drained, acid soil. If you can dig a hole in which water will stand for two or three weeks at a time, that means drainage is too poor for holly growth. Oak-leafmold added each year will keep the soil acid. Also, hollies do not like extremely windy situations. Plant them where a building or a stone wall will shunt the wind, or near an evergreen windbreak.

Hollies like sun, but will bear in shade, although seldom as heavily as in sun. Too much shade causes plants to be scraggly. If you want a good specimen tree, allow plenty of room for growth. You can buy hollies with a ball of earth ready for transplanting in March, April, or May, and also during the fall. With good care, such a tree grows from 6 to 12 inches a year. Top branches grow faster than side branches.

PRUNING: Pruning the American holly is a simple job because it doesn't seem to mind where you cut it. Just make sure your clippers are sharp. Pruning is important because it makes the plant more bushy. If you want it to grow to a tall column or pyramid, trim the sides. You can cut off the top to make a broad bush. It doesn't do a bit of harm to prune at Christmas time for indoor bouquets. Young trees should be pruned at the tops to help them branch out. After the fourth year or so, shaping is needed to get the outline you like.

TROUBLES: *Holly leaf miner:* occasional trouble. Spray with Sevin in early spring.

No berries. If your plants produce no berries it could be due to the plant being a male, or lack of pollination. (There are male and female holly plants.) One male plant will pollinate eight to ten female plants. When plants are three or four years of age, you can expect berries to start forming. Sometimes the blooms of one holly come on at a different time than the other, and pollination does not occur. Sometimes you can chemically make a female bush set, using naphthaleneacetic acid found in garden stores. Use the spray cans, or mix a solution of 1/4 teaspoonful of the hormone to a quart of water. Stir well; spray at least once a day for several days when blossoms are open. A week or two after the flowers fade, green berries begin to form. *Note:* This works only when the female blooms are sprayed. You can't make a male flower produce berries. Incidentally, cut holly branches last longer for decorations if you spray them with the hormone spray just mentioned. Some gardeners use hair spray or "Wilt-Pruf" on cut holly to keep the berries from dropping.

•**Mountain Laurel** (*Kalmia latifolia*) Few evergreens can match the show of mass plantings of Mountain Laurel. Colors run from deep pink to whitish-pink clusters in early June. Plants thrive in sun or shade, and like ample moisture. Mountain Laurel needs an acid, peaty soil (acidity around 4.5). Add peat moss, leafmold, compost to soil before planting.

TROUBLES: *Leaf spot disease. Control:* Dust with Captan.

Green Thumb Tips for Evergreens

*Evergreens are ideal for "specimen" plantings. That means they are useful as highlight trees in a lawn.

*Plant a specimen evergreen and use it for a living Christmas tree outdoors.

*If you plan to landscape your home, first make a sketch, then go to your local nursery and see what the balled or container-grown evergreens look like before you finalize your plans.

*Don't plant a lot of tree-like evergreens in front of your home. Use low spreaders under windows, taller types at the corners; allow at least four feet between plants.

*Water newly planted evergreens two, three, or four times a week, and keep them mulched with any mulch material that's handy.

*Hardy evergreens do not winterkill from freezing. They are affected by the dry winds and sunshine of the fall, winter, and spring months.

*Be prepared to trim evergreens regularly. If you don't they'll grow into a forest and hide your home. It takes less time to trim them than it does to mow your lawn.

*Keep your foundation evergreens neatly trimmed; it will show off your plants better. Plant annuals such as alyssums, marigolds, salvias, petunias, begonias, etc., among your evergreens in summer; plant tulips and daffodils in fall for spring blooms.

*Be prepared to replace old evergreens with new ones every fifteen to twenty years. Evergreens, like wallpaper, drapes, and rugs, get "seedy" looking and should be replaced.

CHAPTER IV

Flowering Annuals
for Summer Pleasure

•

Annuals

Annuals are the cheapest, yet showiest of garden flowers. A dollar's worth of seed produces hundreds of dollars' worth of enjoyment with a minimum of effort.

What is an annual? It's a plant which completes its growth in one year. It is started from seed each year.

HOW TO USE ANNUALS An elaborate color scheme is not necessary. Select two or three good combinations and place them where they'll show off best. Many prefer an old-fashioned mixture, but a more pleasing arrangement is usually to arrange flowers in groups. For example, it is more attractive to have clusters of petunias, salvia, calendulus, zinnias, etc., than to have separate stalks of each scattered haphazardly throughout the planting. Scattered single plants give a spotty effect. Three plants of a kind in a group should be the minimum. In making beds for annuals, don't make them too wide. If against a fence, 4 or 5 feet is handy, and in the open 6 or 7 feet is sufficient. Over greater distances it's difficult to pick the flowers or work the beds. Remember, also, that you should put the taller-growing plants behind those of medium or low growth.

Most flowering plants need at least six hours of sunshine for best bloom. (Petunias, salvia, browallia, and even geraniums will take some shade, but begonias, coleus, and impatiens do best in a shaded situation.)

TIME TO START ANNUAL PLANTS You can sow most annuals out of doors after danger of hard frosts, but those that should be started indoors vary in their rate of germination and development. Other annuals are fall-sown and these are discussed later. At the end of this chapter is a chart which gives starting dates and other useful information.

As for ready-grown annual plants, packs of six, nine or twelve plants are suitable for most folks. If you use a lot of annuals you might persuade your garden store or florist to sell them to you by the "flat" or tray of fifty to one hundred plants. For instant color, buying annuals in pots, already in blossom, will make a quick effect, but they will be much more expensive. Annuals in flats or packs may take a few weeks longer to bloom but what's the big rush? Why pay for a single coleus or petunia in a pot when you can buy a dozen plants in a pack for one-fourth the cost per plant?

A cheaper way to get a lot of plants is to grow them yourself. Build a small hotbed and discover the joy of starting your own plants from seed. Let's say you want to grow a lot of salvia for show. If you bought four packets of salvia seed, you'd have about 200 seeds for what you would spend for about 2 dozen started plants from a garden store. If all the 200 seeds germinated you'd get over 16 dozen plants!

HOW TO START YOUR OWN Most failures in germinating seeds (especially the fussy ones such as coleus and impatiens) are due in part to wrong temperatures. In our greenhouse, we find we get best germination of most annual seeds if they are kept between 70 and 75 degrees F. during the germination period. Seed flats set in sub-irrigation pans (see Chapter XV) are rested on a hotbed cable set into a layer of sand. We use a simple thermometer to keep check on soil and air temperature. There are, however, a few species, such as verbena and hollyhock, which respond to cool temperatures.

Some seeds, such as impatiens and begonias, won't germinate unless they are exposed to light; hence they cannot be covered but must be scattered on the top of the soil. Others require darkness to germinate. A chart is included at the end of this chapter which designates conditions required for most of the annual seeds you would want for your garden.

Another reason for bad luck with seeds is a wrong starting mixture. Most greenhouse operators use one of the prepared mixes containing milled peat moss and vermiculite which are loose, sterile, and excellent for seed starting. Sterility is important because it eliminates danger of damping-off disease, an old enemy of young seedlings.

Moisture is also important. Seeds should be kept moist during the germination process. One drying out can be fatal to seedlings. A pane of glass or sheet of plastic over the seeds will keep temperature constant and prevent drying out, but should be removed as soon as seeds start to sprout. (For complete information on seed starting, see Chapter XV.)

OUTDOOR SOWING: Fast-growing annuals such as zinnias, marigolds, portulaca, and calendula can be sown outdoors. Since they do not suffer the shock of transplanting, they will get off to a quick start and often bloom sooner than plants started indoors. Not all annual flowers may be sown directly in the garden, yet there are many that should be because they are difficult to transplant. These include candytuft, clarkia, cosmos, larkspur, godetia, kochia, linaria, annual lupine, matthiola (evening-scented stock), nasturtium, dwarf phlox, annual poppies, portulaca, salpiglossis, bachelor's buttons, scabiosa.

Control of Diseases and Insects

Annuals and perennials have practically the same pest problems. Good grooming of your plants is the best means of keeping out diseases and insects. As soon as you see a plant showing signs of disease, yank it out and destroy. Also, clean up the flower bed in fall to get rid of diseases and insects which like to winter over on trash.

ALL-PURPOSE SPRAYS: To lick all insects and diseases you can buy all-purpose pesticides or you can make your own. Try this formula: 4 tablespoons Malathion, 25 percent wettable powder, 4 tablespoons nicotine sulfate, one tablespoon of Captan, 50 percent wettable powder; 1/2 tablespoon Karathane (or Mildex). Or you can use sulfur instead of Karathane, 2 tablespoons of the 95-100 percent wettable powder. Mix these with 1 gallon of water for an excellent control that will kill most insects, and most diseases on your flowers (virus, alternaria, fusarium expected).

OTHER MATERIALS TO USE: Sulfur is still one of the best fungicides and is an excellent powdery-mildew fighter. Used in a spray with Ferbam, Zineb, or Captan, it increases their effectiveness against certain diseases like black spot and rusts. It also acts as a miticide and is helpful against tarnished plant bug, leafhopper, and thrips. See section on Control of Insects and Diseases for Organic Pesticides.

Whatever commercial preparations you use, be sure to read the label carefully and follow the manufacturer's recommendations.

The most common pests of annuals are aphids, tarnished plant bugs, thrips, slugs, and snails. For information on their control see Chapter XIV.

Soils and Fertilizers

A sandy loam soil, well supplied with organic matter, is best for most flowers. Use lime to sweeten the soil only when a test shows a need for it. For plants like daisies, lupines, salvia, and others which prefer an acid soil, apply aluminum sulfate, iron sulfate, sulfur or acid peat (see Chapter XIII). An acidity test should be made every two or three years.

The soil should be well drained. If it is heavy and has a tendency to bake or is sandy and dries out quickly, the addition of organic material such as leafmold, compost, or peat will be beneficial. Coal ashes are recommended for heavy clay soils. The more organic matter you can add to a heavy or sandy soil, the better it will be for flowers. Soil improvement is explained in detail in Chapter XIII.

FERTILIZER: Most annuals need feeding when planted, and again about midway in the growing season. The rate of application is based on the fertilizer concentration and, as a rule, the soil should be moist before the fertilizer is applied. If plant food is applied in liquid form, the foliage should not be wet with the solution—unless you are using a type especially designed for foliage feeding. A liquid plant food with a 23-19-17 formula has been a favorite with us for years because it will not burn and can be used with pesticides.

Any dry fertilizer should be measured accurately and spread uniformly over the surface of the soil, keeping it about 4 inches away from the stems of the plants. (For a detailed feeding chart see Chapter XIII.)

Summer Care of Annuals

PRUNING Just about all annuals will perform much better if you give them a summer pruning or pinching. This means simply shortening the growth to make them bushy. At the base of every leaf are one or more dormant growth buds or "eyes," which are forced to grow into side shoots when you snip off the tops. If you pinch the tips of these side shoots again, you will get still more shoots. Pruning will delay flowering a little, but without it the plants will be tall and gangly.

Pinch the tip back with thumb and forefinger when plants are 3 to 4 inches high and continue to snip and prune all summer long. Do only a few branches at a time and begin before the plants look ragged, picking off flowers as soon as they fade to prevent seed-pod formation. Your plants will stay fresh looking and full of bloom much longer with this extra attention.

Later in the season some plants such as petunias, ageratum, and coleus get a bit scraggly and you can cut back some of the old growth.

WATERING ANNUALS You can irrigate or water during the heat of the day—but if you do, about a third of the water never reaches the soil; it evaporates into the air. Plants use more water in July and August than at any other time because days are longer and temperatures are higher. A twenty-day drought in May or October is equal to only ten days of drought in July or August. Soils vary in their ability to hold moisture: sandy soils hold $1/2$ inch of water per foot; loams with sand, 1 inch per foot; loams and clays, about 2 inches. In other words, a loamy soil can go four times as long without water, but requires four times as much to recharge it as a sandy soil. It will take about 350 gallons of water to recharge 1,000 square feet of sandy soil to 1 foot deep, and 1,400 gallons for the same amount of loam soil.

Dry soils will not absorb water as fast as slightly moist soils. By the way, if you have a leaky faucet, fix it! Under average pressure a slow drip will lose from 15 to 400 gallons of water per day! You might better use this water in your vegetable garden or annual beds.

SOME GOOD ANNUALS

Here are the annuals we consider best for the home garden. There are many more to try, but, generally speaking, these will give you plenty of color and show with the least amount of effort.

•**Ageratum** (*Floss Flower*) One of the few good blue flowers, popular for borders, edgings, rock gardens; also indoor pot plants and porch boxes. Grows 8 to 30 inches tall. Also comes in white and off-pink. Blue Horizon is great for cutting.

GREEN THUMB CARE: Plant 6 to 8 inches apart in full sun or semi-shade. Cut off faded flowers to keep plants looking handsome. In dry soils, plants will wilt, but soon after watering they revive.

PROPAGATION: Seed started indoors three or four months before outdoor planting time.

TROUBLES: *Red Spider.* Control: See section on Control of Insects and Diseases.

•**Alyssum** (*Lobularia martima*) A fast-growing, dainty little plant, recommended for use in borders, edgings, baskets, pots, rock gardens, and for cutting. They grow to a height of 3 to 6 inches. The white alyssum is a prolific plant that sows seeds which live over the winter. (The pink and purple varieties do not often self-sow.) There are two types: the dwarf upright, such as Wonderland series and Rosie O'Day, and the procumbent type such as Carpet of Snow and Royal Carpet.

GREEN THUMB CARE: When plants become seedy looking, clip them back within a few inches of the ground. They come back quickly with renewed beauty.

PROPAGATION: Alyssum will produce bloom in six weeks if sown outdoors. Seed is small and should be covered lightly, if at all. Some gardeners cover the row with a strip of newspaper after sowing. Anchor it down with soil along the edges and take it off as soon as the seedlings appear. The newspaper keeps the soil moist and insures a good stand.

TROUBLES: None

•**Asters** (*Callistephus chinensis*) Many summer and early-fall bloomers. Come in all shades of lavender, salmon, crimson, light pink, deep rose, white, and cream. Varieties range from 8 inches to 3 feet tall. Ideal for bouquets, bedding plants and pots.

GREEN THUMB CARE: Likes full sun, does well in partial shade where insect activity is reduced. Should have well-drained, fairly rich soil. Spray with nicotine sulfate or Malathion to check leafhoppers, tarnished plant bugs, and blister beetles, three villains that cause trouble with asters. Also see: Organic Pesticides.

PROPAGATION: Sow indoors in April. After seedlings are about 2 inches high, transplant to a seed flat or to the garden after frost.

TROUBLES: *Aster wilt.* Causes asters to wilt suddenly, turn yellowish-green, and die. The wilt organism lives in the soil from one year to the next, so you should grow asters in a different spot each year. *Control*: Wilt-resistant varieties of aster are helpful but there are many different strains of wilt organism and no one variety of asters is resistant to all of them. But you should always buy wilt-resistant strains in preference to the non-resistant types.

Aster yellows. Leaves get yellow and sickly with a spindly growth, although they do not die. *Control*: Yellows is caused by a virus spread by leafhoppers, so partial control can be had by spraying with nicotine sulfate or Malathion. Since the virus is known to winter over in certain biennial and perennial plants, such as thistle, daisy, and some mums, it's a good idea to plant asters at least 200 feet away from weed borders. Keep weeds mowed around the garden edge and pull up weeds you see in the garden. Weeds harbor viruses and insects which spread diseases.

•**Begonia** (*Begonia semperflorens*) Along with impatiens, hybrid wax begonias are fast gaining on petunias as our number one bedding plant. Although they do not have the color range of petunias, they are more versatile because they can be grown in sun or shade. They provide a neat, bright display all summer long without the gardener's pinching or worrying about seed pods. They come in many shades of red, pink, bicolors, and white, with a choice of bronze or green foliage. The F_1 hybrids start flowering when plants are very small and continue throughout the summer whether it is cool or hot, wet or dry. You can choose dwarfs (3 to 5 inches), intermediate (8 to 10 inches), or tall (about 14 inches). Large-flowered varieties produce blooms up to $2\frac{1}{2}$ inches. Smaller varieties are more profuse bloomers, but all are showy and most are "self-cleaning," meaning they drop their old flowers as new ones come on. There are a few double strains. Of these, Non Stop Hybrid is the best. It is started from seeds but forms tubers. It resists mildew and tolerates adverse conditions.

GREEN THUMB CARE: Begonias like a well-drained soil with humus mixed in. They like to be mulched, so that roots are kept moist and cool, if they are planted in full sun. In hot, dry weather water thoroughly every two or three days or growth will be slowed.

PROPAGATION: Usually from seed in late winter. Some gardeners take plants inside in fall, then in spring take cuttings and root in water, or cut plants back to 2 inches and let them throw out new shoots. We prefer to sow new seed on one of the sterile, soilless mixes (do not cover with soil), water container from below, cover with plastic or glass and keep in a temperature of about 72 degrees F. Seeds are like dust, so it is helpful to mix them with a small quantity of white sand in a salt shaker then shake the mixture on the medium to get even distribution of seeds. Otherwise you wind up with seedlings coming up in dense clumps. Those that have tubers can be started in peat-lite mix.

TROUBLES: Very few. May not bloom indoors in winter due to poor light. Mildew: see section on Control of Insects and Diseases.

•**Calendulas** (Pot or Scotch Marigold) One of the best annuals for the home garden. Will often self-sow and come up the following spring Pacific beauties produce uniformly large, well formed flowers with long, straight stems. See seed catalogs for additional varieties.

GREEN THUMB CARE: Will withstand hot weather quite well, although flowers are larger in cool weather. Cut off seed heads, and flowers will come after frost.

PROPAGATION: Sow outdoors, or start seed indoors and then transplant to open garden after frost. Make a second sowing in early July and you'll have flowers in late summer and fall.

TROUBLES: None

•**Cleome** (Spider Plant) Cleome is a tall, bold annual, 4 to 5 feet in height, and blooms from June until frost. The Rose Queen variety develops huge heads of delightful true pink; equally showy, Helen Campbell is pure white. The four-petaled flowers have an airy appearance because of their unusual long-stemmed stamens and pistils (male and female floral parts). The plant has a rather peculiar odor and does not lend itself too well to arrangements, but is striking as a garden flower in the background of the border. As the plants sometimes get leggy and leafless at the base, it's a good idea to plant other annuals in front of them. A mass planting is most effective. Cherry Queen and Violet Queen add variety.

GREEN THUMB CARE: Grows in poor soils, but flowers are fuller if plants are watered twice a week or so. Very easy to grow.

PROPAGATION: Seed may be started indoors. When you transplant, set the plants at least 2 feet apart. Some gardeners sow outdoors when the weather warms up. Cleome self-sows readily.

TROUBLES: Self-sows and may spread like a weed.

•**Cockscomb** (*Celosia*) A good flower for the gardener who wants something different. Plant breeders have done a fine job of developing new varieties of both the crested types (like a rooster's comb) and the plumed types (*Plumosa*) which are feathery spikes. Both types come in other colors besides the fiery red which is the most popular and makes a dazzling show when used alone or combined with white flowers. Varying shades of gold, yellow, copper, and pink are also available in plants ranging in height from 10 inches to 2 feet. They are most effective when planted in masses. Gardeners also have a choice of foliage color: glossy green or bronzey red.

GREEN THUMB CARE: Needs plenty of space (12 to 18 inches), since close spacing decreases size of heads. For arranging in bouquets, a few smaller flowers are desirable, however.

PROPAGATION: Seed started indoors.

TROUBLES: Cockscomb will bloom prematurely with small heads if growth of young plants is checked. Do not start plants too early indoors as growth will be checked before transplanting. Do not sow outdoors until soil has warmed up thoroughly.

•**Coleus** An easy-to-grow houseplant with leaves as brilliant as a neon sign, coleus is also one of the showiest you can get to grow in semi-shade outdoors. Coleus is nothing new, but the new varieties are something else. Leaves are highly colored, olive, bronze, burgundy, golden chartreuse flecked with green, rose, red, pastel shades, and almost any color or mixture you want. Breeders have developed oak-leaved, fringed, and thin-leaved varieties as well as broad-leaved types. They are easy to grow from seed or slips or cuttings. If your neighbor has a good variety you'll do the plant a favor by asking if you can snip off the top (makes the plant bushier); then root it in plain tap water. Although coleus will tolerate sun, it prefers semi-shade.

Companion plants to grow with coleus in shade include begonias (both annual and tuberous), impatiens or sultanas (which will tolerate extreme air pollution).

Coleus makes a wonderful hanging plant. They'll grow upright, then start to weep over the side of the pot. You can buy a rainbow mixture or separate colors. For a good creamy white and green coleus, grow the Candidum, very showy as a pot plant or in the shaded border outdoors.

GREEN THUMB CARE: Plants should be started indoors eight to ten weeks before they are set outdoors. Nip the plants back when they are 5 or 6 inches tall to induce bushiness. They are not fussy about soil but do best if it is light and humusy. Water during dry spells or they will droop and growth will be retarded. If flower buds appear, pinch them out as soon as they begin. This gives you a stockier plant.

PROPAGATION: Seed can be started in a sand-peat mixture, or any of the soilless mixtures on the market. Sow the seed and *do not cover*. It likes light for germination and a temperature of 72 degrees F. or more, never under 70 degrees F. (See Chapter XV for care of seed box and seedlings.) By the way, when you sow seed of coleus, don't be disappointed when you see the seedlings. They all look green at first, but start showing color when the third set of true leaves appears.

TROUBLES: *Tall, spindly plants.* Prevent by pinching tips out and rooting in plain tap water.

Troubles indoors: Dropping of leaves due to dry soil and dry air. Scorched (brown around the edges) leaves are due to hot sun or hot air. Old plants shed their leaves more readily than young ones. If you grow them in a soil containing lots of humus, shedding of leaves is lessened. You can cut the tops off and root them, then pot up in a good mix. Coleus don't like or need direct sun. Grow them in a bright window and you'll find they produce a minimum of dry, brown leaves.

•**Cosmos** An attractive, airy, background plant. If you are a new home owner and want a quick-growing item while your small woody ornamentals are getting established, consider the cosmos. It grows 2 to 4 feet tall with daisy-like flowers in clear white, pinks, orchid, crimson, orange, and yellow. Fluted, striped and Picotee types add color and variety.

GREEN THUMB CARE: After plants are 2 feet tall, pinch back to induce side branches to form. Pinching delays blooming, so don't pinch too late or you won't get blooms. They like a well drained, gravelly soil, and full sun. Avoid heavy feeding as they don't require too rich a soil.

PROPAGATION: Start seed outdoors in May (after frost). Thin plants to 18 inches apart for nice, husky plants. You can start seed indoors for earlier blooming.

TROUBLES: May break in wind. Staking will prevent this.

●**Dahlia** Hybrids and dwarf annual dahlias as well as large-bloom ones, come in rich and varied colors. Grown from seed, dahlias are earlier to bloom and will form tubers which are handled similarly to the giant dahlias. Flowers are double or semi-double and single, ideal for cut flowers all summer long.

GREEN THUMB CARE: Dahlias need regular watering during the summer months. Keep spent blossoms pinched off for continuous bloom. If stems are dipped in hot water for a few minutes after cutting, the cut flowers will last for days.

PROPAGATION: Sow seed directly outdoors after danger of frost. For earlier bloom start indoors or in a cold frame. The tubers of colors you like may be saved, since separate colors of these dwarfs are not possible from seed.

TROUBLE: *Tarnished plant bug and leafhopper. Control*: Spray with Malathion, or nicotine sulfate. See Chapter XVI.

●**Eustoma** (See Lisianthus)

●**Gerbera** (Transvaal Daisy) If you live in a warm region, gerbera (also spelled geberia) is a perennial. In cold regions it's grown as an annual. Popular with florists as a cut flower because of its strong stems and graceful single and double blooms. Gerberas are ideal in a greenhouse, outdoors in a summer border, or as a pot plant. If you like the double-flower type, grow Parade from seed. It comes 75 percent doubles, and in rose, pink, scarlet, crimson, yellow, white, and many shades in between.

PROPAGATION: Start indoors in February for summer bloom. Sow seed in loose mixture, at 72 degrees F. Transplant to 3-inch pots and set outdoors in warm weather.

TROUBLES: Gerberas have few if any troubles. Sometimes aphids attack, but are controlled with Malathion or nicotine sulfate. See also Chapter XIV.

●**Impatiens** (Day Plant or Sultana) No annual has gained so fast in popularity as this shady lady. If you want a riot of color for shady (or sunny) areas, nothing is better. Impatiens (Im-pay-she-enz) are extremely tolerant of air pollution. Solid colors, variegated, and bicolors in both blooms and foliage produce a spectacular show. Both dwarf and taller hybrids come in shades of crimson, fuchsia, orange, orchid, pink, rose, salmon, scarlet, and white. Double-flowered varieties are also available. All types are suitable for hanging baskets, window boxes, porch pots, and even houseplants. Like begonias, they are self-cleaning so there are no faded blooms to remove.

Handsome New Guinea hybrid impatiens were developed from plants brought to the U.S. by a team of U.S.D.A. plant scientists from New Guinea in 1971. These impatiens, with their striking foliage and flowers, need full sun for good bloom and leaf color. Previously, New Guinea impatiens were propagated from cuttings only. Now seeds are available from some seed companies. One introduction is called Spectra.

GREEN THUMB CARE: Regular impatiens will tolerate a rather poor soil, but all do better in a loose, well-balanced soil. Most varieties can be grown in full sun but regular Day plants prefer some shade at least part of the day. They will *not* tolerate poor drainage. Dwarfs grow to a height of 8 to 10 inches and plants are base-branching, meaning you don't have to pinch them for bushiness. The taller types grow from 12 to 20 inches high, and should be pinched for bushy plants—just snip out the tip and root it in water for another plant.

PROPAGATION: Sow seed in a loose mix such as half perlite, vermiculite, or sharp sand and peat moss or one of the prepared sterile mixes. Do not cover with soil, as they need light to germinate. (See *Sowing Seeds* in Chapter XV.) For transplanting we use a mixture of two parts perlite, vermiculite or sand, 1 part organic matter (peat moss or compost) and 1 part loam. Remember a loose soil mix dries out fast and may need frequent watering. For winter bloom indoors, cuttings can be taken from outdoor blooming plants in early fall and rooted in water. Remove all but a few top leaves so they will not wilt. They do well potted in one part each of sand, peat moss, and loam. Give them a light feeding (liquid plant food) once a month and a temperature about 68 degrees F., and they'll give you a dazzling color display during the short days of the winter months. If plants get sprawly in winter, just pinch the tips back (root tips and give to friends).

TROUBLES: *Red spider mites indoors, aphids outdoors. Control:* Spray with detergent and water, or buttermilk spray for mites or nicotine sulfate for aphids. (see Chapter XIV).

Whitefly. Control: There is a synthetic pyrethroid spray (identified on the label) which works fine on white flies, but this spray should not be used on impatiens as damage to the plants may result. Spray with liquid household detergent, 1 tablespoon to a gallon of water. Be sure to cover undersides of the leaves.

Leaf drop on indoor plants. Due to spider mites, hot dry air, dry soil, or Botrytis blight. Day plants like a cool window. *Control:* Syringe plants once a week to discourage spider mites.

Crystals on leaves. Day plants have nectaries which give off crystals, transparent or sugary droplets on edge of leaves. Also, as the plants take up moisture, they bring up fertilizer salts from the soil; as water is lost from the leaves, the salts are crystallized and left on the edges of the leaves. Sometimes aphids secrete a sweet sticky honeydew material on the surface of leaves. *Control:* Wash them off with soap and tobacco water. (Soak cigar or cigarette butts in water.)

•**Larkspur** (*Annual delphinium*) Lovely branchy stalks of single or double florets, with white, pink, and shades of lavender, 3 feet tall. Ideal for cut flowers. Imperial strain produces large, compact blooms on long stems. Short variety is also available. Hardy larkspur is delphinium, a perennial.

GREEN THUMB CARE: Needs cool weather for good growth; otherwise plants will be stunted. During cool summers, will bloom all season. New varieties do not scatter (lose petals) as easily as older types.

PROPAGATION: Early-spring sowing outdoors or indoors for late summer bloom, or in fall outdoors for June blooms. Needs cool temperature for germination.

TROUBLES: None.

•**Lisianthus** (*Russellianus*) Also called Eustoma, commonly called Prairie Gentian. Parent plants were growing wild on Western Prairies. Japanese plant breeders took seeds and developed a more beautiful cut flower and pot plant. Now available in white and several shades of pink and blue as well as variegated. Currently doubles are more popular than single bloomed varieties. Cut flowers last 1 to 2 weeks in water.

GREEN THUMB CARE: Needs full sun and uniform supply of water.

PROPAGATION: Tiny seeds are difficult to germinate. They take 21 days at a constant temperature of 72 degrees F. and must be kept moist.

TROUBLES: Needs good air circulation to prevent Fusarium and Rhizoctonia.

•**Marigold** (*Tagetes*) Gardeners have a bewildering number of marigolds to choose from: tall mum types, short mum types, carnation-flowered and ball-flowered; large flowered dwarf, dwarf single, and dwarf double-flowering types; the African (*erecta*) and the French (*patula*). Ideal for urns, porch boxes, background plantings, edgings along drives and walks. Few annuals are more dependable. They come in all shades of yellow, orange, gold, bronze, and even white can now be included. Bicolors are prevalent among new varieties.

GREEN THUMB CARE: Thrives in almost any kind of soil, blooms continuously in summer heat—especially the dwarf and semi-dwarf types. Foliage is strong-smelling, but there are odorless varieties. Pick off seed heads for continuous bloom. Some large-flowering marigolds bloom late, so be sure to buy early-flowering types if you get early frosts.

PROPAGATION: Seed sown outdoors; indoors for early bloom.

TROUBLES: *Failure to bloom*. Tall varieties are affected by day length and some won't blossom until days are shorter in fall. Some hybrids will flower earlier, so order these if you want earlier blooms. If dwarf edging marigolds fail to bloom. check buds for thrips and tarnished plant bugs (see Chapter XIV.) Spray with nicotine solution. Spider mites can cause mottled and brown foliage. Look for cobwebs on tips. Spray buttermilk spray, or syringe with water daily. See detergent formulas and other homemade pesticides in Chapter XIV.

•**Morning glories** (*Ipomea*) Although there are red, white, blue and bicolor varieties, Heavenly Blue is still the favorite of this popular annual vine. Thrives in poor soil and grows almost anywhere so long as it has sun. In dull weather the flowers stay open most of the day, but on sunny days they close up about noon, and very hot weather wilts them. Makes a good screening vine.

Moonflowers are a form of morning glory with larger vines, larger leaves and huge, fragrant white flowers. They start to open in late afternoon, stay open all night and close in the morning.

GREEN THUMB CARE: Likes a soil not too fertile and does well without too much moisture. They need a trellis or strings to climb on. Cloudy, wet weather produces lots of runners and leaves, few or no blooms. Will bloom more freely if growing tips are nipped out before buds form. This forces the growth of side shoots which bloom profusely.

PROPAGATION: Seed. Morning glories have a hard seed coat. To aid germination, soak seed overnight in warm water (or file a notch in the seed). Sow outdoors, after danger of frost, in the place where they are to remain, or sow them in individual peat pots indoors, so roots will not be disturbed when planting outdoors. Start two or three weeks before outdoor planting date. Seed germinates irregularly so don't give up too easily. Plant 3 or 4 seeds in each pot. If all germinate, let 2 remain in each pot.

TROUBLES: *Browning and wilting of foliage*, due to fungi in soils. *Control*: Do not grow vines in same spot year after year, or grow in tubs or pots, so you can change soil yearly.

•**Nasturtiums** (*Tropaeolum*, pronounced "tro-pee-o-lum") An old-fashioned plant which remains popular, some folks like the leaves in sandwiches. Ideal for poor soil, hot weather, tolerates semi-shade. The tall type is ideal for trellises and window boxes and to cover walls. Flowers are orange, yellow, red, and variegated. They will climb to considerable height during the summer if given support. Wonderful for hanging baskets.

There are also the dwarf semi-double types with short runners, the globe type, which makes a compact plant, and varieties with variegated leaves. Dwarf Jewel is a dandy, with fragrant flowers well above foliage. If you've got an old stump that needs hiding, plant a few nasturtium seeds in soil on it and let the plants cover the stump.

GREEN THUMB CARE: Don't sow in too rich a soil or you will get mostly leaves and few or no flowers.

PROPAGATION: Sow outdoors in late spring, or start seeds indoors in peat pots, for early bloom.

TROUBLES: *Aphids. Control*: Nicotine sulfate and soap, or Malathion alone will control, but bear in mind these are poisonous materials, so be sure to wash the foliage well if you eat it. See section on Controls of Insects and Diseases.

•**Petunias** Until recently, petunias were the most popular annuals in America. Now they are being challenged by impatiens and begonias. Some of the reasons are that petunias need more care, often get straggly by mid-summer, and do not stand up as well in hot or rainy weather. However, their many colors, types of growth, and the vigor of the many hybrids, especially the double multiflora types, still make them favorites. Whether you want to use them in pots, beds, hanging baskets, or window boxes, there is a petunia which has been developed especially for the purpose.

Petunia classification is so confusing that even expert gardeners have a hard time deciding which kind to select. Here is a general grouping to guide you:

Grandiflora (Giant Flower): The larger-flowered kinds, including those with fringed, waved, and plain edges. This class includes both F_1 hybrids and open-pollinated varieties. White bordered Picotee types are in this class. (See Chapter XV.)

Multiflora (Many Flowered): Smaller-flowered or bedding F_1 hybrids. Blooms in greatest profusion. Includes both single and double types.

Single Floribunda: 2 to 3 inch blooms on compact plants for mass plantings and bedding. Disease resistant and weather tolerant.

Cascade: Replaces old Balcony types. It is ideal for hanging baskets and balcony plantings. Blooms are $3\,^1\!/_2$ to 5 inches on stems which lend themselves to flowing habit.

Double-Flowered: These have more than one row of petals. They include both the large double varieties (grandifloras) with flowers up to 5 inches across, and the smaller kinds, sometimes called carnation-flowered or multifloras (2- to 3-inch flowers).

Impatiens or day plants (also called busy Lizzie) will grow in sun or shade. Ideal as bedding plants, can also be grown in pots or hanging baskets. Avoid overfeeding as it causes plants to stretch up and become scraggly, cutting down on number of blossoms. (*Courtesy National Garden Bureau, Inc.*)

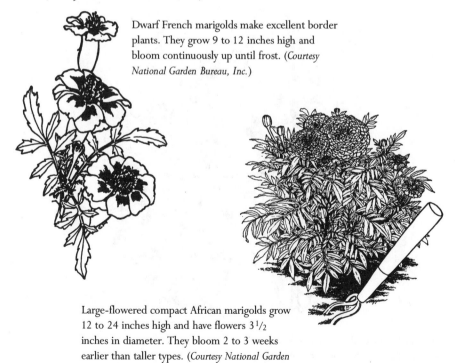

Dwarf French marigolds make excellent border plants. They grow 9 to 12 inches high and bloom continuously up until frost. (*Courtesy National Garden Bureau, Inc.*)

Large-flowered compact African marigolds grow 12 to 24 inches high and have flowers 3 1/2 inches in diameter. They bloom 2 to 3 weeks earlier than taller types. (*Courtesy National Garden Bureau, Inc.*)

Large-flowered, tall African marigolds reach 3 feet in height. (*Courtesy National Garden Bureau, Inc.*)

Petunias are still No. 1 bedding annual, coming in all colors except gold and orange. They bloom from summer until killed by fall frost. (*Courtesy National Garden Bureau, Inc.*)

Pansies make one of the finest cut flowers you can grow. They like full sun and ample moisture. (*Courtesy National Garden Bureau, Inc.*)

GREEN THUMB CARE: Petunias like full sun, ample water in summer. Don't just remove the faded blooms; pinch off the seed pods too to maintain plant vigor. If faded blossoms and pods are picked off, the plants will keep right on blooming.

PROPAGATION: Start indoors in early spring or late winter using a soilless mix. Sow thinly and do not cover; press the seed in lightly and water by submerging the seed flat in a shallow pan. (See Chapter XV for care of seed box and seedlings.)

Since double petunia seedlings develop a little more slowly than the singles, seed should be sown indoors about two and a half months before outdoor planting time.

TROUBLES: Petunias are often attacked by snails which eat holes in blooms and leaves. See Chapter XIV for snails and slugs, flea beetles and other pests.

Damping-off: A real problem in raising petunias. *Control*: Use a sterile mix for starting seed (see Chapter XV) and sow thinly. If crowded, seedling plants do not get enough air and rot sets in.

Botrytis Blight. Another form of damping-off. Air-borne. The leaves take on a watery, glassy appearance and the whole plant suddenly dies. *Control*: Provide good air circulation with an electric fan.

Soil-borne diseases, rhizoctonia and pythium, are controlled by soil sterilization. They cause plants to wilt and die. Do not grow petunias in same spot year after year. If you are a smoker be sure to wash your hands before handling petunia plants, since you are likely to infect with tobacco mosaic.

●**Phlox** (*Drummondii*) Showy, dainty flowers in solid and starred varieties in an unusually wide assortment of colors. Phlox is easy to grow and stands heat well. The dwarf, neat plants are fine for bedding and highly effective in masses; needs full sun and blooms all summer long.

GREEN THUMB CARE: Cut off faded blooms so seed pods cannot form. This extends blooming period and makes plants more compact. Feed and water regularly. Some gardeners shear the plant back after the first blooms fade.

PROPAGATION: Self-sows readily. Fall-sown seed will bloom the following May or June. You can start indoors in March or sow outdoors in April or early May, as it is quite hardy. Self-sown seeds may not produce same colors as parent.

TROUBLES: None.

●**Portulaca** (Rose-moss) A gay and accommodating flower that grows in the poorest and driest ground as long as it gets plenty of sun. It seeds itself and is unrivaled for brilliance among plants of low growth. The flowers open only in full sun, closing at night and on cloudy days. The succulent, needle-like foliage has a creeping habit. It is ideal for lining sidewalks and driveways, around garages, on sunny banks, and even between stepping stones. Some gardeners broadcast the seed over rock gardens to fill them with color. Good also to cover bare spots and stumps. Grows 3 to 6 inches tall. Single and double flowers in red, pink, rose, yellow, white, and shades in between.

GREEN THUMB CARE: Keep weeds out. Avoid heavy watering.

PROPAGATION: Sow seed outdoors after soil is warm. Blooms in six weeks, continuing until frost. Plant self-sows, but the doubles revert to singles even though colors remain vivid. Scatter seed on surface and thin plants later to 6 inches apart. Can also be started indoors 6 to 8 weeks before outdoor planting date.

TROUBLES: None.

•**Salvia** (Scarlet Sage) Few plants are more striking in a mass than a bed of salvia; you'll also like the brilliant red flowers planted among evergreens or in borders. But there is a world of difference in the habit of growth and blooming dates of the several types available. The early dwarfs (8-12 inches tall) bloom from late June until frost. The intermediate type grows about 16 inches high, blooms from mid-July til frost. Late salvia blooms from early-August until frost and grows 24 to 30 inches tall.

GREEN THUMB CARE: Keep watered in summer.

PROPAGATION: Start indoors 8 weeks prior to outdoor planting. Do not plant outdoors until all danger of frost is over. When beginning, do not cover seeds. Simply press them into the top of the soil.

•**Blue salvia** Long, graceful spikes with long stems in a most attractive shade of light blue, ideal for cutting. Plants require the same care as scarlet salvia and will continue to flower right up until late fall.

TROUBLES: Neither red nor blue salvia has any troubles to speak of. White fly may molest them. Spray undersides of leaves with 1 tablespoon liquid household detergent in 1 gallon of water. See Chapter XIV.

•**Snapdragons** (*Antirrhinum*, pronounced "an-tir-rye-num") Available in a variety of excellent colors. Although there are tall and dwarfs, the medium-height varieties are best for general purposes. The more you cut the spikes, the more the plants produce.

Today's hybrids are earlier to bloom, branch more freely and have an upright habit of growth, enabling them to withstand moderate winds without support. Butterfly (open-faced) types have become popular. They are available in tall and dwarf sizes as well as single and double blooms. For an edging, you might want to try the floral carpet snaps.

GREEN THUMB CARE: Plants will be "leggy" unless you pinch them back when 2 inches high. For husky seedlings, grow in a cool place. They will withstand frost after hardening. Grow in sun in a well-drained soil. Dwarf plants produce up to 25 little 3-inch spikes all in bloom at once. Shear each one off after blooming to extend display.

PROPAGATION: Sow indoors 10 weeks before outdoor planting. The seed is fine and has little "pushing up" power. Sow in loose soil and cover lightly (just sift fine peat moss over the seed) or you'll get poor germination.

TROUBLES: Rust. Chocolate-brown puffs on the undersides of the leaves. Rust is the most serious disease of indoor and outdoor snaps. *Control:* Dust with Ferbam, sulfur, or Zineb. If you use sulfur, try to keep it off the blooms, as it bleaches or burns them. Weekly dusting during periods of rain and fortnightly doses during dry weather will do the trick. It's always a good idea to dust when plants are young to prevent rust from getting a foothold. Use rust-resistant varieties also.

Verticillium Wilt. If plants suddenly wilt, pull them up and burn or seal in a plastic bag and discard. Plant in a new location in well drained soil.

Aphids. Control: Spray with Malathion or nicotine sulfate. See Chapter XIV.

•**Stocks** (*Matthiola*) Everyone likes the spicy fragrance of stocks, but not everyone can get this plant to bloom outdoors. Stocks like cool weather and must be started indoors or they may not bloom when warm weather rolls around. The Trysomic seven weeks stocks have been bred for earliness and ability to stand up under summer heat. They

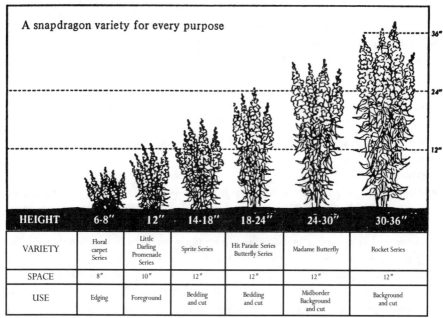

A snapdragon variety for every purpose

HEIGHT	6-8"	12"	14-18"	18-24"	24-30"	30-36"
VARIETY	Floral carpet Series	Little Darling Promenade Series	Sprite Series	Hit Parade Series Butterfly Series	Madame Butterfly	Rocket Series
SPACE	8"	10"	12"	12"	12"	12"
USE	Edging	Foreground	Bedding and cut	Bedding and cut	Midborder Background and cut	Background and cut

Snapdragons are one of the best all-purpose flowers for the home garden. There are dwarfs for borders, and taller types for excellent cut flowers, in all colors of the rainbow. (*Courtesy Geo. J. Ball Co., Inc.*)

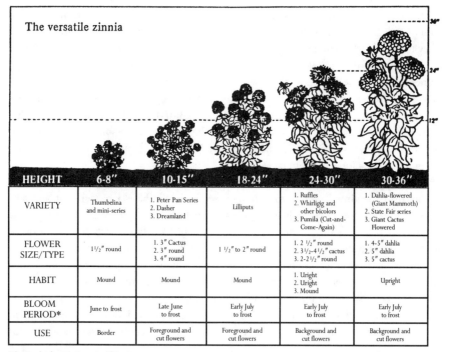

The versatile zinnia

HEIGHT	6-8"	10-15"	18-24"	24-30"	30-36"
VARIETY	Thumbelina and mini-series	1. Peter Pan Series 2. Dasher 3. Dreamland	Lilliputs	1. Ruffles 2. Whirligig and other bicolors 3. Pumila (Cut-and-Come-Again)	1. Dahlia-flowered (Giant Mammoth) 2. State Fair series 3. Giant Cactus Flowered
FLOWER SIZE/TYPE	1 1/2" round	1. 3" Cactus 2. 3" round 3. 4" round	1 1/2" to 2" round	1. 2 1/2" round 2. 3 1/2-4 1/2" cactus 3. 2-2 1/2" round	1. 4-5" dahlia 2. 5" dahlia 3. 5" cactus
HABIT	Mound	Mound	Mound	1. Uright 2. Uright 3. Mound	Upright
BLOOM PERIOD*	June to frost	Late June to frost	Early July to frost	Early July to frost	Early July to frost
USE	Border	Foreground and cut flowers	Foreground and cut flowers	Background and cut flowers	Background and cut flowers

*Blooming date from May 1st sowing-(Chicago)

Popularity of zinnias has been increased by the fact that they come in so many sizes, shapes, and colors. (*Courtesy Geo. J. Ball Co., Inc.*)

grow to 15-18 inches high, producing fragrant spikes, which branch out into bushy plants. The so-called double ten weeks stocks are favorites for outdoor growing and bloom ten weeks after sowing. Longlasting flowers are ideal for vase arrangements, and come in a variety of colors: white, lavender, purple, light pink, rose, red, and cream; all have fragrant blooms.

GREEN THUMB CARE: No pinching is necessary. Remove spent blossoms. When cutting for bouquets, pound the stem ends with a hammer or knife handle to help them take up water better.

PROPAGATION: Seed sown indoors 8-10 weeks before outdoor planting, or directly outdoors.

TROUBLES: None

•**Sweet peas** (*Lathyrus*—pronounced "lath-i-russ—*odoratus*") One of very few fragrant annual flowers. The Cuthbertson type, a spring-flowering strain, is quite heat-resistant. Floribundas and multifloras are free-flowering and long-stemmed. Spencer types are good for the home garden, especially where summers are not too hot. Royal Family has large flowers. Continental is an early bloomer. Plants from 24 to 30 inches tall and produce very fragrant flowers in a full range of colors: salmon, scarlet, rose, navy blue, light blue, and crimson. They are ideal for flower arrangements and need no trellis to grow on. BiJou is a bush type which grows 12-18 inches tall with early, long-lasting flowers in a complete color range.

GREEN THUMB CARE: Sweet peas need sunlight and plenty of water. Being a legume they need lime, applied at rate of half a pound to a 15-foot row. Also add 1 pound of complete plant food to a 15-foot row. Pick flowers daily, or vines will wither. If many seed pods form, the vine will die. Cut flowers in the morning before sun hits them. If blooms wilt after picking, hold stems under warm water and cut off an inch or two. They'll recover in thirty minutes. With trailing types, support vines early, when 4 inches high, because if they topple over they seldom do as well again. Chicken wire or twiggy branches stuck in both sides of the row give good support.

PROPAGATION: Sow seed in fall or early spring. Dig soil deep, work in generous amounts of humus, but never manure (because of Botrytis blight). Sow seeds 2 inches apart in a furrow 2 or 3 inches deep, and cover lightly with loose soil. After plants are 4 or 5 inches high, give a side dressing of 5-10-5. A feeding of liquid plant food when they are in bud gives a longer blooming season.

TROUBLES: *Seed rot. Control:* Treat the seed with Captan. White seeds seem to rot more readily than the tinted ones, and very dark seeds usually have a harder coat and take longer to germinate. Nick each seed with a file before sowing. If your seed rots in the ground, try pre-sprouting it: place the seed in a moist medium, such as wet cotton or shallow pans of water, for three to five days at 70 to 80 degrees F.

Anthracnose. After a good start, leaves suddenly wilt and dry up before blooms have a chance to develop. *Control:* Plant in a new spot. Destroying plant debris in fall removes a fertile source of spores in the spring. Spray young plants with Captan.

Black root rot. Infected plants are dwarf, yellow, and sickly. Diseased plants linger for long periods but fail to bloom. Roots turn black and rot. *Control:* Use a new spot for growing.

Rhizoctonia root rot. Young plants are completely destroyed by damping-off, causing uneven stands. Older plants are dwarfed and die, producing no blooms. Roots decay and turn brown, not black as in black root rot. *Control*: Same as for black root rot.

Root knot. Small galls on roots give a gnarled appearance. Plants dwarf and yellowish. *Control*: None. Remove plants, seal in plastic bag and discard. Do not replant in same area.

Mildew. White, powdery growth on upper leaf surfaces, causing leaves to shrivel and fail. *Control*: Spray with Captan.

Mosaic (Virus). Spread by aphids. Leaves curl and take on a distinct yellowish, mottled effect. Shortened flower stalks, and color of blooms is broken. *Control*: Remove infected plants, spray with nicotine sulfate or Malathion to control aphids. See section on Control of Insects and Diseases.

Bud drop. Caused by lack of light or improper fertilization. *Control*: Feed balanced plant food.

●**Vinca** (*Catharanthus roseus*) Commonly called periwinkle. Has glossy deep green leaves and impatiens-like blooms. Gaining in popularity for pots, beds and hanging baskets. Those with dark color eyes are especially attractive. So far they only come in shades of pink, lavender and white.

GREEN THUMB CARE: Will tolerate hot conditions but needs regular watering; dry soil stunts plants.

PROPAGATION: Sow seeds 12 weeks before planting-out time. Cover lightly with sowing medium and keep seeds in the dark and at 75 degrees F. until germination starts. Grow at 72 degrees until transplanting; then grow at 65 degrees F.

TROUBLES: Rotting due to overwatering or poor drainage. Stunted growth due to dry soil or cold temperature.

●**Zinnia** The zinnia is perhaps the best all-purpose annual in our gardens. In its native country, Mexico, it was called the "eyesore" plant because the original flowers were a dirty orange or a washed-out magenta color. The plant has been dramatized and hybridized so that we now have a bewildering color range (solid, striped, and variegated) and many types to choose from. Zinnias bloom all summer.

Ten years ago if you asked a male gardener what his favorite annual was, nine out of ten would have said "zinnia." It still is a favorite, but discouraging to many because of its susceptibility to alternaria blight, a fungus disease manifested by brown spots which enlarge and cause leaves to parch, eventually killing the plant. There is no chemical control, but breeders have developed some remarkably resistant varieties.

GREEN THUMB CARE: The crown flower (first to appear) can be cut early, forcing the blooms on the side branches to grow larger. Give them full sun. Grow in almost any soil.

PROPAGATION: Seed. Zinnia seeds germinate quickly, from four to ten days, giving you flowers about forty days after sowing. Seed started indoors and potted up in bands may even bloom quicker, although most gardeners have good luck sowing outdoors and transplanting. You can save your own zinnia seed after a frost has blackened the plants. (But do not bother to save seed from hybrids, as they will not come true.) Store seed in glass jars.

WHAT'S THE BEST ZINNIA? Gardeners often ask about size, height, bloom period, etc., of zinnias.

GREEN THUMB NOTE: To avoid alternaria blight, try these disease-resistant types: Lilliputs (pompons), cut-and-come-again types, State Fair (giant-sized).

TROUBLES: Worst trouble is *alternaria leaf* and *blossom blight*.

The Fungus is spread by wind and rain and is known to be disseminated on seed from infected plants. Alternaria is worse in periods of dew, fog, rain, or overhead irrigation. Under such conditions it can spread like wildfire.

Once the soil has become infected, the fungus will survive the winter and infect plants again the following season—even though you start out with perfectly healthy plants. If zinnias are planted in the same area year after year the disease becomes progressively worse and all you have by August is a crop of brown plants. The most conspicuous symptom is spotting and blighting of foliage and blooms. The spots are reddish-brown in color, often having grayish centers. Although the individual spots are usually less than $1/4$ inch, they may become so numerous as to completely ruin foliage and blossoms. In severe cases, the entire plant withers and dies. *Control*: Pull up infected plants and burn, or seal in plastic bag and discard. The small varieties (smaller flowers) are more resistant to alternaria than the large flowering types.

Mildew. White, powdery discoloration of the foliage, starting in late summer. Sometimes causes leaves to curl up or plants to shrivel in dry weather. *Control*: Dust with sulfur, bordeaux, or Karathane. Zenith series and State Fair are mildew resistant.

Tarnished Plant Bug. If blossoms open only halfway, chances are the trouble is due to tarnished plant bug. This pest injects a poison whenever it stings, dwarfing or stunting the plant in the area of the sting. *Control*: See Chapter XIV.

•Other Bonus Annuals The preceding list of annuals was shortened reluctantly. There are dozens of other blue ribbon annuals we'd like to see you grow in your garden. These include Amaranthus (Joseph's Coat); Anchusa (Summer Forget-Me-Not); Balsam (Ladyslipper); Centaurea cyanus (Bachelor's Buttons or cornflower); Chrysanthemum (annual); Clarkia; Datura (angel's trumpet); Dianthus (annual pinks); Eschscholtzia (California poppy); Gaillardia (annual blanket flower); Gomphrena (globe amaranth); Gypsophila (baby's-breath); Helianthus annus (tall-growing sunflower); Helichrysum (strawflower); Hibiscus (annual mallow); Iberis (candytuft); Kochia (summer cypress); Lavatera (loveliness); Lobelia; Mirabilis (four-o-clocks); Molucella laevis (bells of Ireland); Nicotiana (flowering tobacco); Nierembergia (cup-flower); Pansy; Papaver (Shirley poppy); Polygonum Orientale (kiss-me-over-the-garden-gate, or prince's feather); Reseda (mignonette); Ricinus (castor bean); Salpiglossis (painted tongue); Sanvitalia (creeping zinnia); Scabiosa (pin-cushion flower); Schizanthus (poor man's orchid); Statice (sea lavender, a half-hardy annual); Tithonia (Mexican sunflower); Verbena; Vinca (periwinkle).

LOW-GROWING ANNUALS: 6 TO 9 INCHES

Ageratum, dwarf
Alyssum
Anagallis (Pimpernel)
Begonia, dwarf
Impatiens, dwarf
Lobelia, dwarf
Lupine
Marigolds, miniature
Nemesia

Nemophila (Baby blue-eyes)
Nierembergia
Phlox, dwarf
Plumosa, dwarf
Portulaca
Snapdragon, dwarf
Verbena
Virginia stock
Zinnia (Thumbelina)

MEDIUM ANNUALS: 1 TO 2 FEET

Ageratum, tall
Aster
Balsam
Brachycome (Swan River Daisy)
Begonia, tall
Calendula
Coreopsis, dwarf (Calliopsis)
Celosia (Cockscomb), dwarf
Clarkia
Cynoglossum (Chinese Forget-me-not)
Dianthus (Pinks)
Dimorphotheca (Cape Marigold)
Eschscholtzia (California Poppy)
Four-O'Clock
Gaillardia (annual)
Gilia

Godetia, dwarf
Gypsophila (Baby's-Breath)
Hollyhocks (certain varieties)
Hunnemannia (Tulip Poppy)
Iberis (Candytuft)
Impatiens
Larkspur
Marigold, dwarf
Petunia, medium
Salpiglossis
Salvias
Schizanthus, dwarf
Snapdragon, medium
Statice
Stock
Zinnia, dwarf

TALL ANNUALS: 2 TO 3-1/2 FEET

Antirrhinum, tall (Snapdragons)
Campanula (Canterbury Bells)
Celosia, tall (Cockscomb)
Centaurea (Bachelor's Buttons)
Dahlia (annual types)
Didiscus (Blue Lace Flower)
Godetia, tall (Satin Flower)
Gomphrena (Globe Amaranth)
Helichrysum (Strawflower)

Hollyhocks (annual types)
Lupinus (Lupine)
Marigold, tall
Scabiosa
Schizanthus, tall
Shirley Poppy
Sunflower Sweet Sultan
Zinnia, tall

VERY TALL ANNUALS: 4 TO 12 FEET

Amaranthus

Castor Bean

Cleome (Spider Flower)

Cosmos

Helianthus, tall (Sunflower)

Hollyhocks (certain varieties)

Nicotiana (Flowering Tobacco)

Tithonia

ANNUALS WHICH TOLERATE SEMI-SHADE

Alyssum

Aster

Balsam

Begonia

Browallia

Centaurea (Cornflower)

Coleus

Coreopsis (Calliopsis)

Cynoglossum

Godetia

Impatiens

Lobelia

Lupines

Myosotis (Forget-Me-Not)

Nasturtium

Nicotiana

Pansy

Petunia

Phacelia (annual)

Snapdragon

Salvia

Virginia Stock

Vinca (Periwinkle)

Viola

ANNUALS FOR HOT, DRY PLACES

Arctotis

Centaurea (Cornflower)

Coreopsis (Calliopsis)

Eschscholtzia (California Poppy)

Gaillardia (annual)

Ipomoea (Morning Glory)

Phlox drummondii

Portulaca

Salvia

Statice

Zinnia

ANNUALS FOR POOR SOIL

Alyssum

Amaranthus

Balsam

Calendula

Centaurea (Cornflower)

Coreopsis (Calliopsis)

Eschscholtzia (California Poppy)

Four-O'clock

Godetia

Nasturtium

Poppies

Portulaca

ANNUALS FOR SANDY SOIL

Balsam

Cockscomb

California Poppies

Coreopsis (Calliopsis)

ANNUALS FOR SANDY SOIL

Gaillardia (annual)
Marigolds
Nasturtiums
Petunias

Poppies
Portulaca
Summer Cypress
Sweet Sultan

ANNUALS WHICH DO WELL IN WINDOW BOXES

Ageratum
Alyssum
Begonia
Coleus
Dusty Miller (*Centaurea*)
Geranium, carefree
Impatiens
Lobelia
Marigolds, dwarf

Nasturtium, dwarf
Pansy
Petunia
Phlox, dwarf
Portulaca
Salvia, dwarf
Verbena
Vinca (Periwinkle)
Zinnia

ANNUALS FOR ROCK GARDENS

Here are some fool-proof rock garden plants that will give you a continuous show with proper selection.

Botanical Name	Common Name	Remarks
Alyssum	Alyssum	Pink, lavender; summer
Dimorphotheca	Cape Marigold	Orange, white; summer
Gypsophila muralis	Wall Gypsophila	White, pink; summer
Iberis umbellata	Candytuft	Pink, white, red, lavender
Lobelia	Lobelia	White, purple; summer, fall
Nierembergia	Cup-flower	Purple; summer
Petunia	Petunia	Various; summer to frost
Portulaca	Portulaca	Red, yellow, pink; summer, fall
Phlox	Annual Phlox	White, rose, pink; all summer
Sanvitalia	Creeping Zinnia	Yellow; late summer, fall
Verbena	Verbena	Various; summer, fall

ANNUALS FOR A SEASHORE GARDEN

Alyssum
Candytuft
Centaurea (Cornflower)
Coreopsis (Calliopsis)
Dianthus
Eschscholtzia (California Poppy)

Gaillardia (annual)
Geranium
Larkspur
Nasturtium
Phlox

ANNUALS WHICH PRODUCE FOLIAGE EFFECTS

Amaranthus

Bells of Ireland (*Molucella*)

Castor Bean

Cockscomb

Coleus

Euphorbia (Snow-on-the-Mountain)

Flowering Kale

Kochia (Summer Cypress)

Ornamental Grasses

Prickly Poppy

SOME "HEDGE" ANNUALS

Balsam

Celosia

Cosmos

Helianthus (Sunflower)

Hollyhock

Kochia (Summer Cypress)

Mirabilis

Moonflower

Ricinus (Castor Bean)

Tall Marigolds

Tithonia

SOME GOOD ANNUAL VINES

Balloon Vine

Cardinal Climber

Calonyction (Moonflower)

Cobaea scandens (Rosenbergia
  Cathedral Bells)

Cypress Vine

Gourd

Hyacinth Bean (*Dolichos*)

Morning Glory

Nasturtium

Scarlet Runner Bean

Thunbergia

ANNUALS FOR HANGING BASKETS

Alyssum

Balsam, bush flowering

Begonia (*semperflorens*), dwarf

Browallia

Carnation (annual)

Coleus

Dusty Miller

Impatiens, dwarf

Lobelia

Marigold, dwarf

Morning Glory (keep trimmed)

Nasturtium

Nierembergia

Petunia

Portulaca

Verbena

Zinnia, dwarf

ANNUALS FOR FRAGRANCE

Alyssum: Sweet, delicate.

Dianthus (Garden Pinks): spicy.

ANNUALS FOR FRAGRANCE

Heliotrope: Considered the par excellence of fragrance.
Marigold: Intolerable to some, agreeable to others.
Mignonette—Delightful to all.
Nasturtium: Admired by some.
Nicotiana: A delight in the evening.
Pansy: A refreshing fragrance.
Petunia: Heavy.
Phlox, annual: Delicate.
Stock: Fresh, spicy, unusual fragrance.
Sweet Peas: Delicate, enjoyed by all.
Sweet Sultan: Delicate.
Verbena: Some have fragrance of Trailing Arbutus

ANNUALS FOR CUTTING

Anchusa
Antirrhinum (Snapdragon)
Arctotis
Aster
Calendula
Celosia
Centaurea (Cornflower)
Chrysanthemum (annual)
Clarkia
Coreopsis (Calliopsis)
Cosmos
Cynoglossum
Gaillardia (annual)
Gypsophila (Baby's Breath)

Larkspur
Marigold
Nasturtium
Nicotiana
Nigella (Love-in-a-Mist)
Petunia
Phlox drummondii
Scabiosa
Statice
Stocks
Strawflower
Sweet Peas
Sweet Sultan
Verbena
Zinnia

Here are some good annuals you can grow and use for dried arrangements. All can be dried by hanging upside down. (For more information on dried arrangements see *The Green Thumb Book of Indoor Gardening*.)

Acroclinium—white, violet or rose chaff-like heads 1-2 feet

Baby's Breath—White or Pink, dainty, cloud-like masses of blooms

Bachelor's Button or Cornflower (Centaurea)—red, white, blue, pink, feathery round blooms

Bells of Ireland (*Molucella*)—green and white, bell-shaped blooms

Celosia or Cockscomb (Celosia)—Crimson, yellow, pink, either spikes or comb-shaped

Globe Amaranth (Gomphrena)—pink, white, lavender, clover-like flowers

Grasses (ornamental), various types

Honesty (Lunaria)—flat silver seed pods

Job's Tears (Coix-lacryma-jobi)—green or variegated sword-shaped leaves, white bead-like seeds

Larkspur (annual delphinium)—white, pink, blue spikes or spurred flowers

Salvia—1 to 3 foot spires, blue, white, pink, red

Strawflower (*Helichrysum*)—round, many-petaled, pink, rose, salmon, white, yellow straw-like flowers

Sunflower (*Helianthus*)—golden yellow heads 3 to 18 inches across

Winged Everlasting (*Ammobium alatum*)—winged stems, silvery leaves, yellow blooms

ANNUALS WHICH SELF-SOW*

Alyssum	Gypsophila
Anchusa	Larkspurs
Antirrhinum (Snapdragon)	Morning Glories
Balsam	Nicotiana
Calendulas	Petunias
California Poppy	Portulaca
Coreopsis (Calliopsis)	Shirley Poppy
Cornflowers	Snow-on-the-Mountain
Cosmos	Sunflowers
Cynoglossum	Sweet Alyssum

*Self-sown plants usually do not produce blooms resembling the parent plant; most will be inferior.

ANNUALS WHICH BLOOM THROUGHOUT THE SEASON IF SUCCESSIVE SOWINGS ARE MADE

Baby's Breath	Forget-me-not
Bachelor's Button	Love-in-a-mist
Candytuft	Mignonette
Cape Marigold	Petunias
Coreopsis (Calliopsis)	Poppies

Here is a chart to help you have better luck starting seeds of annuals in your home or greenhouse.

SEED STARTING CHART FOR ANNUALS

Plant	Best Germinating Temperature in Degrees F.	Light or Darkness Needed	Average Number of Days for Germination	Time to Start Indoors for Outdoor Planting
Ageratum	70	Light	5 days	12 to 16 weeks
Alyssum	70	Either	5 days	12 to 16 weeks
Aster (annual)	70	Either	15 days	4 to 6 weeks
Begonia (fibrous rooted)	70	Light	15 days	18 to 22 weeks
Browallia	70	Light	15 days	12 to 16 weeks
Calendula (Pot Marigold)	70	Dark	10 days	4 to 6 weeks
Carnation (annual)	70	Either	20 days	12 to 16 weeks
Celosia	70	Either	10 days	6 to 8 weeks
Centaurea (Cornflower)	65	Dark	10 days	8 to 10 weeks
Coleus	70	Light	10 days	8 to 10 weeks
Cosmos	70	Either	5 days	6 to 8 weeks
Dahlia (from seed)	70	Either	5 days	10 to 12 weeks
Dianthus (Annual Pinks)	70	Either	5 days	12 to 16 weeks
Dusty Miller (Cineraria)	70	Light	10 days	12 to 14 weeks
Silver Feather	75	Either	14 to 21 days	18 to 22 weeks
Gaillardia (annual)	70	Either	20 days	12 to 16 weeks
Geranium (seed)	75	Either	5 to 10 days	18 to 20 weeks
Gerbera	72	Light	3 to 4 weeks	15 to 20 weeks
Heliotrope	70	Either	25 days	10 to 12 weeks
Hollyhock (annual)	60	Either	10 days	12 to 16 weeks
Impatiens (sultana or day plant)	70	Light	15 days	9 to 12 weeks
Lobelia	70	Either	20 days	15 to 22 weeks
Marigold (dwarf types)	70	Either	5 days	6 to 10 weeks
Marigold (tall types)	70	Either	5 days	6 to 10 weeks

Plant	Best Germinating Temperature in Degrees F.	Light or Darkness Needed	Average Number of Days for Germination	Time to Start Indoors for Outdoor Planting
Nicotiana (flowering tobacco)	70	Light	20 days	4 to 6 weeks
Nierembergia (dwarf Cup-Flower)	70	Either	15 days	10 to 12 weeks
Pansy	65	Dark	10 days	22 to 26 weeks
Petunia	70	Light	10 days	10 to 15 weeks
Phlox drummondii (annual)	65	Dark	10 days	8 to 12 weeks
Portulaca (Rose Moss)	70	Dark	15 days	6 to 8 weeks
Rudbeckia (Coneflower)	70	Either	10 days	10 to 12 weeks
Salvia Splendens	70	Light	15 days	8 to 14 weeks
Snapdragon	70	Light	10 days	12 to 14 weeks
Stock (Matthiola)	65	Either	14 days	6 to 8 weeks
Sweet Pea	55	Dark	15 days	8 to 10 weeks
Verbena	65	Dark	20 days	8 to 10 weeks
Vinca Rosea (Periwinkle)	70	Dark	15 days	10 to 20 weeks
Zinnia	70	Either	5 days	4 to 6 weeks

Our thanks to Rodale Press, Emmaus, Pennsylvania, for letting us reprint this chart from our book: *Organic Gardening Under Glass*, 1975.

FROST-PROOF ANNUALS

Bachelor's Button	Nierembergia
Calendulas	Pansy
California Poppy	Petunias
Carnation	Phlox
Dianthus	Scabiosa
Larkspur	Snapdragons
Lavatera (Mallow)	Stocks
Mignonette	Verbenas

ANNUALS WHICH MAY BE SOWN IN THE FALL

Alyssum	Cynoglossum
Anchusa	Datura
Antirrhinum (Snapdragon)	Dianthus
Aster	Eschscholtzia (California Poppy)
Calendula	Larkspur
Candytuft	Portulaca
Centaurea (Cornflower)	Shirley Poppy
Cleome	Sweet Peas
Cosmos	

It is wise to place a light evergreen mulch over beds of fall-sown plants. Let it be only an inch or so thick for it must not choke out the seedlings. Although many plants self-sow in the fall, most gardeners prefer to wait until spring to start their seeds.

Green Thumb Tips on Annuals

*If you have fairly good topsoil you can grow practically all annuals successfully.

*Scattered single plants of any one kind of flower give a spotty effect in the garden. Three plants of a kind in a group should be the minimum even in the smallest grouping.

*Annuals are ideal for growing in among a foundation planting of both evergreens and non-evergreens.

*Some annual seeds are fine and difficult to sow. A good idea is to mix the seed with five times its bulk of fine dry sand. Sow sand and all. A salt shaker is a handy dispenser.

*Hard-coated seeds such as sweet peas and morning glories start faster if soaked overnight in a teacup of water.

*Pinching out the centers of annual seedlings when they are 3 or 4 inches high develops stockier, stronger plants.

*Don't work in your flower beds on days when leaves are wet, since your shoes and clothing may spread anthracnose disease spores.

*Most low-growing annuals which flower early (such as alyssum) should be sheared off when the seed heads start to appear "ragged." You'll get a second bloom.

*Annuals in window boxes need water daily. Remove faded blossoms for greater mileage.

*Don't allow most plants to go to seed. It inhibits blooming.

*Flowers cut for indoors should be gathered in late afternoon and arranged in very warm water (110 degrees F.). Then put in a cool spot for one hour.

CHAPTER V

Perennials & Their Care

•

Perennials

A perennial is a plant whose roots live in the ground year after year, even though the tops die down each fall. These nearly ever-living plants are treasured not only for their long life but for their early response to warm spring days which quickly produce a luxuriant growth of leaves, covering the bed with a welcome green that serves as a natural background for the flower display.

Many folks say they would like to have a perennial garden because they want flowers that "come up by themselves and don't take any care." There's no such thing. It takes time and effort to keep a perennial bed neat and attractive, but it is worth it because with proper selection you can have beautiful flowers from early spring until frost. If your time is limited, select some of the best and easiest to grow. If you have time on your hands, you can have a more elaborate perennial garden. Choose carefully for size of plant, harmony in flower colors, foliage habit, and season and length of bloom, using our charts to guide you.

Beginners might start with the eight so-called "backbone" perennials for a continuous flower display. These, in order of bloom, are: daffodils, tulips (see Chapter VI), iris, peonies, delphinium, perennial phlox, hardy lilies (see Chapter VI), and hardy mums. To these you may add others, governed by your space and energy. Just remember that a perennial border can be like a runaway horse if you let it get the best of you.

COLOR AND TEXTURE The colors you select will vary greatly in their effect. For example, orange and scarlet are stimulating colors that will attract attention. Green leaves are quiet and restful. Yellows are warm and invigorating. Blues are cool colors with greatest appeal in the warm mid-summer months. There's no rule for arranging colors harmoniously, but of one thing you can be sure: white is the peacemaker in the perennial garden and makes other colors blend together better. It's better not to have more than two or three colors predominating at one time.

As for texture, the main point to keep in mind is that large-leaved, coarse-branched plants don't look well mixed with small-leaved, fine-twigged plants. One of the real pleasures of a perennial garden comes from rearranging plants from time to time and place to place to get better harmony of color, form, and texture, as well as better seasonal effects.

PLANNING Fall is an ideal time to get the perennial bed in shape for spring planting. Dig up the soil thoroughly, mix in plant food and compost or humus. The more organic matter you can incorporate into a sandy or clay soil the better it will be. Soils that bake hard in the summer or which are poorly drained are apt to give you trouble later on if not corrected beforehand.

Make the perennial bed 4 or 5 feet wide and curve it for effect. A bed 5 feet wide is as large as can be worked without getting into it. Remember that perennials in masses are showier than when set out in a hit-or-miss fashion. And it doesn't do a bit of harm to repeat the same variety in a perennial bed. It will take years to get just the plants you want, so don't try to do it all in one year.

SOILS Hardy perennials thrive in a wide diversity of soils and conditions, but most of those preferred for the home garden do best in full sun and deep loamy soil (See charts at end of chapter.)

Spade as early as the ground allows, but don't work the soil if it is too wet. If it adheres in a lump when squeezed in the hand, it's too wet to work. Tile drains are good for heavy water-logged soils or wet spots (See your County Cooperative Extension Off-ice for instruction.) Work coal ashes, sawdust, peat, or similar materials into heavy soils, as described in Chapter XIII.

CULTIVATING THE PERENNIAL BED While many perennials are well adapted for naturalizing (that is, growing without cultivation), most need timely care for best development. Frequent but shallow cultivation is best for keeping weeds down and the surface soil loose.

WATERING PERENNIALS Perennials do best when plenty of water is made available. An inch of water a week is enough to maintain growth, and a lawn sprinkler can supply this amount in from three to six hours, moistening the soil to a depth of 8 inches or so, enough for a week's growth (except in unusually hot and dry weather). Avoid heavy daily waterings, which make the ground soggy, as well as light sprinklings which encourage shallow root development. Apply as a heavy mist, only as fast as the soil can absorb it. Heavy sprinkling packs the soil and causes water to stand on the surface. Sprinkle during late afternoon rather than in the heat of the day when the sun evaporates much of it. Night watering is to be discouraged, since wet foliage at cool temperatures encourages fungus diseases.

FEEDING To feed a well established perennial bed, make an application in early spring and another in midsummer. Scatter dry plant food around the plants but don't get any on the foliage. Many gardeners like the liquid fertilizers applied to the foliage with sprinkling cans or hose attachments. (See *Liquid Plant Foods* in Chapter XIII).

At dividing time it's a good idea to add a new supply of compost, rotted manure, peat or other forms or organic matter to the soil. Use about 3 bushels per 100 square feet and work it in thoroughly. At the same time, add a balanced plant food such as 5-10-10 or similar analysis at about 3 pounds per 100 square feet.

MULCHING THE BED IN SUMMER A summer mulch not only makes the bed look sharp but cuts down on the need for weeding and watering. When water is not available, a 3-inch summer mulch retains soil moisture and aids growth. (See *Mulches* in Chapter XIII.)

WINTER MULCHING Most hardy perennials like a winter mulch, although many gardeners who don't take the trouble still have success. A winter mulch prevents the alternate freezing and thawing of the soil which causes your plants to heave. Young or newly set plants are more likely to be affected. Protect these with a loose mulch of hay, straw, or evergreen branches applied right around the time of freezing weather. Avoid mulches such as leaves which pack tightly, since they are likely to smother the plants. (For more on mulches see Chapter XIII.)

PRUNING AND TRIMMING PERENNIALS You can lengthen the bloom period of many perennials by removing old flower heads when they fade. Some early-flowering types produce a second crop if tops are cut back following bloom. Any perennial which tends to grow out of bounds should be sheared back to keep it trim. When fall comes, tops are best cut and burned or sealed in plastic bags and discarded, since many insect and disease pests may harbor over winter in them.

(To control flower garden pests, see *Control of Insects and Disease* in Chapter IV.)

TRANSPLANTING A good general transplanting rule is: Flowers that bloom in the fall are transplanted in the spring, and flowers that bloom in the spring are transplanted in the fall. If transplanting in early spring, do so before growth has started so they can become re-established before summer's heat. In northern climates, avoid late-fall planting, because the plants cannot become well established before freezing weather sets in. Flowers that bloom in midsummer may be transplanted in spring or fall. In transplanting, keep as many roots as possible, digging a good-sized ball of soil with each plant, so that the roots are less disturbed.

Set plants firmly in the soil with roots spread out to a depth slightly greater than they originally grew, and water well. Avoid hot, windy days for transplanting. If the perennials have long tops, cut them back about one-half to one third size so they won't droop and look messy.

Propagation

Perennials are increased in many ways. We will describe the basic methods the home gardener can use. For more detail turn to Chapter XV, *Plant Propagation*.

FROM SEED: A good way to get fine plants at low cost. Many can be sown in late fall, if you have a cold frame to keep them over winter where they will remain dormant for an early start in the spring. Don't sow in early fall, since the seed will germinate before winter sets in and you'll have many losses. Wait until October, November, or even December. August is probably the latest date for planting perennial seeds outdoors for bloom the following year if a cold frame is not used.

Many perennial seeds, such as dictamnus, delphinium, and certain rose species, germinate sooner and better if "stratified." This is done by mixing the seed with moist peat, sand, or vermiculite and keeping it in the refrigerator for two or three months at a temperature of 35 degrees F. or so. This gives the same effect as planting the seeds in a cold frame for the winter. (See list of perennials easily started from seed at end of chapter.)

ROOTING STEM CUTTINGS: A simple and practical means of increasing plants. Take stem cuttings when the growth is young and tender, selecting shoots about 3 inches long. With a sharp knife, cut at or just below a node where a leaf joins the stem. Remove the bottom leaves and, if you wish, dip the ends in a root-inducing hormone powder. Place the cuttings about one-third their length in mason's sand, perlite, or vermiculite, press firmly around the base, and water well. Encase the rooting pot or flat in a plastic bag, which acts as a miniature greenhouse. After cuttings have rooted, pot them up or set them directly in the garden or cold frame.

ROOT CUTTINGS: Lift the plant and cut the best roots into pieces 2 inches long. Place them in a sand-peat mixture and cover 1 inch deep. Some which were originally nearest the parent stem will develop shoots at that end and roots at the opposite end. Others will throw out roots and shoots anywhere along the cutting.

LAYERING: Many perennials can be increased by "layering," which consists merely of placing stems in contact with the ground and covering them with soil to encourage rooting. (See Chapter XV.)

DIVIDING: Division is the simplest process for increasing, and it helps keep most perennials vigorous. The best time to divide is also the proper time for transplanting: that is, fall-flowering plants in the spring and spring-flowering plants in the fall. Many, like garden mums, need division annually, while others, such as phlox, iris, and astilbe, should be divided every three years. If you find a hard, woody center when you lift the plants, discard it and use the younger sections, usually found on the outside edges.

Some perennials shouldn't be disturbed unless they are really overcrowded. These include gas plant, bleeding heart, Oriental poppy, and lupine. If they are doing well for you, don't molest them.

Biennials

A biennial is a plant that takes two growing seasons to complete its life-cycle. It makes part of its growth one year, blooms the following year, sets seed, and dies. Examples include hollyhock, English daisy, Canterbury bells, foxglove, and Sweet William. In southern areas these plants live and grow as perennials.

Most biennials are started in a seedbed or cold frame in June or July, although some are best started in August. This gives a long enough season to grow good husky plants for bloom the following year. Biennials usually self-sow, and it's a good idea not to cultivate too vigorously around the plants if you want to save the seedlings. They are generally winter-hardy and need little if any protection, but a cold frame or straw mulch helps to young plants through the winter.

SOME OF THE BEST KNOWN BIENNIALS

Botanical Name	Common	Color	Height (Ft.)	Bloom Date
Althaea rosea	Hollyhock	Various	6	July, August
Campanula medium	Canterbury Bells	Blue, pink, white, purple	3	June, July
Dianthus barbatus	Sweet William	Pink, white, red, lavender, two-tone	1-2	June, July August
Digitalis purpurea	Foxglove	Lavender, peach, pink, purple, rose, white	3-4	June, July

Botanical Name	Common Name	Color	Height (Ft.)	Bloom Date
Lunaria annua	Honesty	Purple, white, rose and white, whitish-blue	3	May, June
Salvia sclarea	Clary	Pink, blue	3	July, August

PERENNIAL FAVORITES

While there are hundreds of perennials available, here are some we have grown and liked in our perennial bed. Many of them we still have after twenty-five years; others we bring back in from time to time. Note: For pest control see Chapter XIV, section on Control of Insects and Diseases.

•**Althaea Rosea** (Hollyhock) A biennial or semi-perennial. Hollyhocks show to best advantage when grouped together in bold masses. Self-sows readily. There are short varieties (2 feet) available as well as tall-growing ones with 5- to 6-foot spires. Seed can be obtained for extra-large, fully double flowers in lovely, delicate shades as well as red, deep pink, and two-tone.

GREEN THUMB CARE: Must have full sun most of the day. Prefers rich, well drained soils but does well in clay soils, too. Since young plants are more vigorous, seed of the semi-perennial types can be sown each summer. Established plants resent being disturbed, but you can transplant young seedlings in the spring.

PROPAGATION: By seed self-sown in August, or you can sow in the cold frame in February. After transplanting into open ground, plants will flower the same year.

TROUBLES: *Hollyhock rust*. Causes leaves to turn yellow, wither, and die. Spreads rapidly up the stalk in wet weather and more noticeable when it's hot. *Control*: In fall, cut down and burn old stems or seal in plastic bag and discard. In spring, dust thoroughly with Zineb or sulfur as soon as leaves start to show and continue once a week throughout the summer. (Sulfur will burn foliage if used in temperatures over 85 degrees F.) Rust overwinters in dead leaves and in a weed known as mallow or "cheeseweed." Eliminate these from the garden or lawn.

•**Aquilegia** (pronounced "a-kwee-lee-gee-a"—Columbine) blooms in May and June. Flowers are blue, yellow, pink, red, white, and bicolor. Ideal for border or rock garden. McKana's giant columbine is an All-America winner which we like. It grows 2 or 3 feet tall and has flowers 4 inches across and spurs almost as long. Good for cut flowers. There are dwarf varieties available and improved strains with deep colors.

GREEN THUMB CARE: Columbines have a tendency to peter out after two or three years. Pinch off the seed heads before they set, since letting it set seed is one reason the plant "disappears." However, you can allow a few seed pods to set to save for planting elsewhere.

PROPAGATION: By seed or by division of clumps in spring.

TROUBLES: *Leafminer insects*. Tunnel between the upper and lower leaf surfaces.

•**Campanula** (Bellflower) There are several *Campanulas* well worth trying. Canterbury bells is a biennial. *Campanula persicifolia* (peach-leaved bellflower) is a noble plant for borders. Blue or white spikes or large, bell-shaped flowers from June to August, ideal for cutting.

GREEN THUMB CARE: Give lots of water during the flowering period for giant stalks blooming at the same time as foxglove, Sweet William, and garden pinks.

PROPAGATION: Sow seed in outdoor beds in late spring or early summer. Move seedlings to their flowering quarters by early fall.

TROUBLES: *Aphids*.

•**Chrysanthemum coccineum** (Pyrethrum or Painted Daisy) Red, pink, and white flowers in May and June. Produces ideal cut flowers when grown in full sun. Two to three feet tall.

GREEN THUMB CARE: Likes a well drained, moderately fertile soil. September is a good time to transplant. Keep faded flowers cut and you'll extend the flowering season.

PROPAGATION: By seed and division. Oddly enough, the double-flowering pyrethrum will often produce single or semi-double flowers the first year after transplanting, but the following year the flowers will be fully double.

TROUBLES: None serious.

•**Chrysanthemum morifolium** (Garden Mums) No other perennial gives so much variation of color and blossom type in the fall, after the blossoming period of most other flowers has passed. Hundreds of good varieties are available, so don't try to grow mums that bloom too late and freeze before the buds have a chance to open. Mums may be grouped according to bloom period as follows: 1) Very early, starting in August. 2) Early, beginning between the middle and end of September. 3) Medium early, beginning the first of October. 4) Medium late, beginning the first and second week of October and 5) Late, starting to bloom after the middle of October. The largest and most colorful mums grow in October when nights are cool and humidity is high. Two to three feet tall.

Chrysanthemums are also classified according to flower types. Here are a few of the most popular:

Decorative or "*double flowers:*" Blooms over 2 inches across, with strap-like rays. Two to three feet tall.

Pompon: Globular or nearly rounded, under 2 inches in size. Blossoms firm and ideal as cut flowers. (*Note:* No such classification as "pom-pom." It's pompon.)

Singles: Daisy-like flowers, all colors. Two feet tall, ideal for cut flowers.

Cushion: Same as "Azalea mum." Low mounded clumps 12 to 14 inches tall, forming "bushels of blooms." All colors available.

Spoons: Rays twisted into spoon-like floral parts. Resembles druggist's spatulas. Two feet high. Some colors are rather late for northern gardens.

Commercials: Lumped together they are called "Football Mums," "English Mums," or "Standards." Some are round, 4 inches or so across, others "half-round." Size depends upon how much they are "disbudded" (see *Disbudding Mums*). Outdoor "Football Mums" seldom reach size and quality of indoor-grown Mums.

Anemone: Outer rays surround central cushion-like pads of "disk" flowers coming in many colors. Ideal for cut flowers. Use early varieties, if you live in cold region.

Buttons: Tiny pompon or button-like flowers $3/4$ inches across. Too late to be of value in cold regions.

"Spider" mums: Spidery, twisted petal rays, resembling thin spaghetti or shoestrings. Bloom in mid- or late October, late for cold regions. Greenhouse Spider mums need heavy disbudding to get the exotic 6-inch flowers you see in florist shops.

GREEN THUMB CARE: Mums like a loose, sandy soil that's neutral or slightly acid, lots of sun and good drainage. Spade in plenty of humus such as compost or well rotted manure (3 to 5 bushels) per 200 square feet. Have the soil worked up loosely with a little peat before transplanting. We like to feed outdoor mums liquid plant food when we set them out, and later when in bud stage.

PINCHING MUMS: The most neglected operation in growing mums is pinching. Without it they grow tall and spindly. Here's all there is to it: when plants are about 6 inches tall, pinch off the top 2 inches of new growth. This stimulates new growth to break out from the first several leaf nodes so that each stem has many stalks. Pinch again when new shoots are 6 inches long, but don't pinch after late July, as they may not bloom before frost. Cushion types or so-called azalea mums need no pinching since they branch naturally.

PROTECT BLOOMS FROM EARLY FROST: Though garden mums can withstand cold weather, frost will damage open blossoms. You can prevent this by covering plants with sheets, burlap sacks, or plastic mulch on frosty nights. When you see the frost starting to melt in the morning, remove the covering.

WINTERING YOUR MUMS: It's been our experience that mums come through the winter with no mulch at all. Although they are not altogether hardy, it's not the cold that kills them, but excessive water around the roots and fluctuating temperatures. If your soil is well drained, your plants will probably winter over successfully without any extra care. If it is heavy and poorly drained, lift the plants with the soil clinging to the roots and place them in a cool, dry place, such as under the eaves of a building or in a cold frame where they can remain until spring. Some gardeners, when their soil is heavy and wet, just dig their clumps and place them on top of the ground. It's a good idea to mulch these lifted mums in case of winter rains. Do not allow the clumps to dry completely, however. Occasional sprinklings will carry them through until spring. A final word: *Do not* cut the tops off in fall. Wait until spring, since the tops catch snow and leaves and serve as a natural mulch.

CARE OF POTTED OR FLORIST'S MUMS: Florist's mums need lots of water and bright light. After blooming, cut plant back halfway and keep in cellar until spring. Set out in warm weather, or divide the plant and grow in pots. Generally speaking, they are not suited for garden plants. There are early, mid-season and late mums. Garden mums are classed in the six- to eight-week response group; florist's mums are in the ten- and 11-week groups, and therefore often freeze before flowering if grown outdoors. Potted mums suited for outdoor growing usually are marked as such. If they aren't marked as garden plants don't attempt to grow them outdoors, as they are not reliably winter-hardy. If you have a florist mum growing outdoors in fall, it can be brought inside and be made to bloom. Dig and pot, even if in bud.

You can cover a late-blooming mum with black plastic sheets or burlap from 6 P.M. to 7 A.M. each night and it'll eventually bloom, but with the large selection available, no reason you can't have early flowering varieties.

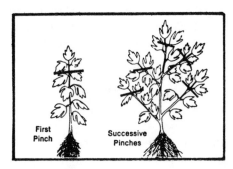

To get nice bushy plants, mums must be pinched. Remove the very tip of each plant as shown, when first set out. Side shoots can be pinched also, as plants develop. Do not pinch later than mid-July, as you may delay blooming.

Stake and tie garden mums early, especially the tall-growing varieties. This will help produce strong stems and well-formed flowers. Use pieces of string, rag, old nylon stocking to tie plants.

Mums are shallow-rooted plants. They won't do well if set too deeply at planting time.

(Courtesy Thon's Garden Mums)

PROPAGATION: By division, cuttings or seed. One reason for poor growth of mums in the garden is that they have not been divided each year to prevent the shoots from becoming too crowded. Cushion mums are divided every second year. In Spring, dig the clump when the young shoots are 3 inches high and separate the strongest ones. Don't use those from the woody center but save the young tender shoots from the outside. The varieties that produce seed will not come true to type. Seeds sown in March or April in cold frames usually produce flowering plants in one season, but we prefer to propagate by cutting or division. We take cuttings in March or April from plants heeled in an unheated greenhouse or cold frame all winter. Simply cut 2 or 3 inch tips from husky growing shoots, making your cut a bit below a leaf joint, and remove the bottom leaves. Insert cuttings in a box of sand, perlite, vermiculite, or other rooting mixture and keep moist. They will root quickly and can be set outdoors or transplanted into pots and allowed to grow larger before planting in the garden. Do not allow them to get dry.

TROUBLES: *Color Change.* Chrysanthemums are subject to diseases, and as with gladiolus, the weaker varieties usually die off due to disease, leaving the stronger colors to survive and multiply. Mums do sometimes exhibit sudden heritable changes called mutations. Strangely, mum mutations are generally reversible and can change back and forth. For example, we have often seen single mums originally thought to be yellow produce blooms with both yellow and white petals. *Fading mum flowers.* Some years mum flowers fade out, while in other years the colors are retained beautifully. Long days and high temperatures are sometimes responsible for fading colors in mums, but these are not the only factors. At high temperatures growth is weakened, and sugar usually used in production of pigments is used up, thus flower color becomes less intense. Pink, bronze, and red varieties tend to fade the most.

Oddly, at low temperatures mum growth is slow and pigment production is higher in comparison. We often see pink protrude on white and yellow varieties, and yellow types tend to be more bronze in color. Anything that affects the production of "food" in the plant alters the production of pigments and may result in changes of flower color. But not all varieties. Heavy infestations of mites and thrips will cause streaking and color loss. Plant diseases also alter flower color. Virus stunt not only produces a stunted plant, but will reduce flower color.

Even pesticides in high concentrations will alter flower color, as will lower soil nutrients. Soils low in potash will result in less intense colors in pink, bronze, and red varieties.

Finally, the age of the flower itself is important. As blooms age and growth slows, pigments become more intense, especially pink. In many varieties, especially white or yellow, pink will appear on outer edges of petals as flowers mature.

Foliar Nematode. Probably the worst pest of garden mums. Nematodes are microscopic eelworms which spread from one plant to another, causing the lower leaves to turn bronze, then black, and die. Nematodes are worse in wet seasons, when they spread more freely. Once inside the leaf, they are difficult to reach, so the best way to deal with them is to avoid splashing water from the soil and to remove dead leaves and burn them or discard them in sealed bags before they fall. Branches with a number of dead leaves should be removed. Also use resistant varieties. For pest control, see Chapter XIV.

Tarnished plant bug. Punches many "shotgun" holes in leaves, stings growing tips and flower buds.

Aphids. Cause twisting and curling of shoots.

Leafrollers. Small worms feed on undersides of leaves, and then leaves curl around larvae, appear as parchment-like films. Upper parts of leaves are untouched. *Control*: Handpick and destroy.

Red spider mites. Hard to see with the naked eye. They infest the tips of shoots and cause curled leaves and stunt growth and mottling of foliage; in severe cases, webbing.

Leafminer. Larvae feed within tissues. Mines appear as white lines or blotches. *Control*: Malathion, one teaspoonful to a quart of water.

Leaftier. Larvae eat soft tissues on underside of leaves, feeding between lightly woven silken webs which tie leaves together. *Control*: handpick and destroy.

Corn earworm. In fall, corn earworms often eat buds. *Control*: Talcum powder.

Chrysanthemum midge. Maggots bore into the stem or flower, causing cone-shaped, $^1/_2$-inch galls.

Thrips. Rasp leaf tissue and are troublesome especially if gladiolus or onions are grown nearby.

Spittlebug or froghopper. Small yellowish-green insects live inside a mass of froth which they generate to protect themselves. They suck plant juices, reducing the vigor of the plant.

Leaf spot. If leaves are peppered with dark brown or black spots, the trouble is leaf-spot disease. It usually appears in July and becomes increasingly worse until fall. *Control*: Start spraying Ferbam or Captan early in July and repeat at seven- to ten-day intervals until bloom. In fall, rake and burn all parts of the plants above ground, since the fungus winters over in debris. Drench plants and soil with Bordeaux or Ferbam.

Precocious blooming. We've seen fall-blooming mums flower in June or July. Hot weather is partly responsible for erratic blooming. It can also slow up bud development. Most garden mums are from the six- to eight-week response group. This means it normally takes them six to eight weeks to flower from time in late summer when days become short enough for flower-bud formation.

Did you know that overhead night lights affect mums? A reader writes: "I had the most beautiful mums for years until my neighbor installed a bright night light. From then on I had no flowers." Mums need a certain number of hours of darkness to flower. They'll flower in the poorest soil if they have time to "sleep."

Rust. Chocolate-brown pustules on undersides of leaves. *Control*: Spray weekly with sulfur or Captan.

Mildew. If leaves look floury, the plant has mildew, common in the cool, moist weather of fall. *Control*: Sulfur spray or dust, Maneb or Bordeaux mixture to which is added two teaspoonfuls of Malathion per gallon. This kills aphids and controls many fungus diseases spread by aphids.

Verticillium wilt. Plants show yellowing, wilting, dying of leaves from base upward. Plants may be stunted, killed. Brown streaks can be detected inside the stems. *Control*: Discard non-resistant varieties, propagate from disease-free cuttings rather than by root division. Sterilize infected soil. No spray is available for controlling wilt disease. Many varieties are completely resistant.

Septoria or black spot. A fungus disease, serious enough to defoliate some varieties. Foliage shows black spots that may turn into blotches. Leaves eventually turn yellowish and fall off. *Control*: Use Ferbam or Bordeaux.

Stunt. A virus disease, very slow to express its symptoms. Infected plants show dwarfing, lighter green foliage, and flowering seven to ten days prematurely. Pink, red, or bronze flowers are faded in comparison to healthy plants. No control known; destroy infected stock and keep aphids in check, as they spread virus diseases.

Grey mold (Botrytis). Brown, water-soaked spots on flower petals. *Control*: Spray plants daily with Captan.

Crown gall. Swollen growths on stems near soil level. *Control*: Use clean stock and a new soil location. Avoid splashing tops of plants. Prune out infected stems, using a knife or scissors dipped in alcohol.

Yellows. Flowers become entirely or partly green. Plants are stunted, leaves show slight yellowing, especially the margins. *Control*: This is a virus spread by leafhoppers. Try not to grow mums near annual asters.

Ray blight or *Ascochyta*. Causes a high proportion of affected flowers to open lopsided. Half the petals turn brown or black and stick together, and rot may progress from a half inch to several inches downward into the flower stalk. A characteristic symptom: falling of the petals when the blossom is shaken. *Control*: Bury or bum all debris or seal in a plastic bag and discard. Sterilize soil with steam or methyl bromide. Leave infected gardens or fields idle for a year or two, preferably fallow, so no volunteer mums or other possible hosts will keep the fungus growing. Do not propagate from infected plants.

•**Chrysanthemum maximum** (Shasta Daisy) Shasta daisy is a chrysanthemum (*C. maximum*), and while it comes in white only, its huge daisy-like flowers are hard to beat. It comes in double as well as single forms, likes a rich, moist ground, will tolerate partial shade, does best in full sun. Esther Read is a double form. Florists get pink, reddish, bluish, or yellow blooms by setting the stems in a solution of dye which is absorbed into the flower heads.

PROPAGATION: Clumps should be divided every two or three years, preferably in spring. Shastas have a way of crowding each other (and blooms get smaller) if left by themselves.

TROUBLES: *Tarnished plant bugs*. Sting buds and cause blooms to be distorted. *Control*: Use Malathion.

•**Convallaria majalis** (Lily of the Valley) Leaves green and broad; delicate flower sprays, pink or white, and highly scented. Six to twelve inches tall.

GREEN THUMB CARE: Tolerates shade or sun. Makes good ground cover on slopes. Aggressive and may need dividing every four years, since roots form heavy mass.

PROPAGATION: Dig and separate roots in fall or spring. Often produces red seeds (which are toxic).

TROUBLES: None serious.

•**Delphinium elatum** (Common Delphinium) A superb, tall accent plant for border or background. Flowers are blue, purple, and white, pure colors with some pink shades. May be single or double, bicolored or solid, and may have a central "eye" or "bee" (anthers) in contrasting colors. Grows 4 to 6 feet tall in rich soil and sunny location. Many gardeners get the terms "delphinium" and "larkspur" confused. Strictly speaking, "larkspur" is the common name for all species of delphinium, but in everyday horticulture, "delphinium" is used for the perennial species and "larkspur" for the annuals.

GREEN THUMB CARE: Any soil that's well drained is suitable. Root rot is worse in heavy soils; soils containing high amounts of organic matter should be avoided. More important is regular feeding with a balanced plant food, either in dry or liquid form. When preparing the soil, work in about 4 pounds of a 5-10-10 brand in each 100 square feet.

Plants can be moved in spring, summer, or early fall, and still make good growth. Move them with a ball of earth and set them in a hole large enough to accommodate the entire clump. Cover the crown lightly (1 inch of soil) and press down firmly. Water each clump thoroughly. Feed delphiniums in early spring and again about June or July when the shoots start growth for the second bloom. Or you can use a liquid food about once a month. Most delphiniums will bloom a second time if plants are cut back to a foot from the ground after first flowers have withered. After cutting a bloom for indoor arrangements, bend over the end of the cut stalk to prevent rainwater from entering the crown. Moisture held around the crown will encourage disease.

You cannot grow good delphinium spikes without staking or fencing the plants. We use tomato stakes, just when the plants begin to bud. Delphinium stalks are hollow and winds or rains are sure to break your spikes if you do not stake them.

PROPAGATION: Mostly by seeds, but also by division and sometimes by cuttings. Good results are obtained by planting seeds in cold frames or deep flats filled with a 50-50 mixture of garden loam and sand. We like to sow in the ground in spring for husky plants next year. Seed germinates best at a temperature of 55 degrees F. and takes about 21 days. Summer-sown delphinium will require a two-week refrigerator treatment. Store seed in the refrigerator at 40 to 50 degrees F. or sow the seed in a small pot and place pot and all in the refrigerator. Faulty germination is due to old seed as it loses its viability in a few months unless properly stored.

For sowing, avoid heavy soils; one of the sterile mixes is ideal. Sow in midsummer as soon as fresh seed is available. After cool treatment, plant $1/4$ inch deep. The soil surface may be kept moist by covering with burlap or by shading with burlap or muslin. Sub-irrigation of flats is excellent. When seedlings have reached their first true leaves, they are potted or planted in boxes and placed in a cold frame for the winter. Larger seedling plants are left outdoors for winter. They are perfectly hardy, although highly susceptible to wet feet. Cold frame plants can be transplanted into their permanent location, the sunniest part of your garden.

Delphiniums can be divided by digging clumps and cutting them into sections, each of which has at least one good eye and well developed roots. This is preferably done in early spring or late summer.

TROUBLES: *Sclerotium* or *crown rot*. A very destructive disease which causes the plant to suddenly wilt and die. The infected spike is blackened at the base and there may be a web-like fungus at the crown. *Control*: Infected plants should be dug up and destroyed. Other delphinium plants should not be set in the same place. Setting the plants on a low ridge so that water drains quickly away from the crown helps to prevent infection. When only a part of the plant is diseased, sterilize the soil around the clump, drenching with a fungicide.

Cyclamen mite. Causes distortion of shoots and blackening of infested spikes.

Mildew. Turns leaves white then brown. *Control*: Keep plants dusted with sulfur or Karathane and don't let them grow too close together. If they are in shade, move them to full sun.

●**Dianthus barbatus** (Sweet William) Fragrant old-fashioned flower with handsome new varieties. Handled as a biennial, seed is sown in spring and seedlings are transplanted in early fall to their flowering quarters. It may self-sow freely. Tall and dwarf types grow from 6 to 18 inches tall, and flower in June or earlier. A medley of color—lavender, red, pink, white, and bicolors—and form, doing best in full sun.

●**D. Latifolius** (Garden Pinks) Another member of the carnation family, worth trying. Comes in white, red, and all shades of pink, as well as variegated. Even the annual types are hardy enough for sub-zero weather if protected with evergreen boughs. Ten to sixteen inches tall. Magic Charms is a profuse single-blooming hybrid.

●**D. Plumarius** (Cottage Pinks) Sweet-scented, double, semi-double, fringed, and single flowers ideal for rock gardens or borders, if in full sun. Shades of red, pink, white. A delight in any garden. Twelve inches tall.

GREEN THUMB CARE: Garden pinks and "carnations" love cool weather. Summer flowers are not ordinarily as handsome as fall blooms, but if you keep the roots cool by mulching and watering, you'll get a good crop of blooms. They prefer a well drained soil, full sun, and a chance to ripen off in fall. Don't feed them after August so that the plants can harden up for winter. They need winter protection, and the best material is evergreen boughs, which allow air to circulate.

PROPAGATION: By seed in spring or fall, also by cuttings or division. Seed sown outdoors in early July will bloom the following summer, or sow indoors in March in shredded sphagnum moss or a soil mixture of $1/3$ sand, $1/3$ leafmold, and $1/3$ loam. Seedlings are transplanted into boxes, spacing about 2 inches apart or into small peat pots. In May, peat pot and all may be set outside. Water after planting and pinch out growing tips to induce branching.

TROUBLES: *Spider mites*. *Control*: Liquid household detergent, or buttermilk spray (see Chapter XIV for control of Insects and Disease.).

●**Dicentra spectabilis** (Bleeding Heart) Grows 3 feet tall with drooping sprays of red and white heart-shaped flowers appearing in May and June. Best in semi-shade but tolerates full sun. Ideal for planting in clumps. Blooms from spring to mid-season, then dies down to the crown. Many other species of Bleeding Heart are available for the home garden.

GREEN THUMB CARE: Large bushes with no bloom means plants are getting too much shade or possibly that soil is too rich or moist.

PROPAGATION: By division. In fall or early spring, chop the clump with an axe into divisions. Replant, supplying ample water. Mulch the first winter with evergreen boughs to prevent heaving, especially if there is clay in the soil. You can also make root cuttings in spring or fall.

TROUBLES: None serious.

•**Digitalis** (Foxglove) Grows 3 to 4 feet tall with big, bell-shaped flowers in June. Colors range from white to pale pink to deep rose, and many of them are spotted. Excelsior hybrids have outfacing bells revealing full markings. Monstrosa has huge campanula-like blooms. Variety Foxy blooms first year from seed.

GREEN THUMB CARE: Thrives in full sun or partial shade and is benefited by a straw mulch after freezing weather sets in. If foxglove does not bloom the second year, it often blooms the third. The drug digitalis, poisonous in overdoses, is obtained from the second year's young leaves. To gather seed, pick capsules from the lower part of the stem as soon as brown and before they shed.

PROPAGATION: By seed sown out of doors in late spring and transplanted in early fall to its flowering quarters. Variety Foxy can be sown indoors in late February and will bloom five to six months later. The coarse foliage remains green all winter.

TROUBLES: *Leaf spot. Control*: Dust with a fungicide.

•**Echinacea** (Purple Cone flower) Often called purple Rudbeckia, or purple black-eyed Susan. The old name of Rudbeckia is no longer valid. Handsome, large flowers with large, bristly cone in center. Colors come in purple to crimson and last all summer long. Stems reach 2 to 3 feet.

GREEN THUMB CARE: Likes well drained soil. Heavy soils kill it. Prefers full sun, but will take partial shade. Plant in fall or early spring. Plants self-sow, so avoid overcrowding by digging up clumps every second year to avoid petering out.

PROPAGATION: Seed sown in fall or spring. Dig up seedings and transplant to permanent spot. Seedlings do not come true to type, but are worthwhile. Divide roots in spring for quick increase.

TROUBLES: Small flowers, due to overcrowding. *Control*: Separate in spring.

•**Gaillardia aristata** (Blanket Flower) One of the showiest and easiest-to-grow perennials. Tall varieties grow 3 feet high in full sun. Plants have large, reddish flowers with yellow borders. Ideal for cut flowers from June through September. Dwarf varieties are available as well as double-flowered annuals. Tolerates hot weather.

GREEN THUMB CARE: If old flower heads are removed and the plant fed and watered regularly, you have one of the most productive plants for cut flowers. It fails to survive the winter if grown in rich, heavy, clay soils. Good drainage is the most important factor.

PROPAGATION: By seed in spring for bloom the same year. Also by division in the spring.

TROUBLES: None.

•**Gypsophila paniculata** (Baby's Breath) Grows 2 to 3 feet tall with fine-textured leaves; most varieties have white flowers in late June, July, and August. There are also pink varieties available. Bristol Fairy has great clouds of double starry flowers in feathery panicles, but is a grafted form not available from seed. All perennial "gyp" varieties ideal for cutting. Most bloom all summer and prefer full sun.

GREEN THUMB CARE: The generic name *Gypsophila*, or "chalk plant," refers to its preference for lime soils. If soil reaction is lower than pH 6, lime should be added so that the reading is pH 7 or more (see Chapter XIII).

PROPAGATION: Both single and double baby's breath may be started from seed in early spring. If you plant seed of double varieties, about 50 percent will be double flowers. You can transplant young plants early in spring, but be sure to get a big ball of earth. If transplanted in the fall, they are apt to heave out of the ground.

TROUBLES: None serious.

•**Hemerocallis** (Day lily) Day lilies have multiple advantages: they are easy to grow, resist heat and dry spells, and wet seasons do not injure the roots. They tolerate shade and are disease-resistant and you don't have to spray them. If you neglect them, they outdo the weeds. A good selection of varieties will produce bloom from early spring to late fall. Tall varieties 2 to 3 feet, dwarf varieties 15 inches.

Day lilies come in a variety of shades of red, orange, yellow, pink, purple, brown, and bicolors. The flowers last only a day but are replaced by new ones the next morning. Give them plenty of room, 2 feet per plant. Dividing them every third year promotes bloom.

GREEN THUMB CARE: Although day lilies are toughies, they do respond to feedings, so apply a little plant food, such as 5-10-5, about 2 pounds per 100 square feet to improve bloom size. They get better and better each year, but like to be kept from overcrowding each other, so if yours are matted together, separate them and they will reward you with better plants and blooms.

PROPAGATION: By division any time. Do not plant too deep, and water well after setting them out.

TROUBLES: None.

•**Heuchera sanguinea** (Coral Bells) A prolific bloomer, fine for hardy border or rock garden. Grows $1\frac{1}{2}$ feet tall with tiny red or pink flowers from May through September. Blossoms have good keeping qualities when cut and lend an airy gracefulness to bouquets. Hummingbirds love them.

GREEN THUMB CARE: Likes a moist, rich, well drained soil in full sun or partial shade. Divide and transplant every three years or when the center of the clump starts to die out. Straw mulch in winter may be needed. Does well in a variety of soil with no special treatment.

PROPAGATION: By seed or division in early spring.

TROUBLES: None.

•**Hosta** (Plantain Lily) A good plant for the shade. Comes in green and variegated, narrow- and broad-leaved types, some with orchid and some with white tubular flowers, highly fragrant. Will grow in sun or shade; likes moist, well drained soil. Hosta is also called funkia.

GREEN THUMB CARE: Plants are carefree, requiring little or no feeding. If you want a solid mass to act as a ground cover on a bank, do not divide them. To grow them in separate clumps, divide every three or four years. Otherwise they will grow quickly and form a dense cluster.

PROPAGATION: By division in fall or spring. Separate the clumps into three or four pieces, plant in a loose soil, recently spaded.

TROUBLES: Holes in leaves, due to snail or slug injury. *Control*: See Chapter XIV.

•**Iris** (Dutch) See chart in Chapter VI, BULBS, CORMS, AND TUBERS.

•**Iris germanica** (German Iris) "German" or tall bearded iris (Fleur-de-lis or Pogoniris) is our most commonly grown garden iris. It offers broad masses of blue, purple, white, yellow, red, bronze, intermediate hues and bicolors, in May and June. Iris can be planted any time from June through September, and you'll get better results if you divide the clumps and reset them every four years. Irises like a sunny, well drained spot. If your soil is mostly clay, add organic matter to encourage fast drainage.

GREEN THUMB CARE: These plants don't need much feeding. Don't use manure or a heavy nitrogenous fertilizer, because of the danger of soft growth which eventually leads to rot. Superphosphate applied two or three weeks before flowering, plus a side dressing of bone meal in late June, is good. If you set out irises in the summer, give some covering with evergreen boughs for winter, removing the covering when growth starts in the spring. The widespread belief that irises need lime is erroneous. They do well in neutral or even slightly acid soils (and repeated heavy applications of lime seem to promote iris rot).

If your irises fail to bloom, chances are the plants are overcrowded. Thin out every three or four years by digging up crowded rhizomes here and there. Those you do not disturb will bloom profusely if others are thinned.

PROPAGATION: In cutting the divisions, remove the old growth, trim the roots back some, and cut the foliage in fan-shaped fashion to make the planting look neater. Avoid deep planting. Set the rhizomes just below the surface of the ground, with roots well spread out. Plant from 8 inches to 2 feet apart. Established irises like to have their rhizomes exposed to the sunlight. However, Bert Porreca, expert iris grower and hybridizer, tells us they should be covered when newly planted in climates where they will alternately freeze and thaw during winter. He recommends covering 2 inches in sandy soils and 1 inch in clay soils, then tamping the soil down firmly. He also recommends leaving on only 2 or 3 inches of root growth. Rhizomes will work up to the surface by the next summer and will be well exposed.

TROUBLES: *Leaf spot*. Oval spots with watersoaked margins. *Control*: Dust with Zineb and remove and burn or seal in plastic and discard the old leaves in the fall. This is an important control factor, since the foliage carries over disease spores and insect eggs.

Iris Borer. Overwinters in eggs pasted to dead leaves. Eggs hatch in May and the larvae crawl up the plants, and make pin-prick holes in the leaves, gnawing their way down the stalks and into the rhizomes, where great tunnels are made, causing serious damage to the plant. *Control*: Look for telltale "sawdust" on stalks or rhizomes; cut borer out with a knife, dust plant and rhizome with sulfur and replant. Spray in the spring with Malathion. Be sure to use a detergent as a sticker-spreader so spray will not roll off the waxy foliage. Trim back and clean up all dead leaves in fall and destroy.

Soft Rot. The whole rhizome except the outer skin becomes mushy. Bacteria live from year to year in infected rhizomes and most new infections take place through wounds. Often borers pave the way for infection. *Control*: Cut leaves back to about 6 inches, and destroy the trimmings. Lift the clumps and cut out and destroy all rotted

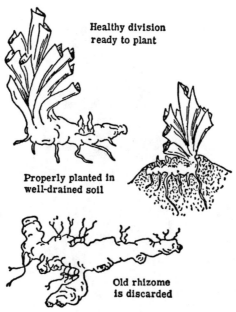

Healthy division
ready to plant

Properly planted in
well-drained soil

Old rhizome
is discarded

Best time to divide iris is after the blooming
season has finished. Divide and replant every 2
or 3 years for best results.

portions. Dust the rot-free parts with sulfur and expose them to sun for a few days to hasten healing over, then plant in a new location. Shallow planting discourages rot.

Color Changes. This is not the result of cross-pollination. What happens when a flower changes color is this: Blue and yellow irises are more vigorous and have been allowed to go to seed. The seed drops to the ground and develops into husky plants which crowd out other (less robust) varieties. So it becomes a case of survival of the fittest. Cut seed pods off before they drop or have a chance to form. Irises will remain the same colors for years if you prevent them from going to seed. Seed formation is a drain on the plant and should be prevented, unless you want to try your hand at hybridizing. Iris hybridizers are working hard to develop more varieties that will bloom in fall as well as spring.

●**Iris kaempferi** (Japanese Iris) One of the best summer-blooming hardy perennials. Grows 3 feet tall, blooms after the "German" or bearded iris, and is at its best in July. The falls (lower petals) are broader and the whole flower has a much flatter character than German iris. Colors usually solid with much less variation.

GREEN THUMB CARE: Prefer a sunny location, although they may exist in some shade. They need plenty of water up until flowering time. Separate every three or four years, as the centers of the clumps usually start to die.

PROPAGATION: By seed sown in early spring for bloom the following year. Also by division in August or September.

TROUBLES: None serious.

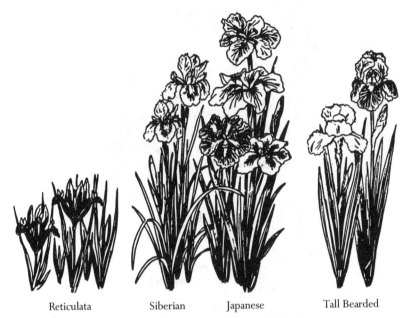

Reticulata   Siberian   Japanese   Tall Bearded

Four types of iris grown in the perennial bed.

●**Iris pumila** (Dwarf Iris) This little beauty, growing from 4 to 12 inches tall, comes in autumn-flowering as well as spring-flowering varieties, in shades of lavender, blue, white, yellow, and red. Good for edging, rock gardens. Has same troubles and care as German iris.

●**Iris reticulata** See chart in Chapter VI, BULBS, CORMS, AND TUBERS.

●**Iris siberica** (Siberian Iris) Hardy beardless iris growing from 2 to 3 feet tall, stately blue, lavender, purple, or white flowers, smaller than German iris. More graceful foliage. Same care and troubles as German iris.

●**Hardy Lilies** (See Chapter VI, BULBS, CORMS, AND TUBERS.)

●**Lupinus** (Lupine) Prefers an alkaline soil but tolerates almost any kind, as long as it is well drained. Pea-like flowers—rose, white, pink, yellow, blue, lavender, red, orange, and bicolors—grows 3 to 4 feet tall on long spikes.

GREEN THUMB CARE: Handsome in arrangements. Cut spikes in early morning and set in warm water to keep them from wilting. After the first bloom is gone, you can cut the plants back and often get a second show of flowers.

PROPAGATION: Sow seed in June for bloom the following June or start indoors in pots of sand and peat in early spring. As soon as the roots start to fill the pot, shift them to their permanent location. Soaking seed overnight before planting is helpful. Lupines are tap-rooted and do not divide or transplant well.

TROUBLES: *Root rot*. Plants wilt and the roots turn brown or black and rot. Root-rot disease is more prevalent in periods of wet weather and in poorly drained soils. Lupines must have a well drained soil. *Control*: Once wilting starts, there's no control. Change to a new spot where the soil is treated with Zineb.

Leaf and stem rot. Bottom leaves and stems are attacked first and become spotted, turning yellowish-green. Leaves die rapidly from the base upward. *Control:* Cut plants back and burn or seal in plastic and discard all fallen leaves. Zineb.

Aphids. Can be a problem on both foliage and roots. *Control:* Spray with nicotine sulfate, 1 teaspoonful to 2 quarts of soapy water, or Malathion, or use a systemic on the soil.

●**Lysimachia punctata** (Yellow Loosestrife) Showy, stout plants with 2- to 3-foot spires of star-shaped yellow flowers. Good as background plant, and in arrangements. Great for spots where hardly anything else will grow.

GREEN THUMB CARE: Will grow in sun or partial shade. Easy to grow in almost any soil. Transplant in spring or late summer.

TROUBLES: None.

●**Lythrum** (Purple Loosestrife) A fine summer-flowering perennial with pink and purple flowers. Actually a perennial shrub, dying back each fall. Morden's Pink grows 3 or 4 feet tall and bears dozens of spikes, covered with deep pink florets from June to late September. Never transplant or start seeds of wild loostrife. It is too aggressive and will take over your whole garden as well as nearby property.

GREEN THUMB CARE: Easy to grow—good for sunny spots, poor soils, or partial shade. Plant in spring or after bloom period.

PROPAGATION: Readily accomplished by root division.

TROUBLES: None.

●**Paeonia** (Peony) There are two broad types of peonies: 1) herbaceous, whose colors range from pink, white, red, and even a yellow with single, double, semi-double, Japanese, and anemone-type flowers; and 2) the tree peony, or the woody shrub type, growing 5 or 6 feet tall. Herbaceous types are easier to grow. Their massive fragrant flowers make them perennial favorites.

GREEN THUMB CARE: Peonies like a well drained soil. Heavy soils can be loosened with peat or compost before planting. The best time to plant is September or October. Depth of planting is important. Do not cover eyes too deeply (about 1 inch). Second year the eyes will be exposed, but this is normal. Peonies planted deeply usually do not bloom. Go easy on plant food. Too much feeding makes lush growth and weak stems, with few or no flowers. You get best stalks if plants are supported with a wire fence. Best blooms are on plants in full sun, but colors last longer when given some shade. Disbudding is not necessary, although if you want larger flowers it's simple. Just remove the side buds (near the base of the large end bud) when they are peasize, leaving the one center bud.

PROPAGATION: By seed or division in fall. Peonies do not need to be divided frequently; about every eight to ten years is enough. Make sure each division has an eye or two.

TROUBLES: *Botrytis blight.* Causes buds to dry or blast. Avoid use of manure. Spray plants in spring with Zineb or Ferbam. Clip off old blooms and remove buds which fail to open. Cut yellowed foliage down in fall and burn or seal in plastic bag and discard. Clean up all debris and dust ground with the same fungicide.

SINGLE   SEMI—DOUBLE   DOUBLE

JAPANESE   ANEMONE

The common garden or herbaceous peony is grouped into five types according to the shape of the petals.

Ants. Harmless, feed on "honeydew" secreted by buds and aphids. Control aphids with nicotine sulfate.

Leaf spot. Controlled by sanitation in fall. Cut off old foliage, rake up, seal in plastic bag and discard. Dust soil with a fungicide.

Failure to bloom. Due to shade, deep planting. All varieties have huge blooms, which require support during rainy seasons. Some cultivars are notoriously weak-stemmed.

TREE PEONIES are a woody shrub growing 5 to 6 feet high. Nurserymen start them from grafts onto the roots of the herbaceous kinds. They like a well drained soil in full sun or partial shade. They can also be started from seed, but it's slow and difficult. They have the same troubles as herbaceous peonies.

•**Papaver orientalis** (Oriental Poppy) A flashy perennial coming in red, pink, and white, 2 to 3 feet tall. The Oriental Poppy is not too hard to grow once you understand its habits.

GREEN THUMB CARE: Poppies resent disturbance, so if they are doing fine, don't touch them unless you want to increase your stock or change the location. The clump gets larger and more blooms are produced as they grow older.

This tough perennial doesn't need a mulch, since cold does not affect it, but it does need a well drained soil to prevent water from rotting the crowns.

Hot, dry periods in summer are required for its dormant period. Remove seed pods as soon as they are formed and cut the foliage when it turns brown. Do not water while dormant as this may cause rot. Green leaves appear in the fall, after the heat of summer is over, and stay green all winter.

PROPAGATION: For spring planting, you can buy plants in pots to avoid transplanting shock. August to September is the best time to handle them, since they start next year's growth after this period. You can dig up and move the entire plant intact. Where plants have some small crowns, these can be easily cut apart and planted. If you divide severely, you won't have any blooms the first year, but lots after that. When roots are 12 to 14 inches long, cut them off 6 inches below the crown and plant these cuttings also. You'll get double the number of plants this way. A 6-inch root as thick as a lead pencil will produce one bloom next spring. Set the pieces about 2 feet apart, making sure the end of the piece nearest the crown is uppermost and about 1 inch below the surface. Fresh green leaves will show up in about a month.

TROUBLES: *Bacterial blight.* Causes black lesions on stems, leaves, floral organs, and seed pods. Tissues between the spots turn yellow, then brown, and the leaf falls. Stems are often girdled and die. *Control*: Destroy plants as soon as you see this. When replanting, select a new site.

Aphids and other pests can be controlled with Malathion.

●**Papaver nudicaule** (Iceland Poppy) One of the best of the smaller perennial poppies and a very-early-flowering type. Two feet tall with wide range of colors; single and double flowers, 2 to 3 inches in diameter. It is not hardy enough to be a good perennial in cold areas, but most self-sow, reverting to more common colors.

GREEN THUMB CARE: If blooms are cut early in the morning and the stems are seared, they make good cut flowers. They will bloom all summer if not allowed to go to seed.

PROPAGATION: In northern areas better grown by seed sown in the spring outdoors. Blooms the first year. In warmer areas plants can be transplanted in spring or after bloom period.

TROUBLES: None serious.

●**Primula polyanthus** (Primrose) Spring bloomer with clusters of small flowers in yellow, blue, lavender, rose, white, cream, pink, red, and bicolors. Plants grow about 1 foot tall and tolerate shade. They are excellent for the shaded, moist corner or north border.

GREEN THUMB CARE: Primroses grow in sun or shade, a soil rich in organic matter and reasonably cool weather. The crowns of the plant should be kept high and dry, but the roots should always be able to reach moisture. Abundant moisture during the summer is essential to good growth for future flowering.

TROUBLES: None.

●**Phlox paniculata** (Garden Phlox) A perfectly hardy perennial and one of the easiest to grow, blooming in late summer and fall. Flowers are in various colors: red, lavender, purple, salmon, white, orange, pink, and "eyed" varieties. So many varieties have been introduced that selection can be bewildering. Beltsville Beauty is one worth trying in any garden. Tall varieties usually grow 3 to 4 feet high, dwarf varieties 1 to 2 1/2 feet.

GREEN THUMB CARE: When a phlox "changes color," when blues or pinks change to a lighter color, it is because faded blooms have been allowed to go to seed, and the seedlings, which never come true with any plant, have crowded out the parent plant. Remove the blooms as soon as they are past their prime; also divide the plants every three years to keep them healthy.

PROPAGATION: Division (in spring) is preferred, since they will not come true from seed. To separate the clumps, lift them and shake the soil loose. They can then be pulled apart, and each stem with its roots, separated from the others, is ready for replanting. Or simply cut the clump into four or more sections with a spade or sharp knife, making sure each division has about four eyes or buds. Reset at the same depth to which they grew and water thoroughly. These divisions will bloom for you next year.

Set phlox about 1 1/2 feet apart and just about 1 inch below the surface. The roots should be planted straight down. When the plants lose their vigor and the flowers their brilliance, divide the clumps again.

TROUBLES: *Powdery mildew*. A whitish mold on leaf surfaces that thrives in damp weather. *Control*: Dust with sulfur or spray with wettable sulfur, 2 tablespoons to a gallon of water, plus 1/3 teaspoonful of detergent. Karathane is also good. The secret is to start control early in the season. Cut old stems back early in the fall and burn or seal them in plastic bags and discard, as the fungus overwinters in old infected leaves.

In spring, just as new growth is coming out, keep it protected with a copper spray repeating once a week until the blooms appear; or use sulfur.

Spider mites. When leaves curl under, look for red spider mites. *Control*: These tiny marauders cannot tolerate moisture and drown easily. A strong hose spray from below breaks up their webs and does a good job of eliminating them. Sulfur dust kills them too. See Control of Insects and Diseases in Chapter XIV.

Leaf spot. Brown spots, first on the lower leaves, which turn brown and die. It works its way gradually up the stem. *Control*: Zineb, Maneb, or sulfur.

Nematodes. Cause stems to swell and crack and leaves to become brown and crinkled. May prevent blossoming. *Control*: Remove plants and surrounding soil and destroy.

•**Phlox subulata** (Moss Pink or Creeping Phlox) Masses of magenta, pink, purple, red, and white flowers. Thrives in dry, unfertile soils in exposed situations and is excellent for rocky slopes or rock gardens. Four inches high.

PROPAGATION: Readily propagated by cuttings or division of clumps any time in spring or fall.

TROUBLES: None.

•**Physostegia** (False Dragonhead) Here's a carefree perennial even one with a "black thumb" can grow. Flowers of purple, rose, or white are produced on stems 3 to 4 feet high, making it a good background plant. Flowers are useful in vase arrangements.

GREEN THUMB CARE: Has a tendency to get "weedy" and must be divided annually for neat effect. Grows well in moist spots or dry soils, in full sun or part shade.

PROPAGATION: Seed sown in spring. Division in spring is best way to start new plants. Lift clumps and separate into small pieces. Plant 2 inches deep.

TROUBLES: Plant is pest-, disease-, and trouble-free. May be weedy if left untended. Divide plants each spring to keep in bounds.

•**Rudbeckia hirta** (Gloriosa Daisy) This glorified offspring of our native blackeyed Susan, which will grow in poor, dry soils, is one of our best perennials. Gloriosa is a giant hybrid tetraploid *Rudbeckia*, growing on stems 2 feet high, and having flowers up to 4 inches across. Blooms are double, semi-double, and single; some solid yellow, some bronze, and varying shades between. Excellent in bouquets. It can also be used as a pot plant.

GREEN THUMB CARE: Plant is a perennial but may be handled as an annual. It takes little care except keeping ground free from weeds while it is becoming established. Plant in full sun for best bloom.

PROPAGATION: Since Gloriosa self-sows, you can get more plants by letting it go to seed. The plants will bloom the second year.

TROUBLES: Mildew during wet, rainy periods or when plant is grown in the shade. Dust with Maneb or Karathane.

•**Salvia farinacea** (Mealycup) A fine blue cut flower for vase arrangement (there are few blue spikey flowers available, making this one useful), spikes 12 to 18 inches long on stems 3 feet high. Flowers also come in white. Ideal in outdoor beds, as border or background plants. Wonderful for drying. Pick spikes and hang upside down in garage.

GREEN THUMB CARE: Likes full sun and good drainage. Plant close together to keep weeds out. Cutting stalks keeps new ones coming on.

PROPAGATION: Start from seed indoors. Plant outdoors in warm weather. In severe winters plants may die out completely. Set out new ones in spring. Plants often self-sow.

TROUBLES: Very few. Scarcity of blooms can be due to excess shade or too rich a soil.

•**Veronica longifolia var. subsessilis** (Speedwell) An excellent item for the border, blending well with other blooms in the garden. Grows 2 to 3 feet tall and blooms from June through September. Its spikes of delicate, deep or light blue flowers are ideal for arrangements. Not aggressive; plant stays neat and compact.

GREEN THUMB CARE: Will grow in ordinary soils, withstands hot weather well. Some varieties have weak stems that need support. Veronicas tend to raise their crowns when left in the same place for three or four years, so it's a good idea to dig the plant every third year and replant to get the crowns closer to the ground.

PROPAGATION: Seed sown in late spring. Also division in fall or spring.

TROUBLES: None.

PERENNIALS WHICH GROW IN SEMI-SHADE

(Nearly all perennials need some sunshine)

Botanical Name	Common Name	Bloom Season (according to species)	Height (Ft.)	Color
Aconitum (various species)	Monkshood	June-Sept.	$3\frac{1}{2}-4\frac{1}{2}$	Yellow, blue, purple
Ajuga reptans	Bugleweed	May, June	$\frac{3}{4}$	Purple, white
Anchusa myosotidiflora	Alkanet	May-June	1	Blue
Anemone hybrid (japonica)	Japanese Anemone (windflower)	Aug., Sept.	2-3	Pink, white, lavender
Astilbe species	Astilbe, Meadow Sweet	July, Aug.	$1-3\frac{1}{2}$	Rose, pink, white
Aquilegia (various species)	Columbine	May, June	$2\frac{1}{2}-3$	Various colors
Aubrietia deltoides	Aubrietia, Rockcress	Apr., May, June	$\frac{1}{2}-1$	Purple, rose, pink
Baptisia species	False Indigo	June	1-2	Blue
Bergenia cordifolia	Saxifraga, Giant Rockfoil	Apr., May	$1\frac{1}{2}$	Pink, purple
Campanula carpatica	Harebell	July, Aug., Sept.	1	Blue, purple, white
Campanula lactiflora	Bellflower	July, Aug.	$3\frac{1}{2}$	Blue
Campanula persicifolia	Peachbell	June, July	2-3	Blue, white
Cimicifuga racemosa	Snakeroot	July, Aug.	3-6	White
Convallaria majalis	Lily-of-the-valley	May	1	White, pink
Dicentra spectabilis	Bleedingheart	May, June	1-3	Red, white
Doronicum caucasicum	Leopards-Bane	June, July, Aug.	$1\frac{1}{2}-2$	Yellow
Epimedium (various species)	Epimedium, Barrenwort	May, June	$1\frac{1}{2}$	White, red, yellow
Eupatorium coelistinum	Mist Flower	Aug., Sept.	3	Purple
Fern species	Ferns	(foliage)	1-4	Foliage green
Geranium maculatum	Wild Geranium	May, June	2	White, blue, purple
Helleborus niger	Christmas Rose	Nov.-Apr.	1	White, purple
Hemerocallis varieties	Daylily	June-Sept.	$1\frac{1}{2}-4$	Yellow, orange, red, pink, purple, brown, bicolor
Heuchera sanguinea	Coralbell	June-Sept.	$1\frac{1}{2}$	Red, pink, white

Botanical Name	Common Name	Bloom Season (according to species)	Height (Ft.)	Color
Hosta (various species)	Plantain Lily	July–Sept.	2–2½	Blue, white, lavender
Iberis sempervirens	Candytuft	May, June	1	White
Liatris scariosa	Gayfeather	Aug., Sept.	5	Purple
Lobelia cardinalis	Cardinal Flower	Aug., Sept.	4	Red
Lythrum salicaria	Purple Loosestrife	July, Aug.	3–4	Purple, pink
Lysimachia clethroides	Gooseneck Loosestrife	July, Aug.	3	White
Mertensia virginica	Bluebells	Apr., May	2	Blue
Monarda didyma	Beebalm	July, Sept.	3½	Red, pink, purple
Myosotis scorpioides	Everblooming Forget-me-not	June, July, Aug.	1	Blue, pink
Primula (various species)	Primrose	Apr.–June	½–1¼	Various colors
Ranunculus repens (var. *florepleno*)	Creeping Buttercup	May, June	1½	Yellow
Sanguinaria canadensis	Bloodroot	April–May	½	White
Veronica spicata	Speedwell	June, July	1¾	Blue, pink
Vinca minor	Periwinkle	May, June	⅓	Blue, white
Viola cornuta	Viola, Tufted Pansy	May–Sept.	¾	Shades of lavender, blue, yellow, bronze, white
Viola odorata	Violet	May, June	¼	Blue, white, pink

Botanical Name	Common Name	Bloom Season	Height (Ft.)	Color
Aruncus sylvester	Goatsbeard	June, July	5	White
Astilbe arendsii	Meadow Sweet, Astilbe	July	1-4	Pink, white, deep rose
Bergenia cordifolia	Giant Rockfoil, Saxifraga	Apr., May	$1\frac{1}{2}$	Pink, purple
Hibiscus hybrids	Rose-mallow	July, Sept.	$5\frac{1}{2}$	White, red, pink, yellow
Iris kaempferi	Japanese Iris	June, July	3	Red, purple, white
Lobelia cardinalis	Cardinal Flower	July, Aug., Sept.	4	Red
Lysimachia clethroides	Gooseneck Loosestrife	July, Aug.	3	White
Lythrum species	Purple Loosestrife	July, Aug.	$4\frac{1}{2}$	Red, purple, pink
Monarda didyma	Beebalm	July, Aug.	$3\frac{1}{2}$	Red, pink, purple
Myosotis scorpioides	Everblooming Forget-me-not	June, July, Aug.	1	Blue, pink
Trollius europaeus	Globeflower	May	2	Yellow
Trollius ledebouri	Globeflower	June	2	Yellow, orange

Botanical Name	Common Name	Bloom Season (according to species)	Height (Ft.)	Color
Aconitum (various species)	Monkshood	June-Sept.	3-4½	Blue, purple, yellow
Alyssum saxatile	Goldentuft	Apr., May	1¾	Yellow
Arabis caucasica	White Rock Cress	Apr., May	1	White
Armeria maritima	Sea Pink	May, June	1	Red, pink
Coreopsis lanceolata	Coreopsis	June-Sept.	2½	Yellow
Coreopsis verticillata	Threadleaf	June-Aug.	3	Yellow
Dianthus barbatus	Sweet William	June, July	1-2	Various colors
Dianthus deltoides	Maiden Pink	May, June	1	Red, pink, white
Dianthus plumarius	Cottage Pink	May, June	1	Pink
Dictamnus albus	Gasplant	June	3	White, purple
Gaillardia aristata	Gaillardia	June-Sept.	3	Yellow, red
Helenium autumnale	Sneezeweed	Aug., Sept.	3	Yellow, red
Hemerocallis (varieties)	Daylily	June-Sept.	1½-4	Yellow, red, orange, pink, purple, brown, bicolor
Heuchera sanguinea	Coralbells	May-Sept.	1½	Red, pink, white
Iris (species)	Iris	Apr.-July	1-3	Various colors
Lupinus polyphyllus	Lupine	June-July	4	Various colors
Lychnis chalcedonica	Maltese Cross	June-July	3	Red, white, rose
Lychnis coronaria	Mullein Pink	June-Aug.	2	Red, purple, white
Rudbeckia lacineata	Goldenglow	July-Sept.	6	Yellow
Rudbeckia triloba (Bi)	Black-eyed Susan	Aug.-Sept.	5	Yellow
Sedum (species)	Sedum, Stonecrop	July-Sept.	½-2	Rose, red, pink, yellow
Veronica (species)	Speedwell	May-Aug. (according to species)	1½-2½	Blue, pink, purple, white

COMMON PERENNIALS FOR THE ROCK GARDEN

Botanical name	Common Name	Remarks
Achillea	Woolly Yarrow	2″ to 6″ high; yellow flowers; May to October
Ajuga	Bugleweed	6″ tall; blue flowers; May til June; sun, shade
Alyssum saxatile	Golden Turf	12″ high; May; spreads fast
Aquilegia	Columbine	24″ high; various colors; sun or shade
Arabis	Rockgrass	8″ high; white flowers; April and May
Arenaria	Arenaria	2″ high; foliage grass-like; sun or light shade
Armeria	Sea Pink or Thrift	Up to 2′ tall; pink flowers; May and some until frost
Asarum	Wild Ginger	12″ high. Forms ground cover; sun or deep shade
Dianthus	Maiden Pink	6″ high; red, pink, white flowers; May to July
Gypsophila repens	Creeping Gypsophila	20″ high; white and pink flowers; May through July
Heuchera sanguinea	Coral Bells	12″ to 18″ high; pink; June through September
Iris pumila	Dwarf Iris	10″ high; blue, yellow, white; May
Myosotis alpestris	Forget-me-not	3″ to 6″ high; blue, white, pink; May to June; tolerates shade
Phlox subulata	Moss Pink	3″ to 6″ high; pink, red, blue, purple, white; May
Primula species	Primrose	8″ to 12″ high; pink, rose, yellow, and shades; April through June
Sanguinaria	Bloodroot	6″ to 12″ high; white flowers, some double-flowered and are best; shade or sun; spring
Sedum album and *S. sieboldii*	Stonecrop Sedum	3″ high; various colors of white, rose, yellow, purple; May through September
Sempervivum	Hens and Chickens	Hugs ground; grown for interesting multiple rosettes of leaves; reddish, green, bronze; June to September
Thymus	Thyme	3″ to 6″ high; white, pink flowers; June, July
Viola cornuta	Tufted pansy, Viola	4″ to 8″ high; violet, yellow, purple flowers; May through September

PERENNIALS FOR APRIL SHOW

Botanical Name	Common Name	Color
Alyssum saxatile	Basket of Gold	Gold
Anemone pulsatilla	Pasque Flower	Purple, white, pink
Anemone sylvestris	Snowdrop Anemone	White
Bellis perennis	English Daisy	White, pink
Bergenia cordifolia	Bergenia, Saxifraga, Giant Rockfoil	Pink
Brunnera macrophylla	Siberian Bugloss	Blue
Eranthis hyemalis	Winter Aconite	Yellow
Helleborus orientalis	Lenten Rose	White, pink
Hepatica (species)	Hepatica	White, pink
Primula polyantha	Polyanthus, Primrose	White, pink, red, yellow, blue, purple, and bicolors
Primula (hybrids)	Dwarf Primrose	Large color range of solids and bicolors
Pulmonaria saccharata	Lungwort	Blue
Sanguinaria canadensis	Bloodroot	White
Viola odorata	Violet	Blue, white, pink

PERENNIALS FOR MAY SHOW

Botanical Name	Common Name	Color
Ajuga reptans	Bugleweed	Blue
Alyssum saxatile	Goldentuft	Golden
Anemone pulsatilla	Pasque Flower	Pink, white
Anemone sylvestris	Snowdrop Anemone	White
Aquilegia canadensis	Wild Columbine	Various colors
Arabis caucasica	White Rock Cress	White
Armeria maritima	Sea Pink, Thrift	Pink
Aubrietia deltoides	Aubrietia, Rock Cress	Purple, rose, pink
Bellis perennis	English Daisy	Pink, white
Bergenia cordifolia	Bergenia	Pink
Brunnera macrophylla	Siberian Bugloss	Blue
Cheiranthus cheiri	Wallflower	Yellow, red, brown
Convallaria majalis	Lily of the Valley	White
Dianthus deltoides	Maiden Pink	Pink, white, red
Dicentra canadensis	Squirrel Corn	White, pink
Dicentra spectabilis	Bleedingheart	White, red
Dodecatheon meadia	Shooting Star	White, pink, purple, red
Epimedium (species)	Barrenwort	White, red
Euphorbia cyparissias	Cypress Spurge	Yellow-green

PERENNIALS FOR MAY SHOW (Continued)

Botanical Name	Common Name	Color
Euphorbia epithymoides	Euphorbia	Yellow
Geum (species)	Geum	Red, yellow, orange
Hepatica (species)	Hepatica	Pink, white
Hesperis matronalis	Dames Rocket	Purple, white
Heuchera sanguinea	Coral Bells	Pink, red, white
Iberis sempervirens	Candytuft	White
Iris chamaeiris	Dwarf Iris	White, blue, purple, yellow
Iris cristata	Crested Iris	Lilac, white
Iris germanica	German Iris	Various colors
Iris pumila	Dwarf Iris	Yellow, blue, purple
Lamium maculatum	Spotted Deadnettle	Purple, rose
Mertensia virginica	Bluebells	Blue
Paeonia lactiflora	Peony	Red, pink, white, yellow
Paeonia suffruticosa	Tree Peony	Red, pink, white, yellow
Phlox divaricata	Blue Phlox	Blue
Phlox subulata	Moss Pink	Pink, white, rose
Polemonium reptans	"Creeping Jacob's Ladder"	Blue
Polygonatum caeruleum	Solomon's Seal	Blue
Primula denticulata	Primrose	Lilac, white, violet
Primula polyantha	Polyanthus, Primrose	White, pink, red, yellow, blue, purple, and bicolors
Primula sieboldii	Japanese Primrose	White, rose, purple
Pulmonaria saccharata	Lungwort	Blue
Trillium grandiflorum	Trillium	Pink, white
Trollium europaeus	Globeflower	Orange, yellow
Viola cornuta	Viola, Tufted Pansy	Shades of lavender, blue, yellow, bronze, white
Viola odorata	Violet	Blue, white, pink

PERENNIALS FOR JUNE BLOOM

Botanical Name	Common Name	Color
Achillea tomentosa	Woolly Yarrow	Yellow
Aconitum vulparia	Yellow Monkshood	Yellow
Aethionema grandiflorum	Persian Stonecress	Pink
Ajuga reptans	Bugleweed	Blue

PERENNIALS FOR JUNE BLOOM (Continued)

Botanical Name	Common Name	Color
Alstroemeria aurantica	Peruvian Lily	Orange, yellow
Alyssum murale	Yellowtuft	Yellow
Amsonia tabernaemontana	Amsonia	Blue
Aquilegia hybrida	Longspurred Columbine	Various colors
Aquilegia vulgaris	European Columbine	Various colors
Armeria maritima	Sea Pink, Thrift	Pink
Aruncus sylvester	Goatsbeard	White
Asperula odorata	Sweet Woodruff	White
Asphodeline lutea	Asphodel	Yellow
Aster alpinus	Rock Aster	Purple
Aubrietia deltoides	Aubrietia, Rock Cress	Pink, purple, rose
Baptisia australis	False Indigo	Blue
Bellis perennis	English Daisy	Pink, white
Campanula glomerata	Danesblood	Pink
Campanula rotundifolia	Harebell	Blue, white, violet
Centaurea dealbata	Persian Centaurea	Lilac
Centaurea montana	Mountain Bluet	Blue
Cerastium tomentosum	Snow-in-Summer	White
Chrysanthemum coccineum	Pyrethrum, Painted Daisy	Various colors
Chrysanthemum maximum	Shasta Daisy	White
Clematis integrifolia		Blue
Corydalis lutea	Corydalis	Golden
Dianthus barbatus	Sweet William	Various colors
Dianthus deltoides	Maiden Pink	Purple, rose, white
Dianthus plumarius	Cottage Pink	Red, pink, white
Dicentra eximia	Wild Bleeding Heart	Rose-pink
Dicentra spectabilis	Bleeding Heart	Red and white
Dictamnus albus	Gasplant	White
Digitalis grandiflora	Yellow Foxglove	Yellow (spotted)
Digitalis purpurea (Bi)	Foxglove	Spotted purple, pink, peach, lavender, white, rose
Dodecatheon meadia	Shooting Star	Pink, white, purple, red
Eremurus (species)	Foxtail Lily	Pink, yellow, white
Euphorbia cyparissias	Cypress Spurge	Yellow-green
Filipendula hexapetala	Dropwort	White
Gaillardia aristata	Blanket Flower	Yellow, red-bronze
Geranium sanguineum	Cranesbill	Purple, red
Geum (species)	Geum	Red, yellow, orange
Gypsophila repens	Creeping Baby's Breath	Pink, white
Hesperis matronalis	Dames Rocket	Lilac, white
Heuchera sanguinea	Coralbells	Pink, red, white
Iberis gibraltarica	Candytuft	Purple
Iris germanica (Pogoniris)	Bearded or German Iris	Various colors

PERENNIALS FOR JUNE BLOOM (Continued)

Botanical Name	Common Name	Color
Iris kaempferi	Japanese Iris	Various colors
Iris sibirica	Siberian Iris	Blue, white
Linum narbonense	Blue Flax	Blue, white
Linum perenne	Blue Flax	Blue
Lunaria annua (Bi)	Honesty	White, lavender
Lupinus polyphyllus	Lupine	White, purple, blue, red, rose, yellow
Lychnis viscaria	Catchfly	Rose, pink
Lysimachia punctata	Yellow Loosestrife	Yellow
Myosotis scorpioides	Everblooming Forget-me-not	Blue, pink
Nepeta faassenii (mussinii)	Catmint	Blue
Oenothera pilosella	Sundrop	Yellow
Paeonia lactiflora (albiflora)	Peony	Red, pink, white, yellow
Paeonia suffruticosa	Tree Peony	Red, pink, white, yellow
Papaver nudicaule	Iceland Poppy	Various colors
Papaver orientale	Oriental Poppy	Red, orange, pink
Polemonium caeruleum	Jacob's Ladder	Blue
Primula japonica	Primrose	Pink, white, purple
Salvia pratensis	Meadow Sage	Blue, rose-pink
Saponaria ocymoides	Soapwort	Pink
Stachys olympica (lanata)	Woolly Lambs-Ear	Pink, purple-red
Symphytum asperum	Prickly Comfrey	Blue, purple
Thalictrum aquilegifolium	Meadowrue	Lilac-purple
Thalictrum minus	Maidenhair Meadowrue	Yellow
Thermopsis caroliniana	False Lupine	Yellow
Thymus serpyllum	Thyme	Rose-lilac
Tradescantia virginiana	Spiderwort	Violet-purple
Trollius ledebouri	Globeflower	Orange-gold
Tunica saxifraga	Tunic Flower	White, rose-pink
Verbascum (Various species) (Bi)	Verbascum, Mullein	Rose, cream, yellow, white
Veronica latifolia (V. teucrium)	Speedwell	Blue
Viola cornuta	Viola, Tufted Pansy	Shades of lavender, blue, yellow, bronze, white

PERENNIALS FOR JULY BLOOM

Botanical Name	Common Name	Color
Achillea filipendulina	Fernleaf Yarrow	Yellow
Achillea millefolium (var. rosea)	Pink Yarrow	Pink

PERENNIALS FOR JULY BLOOM (Continued)

Botanical Name	Common Name	Color
Achillea ptarmica	Sneezewort	White
Aconitum napellus	English Monkshood	Violet
Althaea rosea (Bi)	Hollyhock	Various colors
Alstroemeria aurantica	Alstroemeria	Orange-yellow
Alyssum murale	Yellowtuft	Yellow
Anchusa azurea (italica)	Italian Bugloss, Alkanet	Blue
Anthemis tinctoria	Golden Marguerite	Gold
Aquilegia hybrida	Longspurred Columbine	Various colors
Astilbe arendsii	Astilbe, Meadow Sweet	Rose, pink, white
Callirhoe involucrata	Poppy Mallow	Purple, red
Campanula carpatica	Carpathian Harebell	Blue, purple, white
Campanula glomerata	Danesblood	Purple, blue
Campanula lactiflora	Bellflower	White, blue
Campanula medium (Bi)	Canterbury Bells	White, pink, blue, purple
Campanula persicifolia	Willowleaf Bellflower	Blue, white
Campanula rotundifolia	Harebell	Blue, white, violet
Catananche caerulea	Cupid's Dart	Blue
Centaurea dealbata	Persian Centaurea	Lilac
Centaurea macrocephala	Globe Centaurea	Golden Yellow
Centranthus ruber	Red Valerian	Red
Chrysanthemum maximum	Shasta Daisy	White
Chrysanthemum parthenium	Feverfew, Matricaria	White
Cimicifuga racemosa	Snakeroot	White
Clematis integrifolia		Blue
Coreopsis lanceolata	Coreopsis	Yellow
Coreopsis verticillata	Golden Shower	Yellow
Corydalis lutea	Corydalis	Yellow
Delphinium cheilanthum	Belladonna Delphinium	Blue, white, cream
Delphinium elatum	Delphinium	Blue, pink, white
Delphinium grandiflorum	Delphinium (Chinese)	White, blue
Dianthus barbatus	Sweet William	Various colors
Dicentra eximia	Wild Bleeding Heart	Pink
Digitalis purpurea (Bi)	Foxglove	Various colors
Eremurus (species)	Foxtail Lily	Pink, yellow, white
Filipendula rubra	Queen of the Prairie	Pink
Filipendula ulmaria	Queen of the Meadow	White
Gaillardia	Blanket flower	Yellow, bronze-red
Galium aristatum	Bedstraw	White
Geranium sanguineum	Cranesbill	Purple, red
Gypsophila repens	Creeping Baby's Breath	White, pink
Gypsophila paniculata	Baby's Breath	White, pink
Heliopsis scabra	Heliopsis	Yellow
Hesperis matronalis	Dames Rocket	Lilac, white
Heuchera sanguinea	Coralbells	Pink, white, red

PERENNIALS FOR JULY BLOOM (Continued)

Botanical Name	Common Name	Color
Hosta fortunei	Tall Clustered Funkia	Lavender, white
Hosta fortunei	Tall Clustered Funkia	Lavender, white
Hosta ventricosa	Blue Plantain Lily	Blue
Iberis gibraltarica	Candytuft	Light purple
Iris kaempferi	Japanese Iris	Various colors
Kniphofia (various species)	Torch lily, Tritoma, Red Hot Poker	Red, orange, yellow, white
Lamium maculatum	Spotted Deadnettle	Purple, rose
Limonium latifolium	Sea Lavender, Statice	White, lavender
Linum flavum	Yellow Flax	Yellow
Linum narbonense	Blue Flax	Blue, white
Linum perenne	Blue Flax	Blue
Lychnis chalcedonica	Maltese Cross	Red, white, rose
Lychnis viscaria	Catchfly	Red-purple
Lysimachia clethroides	Gooseneck Loosestrife	White
Lythrum salicaria	Purple Loosestrife	Purple, pink
Macleaya cordata (Bocconia)	Plume Poppy	Cream
Monarda didyma	Beebalm	Red, purple, pink
Myosotis scorpioides	Everblooming Forget-me-not	Blue, pink
Nepeta faassenii (mussinii)	Catmint	Blue, violet
Oenothera missouriensis	Giant Sundrop	Golden
Penstemon barbatus	Beardtongue	Deep rose
Phlox carolina	Phlox Miss Lingard	White, purple, rose
Phlox paniculata	Phlox	White, pink, red, shades of lavender
Platycodon grandiflorum	Balloon Flower	Blue, white
Salvia sclarea (Bi)	Vatican Sage	White, rose, purple
Scabiosa caucasica	Perennial Scabiosa	Blue, white, lavender
Scutellaria baicalensis	Skullcap	Blue
Sedum (species)	Sedum, Stonecrop	Pink, yellow, rose, red
Sidalcea (various species)	Prairie Mallow	Pink, rose
Stachys grandiflora (Betonica)	Betony	Violet, pink
Stachys olympica	Woolly Lambs-Ear	Pink, purple
Stokesia laevis	Stokes Aster	Blue
Symphytum asperum	Prickly Comfrey	Blue, purple
Thalictrum dipterocarpum	Meadowrue	Lavender
Thalictrum rugosum (glaucum)	Meadowrue (Dusty)	Yellow
Thymus serphyllum	Creeping Thyme	Rose-lilac
Tunica saxifraga	Tunic Flower	Lilac
Valeriana officinalis	Garden Heliotrope	White, lavender

PERENNIALS FOR JULY BLOOM (Continued)

Botanical Name	Common Name	Color
Verbascum (various species), *Bi*	Mullein, Verbascum	Rose, cream, yellow, white
Veronica incana	Woolly Speedwell	Blue
Veronica longifolia (var. *subsessilis*)	Speedwell	Royal Blue
Veronica spicata	Speedwell	Blue
Veronicastrum virginicum	Culvers Root	White
Viola cornuta	Viola, Tufted Pansy	Shades of lavender, blue, yellow, bronze, white
Yucca smalliana (filamentosa)	Spanish Bayonet Adam's Needle	Cream

PERENNIALS FOR AUGUST BLOOM

Botanical Name	Common Name	Color
Achillea filipendulina	Fernleaf Yarrow	Yellow
Achillea millefolium (var. *rosea*)	Pink Yarrow	Pink
Achillea ptarmica	Sneezewort	White
Aconitum napellus	Monkshood	White
Althaea rosea (Bi)	Hollyhock	Various colors
Anchusa azurea (italica)	Italian Bugloss	Blue
Anthemis tinctoria	Golden Marguerite	Yellow
Artemisia lactiflora	White Mugwort	White
Asclepias tuberosa	Butterflyweed	Orange
Aster amellus	Italian Aster	Purple
Aster frikartii	Hardy Aster	Blue
Callirhoe involucrata	Poppy Mallow	Purple-red
Campanula carpatica	Carpathian Harebell	Blue, white, purple
Campanula lactiflora	Bellflower	White, pale blue
Campanula rotundiflora	Harebell	Blue, violet, white
Cantananche caerulea	Cupid's Dart	Blue
Centranthus ruber	Red Valerian	Red
Ceratostigma plumbaginoides	Plumbago, Blue Leadwort	Deep blue
Chrysanthemum maximum	Shasta Daisy	White
Chrysanthemum parthenium	Feverfew, Matricaria	White
Clematis heracleifolia		Blue
Coreopsis lanceolata	Coreopsis	Yellow
Coreopsis verticillata	Golden Shower	Yellow
Corydalis lutea	Corydalis	Yellow

PERENNIALS FOR AUGUST BLOOM (Continued)

Botanical Name	Common Name	Color
Echinacea purpurea (Rudbeckia)	Purple Coneflower	Purple
Echinops exaltatus (ritro)	Globe Thistle	Blue
Eryngium amethystinum	Sea Holly	Gray
Gaillardia aristata	Blanket flower	Yellow, red-bronze
Galium aristatum	Bedstraw	White
Gypsophila paniculata	Baby's Breath	White, pink
Helenium autumnale	Sneezeweed	Yellow
Helianthus decapetalus (var. multiflorus)	Thinleaf Sunflower	Yellow
Heliopsis scabra	Heliopsis	Yellow
Heuchera sanguinea	Coral Bells	Red, pink, white
Hibiscus moscheutos	Rose Mallow	White, pink, rose
Hosta lancifolia	Narrow-leaved Plantain Lily	Lavender
Hosta plantaginea	Fragrant Plantain Lily	White
Kniphofia (species)	Red Hot Poker, Torch-lily, Tritoma	Red, orange, yellow, white
Lamium maculatum	Spotted Deadneedle	Purple, rose
Liatris (species)	Gayfeather, Blazing Star	Purple, white
Limonium latifolium	Sea Lavender	White, lavender
Linum flavum	Yellow Flax	Yellow
Lobelia cardinalis	Cardinal Flower	Red
Lobelia siphilitica	Blue Perennial Lobelia	Blue
Lychnis coronaria	Rose Campion	Red
Lysimachia clethroides	Gooseneck Loosestrife	White
Lythrum salicaria	Purple Loosestrife	Purple
Monarda didyma	Beebalm	Purple, red, pink
Myosotis scorpioides	Everblooming Forget-me-not	Blue, pink
Nepeta faassenii (mussinii)	Catmint	Blue
Oenothera missouriensis	Giant Sundrop	Yellow
Phlox paniculata	Phlox	Various colors
Physostegia virginiana	False Dragonhead	Rose
Platycodon grandiflorum	Balloon Flower	Blue, white
Rudbeckia laciniata (var. hortensis)	Goldenglow	Yellow
Rudbeckia triloba (Bi)	Black-Eyed Susan	Yellow
Sedum (species)	Sedum, Stonecrop	Pink, yellow, red, rose
Sidalcea (species)	Prairie Mallow	Pink, rose
Stokesia laevis	Stokes Aster	Blue
Symphytum asperum	Prickly Comfrey	Blue, purple
Thalictrum dipterocarpum	Meadowrue	Lavender

PERENNIALS FOR AUGUST BLOOM (Continued)

Botanical Name	Common Name	Color
Veronica longifolia		
(var. *subsessilis*)	Speedwell, Veronica	Blue
Veronicastrum virginicum	Culvers Root	Blue
Viola cornuta	Viola, Tufted Pansy	Shades of lavender, blue, yellow, bronze, white
Yucca smalliana (filamentosa)	Spanish Bayonet Adam's Needle	Cream

PERENNIALS FOR SEPTEMBER BLOOM

Botanical Name	Common Name	Color
Achillea ptarmica	Sneezewort	White
Aconitum carmichaelii (fisheri)	Monkshood	White
Anemone hybrida (japonica)	Japanese Anemone	Various colors
Artemisia lactiflora	White Mugwort	White
Aster amellus	Italian Aster	Purple
Aster frikartii	Hardy Aster	Blue
Aster novae angliae	New England Aster	Purple
Aster novibelgi	New York Aster	Blue
Callirhoe involucrata	Poppy Mallow	Purple, red
Campanula carpatica	Carpathian Harebell	Blue, purple, white
Centaurea montana	Mountain Bluet	Blue
Ceratostigma plumbaginoides	Plumbago	Blue
Chrysanthemum morifolium	Hardy Chrysanthemum	Various colors
Coreopsis lanceolata	Coreopsis	Golden
Eupatorium coelistinum	Mistflower	Blue
Gaillardia aristata	Gaillardia, Blanket flower	Orange
Helenium autumnale	Sneezeweed	Yellow
Helianthus decapetalus		
(var. *multiflorus*)	Thinleaf Sunflower	Yellow
Helianthus salicifolius		
(*orgyalis*)	Yellow Sunflower	Yellow
Heliopsis scabra	Heliopsis	Yellow
Hibiscus moscheutos	Rose Mallow	White, pink, rose
Hosta plantaginea	Fragrant Plantain Lily	Blue
Lespedeza thunbergii	Bush Clover	Purple
Lobelia cardinalis	Cardinal Flower	Red
Rudbeckia laciniata		
(var. *hortensis*)	Goldenglow	Yellow
Rudbeckia triloba (Bi)	Black-Eyed Susan	Yellow
Salvia pitcheri	Clary, Meadow Sage	Blue

PERENNIALS FOR SEPTEMBER BLOOM (Continued)

Botanical Name	Common Name	Color
Sedum spectabile	Sedum, Stonecrop	Pink, yellow, red
Tradescantia virginiana	Spiderwort	Violet
Viola cornuta	Viola, Tufted Pansy	Shades of lavender, blue, yellow, bronze, white

Here are some good perennials to grow for use in dried arrangements. All can be dried by hanging upside down.

Artemisia (Silvery King): Feathery gray spikes

Chinese Lantern (*Physalis franchettii*): Decorative orange-red "paper lanterns"

Delphinium (*Delphinium*): Tall spikes of blue, lavender, pink blooms

Dusty Miller (*Cineraria maritima*): Silver-gray "cut-leaf" foliage

Globe Thistle (*Echinops ritro*): Blue flowers. Pink globes when green.

Goldenrod (*Solidago*): Tame variety has large, rich, golden trusses.

Lamb's Ears (*Stachys lanata*): Wooly silvery-gray foliage

Lavender (*Lavendula*): Fragrant gray foliage

Onions, ornamental (*Allium*): Large globular clusters of pale pink, blue, white flowers on tall stems

Oriental Poppy (*Papaver orientale*): Pick dry seed pods

Salvia Farinacea (Mealycup): Fine, blue spikey flower.

Sea Lavender or Statice (*Limonium*): A delicate, lacy, plant

Yarrow (*Achillea*): Clusters of yellow, white, or rose flowers on wiry stems

Don't forget there are many other plants and wildflowers you can gather for dried arrangements. These include Boneset (*Eupatorium*), Cattail, Ferns, Goldenrod, seedheads of wheat, oats, millet, and other grains and grasses, *Mullein* (Verbascum), Pearly Everlasting (*Anaphalis*), Queen Anne's Lace (Wild carrot), Sumac, Teasel, and Bull Thistle. See Chapter IV, FLOWERING ANNUALS, for others.

TOUGH PERENNIALS FOR DRY SITUATIONS

Botanical Name	Common Name	Bloom Season	Height (Ft.)	Color
Achillea ptarmica	Sneezewort	July, Aug., Sept.	2½	White
Alyssum saxatile	Golden Tuft	Apr., May	1¾	Yellow
Anthemis tinctora	Camomile (Chamomile)	June–Aug.	3	Yellow
Arabis caucasica	White Rock Cress	Apr., May	1	White
Baptisia australis	False Indigo	June	4	Blue
Centaurea macrocephala	Showy Centaury	July	3	Yellow
Cerastium tomentosum	Snow-in-Summer	May, June	1	White
Dianthus plumarius	Cottage Pink, Grass Pink	May, June	1	Pink
Gaillardia aristata	Blanket Flower	June–Sept.	3	Yellow, red, bronze
Gypsophila paniculata	Baby's Breath	July, Aug.	1½–3	White, pink
Helianthus decapetalus (var. *multiflorus*)	Thin Leaf Sunflower	Aug., Sept.	3½	Yellow
Linum perenne	Flax	June, July	2	Blue, white
Lychnis unclear-chalcedonica	Maltese Cross	June, July	3	Red, white, rose
Lychnis coronaria	Mullein Pink	June, July, Aug.	2	Red, purple, white
Oenothera missouriensis	Giant Sundrop	June, July, Aug.	1	Yellow
Rudbeckia laciniata (var. *hortensis*)	Goldenglow	July, Aug., Sept.	6	Yellow
Rudbeckia triloba (Bi)	Black-Eyed Susan	Aug., Sept.	5	Yellow
Sedum (species)	Sedum, Stonecrop	July–Sept.	½–2	Pink, yellow, rose, red

Botanical Name	Common Name	Bloom Season	Height (Ft.)	Color
Achillea ptarmica	Sneezewort	July, Aug., Sept.	$2^{1}/_{2}$	White
Anemone hybrida (japonica)	Japanese Anemone, Windflower	Aug., Sept.	2-3	Pink, white, lavender
Anthemis tinctoria	Golden Marguerite	July-Sept.	2	Yellow
Aquilegia hybrida	Columbine	June, July	3	Various colors
Aster species	Aster	July, Aug., Sept.	$1-2^{1}/_{2}$	Blue, purple, rose, pink, white
Campanula carpatica	Carpathian Harebell	July, Aug., Sept.	1	Blue, white, purple
Campanula persicifolia	Peachbell	June, July	3	Blue, white
Centaurea montana	Perennial Cornflower	July-Sept.	2	Violet-blue
Chrysanthemum coccineum	Painted Daisy	June, July	$2^{1}/_{2}$	Red, pink, white
Chrysanthemum maximum	Shasta Daisy	June, July, Aug.	3	White
Chrysanthemum morifolium	Hardy Mum	Aug., Sept., Oct.	1-3	Various colors
Convallaria majalis	Lily of the Valley	May	1	White, pink
Coreopsis verticillata	Tickseed, Golden Shower	June, July, Aug.	3	Yellow
Dianthus barbatus	Sweet William	June, July	1-2	Various colors
Dianthus plumarius	Cottage Pink, Grass Pink	May, June	1	Pink
Echinacea purpurea	Purple Coneflower	July, Aug., Sept.	4	Purple
Gaillardia aristata	Gaillardia	June-Sept.	3	Yellow, red
Gypsophila paniculata	Baby's Breath	July, Aug.	$1^{1}/_{2}$-3	White, pink
Heuchera sanguinea	Coral Bells	May-Sept.	$1^{1}/_{2}$	Red, pink, white
Iris germanica	German Iris	May, June	3	Various colors
Iris kaempferi	Japanese Iris	Early summer	$1^{1}/_{2}$	Lavender, orchid, blue, pink
Liatris species	Cattail Gayfeather	July, Aug.	2-4	Purple, white
Lilium candidum	Madonna Lily	June, July	4	White
Lythrum salicaria	Purple Loosestrife	July, Aug.	3-4	Purple, pink

Botanical Name	Common Name	Bloom Season	Height (Ft.)	Color
Monarda didyma	Beebalm	July, Aug.	3½	Red, pink, white
Paeonia lactiflora	Peony	May, June	3½	Red, pink, white
Phlox paniculata	Summer Phlox	July, Aug.	2-3	Various colors
Physostegia virginiana	False Dragonhead	July, Aug., Sept.	3½	White, lavender, purple
Rudbeckia gloriosa	Gloriosa Daisy	July–Sept.	2½	Yellow, bronze shades
Salvia pitcheri	Clary, Meadow Sage	July	3-3½	Blue
Veronica species	Speedwell	July–Sept.	1½-2½	Blue, purple, pink, white

Botanical Name	Common Name	Bloom Season	Height (Ft.)	Color
Asperula Odorata	Sweet Woodruff	May, June	¾	White
Dianthus barbatus	Sweet William	June, July	½-1½	Various colors
Heuchera sanguinea	Coral Bells	June-Sept.	1½	Red, pink, white
Iberis sempervirens	Hardy Candytuft	May, June	1	White
Sedum spectabile	Sedum, Stonecrop	Aug., Sept.	1-1½	Purple, red
Teucrium chamaedrys	Germander or Teucrium	(grown for foliage)	¾	Foliage glossy green
Yucca smalliana (filamentosa)	Bayonet Plant or Adam's Needle	July, Aug.	5	White

Of the evergreen perennials mentioned above, probably *Sedum spectabile* is the showiest. It blooms in late August and September and is an excellent border plant. We like the form with variegated foliage. Flowers vary from rose to purple, pinkish to almost white. The stems and stalks dry up in early winter and in early spring new rosettes appear above ground, later elongating to make dense clumps a foot or more high.

PERENNIALS THAT GROW EASILY FROM SEED

Seeds are produced in tremendous quantities with most perennials, but keep in mind that not all can be expected to produce blooms exactly like the parent plants. Here are some perennials Cornell University recommends as "easy starters" from seed.

Achillea (Yarrow)

Ajuga

Alyssum

Althaea (Hollyhock)

Anchusa (Alkanet)

Anthemis (Golden Marguerite)

Aquilegia (Columbine)

Arabis (Rock Cress)

Armeria (Thrift)

Artemisia (Silver Mound)

Asclepias (Butterfly Weed)

Aster

Aubrietia (Purple Rock Cress)

Bellis (English Daisy [Bi])

Bocconia (Plume Poppy)

Boltonia

Campanula (Bellflower)

Centaurea (Cornflower)

Cerastium (Snow-in-Summer)

Chelone

Chrysanthemum

Coreopsis (Tickseed)

Delphinium

Dianthus (Pink)

Digitalis (Foxglove)

Doronicum (Leopard's Bane)

Echinops (Globe Thistle)

Eupatorium (Hardy Ageratum)

Gaillardia (Blanket Flower)

Geum

Gypsophila (Baby's Breath)

Helenium (Sneezeweed)

Helianthus (Sunflower)

Heliopsis

Hibiscus

Hypericum

Iberis (Candytuft)

Kniphofia (Tritoma)

Lamium

Lathyrus (Sweet Pea)

Lavendula (Lavender)

Liatris

Linaria (Toadflax)

Linum (Flax)

Lobelia

Lupinus (Lupine)

Lychnis

Lysimachia (Loosestrife)

Lythrum (Purple Loosestrife)

Malva

Mentha (Mint)

Myosotis (Forget-Me-Not)

Nepeta

Oenothera (Evening Primrose)

Papaver (Poppy)

Penstemon

Physostegia (False Dragonhead)

Platycodon (Balloonflower)

Polemonium

Polygonum

Potentilla

Primula (Common species) (Primrose)

Pyrethrum (Painted Daisy)

Rudbeckia (Gloriosa Daisy)

Salvia (blue)

Saponaria

Sedum

Sempervivum (Hens and Chickens)

Valeriana

Verbascum (Mullein)

Veronica (Speedwell)

Viola

*There are many others which can be started from seed, but are difficult, or do not come true. These should be propagated by divisions, root cuttings, or offsets.

Ornamental Grasses

Ornamental grasses are a unique group of plants often overlooked in American gardens. There are about eighty types that can be grown easily in many parts of this country, and they should have a greater place in landscape plantings. Ornamental grasses do not spread like weeds and will take abuse from pets and pedestrians. Our friend Mary Hockenberry Meyer, while a graduate student at Cornell, planted 325 grass plants of different species in mid-May in four sections of a municipal parking lot in Ithaca, New York, and all the grasses survived despite adverse conditions from automobile fumes, excessive litter, and people traffic. Here are a few ornamental grasses you might want to try: (Write to Department of Flori-culture, Cornell University, Ithaca, New York, for a complete list of ornamental grasses.)

Botanical Name	Common Name
Arundo donax	Giant reed
Avena fatua	Wild oats
Briza maxima	Big quaking grass
Cortaderia selloana	Pampas grass
Miscanthus sinensis gracillimus	Maiden grass
M. sinensis zebrinus	Zebra grass
Pennisetum alopecuroides	Fountain Grass
Phalaris arundinacea "picta"	Ribbon grass
Setaria italica	Foxtail Grass

Green Thumb Tips on Perennials

*It's better by far to have a few showy perennials than to raise a lot of short-blooming types which require a lot of care.

*Many perennials can be started from seed or divisions. Keep an eye on your neighbor's flower garden and swap plants for a bigger collection.

*Keep your perennial borders neat and sharp!

*Water perennials well in hot summer. An inch of water per week is enough to maintain growth, and automatic sprinklers can supply this amount in from three to six hours, enough for a week's growth.

*When a perennial starts to get out of hand, keep it in bounds by shearing.

*Perennials are showier planted in masses or clumps than when planted in a hit-and-miss fashion.

*Cleaning up the garden in fall will do a lot to control insects and disease pests the following year.

CHAPTER VI

Bulbs, Corms, & Tubers

•

To the average gardener, the term "bulb" includes a wide variety of plants grown from neatly packaged underground storage organs. A dahlia tuber or "toe" is a swollen root. The canna has an underground stem called a *rhizome*. The gladiolus "bulb" is a swollen stem technically known as a *corm*. Narcissus, tulip, and hyacinth plants produce bulbs which are buds (or an embryo flower) surrounded by scaly, fleshy leaves. A busy gardener may not want to concern himself with the correct term for each of these underground food-storage organs, although the botanist would take a different view. All of these parts of plants are lumped into a large group called bulbs, for the sake of simplicity. To make it easier, we have divided them into two groups: hardy and non-hardy bulbs. Just remember as you read that we are including toes, buds, corms, tubers, rhizomes, and all other designations as well.

NON-HARDY BULBS

A non-hardy bulb is one which will not live outdoors over winter in below freezing temperatures. These are usually dug in fall, stored in winter, and started into growth again the following year; or they are grown indoors in pots. Here are some of the most common types, with special green thumb tips to guide you. Because space does not permit us to treat all bulbs in detail, we have included a larger number in a chart at the end of the chapter.

•**Amaryllis** (*Hippeastrum*) Spectacular flowers somewhat similar in form to the Easter lily, but much larger, that come in various shades and markings of red, pink, white, orange, scarlet, rose, and handsome bicolors. The plant often bears flowers before the foliage appears. Ideal for pots indoors in northern areas; in milder climates can be grown outdoors as a perennial.

GREEN THUMB CARE: Place in a 6-inch pot, removing all dead roots. An equal-parts mixture of sand, peat, and garden loam, with a teaspoon of bone meal for each 6-inch pot is ideal. Plant so that the neck of the bulb is above soil surface; water, and place in a cool, light room, but not in the full sun.

A temperature of 50 degrees F. is ideal while roots are forming. Warmer temperatures cause top growth with no roots, giving poor flowers or none at all. A dark room is not necessary. After roots have formed, move the bulb into a room with 70 degrees F. temperature for flowering. Avoid overwatering before growth starts, but once it starts, provide plenty of water. A liquid feeding every three weeks from April to June is good. After the danger of frost is over, set the pots at earth level in a semi-shaded spot in the garden and continue watering all summer. The amaryllis usually flowers once but sometimes it blooms twice a year.

FALL CARE: There are 2 schools of thought on fall care. 1) Bring bulbs indoors before frost and place in a cool room; gradually withhold water for 60 days prior to placing in a bright window. 2) Forget the 60-day cure and water bulbs regularly. Both methods have their proponents.

We leave a bulb in the same pot year after year, scraping off 2 inches of soil and replacing it with a fresh mix each fall until the bulb needs a larger pot.

PROPAGATION: By seed and small bulbs ("offsets"). Sow seed in January in a sand peat mixture. Allow plants to grow for two years before giving them a rest period. From seed, plants take about three years to bloom. Remove the offsets from old bulbs at potting time.

TROUBLES: Failure to bloom may indicate a need for plant food. Scrape soil from surface and add a loose soil mix and fertilizer.

•**Begonia** (Tuberous Rooted) Called the "mockingbird flower" because the blossoms have so many forms resembling other flowers such as camellia, rose, hollyhock, daffodil, carnation, etc. The camellia-type begonia is the most popular, ranging in colors from white, pink, yellow, orange, bronze, and reds, with blooms 5 inches in diameter. The tuberous begonia makes a poor houseplant but is an ideal flowering plant for a semi-shaded part of the garden or border. Hanging-basket types and the newer picotee (bicolor) types are very popular.

The newer Rieger and Non Stop varieties of tuberous begonias are very popular and more disease-free. They are less expensive when started from seed, and do form a tuber.

•**GREEN THUMB CARE:** Tuberous begonias like a rich soil composed of $1/3$ sand, $1/3$ peat, and $1/3$ light loam. This shade-lover will tolerate morning and late afternoon sun, but should be protected from the hot mid-day sun. They like water and should be kept constantly moist, never waterlogged. Single flowers are pistillate (female) and double flowers are staminate (male). Keep spent flowers picked off.

The tubers are flat, shaped like a door knob. Tuber size is not related to age, nor does the age of the tuber affect the quality of the bloom. We've seen some reach the age of twenty years.

Some growers start the tubers indoors in pots from February to April. If you've had trouble with rot, place the tubers upside down and cover with half an inch of moist peat moss. Keep in a cool room (50 degrees F.) for a few days, giving the tubers a chance to take on moisture slowly. Then move into a room of 70 degrees F. or so for two weeks. As soon as they start to form roots on their upturned bottoms, turn tubers right-side up and pot in a humus soil, covering the top with about $1/2$ inch of soil. If rotting hasn't been a problem, plant tubers right-side up with the surface of the bulb showing. If you have long growing seasons, plant tubers directly outdoors. Outdoors, the plants may be given a liquid feeding once a month. When cutting flowers cut only half the stem (the other half will mature and fall off by itself, leaving no wound).

DIGGING: Dig the tubers after a light frost has nipped the stalks and allow to ripen off in an airy, sunny spot. After a month of slow ripening, clean the tubers, dust with sulfur, and store in a half-and-half mixture of dry sand and peat moss at 40 to 50 degrees F. until the end of February.

If tubers are grown in pots outdoors, wait until after the first frost so as to allow the tops to "cure" for a few days. Then cut them off an inch above the bulb and store pot and all in the cellar (or a 50 degree F. room) untit late February, when they can be repotted.

PROPAGATION: From cuttings, seed, and division of tubers. To make cuttings, start the tubers indoors, and when sprouts are a few inches long sever the fleshy stem and root in warm, moist sand. These rooted shoots are potted up and planted outdoors, where they'll bloom the first year. Young cuttings form tubers that can be stored away for another year.

You can cut an old tuber into two or more pieces, but make sure each piece has one or more "eyes." Place the tuber in moist peat moss in February, allowing sprouts to form so you can see them. Then take a sharp knife and divide.

Tuberous begonias raised from seed will bloom in seven months. Sow in January in a light soil mixture. Plants from seed are more compact than those from tubers, and you can buy separate color strains that are 90 percent or better true to color. (Buy seed from a seedsman since your own tuberous begonias usually carry incomplete and nonviable seed.) The seed is fine and must not be covered. Merely press it into the soil.

TROUBLES: *Mildew.* A white, furry growth on leaves. *Control:* Avoid wetting foliage in late afternoon. Dust with Karathane or sulfur.

Leaf-scorch and leaf-curl. Due to too much sun.

Bud- and flower-drop. Means dry soil or too much water.

Lots of growth but no flowers. Can mean too much shade or too much nitrogen in the soil.

Leaf spot disease. Shows up as round, dead spots followed by premature leaf-drop. *Control:* Dust with Captan.

Red spider. Causes leaves to curl and turn pale. See section on Control of Insects and Diseases.

Tuber rot. Due to too much water or grubs in tubers. *Control:* Water with care; dust tuber with Captan before planting. Look for grub in tuber; cut out and dust cut with Captan. Store tubers in peat moss just barely moist.

•Caladium (Fancy-leaved Caladiums) Here's a striking decorative foliage plant: huge, variegated leaves veined, spotted, and margined in exquisitely contrasting colors. Crimson, rose, pink, green, and white predominate. It can be grown outdoors as a bedding plant, but is more popular in the home or on shaded patios, since its brilliantly marked leaves go well with modern decor. Good for sunless room, terrace, or shaded garden.

GREEN THUMB CARE: Caladiums are shade-lovers. Dry soil, too much sun, and dry air may cause leaf burn. Apply a liquid summer feeding and give lots of water at all times. Syringing the foliage once a week keeps plants nice and fresh.

Many commercial growers plant tubers in clean sand, peat, or vermiculite at 80 degrees F. with plenty of water until root action has started. Caladium roots start from the top of the tuber, near the growing point. For that reason, some florists start tubers upside down, lightly covered with peat moss, so that roots start from the part of the tuber deep-set in the soil. They say this gives larger plants. As soon as the roots show, the tubers are potted right-side up in 4-inch pots, using half-peat and half-loam mix. In fall, dry the tuber and store in peat in a cool place until spring when you can repot in a humus mixture.

PROPAGATION: By tubers. Caladium tubers have "eyes" similar to potatoes. The larger the tuber, the more eyes that will develop sprouts and leaves. To increase your plants, cut the tubers into pieces in spring, allowing one or two eyes per section. Dust the cut surfaces with Ferbam, Captan, or sulfur.

TROUBLES: Wilting and dying of foliage. Due to overwatering, which shuts off oxygen from roots. Overwatering may also cause rotting of tuber. The aluminum florists wrap around pots will sometimes trap water and cause this. Punch a hole in the bottom to make sure water is drained. It's natural for leaves to turn yellow in fall. Rotting in storage may be a problem if tubers are too damp. Dust with sulfur and store in peat that is only slightly moistened. A temperature of 55 degrees F. is good.

●**Canna** (Canna) The modern canna is a highly hybridized plant with broad green or bronze leaves and a wide range of flower colors. The canna has staged a comeback in recent years in newer and better colors, in both tall and short varieties. This member of the *Cannaceae* family looks best in masses or groups. Taller plants can be used to screen an outdoor living area, giving an exotic, tropical atmosphere.

GREEN THUMB CARE: Cannas like full sun, rich soil, and plenty of water during dry spells. There are two ways to handle the bulbs: 1) plant directly outdoors, or 2) start them indoors in pots for early bloom. We start ours indoors in 4-inch pots in February, using a half-peat, half-loam mix. Water sparingly until growth has started, then give plenty of water. Outdoors, plant the tuber with the "eye" about an inch below the surface.

Cannas are tropical herbs and cannot tolerate much frost. Dig the same as you do dahlias, following a hard frost. Lift roots and allow to dry in sun for a few hours. Cut stalks to within 5 or 6 inches of roots and store the fleshy roots upside down in the cellar. We dust ours with sulfur and cover with vermiculite to prevent drying. Every now and then take a look to see if they are shriveling or rotting. If too dry, sprinkle lightly with water.

PROPAGATION: Division of roots in spring. With a sharp knife, cut so each division has one good eye, plant in 4-inch pots after dusting with sulfur.

TROUBLES: Non-flowering, usually due to too short a growing season. *Control*: Start plant indoors, about five weeks before planting time. Non-flowering may also be due to lack of phosphorus, too much nitrogen, or excess shade.

●**Dahlia** (Common Dahlia) One of the showiest and most easily grown of tuberous flowers, the common dahlia has come a long way in the past twenty years. There are types, sizes, and colors to suit any fancy. Blooms range from the spectacular 12-inch blooms to 2-inch pompon varieties. They have a full range of colors, solid and bicolor, and almost as many shapes and petal forms as chrysanthemums. Most come in dwarf as well as taller varieties. Some varieties of dahlias are ideal for cut flowers, all are good for beds or borders. Some of the best for cut flowers are cactus types, anemone, pompon, and water lily.

GREEN THUMB CARE: Dahlias do well in a wide variety of soil, so long as drainage is good. If soil is heavy with clay, work in some form of humus in fall and also an application of 5-10-5.

Dig holes 4 inches deep in heavy soils, 6 inches in light soils. Place the tuberous root flat in hole in a horizontal position, with eye facing upwards. At time of planting, put a 4-foot garden stake 1 inch from end of root. The young plant can thus be given support all the time until it reaches full growth. Cover the root with soil and as plants grow, tie the stem to stake using pieces of cloth. Tubers should be planted about 3 feet apart, especially the tall vigorous varieties. Incidentially, don't turn up your nose at a small tuber. Many of the best varieties make small tubers.

Early in summer, hoe to keep weeds down. About ten weeks after planting do no more cultivation, especially when plants are in bud or bloom. We apply a sawdust mulch around our plants in summer to keep weeds down. Apply a handful of a balanced fertilizer or a gallon of liquid plant food solution to each bushel of sawdust.

PINCHING AND DISBUDDING: To get symmetrical plants, pinch when about a foot high, by nipping out the top just above the second set of leaves. Pinching gives a better show of flowers in the pompon, mignon, and bedding types. If large exhibition flowers are desired the plants should be disbudded and side shoots removed. To disbud, merely pinch out all the buds except one central one in each group. Buds usually appear in groups or clusters of three, so you remove the side two. As other buds form, remove them. Pinching develops a shorter, more branched plant, and is done before flowers begin to develop, early in the season. Pinching retards flowering but disbudding does not. Most gardeners neither pinch or disbud and still get lots of blooms.

CUTTING BLOOMS: As cut flowers, some dahlias are discouraging, others are excellent. Large-flowering types usually wilt if cut during the day. Cut them after sundown or very early in the morning, and dip the ends of stems in boiling water for a minute to help keep flowers longer.

DIGGING: Dahlias can be dug any time after the first killing frost. This checks the growth and causes stalks, limbs, and leaves to blacken. Leave them this way for a couple of weeks so juices can flow back to the toes. Then use a digging fork to lift the entire clump, taking care not to bruise the slender necks of the tuberous roots. (If the neck is broken, the result may be a "dud" tuber.) Cut the tops off so that one or two inches of stem remain attached to the crown. Some gardeners leave the soil attached, others hose it off and then allow tubers to dry a few hours before storing in wooden trays or orange crates. A cool, well ventilated cellar is ideal, and it helps to cover the roots with peat moss which has a moisture content of 50 percent. This can be done easily by weighing out ten pounds of peat moss and adding it to 2 1/2 quarts of water. Work the peat over thoroughly.

Sometimes new shoot growth appears after heavy black frosts. When this happens, break off the shoots before storing the tubers, to save strength for next year.

Some gardeners do not dig their dahlias each fall. They cut stalks back to the ground in the fall, cover clumps with a foot of leaves, and place chicken wire over the pile. Their dahlias start flowering earlier and they don't worry about storage problems. With such protection they tell us the tubers have come through winters of 29 degrees F. below zero, but we prefer to dig ours and divide them each year. A little shriveling in storage will not hurt the tubers.

PROPAGATION: By dividing roots in spring, by seed, and by indoor or outdoor cuttings.

Dividing: The best way to divide dahlias is to wait until the eyes start to grow and then with a sharp knife, cut the clump or roots into divisions. The tuberous roots are connected to the main stem at the region known as the crown, where new buds or eyes are produced. Each division should have an eye or bud. To increase stock by indoor cuttings, pot tubers in January, and allow shoots to grow. As soon as a shoot with a second or third set of leaves develops, cut off at soil surface and place in a flat of coarse sand, perlite, or vermiculite and keep moist. In three or four weeks cuttings will root and can be potted up for planting outdoors in shirtsleeve weather.

Outdoor cuttings. You can root shoots by breaking off leaf stalks and inserting them in the open ground, taking care to water regularly. Branches broken by wind or rain can be rooted this way.

Seed. Dahlias do not produce seed in areas with short growing seasons, but you can buy seed for starting plants. Sow seed in March, using vermiculite, peat, or a mixture of sand and peat. Cover lightly and place a pane of glass over the seed box and store in a room at 60 degrees F. As soon as seed has sprouted, remove glass and place the seed box in a bright window. After seedlings have first set of leaves, transplant into three-inch pots and grow on until shirtsleeve weather, when they can be set outdoors. For raising annual dahlias from seed, see Chapter IV.

TROUBLES: *Premature budding.* When plants are only a foot high. Cloudy weather in late spring will initiate flower buds. So will hot dry days. When this happens, cut plants back in July and you'll get new growth for the fall show. Or, you can remove most of the buds or blossoms so plants can develop normal growth and full-size blossoms.

Failure to bloom. Due to too much shade or too rich a soil, factors which sometimes are responsible for no tubers or no flowers, but lots of leaves. Dahlias need at least six hours of sun a day, and good air drainage. If they are planted where air cannot circulate freely they get mildew and many of the buds will abort.

Stunt. A virus which causes leaves to curl and turn yellow. Stunted plants seldom flower, tuber development is repressed, and tubers rot in storage. Destroy such plants.

Insects. Tarnished plant bug causes buds to blacken, or grow lopsided, and flowers to open one-sided or not at all. Thrips feed on open flowers and leaves. Leafhoppers cause leaves to turn pale along the edges and curl, gradually dying. Cornborers cause stalks to suddenly wilt. *Control:* See Chapter XIV.

Snails and slugs. Sometimes eat blooms and foliage during the night. For controls see Chapter XIV.

Change in colors. Dahlias often change colors by a process known as mutation, commonly called "sporting" or "breaking." Mums, azaleas, and many other plants do this. The cause of mutation is unknown, but it can be induced artificially by X-ray, heat treatment, and use of a gout remedy known as colchicine.

•**Freesia** A delightfully fragrant indoor or greenhouse bulbous herb grown for its white, yellow, orange, red, pink, and lavender-blue blossoms, popular with florists who use them in wedding and vase arrangements. A good cut flower for gardeners.

GREEN THUMB CARE: Plant bulbs an inch deep, about a dozen in a 6-inch pot, using plain garden loam. Set pot in a cool (about 50 degrees F.), light place free from frost. Water moderately until tops are 1 to 2 inches high, then increase water gradually. When tops are 6 inches high, increase the room temperature. After flowering, dry off gradually to allow natural growth to be completed. When foliage yellows, place in frost-proof, sunny spot to ripen bulbs. After two weeks, store bulbs in cellar until fall.

PROPAGATION: By bulbs.

TROUBLES: None.

•**Gladiolus** The American Gladiolus Society, polling "glad" growers throughout America, found an overwhelming majority voted to call the flower *gladiolus*, both singular and plural, and not gladioli or gladiola. Glads are one of the most popular summer flowering bulbs. Their long period of bloom and wide range of colors makes them highly desirable as a cut flower. Come in spectacular tall spikes, every color of the rainbow, as well as a full spectrum of dainty miniatures. Solid colors, bicolors, butterfly types, ruffled, and fringed varieties add to their popularity.

GREEN THUMB CARE: Plant corms as soon as you can work the soil. A series of plantings will spread the blooming over a longer season. Early varieties may take from 65 to 75 days to bloom; mid-season varieties 75 to 85; and the late ones 90 days or more, sometimes as long as 120 days.

Corms are graded in six sizes: No. 1, $1\frac{1}{2}$ inches and larger; No. 2, $1\frac{1}{4}$ inches to $1\frac{1}{2}$ inches; No. 3, 1 to $1\frac{1}{4}$ inches; No. 4, $\frac{3}{4}$ to 1 inch; No. 5, $\frac{1}{2}$ to $\frac{3}{4}$ inch; and No. 6, $\frac{1}{2}$ inches and under. Large corms will bloom about 4 days earlier than medium-sized ones and from 10 to 14 days earlier than small ones. Unless you plan to grow for exhibition purposes, you can buy the medium corms, which are often cheaper and will flower well the first year.

Plant glads in rows 18 to 30 inches apart and at a depth of 4 inches in heavy soil, 6 inches in light soil. Glads do not exhaust the soil if you return humus and plant food. The biggest danger of not rotating the land is building up diseases. Do not plant glads near beans, as glads sometimes get bean mosaic. By planting corms of various sizes and varieties of different maturity, you'll have blooms from the middle of July until the fall freeze.

WATERING: First-class spikes come when glads are given an abundance of water from the time leaves appear until they are in full bloom. Water applied to the soil is less apt to spread disease than is overhead watering.

FEEDING: Apply a balanced food between rows while the plants are growing. About one-third of the fertilizer can be used just after the shoots come up, the remainder used in two or three top dressings about three weeks apart. Many growers feel that the fertility under which glads grew the year before has more to do with the growth of the plants than the fertilizer you give them this year.

WEEDING AND CULTIVATION: Shallow cultivation is best for keeping weeds down. There are chemicals that can be applied to soil just before weeds emerge. This treatment kills the germinating weed seeds, but must be applied when the soil is moist. Post-emergence weed-killer treatments, those applied after the weeds are up, should be directed at the bases of the glad plants and not used when the spikes are just emerging. Gladiolus plants tolerate these chemicals both before they emerge and up to the time they are about 10 inches tall. Mulches (see Chapter XIII) are also good for keeping weeds down—black plastic is particularly good.

CUTTING BLOSSOMS: If blossoms are cut in the bud stage, or when two or three florets show color, they'll open up nicely indoors. Spikes can be cut in early morning or late afternoon with a sharp knife. Remember that next year's flowers will be determined by the growth made in the new corm after the flower spike has come and gone, therefore as many leaves should stay on the plant as possible.

WINTER STORAGE: Corms may be dug anytime (it's not necessary for foliage to yellow off). Cut the stalks close to the corm to discard most of the thrips. Destroy stems and leaves of glads to aid in pest control. Dry the corms in a warm part of the cellar or garden for a couple of weeks. Then dust the corms (see below) and place in paper bags or wooden trays. If you can store your glads in 35 degrees F. for two months or 40 degrees F. for three months it will kill all stages of thrips, even eggs, in stored corms. Cool temperatures also help preserve the corms. If you store glads above 40 degrees F. thrips breed and develop in storage. Next spring, you'll plant infested corms.

If you cannot store at 35 to 40 degrees F., then the bulbs can be submerged in hot water (112 to 150 degrees F.) for 20 to 30 minutes. Or in a Lysol disinfectant solution (1 to 1 1/4 tablespoons per gallon of water for three hours) before fall storage.

Naphthalene flakes can also be used for thrip control. Use 4 level tablespoons per 100 bulbs, keep them in closed paper containers for four weeks at 60 degrees F. then air out and store at 40 degrees F. Stored corms may also be dusted with 5 percent Malathion. *Note:* Do *not* remove the papery skins from the bulbs this fall. Leave them on until spring.

PROPAGATION: *By seed.* Not practical unless you are patient and want to experiment. Gather pods and store in sealed glass jars until spring. Sow seeds in loose soil in spring. If you do not want to use the seed, be sure not to allow spikes to develop seed pods.

By cutting corms in half. In spring select corms with two or more buds, then cut the corm through the middle between the buds. Dust with sulfur and plant.

By bulblets. Save the pea-like bulbs or cormels clustered around the large corms. Store in winter and plant in rows in spring. Will bloom in one to two years.

TROUBLES: *Changing colors.* There are several fungus diseases that can kill gladiolus bulbs. Colored bulbs are more susceptible to disease, the whites more resistant. The weak types die out (often completely) leaving the stronger types (such as white) to remain. Thus whenever you grow a mixture, you often wind up with flowers "reverting" to white. It is also true that some varieties, such as Friendship, will flower a normal pink, then will change to red. This is called mutation, and it's nature's way of throwing out a new variety, but it happens only rarely.

Crooked stalks (Saxophone spikes). This is an inherited trait, more annoying to commercial growers than to the home gardener. Select varieties which do not develop crooked spikes.

Mosaic. Causes mottling, spotting, specking, twisting, and crinkling of flowers. Blossoms become hood-shaped. *Control:* Pull up diseased plants and burn, or seal in plastic bag and discard.

Scab. Deep, circular pockmarks on the surface of corms. While it appears ugly, it's not a serious disease. *Control:* Treat infected corms with 1 1/4 Tbsp. of Lysol per gallon of water and sdak for 3 hours. Plant while wet.

Thrips. Worst enemy of gladiolus. Look for white, transparent spots on leaves and blooms, flowers that are mottled and deformed or don't open. *Control:* Keep plants sprayed or dusted regularly using Malathion, starting when leaves are 6 inches high.

Tall and short plants. No one knows why a variety will grow 4 feet tall one year and only 2 feet the next year. Weather, fertility, insects, and other factors enter the picture.

•**Hymenocallis** (*Ismene Calathina*) **Spider Lily, Peruvian Daffodil**. This tropical member of the lily family has fragrant white flowers 6 to 8 inches long, making an ideal pot or outdoor plant.

GREEN THUMB CARE: This summer-bloomer prefers full sun and ample water. Set fleshy roots in spring in shirtsleeve weather and feed once or twice during growing season. In fall, dig roots and store them in the warmest room in your cellar. Cool storage prevents or delays blooming.

PROPAGATION: Division of roots.

TROUBLES: *Failure to bloom.* Due to too much shade, cold storage temperature in winter, or lack of moisture during summer.

•**Ornithogalum thyrsoides** (Chincherinchee or South African Wonder Flower) We've seen three different spellings for this bulbous herb. Chincherichee, Chinkerichee, and Chincherinchee, the last (pronounced "chin-che-rin-chee") being preferred. Clusters of star-like blooms on 16- to 18-inch spikes make an interesting cut flower. They have a long blooming period and are unusually long-lasting in bouquets. The variety Aureum has brilliant yellow flowers, and you can also buy bulbs with white blooms. Bulbs are globe-shaped, 1 1/2 inches thick.

GREEN THUMB CARE: The plant is not hardy in northern areas and must be grown indoors in winter or planted outdoors in summer and given the same care as gladiolus. In September plant bulbs in pots or boxes in a mixture of loam and peat or compost plus sand, barely covering bulb. Avoid overwatering when growth starts; after full growth has been attained, give more water. After the foliage starts to yellow, withhold water and dry the bulbs for another year.

PROPAGATION: Bulbs.

TROUBLES: None.

•**Polianthes** (Tuberose) These summer-flowering tubers are natives of Mexico and a member of the amaryllis family. Their waxy white flowers have a delightful aroma in both single and double forms. This old-fashioned outdoor bloomer makes a fine addition to the summer garden.

GREEN THUMB CARE: Being a tender bulb, it should be planted outdoors after danger of frost is over. Start in pots in early May and plant in a sunny bed for earlier bloom. Dig bulbs in fall and store at about 60 degrees F. if you wish to try keeping them over.

PROPAGATION: We buy new bulbs each year, since bulbs which have flowered are difficult to flower again the following season.

TROUBLES: *Failure to bloom.* Usually due to a shortage of water during the growing season.

•**Zephyranthes** (Fairy Lily) This tender bulb has delicate, funnel-shaped single flowers in white, yellow, pink, and bronze with grass-like foliage. Blossoms come out one or two at a time, fade out, and, oddly enough, can repeat this three times within a year.

GREEN THUMB CARE: Pot bulbs in soil mixture of peat and loam, grow in a sunny window until warm weather comes. Grow outdoors in summer and bring in before frost.

PROPAGATION: Bulbs divided during dormant period.

TROUBLES: None.

Green Thumb Tips on Non-hardy Bulbs

*Lack of moisture during growing season can cause failure to bloom.

*Formation of seed pods will hinder further bloom. Keep them removed.

*Curling leaves may be due to red spider mites.

*Don't be afraid to try new varieties, and replenish your old stock every couple of years.

*Poor soils mean poor growth. Spend time to build up soils. (See Chapter XIII.)

*In winter storage, prevent bulbs from rotting and drying. Dust with sulfur.

*Be on lookout for new "sports." You may have something!

HARDY OR OUTDOOR BULBS

There is nothing more exciting in a gardener's bag of tricks than his ability to stage a show from outdoor-flowering bulbs. The hardy or outdoor bulbs are a big group home owners depend on each year for outdoor display. The awesome selection of tulips and daffodils alone sets a gardener's green thumb twitching. Hardy bulbs are those which can be left in the ground year after year without danger of winter killing. Here are some of the most common hardy bulbs you can grow for maximum enjoyment with a minimum of effort.

•**Colchicum autumnale** (Autumn Crocus or Meadow Saffron) Flowers appear on bare stems the beginning of September. Leaves show up in spring. Flower color ranges from white to rose to lavender or orchid. A double variety is also available. This is the so-called "Mystery" bulb which grows without soil or water as advertisements claim. Ideal for rock gardens, in among ground covers, and between evergreens.

GREEN THUMB CARE: Plant as soon as received or bulbs will bloom inside the package. They will grow in any soil, in a sunny spot. Allow leaves to grow so they can form buds for fall flowering.

PROPAGATION: Dividing bulbs in spring or fall.

TROUBLES: None.

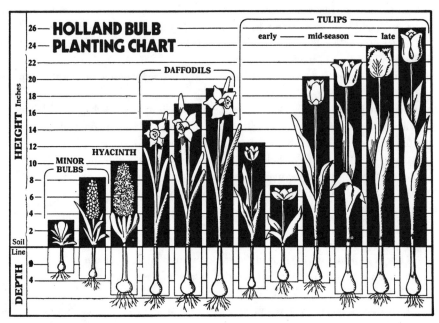

A good rule of thumb to remember is that bulbs should be planted twice as deep as they are round. (*Courtesy Edward Gottlieb and Associates*)

•**Crocus** (Common Crocus) Welcome white, blue, yellow, and striped flowers, appearing in spring, later than snowdrops. Often planted in evergreen borders, in lawns, in rock gardens, and under trees.

GREEN THUMB CARE: If grown in the lawn, do not cut the leaves until they've turned yellow. If mowed when leaves are green the bulbs will die out. To plant in a sod, take a plug of grass roots out, dig a hole 3 inches deep, using a narrow trowel. Set bulb in and cover with loose soil.

PROPAGATION: Plant new bulbs in fall and divide every three years. Be prepared to replace half of your crocus bulbs each year.

TROUBLES: *Vanishing bulbs.* Due to cutting leaves when green.

•**Eranthis hyemalis, E. cilicica** (Winter Aconite) Bright yellow flowers, 2 inches high, resembling marsh marigolds. Good on slopes, rock gardens, and under trees. Appearing same time as snowdrop.

GREEN THUMB CARE: Plant bulbs anytime in fall, 2 or 3 inches deep and same distance apart.

PROPAGATION: Division.

TROUBLES: Prefers to be undisturbed.

•**Fritillaria imperialis** (Crown Imperial) Grows 2 to 3 feet high with a circle of bell-shaped red or yellow flowers beneath a green crown of leaves. Blooms in May. Good in beds where a tall spring bloomer is desired. Blooms susceptible to late spring frosts.

GREEN THUMB CARE: Plant in rich humus soil 4 to 6 inches deep. Will grow in shade.

PROPAGATION: Division.

TROUBLES: Capricious bloomer. Avoid crowding with other plants.

●**Fritillaria meleagris** (Guinea-Hen Flower, Checkered Lily) Interesting checkered purple or maroon, drooping, bell-shaped flowers. Grows 12 to 14 inches high, used to good advantage in rock gardens. A little-known variety comes in white, but the purple shades are more showy.

GREEN THUMB CARE: Plant 3 inches deep in a loose soil which does not bake in summer. Can be grown in semi-shade. In northern gardens they need a light mulch in winter.

PROPAGATION: Division.

TROUBLES: Has fickle blooming habits. Leave undisturbed.

●**Galanthus** (Snowdrops) Fine little white flowers, usually appearing in February or March in spite of snowy weather. Ideal in foundation plantings, under trees, along a shady walk.

GREEN THUMB CARE: Plant in fall, 3 inches deep and 3 inches apart. Do well in all types of soil and will grow in semi-shade.

PROPAGATION: Division in fall.

TROUBLES: None. Leave undisturbed.

●**Hyacinthus** (Hyacinths) Everyone is familiar with this stocky spring bloomer with compact clusters of fragrant pink, white, blue, cream, yellow, red, or peach bell-shaped flowers. Double varieties are appearing. Ideal in borders, masses, around trees, and especially suited for indoor forcing.

GREEN THUMB CARE: Plant in fall in loose soil, four to five inches deep. Bulbs often "peter out" and usually have to be replaced every other year. Outdoor culture is similar to tulips. About two weeks after blooming, we cut hyacinth foliage if it has become droopy and messy-looking.

To force indoors, pot the bulbs in fall in 5-inch pot, water well, and bury in a trench or storage pit or store in refrigerator for six to eight weeks. Then bring to semi-dark room for a week so shoots can turn green and "lengthen." Then bring into direct sunlight in a temperature of 65 degrees F. Many use a hyacinth glass for forcing. Just add a small piece of charcoal in the bottom, set a bulb in the glass so its base almost touches the water. Twist a sheet of paper into a cone, fasten with a pin and cover bulb. Place in refrigerator for six to eight weeks. Then give same treatment as above. "Mother's Day" and "Easter" (florist-forced) hyacinths should be planted outdoors soon after they finish blooming.

PROPAGATION: Multiply by dividing bulbs in fall. Buy new bulbs each year for fall planting. There's no truth to the idea you can produce various-colored blooms by cutting the base of the bulb. (See *Narcissus*.)

TROUBLES: *Blindness, or no flowers.* Due to overcrowding. Dig bulbs each year. Indoors, if flowers come before stems, it means too much light and heat after you bring them out of the cold-storage (root-forming) period. Forced plants should be replanted outdoors after blooming, where they may or may not bloom the following year.

●**Iris** See Chapter V, PERENNIALS AND THEIR CARE.

●**Lilium** (Lilies) The lily family is a large one and hybridizers are constantly creating handsome new varieties. You can have lilies in bloom all summer long by careful selection.

GREEN THUMB CARE: Lilies may be planted any time from autumn until spring, some as late as June. However, fall planting is best. Many foreign-grown bulbs do not arrive here until late in fall, and this makes fall planting impossible in some areas. Some lily bulbs cannot stand much freezing unless well rooted, so if your bulbs arrive late, it's best to hold them over winter and plant in spring. Store the bulbs in sawdust or peat if you plan to carry them over. Dust with Ferbam, sulfur, or Captan at the rate of 1 heaping tablespoon to 1 quart of peat or sawdust and keep them in a cool cellar.

Bulbs planted in fall need a light covering of straw or peat to prevent their being heaved out of the ground. The first season of bloom is often the poorest, as lilies do not flower at their best until bulb has become well established.

Lilies are heavy feeders, preferring a fertile, well cultivated, well drained soil and full sun. Some varieties will tolerate semi-shade, however. Depth of planting depends on whether the lilies are stem-rooting species or those rooting from the base of the bulb. Stem-rooting kinds need deeper planting. The general rule is to plant stem-rooting varieties three times the depth of the bulb. Bulb-rooting sorts may be planted about 4 inches deep. Even in a well drained soil it's a good idea to set the bulb on a cushion of sharp sand. Make the hole sufficiently large so that the bulb may be surrounded by sand. Some of the popular bulb-rooting species are: *Canadense* (Meadow Lily); *Candidum* (Common Madonna); *Giganteum, Testaceum, Chalcedonicum, Pardalinum,* and *Martagon.* By careful selection of varieties you can have blooms from June until frost.

Most popular of the stem-rooting species include the *Auratum, Concolor, Hansoni, Henryi, Japonicum, Longiflorum, Regale, Speciosum, Tenuifolium, Tigrinium, Umbellatum, Willmottiae.* (Lilies have so many different common names most catalogues list lilies by their botanical names.)

CARE OF THE FLORIST OR "BERMUDA" ("EASTER") LILY Botanically known as *L. longiflorum.* Varieties grown by florists, including *giganteum, harrisii, formosum, Erabu* and Creole deserve special mention. This Easter plant likes plenty of water, a sunny window, and a temperature of 65 to 70 degrees F. If you want a pure white bloom that will last longer, pull out the yellow floral parts (anthers, the male elements). This keeps flowers from being pollinated so they last twice as long. After blooming, set bulb in a pernament spot in the garden and it will bloom again in fall. It's hardy outdoors and needs no winter covering.

If you want to grow the lily for Easter, buy "pre-cooled" bulbs, those already given a special cold-storage treatment. If bulbs are not pre-cooled, they must be refrigerated six weeks at 35 degrees F. before potting.

PROPAGATION: By seed, scales, and division of bulbs.

Seed. May be sown in fall in mixture of sand and peat in pots or flats. Do not plant deeply. A flour-sifter makes a fine device for sprinkling soil over seed you sow. You can get a Regal lily to flower nine months after sowing. Others may take longer. Transplant the seedlings to pots and set outdoors in shirtsleeve weather.

Scales. None of the hybrid lilies come true from seed so you can start these from bulb scales, a more rapid method. All lilies grow from bulbs composed of overlapping scales (a special form of leaf). Simply break these scales away and plant them in a sandy soil. Best time is after flowers have faded. Small bulblets form along the bottom of the scale and grow into flowering-size bulbs. It's not necessary to dig up bulbs to get the scales. Simply remove soil so as to expose the bulb, pry off the scales you want, and cover again with soil. We prefer to lift the bulb, remove half the scales, and replant the heart of the mother bulb. In autumn, before freezing, a covering of dry leaves is placed over the flat in a cold frame where the scales are left until spring. The following July the scales will be large enough to plant in the garden. Many will flower the following year.

Many gardeners use plastic bags for starting lily scales. Put a couple of handfuls of slightly moist shredded sphagnum moss in the bottom, and then set the fresh, plump scales in the bags. Shake well to cover the scales. Fold the tops to shut out air. Keep in a dark cabinet at room temperature for three weeks, when you'll notice from one to four or five small bulbs forming at the bases of the scales. By late September or early October these may be placed in a sheltered cold frame for winter rest. Or you can set them out directly from the plastic bag to where they are to flower. A 2-inch covering of leafmold or peat is helpful. By the scale method one healthy bulb can yield up to a hundred flowering-size bulbs within a period of two years.

TROUBLES: *Botrytis blight (gray mold disease).* Brown spots all over blossoms and leaves. *Control:* Dust weekly with Zineb or a copper compound. Zineb alone, 1 tablespoon of 50 percent grade to a gallon of water, plus $1/2$ teaspoon of a detergent makes a good spray. The secret is to keep new foliage and buds covered from the start. In fall, cut back dead stalks and drench plants and soil with Zineb.

Mosaic. The most serious and widespread disease of lilies, mosaic is spread by the melon aphid. Affected plants are stunted, twisted, and mottled. *Control:* Remove and destroy infected plants. See section Control of Insects and Diseases.

Chewing insects. Malathion will banish most of them.

Missing lily bulbs. Due to basal rot, nematodes, and probably insect injury.

Wilting. Due to borers and ants. Malathion or Nicotine Sulphate.

●**Lycoris squamigera** (Hardy Amaryllis, Autumn Amaryllis, Magic Lily) Sometimes listed as *Amaryllis hallii,* this item has green, strap-like leaves that appear in spring, die down, and completely disappear by June. In August, lavender flower spikes, 3 feet long and fragrant, pop up out of the ground. A poor keeper in vase arrangements, *Lycoris* is a fine perennial grown in a mass by itself.

GREEN THUMB CARE: In spring or fall, plant bulbs 5 inches deep in rich, humus soil. They prefer sun or partial shade. The best time to move *Lycoris* is in spring or fall, although it will bloom in the same spot year after year without disturbance. Winter covering is unnecessary.

PROPAGATION: Division of bulbs in spring or fall.

TROUBLES: *Failure to bloom* due to deep planting or overcrowding. Separate bulbs in spring and plant 5 inches deep.

●**Narcissus** (Daffodils) The first major flowers of spring are daffodils, following crocuses in March or April. Daffodils are actually a species of narcissus. The latter is the

Latin name, and daffodil is the English. Recent introductions by breeders have given us beautiful variations of daffodils and narcissus. They range in size from the miniatures, which produce tiny blossoms on 3-inch stems, to those reaching a height of 2 feet or more, with blooms 4 inches across. They include short or long trumpets, frilled edges, doubles and multiple-flowered types in yellows, white, cream, pink, and bicolors. Ideal for naturalizing, growing in beds, borders, and forcing. Plant in drifts near shrubs, or in woodlands.

GREEN THUMB CARE: In fall plant large bulbs 5 to 6 inches deep, smaller bulbs 4 inches. Space 8 to 12 inches apart, and while closer spacing results in quicker mass effect, it also means you'll have to separate the bulbs sooner. Feed a balanced plant food at planting time and each fall thereafter. After plants finish flowering, keep them growing green as long as possible to build up food for next year's crop. Lift and divide the bulbs every three years to avoid overcrowding. After foliage has yellowed three-fourths of the way from the top, dig, divide, and replant. Bulbs may be stored in basement during summer or planted back in ground. Never keep them in basement over winter.

For indoor forcing, the Paper-white narcissus are easiest of all to make bloom, requiring no special cold-storage treatment. Plant bulbs in a bowl of gravel, pebbles, or shells, keep filled with water to slightly above base of bulbs, and keep at room temperature until blooming. Trumpet daffodils and others need cold storage treatment. Plant bulbs in pots of soil with "noses" just sticking out of surface. Place in a cold place (35 to 50 degrees F.) for eight weeks to develop roots. Keep them moist and, around December, bring pots into a temperature of 60 to 65 degrees F. in partial light to "green up" and make stem growth. Then move to a bright window and water as needed. If you have no suitable indoor storage, pots can be buried in a cold frame or in a trench covered with screen to keep out rodents, then topped with leaves or sawdust to keep from hard freezing.

In southern areas, pre-cooled bulbs are often used for planting outdoors or in pots. You can pre-cool simply by putting bulbs in a paper sack and storing in a refrigerator for six to eight weeks, but we feel that bulbs potted before the cool treatment, so they can form roots, have superior blooms.

After flowering, potted daffodils can be planted in border or outdoor flower bed. Do not force them again indoors. The treatment above also applies to tulips, hyacinths, and other hardy bulbs.

PROPAGATION: Separate small bulblets from parent bulb and plant where they can be left undisturbed for a couple of years.

TROUBLES: *Blasting or drying of flower buds.* Due to violent changes in weather, especially hot, sunny days in spring, accompanied by drying winds. *Control:* A mulch of straw, peat, or sawdust conserves soil moisture.

Botrytis blight. Another cause of blasting. *Control:* Cut and burn leaves or seal in a plastic bag and discard when they turn yellow. Keep plants sprayed with Captan or Ferbam, starting in early spring. Overcrowding is another cause of failure to bloom. Dividing and replanting every two or three years will check this.

•**Ornithogalum umbellatum, Star of Bethlehem** Cheerful early bloomer, clusters of showy white flowers with green stripes on petals. Plants grow about 8 inches tall and are good for naturalizing, and in rock gardens. Can become a weed in flower beds.

GREEN THUMB CARE: Plant about an inch deep, 3 or 4 inches apart, in a spot where they can be left to come up year after year.

PROPAGATION: Bulbs.

TROUBLES: None.

●**Scilla** (*Scilla hispanica*, *S. Campanulata*—Spanish Scillia) Numerous tiny, bell-shaped blue, white, purple, or pink flowers appearing in May. Ideal in beds, borders, and rock gardens. Grows 10 to 15 inches tall.

GREEN THUMB CARE: Plant 4 to 5 inches deep.

PROPAGATION: Division of bulbs.

TROUBLES: None.

●**Scilla siberica** (Siberian Scilla or Squills) Long-lasting, six-petalled flowers appearing in early spring on 4- to 6-inch stems. Good for edging or in masses. Can be had in white, but blue is more popular. Easily naturalized and grow well among shrubs.

GREEN THUMB CARE: Plant 2 or 3 inches deep. Tolerates a wide variety of soils.

PROPAGATION: By division of bulbs.

TROUBLES: None.

●**Tulipa** (Tulips) Spring isn't spring without tulips, ideal for beds, borders, mass plantings, and forcing indoors. They are ideal in foundation plantings of evergreens. Color span in solids and bicolors is almost endless. Doubles, singles, lily-flowering, and parrot types (fringed and ruffled), with their variation in blooming dates, make tulips one of our most versatile bulb flowers.

GREEN THUMB CARE: Plant in fall as soon as you receive bulbs. If ground isn't frozen, you can plant as late as mid-December. Plant 4 to 6 inches deep, 8 to 12 inches apart. They must have full sun, will do well under trees or shrubs which leaf out after the bulbs have started their growth. Tulips look best planted in clumps rather than in a single row. Good drainage is essential.

Never use manure because it spreads Botrytis Blight. After bulbs are planted, add 5 pounds of a balanced plant food such as 5-10-10 to each 100 square feet. Old-timers mix bone meal in soil, 10 pounds per 100 square feet. However, it attracts dogs, who dig up bulbs in search of phantom bones. We suggest superphosphate instead, because on the basis of the phosphorus which plants can take up, you're paying nearly three times as much for bone meal as you would pay for superphosphate. Liquid plant food in spring will do a lot to give bigger blooms. Mulching with straw is not necessary, and it may attract mice.

Remove seed pods unless you want to save seed. Pick blossoms before fully open for cut flowers. A few drops of wax in center of bloom keeps blooms from opening wide. We find the double varieties and the parrot types make much longer lasting cut flowers than blooms of other varieties. For indoor forcing, same as for daffodils.

PROPAGATION: By dividing in fall, also by seed sown in sand-peat mixture. Takes three or four years to produce blooms from seed-sown plants. Plant tiny bulblets in garden row in fall.

TROUBLES: *Botrytis (fireblight) or blasting out of buds.* Comes sometimes from using manure. *Control:* Keep bulbs dusted or sprayed with Captan or Ferbam. Cut off old stalks

Spring bulbs are even more welcome when forced to bloom indoors.

    Four steps for forcing tulips:

    (1) Position bulbs so they nearly touch.

    (2) Cover with soil; water well.

    (3) Place in dark, cool place.

    (4) After roots form and leaf tips show, bring into a warm, bright room.

        (*Courtesy Under Glass Magazine*)

below soil level and bum or seal in plastic bag and discard. Do not place on the compost pile if tulips had fireblight.

Spindly flowers or none at all. Means bulbs need transplanting. Dig yours every two years or so to avoid overcrowding. Replant those having a diameter of 1 inch or more for blooms the following spring. Smaller-size bulbs can be planted in a row in the garden to grow for bloom later on.

Mosaic. A virus which causes distortion of color and shape, twisted stems, yellowed or mottled foliage. Aphids transmit the virus. Pull up infected plants and destroy. Do not confuse mosaic-ridden plants with the new parrot tulips which have bizarre patterns.

Rodents. Mothballs and hot pepper flakes among bulb will discourage mice and moles. See Animal Control.

Small flowers. Due to dry soils, overcrowding, insufficient plant food.

Rotted bulbs. At transplanting time, remove bulbs and burn or seal in plastic bag and discard.

Dug bulbs. Due to dogs (looking for bones) or skunks (looking for grubs).
Control: Use superphosphate instead of bone meal.

Green Thumb Tips on Hardy Bulbs

*Failure to bloom is usually due to overcrowding. Most hardy bulbs should be dug and separated every two or three years. Buy new bulbs each year to complement your old stock. It'll pay in extra blooms.

*Tulips coming up with only one leaf in spring means they need dividing.

*Plastic bags make good containers for starting bulbs from seed or scales.

*Don't plant hardy bulbs in outdoor planters. They'll freeze too hard.

*If you can't get manure for your bulbs, be glad! Use balanced plant foods and you won't introduce Botrytis and other diseases carried in manure. (See Chapter XIII.) Soak your bulbs in a liquid plant food one-half hour before planting.

*Fireblight of tulips can be prevented by dusting early in spring using Zineb, Ferbam, or Captan.

*Hot pepper and mothballs scattered in a border do a lot to discourage animals which bother tulip bulbs.

*After tulips, daffodils, and other bulbs have died down, remove foliage and fill in spaces with asters, begonias, violas, dwarf phlox, petunias, salvias, or marigolds.

Common or Botanical Name	Height	Description	Cultural Tips	Use Indoors or Out
Acidanthera bicolor (Sweet-scented gladiolus)	2'-3'	Not a true gladiolus but have small, delicate sweet-smelling blooms resembling glads. White blooms with dark center.	Grows in sun or part shade. Plant in early spring 3" deep, 6" apart.	Dig before hard freeze. Treat same as gladiolus. Good background flower, excellent for cutting.
Achimenes Michelssen Hybrids (For more information see Houseplants)	6"-10"	Masses of long-lasting tubular 2" flowers on compact plant; pink, salmon, blue, rose, red.	Plant corms from Jan. to Apr., 1/2 in. deep, 5 to a 4" container. Keep at 75°, shaded, until sprouts start. Move to light, airy place. Prefer to be watered with warm water.	Ideal pot plant or hanging basket in the home or greenhouse. Bloom begins 2 months after planting.
Alliums Flowering Onions	6"-48"	2-6 inch flower clusters shaped like grapefruit; white, rose, purple, yellow.	Plant in fall in loose soil 3"-4" deep in full sun. Hardy, can be left in ground year after year. Separate every 3rd year.	Flower arrangements, rock gardens, background plants.
Amaryllis (Hippeastrum)	2'-3'	Red, pink, scarlet, rose, white, and bicolor trumpet-shaped flowers. Fall, winter, or early spring.	Plant in 6" pot with neck of bulb above soil. Water and place in cool, light room, not full sun. After flowering, set pot outdoors in summer and bring in before frost. Rest—do not water for 8-10 weeks.	Huge blooms make striking houseplants. Keep bulbs in same pot year after year, changing upper 2" of soil. Flower once a year.
Amaryllis (Hardy) (See *Lycoris*)				

Common or Botanical Name	Height	Description	Cultural Tips	Use Indoors or Out
Anemones	12"–24" or higher	Large flowers. Mixed colors. St. Brigid are doubles, de Caen singles.	Plant in fall 2" deep, 2" apart with 5" mulch. If dug, store in perforated plastic bags of peat moss. Plant in 5" pots for forcing.	Excellent cut flowers and pot plants.
Caladiums, Fancy-leaved	2'–2½'	Large leaved mixed color foliage of pink and green; white and green; red and green.	Start tubers in pots of sand, peat, and loam. For outdoors, set out after danger of frost is past. In fall, dig and store in moist peat. For winter and spring, pot and grow in cool, bright window.	Brilliantly marked leaves go well with modern decor. Ideal for sunless room, terrace, shaded garden.
Calla Lily (*Zantedeschia*)	2'–3'	Broad plain green or green and white spotted leaves.	Plant tubers in 5" pots of equal parts of sand, peat, and loam in March for outdoor bloom; July for indoor bloom.	Grows best as pot plant.
Cannas	Dwarfs 2' tall, standards 4'–5'	Large spikes of red, orange, bronze, yellow. Foliage bronze or green.	Set tubers in loose soil. 5"–6" deep. Full sun. Keep tip 1" below surface. Water well in dry spells.	Background plants, along house foundations, masses in borders. Dig tubers in fall, store in peat moss at 50°.
Chionodoxa luciliae (Glory-of-the-Snow)	5"	Blue, white, pink, flowers in short racemes, ahead of crocus.	Plant in fall, 2"–3" deep 2"–3" apart. Multiply freely.	Good for splash of color, shade or sun. Ideal for naturalizing.
Crocus	1"–3"	Blue, yellow, white, and striped flowers. February through April.	Plant 2"–3" deep in fall, in borders, flower beds, under shrubs.	Ideal for mass planting. Good for forcing indoors.

Common or Botanical Name	Height	Description	Cultural Tips	Use Indoors or Out
Crocus, autumn (*Colchicum*)	3″–4″	Lilac, pink, or white flowers in late summer and fall.	Plant 2″–3″ deep in late summer. Often foliage appears only in spring.	Late summer pickup. *Colchicums* bloom without soil or water. Can be grown in vase of gravel. Do not let children get bulbs; latter are poisonous.
Daffodils (See Narcissus)				
Dahlia	1½′–5′	Any color to suit your fancy.	Plant tubers 4″–6″ deep in full sun in spring. Give ample water. Stake. Mulch with peat, sawdust, etc., to keep weeds down, water in dry spells. Disbud for large blooms.	Background plants or cut flowers for vases, corsages. Dig in fall and store in peat moss at 40°-50°.
Eranthis hyemalis (*E. cilicica*) Winter Aconite	8″	Deep yellow. February or March, followed by lacy green umbrellas lasting until June.	Plant 1″ deep in August or September. Soak overnight before planting.	Earliest of blooms. Good in front of shrubs, in rock gardens.
Erythronium (Dogtooth Violet, Trout Lily)	8″–12″	Turkscap blooms of pink, white, cream, yellow, rose, or lavender in March or April.	Plant 3″ deep in shady, moist spots if possible.	Good near brooks, in woods, for naturalizing.
Freesia	12″–15″	Sweet scented. White, yellow, orange, red, pink, lavender-blue	Plant 1″ deep, about 9 in a 6″ pot. Set pot in cool place (50°).	Fragrant flower for home and greenhouse. Good for arrangements and weddings.

Common or Botanical Name	Height	Description	Cultural Tips	Use Indoors or Out
Fritillaria imperialis (Crown Imperial)	2½'-3'	Circle or red or yellow bell-shaped flowers beneath a crown of green foliage.	Plant 5" deep, 12" apart in groups in well drained, rich soil. Likes sun.	Sometimes touched by late spring frosts, otherwise hardy. Striking background plant.
Fritillaria Meleagris (Guinea Hen Flower)	6"-8"	Drooping bell-shaped blooms of checkered yellow, white, purple, and brown. Blooms in early spring.	Grow in light shade 3" deep, 3" apart. Leave in ground undisturbed for many years.	Ideal in rock gardens, or in groups.
Galanthus nivalis and *elivesi*	8"-12"	Pure white, single or double flowers in March.	Plant 3" deep, thickly, for a good show.	Not a heavy ground cover. Blooms still earlier near foundations.
Galtonia *Summer hyacinth (Hyacinthus candicans)*	3'	White, bell-shaped flowers in long racemes. In summer.	Plant outdoors when soil is warm. Set 3" deep in rich soil. Water during drought.	Not hardy, lift before frost and store at 60° over winter.
Gladiolus	2'-5'	All colors. Summer and fall.	Plant 2"-3" deep in well drained soil in full sun. Series of plantings stretch blooming period. Also use early, mid-season and late types. Dig in fall and store.	Ideal cut flowers for vases.
Gloxinia (*Sinningia*) (For more information on Gloxinia, see Chapter IX, HOUSE-PLANT CULTURE)	10"-12"	Large, bell-shaped velvety blossoms in both doubles and singles cover almost the whole color spectrum; solids, speckled, and bi-colors. Winter and some-times year round.	Plant bulb in 5" pot in fall or late winter for outside use. Also start from seed (takes year to bloom), leaf cuttings.	Excellent pot plants for home or greenhouse, shaded places outdoors. Dry off corms after bloom or keep outdoors until fall. Start watering when growth begins after rest.

Common or Botanical Name	Height	Description	Cultural Tips	Use Indoors or Out
Grape Hyacinth (See *Muscari*)				
Hyacinths	12″–15″	Fragrant white, blue, yellow, pink, red, peach, rose in early April.	Plant 4″–5″ deep in well drained soil. Dig and separate every few years. (See text for forcing indoors.)	Borders, beds, and indoor use.
Hymenocallis (See Peruvian Daffodil)				
Iris (Dutch)	12″–18″	Perky blooms in shades of blue, white, and yellow. June.	Must be mulched in cold areas, preferably with evergreen boughs. Likes sun, well drained soil. Plant 2″ deep.	Can be forced indoors for winter bloom.
Iris reticulata	4″–6″	Purple with yellow markings, fragrant. February or March.	Plant 3″ deep, in dry, sheltered space. Mulch in fall after hard frost.	Not one of most dependable in cold regions, but satisfying where it grows well. Pot in fall for winter forcing.
Ismene Calathina (See Peruvian Daffodil)				
Ixia (Corn Lily)	12″	Red, yellow, pink, rose, and white star-shaped blooms.	Plant 2″ deep, 6″ to a 6″ pot if in North and grow indoors. In South may be planted outdoors in autumn. Can be grown where temperatures go below freezing occasionally, if mulched heavily.	Excellent for cut flowers, for growing in a sunny window or greenhouse.

Common or Botanical Name	Height	Description	Cultural Tips	Use Indoors or Out
Leucojum (Snow Flake)	9"–12"	Glossy white flowers with green-tipped petals.	Likes semi-shade, plant 3" deep, 4" apart. Mulch lightly in cold areas.	Plant in autumn for bloom in April and May. Good for edging.
Lilies (Lilium)	2'–5'	All kinds and colors. June to September. Some have flowers 5" across.	Plant in fall (for depth, see text) in loose, well drained soil, full sun. To force florist type, pot in fall.	Ideal for vases, arrangements. Good background plants.
Lycoris aurea (Spider Lily)	18"–24"	Thin-petalled yellow flowers on tall stems.	Plant 5" deep in partial shade, or full sun. Hardy from Virginia south.	Treat as pot plant in North, or plant as gladiolus for autumn flowering.
Lycoris squamigera and *radiata* (Hardy "amaryllis")	2'–3'	Pink, reddish, and yellow lily-like flowers.	Foliage appears in April then dies down. Flowers from August on. Set outdoors 5" deep in full sun. Blooms year after year. Hardy except in coldest areas.	Splash of color towards fall.
Montbretia (Tritonia)	1'–3'	Panicle spikes of red, orange, yellow, bronze tubular flowers.	Plant 3" deep, 6" apart after last frost in spring. Dig in fall after first frost. Likes sandy loam, sun, or semi-shade.	Hardy south of Virginia. Store and treat as gladiolus. Good for cut flowers or background plants.
Muscari or Grape Hyacinths	6"–8"	Blue or white clusters of tiny round blooms. Mid-April or earlier. Also a fringed variety.	Plant 2"–3" deep and let multiply.	Borders, rock gardens, around trees. Hardy.

Common or Botanical Name	Height	Description	Cultural Tips	Use Indoors or Out
Narcissus or Daffodils	4"–20"	Pale to deep yellows, white. Long trumpets and flat cups of orange, pink, yellow. Select early and mid-season types. Long-lasting singles, doubles, and poetaz (clusters).	Plant miniatures 4" deep, large types 6". Full sun best but tolerate semi-shade.	Ideal in beds, borders, among trees. Dig up every 3-4 years if crowded. If annuals are to be planted in bed, dig bulbs and store in cool place, replanting in fall.
Ornithogalum umbellatum (Star of Bethlehem)	6"	Clusters of showy white flowers with green stripes.	Plant 3" deep in sun or semi-shade.	Plant near spring shrubs, under trees, in rock gardens. Leave undisturbed. Can be weedy in flower garden.
Ornithogalum thyrsoides (Chincherinchee)	16"–18"	White or yellow clusters of star-like blooms.	Not hardy in north. May be grown outdoors in summer. Same care as gladiolus. Can be forced indoors in winter. Plant shallow, 2 per 6" pot.	Especially attractive mixed bouquets. Welcome potted flowers when other winter blooms are scarce.
Oxalis Deppei	10"	White or pink flowers and clover-like foliage.	Plant 1" deep 6" apart in sandy loam. Sun or semi-shade.	Not hardy, grow as pot plant or plant outdoors after frost and dig in fall.
Peruvian Daffodil (Hymenocallis) (Ismene calathina)	1'-1½'	Fragrant white trumpets on spikes in summer.	Plant 3" deep in early sun in spring or early summer. Dig bulbs in fall, store in warm basement. Cool storage prevents blooming.	Ideal as pot plant or in border. Very quick to bloom.

Polianthes (see Tuberose)

Common or Botanical Name	Height	Description	Cultural Tips	Use Indoors or Out
Puschkinia libanotica	5"	Creamy white flowers with blue stripes.	Grow in sun or semi-shade, plant in fall 3" deep, 2"-3" apart.	Leave undisturbed in ground. Can be forced in pots for indoor bloom.
Ranunculus	2"-2½"	Flowers yellow, pink, red, white, and variegated. Double camelia-like flowers among new hybrids.	Same as for anemone.	Some are hardy and can be grown as perennial. Others are not hardy and must be dug in fall or grown as pot plant.
Scilla Siberica	4"-5"	Blue, white bells mid-March or April.	Plant 3" deep, in full sun, or semi-shade. Any soil.	Ideal for naturalizing. Prolific and hardy.
Scilla hispanica (*S. campanulata*)	8"-15"	Blue, pink, or white bells on spikes in late spring.	Plant 4" deep in garden or woodsy soil.	Ideal for borders or naturalized. Long-lived.
Sparaxis (Wand Flower)	8"	Bright multi-color blooms of red, white, yellow, orange, maroon.	Not completely hardy in northern areas. Good in pots, 2" deep, 5 per 6" pot. If outdoors a mulch is helpful.	Good for cut flowers. Make colorful pots when forced indoors or in greenhouse.
Sternbergia lutea	1'-2'	Bright yellow funnel-shaped flowers in autumn.	Plant about 4" deep in a dry, sunny spot. Likes heavy soil.	Good in groups to give color in fall when flower bed needs some show.
Tigridia (Tiger Flower or Shell Flower)	12"-18"	Red, orange, yellow, buff, with spotted center. 3-petaled flowers. Summer to frost.	Plant 3" deep in full sun. Culture similar to gladiolus.	Dig in fall and store as glads. In other areas can be left in ground all winter.
Tritonia (See *Montbretia*)				

Common or Botanical Name	Height	Description	Cultural Tips	Use Indoors or Out
Tuberose	12"	Waxy white flowers, single and double, in summer.	Plant outdoors in May 1"-2" deep. Start in pots and set out for earlier bloom. Dig bulbs in fall and store at 60°.	Ideal as pot plant or for the summer garden.
Tuberous Begonias	12"–20"	Many colors and forms, including camellia, rose, hollyhock, daffodil, and single types. Summer and fall. Winter blooms indoors.	Start indoors in pots in February for outdoor use. Do not cover top of bulb. Likes rich, humusy soil, shade, ample moisture. Frost-tender; dig and store outdoor bulbs indoors.	Good for hanging baskets, porch boxes, tubs, in semi-shade.
Tulips	4"-36"	All colors, sizes, and types. April through May, according to type.	Plant in fall 4" deep, 6" apart for outdoor use in beds, borders, rock gardens. Pot and force indoors.	Greater variety than any other bulbs; for garden, forcing, cutting.
Zephyranthes (Fairy lilies)	12"	White, yellow, pink, red, small, tubular blooms.	Semi-hardy; in northern areas lift in fall and store in moist peat moss or sawdust. Divide before replanting in spring.	Can be used in clusters in foreground of perennial bed.

BULBS SUITABLE FOR ROCK GARDENS

Botanical Name	Common Name	Remarks
Camassia	Camassia	Blue, purple, cream; May
Chionodoxa	Glory-of-the-Snow	Blue, pink; April
Colchicum	Autumn Crocus	Lavender; September
Crocus	Crocus	Various; April
Eranthis hyemalis	Winter Aconite	Yellow; March
Erythronium	Trout Lily, Dogtooth Violet	Yellow; May
Fritillaria meleagris	Checker Lily	Various; May
Galanthus	Snowdrop	White; March
Hyacinthus	Hyacinth	Blue, white, yellow, red; April
Leucojum aestivum	Snowflake	White; May
Lilium pumilum	Coral Lily	Red; June, July
Lycoris squamigera	Resurrection Lily	Lilac, pink; July, August
Muscari	Grape hyacinth	Blue, white; May
Narcissus	Narcissus	Yellow, white; late April, May
Ornithogalum	Star of Bethlehem	White; late May
Scilla siberica	Siberian Squill	Blue, white; April
Scilla hispanica	Spanish Squill	Blue, pink, white; April
Sternbergia lutea	Sternbergia	Yellow; autumn
Tulipa	Botanical Tulips	Various; May

CHAPTER VII

Roses for the Home Garden

•

By almost any method of reckoning roses continue to be the worldwide favorite flower. Over the years and in many lands roses have had the attention of the best gardeners, and as a result one can trace fashions in roses. Many rose types have been developed, flourished, and then declined as enthusiasm passed to another type.

Though hybrid teas are holding their own today, many gardeners are leaning toward masses of blooms rather than the single spectacular bloom of hybrid teas. Miniatures, shrub roses, and floribundas are taking the fancy of rose growers. They give more show for the amount of care and money invested. There is also a marked revival of interest in old-fashioned roses, including moss and cabbage roses. Not only do they have a fragrance long lost in rose breeding but they are often more resistant to insects and diseases.

Rose Classification

Classifications, both old and new, as represented in catalogues are presented in the accompanying charts with brief helpful data for each.

To rose fanciers, hybrid teas are the most important of all roses, and no rose bed would be complete without them. Most of the roses grown for cut flowers in greenhouses are hybrid teas. As a rule, the buds are long and pointed and the individual flowers are larger, on longer stems. Catalogues will usually give detailed descriptions of individual hybrid tea rose varieties.

HYBRID POLYANTHAS OR FLORIBUNDAS These terms are practically synonymous, although floribunda is the more recent term. In this variety, flowers are borne in clusters.

Plants of the floribunda group of small-flowered roses don't grow too tall, have clean foliage to the ground, and bloom over a long season. Floribundas have greater resistance to disease and insects and can readily be used in landscaping. Plants are attractive alone in beds or borders, or along with herbaceous perennials, flowering shrubs, or evergreens. You can use them to line a driveway, an entrance walk, to ring a small pool or a birdbath, or a lawn lamp. They give a splash of color to foundation plantings, and can even be used for a gay blooming hedge, one that stays within bounds. They are well adapted for use around contemporary homes. They are fast becoming the most popular type.

Keep spent roses pruned off and you'll encourage the plants to put their strength into new blooms instead of stems and foliage.

THE GRANDIFLORA This class has large-growing, everblooming plants and big flowers. They are more vigorous growers and need less care than many rose types. Quality grandifloras will produce colorful accents when placed among the other plants on your property. They can be planted in the rose garden with hybrid tea roses, but should be planted a little farther apart and to the back because of their size. They will grow as tall or taller than the largest hybrid teas and will produce more flowers. As specimen plants grandifloras are excellent, producing bright flowers throughout the season, with heavy blooming periods in late spring and fall. Grandifloras are often used with floribundas for landscape effects. Since there are more floribunda varieties, their colors extend over a greater range and offer fascinating contrasts to the grandiflora colors.

MINIATURE ROSES (FAIRY ROSES) Grow about 1 foot high and have flowers 1 inch or less across, single or in clusters. They can be grown as pot plants indoors, or bedding plants outdoors. They are easier to grow outdoors than the other types of roses, and take the same care. Indoors, they need a cool window (greenhouse is ideal) and plenty of light. Spider mites are a problem indoors. Spray with Kelthane if foliage becomes mottled due to mite injury.

TREE ROSES Actually a small tree with a trunk about 4 feet tall, and 1 inch or so in diameter. The top has branches, foliage, and the flowers of a normal rose bush. Nurserymen can take any class of rose and bud or graft it to a tall understock to create a tree rose (often called "standard" rose). Tree roses are very sensitive to winter cold, hence require a special kind of winter protection in cold climates (see *Winterizing*).

ROSA MULTIFLORA HEDGE As a living fence for the farm, the "multiflora rose" may be useful but the average city or suburban property doesn't have the space for this plant. The variety used for fencing grows rampant, is very thorny, and bears white flowers that are not particularly showy when compared with garden ramblers.

Bright red fruits, rose hips (good for rose hip tea) are produced in the fall. Three to four years or more may be needed before the fence is high and thick enough to act as a barrier against animals. Before planting on property lines, you should observe the characteristics of this thorny rose to make sure you'll be satisfied with it once it's established. It can grow to heights of 6 feet and widths of 10 feet or more.

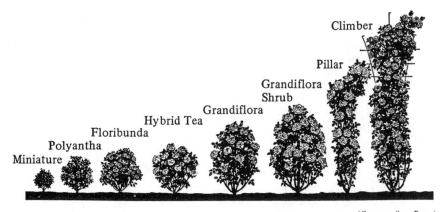

(*Courtesy Star Roses*)

A QUICK GUIDE TO POPULAR ROSE TYPES
(With Growing Tips)

Type (Class)	Description	Uses	Pruning (for more detail see under individual Types)
Miniatures	Grows less than 1′ with blooms 1″ or less. *Examples:* Pixie, Cinderella, Starina	Pots, miniature arrangements, beds, rock gardens.	Trim back in spring, same as hybrid teas, or just cut out dead wood.
Polyantha (Ranunculus flowered roses)	A term largely replaced by floribunda, height 2″. *Examples:* Margo Koster, Karen Poulsen, Carroll Ann	Used for Mother's Day as florist's potted rose. Potted plant can be set permanently in the garden.	Prune to live wood in spring.
Floribunda	Smaller flowers than hybrid teas, but many more of them borne in clusters. Bloom late spring to hard frost in fall. Low-growing, height 2′. *Examples:* Fashion Circus, Bahia, Betty Pryor	Ideal for beds, borders, mass plantings. Good with evergreens in foundation plantings. Good for hedges and potted plants.	Little pruning necessary except to cut out dead wood, because of low habit of growth.
Hybrid Perpetual	Grows up to 6′ or more. Foliage large, thick, and leathery. Blooms brilliantly in early summer, with some flowers throughout summer and fall. *Examples:* Paul Neyron, American Beauty, Frau Karl Druschki	Good in rose gardens, as individual specimens, and background plants.	Prune back to live wood in spring.
Hybrid Teas	Grows 2′-6′. Have large individual blossoms borne on long single stems, or attractive clusters of 3 to 5 flowers. Require much care. *Examples:* Tiffany, Peace, American Heritage	Ideal for rose gardens, individual specimens, cut flowers.	Prune back to live wood in spring.
Grandiflora	New, big, vigorous, tall-growing, 6′. Bloom profusely in clusters, large flowers with individual stems long enough for cutting. *Examples:* Queen Elizabeth, Camelot	Serve well for backgrounds, tall hedges, and screens.	Prune much like hybrid teas in spring.

Type (Class)	Description	Uses	Pruning (for more detail see under individual Types)
Pillar	A bush rose with extra long canes. Glows 8' high or more. Unlike the climber, does not need much support, nor does it grow as tall. *Examples*: Spectacular, Red Fountain	A colorful accent plant, requiring support.	Keep in bounds by training against pillar, post, lamp post, or rural mail box.
Climbers	Bright splashes of color that need support such as trellis, fence, or wall. Height 10' or more. *Examples*: Blaze, America, Don Juan	Ideal against porches, garages, fences, poles, can soften house corners or entrance ways.	Prune after blooming is over. Shorten canes in fall to prevent whipping.
Shrub Roses	A hardy group of wild species, hybrids and varieties. Usually bear single blossoms, have bright attractive fall fruits, glossy, colorful foliage. *Examples*: Yellow Rosa Hugonis, Sea Foam, The Fairy	Some are good for screens, hedges, mixed plantings, and as specimens.	Require little pruning except to keep them in bounds. Prune as you would any shrub.

Planting Roses

In buying roses, home gardeners have a choice of "bare root" plants, i.e., plants which are dug after they have become dormant and have been stored under controlled conditions, or potted roses. Bare root stock is cheaper but mortality rate may be higher if, for example, plants are allowed to dry out in storage. Potted roses come in a variety of containers, and most of them can be planted "container and all" (except metal or plastic), although we do not like to follow this advice. When we plant potted roses we slit the sides of the container, remove the soil ball, and plant it *without* the container (some containers do not break down fast and roots that are too confined cannot get enough water). Some roses come in a plastic sleeve with peat moss inside. Remove the sleeve, snip off tips of roots, and plant immediately.

Plants from reputable nurseries are packed so that they will stand a week or more from time of shipment in the package without serious damage if kept cool (40 to 50 degrees F.).

If it is not possible to set plants out as soon as they arrive, unpack and "heel" in the ground to prevent drying out. Heeling is simply covering roots with soil temporarily until you can plant them. Never let bare roots be exposed to drying winds or sunlight. Plants in containers will survive for several weeks if kept in semi-shade and watered regularly.

However, they should be planted before the end of summer so they can become established before winter.

WHEN TO PLANT Which is better for planting bare-root or potted roses: fall or spring? Nurserymen are still debating this subject although most we've talked to favor spring planting. Their reason: It is practically impossible to get thoroughly dormant bare-root stock early in the fall, especially in areas where there's been a wet summer and prolonged growth due to favorable weather. In a wet fall season the canes may not be hardened enough, and as a result there's likelihood of severe winterkilling. If we had our choice we'd prefer to plant roses in the spring.

If planted in the fall, the soil should be drawn up around the stems, in the manner of "hilling up" potatoes. Straw, evergreen branches, or similar material may be used to cover the entire bed. This treatment applies to all types of roses when fall-planted in cold sections.

LOCATION Be sure to give roses a spot where they will get about six hours of direct sunlight each day. Light shade in the afternoon is an advantage. Never place roses close to trees with matted surface roots, such as some of the maples, willows, elms, and poplars. Although roses should not be planted in a dead air pocket with no air circulation, some protection from high winds is desirable.

SOILS A lot has been said about soils for roses. Actually, these plants aren't too fussy. Experience shows roses will grow in almost any soil. Roses tolerate clay to a remarkable degree, but they do not prefer it to a loose soil. If your soil is heavy, it can be lightened by adding rotted manure, peat moss, or rotted compost to it.

The main thing is to give roses a soil that's well drained, or you may lose plants. Peat creates air spaces in a clay soil. Use 1 bushel of peat to 3 bushels of soil. Well-rotted manure, peat moss, or rotted compost also make good conditioners for a sandy soil, enabling it to hold moisture better.

HOW TO PREPARE THE SOIL If you are preparing a new rose bed, dig the soil to a depth of 18 to 20 inches, and incorporate about 3 pounds of superphosphate or 5 pounds of 5-10-5 (or any balanced plant food) for each 100 square feet of soil before setting out the plants. Peat moss and manure can be used together at the rate of 1 bushel of manure, 2 bushels of peat, to 10 bushels of soil. Never use fresh manure. Horse manure, if well rotted, is as good as cow manure, and even rotted hen manure is usable at the rate of 1 bushel for each 100 square feet.

SPACING Roses need plenty of room for full growth. Hybrid teas should be from $1\frac{1}{2}$ to 2 feet apart in the best part of your garden. The floribundas are somewhat bushier in growth habits—most roses of this class need about the same amount of space as hybrid teas, or a little more. Miniatures can be spaced 12 to 18 inches apart; shrub roses and grandifloras, 3 to 4 feet apart; and hybrid perpetuals 4 to 5 feet apart.

Trim the roots before planting (see illustration) and make large holes so that roots can be spread out. The plant should be placed so that the "bud mark" (knuckle) is at least 2 inches below ground level (this practice is questioned by some rosarians who feel it encourages suckers).

The tops should be cut back when planted and each spring thereafter.

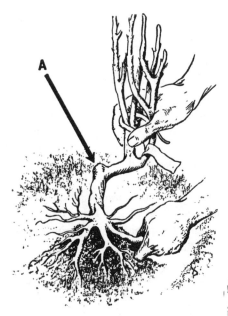

When planting a bare-rooted rose, prune canes back to 6 or 8 inches. Dig hole deep and wide enough to accommodate roots without crowding. Spread the roots out over a cone-shaped pile of soil in bottom of hole. When the plant is set in, the bud union (A) should be about 2 inches below ground level. Crown should be just above soil line.

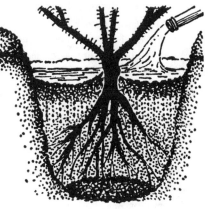

Fill with loose soil and compost or rotted manure well mixed. Firm soil with your foot and water well.

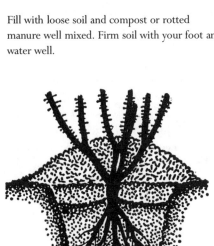

Mound soil up 4 or 5 inches around base of plant to keep from drying until growth starts. Remove as soon as leaf growth starts.

FEEDING ROSES Everyone has his own method of feeding roses. You can fertilize established plants with 5-10-5 at the rate of 5 pounds per 100 square feet each spring. If soil is sandy or porous, larger amounts are needed. Roses aren't fussy, but they do prefer a slightly acid soil. If the soil is very acid, 1 to 2 pounds of lime per 100 square feet will correct the condition. If it becomes too alkaline, 1 pound of sulfur per 100 square feet will be beneficial.

A friend of ours who has good roses feeds 1 rounded teaspoon of 5-10-5 to a square foot (equivalent to 4 pounds per 100 square feet) every three weeks up to the middle of August. For first-year plants, he uses 1 level tablespoon per square foot (3 pounds per 100 square feet) when roses are grown in beds. When grown in rows, he applies 1 pound for each 25 feet of row, putting half on each side of the row.

For foliar feeding, you can use a liquid plant food applied with a garden hose attachment, every three or four weeks. If you foliage feed, do so in early morning (so leaves can dry before night) and include fungicides and insecticides in your fertilizer solution.

Many gardeners find fish emulsion and "liquid seaweed" superb plant foods for roses.

For prize-winning roses, you have to follow a more ambitious feeding schedule than rough-and-ready gardeners may be willing to undertake. Rose experts Elmer Haley and Al Picciocchi of Rochester, New York, combine chemical fertilizers with organic ones with excellent results. Mr. Haley has given us his feeding schedule:

Mid-April, 2 tablespoons of a high-nitrogen fertilizer to each bush. *First week in May*, 1/2 cup per bush of any rose food plus 1 tablespoon of epsom salts, watered in well. *Third week in May*, feed each bush 1 tablespoon of fish emulsion and 1 teaspoon of chelated iron in one gallon of water. *First week in June*, give each bush 1/2 cup of any rose food. *Second week in June*, put on a mulch of well rotted manure or any organic mulch material. (See *Mulches* in Chapter XIII.) *A few days later*, feed a liquid plant food, about a gallon of solution per plant. *About four weeks later*, feed 1/2 cup of any rose food per bush. *First week in August*, use a tablespoon of fish emulsion and 1 teaspoon of chelated iron in a gallon of solution for each bush. *Do not feed after first week in August*, since it may make soft, succulent growth which may winterkill.

Drought can do considerable damage to roses. Many are so weakened they are apt to winterkill. By maintaining fertility of the rose bed, you can do much to toughen up plants. Far more roses starve than are overfed. But neither should you overfeed your plants, since they may grow too much and retard proper ripening of the wood in the fall.
WATERING Roses like plenty of water. Soak the beds once every week or ten days during dry spells so that water may reach the roots. Avoid wetting the foliage in the evening, for this encourages black spot and spreads mildew diseases. Give your roses a good mulching to conserve moisture when hot weather comes.

Plants are easily started from "slips," the home gardener's method for starting roses and other shrubs. Leave the cuttings under the glass "greenhouse" jars all winter, remove jar in spring. Add a clump of earth on top of the jar to shade the cutting while rooting.

PROPAGATION Roses are started by seed, budding, grafting, layering, and cuttings. One of the easiest ways is by taking a "slip" or a "greenwood" cutting, or you can use mature wood ("hardwood"). In summer take a cutting about 4 inches long, insert it in soil or sand, and cover with a glass jar, after watering. The jar acts like a small greenhouse and maintains proper humidity. Leave the cutting there all winter, and in the spring you can remove the glass and plant the rooted cutting.

Cuttings are taken in different ways: Some gardeners pull the shoot off, leaving a little "heel" at the base for roots to form. Others make the cutting anywhere along the stem (either between the node, or at the joint or node) and get a good response. You can dip the ends in a rooting hormone or not (see *Hardwood Cuttings*, Chapter XV).

PRUNING We're going to try to eliminate much of the mystery in pruning. Although these tips may not jive with rules set down in many rose books, they do work for us. Until recently, it was believed that roses should be pruned severely; now, many think roses should not be pruned heavily because the more wood on the plant, the more food reserves it provides for blooms.

CLIMBERS AND PILLARS: Climbing and pillar roses are pruned in midsummer just after the blooms have faded. At that time the old canes which have just produced flowers are cut close to the roots of the plants. New canes for next year's bloom will be several

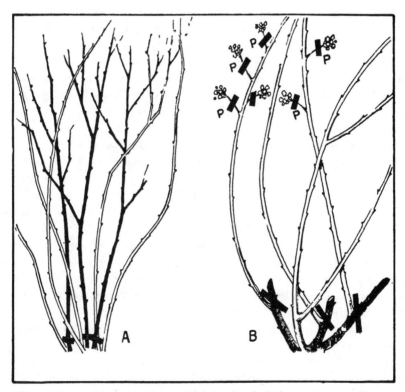

When pruning rambler roses, thin out old dark-colored, thick canes in spring. Remove any seed pods that still remain. (*Courtesy University of Maine*)

feet long. Care should be taken not to break or bruise these in the pruning process. Thiskind of pruning is practiced on such varieties as Dorothy Perkins, Paul Scarlet, and American Pillar. Such semi-climbing varieties as Dr. Van Fleet, Dr. J. H. Nicolas, and others should have older flowering wood removed only.

What should be done with long rambler canes in fall? If they windwhip or have grown longer than their space allows, it's best to break a few rules and shorten the canes to prevent rubbing on the house. The only time climbers are cut back completely is when they have been neglected to the point that it's almost impossible to separate and cut out the old wood.

HYBRID TEAS: Prune in spring after all danger of winter injury has passed. Hybrid tea roses or "monthly roses" can be pruned once winter protection has been removed. Any wood that has blackened can be cut off to the nearest live bud. Trim out any weak branches, and weak and spindly growth which is smaller than a lead pencil in diameter, provided two or three more vigorous canes are left. The vigorous living canes should be cut back to live tissue. Some growers still prefer to cut the entire bush back to 9 to 12 inches above the ground. This may be necessary because of winterkilling, but may be too severe in milder climates. If there is little winterkilling of canes, you can cut your roses back to a height that is satisfactory to you. Many rose growers today feel that leaving the canes longer when pruning in spring produces longer and better stems for cut flowers.

To sum up tea rose pruning: 1) Cut all dead and injured wood. 2) Remove weak shoots. 3) Cut back the largest canes to 9 to 12 inches above the ground—longer if you prefer. Make cuts slanting and about 1/4 inch above a bud that points outward.

SUCKERING ROSES: Be sure to remove suckers or sprouts which arise from base of grafted or budded roses. These may overtake and crowd out parent plant. Put on your gloves and remove the sucker at the point from where it emerges by giving it a quick, sharp pull! Cutting them off at ground level is only a temporary measure.

WINTERIZING ROSES

WITH SOIL: If you live in cold regions, mounding or hilling tea roses with extra soil, 8 to 12 inches high, is protection from changing temperatures. Do not take earth from between the bushes, as it may expose the roots. A covering of straw over the mounds is added protection. Some gardeners make "cones" from tar paper and put leaves inside; however, we feel you can't beat soil mounding for protection. In spring we cut the long canes back to live tissue and get bushels of blooms (see illustrations).

Tree roses must be covered or they will succumb. Dig a narrow trench on one side of the plant, remove some soil near the root ball, gently bend the plant over into the trench (being careful not to injure the roots), peg it down, and completely cover it with about 12 inches of soil. Climbing roses can be pegged to the ground, although many gardeners (including ourselves) do not take the time.

Never wrap roses with plastic sheets, as sunny winter days can "cook" them with heat trapped inside.

IN POLYSTYRENE: Some gardeners who have tried polystyrene hoods or cones to cover rose bushes have told us they wound up in spring with dead bushes. This is due to a lack of ventilation. Anyone who uses rose cones *must* take off all the leaves when plants are cut back in fall. The cones need ventilation; without it, the leaves get wet and rot sets in. They also need weights on top to hold cones in place, since they are lightweight. Holes should be drilled into the cones to allow for ventilation. Drill two holes $1/2$ inch in diameter on two sides of the cones, $1\,1/2$ inches from the top. Place cones so that holes will not get in the path of the prevailing wind. For example, if the wind is mostly from the west, place the cone so that one hole is facing south and other facing east. The best rose growers suggest tying the canes with garden twine, spraying the cut bushes with Captan, 3 tablespoons per gallon of water, allowing them to dry, and then putting the cones over. Properly used, cones can do a fine job. Elmer Haley suggests that cone users give them a quarter turn in early spring to break the seal at soil level. Then make a narrow 1-inch groove in the soil with a trowel on each side of cone to give ventilation. This prevents premature leaf growth.

Diseases and Insects of Roses

BLACK SPOT Black spot, the worst disease of roses, causes leaves to spot, turn yellow, then drop. Control is not easy, but one thing you can do is to pick up fallen leaves and burn them or seal in plastic bag and discard. In spring, cut back the old canes as far as possible, since the spores overwinter in them, as well as in dead leaves. Growers we know spray roses two or three times a week to prevent black spot, and that takes a lot of joy out of rose growing. If you don't spray, the canes often become denuded by the ethylene gas given off by the fungus (*Diplocarpum rosae*). which causes black spot.

Unlike powdery mildew, which lives on the surface of the leaf and is checked readily with Phaltan or sulfur, the black spot organism invades the leaf and lives between the upper and lower leaf surfaces. Because the fungus is inside the leaf, no fungicide can kill it without also killing the leaf. That's why *prevention* is more important than eradication. If rose foliage is unprotected by a fungicide for as little as six hours, especially after a rain or in muggy weather, you can expect black spots on your leaves.

CHEMICAL CONTROL: 1) Try a dormant spray of lime sulfur in early spring just before growth begins. 2) Spray at least once a week with a fungicide such as Ferbam, Maneb, Phaltan, Zineb, or sulfur-copper mixtures. Some growers like to alternate with weekly sprays.

ORGANIC CONTROL: If you don't like to use chemical sprays, try using crushed tomato leaves (see recipe in Chapter XIV). Or you can grow tomatoes in with your rose

Black spot disease is the most common problem of roses. Sanitation, plus regular spraying with a fungicide, will prevent black spot disease.

bushes. How do tomato leaves fight black spot? The leaves secrete solanine, a chemical that has an inhibiting effect on black spot fungus.

Another control for black spot and powdery mildew is the following: 1 tablespoon of baking soda (bicarbonate of soda) plus 1/4 teaspoon of liquid dishwashing detergent per gallon of water, applied weekly or as needed.

BUDS FAIL TO OPEN What makes buds start to come out, then fail to open? One reason is the work of the rose midge, a small fly rarely seen except by trained entomologists. The midge causes rose buds to crook or flop over at right angles, without opening. The small flower buds "blast" or abort, and later in the season the tips of new shoots die when they are about an inch or so long. Flowering practically stops. *Control*: Spray with Malathion. It's best to start early in spring when young growth is about 6 to 12 inches long. It's also a good idea to treat the soil, since the midge passes part of its life-cycle in the earth.

ROSE SLUG If something is skeletonizing your rose leaves, it's probably the rose slug, the immature or larva stage of the rose sawfly. Slugs (nothing to do with the common garden slug) are greenish, caterpillar-like worms that feed on the undersides of leaves. They skeletonize them or carve out conspicuous holes in the foliage. *Control*: Spray with Malathion or nicotine sulfate.

Best way to check most diseases and insects is before they get started. You can buy all-purpose rose dusts or sprays or you can make your own.

Here's a spray schedule given to us by two rosarians. *As soon as cones or covers are removed in the spring*, spray with phaltan or other fungicide. (Covering should be kept handy in case of late severe frost.) *In mid-May*, apply a systemic insecticide and use 1/2 tablespoon of Captan.

Daily syringing with a hose is also helpful. *In Mid-July*, rose midge is controlled by using methoxychlor or Diazinon. After first blooming, spray ground around plants once a week, for three weeks, to get Japanese beetles and other insects. Or use beetle traps. *In Mid-November*, cut canes back to 16 inches and remove foliage. Tie canes together with garden twine and spray with captan—3 tablespoons per galloon of water. Then let dry before covering. See chapter XIV for more Organic controls.

WHEN ROSES CHANGE COLORS Many complain that their yellow roses (and white ones) bloomed to a red or other color.

Roses do not often truly change color. Some do mutate, as do other plants, but what usually happens is this: Since roses are budded on understocks, the top or budded part dies, leaving the understock to carry on. Many roses are budded on an understock known as Dr. Huey (a maroon red), an old variety commonly used for budding. Winter disease, or insects kill the top or budded rose (white, yellow, etc.) and the understock (very vigorous) takes over. When this happens you often see a lot of long canes coming up from the base of the plants.

All rose blooms change color with age. A partially opened bud will be a much deeper colothan the fully opened bloom. Peace, one of the most popular roses ever delevoped, changes shades many times during its stages of bloom.

A QUICK KEY TO ROSE TROUBLES:

(Prepared with assistance of Dr. R. C Allen, noted rosarian)

Leaf Symptoms	Some Common Causes	Control: see section of the Control of Insects and Diseases (Ch. XIV)
Prominent black spots	Black spot disease	Captan, Maneb, sulfur, Phaltan, clean-liness (see black spot section, organic control of Black Spot).
Holes chewed in leaves and and petals	Japanese beetles, rose chafers, or various cater-pillars, leaf cutter bees, raspberry cane borer	See Chapter XIV
Tips turned brown	Spray or dust burn	Avoid too heavy dosage when spraying
Margins brown	Spray burn or potash deficiency	Avoid too heavy dosage when spraying. Feed regularly
Leaves skeletonized	Rose slugs	Malathion; see Chapter XIV
Strong yellow mottling of leaves	Soil too alkaline	Have soil tested, add sulfur
Faint yellow stippling of foliage	Spider mites or leaf-hoppers	Miticide, Malathion for leafhoppers
White moldy patches on leaves, stems	Mildew	Karathane, sulfur, fixed copper fungicide
Pale green or yellow appearance	Nitrogen deficiency	Add complete plant food
Wilting of foliage (overall)	Drought	Add water
Wilting of foliage (tips)	Borers in stems	Keep canes sprayed with Malathion; see Chapter XIV
Shedding	Drought Black Spot Other causes of foliage shedding include nutrient deficiencies, spray and dust injury, and spider mites	Add water; See Chapter XIV Check each for cause

Stem Symptoms:	Some Common Causes	Control
Brown patches in spring	Brown canker	Dormant spray lime sulfur (in April)
Dark brown patches on stems	Common canker	Dormant spray lime sulfur (in April)
Entire stem dark brown in spring	Winter injury	Prune out black canes
Hollow areas in stems after pruning	Rose slugs	Malathion or other controls as detailed in Chapter XIV
Failure to elongate, remains stubby	Rose midge	Malathion
Grayish white, moldy patches on young growth	Mildew	Sulfur
White dots in summer	Brown canker	Dormant spray (in April)
Thick concentrations of small soft-bodied, green, pink, red, black insects on tops or tips	Aphids or plant lice	Nicotine sulfate (1 tsp. to 2 qts. water) or Malathion Also see Chapter XIV.
Rough, tumor-like growth on stem near soil or on roots	Crown gall, a bacterial disease that gains entry through wounds made by cultivating	Disease is so infectious that you should dig up plant and burn (or seal in plastic bag and discard). Disinfect tools by dipping in full-strength household bleach.
Buds covered with grayish mold	Mildew	See Mildew in section on Control of Insects and Diseases.
Tiny buds turn brown	Rose midge	Methoxychlor or Sevin (see Chapter XIV.)
Holes in buds	Chewing insects, such as rose budworm	Methoxychlor or Sevin (see Chapter XIV)
Large buds fail to open	Thrips, wet weather	Malathion and other controls in Chapter XIV.
Petals riddled	Chewing insects (see "Holes in Leaves" under *Leaf Symptoms*)	Malathion; Chapter XIV.

Note: Do not spray Sevin on open blooms as it kills bees.

Longer Life for Cut Roses

Here are a few hints on extending life of cut roses; 1) Cut them in bud stage, just when the first outer petal starts to unfold. Use a sharp knife or sharp shears, and cut so five or more leaflet leaves are left on the plant below the cut. 2) Remove any leaves from the lower part of the stem that would be under water. 3) Place cut rose immediately in deep, *warm* water, covering the lower two-thirds of the stem. 4) Use a floral preservative in the water at the strength recommended on the package—no stronger. 5) Condition them in a cool place (40 or 50 degrees F.) for two to four hours, to allow them to absorb water readily. 6) Arrange in deep vases so that at least one-fourth to one-half of the stem is submerged. Many rose growers even suggest cutting 1/2 inch from the stem end while it's in water so that an air bubble is released. If the stem is cut outside of water, this "gas" bubble will block the water flow. For a cut flower preservative, researchers at the College of Agriculture/Texas A&M, recommend 2 ounces of Listerine mouthwash per gallon of vase water. Listerine contains sucrose which is a food source for flowers, and a bacteriacide. Further, its acidity facilitates quick uptake of water by the stem, thus extending the life of cut roses and other flowers.

If you happen to use florist's porous foam blocks for arrangements, be sure to saturate the foam thoroughly in advance in clean water containing a floral preservative. Inserting stems into dry "foams" will shorten the life of the flowers. Most foams should not be reused. 7) Crumpled "chicken wire" makes a good holder to keep stems in position. 8) When removing thorns, be careful not to scrape or injure the stem. Use a glove or cloth and simply pull it down over the stem. The water-conducting tissues are just below the bark; if they are severed, the flower cannot take up the water necessary to maintain it.

Wilting is not necessarily a sign that the rose is old. It often happens if the bud has been cut before sufficiently mature, or if a cut has been made through the bark. When a rose "flops" or wilts, cut the stem off one inch, and insert the stem in a vase of very warm water (about 120 degrees F.). When the rose revives, replace it in the arrangement and it will be "good as new."

CHAPTER VIII

Container Gardening

•

Container growing, pot growing, raising plants without a garden, call it what you will, container gardening is the perfect answer for the apartment dweller, mobile-home owner, townhouse occupant, or owner of a postage-stamp backyard. Mini-gardening has become so popular that plant breeders have developed mini-vegetables especially for growing in containers and small spaces. Many standard-size vegetables can be adapted to containers if they are watered, fed frequently, and given support.

Summer, winter, spring, or fall—you can grow edible crops as well as flowers in tubs, pots, baskets, boxes, tanks, barrels, pails, window boxes, wagons, wheel-barrows, urns, and anything else that will hold potting soil.

One big advantage of farming in a window sill, balcony, rooftop, or door-stop is the small outlay of cash. You don't need to hire a tractor or plow, and there's no need for bags of fertilizer or a tool shed full of implements to work the plants. Yet it's surprising what this "concentrated" gardening can produce, whether it's vegetables, herbs, or fruits, growing in containers.

Pot gardens can be ornamental as well as edible.

Another big advantage of container gardening is mobility. Most vegetables need at least six to eight hours of sun a day; containers can be moved as the sun moves. Also, by placing mirrors or other reflecting surfaces in strategic places you can grow vegetables in otherwise shady spots. White houses, white walls, and overhangs add reflected light as does a white gravel mulch.

Your front entrance can be "plant-scaped" with a couple of pots (a 12-inch diameter is large enough) of tomato plants trained to a stake. If grill-work is present, let them ramble up the metal and use old nylon stockings to fasten them. For a touch of extra color, place a petunia plant, dwarf marigold, portulaca, or sweet alyssum toward the front of the pot. Tomatoes will bear fruit all summer long and the flowers will provide a show throughout the season. Either standard-size tomatoes (which must be staked or tied for support) or a dwarf type called Patio with good-sized fruit on 24-inch plants are successful. A number of small fruited varieties are prolific and attractive. Some we've tried with good results are Presto, Pixie, Small Fry, Gardener's Delight, Sweet 100, Tiny Tim, Sweet Million, Chelsea, and several varieties with yellow and red pear-shaped fruit.

Types of Containers

Almost any vegetable lives comfortably in a container. Cucumbers do especially well, as do eggplants, peppers, lettuce, and beans. We grow mini-melons and summer squash in boxes $2' \times 22'' \times 2'$; bushel baskets will serve as well. We grow carrots, beets, lettuce, and onions in boxes which are $2\frac{1}{2}$ feet long, 18 inches wide, and 1 foot deep because we had a windfall of old grape-picking trays of these dimensions. Take advantage of any available container that has a depth of 6 to 8 inches or more: pots, tubs, baskets, boxes, water tanks (split lengthwise with a torch), galvanized pails, plastic waste baskets or dishpans, old wheelbarrows, children's wagons, and window boxes. We're delighted to see urban houses with window boxes filled with red petunias in front for show and bush beans in the back for easy picking. A boy we know grows attractive hanging baskets of beans attached to the sunny side of the porch with brackets.

Whatever you use, make sure drainage holes are provided or roots will suffocate from lack of oxygen. We like to use pieces of $2'' \times 4''$ blocks under the corners of containers to raise them and allow air circulation. Other Containers You Might Want to Try Are:

GUTTER PIPE Your lumber yard has the "K" or standard half-round eaves trough, both simple to use for crop growing. You need only to solder the end caps on desired length of trough and drill holes in the bottom for drainage. Fill with a soil mixture of 1 part each of sand, peat, and loam. Then place the trough on the edge of your patio, balcony, or sidewalk in a spot that gets full sun. Keep the soil moist but don't let heavy rains flood the trough.

CEMENT BLOCKS For cheap containers to grow herbs or vegetables, pick up some cement blocks from your lumber yard. They come in all sizes, but an $8'' \times 8'' \times 16''$ is easy to handle and holds moisture well. Lay the blocks end to end so the openings face up. Fill openings with soil and set plants or sow seeds in them. You'll be surprised to see how well the plants grow. On hot days, you might have to water them daily.

METAL OR WOOD BARRELS Keep an eye open for discarded metal or wooden barrels. Old wine barrels, nail kegs, etc., painted to harmonize with the setting, make excellent containers for shrubby ornamentals (and vegetables and fruits as well). Make sure the barrel is free from harmful chemical residues by scrubbing the insides with ammonia water and soap suds and rinsing. A garage man can cut a metal barrel in half and be sure to have him burn holes in the bottom for drainage. This is *important*, since metal does not breathe. A wooden barrel can be cut in half with a circular saw or a saber saw. Make a chalk mark around it first, so you won't end up with one half of the barrel taller than the other. If the bottom is rotten or lacking, don't worry. Just set it on the ground. Fill the barrel with your regular potting mix and sow seed of small vegetables directly in the soil, or set out tomato plants, 1 foot apart. Train them on a wire corset or trellis. Best material for this is 4-inch concrete reinforcing wire. Just roll it into a cylinder and place it around the inside of the barrel or wrap it around the outside.

Not all plants require a trellis. Plants such as blueberries, eggplants, or broccoli support themselves very adequately.

WOODEN BOXES Any kind of wooden box will grow crops. For growing tubbed evergreens or flowering shrubs and fruit trees, you will need larger boxes than for vegetables. If you're handy, make your own. Naturally, redwood is the best because it is rot-resistant but it is expensive. Cedar or cypress are also long-lasting. You can make boxes out of hemlock, pine, or other materials and stain them to resemble redwood. If you use other wood, treat with a "rot fighter" such as used by greenhouse people. Watch out for creosote and other materials: their fumes can kill plants. Make the boxes about 10 to 12 inches deep, using galvanized or zinc-coated nails to prevent rust, and don't forget drainage holes, five or six inches apart. Put a layer of pebbles, crushed stone, pieces of broken pots, or charcoal in the bottom for drainage, and add the standard 1 part each sand-peat-loam soil mix. Sow seed directly in the box or place started plants.

Wood containers lose moisture faster than metal or porcelain types, so you should water them more often.

INDOOR PLANTER BOXES Almost any kind of flower or vegetable plant (as well as houseplants, etc.) can be grown in home-made indoor planter boxes. These can be made of wood or rust-resistant metal (or simply use a regular "outdoor" window box) and placed on windowsills, tables, floors, pedestals, anywhere that has light. (If you don't have much light, choose your plants accordingly. See Chapter IX, HOUSEPLANTS CULTURE.)

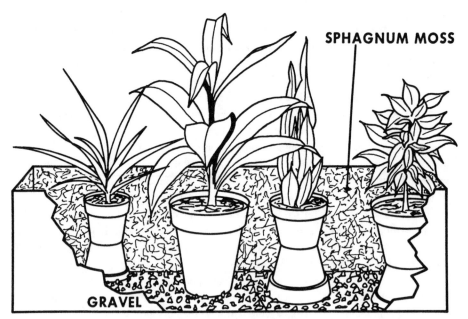

Cross section of a planter box with plants left in their pots. A layer of gravel is placed on the bottom and remaining space is filled with damp peat moss to within an inch of the top. Smaller plants are set on inverted pots. (*Courtesy of USDA*).

We've tried several different methods for filling indoor planters and here's what we recommend: 1) Make the box at least 8 inches deep. 2) Line the bottom with some water-resistant material to prevent dripping and leaking. 3) Place a layer of gravel in the bottom for drainage. 4) Fill the box with moist peat moss up to within an inch of the top. 5) Place plants in the peat moss, pot and all, rather than knocking them out of the pot and planting directly. (It isn't likely to happen, but if a plant should die, all you have to do is to lift out the pot without disturbing the plants nearby.) 6) When you apply water, add a small amount to the surface of each pot and also keep the peat moss slightly dampened at all times.

A common mistake is to plant "dry" plants along with those which need a fair amount of water. The same goes for light. Some plants can tolerate a lot of light while others need very little.

Care of Plants in Containers

DRAINAGE One of the big secrets for the good growth of all container plants is good drainage. No fruit or vegetable can take wet feet. If water builds up from overwatering or a heavy rain plants will suffocate. Regardless of which container you use, be it wood, metal, or earthenware, be sure to drill at least three or four holes in the bottom for good drainage, if the container does not already have drainage holes. An electric drill will do the job. *Note: Never drill if water is in the container, as it can be dangerous.* It's also a good idea to put pieces of broken crocks, pebbles, or crushed stone in the bottom for better drainage (a few pieces in a small container, an inch or more in a large container.

WATERING Plants in tubs or boxes need water more often than those growing in the garden, especially during dry spells. Glazed or metal containers do not dry out as quickly as wooden or porous types, so should *not* be watered as often. Feel the soil; it should be slightly damp—*not soggy*—at all times. If you are using the containers indoors or on a porch, set trays or large saucers under them so water won't drain on the floor.

SOIL A good standard soil mixture for anything you grow is one part each of sand, peat (or rotted compost or rotted manure), and loam or ordinary garden soil. If you buy packaged potting mix make sure it is not just plain muck. Add perlite, vermiculite, or peat moss to such soils. We like to dilute all potting soils with perlite, about one-third by volume. Perlite loosens it, latches on to any excess fertilizer salts the mix may contain and prevents burning of roots.

FEEDING Since plants in containers are confined to a small space they need feeding oftener. We fertilize outdoor containers every two or three weeks during the growing season, using a liquid plant food. If you prefer you can use slow-release plant foods mixed with the soil. Be sure to follow manufacturer's directions.

Vegetables in Containers

You can buy started plants, or start your own (see *Seeds* in Chapter XV). Container gardening lends itself to growing smaller, compact plants such as patio cucumbers, mini-melons, dwarf eggplants, tomatoes, lettuce, radishes, onions, beans, beets, turnips, and herbs. Avoid heavy-rooted crops such as corn (unless you use the dwarf), pumpkins (except bush types), and the like as they need more space for root growth.

The following chart should help in determining the space needed for each vegetable. Containers should not be less than 8 inches deep for most vegetables.

SPACE NEEDED FOR MOST POPULAR VEGETABLES IN CONTAINERS

(For herbs see Chapter X)

Bush Beans 3 or 4 plants per square foot of space.

Pole Beans 2 plants per 12-inch pot.

Beets Sow seeds 3 inches apart (beets are a compound seed) and thin plants to 12 per square foot.

Carrots Sow 3 or 4 seeds per inch and thin to $^3/_4$ inch apart.

Chard (Swiss) Sow 1 to 2 seeds per inch, thin to 4 inches apart.

Cole Crops (cabbage, broccoli, brussels sprouts, kale, collards, kohlrabi, cauliflower) Allow 8 to 10 square inches per plant.

Corn Grow the midget varieties. Plant in clusters so plants are 4 to 5 inches apart.

Cucumbers Allow 8 to 10 square inches per plant.

Eggplants Allow 1 square foot per plant.

Lettuce Sow 2 or 3 seeds per inch; thin to 5 inches apart for leaf lettuce, 6 inches apart for semi-head lettuce.

Muskmelon Allow 1 square foot per plant.

Onion For green scallions sow seed $^1/_2$ inch apart; for mature onions thin to 2 or 3 inches apart.

Peas Sow about 15 seeds per square foot.

Peppers Allow 1 plant per 8 to 10 square inches.

Pumpkins (Midget) Allow 2 square feet per plant.

Radishes Sow 2 or 3 seeds per inch, thin to 1 inch apart.

Spinach 2 or 3 seeds per inch, thin to about 6 square inches per plant.

Squash For summer and bush Winter squash, sow seed 2 or 3 per square foot and thin to 1 plant per square foot.

Tomatoes Allow 1 plant per square foot.

Turnip Sow 4 seeds per inch, thin 2 inches apart.

Note: Do not throw away thinned seedlings; transplant them to another area or give them to a neighbor.

For more detailed information see our book *How To Grow Vegetables Without a Garden*.

Vegtables for Indoor and Outdoor Flower Arrangements

Many "container farmers" grow vegetables that can be used for indoor arrangements. For example, a pretty table decoration can be made by digging up a beet, cutting it in half, and placing the upper part in a bowl with colored stones. If a little water is added, green and red leaves soon appear and last for a long time. Regular kale, growing in pots or among foundation shrubs, produces a beautiful foliage which can be picked and used in bouquets. Ornamental kale, with soft cream, pink, lavender, and green shading, plus crinkled and frilled edges, looks beautiful along a walk or tucked into the foundation planting. Purple basil varieties are fine herbs with reddish-purple leaves and spikes of blue flowers. Dwarf eggplant offers an exotic show with its glossy purple fruit.

There are several ornamental peppers with bright yellow and red fruit on perky dwarf plants. All are edible, but most are hot. Rhubarb chard has crimson stalks and veins, artistically "crumpled" leaves, good in summer arrangements. Bronze ("ruby") lettuce is a handsome border for door entrances and the leaves are edible as well as ideal at the base of flower arrangements. If leaves are picked, rather than the whole plant pulled, the lettuce will keep producing all summer. The cream-yellow blooms of okra are interesting enough to start a conversation at any dinner table.'

Highly colored gourds, while not edible, add a bright touch inside the home during fall and winter as well as providing attractive vines and blooms during the summer.

Gardening on a Fence

While fence gardening isn't exactly container gardening, it's still making the most of a small area. For example, you may have a wooden or iron fence on your property ideal for supporting cucumbers, gourds, tomatoes, eggplants, melons, pole beans, or ornamental scarlet runner beans (which produce edible beans). The fruit of melons grown vertically must be supported by "slings" made of any soft material such as a nylon stocking. Bonded materials have a built-in cushion; knits have a handy two-way stretch. Small varieties of pumpkins (Spookie is a good one) can be grown this way also, if fruit is supported.

Space Savers for Strawberries

If you hanker for a few fresh strawberries, grow some in a hanging basket or two on your sun porch (see later in this chapter for how to prepare a hanging basket) or in a strawberry barrel. If you have a bit more space, try a strawberry pyramid. You can buy a complete pyramid "kit" from a garden catalogue or make your own. The bands or metal edgings should be 5 inches deep. The bottom ring is filled with soil and leveled off, then a smaller ring is added on top of the soil, filled with more soil, and then an ever smaller ring is added. For soil mixture, use two bushels of topsoil mixed with a bushel of peat moss or compost.

Vertical Gardens and Bag Gardens

Strawberries and other crops can be grown in these. Tower or vertical gardens are constructed by standing on end a cylinder made of wire fencing (2- by 4-inch mesh). The cylinder is lined with sisal kraft papers, and filled with a moistened soilless mix. Holes are cut in the cylinder at 4 or 5 inch intervals and plants or seeds are inserted in the mix. Bag gardens can be black plastic or burlap. Moistened soilless mix (or any good potting mix) is stuffed inside, the bag is laid flat and holes are cut at appropriate intervals. Plants or seeds are inserted in the medium. Remember that transplants should be watered when they are set out even if the soil is moist.

Other Fruits in Containers

Dwarf oranges, lemons, limes, and grapefruits can be grown in tubs or large pots both indoors and out. Outdoor pots can be designed to move indoors easily if you live in a cold climate where they need protection during winter. These little beauties grow about 2 to 3 feet high and produce edible fruits. Foliage is handsome and the blossoms are fragrant, appearing several times a year, followed by brilliant fruit that will remain on the tree for months. All citrus prefers a cool night temperature of 50 to 60 degrees F., but full sun in the day. You can buy started plants from a nursery, but if you want an ornamental effect only and are content with small "wild sour fruit," start seeds in a pot. They'll grow into handsome bushes. Syringe leaves of all citrus every day or so as they like high humidity. This also keeps dust off foliage and protects against insects. We like to grow our dwarf citrus with the tubs standing on pans of pebbles with water covering the pebbles, which increases the humidity in the room. (See Chapter XVI for more detail on growing citrus.) You can also grow other fruits in containers, especially dwarf peach, bush cherries, beach plums, blueberries, currants, gooseberries, avocados, figs, and pineapples.

How to Make a Porch or Window Box

Porch or window boxes are useful for growing plants indoors and out, 12 months out of the year. During spring and summer all kinds of plants can be grown in them outdoors, and when frost threatens, the boxes can be brought indoors to grow herbs, flowers, and vegetables for winter harvest. Window or porch boxes can be made of copper, zinc, or galvanized metal or wood. Make them at least 8 inches deep (inside measurement), with the length depending upon space available. For a standard single window, a box 3 1/2 feet long, 8 inches deep, and 10 inches wide is a good size. Measure your window and make your boxes to fit. If made of wood, brass or galvanized screws are best because they resist rusting and fertilizer burn.

To prevent decay, the inside boards should be painted with a safe wood preservative (i.e., non-toxic to plants; your garden store will have one). A hole every 6 inches is needed for drainage in a wooden box. Metal containers are usually provided with false drainage bottoms, and they do not need to be painted unless for decoration. Broken pieces of pots or pebbles can be placed in the bottom of any container to improve drainage.

Boxes can be attached to the houses by means of metal or wooden brackets. You will probably find a subdued color like dark green easier to live with than a bright color. Ordinarily, the color of the flowers and foliage should harmonize with the color of the house, but of course, you can select any kind of plants you want.

SOME PLANTS SUGGESTED FOR PLANTER USE
(Outdoor annuals not hardy for year round use)

The following plant combinations have been chosen for pleasing combinations of color, growth habits, and leaf texture.

Taller plants, which you can use for the center or back of window boxes or other planters, are listed first. Others are low growing, which you may group around the center plants,

---

For Full Sun

French marigolds and Ageratum (Blue Bedder)
Scarlet sage, *Salvia splendens*; "St. Johns Fire," and Dwarf Snapdragon, *Antirrhinum* (white and yellow)
Zinnia (scarlet); French marigold, *Tagetes* (yellow); Creeping Zinnia, *Sanvitalia procumbens flore-pleno* (yellow)

Bedding-type Snapdragon, *Antirrhinum*; Dwarf Celosia, *Plumosa*; Verbena (scarlet) with Variegated Periwinkle, *Vinca major variegata*

Annual Phlox (red, pink, and white); Ageratum (blue); Sweet Alyssum (white)

Geranium (white); Balcony Petunias (dark purple)

Geraniums (pink); Balcony Petunias (white and crimson pink)

Heliotrope (blue); French Marigold, *Tagetes* (yellow with maroon); Dwarf Nasturtium, *Tropaeolum* (scarlet)

Lantana camara (orange); Verbena (purple); Variegated Periwinkle, *Vinca major variegata*

Geranium (salmon pink); Balcony Petunia (deep blue)

French Marigold (yellow); African Marigold (deep orange); Ageratum (blue)

Scarlet sage, *Salvia splendens* (red); Dwarf Celosia Plumosa (gold); Portulaca (golden yellow and scarlet)

Petunia (scarlet); Verbena (dark purple); Verbena (blue or white)

Rainbow pink, *Dianthus chinensis heddewiggii* (dark scarlet); Marigold, *Tagetes tenuifolia, T. signata* (orange); Ageratum (blue)

Petunia (white, striped red); Dwarf Morning Glory, *Convolvulus tricolor* (deep blue with white throat); Variegated-leaf (Ivy) Geranium, *Pelargonium peltatum*

For Light Shade

Begonia semperflorens (red, pink and white); Hanging Lobelia, *Lobelia* (blue with white eye)
Geranium (dark scarlet); Geranium (salmon); Geranium Variegated Foliage with Variegated Periwinkle
Torenia fournieri compacta (deep blue with white); Cup Flower, *Nierembergia*; Purple Robe (purple); Sweet Alyssum (white)
Variegated-leaf Geranium, Dwarf Geranium
Coleus (all colors) with Impatiens (all colors in variegated or green leaves)

For Northern Exposure

Fuchsia or "Tom Thumb" (red and blue); hanging basket fuchsias such as Trailing Queen or Cascade
Begonia semperflorens (red foliage, scarlet flowers)
Lobelia (blue, white, lavender) with Impatiens or Coleus
Tuberous begonias (all colors and types)
Small-leaved Periwinkle, *Vinca minor*
Coleus (all colors) with hanging begonias
Impatiens, "Day Plants" (all colors) with Vinca

SOIL MIXTURE: A common mistake is to make soil too rich for porch boxes, and as a result to get all "bush" and no blooms. A good mixture is one part garden loam, one part peat moss or finely sifted humus, and one part sand. To this add an ounce of balanced plant food like 5-10-5 in each bushel. Soil should be changed once a year for best growth. To fill the box, a $1/2$- to $3/4$-inch layer of sand is placed over the false bottom. The soil mixture is then added to within one or two inches of the top.

LOCATION: Most porch boxes are exposed to a relentless midsummer sun, hence need plants which will tolerate sun. Select plants according to exposure from the list "Some Plants Suggested for Planter Use" earlier in this chapter.

PLANTING: Plants should not be crowded. If the box has a surface area of four square feet, for instance, the right proportion would be five erect plants, such as geraniums, and three vines, such as vincas, or tradescantia. The wider the box, the more plants can be grown. The more soil there is, the less liable are the plants to become dry in hot summer weather. Plants can be set directly into the soil or be allowed to remain as potted in the box.

WATERING AND FEEDING: Water is the most important item in maintaining a porch or window box. Exposed to sun and wind, window and porch boxes should be checked for water every day. If weather is rainy and cool, water is applied less frequently. If plants such as petunias or marigolds are allowed to go dry, they quickly turn brown and go to seed, and the box becomes unsightly. When plants are well established, one or two applications of a water-soluble fertilizer, a month apart, should be sufficient to carry them through the summer.

SUMMER CARE: The growing tips of the plants should be nipped off now and then to keep them bushy and attractive. Faded blossoms should be removed before they go to seed. Seed pods are a drain on the plants and make them unsightly.

Be on the lookout for red spider mites, the most offensive pest of window boxes. Frequent syringing with a garden hose will help control these pests. For more pest controls, see section on Control of Insects and Diseases.

WINTER CARE: In winter, porch or window boxes need not be bare. Instead of storing them, fill them with evergreen trimmings. All kinds of greens can be used, although some kinds are better than others. Australian pine, red pine, Colorado blue spruce, Swiss mountain pine (mugo pine) are all good candidates. Norway spruce is showy for a little while, but the needles drop or become yellowish. Balsam is one of the best for color and persistence of needles.

It's better to use one kind rather than branches of two or three different varieties. Put the taller branches in the center and shorter ones in front or on the ends. Soak the soil in the window box, sharpen the ends of the branches to a point and insert into the soil. Water the box and the soil will freeze, holding the branches in place all winter. We like to string Christmas tree lights on ours, and they're showy when snow falls on them. Cones (natural or painted) can be wired to the branches. A few branches of red ruscus from your florist make an attractive addition. The foliage of evergreens (or laurel branches) can also be spray-painted for effect.

Window boxes can be used for tulips, hyacinths, and other bulbs in spring before the regular season of bedding plants. Bulbs planted in the boxes in fall, stored in cool cellar or cold frame, and brought into a warm window in spring, will bloom indoors.

Some gardeners bring window boxes indoors and grow herbs, onions, snap beans, tomatoes and lettuce. This makes a good winter project for kids.

Exterior Decorating with Tubbed Plants

With the increased use of patios and outdoor "living rooms," tubbed plants are being used more and more as a flexible, inexpensive way to concentrate color where you want it. Plants in pots or tubs can be moved from one place to another to highlight terrace, porch, house entrance, balcony, or what have you. Foliage and blooming plants in tubs, pots, or boxes, can be rearranged or moved just as you would furniture. Your own terrace, lawn, or porch will dictate how you arrange your "living exterior decoration."

TUBBED FLOWERS For colorful flowers to cheer you, you can choose from a huge selection. If sunlight is scarce, try coleus or caladium for dazzling foliage, or grow impatiens, begonias, browallia, and lobelia. Sunny spots can support almost any flower. Dwarf cannas provide bold, glossy green leaves; and we especially like dwarf asters, dwarf zinnias, marigolds, salvia, calendulas, and double petunias (you probably will want to avoid tall upright types such as cosmos or larkspur). Vining flowers like nasturtiums, browallias, lobelias, verbenas, and lantanas are excellent for hanging baskets. For other possibilities see Chapter IV, ANNUALS, Chapter IX, HOUSEPLANT CULTURE and Chapter VI, BULBS, CORMS AND TUBERS.

TUBBED VINES If you have a post or pillar and want to make it less conspicuous (or you want to dramatize it) encourage vines such as German ivy, clematis, vinca, English ivy, Baltic ivy, etc. to entwine it (see *Vines* in Chapter II, Chapter IX, HOUSEPLANT CULTURE). Place a gallon can inside a nail keg on a layer of sand or gravel. Punch holes for drainage, and if you like, paint the kegs to harmonize with the setting. Some vines are rampant growers, so don't hesitate to nip them from time to time.

LARGE POTTED FOLIAGE PLANTS Palms, schefflera, spikes (Dracaena), and other upright foliage plants give a flair to tubs or boxes (and can be a source of instant exotic atmosphere). Today's selection is greater than ever before, and there is a foliage plant to meet every need (see Chapter IX).

TUBBED EVERGREENS AND SHRUBS Tubbed evergreens such as yew, euonymus, hardy boxwood, and also clipped privet, hydrangeas, red spirea, and floribunda roses are suitable to accent the opening to a doorway or terrace. (For more flowering shrubs see Chapter IX.) These shrubs may already be potted in metal or paper maché. It is alright to grow them in these containers (we suggest setting the "nursery container" inside a larger, fancier tub) the first season, but they should be planted in a larger container the next year. For the winter, it's a good idea to set the tubs in the ground and mulch with leaves or straw, as they may winterkill if left on an open terrace (they desiccate or dry out due to winds and lack of moisture in the confined tubs). These pots can be used to soften the appearance of bare steps. Feed them once or twice a year and be sure to give them ample water, especially during the summer, as they have very little moisture and soil to live on.

Green Thumb Hints on Container-Grown Shrubs

Start with the right plants. Shade lovers need shade; sun lovers need sun. Before you buy, check your light situation, for there are plants for every location. Tubbed evergreens, including dwarf spruce, mugo pine, Japanese yew, euonymus, and hardy boxwood are all ideal for accenting the opening to a doorway or terrace. Also, try clipped privet, floribunda roses, and miniatures. If you want a good show during the sizzling heat of July, August, or September, wonderful shrubs for container-scaping include althea, hibiscus, spirea Anthony Waterer, lily-of-the-valley shrub (Pieris or andromeda), coral berry, and snowberry. Others include butterfly-bush, vitex, crepe myrtle, blue mist spirea, and potentilla. Most of these will freeze back in winter, but if you move them to a basement, they'll live over the winter nicely. Whatever you do, avoid giant or aggressive plants. And don't hesitate to start with smaller sizes. They'll take off quicker than larger ones and can acclimatize more easily.

Whether summer or winter, there are a few pitfalls to avoid at planting times:

1. Try not to loosen the soil ball when planting. If the plant is in a paper or tarpaper pot, slit the sides with a sharp knife, then gently lift ball and all, and insert it into the container. Plant it at same depth it grew in the nursery container.
2. Make sure the container is large enough to accommodate the plants nicely. Don't try to jam a $25.00 plant into a $2.00 hole.
3. Firm the soil around the base before you water it.
4. If nursery container is metal, lift it upside down and take out ball and all. Sometimes you have to use a pair of tin shears to remove the sides before lifting out the soil ball.

Note: Watch out for plastic wraps around the ball. Some look like burlap and may fool you into planting wrap and all. Plastic does not break down and the plant will die from lack of water or air. Burlap can be planted with the soil as it rots down, but watch out for plastic substitutes.

MULCHING: A mulch not only helps to prevent moisture loss; it adds beauty to your container-grown plant. White gravel, marble chips, wood chips, bark nuggets all look neat and allow water to seep in readily.

FEEDING: Feed liquid plant food once every three or four weeks while watering. Avoid hot, dry fertilizers with container-grown plants.

TROUBLES: If insects show up, hand picking is effective; so is spraying with any good all-purpose pesticide. Yellow foliage could mean overwatering or poor drainage. If water does not drain fast, drill a couple more holes in the container. Mottled foliage could mean red spider mites. Syringe foliage with a fine mist to keep mites in check. Syringing or watering can be done any time of day or night.

WINTERIZING YOUR PLANTS There are a variety of ways to bring your plants through the winter:

1. Set tubs of hardy plants in the ground and mulch them with leaves or straw. Evergreens and woody ornamentals seldom die from freezing—it's desiccation, or drying out, due to wind, sun, and lack of moisture in the confined soil area.
2. Your plants need only a small amount of light in winter. Move the tub into a garage and out of the wind and sun until spring, when it can be moved back to your terrace or patio. A small platform on wheels makes it easy to jockey your container any place you wish. Wheels from an old lawnmower make a good container dolly.
3. Wrap the entire plant with burlap or cloth screen to keep out hot sun and drying winds. *Never* wrap evergreens or woody ornamentals with plastic sheets, since they trap heat inside and cook the plants. Miniature roses and hybrid teas can be covered with polystyrene cones, but if no holes are in the top, be sure to drill a few for air drainage.
4. Spray plants with anti-desiccant (also called an anti-transpirant) to cut down on winter injury and summer scald.

5. Make sure the soil ball goes into the winter in a moist condition. If it freezes while the roots are dry, the plant will die. On mild winter days, add water to the soil ball if needed.

"SUMMERIZE" YOUR PLANTS Having brought them through the winter, here are some summer tips:

1. "Acclimatize" newly set plants daily for a week by syringing foliage on hot days. This minimizes the shock of transplanting, helps plants become established (and accustomed to being outdoors), keeps down insects, and washes off dust. Water plants at the base as often as needed. Regular syringing in hot weather is a good practice.

2. Groom plants by removing dead twigs, leaves, etc. Shear to give shape (see Chapter III, EVERGREENS, and Chapter 11, LANDSCAPING for pruning tips).

Hanging Baskets

Hanging baskets are back in style. Years ago it was common to see baskets on porches, balconies, and in kitchens. Now they are used everywhere—in windows where there's no room for plant stands—even in bathrooms. Growing plants "in space" by means of hanging baskets is smart and stylish. These suspended containers are popular as a pleasant addition to porch, patio, breezeway, and even trees. They can be used for growing vegetables, fruits, and herbs as well as ornamental plants.

Containers come in many types: solid, perforated, or mesh sides, many plastic. Many gardeners attach wires, cords, leather strips, chains, or ropes (braided, crocheted, woven, macraméd) to flower pots or other containers and make their own hanging baskets. Any receptacle can be used, provided it is not too heavy and has good drainage. A wire frame lined with sphagnum moss, a wooden or plastic basket, a clay pot, or even a kitchen colander or old teakettle works out fine.

Here is a great place to use your imagination. We have seen "pillows" of sheet plastic stuffed with sphagnum moss mixed with one of the soilless mixes. Holes were punched at regular intervals and plants carefully tucked into the holes. They were watered by inserting a small piece of hose in the top. Others we have seen include hollow pieces of wood, large gourds, old-fashioned water dippers, quart berry baskets, cleverly planted plastic jugs with openings cut in the sides, iron kettles, and tin pails, just to name a few. Florists sell many attractive plastic, pottery, woven, and styrofoam baskets ideal for hanging plants.

A hanging pot should always be suspended from a strong hanger or a substantial support. Hardware stores have all sorts of supports that can be adapted to this use.

Indoors, baskets with solid walls should be used to prevent water from dripping onto the floor. Outdoors, mesh containers are okay. Some use a lining of plastic (with small holes for drainage), sphagnum moss, burlap, or leaves in mesh containers to hold soil and moisture.

Remember that good drainage is important, so use pieces of broken pots, pebbles, coarse sand, or charcoal in the bottoms of pots. Holes in the bottom are almost a must. Clay pots slipped into other containers are ideal if care is taken in watering.

SOME PLANTS FOR HANGING BASKETS

Although almost any plant can be adapted to a hanging basket, the following are some of the best candidates. For more information on ferns, see Ferns under HOUSEPLANTS.

Plant Name	Sun or Shade	Adaptability for Summer Growing Outdoors and Winter Care Indoors
Ageratum	Sun	Do not keep over winter. Start new plants from seed.
Artillery plant (*Pilea*)	Shade	Outdoors or indoors. Can be carried over in home
Asparagus plumosus (fine-foliaged Florists' Asparagus Fern)	Semi-shade	Indoors or outdoors. Likes moist, warm atmosphere.
Asparagus sprengeri ("needled-foliage" Asparagus Fern)	Sun or shade	Easier to grow than A. plumosus, Indoors and outdoors, if given enough moisture.
Begonia: Rex	Shade	Hanging types do well outdoors and indoors if left in shade. Likes yearly repotting.
Rieger	Shade	Does well indoors if nipped back severely after bloom period.
Tuberous	Shade and semi-shade	Better outdoors: bulbs need a 3- or 4-month rest over winter.
Wax (*B. Semperflorens*)	Shade or sun	Do better outdoors. Tend to get scraggly indoors if carried over.
Boston Fern (*Nephrolepis*)	Shade	Indoors and outdoors in shade. Leaflets shed if air or soil is too dry.
Browallia	Sun or semi-shade	Peters out indoors after summer bloom. Start new plants in spring or take cuttings.
Caladium	Shade	Give corms a rest period during winter by storing in peat moss.
Christmas Cactus, Easter Cactus, Thanksgiving Cactus	Sun, semi-shade	(See Chapter IX.)
Coleus	Sun or shade	Sheds leaves indoors if air is too dry. Handsome colors in shade. (See Chapter IV.)

SOME PLANTS FOR HANGING BASKETS (Continued)

Plant Name	Sun or Shade	Adaptability for Summer Growing Outdoors and Winter Care Indoors
Creeping Fig (*Ficus*)	Sun or semi-shade	Keep soil uniformly moist but not soggy. Indoors.
Dallas Fern	Shade	Same care as Boston Fern.
Dusty Miller (*Dwarf variety of Boston Shade*)	Sun or shade	Can be carried over. Make new plants from cuttings. Fairly hardy indoors or out.
English Ivy (Hedera)	Sun or shade	Hardy outdoors but will grow indoors. Start new cuttings from tips. Syringe foliage to keep down red spider mites.
Fuchsia	Sun or shade	Should be cut back in fall as it prefers rest period from fall to February. Start new plants from tips.
Geranium, Ivy (*Pelargonium*)	Sun or semi-shade	Shy bloomer indoors until after spring.
Grape Ivy (*Cissus*)	Sun or shade	Indoors or outdoors, but must be brought in before frost.
Impatiens	Sun or shade	Indoors leaves shed due to hot air or dry soil. Syringe to check red spider mites. (See Chapter IV.)
Lantana	Sun or semi-shade	Nip tips back to encourage new growth indoors.
Lobelia	Sun or shade	Start new plants in spring. Gets ratty looking indoors.
Marigold (dwarf) (*Tagetes*)	Sun	Does well carried over if you can keep it free of red spider mites.
Morning Glory (*Ipomoea*)	Sun	Fast twiner. Should be nipped in winter to keep it from getting scraggly indoors. May not bloom during winter.
Nasturtiums	Sun	Skimpy bloomer indoors, but foliage of variegated varieties attractive in winter.

SOME PLANTS FOR HANGING BASKETS (Continued)

Plant Name	Sun or Shade	Adaptability for Summer Growing Outdoors and Winter Care Indoors
Pansy and Viola	Sun or shade	Tends to get sprawly during winter if carried over. Start new plants in spring.
Pepper (ornamental)	Sun	Handsome hot peppers (edible). Save seed to start new plants.
Petunia	Sun or semi-shade	In fall cut plants back $1/2$ and bring indoors. Keep seed pods removed.
Philodendron (several types)	Sun or semi-shade	Fast growers indoors or out.
Picka-back plant (Piggy back) (*Tolmiea*)	Sun or shade	Bring indoors; divide, if overgrown, in fall.
Plectranthus (Swedish Ivy)	Sun or shade	Outdoors or indoors, not hardy. Good as winter vine.
Portulaca	Sun	Okay for summer outdoors in full sun. Do not carry over indoors. Start new plants in spring.
Pothos (Devil's Ivy) (Also listed as *Scindapsus* or *Epiprimum*)	Shade	Not hardy. Ideal indoor vine.
Shrimp plant (*Beloperone*)	Sun	Bring indoors, trim back heavily. Start new cuttings for next year.
Spider Plant (Airplane Plant) (*Chlorophytum*)	Shade or semi-shade	Works well outdoors and indoors. Does not form plantlets indoors if given too much artificial light at night.
Strawberry Begonia (*Saxifraga tomentosa*)	Semi-shade or shade	Good indoors or outdoors. Prefers semi-shade to form plantlets.
String bean (snap bean)	Sun	Do not bring indoors in fall. Start new plants from seed. Enjoy fresh beans in winter months.
Sweet Potato	Sun or shade	If plants get scraggly start new plant from another potato.

SOME PLANTS FOR HANGING BASKETS (Continued)

Plant Name	Sun or Shade	Adaptability for Summer Growing Outdoors and Winter Care Indoors
Tomato	Sun	Cascading varities called Sweet Million and others are ideal for hanging baskets. Year round indoors and out. Start seed anytime. To keep free of white fly and red spider mites see section on Control of Insects and Diseases.
Tradescantia ("Wandering Jew")	Sun or shade	Bring indoors. Fast grower. Nip tip back and start new plants. Small-leaf variety not suited for outdoors in sun. Likes shade.
Zebrina ("Wandering Jew")	Sun or shade	Same as for *Tradescantia*.
Zinnia, Creeping (*Sanvitalia*)	Sun	Do not carry over indoors. Start new plants in spring.

Care of Hanging Baskets

SOIL: Soil for hanging baskets should contain a high percentage of organic matter. Try using half soil and half peat moss, and to each gallon or pail of mix add 1 tablespoon of lime and 1 tablespoon of garden fertilizer, either organic or inorganic, and mix thoroughly. Perlite or vermiculite added to the mixture will help loosen it for good drainage.

WATERING: After the container has been planted, water it thoroughly. Baskets hanging in the sun will dry out fast and may have to be watered daily. Indoors, they may need watering just as often. When watering, give a good soaking. Mix a little water-soluble or liquid plant food with the water every three or four weeks. Make sure water doesn't stand in the bottom following a heavy rain.

FEEDING: Plants confined in a small space use up nutrients readily. Also, daily watering removes many nutrients (by leaching). One of the best ways to replace lost nutrients is to feed a liquid plant food once a month. Slow-release fertilizers are available and do a good job, also. Watch out for ordinary dry fertilizers, which may burn the plants.

GROOMING: Since hanging baskets are quite conspicuous in their setting, go over your plants once a week and cut out dead leaves, old flowers, and seed pods. If your plants are getting too leggy (as petunias or coleus often do) cut them back a few inches to make new growth.

WINTER CARE: Many folks want to bring their hanging basket plants indoors for the winter after having enjoyed them outdoors during the summer months. There are three things you can do for winter: 1) Continue to grow the plants for a winter show; 2) Let the plants go dormant until late winter or early spring and then start them up again; 3) Discard the plants and store the baskets until the following spring. Whatever you do, do not leave plastic containers in cold spots, as they will crack when frozen.

Plan 1 calls for shaping the plants by removing several inches of the end growth. Simply pinch or snip the tips back about half. Remove old seed pods, flowers, and dead material which can be unsightly and encourage disease and insects. Most plants will benefit if cut back quite a bit. Plan 2 means storing the baskets in a cool basement or attic where there's some light. You'll have to keep the soil moistened from time to time to keep the plants alive. Plan 3 is best if your plants are ragged and the soil is petered out.

You can take cuttings of your favorite plants such as coleus, impatiens, and others and use them in the baskets next spring. Ferns, ivies, hard-leaved foliage plants can be kept for next year.

TROUBLES: Outdoors, hanging baskets have few insects or disease problems. They may get scraggly but grooming (see above) takes care of that.

When plants are brought indoors, be on the lookout for red spider mites, aphids, scale or mealybugs. Warm, dry air in homes favors growth of these pests. Grooming discourages diseases and insects. See Chapter XIV for ways to deal with these pests.

CHAPTER IX

Houseplant Culture

•

Rare is the house or apartment without some flowering or foliage plant, even in hard times. Plants, like pets, give comfort to the human soul. You can tell much about a person's nature and temperament by the plants he has in his home. People who enjoy plants have a better insight on life, and seem to be more understanding than those who have no use for plants.

The farther modem society is removed from nature, the greater the demand for living plants as soothing, silent companions in homes, apartments, hotels, offices, airports, and other public buildings.

The National Aeronautics and Space Administration (NASA) told the world that there's a good reason to grow house plants: They remove formaldehyde and other health-threatening pollutants from indoor air. Plants are green living filters. We spend 90 percent of our time inside energy-efficient houses where air is two to five times more polluted than the air outside. Plants are the answer to the high-rise or sick building syndrome. NASA studies on using house plants to reduce indoor pollution found that the following species reduced the levels of three common household pollutants—formaldehyde, benzene and trichloroethylene.

Aloe barbadensis (A.vera), or medicine plant

Chamaedorea seifrizii (bamboo palm, reed palm)

Chlorophytum elatum vittatum (or spider, air plant)

Chrysanthemum morifolium, pot mum or florist's mum

Dracaena deremensis "Janet Craig" (Janet Craig dracaena)

Dracaena deremensis "Warneckeii," Warneckeii dracaena

Dracaena marginata (Dragon tree)

Gerbera jamesonii (African daisy, Gerbers daisy, or Transvaal daisy)

Hedera helix (English Ivy)

Musa or banana tree (dwarf)

Philodendron oxycardium (heart-leaf philodendron or P. Cordatum)

Philodendron selloum, lacy tree philodendron

Sansevieria trifasciata ("Laurentii") Bowstring hemp, snake plant, and mother-in-law's tongue

Spathiphyllum "Mauna Loa," peace lily, spatheflower, or Mauna loa plant

While the data from NASA is only the beginning, it is a good start for the argument that common indoor plants can be a very effective way to provide pollution-free homes and workplaces ... to say nothing of the comfort we get from watching them grow.

Houseplants are divided into two groups: the flowering types and the foliage types. Once you understand the basic principles of houseplant culture you should get more mileage from both of these.

Basic Principles of Houseplant Culture

LIGHT To some plantsmen, no other factor is more important in governing the growth of plants. Indoors, most plants do best in a southwest window. Intense light but not necessarily direct sunlight is needed to produce flower buds on nearly all flowering plants, some needing less light than others. Most foliage plants are of tropical origin and need less light (they are used to being shaded in the jungle). Some plants need a short day to produce blooms, and they are called short-day plants. Others need a long day before they'll bloom. Mums will set flower buds, and bloom only when the day length is short. That's why your mums do not bloom in June when the day is long. By influencing the length of day, greenhouse owners can produce chrysanthemums the year round, even though the plants are normally fall-blooming.

TEMPERATURE Plants make their food during the day, but they "digest" it during the night hours. When greenhouse operators talk about temperatures, it's the night temperature they refer to; day temperatures aren't considered vital.

Plants vary in their requirements. Some like it hot, some like it cold. Probably the best temperature for most plants in winter is 70 degrees F. in day and 55 degrees F. at night, with a few exceptions such as African violets. A high night temperature causes food in plants to be used up too quickly, followed by yellowing of foliage. You can have a day fluctuation between 45 and 80 degrees F. with no serious results, if your plants have a low night temperature. That's why it's a good idea to place your plants in a cool room at night, or turn the thermostat down. One reason why our grandmothers grew better houseplants than we do is because room temperatures then were lower, especially at night. Bedrooms were seldom heated. If your houseplants have soft, spindly growth, pale foliage, and the buds blast or drop prematurely, you will usually find that the temperature is too high. At night put your plants in a cool room, 60 degrees F. or lower, and see how much difference it makes in prolonging their life and improving their appearance.

HUMIDITY Although most modern homes are too hot and dry, it's still possible to raise good flowering plants by resorting to some green thumb tricks. While the proper relative humidity in the home is from 35 to 40 percent, the air indoors often goes as low as 12 percent. This is 8 to 11 percent lower than the average relative humidity in the Sahara Desert in the summertime, much too dry for human or plant comfort. Plants grow best when the humidity is from 80 to 90 percent, although we cannot (and probably wouldn't want to) maintain this in our homes. In a greenhouse the relative humidity is usually 60 percent or more. This explains why plants start to turn brown around the edges, flowers drop and buds shed, soon after being moved from the moist atmosphere of the greenhouse or even from the garden, in the fall.

You can increase the humidity in a room by putting a pan of water on the radiators or register. Also place a galvanized or zinc tray on the windowsill for your plants, and fill with pebbles, then add water to the tray until it barely covers the pebbles. Syringing foliage increases humidity if done once or twice a week. And don't forget the old kitchen teakettle. It used to sing songs and make plants happy with extra humidity. Plants themselves help release moisture into the room, and thus are healthy for humans. For example, the leaves of an average-sized cineraria give off as much as three times more water as would be evaporated from the surface of a 4-inch pan of water.

WATERING Watering is an art. A greenhouse operator will tell you that the man with the hose determines the profits and losses. One reason home gardeners have so much trouble watering plants is due to the pots themselves. Plastic and glazed pots are trickier to use than the old-fashioned florist clay pot. They are non-porous and do not "breathe" or allow air to enter. Thus the soil does not dry so fast, and when plants are watered with the same frequency as those in clay pots, the result is overwatering. Water accumulates, shuts off oxygen to the roots, and causes stunting, yellowing of foliage, and shedding of buds.

Why do new houseplants do poorly after being in the home for a few weeks or months? When you first get the plants they are nice and green. That's because the commercial grower grew them under high humidity, gave them good lighting, and regular feeding and watering. Now, when these plants are placed in the low humidity common to most building interiors, many older leaves become yellow or brownish and drop. This leaf drop occurs even though "I watered the plant regularly." These plants haven't developed a sufficient root system to take up enough water to keep proper moisture levels within the plant tissue under the conditions of the average household environment, so leaves drop. Most of us either overwater or underwater. A moisture meter is handy, but without one, here are a few tips to go by to tell if plants need water:

1. Feel soil surface with your fingers. If soil is dry down about one inch it's starting to get dry. This system is quite accurate for any size plant.
2. For clay or plastic pots, insert a dry toothpick into the soil. If some soil or moisture sticks to it when the pick is pulled out, no watering is needed.
3. Tapping any pots with metal. If you tap a pot with a spoon or hose nozzle and get a dull sound, it means there's enough moisture present. If you get a hollow ring instead of a thud, you'll know the soil is dry.
4. Look at the plants. If leaves are slightly droopy and top of soil is dry, it usually means they need some water.

Best time to water is in the morning and it can be done from top or bottom, as long as you are careful not to splash water all over the leaves.

When you water plants give them a good soaking. Don't tease them with a sprinkling. Remember plants in small pots dry out fast because of limited soil volume. They may need watering daily. When soil dries out in a pot, the earth shrinks away from the sides of the pot. Then when you apply water, most of it actually runs down the inside, and is lost before it can be absorbed. That's why a plant can be dry even though you think you gave it lots of water. *Note:* If you repot a plant it should be watered immediately.

A plant that has drooped from lack of water usually can be revived by placing the pot in a pan of warm water until it perks up. In fact some plant lovers feel that a good way to water is to set the plant, pot and all, half-submerged in a dish or pan. After the plant waters itself completely, allow surplus to drain off. Keep in mind that pots with drainage openings need more water than those without openings. Glazed decorative pots without drainage facilities can be made more suitable for growing by placing small pieces of charcoal or stones in the bottom. Even then you are apt to overwater and suffocate the plant. We much prefer double potting when there is no drainage hole. All this means is that you pot the plant in a well drained pot and set it in the decorative pot. You can pack peat moss in between the two pots. Keep the peat moss moist and the plant is watered automatically.

Also note that a plant in a clay pot loses 50% (half) of the water you give it to evaporation. Water does not evaporate in plastic pots so you can cut your watering in half.

WATERING PLANTS WHILE YOU VACATION: Your plants need not go dry while you vacation away from home. One helpful trick is to lay a few building bricks in the bathtub with about 1 1/2 inches of water. Pots placed on the bricks are automatically watered for at least two weeks. Another trick is to place several thicknesses of newspapers in a pan, saturate them well, and place the pots on these. Other gardeners sink their pots in vermiculite, wet peat, or sawdust. Saturate these materials and water the plants first before packing the pots to their rims. Plants will keep three or four weeks in this manner. Another trick worth trying: Place plastic bags over the plants and tie them securely around the pot. This forms a vapor-tight terrarium which makes a fine "plantsitter" for three or four weeks. Some plants such as begonias, saxifraga, pilea, and many "soft-leaved" plants, do not tolerate the excess humidity inside the plastic sheet, but it's worth the try, especially for most foliage plants.

HARD WATER VS. SOFT WATER: Some gardeners prefer rainwater or melted snow for their plants. Azaleas and other "acid-loving" plants do not like hard water and nearly all water coming from wells in limestone areas will have some degree of hardness. Hardness is caused when water containing dissolved carbon dioxide comes in contact with limestone in the soil, forming a carbonate. If your soap curdles or doesn't lather well, chances are your water is hard. Another simple test is to look for a scaly deposit adhering to the inside of the teakettle. Or you can test water with litmus paper, available in drugstores. If it turns the litmus paper blue, the water is alkali or hard, and if it turns red, the water is acid and is not likely to be hard.

IS A WATER SOFTENER HARMFUL TO PLANTS? In most cases water passing through mechanical softeners does have a harmful effect on plant growth. Hard water contains large amounts of calcium and magnesium. Softeners exchange the calcium (harmless to plants) for sodium (harmful to plants). Sodium has a tendency to puddle the soil (make it sticky) or "deflocculate" it, leaving such soils in poor physical condition. In addition, sodium is taken up by plants, forming a toxic substance. Our water softener is hooked to the hot-water line only. However, the newer softeners appear to have no adverse effect. One reader wrote us: "I have used water which goes through our softener for three years and we have beautiful houseplants. However, I don't just draw the water and use it at once. I water my plants once a week (or as necessary) and I keep 3 gallons of water in plastic jugs to which I have added $1/8$ teaspoon of a liquid plant food per gallon. I use this water and immediately refill the jars for use the following week, so that it has settled for a week before being used. No problem at all."

IS CHLORINE IN WATER HARMFUL TO HOUSEPLANTS? Probably not, although many of our friends emphatically state that chlorine-treated water is harmful to plants. Perhaps the greatest concentration of chlorine is early in the morning when the water is first turned on, after standing all night in pipes. To be on the safe side, allow tap to run a few minutes before gathering water, since chlorine disappears rapidly upon aeration. Or better still, allow tap water to remain in a pail overnight before applying to plants. However, fluorine does not dissipate.

There are some plants that show reaction to fluorine in tap water. Some foliage plants in certain areas of the country show tip burning when the soil or water contains as little as $1/10$ ppm of fluorine. Since some municipal water supplies have as much as ten times this amount (added to reduce tooth decay) rainwater, well water, or water from a defrosted refrigerator should be used instead for these plants. Be sure your rainwater is not acidic.

If there is a suspicion that water treated with fluoride is a troublemaker or if your soil mixture has fluorides, don't be alarmed because it's easy to correct. Simply add some limestone or gypsum to counteract it. Use gypsum at the rate of 1 teaspoon per 5-inch pot of soil, or lime, 2 teaspoons per 6-inch pot. It's also a simple matter to offset fluoride in tap water. We use a "Hydrion" paper dispenser, to test the pH or acidity. If the water tests acid, we add a little lime to sweeten it up to around pH 6 or 6.5 (almost neutral). In this range fluorides are tied up and plants will not absorb them. A simple litmus paper test (see Chapter XIII) can be used to determine the acidity of your water or potting soil.

SOIL MIXTURES You cannot go out in your garden and scoop up soil for houseplants. Good soils are made, not born. The new "soilless soil mixtures" or "peatlite" mixes, perfected by Cornell University, University of California, and other state colleges, are a boon to commercial and home growers who want to start plants from seeds and cuttings, and who want to repot plants. These mixes are sterile, weed free and provide ample drainage. Good drainage means good growth. Plants in a heavy soil will turn yellow due to poor drainage and a lack of oxygen around the roots. These mixes are ideal for all types of plants except cacti, which like sand added, and acid lovers, which need more peat moss. Complicated soil mixes for specific plants are not necessary.

A good soil mixture for most houseplants is made up of 1 part sphagnum peat moss (or compost), 1 part sand, 1 part garden loam and 1 part perlite or vermiculite. The only plants to benefit from a larger amount of peat are gardenias, azaleas, some citrus and other acid-loving items.

Many "store-bought" black potting mixes are not satisfactory, as they may be pure muck and not drain well. Some of these mixes have been sterilized, others have not. Some hold moisture too long, causing roots to rot, or plants to suffocate.

To offset this, we recommend adding perlite to most packaged mixes at least $1/3$ by volume. Perlite (a volcanic ash) increases the porosity of the soil, allowing air to enter to the roots and promotes better drainage.

Packaged soil mixes sometimes stand in stores at room temperature for long periods of time. Stacked on top of each other or near a radiator, the mixes are moist enough to permit bacterial activity inside the bag. In the process, heat is generated and organic material is broken down, releasing plant nutrients. Added to the fertilizer already put in by the manufacturer, these could make it "hot" for plant roots. That's why we recommend the addition of perlite to potting mixes. Each particle of perlite absorbs water, helping to keep roots cool and moist, and at the same time taming "hot" or soluble salts.

CHARCOAL, A PURIFIER: "Musty" or moldy soils mean poor drainage and usually additions of charcoal, sand, or perlite will help prevent this. While charcoal contributes very few plant nutrients, it is a valuable soil conditioner and purifier. Small pieces of charcoal in the soil aid drainage and absorb impurities from the soil solution. Charcoal briquettes should not be used in place of wood charcoal to sweeten potting soil. (Briquettes are held together with chemicals.)

If you're interested in sterilizing soil of houseplants, see Chapter XV, PLANT PROPAGATION, and Chapter XIV, ORGANIC GARDENING.

FEEDING Nearly all plants respond to regular applications of plant food, applied preferably in liquid form and in light doses. Coffee grounds, tea leaves, eggshell water (eggshells soaked in water), castor oil, etc., offer only mild encouragement to starved plants. Liquid plant foods are increasingly popular for all types of houseplants because they are safe and easy to use. Our house and greenhouse plants are fed with a liquid food at the rate of 1 level teaspoon to 2 quarts of water, and applied every three or four weeks. Many good gardeners swear by fish emulsion as an excellent plant food for indoor and outdoor plants alike. Slow release plant foods are popular but be careful not to add other fertilizers to soils containing them or plants get a double dose which may burn roots. While many plants are dormant in winter, it's still a good idea to feed them lightly to maintain color. Be safe and avoid "farm fertilizers" for houseplants unless you know what you are doing.

WHY HOUSEPLANTS LEAVE HOME: Some people burn their plants up with fertilizers. If plants aren't doing well, it doesn't necessarily mean they need feeding. Plant foods are *not* a cure-all and are not a substitute for good culture. Quite often, too much feeding will cause concentration of salts (including potassium, calcium, nitrates, phosphate, sulfates, and chlorides) to build up in the soil. The college term "soluble salts" refers to the particles (ions) which are found in the soil and which dissolve easily in water. Too many salts damage the roots, cause chlorosis (yellowing of foliage), wilting, leaf burn ("necrosis"), stunting, slow growth of seedlings or cuttings, and actual death of the plant. Here's how a plant gets too many salts: 1) Heavy doses of fertilizer. Use liquid plant foods. Light, infrequent applications are better than heavy doses. 2) High concentrations of salts in the water supply. Use rain water. 3) Poor drainage or plugged drainage holes.

REPOTTING DRACAENA.

Matted roots show need of repotting.

Plants need repotting from time to time. Sometimes if leaves show an abnormal symptom, it's good idea to look at the roots. To do this, tip plant upside down, and tap or "tunk" ridge of pot against the edge of a table. Remove some old soil and replace with fresh mixture of one part each sand, peat, and loam.
(*Courtesy Under Glass Magazine*)

If you see white salts on the surface of your soil, loosen up the soil with tines of a fork. Water the soil heavily; then repeat in a half hour. The first watering dissolves the salts, the second flushes them from the soil. Florists call this 'leaching," an effective method of reducing heavy salt concentrations. Or you can scrape off the surface soil and replace with fresh soil.

REPOTTING Sooner or later all houseplants become "potbound" (the roots fill the pot). A little "potboundness" is desirable in that it encourages blooming and keeps plants from growing out of bounds too rapidly. In fact, you should avoid "overpotting" or moving to too large a pot for this reason. However, too much potboundness is followed by stunted growth, falling leaves, and a generally unsightly plant. No hard and fast rule can be made for repotting, since plants vary greatly in their habits. The pot size is determined by the growth habit. For example, slow-growing items such as cacti do not need large pots, nor frequent potting. Rapid-growing plants such as begonias need repotting more often. Repotting should always be to a slightly larger pot, for example, from a 4-inch pot to a 6-inch size. When repotting, remove a small portion of the old soil and matted roots: this stimulates development of new roots. You should also replenish the old soil with new mixture.

Potting soils should be moist but not wet, since such soils often pack too hard. And keep in mind that finely sifted soils are okay for seedlings, but not acceptable for houseplants. Finely prepared soils bake, crack, and often become hard.

STERILIZING USED POTS: Both clay and plastic pots are expensive, and while used ones may have fungi or bacteria on them, they need not be discarded. If you want to guard against contamination, scrub the pots with a brush and soak them for ten to fifteen minutes in a solution of household bleach at the rate of 1 part bleach to 9 parts water. A fresh solution of bleach should be made for each batch of pots and it's best not to use a solution for longer than a half hour. Better wear rubber gloves while dipping the pots. The residue on the treated pots is effective against stem rot of geranium, dieback organism, and root rots, but never use this solution directly on plants.

Pots can also be put into boiling water for twenty minutes, or washed in your dishwasher. Plastic pots will melt in water over 160 degrees F., so it's best to treat them differently.

Fertilizer salts on pots can be removed by brushing with a wire brush. Boiling detergent solutions will often help remove the fertilizer salts found on the inside and outsides of pots.

PINCHING PLANTS One reason houseplants are tall, spindly, and lopsided is that they are never pinched back. Most greenhouse operators would go out of business if they never pinched their snapdragons, mums, and other crops. Pinching merely consists of removing the tip of a plant after it has developed anywhere from four to six leaves. To pinch you simply take your thumb and forefinger and pinch out the tip. This makes your plants nice and bushy, so they'll branch out instead of growing straight up. In most instances, the pinched tips of houseplants may be rooted in moist sand or tap water to make new plants. See Chapter XV.

SUMMER CARE OF HOUSEPLANTS Although some houseplant growers won't agree we feel that summer's a fine time to give many of your plants a vacation outdoors, as it helps build up vigor for winter growth. Sink the plants in the ground up to the rim of pot, in shade or semi-shade and water them once or twice a week. If you have a shady back porch or terrace, try moving house ferns, gardenias, begonias, and other shade-lovers there. A gentle misting once every week or so will give these plants a new lease on life.

One of our readers tells us when she sets out flower pots in the garden in summer, she first places a piece of nylon net (double thickness of old nylon stockings) under the pot and folds it up around before sinking the pot into the ground. This prevents worms and insects from getting in the drainage hole and roots from growing through it. In this way you do not have to turn the pots and they lift out easily. Often when plants such as poinsettia, Christmas cactus, or hydrangea are lifted out of their summer resting place, the leaves will drop or wilt because the roots are broken off. The nylon net eliminates this. Inspect your plants when you bring them back in to be sure no insects, eggs or larvae are on leaves or stems.

How to Increase Your Houseplants

Houseplants are increased by three common methods: Seeds, leaf and stem cuttings ("slips"), and by division. For details on these methods, see Chapter XV.

Be Your Own Plant Doctor

Houseplants fall heir to physiological troubles, as well as to insect and disease pests. Armed with a few green thumb facts you can track down most houseplant ailments and correct them. The following are a few of the common physiological problems you're apt to come across with your flowering plants.

BLINDNESS: This is failure of plants to produce flower buds. Environment is likely to be the cause. Look for poor light, low or high temperature, improper nutrition. African violets will not set buds readily if kept too cool (below 65 degrees F.), whereas azaleas prefer a cool temperature for bud formation and flowering (40 to 65 degrees F.). Many plants have "hidden" requirements which must be met before buds set.

CHLOROSIS: A sickly, yellowed appearance of plants is often due to a lack of nitrogen or a lack of iron. Balanced feeding of iron chelates correct this. (See Chapter XIII, SOILS AND FERTILIZERS.)

LEAF SCORCHING: A dry browning of the tips or edges of leaves is found among ferns, begonias, and hundreds of other items. This can be a sign of inadequate water, excess fertilizer, sun-burning, or not enough humidity.

STUNTED GROWTH: Poor growth accompanied by dark, undersized leaves are often signs of lack of phosphorus. Balanced feeding corrects this. A lack of moisture will cause the same type of growth. Soft growth during winter is generally due to a combination of high heat and insufficient light.

EFFECT OF GAS FUMES ON PLANTS: Artificial or manufactured gas and coal gas have a bad effect on many houseplants. Natural gas isn't as hard on plants. Quite often a concentration so small as to be undetected by the human nose will cause carnations to "go to sleep." Many plants will lose their foliage from leaking gas or gas fumes, especially in winter because rooms are poorly ventilated.

Natural gas is more difficult to detect indoors because it works differently on plants. Usually the stems start to harden, or plants make poor or slow growth, as if stunted, and leaves will yellow or distort. If you cook by gas, light the burner immediately because each time you turn it on before lighting a match you allow some gas to escape into the room. Ventilating as much as possible is the best way to cope with gas fumes.

INSECTS THAT ATTACK HOUSEPLANTS Houseplants are subject to attack from insects and disease 365 days out of the year, but fortunately, we have methods to combat them that are safer and better than ever. We've advocated using 1 tablespoon of liquid household detergent in a gallon of water for spraying leaves. Now we have Safer and Murphy Soap solutions which can be mixed in your kitchen sink. These also come ready-to-use. Even cooking oil (safflower, peanut oil, sunflower oil, etc.) mixed with detergent and water is good for fighting indoor pests, according to USDA tests.

Some gardeners dip small houseplants into a bucket of the solution. Put a collar around the pot, covering the soil surface with plastic wrap or aluminum foil to keep soil from falling into the bucket. Two treatments a week apart should control pests. Pushbutton spray cans are handy, but make sure the material is for use on plants; otherwise you may "burn" them. Hold spray can about 18 inches from the surface of leaves and cover both top and undersides.

Nicotine is an excellent aphicide. Tobacco (from which nicotine sulfate is made), soaked in water until the color of strong tea, is good for pouring on soil to get rid of such insects as symphilids, spring tails, and fungus gnats. Caution: do not leave solution where someone might drink it. Can be toxic. Also, spray in well ventilated area and do not breathe in fumes.

For a chart of both organic and chemical controls of insects and detailed information on relatively safe homemade and commercial pesticides, See. Chapter XIV, Section on Control of Insects and Diseases.

HOW TO DISCOURAGE INSECTS: One way to keep insects and diseases from plants in your home (or greenhouse) is to practice sanitation and segregation. Watch out for the friend who wants to give you plants, or wants you to "babysit" for his plants while on vacation: your "boarder" plant could be a source of noxious insects. For example, fuchsia could harbor red spider mites or white fly; coleus could harbor mealybugs, aphids and white fly; citrus plants could harbor scale, mealybugs, and white fly; palms could be a haven for scales, mealybugs, mites, and thrips; gardenia is favored by mealybug, white fly, and red spider mites, etc.

If you must bring a plant into your home or greenhouse, be sure to inspect it first with a hand lens. It will help you detect tiny insects and eggs. As an added precaution, spray (covering undersides of leaves as well as topsides) or dip plants in one of the previously mentioned pesticides.

HOUSEPLANT DISEASES Houseplants are subject to a number of diseases. You can keep them to a minimum by good grooming (removing dead leaves immediately), using a good soil mixture (one that's well drained), and by not overwatering. Overwatering is probably the greatest single cause of plant diseases. If you use your own soil to mix with sand and peat moss, baking it at 180 degrees F. for a half hour will take care of most of the harmful organisms. Washed sand from a lumber yard and peat moss don't need to be sterilized. Don't forget to treat used pots, either by boiling (not plastic, of course) or using household bleach (see *Sterilizing Used Pots*).

Nowadays, foliage plants appear to be afflicted with more diseases than flowering plants. One of the reasons is related to the "green plant boom." Southern growers are shipping tropical foliage plants to all parts of the country via air, truck, and train.

To fill demands, the growers "force" plants by giving them plenty of heat, moisture, and fertilization. These conditions are good for plant growth, but they're also conducive to the development of plant disease. Some of these plants have a poor root system, and most of them have not been "acclimatized"—conditioned to grow in a home, office, or shopping mall. And often the customer does not get sufficient cultural information. Many troubles could be eliminated if the customer knew something about the requirements of the plant he purchased. Most of the problems that arise are due to improper watering—either too much or too little.

For easier identification, we have divided the diseases into two groups: Those common to flowering plants, and those that more commonly affect foliage plants. Occasionally a flowering plant will fall ill to a disease in the second group, or vice versa.

If after reading the charts you can find no apparent cause for trouble, knock the plant out of the pot and check for soil insects around the roots, and also drainage. If insects are present, dunk soil ball in solution of nicotine (see section on Insect & Disease Control).

Naturally, there's more to fighting foliage diseases than we've presented. The subject is complicated, but to grow healthy plants in your home remember these rules: 1) Practice sanitation. 2) Don't overwater. 3) Don't overfeed. 4) Use a sterile soil mix, and sterilize used pots. 5) Be sure to provide good drainage.

SOME COMMON DISEASES OF FLOWERING PLANTS

Disease	Damage	Control
Botrytis or "fireblight"	Buds and blossoms dry up and die.	Good air circulation. Dust with Captan. Pick off brown or shrivelled buds, blossoms and leaves, and destroy.
Crown rot or Stem rot	Fungi or bacteria cause foliage to yellow or rot at soil level.	Avoid overwatering. Use good drainage, sterilize soil. (See Plant Propagation, Chapter XV.) Dust plant and soil with Ferbam, Captan, or Benlate.
Damping-off disease	Seedlings rot at base and topple over.	Use sterile soil mix, do not sow seed too thickly; give good air circulation. Dust soil with Captan or Ferbam, when seedlings first appear.
Mosaic virus ringspot, leaf spot	Yellow spotted or mottled foliage, stunted growth.	None. Destroy plant.
Powdery mildew	White, fuzzy spots on leaves and stems. Eventually leaves turn brown and drop off.	Set in sun, give good air circulation. Turn on electric fan on cloudy days to get air circulating. Dust weekly with sulfur or Karathane.

Disease	Damage	Control
Rhizoctonia root rot	Sudden wilting of tips, followed by collapse of entire plant.	Use sterilized soil mix, or pasteurize your own. (See "Sterilizing your Soil," in Chapter XV.) No chemical control once disease sets in.
Verticillium	Same damage and control as Rhizoctonia.	

We have divided foliage plant diseases into two parts: leaf or foliage diseases and soil-borne diseases.

LEAF OR FOLIAGE DISEASES

Disease	Damage	Control
Alternaria blight	Small circular black lesions. Often a halo is seen around the diseased area. Found often on schefflera (*Brassaia*)	Always keep foliage dry. This helps control all foliage diseases.
Brown leaf spot	Small yellow lesions that enlarge, then turn brown. Worst on dieffenbachia.	Keep leaves dry.
Cercospora leaf spot	$1/4''$ spot on leaf like a frog's eye. Found on rubber tree, peperomia, etc.	Do not overwater.
Dactylaria ("White leaf specks disease")	White stippling of foliage. Resembles work of thrips. Found often on philodendron.	Scrub leaves with soft toothbrush and soapsuds. If it doesn't clear up, discard plant.
Fusarium leaf spot	Worst on dracaena. Leaf spots begin as small pinpoints, enlarge, become watersoaked.	Keep water off foliage.
Phytophthora leaf spot	Mushy, shiny, water-soaked spots. Worst on philodendron, dieffenbachia, etc.	Dust with Benlate or Captan. Avoid water on leaves.
Rhizoctonia foliar blight	Found on ferns, syngonium, schefflera, etc. Brownish, wet rot, with reddish-brown thread-like tufts.	Keep foliage dry.

Disease	Damage	Control
"Shotgun" fungus disease	Common on nephthytis on Chinese evergreen and others. Leafspots as numerous as if hit by a shotgun blast.	Keep foliage dry.

SOIL DISEASES OF FOLIAGE PLANTS

Disease	Damage	Control
Fusarium	Mainly a stem rot disease, worst on dracaenas.	Repot, cut out rotted portions. If entire plant is rotted, destroy. If healthy tips remain, start new plants in sand, peat, or perlite.
Phytophthora	Similar to pythium. Causes serious foliage blight and stem rot, especially on dieffenbachia and others. Look for stem lesions.	Repot, using fresh soil mix. Select clean stalks and root. Discard remaining stem. Dust soil with Benlate.
Pythium	Causes roots to turn black and rot, plants to collapse. Affects dieffenbachias, Christmas cactus, pothos, gardenias, scheffleras, and many others.	Repot. If roots are completely black, discard. Avoid overwatering. Disease is spread by hands, infected tools, etc. Wash tools and pots in diluted household bleach. Scrub hands well with naptha soap.
Rhizoctonia	Called "the king" of the soil-borne diseases attacking foliage plants. Attacks young plants and seedlings at or near the he soil line. May spread to leaves, causing collapse. Works on aglaonemas, aphelandra, gardenias, gynura, philodendron, pothos, Scindapsus, and others.	Avoid overwatering and poor drainage. Dust soil with Captan.
Sclerotium	Look for white fungus growth on soil surface and on affected plants. Produces small structures the size of mustard seed on leaves and stems.	Repot, cut out affected portions and destroy. Dust with Captan.

THE THRILL OF GETTING PLANTS TO BLOOM INDOORS Flowering plants are more of a challenge to grow than are foliage plants. Not only do you need the right conditions for attractive leaves but you must provide the proper care for flower buds to form and burst into bloom. However, once you've produced your first gloxinia bloom from seed or tuber, or managed to have your poinsettia or Christmas cactus bloom on time, you'll agree that flowering plants are worth the effort.

Lack of windows for light is no longer a valid excuse with the number of fluorescent fixtures now on the market. Dry air in homes during the winter months can easily be offset by simple methods. We recommend that anyone who has been discouraged by previous failures try again with new expectations. You'll be thrilled with what you can do to brighten up your home with blooms.

Flowering houseplants are so numerous that it would take volumes to cover the subject. The following are some of the most common. Asterisks (*) denote plants we are most often asked about. They are discussed more fully in a special section.

Flowering Plant	Green Thumb Tips	Propagation	Troubles
ACHIMENES (species and hybrids) Velvety leaves, tubular flowers, pink, rose, red, violet, blue, purple	Grow from scaly cone-like rhizome planted in spring. Flower in summer. After flowering, soil should be dried gradually and pot placed in cool, dark place. In February, remove old soil and repot. Likes 80° temperature.	Division of roots.	Failure to flower due to lack of rest period in summer. Aphids, use Malathion or nicotine sulfate.
*AFRICAN VIOLET (*Saintpaulia* species and hybrids) Violet-shaped blooms white, pink, rose, blue, violet, purple and bicolored.	Detests direct sun, will not flower in poor light. Likes humusy soil and 70° temperature. Water from above or below, making sure of good drainage.	Leaf cuttings and seed, cuttings in vermiculite, perlite, or water. Seed in peat-lite mix.	Aphids. Leaf or crown rot due to overwatering. Lack of blossoms due to poor light. Spots on leaves due to water splashing.
AMARYLLIS (see Bulbs) (*Hippeastrum* species and hybrids) Large showy trumpet-shaped flowers, orange, white, red, shades in between and bicolors.	Needs summer outdoors. In fall, bring in and keep in cool basement for 8-10 weeks without water. 70° until growth starts, watering regularly until fall.	Bulbs.	Failure to bloom due to lack of good "rest cure" in fall or summer care.
AZALEA (*Rhododendron indicum and R. obtusum amoenum* — many hybrids) Pink, red, white blooms on woody plant	Prefers acid soil. If your water is hard, apply vinegar, 1 teaspoon per quart every 3 weeks. Grows outdoors in summer, move indoors in fall, keeping in a cool window until January 1, then move it into a bright window. Likes 65° day, 40-50° night.	Cuttings in July. Also by seed sown in sphagnum moss.	Nonflowering due to no cool period in fall. Red spider mite and chlorosis of foliage.

Flowering Plant	Green Thumb Tips	Propagation	Troubles
BALSAM (*Impatiens sultanii* and *I. holstii*, hybrids of same) Pink, white, orange, red, lavender, bicolors.	Grown as housplant and outdoor annual. Ideal for sun or shade. Likes it cool indoors, 65°	Seed started in sand-peat mixture, also by cuttings in plain water.	Aphids and red spider mites.
*BEGONIA (*Begonia* species and hybrids including Rieger, a cross between Christmas begonia and tuberous begonia).	Among the most versatile houseplants. All like humusy soil, warm temperature, bright light, but never direct sunlight. 60° at night, 72° during day.	Seeds, stem and leaf cuttings. Calla begonia is most trying to root. Try greenest tips in moist perlite, tuberous begonias by seeds, cuttings, division of tubers.	Leaf scorch, bua drop due to hot, dry rooms. Mealybugs, scale. Nematodes (eelworms). See Chapter XVII, INSECTS IN AND AROUND THE HOME.
BIRDS OF PARADISE (see *Foliage Plants*)			
CALCEOLARIA (*Calceolaria intergrifolia*) Spotted pouch or "pocketbook." Flowers yellow, white, red.	"Pocketbook" plant likes full sun. 70° in day and 60° at night. Cut plants back to within 4″ after blooming for new growth. Keep below 60° for bud formation.	Seeds.	Dropping of buds due to poor ventilation (this item can gas itself and nearby flowers, though harmless to humans). Red spider mites.
CALLA LILY (*Zantedeschia aethiopica*-white; *Z. elliottiana*—yellow; *Z. rehmannii superba*—pink; *Z. albo maculata*—white with mottled leaves).	Both yellow and white callas need full sun and ample water. Dry the yellow tubers off in June, repot in August. Yellow callas should be left until November before re-potting. 65°.	Offsets of the fleshy storage organs.	Mealybugs and spider mites. Nonflowering due to lack of light or dry soil.

Flowering Plant	Green Thumb Tips	Propagation	Troubles
CAMELLIA (*Camellia japonica*) Pink, white, rose flowers.	Not an ideal houseplant. Likes a temperature of 50° at night and 60° in day. Bright window. Set outdoors in summer.	Cuttings.	Same as gardenias (see *Gardenias*).
*CHRISTMAS CACTUS (*Schlumbergera bridgesii*) Thanksgiving Cactus (*S. truncata*); Easter Cactus (*S. gaertneri*)	Likes full sun and night temperature around 65°. Should not be kept dry as with other cacti. Buds form in October and will flower through winter. Place plant outdoors in summer.	Cuttings.	Failure to bloom; due to too high night temperature or too long a day. Bud drop, too much or too little water. Thanksgiving and Christmas Cactus buds form in fall, when days are shorter. At 50° to 55° night temperature buds will form, regardless of day length. No flowers will form if night temperatures are consistently above 70°.
CHRISTMAS PEPPER (*Capsicum frutescens conoides*) Flashy houseplant has edible (hot!) peppers; fruits are yellow, red.	Needs full sun, lots of water. Discard after fruiting and start new plants from seed. 72°. Keep pods away from children; can cause severe irritation.	Seed sown in June or July will produce flowering plants by Christmas.	Red spider mites.
*CHRYSANTHEMUMS (*Chrysanthemum coronarium* and *C. carinatum*) White, pink, orchid, yellow, bronze, red.	May be dug in garden and potted for indoor flowering. Plants need full sun and ample water. Potted florist mum is often too late-flowering to be planted outdoors. Set pot outdoors in summer, bring in before frost. Likes sun, 65° night temperature.	Division and cuttings.	Red spider mites, aphids, and white flies.

Flowering Plant	Green Thumb Tips	Propagation	Troubles
CINERARIA (*Senecio cruentus*) Daisy-like purple, blue, red pink, white, bicolors.	Prefers full sun, lots of water, cool night temperature (50°). Discard after flowering.	Seeds.	Aphids, red spider mites.
CITRUS PLANTS (see under foliage plants)	A large group including lemon, orange, grapefruit, limes, and others. Flowers, fruits, and foliage are handsome. Keep plants outdoors in summer, bring in before frost. Sunny window, 70°	Seeds, cuttings and grafting. Buy grafted types from nursery for large, handsome fruit.	Capricious blooming habit, due to hot, dry rooms. Red spider mites and scale.
CYCLAMEN (*Cyclamen indicum*) Shooting-star-like flowers, white, red, lavender, pink.	Prefers full sun in day at 70° and night temperature of 50°. Keep soil moist at all times. After blooming, dry off corm and place in cellar until summer when it can be repotted for another show. Some grow year round.	18 months from seed to a flowering plant.	Yellow leaves and buds blasting, due to high room temperature or lack of light. Cyclamen mite, red spider mites. Leaves flop from lack of water. Set in pan of warm water in a cool spot.
EASTER LILY (*Lilium longiflorum*) Fragrant, white trumpet-shaped flowers.	Prefers bright light and a good supply of water. After flowering, plant bulb out-doors in permanent place in garden and it will bloom year after year. 65°.	Bulblets, scales, and seed.	Leaves turn yellow due to lack of light, root rots, poor aeration, highly soluble salts.
FLOWERING MAPLE (*Abutilon megapotamicum*) Maple leaves will balloon-shaped flowers, yellow, orange, peach.	So-called because of maple-ike leaves. Likes a cool room, is a fast grower. Must be pinched to induce squattiness. Deserves renewed interest. 65° to 70°	Cuttings and seed in sand-peat mixture or peat-lite.	Yellow leaves due to lack of nitrogen. Red spider mites.

Flowering Plant	Green Thumb Tips	Propagation	Troubles
FUCHSIA (*mostly hybrids of species*) Bell-shaped flowers, purple, lavender, white, pink, bicolors.	Will grow in full sun or semi-shade. Likes a moist, humusy soil, temperature of 70°. Flowering stops in summer due to high temperature. Ideal for window boxes and hanging baskets.	Cuttings from young growth. In fall, cut old plant back and start new plants in perlite.	Flower drop due to high room temperature or poor light, or poor drainage. White flies, aphids, and red spider mites.
*GARDENIA (*Gardenia jasminoides fortuneri*, hybrids of same) Fragrant white camellia-shaped flowers.	Not a satisfactory houseplant, though a challenging one. Needs full sun, night temperature of 60°, day temperature of 70-°80°. Feed ammonium sulfate, 1 tsp. to quart of water, once monthly from March to November. Grow outdoors in summer. Mist regularly indoors.	Cuttings taken in winter. Use sand, peat, perlite or vermiculite.	Bud drop due to high night temperature. Yellow foliage due to non-acid soils and low temperatures. Mealybugs, red spider mites.
*GERANIUMS (*Pelargonium hortorum* and *P. domesticum*, hybrids of *hortorum* and many species) Pink, white, red, lavender flowers in clusters.	All like a cool temperature (60° or so), full sun, and plenty of water. Too much shade and high temperature causes spindly plants. Pinch back the growing tip to make them bushy. Available in many varieties, some valued for odor of foliage. Plants may be kept over winter by hanging upside down in cellar in polyethylene bags, or putting roots in moist peat moss.	Seed sown in a shallow box. Also cuttings taken in autumn and stuck in sand or perlite. Pour boiling water on sand first to sterilize it. Plastic bags over cuttings favor rooting. Ideal for storing mother plants over winter.	Failure to flower due to lack of light, low humidity, or too high a room temperature. Yellow leaves due to lack of light, dry soil, too little nitrogen, or poor drainage.

Flowering Plant	Green Thumb Tips	Propagation	Troubles
*GLOXINIA (*Sinningia speciosa*) Velvety bell-shaped flowers, purple, white, lavender, pink, red and bicolors.	Prefers humus soil, with charcoal for drainage. Night temperature 62°, day temperature 70°. Avoid direct sun, but provide bright light. Tubers planted in March will bloom in summer. After flowering, soil can be kept dry until foliage wilts and dies, then store in basement until next fall or spring when it can be repotted. Some gardeners grow them year round without a rest period.	Tubers do not multiply, but get larger as they get older. Split tubers so each piece has an eye. Or root stems in water. Small tuber will form at end with roots. Sow fine seed in box of peat. Also, leaves can be pinned to perlite or vermiculite.	Leaf curl due to poor drainage or red spider mites. Bud failure due to overwatering, Botrytis blight, thrips, lack of humidity. Failure to bloom is due to lack of light as are spindly stems. Rotate plants every 3 or 4 days to prevent lopsidedness.
HYDRANGEA (*Hydrangea macrophylla*) Large flower clusters, white, pink, blue, lavender.	Prefers bright window, lots of water. After blooming, cut tops back 2" above pot and plunge into garden until September, when it is brought in and left in cool, dark basement until January 1, when it can be brought into bright room. 65°–70° night and day. Changing colors due to soil acidity. If you want to change yours from pink to blue, water with aluminum sulfate solution several times during growing season. For pink flowers add lime.	Cuttings.	Plants are not hardy outdoors. Non-flowering due to pruning. Prune *after* flowering or not at all. Yellow between veins means alkaline (sweet) soil.
JERUSALEM CHERRY (*Solanum pseudo-capsicum*) Orange berries size of cherry on a dwarf, tree-like plant.	Likes cool bright window and lots of water. Give 70° daytime temperature and 60° at night. Fruits poisonous when eaten.	Seeds and cuttings taken in summer.	Fruit dropping, due to old age, lack of water, or poor light. If plants get too leggy, prune them back for size and shape.

Flowering Plant	Green Thumb Tips	Propagation	Troubles
KAFIR LILY (*Clivia miniata*) Strap-like leaves, clusters of very fragrant tubular flowers, orange, peach.	Does well indoors in same pot for years. Likes cool room and good light in winter, and should be outdoors in summer. 65° night and day.	Start new plants from seed or offshoots.	Failure to flower due to lack of light.
KALANCHOE (*Kalanchoe blossfeldiana*) Glossy green leaves, clusters of tiny flowers, red, yellow, orange, white and pink.	Handsome, tough little plant which should be raised more. Flowers in bright light from Thanksgiving until May.	Seeds and leaf cuttings any time of the year. Sow seed in peat-lite mix.	Failure to flower due to poor light. Aphids.
LANTANA (*many species*) Quarter-sized clusters of pink, white, lavender, yellow flowers.	Ideal for hanging baskets, porch or patio. Needs full sun and average soil. 55° night; 65° during day.	Cuttings from summer flowering plants will bloom in winter.	Lack of blossoms due to rich soil and not enough light. Red spider mites.
LEOPARD PLANT (*Ligularia kaempferi*) Spotted foliage and yellow flowers.	Grandma grew this handsome plant for its spotted foliage and yellow flowers. Likes cool temperature, full sun, or semi-shade; moist, peaty soil. 55°-60° night and day.	Dividing old plant, or by taking stem cuttings in the spring.	May get leggy if not pruned. Also subject to red spider mites.
LILY-OF-VALLEY (*Convallaria majalis*) Fragrant pink or white bell-like flowers ideal for forcing.	"Pips" (rootstocks) are dug from garden after foliage dies, stored at 30°-40° until January, when they can be planted in sand or peat moss and forced to flower merely by keeping them wet.	Divisions.	Failure to flower due to poor light or lack of cool storage period.

Flowering Plant	Green Thumb Tips	Propagation	Troubles
OLEANDER (*Nerium Oleander*) Pink, lavender, funnel-shaped flowers, leaves poisonous.	Tubbed plant grown for foliage and white, pink or reddish-purple flowers in spring. Keep outdoors in summer; bring indoors in fall and keep dry until March 1. Give bright light and ample moisture. 70°.	Cuttings.	Failure to flower due to lack of moisture. Tall plants get out of bound. Nip back old growth *after* flowering.
*****ORCHIDS** (many species and varieties)	Orchids are more difficult to nurse than most houseplants indoors. Cattleya is the most popular and easiest. All may be grown if humidity is high. Likes full sun in winter, osmunda moss or shredded bark for potting "soil." Likes bright light but not full sun in summer. 70°.	Seeds and by division of "pseudo-bulbs."	Failure to flower due to poor light or low humidity. Red spider mites, scale, and aphids.
PASSION FLOWER (*Passiflora* species and hybrids) Lavender, pink, white flowers, 4″ across.	In early winter plant likes to rest, so give cool window and withhold water. In late winter give more water and temperature of 72°. Keep plant watered in summer outdoors. In fall, cut vine back to 10″ and bring indoors.	Cuttings in water, sand, or perlite. Also seed sown indoors in February or March. Seed is slow to germinate.	Yellow foliage due to red spider mites. Failure to flower due to early winter rest period.
*****POINSETTIA** (*Euphorbia pulcherrima*) Popular Christmas plant. Large red, pink, or white bracts (miscalled flowers), framed with large green leaves.	Likes bright window at 70° and plenty of water. After blooming, cut to 5″ in May and set pot in garden all summer. Bring indoors September 1. Put plant in dark room each night until after Thanksgiving. Pink varieties come about in two ways: either by crossing a white and a red type, or by mutation or "sport." For example, "Mikkelpink" is a mutation (sudden change) of the red Paul Mikkelsen poinsettia.	Cuttings taken in summer. Use sand, perlite, or vermiculite.	Leaf drop due to poor light, drafts, or high temperature. Failure to flower due to lack of long-night treatment. Mealybugs and red spider mites.

Flowering Plant	Green Thumb Tips	Propagation	Troubles
RED-HOT CATTAIL (*Acalypha hispida*) Chenille-like hanging flowers, pinkish white or red.	Heart-shaped leaves and red "tails" for blooms. Prefers bright window. Shade during hot summer. Pinch soft foliage to make them branch. 70°.	Put cuttings in sand-peat mixture.	Legginess. Pinching soft growth produces compact plant.
TWELVE APOSTLES (*Neomarica northiana* and *N. gracilis*) Sword-shaped leaves, yellow, white, and blue flowers 2" to 3" across and iris-like, short-lived. New flowers unfold in quick succession over period of several weeks.	Bright window and ample moisture. 70°.	Set old plant in garden in May. Bend flower stalk to earth and anchor. By autumn it'll be rooted and can be separated from the old parent plant.	Failure to flower due to dry soil, poor light. Spider mites.
WILD ORCHID (*Bletilla striata*) Dainty orchid blooms.	"Oriental Orchid" of Japan. Potted in November, will bloom in February, with 6 or 8 dainty orchid blooms on a 12" stem. Blooms for 6 weeks. 65°.	Rhizomes. By division.	None.

Plantscaping with Foliage

The green plant boom is on—and it's going to be with us for years to come. Modern homes use plants as room dividers. Portable planters on rollers are handy and practical. You can load them up and get the feeling you're in a cool, moist jungle. A tea cart full of plants makes a good mobile divider and what a selection you have! Ferns, Norfolk Island pine, sunset ivy leaf geranium, Chinese evergreen (Aglaonema), Aralia, peperomia, episcia, to name a few.

Don't worry if a shortage of sunshine is a problem. Plant hunters all over the world have been seeking out plants that grow in sun, shade, or desert conditions; you can find

Showy foliage plants with variegated leaves

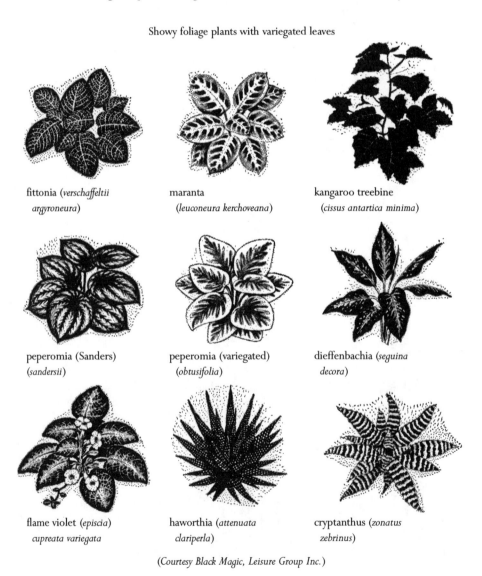

fittonia (*verschaffeltii argyroneura*)

maranta (*leuconeura kerchoveana*)

kangaroo treebine (*cissus antartica minima*)

peperomia (Sanders) (*sandersii*)

peperomia (variegated) (*obtusifolia*)

dieffenbachia (*seguina decora*)

flame violet (*episcia*) cupreata variegata

haworthia (*attenuata clariperla*)

cryptanthus (*zonatus zebrinus*)

(*Courtesy Black Magic, Leisure Group Inc.*)

Showy foliage plants with variegated leaves

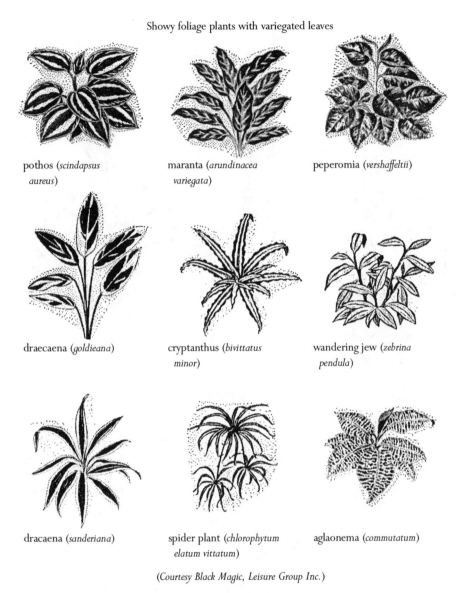

pothos (*scindapsus aureus*)

maranta (*arundinacea variegata*)

peperomia (*vershaffeltii*)

draecaena (*goldieana*)

cryptanthus (*bivittatus minor*)

wandering jew (*zebrina pendula*)

dracaena (*sanderiana*)

spider plant (*chlorophytum elatum vittatum*)

aglaonema (*commutatum*)

(*Courtesy Black Magic, Leisure Group Inc.*)

a plant tailored for any room in your house. And modern fluorescent lighting enables you to supplement natural light so you can enjoy plants even more.

The big thing to watch out for is not to mix "opposites" together. For example, do not grow cacti with types which need lots of moisture, or geraniums (which like sunlight) with schefflera, which cannot tolerate direct sun.

Requirements of most foliage plants are not complicated: a humusy, well drained soil, diffused light, and the highest humidity possible. Probably more foliage plants die in dish gardens and planters from overwatering than underwatering. Plastic or metal con-

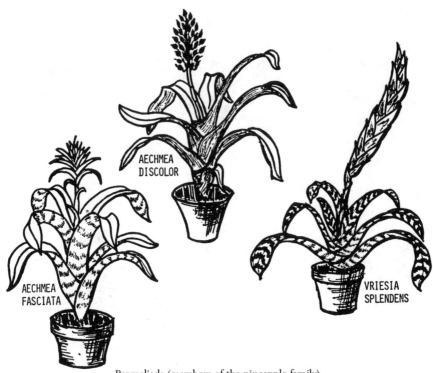

Bromeliads (members of the pineapple family) are striking and easy to grow indoors. (*Courtesy Fennell's Orchid Jungle*)

tainers are trickier to use because they do not dry out as fast as clay pots and therefore plants in them are usually overwatered. This causes stunted growth, yellowed leaves, and musty soil. For the most part, the soil and water requirements for foliage plants are similar to flowering plants. The big difference in culture is that the foliage plants usually need less light than do the flower-producing plants.

You don't need a lot of fancy soil mixtures to grow foliage plants. Stick with an old standby; 1 part each of sand, perlite, peat, and garden loam, or you can use a soilless mix. Add a few pieces of charcoal to the mixture, and a few pieces of broken pots or a half inch of pebbles in bottom of container for drainage.

For use in planters, we set pot and all in peat moss rather than remove the plant from the pot. If a plant conks out, you simply put a new one in its place. Also, roots remain confined to the pot and do not ramble throughout the entire planter. (See Chapter VIII for more detail on pots in planters.)

GROOMING "HARD-LEAVED" FOLIAGE PLANTS To make foliage on your vines and other indoor plants look shiny and well scrubbed, try a trick florists use. Put a few drops of glycerine on a cloth and swab the leaves. This brings out the plants' natural colors and appearance, and at the same time eliminates the dull, dusty look. Glycerine is safe to handle, does not harm plant life, and is also usable on gourds for brighter effect. Never use olive oil, as it collects dust and plugs up the leaf pores. If leaves are quite greasy or dirty, you can add a few drops of cider vinegar to the water. Some gardeners wash their leaves with tepid water, soft soap and water, detergent water, milk and water (1 teaspoon milk in 1 cup water), or skimmed milk alone (gives a semi-glossy effect). Do not use cooking oils, butter, greases, etc. for shiny effect on plants. And if you use commercial plant shines, be sure not to overdo it, or you will clog the pores of leaves.

We list in this chapter some well known foliage plants, with their temperature, moisture, and light requirements for interior plantscaping (based on information from our Cornell University classmate, R. C. Mott, who worked for years at the L. H. Bailey Hortorium and in the floriculture greenhouses).

GROWING VINES ON TOTEM POLES "Moss sticks" or "totem poles"—slabs of bark with sphagnum moss wrapped around them—are used for growing house ivies such as philodendrons, grape ivy, English ivies, and dozens of others. Roots grow into the bark and moss and receive added nourishment. To water the plant you simply add water (with liquid plant food added) to the bark and moss, and any excess water will drain to the pot, since the moss stick is sunk deep into the soil where it is anchored.

TERRARIUMS A terrarium is nothing more than a glass or plastic container used for growing live plants. Inside this glassed-in garden conditions are just perfect for plant growth: humidity, temperature, and light. Many interesting plants can be grown in this miniature greenhouse (see *Plantscaping with Foliage* for cultural tips).

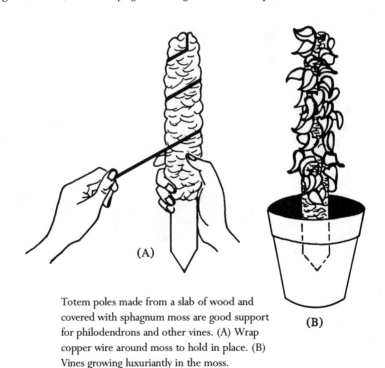

(A)

(B)

Totem poles made from a slab of wood and covered with sphagnum moss are good support for philodendrons and other vines. (A) Wrap copper wire around moss to hold in place. (B) Vines growing luxuriantly in the moss.

An iced-tea spoon is a good shovel for mini-gardens. Tamping mix around the roots anchors plants firmly. Water carefully so soil is just moist—not soggy.

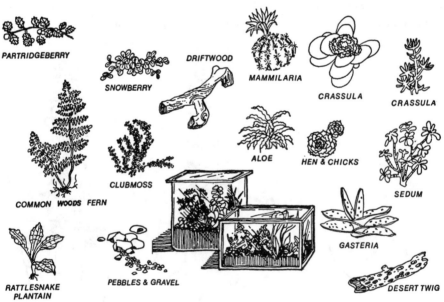

PARTRIDGEBERRY

SNOWBERRY

DRIFTWOOD

MAMMILARIA

CRASSULA

CRASSULA

ALOE

HEN & CHICKS

SEDUM

COMMON WOODS FERN

CLUBMOSS

GASTERIA

RATTLESNAKE PLANTAIN

PEBBLES & GRAVEL

DESERT TWIG

These plants, which grow in a moist situation, can be used to simulate a woodland scene.

These plants will tolerate neglect and can be grown in plain sand. Good for desert terrarium or planters.

(Courtesy Black Magic, Leisure Group, Inc.)

The main reason plants grow so well is the humidity. It runs around 60 to 80 percent, as compared to the low (as low as 12 percent) humidity often found in homes today.

It's easy to make your own "glass garden." First, select your container. It can be any kind of a clear glass or plastic jar, bottle, box, or dish, or you can buy one of the fancy models (either glass or plastic) from your local flower shop or department store. (Fish tanks make great terrariums.) A terrarium should usually have some sort of removable top (or you can use clear plastic wrap).

Start with the right soil mix, which can be purchased or home-made. A simple mix is 1 part each of sand, peat, and loam. Soil must be loose and tight, not heavy and soggy. Place a layer of charcoal or pebbles on the bottom, then a 2-inch layer of soil.

Plants that go into the terrarium can be selected from the woods or purchased. No law says you can't mix the two. But don't mix moisture-loving plants such as African violets with desert types such as cactus (which in a terrarium take almost 100 percent sand, no cover, and only tiny amounts of moisture). If gathering your own, select small plants and seedlings—they'll grow soon enough—and probably larger than you want. Use a little imagination and gather little pieces of bark, twigs, pretty stones, lichens, moss, pieces of mirror for a lake, small, colorful, tiny bridges or figurines.

Vent your terrarium from time to time by simply leaving the top open. This prevents moisture from gathering on the sides and shutting off the view.

Here are a few plants to try for your terrarium:

Native Plants	Store Bought Plants
Rattlesnake plantain (*Goodyera*)	African Violets (*Saintpaulia*)
Partridgeberry (*Mitchella*)	Acorus (*Acorus gramineus*)
Rock Polypody (*Polypodium*)	Podocarpus (*Podocarpus*)
Pipsissewa (*Chimaphila*)	Dracaena (*D. Sanderiana* and *godseffiana*)
Wood Anemone (*Anemone*)	Miniature peperomias (*Peperomia*)
Hepatica (*Hepatica*—may be illegal)	Creeping Fig (*Ficus pumila*)
Foam Flower (*Tiarella*)	Scindapsus (or *Pothos*)
Wood Violets (*Viola*)	Croton (*Codiaeum*)
Pussytoes (*Antennaria*)	Wandering Jew (*Zebrina* and *tradescantia*)
Hawkweed (*Hieracium*)	Hahn's Sansevieria (*Sansevieria*)
Wild Strawberry (*Fragaria*)	Syngonium (*Syngonium*)
Wintergreen (*Gaultheria*)	Philodendron (*Philodendron* species)
Goldthread (*Coptis*)	Bromeliads (*Cryptanthus, Billbergia, Aechmea,* and others)
Woodbetony (*Pedicularis*)	Pteris (*Pteris*)
	Selaginella (*Selaginella*)
	Ivy (*Hedera helix*)
	Prayer Plant (*Maranta*)
	Crassula (*Crassula*)
	Kalanchoe (*Kalanchoe*)
	Echeveria (*Echeveria*)

TEMPERATURE, MOISTURE, & LIGHT
CONDITIONS FOR INTERIOR PLANTS

Key:

Temperatures

(C) Cool: 60°F (55°-70°F range) Conditions commonly found in shopping malls, hotels, foyers, lobbies and other entryways.

(W) Warm: 75°F (65°-85°F range) Generally found in homes and offices.

Moisture

(M) Moist: Plant requires frequent watering, surface of soil should never dry out.

(D) Dry: Plant requires less water, soil should become dry to touch from surface to 1 inch deep between waterings.

Light

(H) High: (400 footcandles) Highest natural light intensity possible exclusive of direct sunlight.

(L) Low: (150 footcandles) Light intensity equivalent to fair reading light.

| | CONDITION | | |
Plant Name	Temperature	Moisture	Light

Aglaonema commutatum, A. crispum,
  A. modestum (Chinese Evergreen)
  (CV White Rajah)
	W	M	L

Aphelandra squarrosa (Zebra Plant)	W	M	H
Araucaria heterophylla	C	M	H
Ardisia crisps (False Holly or Coral Berry)	C	M	H
Asparagus adantinoides ("Sprengeri" Sprenger Fern)	C	M	H
A. plumosus (Asparagus Fern)	C	M	L
Aspidistra elatior (Cast Iron Plant)	W	M	L
Aucuba japonica (Gold Dust Plant)	C	D	H
Begonia masoniana (Iron Cross Begonia)	W	M	L
B. rex-cultorum (Rex Begonia)	W	M	L
B. semperflorens (Common Begonia)	W	M	L
Carissa grandiflora (Natal Plum)	C	M	H
Chlorophytum capense (Spider Plant)	C	M	L
Cissus antarctica, C. rhombifolia (Grape Ivy)	C	M	L
Clusia rosea (Signature Plant)	W	D	H
Codiaeum variegatum, var. pictum (Croton)	W	M	H
Cordyline terminalis (Ti Plant)	W	D	H
Crassula argentea (Jade Plant)	W	D	H
Cyperus alternifolius, C. papyrus	W	M	H
Dieffenbachia sp. (Dumb Cane or Dumb Plant)	W	M	H
Dizygotheca elegantissima (False Aralia)	W	M	H
Dracaena godseffiana, D. marginata	W	M	H
D. deremensis, D. fragrans, D. sanderiana	W	M	L
Epipremnum aureum (Devil's Ivy, Pothos)	W	D	L
Euonymus japonicus (Euonymus)	C	M	H
Fatshedera lizei (Tree Ivy)	C	M	H
Fatsia japonica (Japanese Aralia)	C	M	H
Ficus elastica (Rubber Plant)	W	M	H
F. benjamina (Weeping Chinese Fig)	W	M	H
F. lyrata (Fiddleleaf Fig)	W	M	H
Fittonia verschaffeltii (Mosaic Plant)	W	M	L

Plant Name	CONDITION Temperature	Moisture	Light
Geogenanthus undatus (Seersucker Plant)	W	M	L
Gynura aurantiaca (Velvet Plant)	C	M	H
Hedera helix (English Ivy)	C	M	H
Helxine soleirolii (Baby's Tears)	W	M	H
Hoya carnosa (Wax Plant)	W	D	H
Malpighia coccigera (Miniature Holly)	W	D	H
Maranta leuconeura (Prayer Plant)	W	M	L
Monstera deliciosa (Split-Leaf Philodendron)	W	M	H
Myrtus communis (True Myrtle)	C	M	H
Pandanus veitchii (Screw Pine)	W	D	H
Peperomia argyreia (Watermelon Peperomia, *P. sp*)	W	D	H
Philodendron scandens spp. *oxycardium* (Heart-shaped Leaves)	W	M	L
Pilea cadieri (Aluminum Plant, *P. microphylla*—Artillery Plant)	C	M	H
Pittosporum tobira	C	M	H
Plectranthus australis (Trailing Coleus or Swedish Ivy)	W	M	H
Pleomele reflex, P. thaloides	W	D	H
Podocarpus gracilior, P. macrophyllus var. maki	C	M	H
Pothos (See Epipremnum or Scindapsis)			
Rhoeo spathacea (Moses-in-a-Boat)	C	D	H
Sansevieria trifasciata (Snake Plant)	W	D	H
S. Trifasciata "Hahnii" (Bird's Nest Hemp)	W	D	H
Saxifraga sarmentosa (Strawberry Geranium)	C	M	H
Schefflera actinophylla (Umbrella Plant)	W	D	H
Scindapsis (Pothos or Epipremnum) *Spathiphyllum sp.*	W	M	L
Snygonium podophyllum, S. wendlandii (Arrowhead Plant)	W	M	H
Tolmiea menziesii (Piggy-Back Plant)	C	M	H
Zebrina sp. (All three (3) commonly *Tradescantia* sp. called Wandering Jew. Dis- *Commelina* sp. tinquished most easily by color of the leaves.)	W	M	L

Selected Succulents

Plant Name	CONDITION Temperature	Moisture	Light
Agave americana (Century Plant)	W	D	H
Bryophyllum tubiflorum (Air Plant)	W	D	H
B. Pinnatum (Madagascar Air Plant)	W	D	H
Euphorbia splendens (Crown of Thorns)	W	D	H
Gasteria sp. (Deer or Ox Tongue)	W	D	H
Kalanchoe sp. (Kalanchoe)	W	D	H
Opuntia sp. (Prickly Pear)	W	D	H
Schlumbergera bridgesii (Christmas Cactus, see text for further information)	C	M	L
Stapelia sp. (Star Fish)	W	D	H

Asterisks (*) denote plants we are most often asked about. They are discussed more fully in a special section.

Foliage Plant	Green Thumb Tips	Propagation	Troubles (For controls see section on Insects and Diseases in this chapter.)
ALUMINUM PLANT (*Pilea cadierei*)	Silver blotches as if aluminized. Sensitive to overwatering; will rot if soil is soggy. Filtered sunlight. Pinch back regularly.	Tip cuttings.	Rotting of stems due to poor drainage.
ARTILLERY PLANT (*Pilea microphylla*)	Anthers (male elements) burst open and discharge little puffs of pollen, resembling smoke. Likes ample water, but not soggy soil, bright light. Won't do well in temperatures below 55°.	Seeds and cuttings.	Light foliage due to lack of nitrogen.
ARALIA (False) (*Dizygotheca, or Polyscia*)	Fussy item. Grows on foot-long stalks, with narrow and toothed leaves. Warm, moist atmosphere and plenty of water.	Seed.	Will lose leaves quick if not given warm temperature days (80°), 65° at night. Poor drainage causes tip burns on leaves, as will direct sun.
GOLD DUST TREE (*Aucuba japonica*)	Variegated leathery leaves, some with yellow spots. Likes cool, bright window. Keep dry.	Cuttings.	Browning of edges due to hot, dry rooms.
BABY'S TEARS (*Helxine soleirolii*)	This rambling plant makes a solid mat, often called "Paddy's Wig." Likes bright light, ample moisture, but avoid overwatering. Be sure soil is well drained.	Cuttings. Division of plant.	Browning due to overwatering or poor drainage.
BIRD OF PARADISE (*Strelitzia reginae*)	Nice foliage but hard to get flowers. Prefers 60° at night, 70° in day. Takes up to 3 years for plants to bloom. Avoid excess watering in winter, as plants are semi-dormant.	Seed in sand peat mix, also by division.	Failure to flower due to immaturity and poor light. Scale and mealybug.

Foliage Plant	Green Thumb Tips	Propagation	Troubles
BRASSAIA (see *Schefflera*)			
BROMELIADS: A large group of houseplants, some with showy flowers and leaves. Pineapple is member of the Bromeliad family.	All like a soil mix of 1 part each of sand, peat, and loam. Foliage syringed from time to time. Bright window. Some such as Vriesia, or "Living Vase Plants," have leaves which form in rosettes and catch water. These are watered in the "cups" formed by leaves.	Cut off suckers and root in sand, perlite, or plain tap water.	Yellow leaves due to overwatering or cold temperature. Most bromeliads are tropical and like 72° in day, 65° at night. Give full light.
*CACTUS (many genera)	Most cacti like 70°, bright light, and a dry soil. Avoid plastic or glazed containers and excess watering. Sandy soil is best.	Seeds, grafting, and cuttings.	Rotting due to excess water or poor drainage. Make sure plants are well drained. Mealybugs and scale.
CHINESE EVERGREEN (*Aglaonema modestum*)	Handsome, arrow-shaped leaves, green and white or solid green. Grows well in water, soil, light or dark room. Tolerant of dry rooms, does not like to be overwatered if in soil.	Cuttings and division.	Yellow leaves due to too much light and overwatering. Mealybug and scale. Use Malathion.
COLEUS (*Coleus blumei*; many varieties) (See also under Annuals)	Likes warm room, rich soil, and ample moisture. Bright light or shade.	Seeds or tip cuttings rooted in water.	Mealybugs. Pale color due to lack of light. Tall plants due to failure to pinch.
CROTON (*Codiaeum variegatum pictum*)	Multicolored, shiny red, pink, brown, yellow, highly ornamental foliage. Likes rich soil, warmth, and high humidity. Good light for best coloring. Prefers semi-shade in summer.	Cuttings.	Leaf burn due to direct sun. Wilting foliage due to dry soil or dry air. Leaf drop due to poor drainage. Mealybugs and scale.

FAVORITE INDOOR FOLIAGE PLANTS (Continued)

Foliage Plant	Green Thumb Tips	Propagation	Troubles
DUMB CANE DIEFFENBACHIA (many species)	One of the best foliage plants. Large green and white leaves have acrid juice which can cause temporary loss of speech if chewed. Bright window, ample moisture and 70° is best.	Cuttings. Cut stem in 3" pieces and root in pan of peat.	Tendency to grow tall. Cut top off and root in jar of water or moist sphagnum moss. Can be wrapped around a slit in stem (see *Air Layering* in Chapter XV, PLANT PROPAGATION).
*DRACAENA	Many species. Tolerate much abuse. Prefer soil on the dry side. Sun or shade.	Cuttings.	Rotting due to excess moisture.
EPISCIA	Rich variegated green bronze, pink foliage, pink or red flowers. Ideal for hanging baskets, with culture same as for African violets. Rich loam soil, bright window but not direct sun as it will burn foliage. 65°-75° temperature best.	Cuttings.	Rotting due to excess moisture. Red spider mite.
*FERNS (many genera)	All ferns like a peaty, moist soil, a cool window, and freedom from direct sun. Remove dead twigs and blind runners. Hose off fern in summer, and apply weak liquid plant food every 3 months. Repot yearly.	Division of roots, done any time of year. Spores form black dots on back of leaves. (Do not confuse these with insect pests!)	Scale, red spider mite. Brown tips due to hot, dry rooms. Yellowing of leaves due to poor drainage, standing in jardiniere, lack of nitrogen or too much sun.
FITTONIA (*Fittonia verschaffeltii*)	A real darling of the plant world, having handsomely veined foliage. Likes plenty of moisture but well drained soil and semi-shade, 70°.	Cuttings stuck in sand or water.	Wilts badly in dry soil, turns brown in direct sun, yellow in temperatures below 55°.
GRAPE IVY (*Cissus rhombifolia*)	Trailing vine with grape-like leaves. Tolerates neglect. Will grow in dry soil. Likes bright windows without direct sun. Grows in soil or water, and temperature 55°-85°.	Cuttings stuck in water, moist sand, or perlite.	Drying of foliage due to hot rooms. Red spider mite, aphids, and scale.

Foliage Plant	Green Thumb Tips	Propagation	Troubles
IRESINE HERBSTII (Bloodleaf, "Chicken Gizzard" Plant)	Highly colorful foliage plant, deep crimson, red, and yellow-green leaves shaped like chicken gizzard. Likes cool room, 65° or so, full sun or semi-shade. Soil: equal parts sand, peat, and loam. Good in hanging baskets, tubs, pots, urns, and outdoor borders.	Take tip cuttings any time of year and root in water, or sand-peat mix, perlite or vermiculite.	Red spider mites.
JADE PLANT (Crassula argentea)	Treelike plant with small thick oval leaves. Old favorite; will tolerate shade and neglect, but does best in bright windows and in barely moist soil. Needs good drainage. Place outdoors in summer; bring in in fall.	Leaf cuttings in sand, perlite, or vermiculite	Leaf drop due to poor light or excess water. Mealybugs and thrips. Wilted leaf due to anthracnose, dust with Captan. Root rot due to poor drainage.
KALANCHOE (Kalanchoe blosfeldiana)	Can be grown for leaves as well as flowers, which are brick-red, yellow, or pink and numerous; leaves green and leathery, making it an ideal foliage plant. Needs full sun and moist humus soil.	Seeds and leaf cuttings in sand, perlite, or vermiculite.	Lack of flowers due to poor light or high temperatures. Mottled foliage due to thrips. Dropping of foliage due to poor light or old age.
KANGAROO VINE (Cissus antarctica)	Has 3 leaflets resembling poison ivy (unrelated). One of the most durable foliage plants.	Cuttings in sand, perlite, vermiculite, or water.	Leaves turn brown or are scorched at edges, due to lack of water, or red spider mite.
KENILWORTH IVY (Cymbalaria muralis)	A delicate vine ideal for hanging baskets. Grows in sun or shade. Tolerates temperatures of 50°-85°. Likes humidity.	Cuttings, and it also self-sows.	None, if given good drainage.
MIGNONETTE VINE Maderia Vine (Boussingaultia baselloides)	Tall, fast-growing vine with tuberous roots; leaves are heart-shaped and tiny white flowers are fragrant. Grows in sun or semi-shade. Likes warmth, 70°-80°.	Seed, root divisions and small tubercles found on stems.	Unusually free from troubles.

Foliage Plant	Green Thumb Tips	Propagation	Troubles
NIGHT-BLOOMING CEREUS (Cacti family: *Hylocereus undatus*, *Selenicereus undatus*, *Nyctocereus serpentinus*)	There are several night-blooming plants. Most detest overwatering. Prefer bright light, well drained soil. Take many years to bloom. Flower in summer, rest in winter.	Cuttings.	Stubborn blooming habit. Give light and plenty of water in summer, less in winter. Don't force it during winter rest period.
NORFOLK ISLAND PINE (*Araucaria heterophylla*)	A charming evergreen for indoor culture. Likes cool window, ample moisture at all times, and a fairly heavy soil. Likes syringing once a week, dappled shade, and a temperature of 60°-70°.	Seeds, or cuttings taken from the tip growth and rooted in sand, perlite, or vermiculite.	Red spider mites. Brown leaves due to hot sun, or may be due to excess watering.
PALMS (many genera)	There are many true palms, but one used often is Paradise Palm (Kentia), found in hotels, lobbies, offices. Try these single-stem palms for containers: Fish Tail, Parlor, Coconut, Belmore Sentry Palm, Forster Sentry, Chinese Fan Palm, Pigmy Date Palm, Chamaedorea, and the Christmas Palm. Soak well when watering, give filtered light. Syringe foliage regularly to rid dust. Provide good drainage.	Seeds; slow to germinate (3 to 16 months). Buy fresh palm seed because it does not mature properly indoors.	Yellow leaves from poor drainage, or bright sun. Burning at tips or edge of leaves due to hot, dry room or fertilizer injury.
PEPEROMIA (many genera)	Will not tolerate heavy, soggy soils, prefers loose peaty type. "Little Fantasy" is a hybrid with crinkled leaves. All prefer filtered or subdued light, dry soil.	Leaf and stem cuttings.	Stem and crown rot due to overwatering or poor drainage, or heavy soil.

Foliage Plant	Green Thumb Tips	Propagation	Troubles
*PHILODENDRON (many species)	A large group and one of the most popular. They prefer subdued light, and temperature of 60°-70°. Humus soil is best and they prefer to be grown on "totem poles" (see). *P. corda-tum* is extremely tolerant of neglect. Cutting off the aerial roots does not harm the plants but be sure to use a clean instrument. (You can dip a razor blade in alcohol or boiling water.)	Tip cuttings in sand or water, also from seeds.	Smaller leaves due to lack of light, hard soils. Failure of slit-leaved types to develop holes or slits—lack of light. Yellow leaves due to overwatering, dry soils, or too much plant food. Tip burn and leaf-scorch due to dry room or dry soil.
PICK-A-BACK PLANT (*Tolmiea menziesii*) Also called "Youth-on Age."	Tiny plantlets form on axils of leaves. Endures dry air, dust, and gas fumes in most homes. Likes bright light and ample moisture. Regular houseplant soil is suitable. Feed once a month with liquid plant food.	A self-propagating type, producing small plantlets which will root if pinned on surface of soil in a pot or set in shallow bowl of water.	Leaves turn yellow due to direct sun or lack of nitrogen.
PILEA includes Aluminum plant (which see); *P. involucrata*, Friendship Plant; Pilea, Moon Valley Plant, which has been incorrectly listed as *P. involucrata*, but has not been given a species name at this writing.	A handsome group of plants useful in hang-ing baskets, shelf pots, terrariums, and on coffee tables. Likes humusy soil, warmth (70° or so) and night temperature no less than 55°-60°. Avoid direct sun, but give bright window.	Tip cuttings rooted in perlite, sand or vermiculite.	Rotting at base of plant due to poor drainage or overwatering. Leaf scorch due to direct sun, or hot dry room.

Foliage Plant	Green Thumb Tips	Propagation	Troubles
POTHOS (*P. argraeus*) Also listed as Scindapsus, or Epipremnum, commonly called Devil's Ivy	Heart-shaped leaves, solid green or splashed with yellow. A handsome trailing vine, more handsome than philodendron. Keep out of direct sun. Likes humus soil.	Leaf or stem cuttings.	Crown rot due to poor drainage or overwatering.
PRAYER PLANT (*Maranta leuconeura*)	Oval, dark green leaves with brown spots, leaves folding up at night. Likes it warm; avoid direct sun.	Divisions or cuttings in sand, perlite, or vermiculite.	Scorched foliage due to dry air or hot sun. Crown rot due to overwatering.
ROSARY VINE (*Ceropegia woodii*)	String of heart-shaped leaves makes this ideal for hanging baskets. Does best on dry side; likes warm room and filtered sunlight.	Root cuttings in sand, perlite, water, or vermiculite.	Rotting due to overwatering or poor drainage.
*"RUBBER" PLANT (*Ficus species*)	Glossy green leaves, elliptical or fiddle-shaped. Likes semi-shade, good drainage. Pot in one part each sand, peat, loam soil. Will tolerate dry soil. Slow grower, resistant to dry air in the home.	Tip cuttings and air-layering. Takes 2 months to root.	Leaf-drop due to poor light, too much water. Spots on edges due to dry soil or leaf spot disease, overwatering.
SCHEFFLERA ACTINO-PHYLLA (correct name is *Brassaia actinophylla*, Australian Umbrella tree)	Prefers bright, sunless windows. Temperature 70°-75°. Soil mixture 1 part each sand, peat, and loam. Must be well drained. Keep out of direct sun. *Do not overwater*—causes leaves to turn brown and drop.	Seeds, and rooting of tip.	Brown leaves, due to overwatering. Grow on dry side. Make sure drainage is good. Pinch tip back to induce bushier plant. Syringe foliage in tub or outdoors.
SCREW PINE (*Pandanus veitchii*)	Stiff, spikey leaves need ample room. Tolerates shade; should be watered sparingly and soil must be well drained. A rugged foliage plant for the "Everything-I-touch-dies" gardener.	Offshoots or suckers.	Scorched leaves or burning around edges due to hot sun or dry air.

Foliage Plant	Green Thumb Tips	Propagation	Troubles
SENSITIVE PLANT (*Mimosa pudica*)	Feathery-leaved curiosity valued for its ability to droop when touched. Likes loose soil, ample light, and warm temperature.	Seeds, which are tricky to start. Soak overnight in water to soften seedcoat to hasten germination.	Yellowing of foliage due to excess water.
SHAMROCK (*Oxalis species*)	The term Oxalis is common name for both Oxalis and white clover. No such thing as a true shamrock. Oxalis is a bulbous perennial grown in pots. Loose soil and good light are main requirements.	Seed and bulbs. Bulbs started in October will produce by Spring.	Avoid overwatering or will turn yellow. Red spider mites.
SNAKE PLANT (*Sansevieria* species) Also called Mother-in-Law's Tongue, or Leopard Lily	Handsome new varieties make this spikey grower a popular foliage plant today; grows in most soils, bright light or shaded window. Tolerates dry soils and much neglect. Blossoms when given good care.	Cuttings and divisions. Divide every 3 or 4 years. Cuttings from variegated type will not come true. Divide these plants.	Yellowing of leaves due to over-watering. No pests to trouble it.
SPIDER PLANT (*Chlorophytum comosum*) Also called Airplane Plant	A tuft-forming, grassy-looking plant with green or white striped narrow foliage. Sends out baby plantlets on narrow stems. If baby plantlets come in contact with soil they'll root. May not form plantlets if plant gets more than 12 hours of light per day. Keep out of artificial light at night to stimulate production of baby plants.	Snip off aerial plant-lets and place in pot of loose soil and keep moist. Will also root in water. Divide plants any time of year.	Red spider mites. Yellow foliage due to heavy soil or poor drainage. Brown tips due to dry air or fluoride injury. Two teaspoons lime per 6" pot corrects fluoride.

Foliage Plant	Green Thumb Tips	Propagation	Troubles
STRAWBERRY GERANIUM (*Saxifraga sarmentosa*) Mother-of-Thousands	Tiny plants borne on runners. Leaves round or heart-shaped. Happy in a cool, well lighted window without sun. Rich soil with ample humus. Water moderately.	Pot the young plants or root in shallow bowl of water.	Leaf scorch due to bright sun.
SYNGONIUM (*Syngonium podophyllum*) Trileaf Wonder	Leaves rich green and arrow-shaped; prefers moist soil and indirect light.	Cuttings.	Yellow leaves due to poor drainage, scorched tips from direct sunlight.
SWEDISH IVY (*Plectranthus australis*) Miscalled Creeping Charlie and Pilea	Waxy green, scalloped leaves, the size of a quarter and some variegated; white flowers. Wonderful for hanging baskets in sun or shade. Several good varieties. Takes same care as coleus. More tolerant of poor lighting.	Cuttings rooted in a terrarium, or plain sand and peat moss, or tap water. Plant gets rather leggy and should be pinched back. Use the clippings for starting new plants.	Yellowing of leaves due to lack of nitrogen. Feed a liquid plant food once a month.
TREE IVY (*Fatshedera lizei*)	Grows upright; leaves resemble maple foliage. Does well in sun or dull window. Soil must be kept moist.	Cuttings.	May get scale or mealybugs. Yellow foliage due to wet feet.
TROPICAL FRUITS Avocado, dates, olives, figs, etc.	All prefer humus soil, ample light and a warm temperature.	Seeds and cuttings. Buy started plants from a nursery if you want edible fruit.	Failure to set fruit is natural, as they are meant for outdoor growing. Red spider mites, scale.
WANDERING JEW (*Zebrina* and *Tradescantia* species)	Ideal for porch boxes, planters, terrariums, and hanging baskets. Shade from bright sun. Likes loose soil.	Root shoots in water or perlite.	Tips take on a scorched appearance, due to dry soil.

Foliage Plant	Green Thumb Tips	Propagation	Troubles
WAX PLANT (*Hoya species*)	Prefers bright window, rich, well drained soil. If pot-bound somewhat, plant will bloom well. Keep cool and dry in fall and winter. Tolerates neglect.	Cuttings.	Failure to bloom due to lack of light.
ZEBRA PLANT (*Aphelandra squarrosa*)	Shiny green leaves, strikingly veined white. Flowers orange-scarlet or yellow. Likes semi.-sunny window. 72° . Soil mix 1 part peat, sand.	Cuttings.	Brown leaves due to dry soil. Tall plant due to lack of pinching.

POPULAR FLOWERING AND FOLIAGE PLANTS

There are too many foliage and flowering plants to treat each one in detail in a book of this type. However, we will elaborate on a few, which, according to our mail, are the most popular.

The Top Five Foliage Plants

•**Cactus** You're either a cactus lover or you aren't. Once you start, though, you're likely to become a compulsive collector. Cacti are great for the busy (or forgetful) plant-lover. And the selection is almost endless. If you've never grown a cactus, your best bet is to start small and go from there. Try the barrel cactus (*Echinocactus*), or the Easter lily cactus, or one of the night-blooming types such as Epiphyllum. One of the best known is the Opuntia, rabbit ears or pad cactus, found frequently in dish gardens. The popular and cantankerous Christmas cactus (which see) is a handsome but finicky one to grow and bloom. The group known as Mammillaria contains a great many varieties grown as houseplants.

CULTURE: Most cacti prefer a loose, humusy soil, good drainage. We use our standard potting mix (equal parts sand, peat, and loam) even for cacti. Some use half sand and half loam. The sod must be well drained, so incorporate a lot of sand in the mixture, even if you have to cut down on the peat moss. Cacti grow best in clay pots (though you can grow them in glazed pots if you are careful not to overwater). Temperatures of 60 to 75 degrees F. are best; below 50 degrees F. can be a bit tricky for them. Direct sunlight is not needed, but give them the brightest window in the house. More important is the way you water. In winter, most cactus plants are in a rest period and should be grown on the dry side. Cacti do not need much feeding, so go easy on fertilizer (if you fertilize at all). By nature they are designed to grow in "deprived" conditions.

Buying plants (especially larger specimens) can be a costly proposition. Expand your cactus collection from seeds. Grow seedlings in a sandy mix, and on the dry side (don't overwater). Cactus seedlings are slow-growing. When they've reached a half inch or so remove (with tweezers) to individual pots. Later, when you've mastered them, try grafting and growing them from cuttings. The easiest way to multiply your plants is by cuttings. Let the cut end dry a bit in the sun, then insert in a box of sand or a well drained mixture of soil, sand, and peat.

Cacti are interesting even without blooms, but blooms are an added bonus. Some varieties bloom better than others, and all need a sunny exposure to blossom.

TROUBLES: Most beginners have trouble with their cactus plants rotting. This is due to overwatering, especially during the dormant winter period. Most cacti don't need watering oftener than once every ten days or so. Some kinds can go a month or so without any watering. Take great care if you water from above, especially those cacti which have a depressed crown. Some folks water with an eyedropper. Sudden wilting is also due to excess water. Cut plants back and repot in a sandy soil mix.

Mealybugs. White, cottony masses found on stems. Try to wash them off with a soft toothbrush and soapy water. This is also a good method for checking scale. Be sure to wash them in the morning and put them in a well ventilated, sunny spot to dry.

● **Dracaena** Dracaenas are some of our most handsome foliages. Most of them are gluttons for punishment. They will grow in poor light, dry soil, and dry atmosphere, although they will be more lush if they are given an evenly moist soil and plenty of humidity. Some of these decorative plants have strap-like leaves resembling corn plants, hence they are commonly so-named. *Dracaena sanderiana* is a small plant resembling a miniature corn stalk. It has long, narrow green leaves with white margins. *D. marginata* has reddish veins and margins, an interesting "tortured" habit of stem growth. The ti plant (*Cordyline terminalis*) is also listed as dracaena. A relative of the florist's spike (used in urns and porch pots), it has the common name of Hawaiian ti (pronounced "tee"). Larger corn types include four varieties of *Dracaena fragrans*, all very striking, alone or in groups.

Broad-leaved types are also popular. Some of the most common are varieties of *Dracaena godseffiana*, having pale green or white foliage speckled with gold dust. They are good in terrariums and dish gardens.

CULTURE: Dracaenas prefer a moderately moist soil, but it must be well drained. Best temperature is around 72 degrees F. For the brightest show of color grow them in a very bright window, even in partial sun.

For best growth, give a soil mixture of equal parts sand, peat, and loam. Avoid growing them in plastic or glazed containers, as the plants need plenty of air around the roots. Syringe foliage with soapy water once a month or so to discourage build-up of red spider mites.

PROPAGATION: You can start new dracaenas from stem cuttings, by root division, or air layering. Place sections in a pot of moist sand and peat moss.

TROUBLES: Red spider mite is the only pest. Syringe foliage regularly or wash off in bathtub once every two or three weeks to prevent recurrence of spider mites.

Tall growth due to lack of light. Cut top off and root it in a jug of plain tap water. If stalk is naked, with only a bunch of leaves at top, cut off top, root it, then cut the section up into pieces and root each in a pot of moist sand and peat moss, perlite, or vermiculite.

● **Growing ferns indoors** In the day of the parlor, ferns were common in homes. Indoor ferns flourished in great-grandmother's day because the old-fashioned home had more humidity, with the tea kettle and clothes boiler releasing moisture into the air. With the advent of central heating, ferns took a leave of absence with the exception of the hardy, tolerant Boston fern. Today, ferns are making a comeback. Ferns give a cool effect in the summer, and in winter they provide the tropical look people long for when snow is on the ground. Generally speaking, non-hardy ferns, being tropical in nature, like the same conditions. Here are the highlights of fern culture:

SOIL: Just about all ferns like a mixture with high amounts of organic matter such as peat moss, leafmold, ground sphagnum, or rotted manure. Roughly speaking, 2 parts peat moss (or rotted compost or equivalent), 1 part sand, and 1 part garden loam is suitable. Add 1 teaspoon of ground limestone per quart of mixture, or 1 tablespoon to 1 gallon. Mix ingredients thoroughly. Charcoal chips or pebbles in bottom of pot help give any mixture good drainage.

HUMIDITY: Today our homes are dry, but countless gardeners have found ways to increase the humidity in their homes to the satisfaction of ferns. Humidifiers relieve dry noses and benefit ferns. Another idea is to use saucers or trays filled with gravel, crushed stone, or sand. The ferns are placed on the trays and water is added to increase humidity around the plant.

In winter you can do ferns a favor by misting or syringing them in the bathtub. This helps prevent leaf scorch or tip burn, especially when heat in the house lowers the level of air moisture. Never try to grow ferns near a fireplace or a radiator, on a TV set, or in a bright, sunny window.

LIGHT: Most ferns do best out of direct sunlight. Fortunately, there is a fern for almost any room in your house. If your window is too sunny, cut down the light by means of venetian blinds, drapes, or curtains. This is important in the summer when you might have to shut out the light in an east or west window by 40 to 50 percent. Many ferns turn yellow in bright, sunny windows. Asparagus fern, *A. Sprengerii* (which isn't a fern, but a member of the lily family), will grow in a sunny window anytime.

TEMPERATURE: While tropical in nature, ferns strangely enough like it cool—70 degrees F. (or cooler) in the day, and 50 to 60 degrees F. at night, if possible. If you "summerize" your ferns, keep them on the north side of your house or the coolest part of your garden, in shade. They don't like the summer heat or summer sun.

WATERING: Large ferns are water hogs, while small ones can turn yellow or shed leaflets if plants are overwatered. A safe rule of thumb is to keep the soil uniformly moist (not soggy) all the time. Overwatering (poor drainage) is rough on ferns and may cause leaves to shed or yellow. Use ordinary tap water and apply from top or bottom. When you water, make sure the soil is soaked, then stop.

FEEDING: Ferns are not heavy feeders. Avoid putting "hot" dry fertilizers around the base of the plants. It's much wiser to apply a liquid plant food (such as 23-19-17), 1 teaspoon to 2 quarts of water, every two or three months. Some gardeners make a weak "tea" of rotted manure and apply it to ferns. Others use dishwater to which a little ammonia has been added. And some use water from their goldfish bowl or aquarium; others, fish emulsion.

GROOMING: Ferns like to be "groomed" from time to time. That simply means snipping off dead leaves, fronds, and browned tips.

REPOTTING: Ferns do get potbound, and some, like the Boston fern, will "rise" (the entire root-and-soil mass will lift up) out of the pot. This is a sign they need repotting. However, don't over-pot. A small fern needs a small pot, and as it enlarges, increase the size of the pot. Plastic pots are fine, *provided you don't overwater.*

Most ferns can stand to be slightly pot-bound, but if plants are yellowish, in spite of good feeding, be suspicious that they need repotting. Tip the pot upside down and tap the edge of the pot on the edge of a table. If roots are a tangled mass, it's time to divide or repot.

DIVIDING: Often your best bet is to take a sharp knife and divide the entire ball into two or three sections. Don't be bashful about dividing your fern. You can't hurt it. Just make sure that when you repot the sections you use a loose soil mixture and water the plants thoroughly until they become established. If you don't want to divide a fern, shift it to a next-size-larger pot.

STARTING FERNS FROM SPORES: Many seed houses sell fern spores ("seed") which can be started indoors. Spores are as fine as dust. Scatter the spores on a box of peat moss, carefully sprinkle with water until moss is saturated, and cover with a pane of glass or sheet of plastic. Keep out of direct sun and keep moist. Best germinating temperature is around 70 degrees F. Have patience, as germination takes quite a while—a couple of months. Remove plastic immediately after sprouting. When plants are large enough, transplant to 2 $1/2$-inch pots of 1 part each of sand, peat, and loam.

INSECT AND DISEASE TROUBLES: Ferns have few diseases, but they do have some tough insect pests, the worst being the fern scale, hemispherical scale, and the mealybug. If a friend gives you a fern or you bring one home from the florist, check it over for scales—hardshelled bodies which do not move. Scales are usually brown (some whitish), and they are sap-suckers. They secrete a sticky syrup ("honeydew") which attracts a black mold-like algae or fungi, which gives the leaves a "coal dust" appearance. You find scale under leaves, on axils, and on stems. *Control*: Not easy, since pesticides roll off the waxy shell. Take a pair of tweezers and pick them off, or use a cotton swab with rubbing alchohol. Also see section on Control of Insects and Diseases.

Note: If you see straight rows of tiny dots on undersides of fern leaves, don't panic. The dots are spores ("seed"—ferns do not flower and set seed; they produce spores).

Mealybugs are fond of certain ferns. This pest is snow white, like tiny fluffs of cotton. It too produces a sticky "honeydew" material which attracts the sooty mold. Control is same as for scale. (See also section on *Insects and Disease*, Chapter XIV.)

Tip burn (brown tips) on leaves is due to hot, dry air or lack of water. Mottled foliage can be due to red spider mites. Syringe foliage and use buttermilk spray or other good miticide. (See Chapter XIV.)

AIR FERN The so-called "air fern" (also called "Neptune Fern") is not really a fern but a marine animal (a member of the *Phylum coelenterata*, to which corals and sea anemones belong). Air fern is found off the coasts of eastern North America and Western Europe, and is gathered by raking the sea floor to pick up colonies of the spineless animal. Then material is treated, dyed and packaged. So it's not a fern, not a plant, and it's no longer alive (no wonder it "doesn't need soil"!)

Here are some common ferns used in homes and offices (our thanks to the University of Georgia College of Agriculture for their assistance):

ASPARAGUS FERN *A. plumosus*	Delicate dark green foliage used as bouquet backgrounds.

ASPARAGUS SPRENGERII
  Florists' "asparagus fern"
  A. Meyeri (Meyer's Asparagus)
  a sport
	Bright green inch-long needles on thorny stems.

BIRD'S NEST FERN *Asplenium nidus*	Wide fronds which rise in rosettes, like a bird's nest.

BOSTON FERN	See Nephrolepis below.
BUTTON FERN *Pellaea rotundifolia*	Handsome dark green fronds 1 to 2 inches long.
DALLAS FERN	A beautiful, compact sport of Boston Fern.
FLUFFY RUFFLES *N. exaltata "Fluffy Ruffles"*	Dwarf and compact, 2 feet tall, fronds full and fluffy. A sport of Boston fern.
HOLLY FERN *Cyrtomium falcatum* *"Rochefordianum"*	Glossy, leathery, dark green leaves resembling holly.
MAIDENHAIR FERN *Adiantum cuneatum*	Dainty green leaflets on thin wiry stems.
NEPHROLEPIS EXALTATA *Bostoniensis*	Coarse "sword" fern with fronds 2 to 4 feet long.
PETTICOAT FERN (A sport of Boston fern) *Nephrolepis exaltata*	Similar to fluffy ruffles, very dainty.
PTERIS FERN *Brake fern*	Long slender fronds with irregular indentations
RABBIT'S FOOT FERN *Davillia fejeensis*	Wiry stems, creeping "fur"-covered rootstock.
STAGHORN FERN *Platycerium bifurcatum*	Smooth broad foliage resembling staghorns. Broad-leafed fern which can be grown in a pot of bark nuggets or on a slab of wood or a stump to which is wrapped a wad of sphagnum. When you water, syringe the moss.
SWORD FERN *Nephrolepis exaltata*	A sport of the Boston fern.
WHITMANII *Nephrolepis exaltata* *whitmanii*	Airy lace-like foliage; a sport of the Boston fern.

•**Philodendrons** People like philodendrons because they can take abuse, and produce a jungle of greenery with very little care. The only thing they are fussy about is drainage. If overwatered, or if the soil is poorly drained, the roots suffer from a lack of oxygen and the leaves turn yellow. Perhaps the most popular philodendron is *P. oxycardium*, also known as *P. cordatum*. The Swiss cheese plant is called *Philodendron pertusum*, but rightfully it is *Monstera deliciosa*.

SOIL: The best soil mixture is 1 part each of sand, peat, and loam. Also, put some pieces of broken pottery or a layer of pebbles in the bottom to help drainage.

SOIL: The best soil mixture is 1 part each of sand, peat, and loam. Also, put some pieces of broken pottery or a layer of pebbles in the bottom to help drainage.

LIGHT: Bright light gives the best growth. If the light is too weak, plants grow smaller leaves, and vines become stringy. A pale yellowish leaf color in an otherwise healthy plant indicates too much light. Monstera or Swiss cheese plant needs more light than true philodendrons or the leaves will fail to develop split.

WATERING: Philodendrons should not be watered too heavily; soil should be moist but not soggy. You can give a light feeding of liquid plant food every four to six weeks.

PRUNING: All philodendrons need some pruning from time to time. The vine types can be trained on a totem pole, using wire twistems. If the tips grow above the pole you have two alternatives: 1) train the tops to grow back down again, or 2) cut the tip out and root it in tap water. Aerial roots grow into bark to gather moisture and nutrients. Prune off the aerial roots which stick out in mid-air, or try to get them to grow into the moss bark.

Some gardeners handle a gangly philodendron by detaching it from the bark slab and making two 180-degree turns in the stem, automatically concentrating all of the foliage in one-third of the original area. One-third of the leaves will be upside down but they will gradually rearrange themselves.

GROOMING THE LEAVES: If you like the glossy look in philodendrons plain tap water with a little soap once a week is enough to keep the leaves clean. (See *Grooming Hardleaved Foliage Plants* earlier in this chapter for some other "safe" plant shines.) There are commercial plant shines on the market, but *use with care*. A little once every month or so is fine, but do not apply weekly as it's apt to harm the plants or slow down growth.

PROPAGATION: Root tips in water or perlite. Tall plants can be cut back and the cuttings rooted to make new plants.

TROUBLES: If leaves do not split, plants are not getting enough light. Move to a brighter window.

Brown leaves. Leaves with brown spots on edges. Due to overwatering or poor drainage.

Mealybugs and Scale. Check with soft toothbrush and soapy water. Enclose plant in plastic bag with no-pest strip for ten days.

Wilting. May be due to poor drainage, root rot (aggravated by poor drainage), or grubs in soil. Check and see which is the cause. For poor drainage, repot plant, adding a layer of pebbles for drainage and fresh soil. For grubs, drench with nicotine solution. See Chapter XIV, section on Control of Insects and Dieases.

●**Rubber plants** The rubber plant (*Ficus*) is actually in the fig family. The plants have green, leathery foliage, some variegated. As foliage plants, figs or rubber plants are among the best for homes, offices, and lobbies (and can grow from 3 to 50 feet).

They like a soil mixture of 1 part each of sand, peat, and loam, with pieces of crocks or a layer of pebbles in the bottom for drainage. *They must have good drainage.* Rubber plants will stand a surprising amount of abuse, but the worst thing you can do is to overwater. Never use a glazed or plastic pot because they do not "breathe." Water the plant once a week and you won't run the risk of overwatering.

Full sun is not needed. They do better in a partially-shaded window. Too much sun will scorch the leaves. They tolerate room temperatures anywhere from 60 to 80 degrees F., although a warm, moist condition seems to favor growth.

Rubber plants don't really need feeding. A liquid feeding once every year or two is ample.

ALL-TIME POPULAR FLOWERING HOUSEPLANTS

•**African Violets** (Saintpaulia) The African violet is still the Number One flowering houseplant, mainly because it's so easy to grow, and under proper conditions is in blossom twelve months of the year. This is especially true of Fischer Ballet hybrids, which seem to bloom even under adverse conditions.

GREEN THUMB CARE: Likes a soil mixture of 1 part each of sand, peat, and loam. Be sure to add pieces of crocks, pebbles, or charcoal in the bottom for drainage. If you use plastic pots do not overwater or crown rot will set in.

African violets like a bright window, but not direct sun. Too little light causes plants to be shy bloomers, or have no blooms at all. Too much light will cause the leaves to turn gray. If the stems are long and leggy you can be pretty sure of insufficient light.

Watering is a trick for most violets. You can water from below by placing pots in a tray of water, or setting each one in a shallow saucer. It's a good idea to water them from above from time to time. Use water at room temperature. If you splash water on the leaves which is either cooler or warmer than room temperature, it causes spots. White salts on soil surface are fertilizer salts. Loosen up soil with tines of fork, and wash fertilizer salts back into the root zone where they belong.

Violets are not heavy feeders. Every four or six weeks you can give them a weak solution of any good liquid plant food at the rate of 1 teaspoon to 2 quarts of water. Repot once a year: remove most of soil and repot plant in new soil.

PROPAGATION: You can start new plants by placing leaf stems in plain tap water, or in moist vermiculite or perlite. Roots will form at the base of the plants in three or four weeks, and soon a small rosette of leaves will appear. Pot these up in a good mix (1 part each sand, peat, and loam) and you'll have flowers within six or eight months.

TROUBLES: *Wilting or curling of leaves.* Due to hot fertilizer salts, poor drainage, or crown rot. If crown rot is present, cut off the diseased portion, dust with Captan, and repot in clean mixture. Failure to bloom is due to insufficient light for flower-bud formation.

Dropping of buds. Due to low humidity, hot, dry air, or gas fumes. Avoid sudden drafts and provide a warm, moist atmosphere and ample water in summer, but less in winter.

Wilting of lower leaves. Sometimes fertilizer salts collect on rims of clay pots. Succulent stems touching these areas often rot. If moisture collects on rims of clay pots the same problem results. Prevent by covering rims with aluminum foil or by dipping rims in hot wax to coat before potting plant.

Spider mites. Cause "glassy" or mottled leaves. Spray with buttermilk spray. If infestation is heavy, discard plant.

Cyclamen mites. Cause brittle, stunted leaves. Also see section on insect and disease control. Isolate plant. If symptoms persist, discard plant.

Mealybug. Fluffy, white, cottony insects suck sap, stunt growth.

Scale. Look for brown elliptical or circular pest under leaves or on stems. For controls see Chapter XIV.

●**Begonias** Begonias, "queen of houseplants," constitute one of the largest and most handsome groups of indoor plants, distinguished by both their flowers and their foliage.

Begonias are classified according to the type of roots they have—fibrous, rhizomatous, or tuberous. (For tuberous begonias see Chapter VI.) The most common types grown indoors include the angel wing (lopsided leaves resemble an angel's wings), Rex begonia (speckled multicolored leaves, very showy), and calla begonia (called "youth and old age"). The calla is one of the most striking, but difficult to grow because it has only a limited amount of chlorophyll, reducing the plant's stamina and vigor. Beefsteak begonia has blood-red coloring on the back of smooth, shiny leaves.

And then there's the wax begonia—a fibrous-rooted type which can be grown by anyone. This is the one used in porch and window boxes, and in shady borders outdoors. It bears in rain or shine, sun or shade, and is self-cleaning.

To some, the newest member of the begonia family, the Rieger type, is the showiest of all. *Rieger elatior* (elatior means "exalted") has semi-double flowers and grows larger than regular begonias. It's the result of nearly one hundred years of hybridizing, involving the work of French, British, Scandinavian, and German growers. Rieger is a cross between the showy Christmas begonia (*Gloire de Lorraine*, or "busy Lizzie") and tuberous begonias. The result is a fibrous-rooted type with sterile flowers. That means they are not propagated by seeds because they don't produce seed. They are propagated by cuttings. They're patented, so it's not legal to propagate them for sale.

There are two types of Rieger begonias: upright, or Schwabenland, and the hanging or procumbent sort (Aphrodite). Both types have single or double flowers and intermediates in shades of red, pink, rose, orange, and yellow.

GREEN THUMB CARE: All begonias like a loose, humusy soil. We grow ours in the 1 part sand, peat/compost, and loam mixture. Commercial growers use a special mixture of 10 percent loam, 45 percent perlite or vermiculite, and 45 percent peat for Rieger.

In summer, do not give begonias direct sun, but the rest of the year they can get morning sunlight (except the touchy calla). Direct sun will scald the flowers and may burn the leaf edges. Shade the plants in summer and keep the soil moist. Begonias prefer to be uniformly moist at all times but never soggy, as this encourages rot.

Never splash or wet the foliage on any begonia, as it encourages diseases such as mildew and Botrytis.

FEEDING: No begonia is a heavy feeder, so go easy on plant foods. A light feeding once every eight to ten weeks is ample. Plants with thick foliage produced by heavy feeding do not produce as many flowers as plants grown slightly on the hungry side. For rex begonias grown mainly for foliage effect, feeding more often is all right.

Most fibrous-rooted begonias grown as pot plants (including the Rieger) have a tendency to get leggy and should be pinched back. Rhizomatous species grow more compactly.

PROPAGATION: All begonias can be started by leaf cuttings with stems 2 inches long inserted in moist sand. Some people cut the leaf into triangular pieces (see *Leaf Cuttings*

Hundreds of varieties of fancy-leaved begonias are available. They can be started from seed or cuttings. (*Courtesy Geo. W. Park Seed Co.*)

in Chapter XV). Or you can take a leaf with a piece of the stem and make small cuts across the back over the main veins. Insert the stem into moist sand so the leaf rests cut-side down on the sand, and pin the leaf down against the sand. New plants will develop at the cuts. You can also start most begonias (except Rieger) from seed. It's exceedingly fine, almost dustlike. Mix it with a tablespoon of white sand in a salt-shaker. Sprinkle it on top of finely-powdered, moist peat moss and sand (see *Sowing Seed* in Chapter XV).

TROUBLES: *Mildew* is the worst problem of the Rieger, wax, and other shiny-leaved begonias. Never get water on foliage, as it encourages mildew and Botrytis blight. *Control*: Wipe off white fuzz with cloth and dust foliage with sulfur. Try Karathane for mildew.

Leggy growth. Cut plants back about half and let new growth come on.

Dropping of buds. Due to lack of light, too dry a room, or lack of sufficient moisture. Most begonias like a temperature of 55 to 65 degrees F. Gas fumes may also cause buds to drop.

Failure to bloom. Due to excess nitrogen in soil, or lack of light.

Mottled foliage, crinkly or brittle leaves. Look for mites, cyclamen, or red spider mites. Dust with sulfur, or other controls as listed in Chapter XIV.

Sugary substance on leaves. Sooty mold, crinkled tip shoots: Aphids. Spray with Malathion or nicotine sulfate. Also see section on Control of Insects and Disease.

Stunted growth. Look for grubs in soil or in roots. Remove grubs with knife. Also see section on Control of Insects and Diseases.

Brown spots on leaves. Due to dry soil, sudden changes in soil or air temperature, foliar nematode, or fungus disease. *Control*: by keeping soil uniformly moistened, removing brown leaves, and keeping foliage dry.

Yellow or dwarfed plants. Look for small lumps on roots caused by nematodes. If present, discard plant as there is no good control for nematodes.

•**Crab cactus** (Christmas Cactus, Easter Cactus, Thanksgiving Cactus) If you think you've got it tough, try keeping straight the difference between "Christmas Cactus," "Easter Cactus," and "Thanksgiving Cactus"; we get many letters from gardeners asking why their crab cactus doesn't bloom at Christmas time. To explain we have to resort to jawbreaking names. First, the so-called Christmas cactus isn't what it used to be. Formerly known as *Zygocactus truncatus* (it is still called that by many writers) or *Epiphyllum truncatum*, it's correctly identified today as *Schlumbergera bridgesii*. A related species is *Schlumbergera truncata*, commonly called Thanksgiving cactus. And there's the Easter cactus, *Rhipsalidopsis gaertneri* (also called *Schlumbergera gaertneri* and *S. makeyana*). The Easter cactus is a spring-flowering relative of the Christmas and Thanksgiving cacti.

So you can see there are *three* different crab cacti, all blooming at different dates. The Christmas cactus has jointed stems with rounded leaf segments and it flowers "around" Christmas, which is how we remember it. The Thanksgiving cactus has jointed stems and leaf segments with very pointed teeth. The Easter cactus comes in varieties with rounded and pointed-tooth leaf segments.

CULTURE: For flowering, both the Thanksgiving and Christmas cacti start to form buds during the fall when days become shorter and the temperature lower. At 50- to 55-degrees F. night temperatures, flower buds will form, regardless of day length. *No*

Christmas Cactus   Thanksgiving Cactus

flower buds will form if night temperatures are above 70 degrees F. If you cannot give a night temperature of 55 degrees F., give the plants a temperature of 60 to 65 degrees F. (night temperature), plus thirteen hours of complete darkness, which means you must shade the plants (or put them in a dark room til next morning, til buds start). After the buds start to form, they'll flower regardless of day length or night temperature.

All crab cacti like a soil mixture of 1 part each sand, peat, and loam. They like good drainage and a bright window. After flowering period is over, you can set the plants outdoors on a semi-shaded side of your home. Keep watered until fall, and bring indoors before frost. Some people leave their crab cactus in a cool, bright bedroom during summer.

TROUBLES: *Non-flowering.* The biggest complaint. It's due to too high a night temperature, or too long a day length (see above explanation).

Bud drop. Due to excessive water, too little water, exposure to drafts. Water plants once a week and make sure drainage is good. Too much water will cause shrivelling of leaves. After bloom, the plants will produce new growth, and during this period of active growth, you can feed a liquid plant food of fish emulsion and give a little more water.

●**Geraniums** Next to African violets, geraniums are probably the most popular houseplants. Geraniums flower dependably outdoors, and can be brought indoors for winter show. There are trailing geraniums, tree geraniums, variegated and scented types, miniatures, as well as the common "Memorial Day" type. The trailing geranium is handsome in a hanging basket, but does not bloom well indoors in winter. Tree geraniums are trained from the regular "Memorial Day" geranium by pinching off the side shoots and training the stalk to grow up a support. Sweet-scented geraniums are old-fashioned beauties making a strong comeback. Here are a few:

The rose-scented group (*Pelargonium graveolens*) has deeply-cut foliage. The peppermint group (*P. tomentosum*) has large soft, deeply-cut foliage. The pinescented type (*P. denticulatum*) has deeply-cut leaves and pink blooms. The apple, nutmeg, and old-spice groups (*P. fragrans*) have smaller leaves and a strong scent. The lemon-scented group (*P. crispum*) has small, ruffled leaves and pink blooms. Culture for these is practically the same as for other geraniums.

CULTURE: Indoors, geraniums like a cool temperature, 55 to 65 degrees F. Give them plenty of water and elbow room. Plants grow best in full sun. Too much shade and high temperatures cause spindly growth. It is difficult to grow the Martha Washington type in the home because high temperatures often prevent flowers from forming.

Best soil mixture for all geraniums is 1 part sand, 1 part peat, and 1 part loam. Feed them a liquid plant food in spring, applying around the base of the plant. You can also use a dry fertilizer such as 5-10-5 at rate of $1/4$ teaspoonful per 4- or 5-inch pot. Be careful not to get any directly on the plant.

PROPAGATION: Propagation by seed is simple. With new varieties you can have flowering plants by Memorial Day. Sow seed in January in a box of moist sand and peat moss, or Jiffy-Mix (or any of the other sterile mixes on the market; see *Starting Seeds* in Chapter XV). Be patient, since some geranium seed germinates a bit irregularly. After seedlings are up (about three weeks later) transplant each to a 2 $1/4$-inch peat pot or Jiffy 7 pellet when seedlings are 1 inch high. Grow these in a bright window and never allow them to dry out. Avoid temperatures over 80 degrees F. Around the middle of March shift the plants to 4-inch clay pots. If you have a home greenhouse, you'll find that most plants will be in color at the end of May, the balance in bud. Seed can also be started in midsummer for winter bloom.

After potting, the plants need all the light they can get. Best day temperature is around 70 degrees F. and night temperature is around 60 degrees F. Feed every three weeks. You'll find that as the plants go into July and August, these "seed" geraniums will flower just as well as those strains started by cuttings. And you'll have a matchless range of colors.

Cuttings. If you want to start plants from cuttings, select healthy mother plants and take cuttings 3 or 4 inches long anywhere on the branch. Take all leaves off lower half and insert cuttings into your favorite rooting material (see Plant Propagation) or plain tap water. Insert cuttings into rooting material to a depth of 1 inch and keep cuttings moist, but not too wet, until rooting takes place (about three weeks). After roots have formed, put the cuttings up in 3- or 4-inch clay pots, using a regular mixture. Grow plants in a bright, cool window, and keep the soil moist. Another way to start geranium cuttings is with Jiffy 7 pellets (see Chapter XV).

OVERWINTERING GERANIUMS: There are various ways of overwintering geraniums:

1. Take cuttings from mother plants and start new ones for next year's show, as mentioned above.
2. Remove plants from pots, shake soil from roots, and hang plants upside down in plastic bag, with a few air holes in it. Add a little moist peat moss to keep plants alive during winter. Some gardeners soak a piece of rag in water and slide this inside the bag once a month. Sometimes the geraniums bloom inside the bag!
3. Cut the plants back and store them in a bright cellar, attic, or kitchen window or sun parlor, where the temperature is as cool as possible.
4. Store plants in tubs filled with peat moss kept slightly damp in the basement. Add a little water now and then to keep the plants alive during the winter months. In spring, cut tops back and pot the plants. Watch how quickly the "dead" stalks put forth new life.

TROUBLES: *Lack of bloom*, a common complaint, is due to too rich soil or insufficient light. Botrytis blight can cause buds to turn brown and "blast." *Control*: Remove dead leaves and destroy. Keep infected flower heads picked off. Give good air drainage, even if you have to put a tiny fan in the window.

Pythium (Black leg). Look for coal-black, wet sheen on stems. Disease spreads by infected rooting and potting materials. *Control*: Bake soil before rooting and potting or use sterile medium.

White fly (see Insect Control chart): Insects congregate on undersides of foliage, suck juices, and secrete a sticky substance which attracts a black, sooty mold. Spray plants with detergent, 1 teaspoon to 2 quarts of water. Cover undersides of leaves.

Spider mites. Cause stippling of foliage, webs on tips. Spray with buttermilk spray (see Chapter XIV).

•Gardenia Though gardenia culture can be tricky, people grow gardenias for the same sorts of reasons they climb Mt. Everest, and anyone who has smelled a fresh gardenia will understand why. The florist's gardenia (*G. jasminoides*) is a tropical item, meaning it likes warmth and humidity. It likes a soil mixture of 1 part each of sand, peat, and loam, plus pieces of pottery or a half inch of pebbles in the bottom for drainage.

During winter months the plant likes a southern exposure, where the day temperature runs from 70 to 80 degrees F. Night temperature should range between 62 and 65 degrees F. If lower than this, the plants are apt to grow slowly and the foliage is likely to become yellow-green. *Note*: Night temperatures above 65 degrees F. seem to be responsible (at least in part) for dropping of buds. Any sharp change in temperature will cause buds to drop.

WATERING: Always keep the soil moist. A dry soil can cause bud drop. Occasional feeding is helpful. Use ammonium sulfate, 1 level teaspoonful in a quart of water. Apply 1 cupful of the solution to the soil once a month from March to November. Avoid feeding during dull, short days of the winter months, as it stimulates growth.

SUMMER CARE: Important. If you live in a cold section of the country, gardenias can be put outdoors from June to September. Move tub and all out and keep in a spot getting morning sunshine and some afternoon shade. Do not neglect watering in summer, as this may cause leaves to turn brown and drop. If plant has not been repotted within the past three years, do it no later than August 1. Use equal parts of peat moss, sand, and loam.

PROPAGATION: You can start new plants by rooting slips (cuttings) in a terrarium, or a jar of sand, peat, or perlite. Grow the rooted cutting indoors during winter.

TROUBLES: *Shedding of buds*. Due to reasons mentioned above, and to hot, dry air. Syringe foliage daily, and enclose plant in clear plastic bag to trap humidity inside.

Yellowing of foliage. A common problem. May be due to low temperature, or a lack of iron in soils. Alkaline soils tie up iron so plants cannot take it up. Acidify the soil by scraping into the surface a small amount of any one of the following materials: aluminum sulfate, iron sulfate, or sulfur dust. Repeat at six- to eight-week intervals.

Red spider mites. Cause mottling of foliage, webbing of tip shoots. *Control*: Syringe leaves daily, and if they persist, dip into a solution of soap and water until cleared up. Spray with buttermilk spray. More controls listed in Chapter XIV.

•**Gloxinia** Gloxinia (correctly called *Sinningia*), in the same family as the African violet, is one of our showiest houseplants. Today's spectacular, vigorous, easy-to-care-for hybrids produce their large, flared, funnel-shaped flowers six to eight months of the year. The so-called slipper-type gloxinia is a different group of hybrids. These include the white slipper flowers (*Sinningia eumorpha*) and a miniature (*S. pusilla*) with half-inch lavender flowers on one-inch stems.

CULTURE: Give a soil of 1 part each sand, peat, and loam, and feed once every three or four weeks with liquid plant food. Grow in the brightest window possible, even one with sun. Gloxinias tend to get leggy if the light is not sufficient. If the leaves curl under around the edges, it's a good sign the plant is not getting enough light, or else the air is too dry.

After your plant has finished blooming, you can dry it off by gradually withholding water. Place pot and all in a basement or cool room without giving it any water. (Some of the newer types just don't want to "go to bed" and will continue to blossom. If they're inclined that way, just keep on watering and feeding them.) After your tuber has been dormant a month or two, check to see if any growth has started. When you see a sprout and some leaves appearing, it's a signal to repot in a fresh mixture and start growth all over again.

PROPAGATION: Can be started from tubers or leaf cuttings. Set tuber in a 5-inch clay pot of soil with 1-inch layer of broken pieces of crockery in the bottom. You can let the tip of the tuber stick out above the soil. Moisten the soil and set in a room of 70 degrees F. *Do not water* too heavily until roots form, or tuber will rot. After sprout shows up, place in a bright window and step up the watering schedule. As growth continues, be sure to turn the pot a little each day so plant will grow symmetrically.

TROUBLES: *Lack of buds or blossoms.* Due to insufficient light. Grow under lights, or in a sunny window.

Spindly stalks. Lack of light (see above). Turn plant once every two or three days to shape up plant.

Blasting of buds. Due to hot, dry air. Put pot inside a larger pot and place moist peat moss in between the two pots. This releases moisture and helps buds develop. Some gardeners put a plastic "tent" over the gloxinia to prevent buds from dropping or blasting and provide the moisture necessary to develop buds.

Curled leaves. Look for spider mites. Dip plants in soapy solution once every three days. Use buttermilk spray. Badly infested plants should be discarded. Also caused by insufficient light, dry soil, or dry air.

•**Orchids at home** When you think of orchids you think of steaming jungles, but actually orchids do very well in homes if a few simple provisions are made, even though the air in most homes is dry.

To get started in the orchid "business" you should buy bulbs or "pseudo bulbs" from a grower. Start out with the easy kinds such as the *cattleyas* (the florist's white and lavender type), or the long-lasting (but less showy) *cypripedium*. Most orchids like a humusy potting mixture such as osmundine (a fern fiber in which orchids do beautifully), bark, and other materials of a porous nature. Shredded bark (fir, pine, cedar, or birch bark) and certain porous stones are used because osmunda fiber has been so hard to obtain. Perlite is also used.

CULTURE: Orchids need not be grown in pots; they do very well in wire cages filled with osmunda, or in hanging baskets. The important thing is good drainage, so if you use a pot it *must* be a clay pot. Prepare the bark or fiber by soaking in water overnight. A small amount of household detergent added to the water makes the bark easier to wet. Whatever you use, the potting material should be coarse to allow fast drainage and good circulation of air so roots can dry out between waterings.

Orchids like a bright (south) window, but protect from direct sunlight from April until October, because during that period too much sun may cause the foliage to turn yellow. You can leave your orchids indoors in summer, or place them out where they do *not* get full sunlight. Suspend the potted plants from a tree or vine-covered pergola, or put them on the shady side of the house. They need to be watered more frequently outdoors, especially in dry weather.

The best way to water orchids is to syringe or mist the potting medium (you can do it as often as every other day). Many people set orchids on trays of pebbles filled with water for extra humidity, which orchids like.

When it comes to feeding, go easy. A liquid plant food of fish emulsion every three or four weeks is ample.

REPOTTING: The time to repot an orchid is usually when the roots start to push out from the base of a mature bulb, or from the base of new growth.

PROPAGATION: By seeds planted in agar solution or by division of pseudo bulbs (thickened stems).

TROUBLES: Look for scale and mealybugs. With soft brush or cloth, wash off with detergent solution. Slugs, sowbugs, and garden centipedes may get into the soil. Pour a "tea" of cigar butts or cigarette butts soaked in water over the soil surface. Malathion will check most insects that attack orchids.

•Poinsettia Look what they've done to our most popular Christmas plant! The new varieties keep much longer, are easier to care for, and the colors are brighter than ever, and the plants are stockier and better shaped.

CULTURE: Give a bright window, not in direct sun, and a temperature of 70 degrees F. by day and not less than 60 degrees F. at night. Dropping of leaves is caused by poor light, so give it the brightest window in the house.

Poinsettias like a daily watering. Keep soil uniformly moist at all times—but not soggy, as this will cause leaves to yellow. If soil goes dry, leaves start to curl and drop off. With proper watering your plant will last beyond August.

When your plant begins to fade, you can rehabilitate it for another Christmas show. Put the plant in the cellar or a cool room and gradually withhold moisture, giving it just enough to keep growing. Or you can set it in the ground outdoors during the summer months. *Note:* Give the pot a twist weekly to break off any roots that might grow through the hole in the pot. If you don't, leaves turn yellow and drop in the fall after you yank the pot out of the soil. Some gardeners stretch a nylon stocking over the bottom of the pot to confine roots.

Cut the plant back to within 4 to 6 inches when setting it out. Root the tips in plain tap water or vermiculite for extra plants. Keep the plant watered outdoors. Bring indoors in fall before frost; repot using 1 part each sand, peat, loam and perlite.

If you want your poinsettia to blossom for Christmas, place the plant on a short-day, long-night schedule, starting in September and ending around Thanksgiving. You must keep the plant in total darkness from 6:00 P.M. until 8:00 A.M. the next day.

Ten hours of daylight each day is enough for the poinsettia. Any extra artificial light coming from overhead lights, or even from a street light, can delay flowering. We place a black plastic sheet around our poinsettia at night and it does a great job shutting out artificial light.

TROUBLES: *Lack of "blossoms."* Due to excess artificial light at night. Follow steps mentioned above and you'll make Christmas blooming.

Yellowing of leaves. Due to poor light, dry soil, high room temperature. Keep soil uniformly moist for longer life.

Mealybugs. Remove with cotton swab dipped in alcohol or soapy water.

●**The "Hearty Dozen"** If you haven't a green thumb but still want to enjoy green plants in your home, we've got just the ones for you. Here are a dozen tough, easy to grow, foolproof foliage plants anyone can grow. (These will generally tolerate a wide temperature range, but the figure in parenthesis is the best or *ideal* temperature.)

1. *Agave americana* (American century plant). Has toothed, fleshy swordshaped leaves, hard, tough, and tolerant. Some have yellow markings on blue-gray leaves. Bright window, well drained soil. Avoid overwatering. (70°)

2. *Crassula argentea* (jade plant). Tree-like succulent fleshy brown "trunk," with fleshy oval leaves. Needs bright window. Avoid overwatering. Too much water causes leaves to drop, as does poor drainage. (72°)

3. *Aspidistra elatior* (cast iron plant). A tough one you used to see in hotels and saloons. Tolerates foul language, bad air, all sorts of neglect. Try the variegated sort, with yellow stripes down the margins of leaves. Grows knee-high. (55°-72°)

4. *Sansevieria trifasciata* (snake plant or "mother-in-law's tongue"). Takes abuse, tolerates dry soil to a remarkable degree. There are some good ornamental strains much more attractive than the solid green types. Try the dwarf, "Hahnii," in planters. Keep soil uniformly moistened. Plants do best in bright window. (70°)

5. *Cissus incisa* (grape ivy or kangaroo vine). Has twining stems and handsome foliage. Does well without sunlight; good for offices and homes alike. Likes it moderately cool, and soil kept evenly moist. (55°-70°)

6. *Senecio mikanioides* (German ivy). Good for chilly windows, foliage star-shaped, light green; small yellow flowers. Easy to slip from cuttings (55°-70°)

7. *Araucaria excelsa* (Norfolk Island pine). Evergreen tree with bright green needles. Likes strong light, syringed foliage, uniform watering. (70°)

8. *Cordyline terminalis* ("dracena"). A big family, called "dracenas," but aren't. Bright window and uniform moisture. (70°)

9. *Ficus benjamina* (Java fig tree). Potted or tubbed specimens fine for lobbies, etc., where height is important. Likes sand, peat, and loam mix, soil kept barely moist. (60°-72°)

10. *Chamaedorea elegans* (parlor palm). Graceful, feathery palm. Likes strong light (not direct sun), ample humidity and well drained soil. Do *not* overwater. (70°)

11. *Howea fosteriana* (Kentia palm). Leaves seen in churches on Palm Sunday. Same care as parlor palm. (72°)

12. *Philodendron cordatum*. Heart-shaped leaves 2 to 4 inches long on traffing vines. Will stand neglect. Can be grown in soil or water. Easy to train up a "totem pole" of moist moss. Likes filtered sunlight. Will tolerate a dry soil but prefers a barely moist soil which is well drained. Cannot stand overwatering. (65° to 75°)

HOUSEPLANTS WHICH CAN BE USED FOR HANGING BASKETS

Listed below are some of our favorite selections for hanging baskets. This list is by no means complete, because there are hundreds of flowering and foliage plants to choose from. For more complete information on hanging baskets and their care see Chapter VIII.

Sunny Window:
Abutilon megapotamicum variegatum (Flowering "Maple")
Campanula isophylla (Star of Bethlehem)
Hoya carnosa variegata (Wax or Parlor Plant). All wax plants, variegated and solid leaves.
Kalanchoe (trailing type)
Lotus bertholetii (Winged Pea)
Passiflora caerulea (Passion Flower)
Sedum morganianum (Burro's Tail)

Filtered Light
Achimenes (all types)
Begonias (all hanging types, including Rieger Begonias)
Cissus (Kangaroo Vine or Grape Ivy)
Columnea arguta (Columnea)
Episcia ("Flame" Violets)
Ferns, many varieties (See section on ferns)
Helxine soleirolii (Baby's Tears)
Maranta massangeana (Rabbit Track Plant)
Pellionia (Pellionia)
Philodendrons (all vining types)
Pilea (all trailing types)
Smilax
Syngonium (trailing kinds)

Filtered Light (Cool)
Chlorophytum elatum (variegated and green-leaved Spider or Airplane Plant)
Cymbalaria (Kenilworth Ivy)
Fuchsia (hanging basket types)
Hedera Helix (English Ivies—all varieties)
Lantana (Lantana)
Lobelia (both blue and white types)
Nepeta (Green and variegated gill-over-the-ground)

Oxalis (both green- and red-leaved types)

Pelargonium (try the Ivy Geranium and scented types)

Saxifraga sarmentosa (Strawberry Begonia or Strawberry Geranium)

Senecio mikanioides (German or "Maple" Leaf Ivy)

Tolmiea menziesii (Pickaback or Piggyback Plant)

Filtered Light (Warm)

Ficus pumila (Creeping Fig)

Peperomia (many varieties)

Plectranthus (variegated and green Swedish Ivy)

Pothos (also called *Scindapsus* and *Epipremnum* — Devil's Ivy)

Tradescantia (Inch Plant or "Wandering Jew")

Zebrina (Also called Inch Plant or "Wandering Jew." Both have many handsome varieties, small-leaved, large-leaved variegated, striped, bronzed; white, green and pink. Easy to grow.

CHAPTER X

Herbs Indoors & Out

•

Herbs Add Spice to Life

Herbs do a lot to pep up a jaded appetite. Their culture is simple and their uses are many. Few twentieth-century cooks can operate without a dash of herbs, even in the simplest of dishes. The ideal location for a pot or box or bed of herbs is near the kitchen, whether you grow them on the patio, window sill, or "kitchen garden."

Outdoors, most herbs are started by seed sown in spring or fall. Fall-sown seed lies dormant until spring, and germinates earlier and often better than spring sown seed. Or you can start herbs indoors and transplant them to outdoor locations. When spring comes along, you can grow them in window boxes, crocks, tubs, any kind of container, or directly in the ground. You don't have to give up precious vegetable space for herbs—they can be squeezed in anywhere: flower beds, foundation plantings, among evergreens, even in hanging baskets.

Outdoors, nothing grows better herbs than the ordinary cement building block, 8″ × 8″ × 16″. Place the block so that the opening is facing the sky, then fill with loose soil. Set the seeds or plants in and watch them grow. Any that do not grow over 2 feet tall are fine for cement blocks. You can sow several seeds per opening, leave one or two seedlings, and transplant the rest to other spots. They can be fed when they are 2 or 3 inches tall, then again four or five weeks later. The only other care is watering. On hot days the blocks may need daily watering. Snip off any foliage that gets dry around the base of the plant.

Winter months need not be drab. A few pots in a well lighted window will allow you to cultivate, among others, rosemary, lemon verbena, lemon balm, thyme, parsley, sage, sweet marjoram, oregano, savory, and many different mints for delightful teas. In addition, you might try sweet basil, chives, chervil, tarragon, and some catnip for your felines. Glass shelves bracketed to the window frame will hold pots for your herbs. Or you can build a metal pot tray and set it on the window sill. Add a layer of pebbles to the tray and add water until it reaches the top of the pebbles. The humidity generated as the water evaporates counters the dry air in your home. Rotate pots about once a week so they will grow symmetrically. A 4- or 5-inch pot is large enough to grow most herbs. Start seeds in clay or plastic pots or a kitchen window box using a $1/3$ sand, $1/3$ peat, and $1/3$ loam mixture. In the bottom of the pot provide drainage with gravel or broken pots. Keep the plants watered uniformly, provide a bright window, and feed them lightly from time to time.

Sweet Basil   Sage   Sweet marjoram

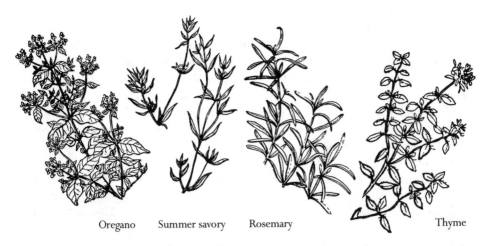

Oregano   Summer savory   Rosemary   Thyme

Herbs which grow on the patio, porch, or terrace in summer can be brought indoors in fall. You can prune them back to 3 or 4 inches before bringing them in and they will branch out into fresh new growth. Herbs will take more abuse than many houseplants, but they do rebel at the desert-like dryness of indoor winter environment unless humidity is provided.

Herbs have few problems because most insects are not attracted to them. White flies, aphids, or spider mites sometimes bother. Several washings in detergent water will usually eliminate them. Hold the pot and soil ball firmly with your fingers. Then immerse it in a container of 1 tablespoon of detergent or fels naptha soap to 1 gallon of water. Swish it up and down vigorously to dislodge them. If aphids persist, add a tablespoon of hot pepper to the solution. For spider mites see Section on Control of Insects and Diseases.

Curing

QUICK-DRYING HERBS If you have a gas stove, the heat from the pilot light alone is enough to dry herbs. Place them on a flat pan and leave them in the oven for a day, using only the pilot light for heat. We strip leaves from stems, distribute evenly over cookie sheet and dry in an electric oven set at lowest heat, with door ajar. They dry quickly, from one to two hours, and must be watched to prevent overdrying. Microwave ovens can be used also. Refer to instruction book for timing.

SLOW DRYING If you wish, you can cut stems and dry by hanging upside down. Sometimes if herbs are dried too slowly they will turn dark or mold. For this reason a well ventilated darkened room, such as an attic or airy garage, furnishes ideal conditions for curing. Dry them away from light if you want to retain their green color, especially those which have a high moisture content. Once herbs have dried, remove leaves from stems and crush with your fingers or a rolling pin. Store in air-tight containers and keep in a cool, dry place.

FREEZING Herbs are also preserved by freezing. Wash parsley, basil, chives, savory etc., and while still wet roll them into "cigars" and wrap aluminum foil around them. Place in the freezer. When ready to use, unroll the foil and slice off the amount you want to use. Rewrap and place rest back in the freezer. Some people chop herbs into small pieces and place into slender spice or olive jars or plastic bags. Jars are capped, or bags are tied with twistems, then labeled and frozen quickly in freezer compartment. You can shake out a few when needed and pop the bottle or bag back into the freezer.

TO MAKE HERB VINEGAR Simply place stem with fresh leaves of basil, dill, marjoram, chives, tarragon, etc. in vinegar and let stand for about a month. You can filter out the herbs before using the vinegar. The ornamental purple basil colors up vinegar beautifully.

HERB BUTTER Take slightly softened butter or margarine, add an equal amount of chopped herbs such as tarragon, marjoram, parsley, chives, basil, etc.; mix well with a fork. Cover and place in a refrigerator so they'll blend, then freeze if you wish.

In chart form are some of the most common herbs to grow for fun, food, and ornamental effect. You can buy seeds or plants from seedhouses and get started building up your herb garden.

Note: The planting time and soil preference under "Green Thumb Tips" refers to outdoor care. Try growing all but the tall ones indoors. Indoors, seed can be started anytime. A satisfactory soil mixture for all herbs in pots or other containers is one part each of sand, peat and loam, or you can use one of the soilless potting mixes. Fine seed should be covered very lightly. Larger seeds should be covered about three times the diameter of the seed.

Herb	Green Thumb Tips	Description and Outdoor Uses	Principal Indoor Uses	Harvesting for Curing
Angelica (*Archangelica*)	Start from seed or buy started plants, grow in light shade. Sow in fall and transplant in spring.	Grows 6' tall, ideal background plant. Cut flower heads off after blooming for longer life.	Use young leaves with fish, seed for cookies and candies. Stems can be candied.	Cut seed head before dry. Cut stems before plant blooms.
Anise (*Pimpinella anisum*)	Plant seed in May in well drained soil, full sun. Sow seed direct without transplanting.	2' annual, sprawling and rather slow-growing.	Fresh leaves in salads, soups, and stews. Seeds in cake, cookies, and fruit pies.	Fresh leaves anytime. For seed, clip umbels when gray-green.
Basil (*Ocimum basilicum*)	Sow seed in well drained soil after last frost. Likes full sun and ample water. There are at least 12 varieties of basil: Spicy Globe, Lemon, Licorice, Sacred, Thai, Cinnamon, to name a few.	Green varieties include: Large green—2' tall; Bush green—14"; Lettuce Leaved—18". Attracts bees. Ornamental basil has attractive purple leaves. Good for borders. Not as tasty as green varieties.	Use fresh or dried leaves in eggs, meat, salads, and vegetables. Purple variety makes beautiful houseplant.	Cut 6" above ground when plants flower. After drying strip leaves and flower tips. Can also be frozen.
Borage (*Borago officinalis*)	Will grow in poor dry soil, full sun. Thin to 12" apart.	3' annual, star-shaped blue flowers. Good in rock garden. Hummingbirds love blooms.	Herb teas, vegetables. Fresh or dried.	Pick flowers and leaves anytime.
Caraway	Sow seed in spring or fall in dry light soil. Germination is slow.	A biennial 2' tall, white flowers. Useful in back border.	Leaves in meat, salad, soup. Seeds in rye bread, cheese, cookies.	Cut seed heads before dry. Cut leaves anytime.

Herb	Green Thumb Tips	Description and Outdoor Uses	Principal Indoor Uses	Harvesting for Curing
Catnip (*Nepeta cataria*)	Easily grown from seed or division of clumps in spring. Not soil-fussy. Grows in sun or semi-shade.	Perennial about 12"-15" tall; velvety aromatic leaves loved by cats.	Can be grown in pot for your cat or dried and stuffed inside kitty toys.	Cut and dry stems and leaves anytime.
Chamomile (*Anthemis nobilis*)	Sow seed in spring or late summer in sunny spot. Thin to 10" apart.	Hardy perennial 12" tall. Useful in border or as ground cover.	Herb tea often used as tonic.	Cut flower heads in full bloom.
Chervil (*Anthriscus cerefolium*)	Sow seed in spring, grows best in shaded, moist spot. Thin to 4" apart.	Hardy annual, 2' tall. Handsome deep-green foliage ideal in back of border.	Use fresh or dried, like parsley.	Cut leaves and dry quickly.
Chives (*Allium schoenoprasum*)	Sow seed in spring or fall, or use divisions. Likes full sun, loamy soil indoors or outdoors. Divide clumps every 3 or 4 years.	Onion-like perennial in 10" clumps, with lavender blooms. Good in rock gardens.	Use in omelettes, salads, cheese, appetizers, and soups.	Cut leaves as needed.
Coriander (*Coriandrum sativum*)	Sow seed in late spring, in well drained soil; full sun. Thin to a foot apart.	Handsome annual, 12" tall; do not disturb the roots when weeding or cultivating.	Meats, cheese, salads, soups and pickles.	Snip stalks when seeds are ripe.
Costmary (*Chrysanthemum balsamita*)	Start from seed or root division in spring. Likes semi-shade, division every 3 or 4 years.	4' perennial with yellow flowers. Shade produces nice green leaves, but will not bloom unless in full sun.	Use dried leaves in linen closet; or as flavoring for cakes and meats.	Cut leaves before flowering and dry.

Herb	Green Thumb Tips	Description and Outdoor Uses	Principal Indoor Uses	Harvesting for Curing
Curly Cress Garden Cress (*Lepidium sativum*) Curly is a curled leaved variety of Garden cress also called "Pepper grass"	Sow seed in spring as soon as ground can be worked or in containers of 1 part each sand, peat, loam. Leaves ready in 5-8 weeks. Successive sowings can be made through August, for fresh tender leaves throughout season.	Low growing round, or curley leaved plant in mustard family with nippy taste similar to watercress.	Used fresh good for garnish, salads, sandwiches, egg dishes.	Cut fresh tender leaves anytime. Old tough leaves develop unpleasant taste.
Dill (*Anethum graveolens*)	Sow seed in spring or late fall in full sun. Do not transplant.	4' annual which may need fencing for wind protection.	Crushed leaves and stems in soups, salads, cheese, eggs, gravies. Seeds in pickles and vegetables.	Pick whole sprays and hang upside down to dry.
Fennel, Common (*Foeniculum vulgare*)	Sow in rows in May and thin to 6" apart. When plants are half-grown, draw earth up to them to blanch the bulbous stalk.	Grown as an annual. 4'-6' tall.	Valued for its anise-like flavor. Cooked or in salads. Seed and crushed leaves used in cookies, cheese and with vegetables.	Fennel plants mature in 60 days and are then dug. For seeds, harvest when ripe.
Fennel (*Foeniculum vulgare*, var. *dulce*) Florence Fennel or Sweet Fennel	Florence fennel or sweet fennel has same care but grows only half as tall.			

Herb	Green Thumb Tips	Description and Outdoor Uses	Principal Indoor Uses	Harvesting for Curing
Garlic (*Allium sativum*)	Separate cloves and plant base down, 2" deep in very early spring or fall. Likes full sun, ample water. Needs loose humusy soil.	Bulbous annual, 2' tall with tiny whitish flowers. Ideal as back border.	Used widely in cooking, meats, sauces, stews, tomato dishes, eggs, and salad dressing. Anywhere a bit of zip is needed.	When top yellows off, pull up clumps and dry in sun 3 days. Remove foliage and store in dry place. Can also be chopped then dried or frozen.
Horehound (*Marrubium vulgare*)	Plant seeds or root division in spring. Tolerates poor soil, likes full sun.	Coarse perennial 2' tall, forms bush for background foliage.	Fresh or dried leaves in cakes, cookies, candy, sauces, and meats.	Cut just before flowering
Horseradish (*Armoracia rusticana*)	Plant root cuttings in deep, moist soil in early spring 5" deep	Perennial; foliage is coarse, so plant in inconspicuous spot at one side of the garden.	Ground roots blended with vinegar pep up meats and salad dressings.	Dig roots in late fall or early spring and grind, mix with white vinegar and store in glass jars in refrigerator.
Lavender (*Lavendula spica*)	Can be started from seeds or divisions in spring. Grows well in dry, stony places but will grow anywhere with good drainage. Thin dead stalks out occasionally.	Shrubby perennial with small lavender flowers in clusters, narrow grayish felty leaves. Grows 1'–3' tall. Good in perennial bed if kept trimmed and confined.	Dried leaves and flowers used in sachets and potpourris.	Cut leaves and flower heads when plant in full bloom. Dry quickly out of sun.
Lemon Balm (*Mellisa officinalis*)	Hardy perennial; sow seed in summer, in full sun.	Good border plant 3' tall. May be a pest if allowed to self-sow.	Dried leaves and flowers in teas and sachets.	Cut tips 2 or 3 times a season.

321

Herb	Green Thumb Tips	Description and Outdoor Uses	Principal Indoor Uses	Harvesting for Curing
Lemon Verbena (*Lippia citriodora*)	Start from cuttings in sand; full sun and ample water.	Fine perennial. Normally 4' high but can be kept 1'-2' high by regular pinching.	Sachets, perfumes, toilet water. Flavors fruit salads, jellies, and beverages. Good houseplant.	Pick tender leaves.
Lovage (*Levisticum officinale*)	Sow seed in spring or fall in moist soil, full sun.	Tall (5') perennial, ideal as background plant.	Leaves and stems used in soups and stews.	Use fresh or dry the leaves.
Sweet Marjoram (*Marjorana hortensis*)	Start seed early and transplant out in spring in dry, well drained soil.	Annual 15" high with gray foliage, white flowers. Front border.	Eggs, sauces, soups, stuffings.	Use fresh, or dry, or freeze leaves.
Oregano (*Origanum vulgare*) (often called marjoram)	Can be started indoors in early spring and transplanted outdoors when weather permits; prefers well drained soil.	Annual 15" high with gray foliage like marjoram, white flowers. Does well in pots.	Eggs, sauces, soups, Italian dishes.	Use fresh or dry or freeze leaves.
Parsley (*Petroselinum crispum*) Many varieties ranging from loosely curled to finely cut and tightly curled.	Soak seed in warm water for a day, plant in rich soil. Full sun. No one should be without parsley.	Neat plant 12" tall, used in front border or edge. Bring indoors in fall and keep in bright window; or sow new seeds in pots. Biennial grown as annual.	Garnish in egg dishes, meats, sauces, salads. High in vitamins. *Parsley tea:* To a cupful of potato water (or tap water) add 2 rounded dessert spoons of dried parsley, or 4 spoons chopped fresh parsley and steep about 10 mins. Add salt, pepper and butter to taste.	Cut as needed; dry or freeze leaves and stems.

Herb	Green Thumb Tips	Description and Outdoor Uses	Principal Indoor Uses	Harvesting for Curing
MINT Peppermint (Mentha piperita)	Plant roots or runners in spring; sow seed anytime. Shade and wet soils are preferred. Takes little care.	Fragrant 15″ perennials spread fast, keep in bounds with metal edging strips. Set in back border.	Fresh or dried leaves in jellies, desserts, beverages.	Cut as needed; dry or freeze leaves and stems.
Spearmint (Mentha spicata)	Same as for peppermint.			
Rosemary (Rosmarinus officinalis)	Start seeds indoors in cool temperature (65°) in spring, or root cuttings. Full sun. Tolerates poor, alkaline soils.	Perennial 4′ high, blue flowers. Needs winter protection. In cold areas, better grown in pots and moved indoors.	Fresh or dried leaves in poultry, meats, seafoods.	Cut leaves just before blooming period. Freeze or dry.
Sage (Salvia officinalis)	Sow seed or start cuttings in spring. Full sun and drained soil. Mulch in winter, remove dead wood in spring.	Shrubby perennial, 2′, light bluish flowers, fine addition to border.	Chopped, fresh leaves in cheese, pickles, sausage. Powdered leaves in stuffings.	Cut young tips. Freeze or dry.
Savory (Summer) (Satureia hortensis) Savory (Winter) (Satureia Montana)	Sow seed in spring, in loamy soil, full sun. Grows fast. Winter Savory has same care and uses; it grows in most areas as a perennial.	Annual 18″ high, bushy. Pinkish flowers.	Fresh leaves in green vegetables; dried leaves in meats, turnips, cabbage.	Cut anytime; separate leaves from stems after drying. Strip leaves before freezing.

(Other mints such as apple, lemon, and pineapple may not be hardy and are better grown in pots so they can be moved indoors. All can be started from seeds or cuttings.)

Herb	Green Thumb Tips	Description and Outdoor Uses	Principal Indoor Uses	Harvesting for Curing
Shallot (*Allium ascalonicum*)	Start from new shoots or cloves in spring. Rich, moist soil.	Bulbous annual in the onion family, bright green foliage.	Use in same manner as onion or garlic (has a much more delicate flavor).	Pull up when tops yellow; dry 2 or 3 days. Cut off tops and store cloves in trays. Can be chopped and frozen.
Sweet Cicely (*Myrrhis odorata*)	Sow seed in fall or spring, or divide parent plant. Partial shade, any type soil. Slow to germinate.	Fern-like leaves, fragrant white flowers; 2' to 3' tall.	Spicy-tasting seeds used with other herbs in salads. At one time, seeds were ground to perfume furniture polish.	Pick seeds when green. Use fresh or dried.
Sweet Woodruff (*Asperula odorata*)	Take root divisions in spring, plant 12" apart in dense or partial shade. Likes moisture.	Creeping perennial 12" high; ideal ground cover for shade.	Fragrant sachet, use fresh or dried leaves for garnishing.	Pick stems in spring and dry.
Tarragon (*Artemisia dracunculus*)	Root cuttings in spring. Well drained soil, full sun, or semi-shade. Divide every 3 years.	Graceful 15" plant with greenish-yellow blooms.	Fresh or dried leaves in salads, vinegar, poultry, and appetizers.	Cut leaves and stems anytime. Dry or freeze.
Thyme (*Thymus vulgaris*, and others)	Sow seed in spring in full sun. Renew planting every 2 or 3 years as plants get woody.	8" tall plant with fine leaves. Some varieties with variegated foliage. Enhances the border. Some varieties are hardy.	Flavors sauces, salads, seafoods, stuffings.	Cut leaves anytime and hang in loose bundles, or use fresh

Herb	Green Thumb Tips	Description and Outdoor Uses	Principal Indoor Uses	Harvesting for Curing
Watercress (*Nasturtium officinale*) or *Sisymbrium: Nasturtium aquaticum*	Grows best in moist soil in sun or shade. Start from seeds or cuttings in spring.	Low, creeping, round-leaved hardy perennial good for moist areas. Nippy, refreshing taste.	Difficult to grow indoors unless in well drained moist situation. Pot of sand in pan of water or a moist terrarium sometimes works. Also can be grown as a vine in a vase of water in the window. Use fresh for salads, sandwiches, garnish egg dishes and cottage cheese.	Pick fresh tender shoots anytime.

CHAPTER XI

Vegetable Gardening

•

Few enterprises about the home give as much satisfaction and as big a net return as the vegetable garden. Studies show that for time spent in the garden, you get a net return from $5.00 to $7.00 an hour. You also get the added bonus of high-quality crops you pick right in your own backyard—when you want them. A well managed plot 20' × 50' (1,000 square feet) will be sufficient for a small family with produce left over for freezing and canning. Even less space is required to grow the same amount of food if tomatoes and vine crops are grown on trellises.

For an indication of the value of vegetables in the diet, scientists studied the food habits of people in the Caucasus mountains on the eastern shores of the Black Sea. According to an article in *National Geographic*, the number of active people over 100 years of age in this region is estimated at 5,000 (and a good disposition seems to be a common characteristic among the older people).

Significantly over 70 percent of their diet is of vegetable origin, particularly lettuce, cabbage, beans, spinach, corn, celery, and parsley. Corn mush, eaten with red pepper sauce, and fresh green vegetables are a major part of every meal.

Americans can take a tip from these mountain people and do more vegetable gardening for health's sake.

The fresher the vegetable the tastier it is, a valid argument for growing your own. Also, all fresh vegetables are high in vitamins and nutrients, but it isn't generally known that different parts of vegetables differ in nutrient content. For example, the leaf part of collard greens, turnip greens, and kale contain much more vitamins than the stems or midribs (but even these parts have some nutrients and are good for roughage). The outer green leaves of lettuce are coarser than the inner leaves, but they have high calcium, iron, and vitamin A value. The core of cabbage is high in vitamin C and so are cabbage leaves. Broccoli leaves have higher vitamin A content than the stalks or flower buds. If broccoli leaves are tender, why not eat them?

To conserve nutrients, keep vegetables cool and moist until you can prepare them. And when you boil beans don't throw out the water. Use it for making soups, stews, gravies, etc., because the water is loaded with vitamins. Whenever we make bread or pizza crust at least a cup of potato water is used instead of plain water; it makes the bread more tender and moist as well as more delicious.

When harvest season rolls around, an important point to remember is to pick vegetables at their proper stage. Try to pick your vegetables just before you are ready to prepare them. Cook them as little as possible, preparing them in their skins if you can. If you do peel vegetables, just scrape or pare them thinly.

Vegetables make attractive additions to the foundation planting. Small-fruited tomatoes are good for trellises. Peppers and eggplants are showy for entrance-ways. Ornamental kale and cabbage keep growing long after frost, when they can be eaten, after making a beautiful display all summer and fall.

Planning the Vegetable Garden

Plan your garden according to the space available, the size of your family, the time you have to work your garden, and the type of crops that please your palate. If it's your first attempt, "Don't bite off more than you can chew" is still good advice. Where space is a problem, you can stick to salad greens, a few onions, radishes, and a couple of tomato plants. If you have space that adds up to about 300 square feet then you can add beans, beets, carrots, and more tomatoes. One of our plots is about that size and we grow all these plus a dozen pepper plants, several herbs and extra onions in the holes of cement blocks surrounding the area. We also have four half-barrels, one at each corner; we grow tomatoes in three of them and Burpless cucumbers in the other. Oil drums cut in half and washed clean are fine substitutes for barrels, but be sure you have seven or eight holes drilled in the bottoms. After our beans are through producing (we make two sowings to stretch their season), we pull them up and sow turnips and Swiss chard. This is called double cropping.

If you have a plot that's 40 or 50 square feet larger (or more) you can plant corn with squash in among the rows. You can squeeze in more if you hand-work your garden (machinery takes wide rows) and utilize mulches to keep weeds down. It makes no difference which way the rows run, although running them lengthwise of the garden makes it easier to cultivate. If they run east and west, plant your large crops on the north side of the garden so that they will not shade the small crops. You don't have to stick to rows. You can plant in any pattern that suits your space as long as you leave room enough to walk between groups of plants for weeding and harvesting.

Remember that all vegetables need at least six hours of sun daily, so if your yard is shaded, take note of the amount of sun each spot gets before you plant. Some folks get around this problem by planting in containers set on movable platforms.

We have found that by making use of mirrors, aluminum foil, white gravel mulch, and a white painted background, plants can be grown in shady corners and beneath the overhang of our house. (These tricks are also handy indoors in winter when most windows do not get enough direct sunlight.) Aluminum foil is especially useful: applied as a mulch it becomes a reflector and an aphid repellent as well. Gardeners with white painted houses have found that they can grow vegetables successfully in semi-shaded areas next to their houses, whereas those with darker painted houses cannot.

IF YOU MUST SAVE SPACE Gardeners can also make use of other space-savers like the following (for more ideas see Chapter VIII, CONTAINER GARDENING): If you have a wooden or metal fence on your property, why not grow climber vegetables such as cucumbers, tomatoes, melons, squash, and pole beans on it? You can also grow these types of vegetables around trees and let them climb up the outside of the branches. The trees should be narrow-based with branches close to the ground, such as an evergreen or clump birch. We have grown buttercup squash and cucumbers in this manner by setting the plants at the edge of the branches so they have full exposure to the sun. First vines may have to be fastened with twistems, and melons would have to be supported with slings of nylon stockings. Be sure to keep the plants watered, as the trees take up a great deal of moisture.

We have a compost pile enclosed by cement blocks. We put soil in the holes in the blocks and sow radish and lettuce seeds, and even plant onion sets in the holes. These waste holes produce fine crops if you keep them watered during the summer months.

SEED CATALOGUES CAN HELP Don't forget that seed catalogues are invaluable sources of information when it comes to planning your garden. You'll find the number of days it takes a variety to mature; the number of seeds per packet or ounce, etc., how many feet of row certain quantities of seed will sow; what should be started indoors; disease-resistant varieties. Study them and order accordingly. Seed houses are more than willing to assist gardeners with questions.

A few more suggestions on mini-gardening:

Kentucky Wonder pole beans can be grown in the corn patch. Let the beans climb the corn stalks, eliminating bean poles. Kentucky Wonders are tender, and can't be beat for flavor.

Lettuce, onions, and radishes can be started indoors in pots in winter, moved outdoors in spring, and you can eat these in April or May, and then all summer, every time some are pulled, drop in more seed to replace the ones you've pulled.

When thinning out beets, turnips, lettuce, onions, carrots, radishes, and chard, remember the young plants pulled make good greens. Don't throw them away.

When lettuce, Swiss chard, mustard, etc., are ready to harvest, leave roots secure and cut leaves off about 2 to 3 inches from ground, and plants will grow more leaves for future meals.

WHAT VARIETIES TO CHOOSE Plant breeders are doing a tremendous job of producing better varieties. Each variety has its strong points. Be sure to choose varieties that are adapted to your area. For example, northern gardeners should steer clear of California Wonder pepper. The growing season is too long for it to produce peppers in northern areas. Choose an early variety. The same applies to tomatoes.

Hybrid varieties of vegetables (and flowers) are being bred with disease resistance in mind. Most hybrid sweet corn varieties are resistant to bacterial wilt. A number of cabbage, tomato, and celery varieties are resistant to fusarium yellows or wilt. Some cucumbers are resistant to mosaic virus and several tomatoes are resistant to both verticillium and fusarium wilt (designated by the letters VF in seed catalogues). Keep your eye out for these because it may make the difference between success and failure. We mention many of them under the individual vegetable entries that follow.

If you have had good luck with a certain variety and it is stfll listed in the catalogue, don't discard it in favor of something more enticing until you're sure the new variety will be more satisfactory. Retain some of the older variety whhile giving the other one a try. On the other hand, don't be so stubborn that you refuse to plant anything else. When we were in the bedding plant business we had customers who became angry when we told them that John Baer or Earliana tomatoes were no longer available. If you don't find a certain old-time variety when looking over your seed catalogue, chances are it has been discontinued and replaced by a better one.

The Soil

FITTING THE SOIL Get your soil in shape as soon as the ground permits. This operation starts with turning the soil over to a depth of 8 inches as soon as it is dry enough. Here's a simple test for soil fitness: Grab a handful of earth and squeeze it tightly for ten seconds; if the soil breaks in several places when dropped from a 3-foot height, it's workable. Soil that forms a mudball is too wet to work. Heavy soils (clay types) are slow to dry out in spring and should not be worked when wet. To improve such soils add plenty of humus each year. Sandy loam soils are ready to work early in the year because they are better drained (for details see Chapter XIII).

There are three ways you can break up the earth for spring planting:

1) Hand spading, great for small gardens. Plunge your fork 8 inches into the earth, lift, and flip the slice back down. 2) Rototilling. You can borrow or rent a rototiller, which does a fine job of breaking up the earth. 3) Plowing. Many small garden tractors are equipped with a plow which can turn up an 8-inch slice of earth. They're equipped with a drag to smooth the surface.

Break up the clumps and rake the soil over after the ground has been broken. Don't fret over small stones. Leave them in: they act like a mulch and hold moisture.

TREATING THE SOIL If you've been plagued with soil pests such as wireworms, centipedes, grubs, etc., you might want to treat the soil with pesticide in fall, after plowing. Most recommended pesticides have directions and rates to use. Be sure to read the label. There's no practical way to treat soils chemically for diseases such as fusarium or verticillium. A good fall clean-up will do more than anything else to keep insects and diseases from flaring up. Rake up debris after the fall harvest and remove nearby weeds and you'll prevent many insects and diseases from wintering over.

ADDING NUTRIENTS Good growth of plants is dependent upon ample amounts of nitrogen, phosphorus, and potash in the soil, elements offered in a complete plant food. With "average" weather conditions, most vegetable gardens produce best when a balanced fertilizer such as 10-10-10 is added at the rate of 4 pounds per 100 square feet. Half of this can be applied before planting in spring, the other half applied as a "side dressing" (along the rows) halfway through the growing season. Lime helps make better use of fertilizer, and usually should be applied every three or four years at a rate of 5 pounds per 100 square feet. A simple soil test is your best guide (see Chapter XIII).

Most vegetables enjoy a "summer snack," since plant growth and rains combine to take nutrients from the soil. A popular way to boost droopy, parched plants along in midsummer is to irrigate and apply a liquid fertilizer. Complete plant foods are available which are mixed with water and applied along the soil row. Homemade plant boosters are apt to burn roots and leaves if care is not taken. If you use a handful of nitrate of soda to a 12-quart sprinkling can of water, and apply it to the soil, little burning is likely, or use 1 level tablespoon of a balanced fertilizer such as 5-10-5 or 10-10-10 with each gallon of water. Dig a ring around each plant and apply a cup of solution, or apply in a stream along the row so it will penetrate the soil.

Commercial liquid "foliage-feeding" formulas such as 23-19-17 are available and these are safe enough to sprinkle over the plant, so that the foliage as well as the roots absorb some of the nutrients. (See *Foliage Feeding* in Chapter XIII.)

Planting The Vegetable Garden

STARTING YOUR OWN PLANTS (For more information see *Sowing Seed Indoors* in Chapter XV, PLANT PROPAGATION; Fo complete and detailed information on seed, consult Doc and Katy Abraham's *Growing Plants From Seed*, published by Lyons & Burford.) One reason home gardeners like to start their own is that they can be sure of the variety. There are some varieties that are hard to buy as started plants, but seed is available in many cases. Also, it's hard to believe, but some growers or store operators will run out of a certain variety and solve the problem by just switching labels. This happens often with hybrid tomatoes. Reputable garden centers and most successful growers don't switch labels, fortunately.

Tomatoes, peppers, eggplants, melons, cabbage, and other cole crops are vegetables that require long growing seasons and can be started indoors. This is discussed in full in Chapter XV. We'll only repeat here that the secret for getting a good start is to use a sterile starting material such as vermiculite, perlite, or sphagnum moss. We use a sand-peat-vermiculite-perlite mixture because the seedlings are moved from it so readily. Never use soil for starting seed, unless you sterilize it (see Chapter XIV).

Most vegetable seeds are not as fussy to germinate as flower seeds are. They like a loose soil mixture, constant (day and night) temperature of 68 to 72 degrees F., and uniform moisture at all times. They are easily started in various tyes of boxes or individual containers such as peat pots, Jiffy 7, Kys-Kubes, clay pots, etc. Melons—both muskmelons and watermelons—should be started in individual pots, three or four seeds per pot, since they do not like to be transplanted. If all germinate, snip off all but the two most promising and let them grow.

Melons, peppers, and eggplants like a germinating temperature of 72 to 80 degrees F. Tomatoes and most cole crops do fine at 70 to 72 degrees F. After germination, they can be moved to a cooler area (65 to 68 degrees F.). See use of heat cables for good germination in Chapter XV.

Don't sow seed too thickly or you will get spindly plants. Plan to sow about seven to ten small seeds or four to seven large seeds per inch of row. All vegetable seeds should be covered. Tomatoes, peppers, eggplants, and cole crops are covered lightly. Vine crops can be covered $1/4$ inch. A sieve or flour sifter is a handy gadget for spreading peat moss (or other starting media) lightly over the seeds. Usually, seed is treated with a fungicide. If the mix is extremely dry it should be dampened before sowing seed. (See Chapter XV for general care of seedbox and seedlings.)

The seedlings should be transplanted into small (peat or clay) pots and allowed to become established. In a greenhouse or in a home, growth is apt to be soft and "leggy," so your job is to toughen or "harden off" the plants in a cold frame, before planting outdoors. By subjecting them to a cooler temperature and giving them less water, seedlings slow down in growth and are better able to withstand the shock of transplating into the garden.

BUYING PLANTS IN FLATS OR POTS Commercial growers who raise bedding and vegetable plants try to keep their stock as clean as possible. Sometimes space is a problem and they have to crowd plants; this brings on troubles. Here are a few tips on selecting good plants:

1. Look for nice green foliage. Yellow leaves could mean plants have been neglected.
2. Reject any plants covered with aphids, or that have light-yellow-stippled leaves (which means spider mites). You'll only add to your problems if you bring them home.
3. A short, squatty plant will take off quicker than a tall, spindly one. Plants that have been checked in growth become tough-stemmed and may take a long time getting started. If you can't plant the stock right away keep them watered, and in a semi-sunny, windless spot. If allowed to dry in the sun, they become woody and worthless.
4. Potted plants are much more expensive than the kind you buy by the dozen. If you have a large garden buy plants by the flat or dozen. They'll yield just as much as the potted ones, but perhaps not as early.

PLANTS LIKE ELBOW ROOM Whether you start your plants indoors and transplant them or you start them directly in the garden, remember each must have room enough for natural growth. A weed is just a plant out of place—even a vegetable can become a weed if plants are crowded. If you leave two plants to occupy the space needed by one, each is likely to produce poorly. Hand thinning is a tedious but necessary step. It's impossible to avoid the need for thinning by sowing just the right amount of seed. Even with high-germinating seed it's a good idea to sow more than you need. To thin your plants, pull out extra seedlings until the remaining ones are the proper distance apart. Most seed catalogues and packets have this information (also, see our chart). We are not sold on seed tapes, but you may want to try them, or pelleted seed, which make seed spacing easier.

WEED CONTROL AND CULTIVATION The best weed killer you can have in the vegetable garden is a hand hoe or cultivator. Some gardeners prefer to use a mulch of straw, hay, shredded cane, sawdust, wood chips or shavings, or plastic sheets. These keep the soil warm, weeds down, and water in. But they should do a thorough weeding

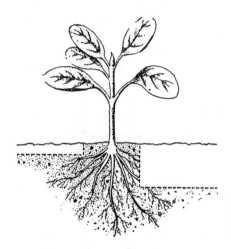

When cultivation is too deep it cuts roots and stunts the plants. Left side, just right; right side, too deep.

job first. (For detailed discussion, see *Mulches* in Chapter XIII.) A garden plot 50′ × 50′ has about 170 pounds of weed seeds in it, and the best way to lick these future bandits is to get them while they are small. You don't gain a bit from deep cultivating, just enough to break the crust is all you need. Never hoe or cultivate too close to the plants, especially in a season of plenty of rain. When there's lots of moisture in the ground, roots are likely to be near the soil surface, and deep cultivation near the plant may cut off as many as half of the feeder roots. A good rule of thumb: cultivate shallow, just deep enough to cut off the weeds below the surface of the ground, then apply a mulch.

In the home garden chemical weedkillers should be used with extreme caution. There is danger of drifting because of the small space plants are grown in. Also, some weedkillers persist in the soil for considerable lengths of time. Even oil sprays from the highway can drift to gardens and cause damage to sensitive crops such as cabbage, lettuce, and tomatoes. Avoid using "Weed and Feed" lawn fertilizers on your ornamentals or vegetables. Never apply them to lawns on a windy day, and never use the same applicator for fruits, vegetables, or ornamentals (weedkillers can persist in a sprayer and injure your plants).

WATERING THE VEGETABLE GARDEN All growing plants must have water, and throughout the hottest part of the season most garden crops benefit by at least one inch of water a week. Sprinkling is good but not necessarily the best way to irrigate the garden. If it does not wet down at least 3 inches it's likely to do little good and may be even harmful. To apply the equivalent of 1 inch of rainfall requires about 2/3 gallon of water to each square foot of soil. (Set a rain gauge under the sprinkler.)

The soaker hose is a good way to prevent soil erosion and it keeps plant leaves dry. Whichever method you use, apply sufficient water to wet down several inches into the soil. Incidentally, did you know dew works for you? Dew can often total as much as 10 inches of water a year, so even if your soil seems bone dry during the day, the plants may still be getting moisture in the form of dew overnight.

One way to save soil moisture is to avoid unnecessary deep hoeing or heavy cultivation in dry weather. Yank out moisture-robbing weeds. A wide variety of mulches can be used to keep roots cool, prevent leaf curl and blossom-end rot on tomatoes, and save moisture. (See *Mulches* in Chapter XIII.)

In some areas water is so scarce some gardeners use dishwater or laundry water for their flowers and vegetables. Nothing wrong with this, even if they contain detergents, soaps, ammonia, borax, and other household chemicals. The ammonia supplies nitrogen, soaps are harmless, and detergents actually make water wetter, more able to penetrate. So, if water is scarce, use wash water on vegetables, fruit trees, and ornamentals.

Rain and snow water for plants: Rain water is usually better for watering plants, and it can also improve insecticide efficiency. Why? Because municipal water supplies are generally alkaline and reduce the effectiveness of many pesticides, according to a Texas agricultural entomologist.

FIGHTING INSECTS AND DISEASES The best advice we can give gardeners is this: Don't be jittery every time you see a bug on your plants. You're not going to liquidate them no matter how you approach the task—chemically or organically. We don't approve of constantly plastering plants with pesticides. If you do spray or dust, a light application is just as effective as a heavy dose. A little pesticide goes a long way.

Thousands of gardeners raise vegetables and don't even own a spray gun. True, they do have some insects but in a world where insects are here to stay (and they'll be the last to leave) you'd better make up your mind to raise enough crops for your family and for bugs too.

Furthermore, a lot of the bugs you "knock off" are good ones—they feed on bad bugs. Pesticides don't differentiate between good and bad. We hesitate to eat produce thickly coated with pesticide residue.

The secret of growing pest-free vegetables (or nearly so) a is to apply a treatment plants as soon as you see the insects. Use an all-purpose spray or dust. See section on Control of Insects and Diseases. Dust or spray both top and bottom sides of leaves. Usually, an application once every two or three weeks is sufficient. *Do not* apply any chemical pesticide to edible portions of vegetables within seven days of harvest.

The best pesticide you can have is a good fall clean-up. Early removal of crop residues and fall composting does a lot to reduce the garden pest population. Fall plowing is also helpful. Don't count on cold winters to kill insects. They won't, because the bugs are too tough! For small-animal damage see section on Animal Control.

SOME IMPORTANT VEGETABLES FOR THE HOME GARDEN

We have not attempted to list many varieties because they change so rapidly. Your annual seed catalogues are the best authorities on what will grow best in your area. At the end of this chapter we have included a chart of vegetable planting information which tells: estimated yield for amount of seed planted, number of days to maturity, rate of sowing per foot, how much to thin plants, depth to plant, and when to sow seed indoors for transplanting outdoors.

Note: If you want to raise vegetables in containers, refer to Chapter VIII for spacing of plants and seeds.

•Asparagus

GREEN THUMB CARE: Asparagus does best in well drained soil. Spring is the best time to set out a patch and a 15-foot row will furnish enough spears for one person a season. You can plant seeds but they will take a year longer to produce. One- or two-year-old plants are best for planting. Dig a trench 10 inches deep, push some loose soil into the bottom, and place plants 6 or 8 inches below ground level if soil is sandy. Shallower planting is needed if soil has a high clay content. Firm soil around the roots, but do not fill trench completely. After young shoots are above ground, fill in the soil around them.

Cut no spears the same season of planting. Wait until the second, then cut only a few. It is usually better to wait until the third season. Stop cutting after first week in July. Snapping off the spears with fingers is recommended over cutting them with a knife. In fall, after foliage has yellowed, cut stalks back to ground, or wait until spring. In summer a few sprigs of lacy green foliage can be used in bouquets after the bed becomes established. Feed a well balanced plant food in spring and again in midsummer.

TROUBLES: Asparagus beetle lays black eggs on stalk. Control with 1 percent rotenone dust during cutting season. Rust can be prevented by planting resistant varieties: Mary Washington, or the Roberts strain of this variety.

The old and still persistent idea that salt is good for weed control on asparagus has been pretty much discredited. Still, many swear by it. If you want to try salt as a weed killer, use a solution of two pounds per gallon of water when weeds are 2 to 3 inches high.

•Beans

Beans yield heavily for the space they occupy. Snap beans, green or wax, are capable of growing in a wide variety of soils. Pole beans are ideal for small gardens because they do best on trellises or poles, and their yield per square foot of ground area is greater than the bush beans. Lima beans need a longer and warmer growing season. The bush or dwarf type lima matures earlier than the pole type, and all can be grown in the same garden, provided the soil is well drained.

GREEN THUMB CARE: Beans are a warm weather crop. It's a waste of time to sow seed when the soil is cold. Lima beans are more sensitive to soil temperatures than snap beans and should be planted even later or they will rot. Bush limas should be sown 2 inches apart. Pole limas and pole snap beans can be sown around a pole. Plant 4 or 5 seeds and thin to about 3 or 4 inches apart.

For a continuous supply of beans, plant at ten-day to two-week intervals until late July. Bean pods should be picked while young and succulent before seeds start to mature. Pick them daily to keep the plants producing freely. If beans have overmatured, dry the pods and use the seed for soups or bean dishes.

Fava bean (also called English broad bean, or "horse bean") is often used in place of pole limas where growing seasons are short. Culture is same as for pole limas. They like cool weather and can be sown in the ground in spring as soon as the soil can be worked. Fava can be cooked in the same way as lima beans are. *Note*: Some people are allergic to fava beans.

Europeans and Orientals have long recognized the soybean as a tasty, staple vegetable; now this high protein, low cholesterol vegetable is finding its way into home garden seed catalogues. A good variety is Early Green Bush soybean, which can be sown at about the same time as lima beans for an end-of-August crop. If you want to harvest it earlier it should be sown between April 15 to May 15 in peat pots and transplanted into the garden when it is warmer. Early Green Bush needs a fairly long season, 85 days, to mature. You can harvest the green pods as you do limas, or wait until pods are dry. Roast the beans like peanuts, or use as dry shell beans. From one packet of seed we got 5 pounds of dry beans. Soybeans contain 37 percent protein, amino acids, calcium, B vitamins, a small amount of sugar, and no starch. They are the best substitute for meat anyone can eat! Just be sure to plant an early variety if you live in a cool climate, or they will fail to mature.

TROUBLES: All beans have the same troubles. The worst pest to beans is the Mexican bean beetle. Watch for orange-colored egg masses on the undersides of leaves. Hand pick and destroy. Dust rotenone on undersides of leaves.

Anthracnose ("bean rust") and bacterial blights are serious diseases of snap and dry beans, spread by splashing rain and cultivating while plants are wet. Never pick, cultivate, or even walk in a bean patch while the plants are wet, as they are liable to wilt completely.

The bean weevil troubles stored beans. Store beans in tight cans in an unheated place if possible.

• **Beets** Beets are a "double-header" vegetable because of their edible tops and fleshy roots. Easily grown, yielding heavily, they are hardy enough for sowing in the ground as soon as soil warms up to 50 degrees F. *Caution*: Each compound seed has one to four seeds within it, so avoid heavy seeding. Twelve seeds to every foot is plenty.

GREEN THUMB CARE: When plants are small, thin to ten or twelve plants per foot. Then thin again as soon as plants are large enough for greens, leaving four or five plants per foot to mature. If you are a beet-green lover you can make successive sowings up to midsummer. You can buy varieties especially for greens as well as for storage qualities. Long Season is a good winter keeper, roots far more tender and sweet than any other beet (and they stay that way all winter). We dig ours, put them in a pile, and cover them with a foot of straw weighted down with boards for winter use. Or, you can leave them in the row and cover with a foot of straw.

TROUBLES: Beets have few troubles in the home garden: all tops, no bottoms (or small bottoms), due to close planting, lack of thinning or lack of boron. Use borax solution around roots, 2 teaspoons to 1 gallon of water. Yellow, stunted, off-color plants: test soil for acidity, and add lime if needed (beets are lime-lovers).

• **Broccoli**

GREEN THUMB CARE: Broccoli is hardy, nutritious, and easy to grow. It has the same general care as cabbage (see). Seed may be sown directly or started indoors six weeks before they are to be planted in the garden. The edible heads should be picked just before the yellow flowers come out of the green buds. Plants will produce green flower buds way into the fall. Plant Green Mountain for a spring crop or Waltham 29 for a fall crop.

TROUBLES: Aphids, cabbage worms. (See *Cabbage*)

●Brussels Sprouts

GREEN THUMB CARE: Though not as easy to grow as cabbage, Brussels sprouts will be productive if plants are started early indoors or in a hotbed. Instead of developing one large head, the stalks produce a number of small heads the size of walnuts. When sprouts have formed, break off the lower leaves to allow more room for the sprouts to develop. Do not remove the top leaves. They are needed to produce food for the plant.

Pick the largest sprouts at the bottom, and eat them as soon as they are large enough. Sprouts are best if allowed to freeze once or twice in the open ground. When severe freezing weather comes, pull the plants or cut them close to the ground, and bunch tightly together in a cool cellar. In mild winters, we've eaten fresh sprouts from the garden as late as February, having left most of the leaves on the plants, which protected them from cold.

TROUBLES: Aphids, cabbage worms. (See *Cabbage*)

●Cabbage

Cabbage, valued for its high vitamin content, is a truly international vegetable, appearing in recipe books throughout the world. Since most home gardeners can use only three or four heads of cabbage a week, it's a good idea to plant a few of each of several varieties, using early, midseason, and late types. Red varieties (actually, the color is purple) are just as flavorful as green and are better to pickle, but we prefer the green for sauerkraut. Chinese cabbage (sometimes called "celery cabbage") has longer, thinner heads and a more delicate flavor and is excellent in salads. Savoy cabbage also has a milder flavor than regular cabbage. It forms a beautiful head with crinkled leaves and a slightly golden tint in the center.

GREEN THUMB CARE: For cabbage, the only requirements are ample moisture, plant food, and a soil that's about neutral.

For early plants seed can be sown indoors in April, or started plants can be purchased and set out in early May. Plants from early seed sown outdoors in April will form mature heads in midsummer. If you want cabbage for storing, sow seed of late cabbage in early June and transplant the plants to a permanent spot in late June or early July. Or seed can be sown in the row where they are to remain, then thinned to about 15 inches apart.

TROUBLES: Since the many "cole" crops in the cabbage family all have the same problems, we'll mention many of the problems this important family gets.

Cabbage maggot. Roots damaged by a white maggot. *Control:* Before planting, dust or spray soil with nicotine. Plant roots wet. Sprinkle wood ashes in the planting hole. Lay tarpaper square on soil, make hole in center and insert plant.

Cutworm. Cuts off stems at soil level. *Control:* Put paper collar around plants. Dust with rotenone.

Cabbage lice (aphids). Use nicotine sulfate (no closer than seven days before harvest), or use natural controls (see Chapter XIV).

Cabbage worms. Velvet green looper feeds on foliage. Use bacillus biological control (see Chapter XIV). Lightly sprinkle kosher salt on head of cabbage.

Cabbage yellows (stunted plants). Black leg or black rot. (Stems turn coal black and mushy.) Start with clean plants. Avoid planting where drainage is poor.

Clubroot (finger-and-toe disease or slime mold). A fungus that persists for many years in acid soils. Symptoms are large, irregular swellings or "clubs" on roots and stunted plants. Liming of soil before planting helps minimize clubroot, since it thrives in acid soils.

Split heads. Due to a soaking rain following several weeks of late summer drought. Excess fertilizer and insects also may be responsible. All varieties are susceptible, although the later varieties have less tendency to burst open. You can prevent bursting by seizing head of the plant and giving it a slight pull until you feel the roots give way slightly (but not pulling all the way out of the ground).

●**Carrots** This vegetable takes only a small spot in the garden for a season's supply. Carrots like a loose, well drained soil. Heavy, wet soil makes them poorly shaped. For a continuous supply of tender carrots make two or three sowings, one early in spring, another about three weeks later and a third in mid-July for storage.

GREEN THUMB CARE: Sow seed thinly and thin plants to 2 inches apart. Thin when they are about the size of your little finger, so you can eat the thinnings. Some gardeners make a raised bed of loose soil surrounded by cement blocks or boards. This method is especially helpful if your regular garden soil is stony or not loose enough. While carrots will tolerate a considerable amount of dry weather, regular watering produces a tastier and bigger crop.

Store carrots in a galvanized garbage can sunk in the ground and covered with straw and leaves (see *Apples, Storage,* Chapter XII). If you use sand for storage keep it moist at all times; otherwise it will draw moisture from the root. We like to store carrots in a crock. Wash them, allow to partially dry, then pack in sawdust or leaves, dampened a bit from time to time during winter. You can also store carrots in a garbage can lined with a plastic bag. (See *Storing Your Vegetables* at the end of this chapter.) If you want to wash and store them in a plastic bag in your refrigerator that's fine, but ventilate with a few holes so they don't rot. Another trick is to leave the carrots in the ground all winter. Cover with 1 foot of straw and some boards.

TROUBLES: The carrot rust-fly burrows into the roots. Best control is to harvest carrots in early September. Also, use Sevin in the row at planting time. Organic gardeners often use ashes in the row. Forked roots are due to rocky or stony soils. Add lots of organic matter if the soil is heavy.

●Cauliflower

GREEN THUMB CARE: Cauliflower grows best in cool, moist weather, but unlike cabbage will not withstand freezing or extreme heat. Feed at planting time and again in mid-season. If you like the white "curds" or edible heads you must blanch most varieties by tying the outside leaves together over the curd when it has reached a diameter of 2 or 3 inches. The variety called "self-blanche" does not require tying, since leaves curl over heads naturally. Harvest the curds when they are still compact, not open and "ricey." You'll have more luck with a late crop than one planted for early harvesting.

TROUBLES: Heading when plant is only 2 to 3 inches tall. This is due to hot, dry weather. The plants should be watered regularly; if growth is checked plants will be stunted. It is better to set plants in late June or July so plants will head during cool weather. Other problems of cauliflower are same as cabbage (see).

●**Celeriac** Celeriac (turnip-rooted or "knob celery") produces a large turnip-like root with a celery-like flavor. The top $1/3$ of the root is not eaten. Store for winter as you would other root crops. Seed directly in the garden in early spring, and thin plants to 6 inches apart.

TROUBLES: None.

●**Swiss chard** This is one of those useful vegetables not grown enough. Chard does well in pots, tubs, boxes, and small spaces; some people even grow it in flower beds, especially the colorful "rhubarb" chard with red stalks and heavily crumpled leaves.

Chard takes both hot and cold temperatures, rainy or dry weather. Many people who like chard better than spinach call it a beet grown for its leaves. Surplus chard leaves can be cooked and frozen.

GREEN THUMB CARE: Since chard is closely related to the beet, it is grown in much the same way. It likes a soil that's loose and well drained. Sow seed in marked rows and thin to 4 inches apart the first time. As growth progresses, pull every other plant for use when they are about 10 to 12 inches high. Of the remaining plants you should cut only the outer leaves as they become large enough and leave the centers to produce a continuous crop for use right up until hard frost.

TROUBLES: Chard has very few troubles. It produces so heavily that leaves damaged by insects can be discarded and you can still have plenty to eat.

Thin stalks. Due to planting too thickly and not thinning enough after seedlings are up.

Slugs will bother sometimes during prolonged wet spells. (See Chapter XIV.)

●**Celery** Many people don't know you can grow celery in the home garden. Some who grow it for summer harvest find the celery tough, stringy, and bitter, lacking in crispiness and flavor. If you grow the wrong variety for your area this will happen. Summer Pascal is good for home garden use and is recommended for earlier crops. Another variety, Tall Green Light, is recommended for fall harvest but if Green Light is grown too dry or started so early that it matures in hot weather, you are apt to get a bitter crop.

GREEN THUMB CARE: Celery likes a rich, moist soil well supplied with organic matter such as manure. Seed may be started indoors and planted out in warm weather or better still, buy started plants. Celery is slow-growing and has a small root system so it needs frequent cultivation, as the plants cannot compete with weeds. Watering is essential for a good crop, and the soil around the roots should be soaked each week in July and August. Watering several days prior to harvesting produces a crispier product. There's no need to "blanch" celery by banking with soil or boards during the growing period. The green varieties which now dominate the consumer market prove there's no need for it.

TROUBLES: *Dwarfed, yellow plant.* Due to a yellows disease. Control leafhoppers which spread the disease. Also, grow resistant varieties. For leafhoppers spray with Malathion weekly.

Early and late blight (brown wilted stalks). Use Manzate every ten days all season.

Tarnished plant bug. Spray with Malathion.

•**Sweet corn** Fresh-picked corn from the garden has far more sweetness and flavor than any you can buy. Corn loves hot weather, yet can withstand more cold than can cucumbers, muskmelons, pumpkins, or squashes. Plant breeders have given us increasingly more delicious corn in all types, yellow, white, and bicolor. Gardeners should plant early, mid-season, and late varieties for a supply of fresh corn for the table from midsummer until frost.

Popcorn and ornamental corn take the same culture as sweet corn, but care must be taken not to plant either of these with late varieties of sweet corn which mature at the same time, or they will cross-pollinate and the sweet corn may lack flavor.

GREEN THUMB CARE: Sweet corn is best planted in small blocks of at least three rows side by side, rather than in a single row, so as to get better pollination. Each silk must be fertilized by pollen from the tassel to form a full ear of kernels. Corn is a "gross-feeder," and should be fed about 10 pounds of a balanced plant food per 100 feet of row in summer. It needs plenty of water to form silks and juicy kernels, especially during dry spells. Keep weeds out, as they rob moisture.

There's no advantage to "suckering" (removing side shoots from the base of the stalk) or removing tassels for earlier corn. Hoe around plants to remove weeds and aerate soil until plants are well established.

Kernels have maximum sweetness when they are filled out, but still spurt "milk" when punctured with a thumbnail. Try to eat your corn within an hour after picking. If you cannot eat it immediately then store it cool. Sweet corn loses 50 percent of its sweetness when kept a day at 86 degrees F. It only loses 8 percent when stored at 32 degrees F. If you have to keep corn for a couple of hours and cannot refrigerate it, fill a pan with water and stand ears upright in the pan. Put the pan in as cool a place as possible.

Don't overcook corn ears! Four minutes of boiling is ample, and for something different, try buttering the ears, wrapping them with aluminum foil, and broiling in the oven eight to ten minutes. To freeze corn on the cob, select small ears and blanch in boiling water for six minutes, then cool immediately in ice water. Seal the ears in freezer bags and place in the freezer. Flavor is improved if a few inner husks are left on. To prepare for table use, remove ears from bags, place in a shallow tin and heat in a 350-degree oven for thirty minutes until ears are warmed through to the center.

TROUBLES: *Black Smut boils on ears and stalks.* Pick them off and destroy. Get your neighbors to do the same.

Ear worms and cornborers. Dust silk on ears and tassels with talcum powder. Start treatment as soon as the corn is 18 to 24 inches high, and as soon as it comes into silk. Cut down and destroy infested stalks after harvest.

Ants on tassels or silk do no harm. They are seeking food ("honeydew") secreted by aphids. Spray with Malathion to check the aphids.

Unfilled ears. Due to poor pollination during hot, dry weather or periods of steady rain. High temperatures dry up the silks (female), and pollen (male) cannot reach the ovary. (For animals and birds bothering your corn, see Chapter XVII.)

•**Cucumbers** Cucumbers are a warm-season, frost-sensitive crop prized because few plants produce such a large number of fruit. There are a number of good varieties, including gynoecious hybrid (all female) cucumbers. These produce mostly female blossoms, hence a heavy yield of cucumbers.

Long varieties are used for slicing (and pickling if the fruit is removed when small). Pickling varieties are blunt-ended when small and preferred by most gardeners who like pickles. Cucumbers which become too large and tough for the table, even ripe ones, can be sliced and pickled using a watermelon rind recipe.

If you can't eat regular cucumbers, try the Lemon, a yellow variety which is mild and burpless. Bitterness is an inherited trait, and hybridizers are working hard to produce bitter-free cucumbers. The variety Burpless is bitter-free and mild, as are Sweet Slice, and Marketmore 70 and Tablegreen 65, two good slicing varieties.

GREEN THUMB CARE: Sow seed in hills or rows, four seeds per hill or five to seven seeds per foot in rows, as soon as danger of frost is over. Cucumbers can also be grown in pots or tubs. A dozen hills should produce enough for slicing and pickling to satisfy the needs of five. You can start cucumbers in peat pots two weeks before planting, but disturb as little as possible when setting outdoors. Never try transplanting cucumber seedlings. If you thin plants, discard them. Harvesting is important. Pick the cucumbers every two or three days. If large cucumbers are allowed to develop and ripen, the vines soon start to decline. Give a liquid feeding in midsummer, provide ample moisture, and do not disturb vines while harvesting. Also, do not pick cucumbers when vines are wet, since this will help spread mildew and mosaic.

TROUBLES: *A poor set of fruit and "nubbins" (misshapen fruit).* Due to improper pollination. Rain and cloudy weather hinder pollination.

Striped cucumber beetle. Riddles foliage. Spray or dust with Malathion.

Shrivelling of vines. Due to bacterial wilt or anthracnose (blight). Rotating with other crops and keeping vines covered with copper spray are sound control practices.

Yellow-green leaf color. Means mosaic, a virus spread by aphids and leafhoppers. Plants are stunted and wrinkled; fruits are runts instead of being nice and juicy. The virus lives in milkweed, catnip, burdock, wild cucumber, horsenettle, pokeweed, phlox, marigold, petunia, hollyhock, and many other plants. *Control*: Pull up affected plants and nearby weeds and destroy. Plant mosaic-resistant varieties such as Wisconsin SMR or Challenger, Saticoy Hybrid, or Tablegreen. No chemical control available.

•Eggplant Eggplant, considered a difficult vegetable, has about the same culture as peppers. Six plants will provide all the fruit an average family of five will need. A rich, warm, sandy soil produces the best eggplants and the most fruit.

GREEN THUMB CARE: If possible plant where no tomatoes, potatoes, peppers have been grown, to avoid verticillium. Start plants indoors (or buy started plants), as it takes about eight weeks to grow plants to proper size before setting out. Seed will not germinate unless temperatures are kept between 72 and 90 degrees F. (see Chapter XV). Plants are frost-tender so do not plant until danger of frost is over. Do not let plants become dry during growing season or fruit will be small.

TROUBLES: *Verticillium.* Causes leaves to shrivel, plants to wilt and droop; there's no control for it (see Tomatoes).

Leaf spot and fruit rot. Two diseases encouraged by too heavy feeding of nitrogen. A covering of copper fungicide helps to prevent diseases.

Poor blossom-set and blossom-drop. Due to low night temperatures, hot dry winds, and lack of water.

●**Endive** Endive (or escarole) is one of the finest salad crops you can grow. You have a choice of finely curled or broad-leaved varieties. Plant it any time from early spring until about the first of July in the North. If you want salads for autumn and winter, sow seed in early July.

GREEN THUMB CARE: Seed can be planted shallow, $1/4$-inch deep, and thinned to 8 to 10 inches apart. If you like the hearts nice and white, plants can be "blanched;" i.e., gather the outer leaves together over the heart and tie with a string or rubber band. It takes two weeks to blanch a head. Aside from making the center white, blanching improves the texture and prevents bitterness.

TROUBLES: *Holes in leaves.* Due to snails or slugs. (See section on Insect and Disease Control)

Bitter taste. Can be due to excess green pigment. Blanching (described above) prevents it.

●**Garlic** (See Chapter X, HERBS INDOORS AND OUT).

●**Gourds** Gourds are not edible, but decorative and fun. A packet of gourd seed brings bushels of fruit for a fall show, and you can even make pin money besides. Here are some gourd varieties to try in your garden or greenhouse: Striped Pear, Hedgehog, Nest Egg, Apple; multi-colored types: Miniature Pomegranate, Small Bottle, Spoon, Orange, Aladdin's Lamp, Crown of Thorns, Warted Hybrids, and Queen's Pocket Melon Gourd. All can also be purchased in mixtures. There are large gourd varieties which you can train up a trellis: Hercules, Penguin, Tobacco Box, Dipper, Dolphin, Half Moon, Star, Long Marmorata, Turk's Turban, Chinese Water Jug, Bird's Nest.

GREEN THUMB CARE: Gourds have about the same culture as pumpkins. They must be allowed to mature before picking or they'll rot. Don't use the "fingernail" test for maturity, as a scratch on the shell of an unripe gourd defaces the surface and may cause rot. Leave gourds on vines until frost threatens, and harvest in the afternoon of the first clear day that portends frost. Cut stems with sharp knife, leaving a few inches of stem attached to avoid bruising in handling. The stem usually drops off as the gourd dries. Large or immature gourds will dry faster if you drill a $1/4$-inch hole through the blossom end of the gourd—well into the seed cavity. This lets air in and prevents rotting. It takes from two to four weeks for gourds to dry on the inside. Green or immature gourds often last only a few weeks at normal house temperature before they dry up or mold, but if you take the time to dry them thoroughly, they'll last a lot longer.

Spoiling can be further reduced if you wash gourds with a household disinfectant both before and after curing. Then after the gourds are *dry*, varnish for a shiny finish or wax for a soft finish (varnish and shellac have a tendency to discolor them somewhat).

TROUBLES: None. Insects don't like bitter taste.

DISHRAG GOURD The so-called dishrag gourd, also called Japanese Bottle Luffa or just plain Luffa, makes an ideal bathing or kitchen sponge. It requires a long growing season, which means you should start the plant in peat pots indoors eight weeks before outdoor planting and set out after danger of frost has passed, or you can grow them in your greenhouse. Sow two or three seeds per pot or hill. During dry weather keep them well watered as they need plenty.

Removing the "sponge" from the gourd is a bit of a trick. We simmer ours in a roaster until the outer skin is tender, or you can pressure-cook pieces of them about ten minutes at ten pounds pressure. The outside skins have strings which you can pull to "unzip" the sponge. Remove the seeds by swishing and squeezing several times in a pail of water. To make them white some people bleach their Luffa gourds in a solution of household bleach, one tablespoon per quart of water.

●**Kale** Kale is loaded with vitamins and minerals, and yet not many people will raise it. Culture is similar to cabbage. It withstands cold weather very well and can be used from the garden until early winter. Harvest by cutting only the outer leaves as they mature, or by cutting the entire plant.

There is an ornamental kale (also edible) that produces white, crinkly leaves surrounded by blue-green ones. Another variety with a pink center is equally beautiful. Both varieties (both also called flowering kale) are worth growing for the show alone.

TROUBLES: Same as cabbage.

●**Kohlrabi** Kohlrabi produces a thickened stem that looks and tastes like a turnip. Stems are cooked like turnips but can be eaten raw.

GREEN THUMB CARE: Kohlrabi has the same general culture as cabbage. Two or three sowings can be made in early spring directly in the garden, or plants can be started inside and set out about the middle of May. A planting can be made in late July for fall use. Thin plants to 6 inches apart. Kohlrabi from a late planting can withstand mild freezing, then it can be dug and kept in basement for winter use. (See *Storing Your Vegetables* in this chapter.)

TROUBLES: Same as cabbage (see).

●**Lettuce** Lettuce is one of the easiest and most satisfying vegetables to grow in the home garden. There are three types to select from: looseleaf lettuce, head or semi-head, and upright.

Looseleaf varieties are good for the inexperienced gardener and there are some excellent ones on the market. Your seed catalogue will tell you which varieties hold up best and will not "bolt," go to seed or become tough and bitter. Head lettuce is more difficult to grow, but there is a semi-head type, Buttercrunch, which is not only easy to grow but one of the best for the home garden. Summer Bibb is another good one.

The upright type is called Cos or Romaine, and the leading variety is Parris Island. With all leaf lettuce and semi-head types, you can pick off the individual leaves and the plants will keep on producing tender, sweet lettuce for a long time.

GREEN THUMB CARE: Because it is a cool-season crop, lettuce can be sown any time from early spring until July. If you have trouble getting seed to germinate in hot weather, try putting it in a refrigerator for 24 hours prior to planting.

Lettuce likes a loose soil. Sow outdoors as soon as the ground can be worked and make successive plantings every two weeks for a constant supply of crisp greens. Some gardeners like to make two or three plantings of leaf or semi-head lettuce during the season and then instead of cutting the whole plant, cut just the outside leaves. The plants continue to produce over a long period if they are given a midsummer snack with a balanced plant food and watered regularly.

TROUBLES: *Bitterness and browning of leaf edges.* Due to hot, dry weather. Plant resistant varieties. Some feel that ozone has much to do with browning (see ozone damage in Chapter II). Tough leaves can be eliminated or prevented if you water and harvest the crop daily. It's also a good idea to make successive sowings for tender, non-bitter crops.

Chewed leaves. Woodchucks and rabbits. (See ANIMAL CONTROL in Chapter XVII.)

Snails and slugs. Worse in wet weather. Never mulch lettuce except with black plastic. See Chapter XIV for information on Insect and Disease Control).

•**Melons** Generally speaking, the care for melons, whether muskmelons, honeydews, cantaloupes, or watermelon, is all the same. There's no use being bogged down in classification of melons. Roughly speaking the varieties known as cantaloupe, honey-dew, casaba, and Persian melon are all muskmelons. Some are netted, and some are smooth-skinned. All melons need a well drained soil with plenty of moisture. Although they are a warm season fruit, it's amazing how sweet and tasty they can grow in northern gardens.

The secret is to select a variety with care, especially if you live in the North. There are several varieties of the "netted" melons we have grown in New York State and have found absolutely superb, including Ambrosia, Gold Star, and Harper Hybrid, with orange flesh. The smooth-skinned "gourmet" melons we've grown include Burpee Early Hybrid Crenshaw (salmon-pink flesh), huge (15 pounds) and as tasty as any melon we've ever eaten; and Honey Mist, with light green flesh and superior sweetness and flavor. Both of these melons mature in about 90 days, but maturity is hastened along if you use black plastic mulch.

GREEN THUMB CARE: To get a head start, it's a good idea to sow seeds in plant bands, peat pots, or Jiffy 7 Pellets three to four weeks before planting outdoors.

Place three or four seeds in each container, covering lightly with peat, vermiculite, or perlite. Water well and keep in 75 to 80 degrees F. Heat is *important* for germinating melon seeds. If all germinate, thin to two per pot. Gardeners who do not start seed indoors should wait until the soil warms up before sowing seed or use Hotcaps to trap heat inside. Never disturb the roots of cucurbits (melons, cucumbers, squash) as it checks growth.

After all danger of frost is past, set plants (pot and all) in the ground. From eight to ten hills are needed for a family of five. Black plastic mulch can be used between the rows or laid in solid strips, with plants placed in soil through holes cut in the plastic. This is a real boon for hastening maturity of melons because it traps heat in the soil, holds moisture, and keeps weeds down. A feeding in midsummer helps fruit growth. If weather becomes hot and dry see that plants do not suffer from lack of moisture.

A mature muskmelon will separate easily from the vine with a light pull, but it's better to pick them before they completely separate from the vine naturally.

As a muskmelon ripens, the background color between the netting changes from green to light yellow. At this stage, the fruit is reaching maturity and is ready to pick. If the blossom end is still firm, hold the melon at 70 degrees F. for a day or two to finish ripening, which will be indicated by softening of the end.

TROUBLES: *Tasteless melons.* May be due to cloudy, dark weather, diseases (mentioned below) or a lack of magnesium or boron in the soil. Such soils can be corrected by giving them a dose of epsom salts and ordinary household borax. Mix $6\frac{1}{2}$ tablespoons of epsom salts to $3\frac{1}{2}$ tablespoons of borax to 5 gallons of water and spray when vines start to run and again when fruit is about 2 inches in diameter. Melons do not cross with cucumbers or pumpkins, so you cannot blame flat taste on cross-pollination.

Aphids and striped cucumber beetles. Malathion banishes these (or see Chapter XIV, for natural controls). Captan added to the above spray will do a lot to check *damping-off, bacterial wilt, downy mildew and blossom-end rot.*

●**Mushrooms** You won't get rich raising mushrooms in your cellar, but it can be a satisfying experience. Mushroom spawn is available in prepared trays, or you can buy a bag of spawn—whichever is more economical. Half a pound will cover 35 square feet of bed. An excellent medium for spawning is rotted horse manure, which must be kept moist, but not wet.

GREEN THUMB CARE: Your cellar (or spare room) temperature must be between 50 and 60 degrees F. Darkness is not essential. The most common failure with mushrooms comes from high temperatures or dry air. If held over 75 degrees F. for as much as 24 hours, failure will result. Never allow the beds to dry out. Sometimes spent spawn discarded on the compost will produce mushroom buttons, even outdoors; however, for a successful new crop use fresh spawn.

If you're a mushroom enthusiast, be leery of the wild types popping up in fields. Some are edible, others are not, and there's no dependable test for determining which is which. For more information see *The Green Thumb Book of Fruit and Vegetable Gardening.*

TROUBLES: Failure to produce can be attributed to drying out of spawn or high temperature.

●**Onions**

GREEN THUMB CARE: Onions are started from seed, plants, or from "sets" (small onions grown from seed the previous season). They can be grown from seed sown directly in the ground just as soon as it can be prepared. All onions like a rich, sandy loam soil. They respond to additions of compost and rotted manure. So-called big "hamburger" onions (such as Sweet Spanish and Bermuda) can be set out as seedling plants early in spring. (They can be bought in bunches from mail-order catalogues.) Set 4 to 5 inches apart in rows. You can sow seeds of hamburger types indoors in February, instead of buying plants. If you sow seed of any type of onion, allow 3 or 4 per inch and then thin. Hamburger onions need more space than the smaller plants. Mild onions such as Walla Walla, Vidalia, and others can be grown satisfactorily only in certain areas of the country. Best to try a few seeds as a test. If you live in an area where "eat-out-of-hand" onions cannot be grown, try a variety called Sweet Sandwich.

Onion "sets" (small ones seem to do best) should be planted 1 inch apart, or closer. We like to dig a trench and scatter onion sets in the trench, cover with 1 inch of soil, then thin out green onions for the table and leave the rest to mature. Onions make best growth in the cool, early spring, so get them into the ground as early as possible. To have several crops of fresh green onions make several sowings of seed from early spring to midsummer.

As the tops start to die down in late summer, they can be pulled and left to dry a day or so in the sun. After that, cut tops off, leaving an inch of the stem on the bulb.

We store onions in a dark storage room around 40 degrees F. We leave some small onions in the garden all winter, and when spring comes we have tender scallions at a time when fresh produce is rare.

TROUBLES: *Onion maggot.* Small grubs burrow into bulbs and cause mushiness. Dust soil and seed with Sevin after planting.

Thrips feed on leaves, causing stippling. Spray with Malathion.

Poor storage quality. Onions with low pungency don't keep as well as those that make you "cry." The sweeter the onion the higher sugar content, and that means they spoil more quickly in storage.

Neck rot. A soft watery decay around the neck. Control by drying harvested onions for a couple of days in the sun before storing.

Hot onions make you cry? Some readers tell us the onions they raise are almost too hot to eat. What's the reason for hot onions? Overcrowding. Planting them too close together (or low soil fertility, or insufficient moisture) will slow their growth and make them hot.

•Parsley Parsley takes little space in the garden and is always appreciated for garnishing and flavoring. Sow in spring or summer where plants can be left until following spring. Some plants can be transplanted into pots and grown indoors for winter use. (See Chapter X, HERBS INDOORS AND OUT.)

TROUBLES: Outdoors: none. Indoors: *yellowing of leaves.* Due to too-high temperature or overwatering.

Aphids. Spray with detergent water or use aluminum foil. (See *Natural Controls* in Chapter XIV.)

•Parsnips Parsnips have a unique flavor and give variety to meals in winter and early spring.

GREEN THUMB CARE: Since they take a long season, sow seed as soon as the soil can be fitted. They prefer a rich, loamy soil that has been spaded deeply so roots can penetrate easily. Because parsnips have little pushing-up power cover very lightly, not over 1/4-inch deep. Thin plants to 4 inches apart. Radish seed mixed with parsnip marks the rows, breaks the soil crust (and provides an extra crop in the same space). Freezing improves the flavor of parsnips, and that's why many gardeners leave them in the ground over winter to use them in early spring before the plants start to grow again. Or you can dig in late fall and store as you would store carrots or other root crops.

TROUBLES: *Carrot Rust Fly.* Roughens up roots. Control by applying Sevin to the soil at planting time.

Celery blight. Causes mottling and browning of tops. Apply bordeaux mixture.

Rust spots. Due to a fungus canker which is controlled by hilling parsnips with soil during the latter part of the growing season. A worse problem in cool, wet seasons. Spray or dust with bordeaux mixture, 4 to 6 tablespoons to 1 gallon of water.

•Peas Peas are a cool-season crop. The best way to get a succession of peas is to plant three or four varieties of different maturing dates. Wando is a heat-resistant pea which can be planted as late as July 1 and still give good, tender peas even in the fall.

Dwarf peas are preferred over tall-growing ones that mat on the ground unless trained on strings or on a fence or netting. For a delectable treat, grow Sugar Peas, also called Snow Peas or edible-podded peas. They can be cooked and eaten whole like snap beans. If pods get too mature, shell and eat like regular peas. Same care as regular peas.

GREEN THUMB CARE: Peas trained on a fence, etc. can be mulched between the rows. Although peas prefer an alkaline soil as do all legumes, they will produce in almost any soil as long as it is well drained. A feeding of a balanced plant food at planting time is sufficient. If soil is very acid add lime at the rate of 6 pounds per 40 square feet. Harvest peas when pods are filled out but peas are still sweet and tender, and eat or preserve them as soon as possible after harvest. High temperature changes quality fast (within a few hours) and it may spoil your efforts.

TROUBLES: *Seed rot and root rot.* Dust seed with Captan before planting, and rotate planting site. Plant resistant varieties.

Aphids. Check with Malathion.

•**Peppers** The culture of both hot and sweet peppers is similar to that of tomatoes. Pepper plants are started indoors in March, ten to twelve weeks before outdoor planting, because peppers are slow growers. Seeds need a germinating temperature of 72 to 80 degrees F. With new hybrids there are varieties which can be depended upon for heavy bearing year after year. Weather, temperature, and locality all make a difference in crop performance.

GREEN THUMB CARE: Peppers are self-pollinating and they like a well drained soil, not too rich. A plastic or grass-clipping mulch helps hold moisture. Avoid deep cultivation, as they are shallow-rooted.

All red peppers are green before they are ripe, the red pigment being masked by the green. Pepper seed may be saved, provided hot pepper plants are not growing nearby. Hots will cross with sweet ones, and you may wind up with a "sweet" looking pepper with fiery hot flesh. Remember also that hybrids are not likely to have the same characteristics the next year.

By selecting the right varieties you can avoid the aggravation of "lots of bush and no fruit." We have raised all kinds of peppers and are convinced the following are excellent sweet varieties which do well even for short seasons: Vinedale (62 days), 3 inches long, blunt-nosed, glossy green to scarlet, and dependable, but not as thick-skinned as others. Cubanelle (68 days), 6 inches, bright yellow-green, tapered, heavy producer. Canape, an early hybrid (62 days), 3 1/2 inches long and high-yielding. Sweet Banana (72 days), another dependable and heavy producer, 6 inches long, looks like a hot pepper. Charles Wilson, formerly of Jos. Harris Co. recommends Staddon's Select if you want a large, blocky pepper for extra early crops (70 days). Lady Bell is also a dependable bearer.

Most hot peppers are better bearers than sweet ones. For some goods ones try: Hot Portugal (64 days), 6 inches long, red, and a heavy yielder. Rumanian Wax is a hot yellow-fruited pepper, 5 inches. Flesh is sweet but the ribs are hot. Turns bright red. Hungarian Wax (70 days) is yellow-fruited and very prolific (looks like Sweet Banana, but watch out!). After being "burned" several times our friend Robert Mann discovered that on a bush you can tell sweet from hot ones this way: Yellow banana-fruited types such as Sweet Banana grow or point down. Hot banana-shaped peppers point or grow upward as if pointing to the hot sun.

TROUBLES: *All bush, no fruit.* Due to loss of water from soil, low relative humidity, or hot drying winds at blossom or bud time. Irrigation and mulching are recommended. Also, in cooler climates an early bearer must be grown. Use the varieties we mentioned, as they are not affected by the vagaries of weather.

•**Potatoes** Potatoes are fun to grow because it's always exciting to find the "hidden treasure" of tubers at harvest time. Many home gardeners like to raise their own because potatoes lose flavor if stored too warm and turn green when exposed to light, and these are hazards of some produce counters.

GREEN THUMB CARE: Potatoes like a loose sandy loam and a slightly acid soil for best growth. Compost worked into the soil is good, but avoid poultry and rabbit manure because it encourages scab, a seed- and soil-borne disease. Do not let potatoes grow dry, or most of the tubers will be small.

Small potatoes, $1\frac{1}{4}$ to 2 ounces, are planted whole, or larger ones cut into blocky pieces with an "eye" or bud on each may be used. Plant as soon as soil can be worked in spring, covering 4 to 5 inches deep. If potatoes are peeled thickly in spring at planting time they can be saved up for three or four days and then planted to produce a crop. Each peeling must have an eye. To produce about 5 bushels of late potatoes from tubers, you need about 10 pounds of "seed pieces" (potatoes with eyes or sprouts). For early potatoes you would need 10 pounds for 1 bushel. Seed potatoes must have an eye or sprout on each piece.

Have you ever grown potatoes using wood chips? Loosen the soil a bit and place the seed pieces on the ground, then put on some decayed wood chips, about 4 or 5 inches deep. After the green plants are up to a height of about a foot, fill in between the rows with about 6 inches of the wood chips. As the plants spread out, scatter a little balanced plant food on the chips in the middle of the rows.

Potato bugs seem to have very little truck for wood chips, and chips hold the moisture, keep the soil cooler. There's a big difference in the flavor of potatoes grown this way.

Many people use straw to grow potatoes. The soil surface is loosened a bit, seed potatoes are planted and covered with straw, or they are laid on the ground in rows and gently pushed into the soil, which has been worked, and covered with straw to a depth of 8 to 12 inches. Avoid letting the potatoes become exposed to the light (the skins will turn green, causing a bitter taste which also may be toxic). During the season some of the straw will rot away, so it's better to have a deep covering to start with. Straw-covered potatoes mature faster, and the tubers are always at your fingertips. As soon as potatoes have developed just lift up the straw and there they are, so clean they need no washing.

STORAGE: Potatoes keep best at temperatures between 36 and 40 degrees F., an impossibility in modern homes (see *Storing Your Vegetables and Fruits* at end of this chapter). Cover containers with opaque material to keep out light and prevent greening. If potatoes start to sprout be sure to gouge out eyes, as sprouts are poisonous.

You can keep stored potatoes from sprouting by mixing apples with them. Tests at Ohio State University have found that apples give off ethylene gas, which halts sprouting. One apple per bag, if the bag is paper or paper-lined, is enough. You can use about 10 pounds of apples per bushel of potatoes if the spuds are stored loose. Potatoes and apples, incidentally, shorten the life of cut flowers, so don't keep posies in their vicinity if you want them to last.

TROUBLES: *Scab.* The most common trouble with potatoes is scab, or pits on the tubers. Scab is a bacterial disease, seed- and soil-borne. It's worst in sweet or alkaline soils and is stopped in soils that are acid (pH below 5.6). Too much chicken or barnyard manure or too much lime or wood ashes produces scab. *Control:* Grow scab-resistant varieties such as Ontario and Cherokee (but these lack the quality that scab-prone potatoes have). Your best bet is to test your soil with a simple test kit (see Chapter XIII) so that you can get the pH reading below 5.6. If your soil is sweet (alkaline), sulfur will lower the pH to the point where the scab organism cannot thrive.

Green skinned tubers. Due to sunburn in the garden or too much light in storage. If potatoes become exposed, cover roots and tubers by hilling up soil from between the rows to exclude sunlight. Usually if potatoes are planted 4 to 5 inches deep they have enough soil cover. Store potatoes in a dark room or covered with a dark cloth.

Potato beetles. If you have only a few potato plants the old-fashioned way still works. Take a pan with a little kerosene in the bottom. Paddle or knock the beetles into the pan. If you want to spray or dust use Methoxychlor or Malathion.

Potato leafhopper and flea beetles. Dust with all-purpose garden dust or talcum powder or use other organic sprays (see in Chapter XIV).

•**Pumpkins** Pumpkins take up so much space it doesn't pay to grow them in the small garden. Jackpot is a full-size pumpkin which grows on compact vines, but even so it takes up considerable space. If you want to raise a small pumpkin try Spookie, only 6 inches in diameter. Its thick flesh is great for pies.

If you're a pumpkin-seed eater and are tired of removing the hulls, grow Lady Godiva. It produces naked (hulless) seeds, ready to eat raw or toasted, without tedious shelling. Pumpkins weigh about 6 pounds, but the flesh is not of table quality.

GREEN THUMB CARE: Culture of pumpkins is the same as for winter squash. They like a well drained, sandy soil. Plant compact types 4 feet apart each way. Space hills of the large vining types 6 to 8 feet apart each way. Plant six seeds to the hill, and thin to three when they start to come up.

To prevent lopsided pumpkins, set the young ones in an upright position. Do this when they are about 6 or 8 inches across, even propping them up with a couple of small stones—anything to keep them resting in an upright position. If you don't, one side of the pumpkin will be 4 or 5 inches higher than the other, not too satisfactory for Halloween.

TROUBLES: Same as squash (see).

•**Radishes** Radishes are hardy, easy, and quick to mature. They do best in cool weather, become pungent in hot weather. Small, round varieties mature more quickly than long ones. Cherry Belle matures in 24 days, has white flesh and is as round as a marble. Icicle is a good white radish, 4 or 5 inches long, and mild. Champion is another good radish which stays firm and lacks pithiness.

GREEN THUMB CARE: All radishes like a loose, rich, and moist soil. Make successive plantings for young, tender radishes; irrigate every third day. A few feet of row sowed every ten days throughout the summer will give you a continuous supply. Midsummer plantings may be a bit bitey, but if you marinate slices in oil and vinegar for two hours it takes the sting out. They are delicious in salads.

TROUBLES: *Hot taste.* Due to dry soils and hot weather.

All tops, no bottoms. Due to planting close together without thinning, or lack of boron.

Flea beetles. Checked by dusting with talcum powder or Malathion. To avoid root maggots, soak seed in kerosene 15 minutes.

Pithiness. A common annoyance. Due to heredity, aggravated by hot, dry soils. Grow a pith-resistant type such as Champion.

●**Rhubarb** Pie-plant or rhubarb likes a deep, rich, well drained soil with plenty of moisture and heavy feeding to keep it tasty. A rhubarb patch will last as long as your house. Varieties to try: McDonald and Valentine.

GREEN THUMB CARE: Plant root divisions in fall or spring, setting crowns 2 to 4 inches below soil level, 3 to 4 feet apart. Don't harvest any stalks until after the third year. Remove flower stalks as soon as they appear to conserve the plant's strength. Never cut stalks; rather, pull them. Some gardeners confine feeding to chemical plant foods, as manure may encourage disease problems. Organic gardeners disagree, and favor the use of rotted manure on the rhubarb patch. Authorities say to divide the roots in your patch every five or six years, but most gardeners do not bother to do this and they have all the "pie-plant" they can eat!

TROUBLES: *Curculio.* A snout beetle attacking stalks. Dust with rotenone when stalks are 2 to 3 inches long and leaves have started to unfold.

Thin stalks. When stalks are pencil-thin it's a sign the plants need division. If plants are not husky, and are slow-growing, add fertilizer (or rotted manure) in fall. If that doesn't work, divide the plants and set crowns in a new spot.

●**Rutabaga** The roots of this plant, also called Swede turnip, have a coarse appearance but a smooth texture and agreeable spicy flavor. Turnips grow in almost any soil that is well drained.

GREEN THUMB CARE: Sow seed June 15 to July 1, and thin plants six to ten inches apart in the row. They develop an excellent flavor after a few frosts but should be dug before ground freezes. They keep well most of the winter. (See *Storing Your Vegetables and Fruits* at the end of this chapter.)

TROUBLES: *Flea beetles.* Dust with wood ashes or talcum powder.

Cabbage maggot. Dust or spray soil at planting time with Sevin, or soak seeds in kerosene for 15 minutes before planting.

●**Shallots** (See Chapter X, HERBS INDOORS AND OUT).

●**Spinach** Spinach is an early spring and late fall crop. Late spring and summer sowings will almost always send the plants to seed ("bolt").

GREEN THUMB CARE: Sow seed in rows spaced 18 inches apart and thin plants to stand 3 to 6 inches apart. Culture is like chard (see).

TROUBLES: Leaf miners can be a problem. Spraying is difficult as the tender leaves are the part you eat. Early spring or fall plantings usually escape damage.

•**Squash (summer and winter)** It's gratifying to note a new respect for a vegetable (summer squash) at one time frowned upon by a large number of Americans.

To be technical, the hard-skinned winter squashes (Acorn, Butternut, Hubbard, etc.) are the true squashes. So-called "summer squashes" should be correctly called summer pumpkins. Regardless of what you call them, they are here to stay because many have discovered the value of this prolific, versatile crop.

If you have a small garden you can grow bush squash instead of long, rambly vines. Patty Pan bush type hybrids resemble scalloped frisbees. They come in white or green, are abundant yielders, and are extremely tasty. Regular zucchini and yellow summer squash have to be picked and eaten as soon as they are 6 to 8 inches long or they will lose much of their flavor. Patty Pan, however, keeps well and doesn't have to be picked daily (though regular picking increases production).

Along with the green zucchini, we have a golden type. Kept picked, they yield large numbers of fruit all season long. Butterbar also merits high marks.

GREEN THUMB CARE: Five or six seeds of bush types can be sown in hills 4 feet apart. Also they can be planted one foot apart in rows. Non-bush types can be sown five or six seeds in hills every 7 feet. Later thin the plants to three in a hill.

Winter squash needs more space to grow than summer squash. Plant rows 6 or 7 feet apart for smaller types such as butternut, acorn, and buttercup, and rows 9 feet apart for the larger types such as hubbard. Plant in hills 4 feet apart in the rows, with eight to ten seeds to the hill, then thin to three plants per hill after plants are up.

For earlier squash you can sow seeds indoors in Jiffy 7 Pellets or peat pots, four weeks before time to set outdoors (see the beginning of this chapter, Chapter XV). When setting out, try this trick: dig a hole a foot deep, half fill it with rotted manure, add some soil and set the plant in. Firm soil around the base.

All kinds of squash will grow best in a deep, well drained soil. Working a couple of handfuls of 5-10-5 into the soil around each clump of plants is beneficial, and it will last all season.

Pick winter squash before frost. They will take a light frost but don't take a chance.

TROUBLES: Summer and winter squash and pumpkin troubles are the same.

Squash vine borer. Causes wilting and death of vines. Small piles of a sawdust-like material (frass) on ground indicate presence of borers. Spray vines during late June and early July (after the blossom shucks have fallen) using 2 tablespoons of 50 percent Methoxychlor to a gallon of water, giving two or three doses seven days apart. Borers already inside a stem may be stabbed with a penknife. Carefully slit stem on one side and remove the borer. The wounded stalk is then placed on the ground and covered with soil for root formation.

Squash bugs. A nuisance, causing leaves to shrivel. They can be controlled by Malathion. Clean up and burn or seal in plastic and discard all vines and trash in fall. Organic gardeners should try garlic-red pepper spray. (See Chapter XIV.)

Blossom drop. Blossoms which dry up are *no* cause for alarm. Squash and pumpkins produce five to ten male blossoms to one female, and only a small percent of the female blossoms naturally develop into fruits. Nature produces more male blooms to make sure

Bush Limas are productive and dependable, and are earlier than pole types.

Pole beans are heavy producers. Especially good for small-space gardeners since several plants can be grown around one pole, on a trellis or boundary line fence.

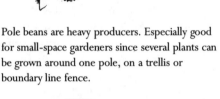

Acorn squash at various stages of maturity. Do not pick too early and be sure to pick before a heavy frost.

The new "bush" types of winter squash grow on compact vines that take up less space than the non-bush types. Bush squash are ideal for gardeners with limited space.

Squash produce 5 to 10 male blossoms to 1 female. Only a small percent of the female blossoms develop into fruits. Allow plenty of space to grow, and be sure to pick daily for a continous supply.

(Courtesy National Garden Bureau, Inc.)

there is enough pollen to fertilize the female blossoms. So those blooms which come out in profusion, then dry up and drop off are the males, and they wouldn't produce any fruit anyway.

•**Sunflowers** Sunflowers may not be a vegetable in the usual sense, but they're loaded with nutrients, vitamins, and proteins. A row of sunflowers makes a fine "living fence" as well as a snack bar for the birds.

GREEN THUMB CARE: Sunflowers grow in any kind of soil. They prefer full sun and plenty of moisture. Sow seeds two per foot or sow in hills, three or four per hill, and cover with a half inch of soil. Thin so that plants are about a foot apart. Seed germinates quickly.

Keep plants watered during dry spells if you want exhibition sunflowers.

TROUBLES: *Mildewing of seed heads*. Prevent by picking heads when seeds first start to ripen (just before they shed). A friend of ours uses a stiff bristle brush or a curry comb to dislodge the seeds. He puts them on a screen and dries them in a very warm airy place. Better still, dry them off quickly by placing seeds in front of an electric fan to drive off moisture.

Bird damage. Most people would rather have sunflower seeds available for birds in winter instead of fall. Cover seed heads with muslin or cheese cloth if you want to keep birds out.

•**Sweet potatoes** While sweet potatoes are generally a warm-climate crop, you can grow them almost anywhere tomatoes will grow if you use a black polyethylene sheet around the base of the plant. The plastic raises the soil temperature and hastens growth. Being a root crop, sweet potatoes like a deep, sandy soil.

GREEN THUMB CARE: For best results buy sweet potato plants from a seedsman and set outdoors 15 to 18 inches apart as soon as frost danger has passed. Sweet potatoes take a long growing season. Some gardeners buy a sweet potato in January, start it in water, take cuttings from the vines and pot in a loose soil mixture. They can be making good growth indoors until soil has warmed up enough so they can be planted outdoors in May or June.

To harvest, dig a short time before frost (a little frost damage may "scorch" the vines, but won't harm the tubers). Let the roots dry in the sun for two or three hours, then place in 60 degrees F. storage. Some gardeners like to "cure" their tubers for 15 days by putting them in 80 degrees F. storage near a furnace or radiator. After curing, move them to a cooler room.

TROUBLES: *Failure to mature*. Due to cold weather, short growing season.

Rotted tubers. Any time sweet potatoes are subject to temperatures below 50 degrees F. for more than 48 hours, they are subject to decay.

•**Tomatoes** By anybody's survey, tomatoes are the No. 1 vegetable. They're popular because they are so easy to grow (giving even the most indifferent gardener "something to show" for his efforts) and have such wide uses, fresh or canned. They grow in almost any well suited soil, can be used in a hanging basket, porch box, or in tubs—among a wide variety of space-saving ways.

When it comes to varieties, the list is long. Never before have we had such a large selection of early, midseason and late tomatoes, in both hybrids and nonhybrids. Greenhouse operators, garden centers, and fruit stands sell plant-paks, flats, and potted tomatoes, started indoors six to eight weeks ahead of outdoor planting time. One of the drawbacks of buying started plants is that you don't always get what you ask for. Some sellers switch labels and you may end up with a variety that is not suited to your locality.

Pick out stocky plants when buying them (see *Buying Plants in Pots and Flats* earlier in this chapter). Potted ones bear earlier because they have small fruits already formed. Tomatoes bought "by the dozen" are cheaper and will not only produce as much, but will eventually catch up with potted tomatoes in growth and yield.

Being sure of the variety and being able to grow varieties not commonly available as started plants are two reasons you may want to start your own plants indoors. Hybrid seed and plants cost more, but the extra price is usually justifiable in higher yields and quality.

Look over three or four seed catalogues, and pick some good varieties. After you've tried them, stick with those that work best in your own garden. An important thing to look for is disease resistance. Most home gardeners can't rotate their crops as farmers do, and must plant in the same area year after year. This tends to build up various diseases in the soil, including fusarium and verticillium wilt, discussed under *Troubles* later on.

Start your tomatoes indoors in Jiffy 7 Pellets, peat pots, clay pots, or boxes. We sow seed in flats and when 2 inches tall, transplant into individual pots where they are grown until planting-out time. (for more detail see earlier in this chapter, and Plant Propagation.)

SETTING OUT THE PLANTS, IMPORTANT: Before you handle any tomato plant (or any member of the family such as peppers, eggplants, petunias) always wash your hands with soap and water if you are a smoker or use tobacco in any form. Tobacco mosaic can be spread to your plants unless you deactivate the mosaic virus with a good soap (Naptha is fine). Or you can use milk on your hands, either fresh or powdered, before planting.

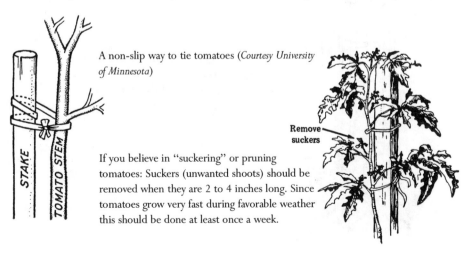

A non-slip way to tie tomatoes (*Courtesy University of Minnesota*)

STAKE

TOMATO STEM

Remove suckers

If you believe in "suckering" or pruning tomatoes: Suckers (unwanted shoots) should be removed when they are 2 to 4 inches long. Since tomatoes grow very fast during favorable weather this should be done at least once a week.

Tomatoes not grown on a trellis can be grown staked or unstaked. If you stake and prune tomatoes, set them 2′ × 2′, and apply a mulch such as straw, sawdust, etc. If you let your plants ramble on the ground, unstaked, plant them 3′ × 4′ apart. Staking gives you earlier, cleaner fruit, less snail injury, and fruit is easier to pick and spray. Disadvantages to staking: More sun-scald, blossom-end rot, and a little extra cost and effort. Whether you stake or not, mulching reduces fruit cracking and dry blossom-end rot, that black, leathery condition you see on the bottom of tomatoes.

TRELLISING TOMATOES: If you're limited on space or are bothered with snails, try the "Chinese" or "Japanese" tomato ring (or corset) methods for growing bumper crops. Or grow your tomatoes on a fence, supported by a post on each end. Either method keeps the plants off the ground, keeps out snails, keeps diseases down, and makes picking a snap. Tests show you get 10 percent fewer cull fruit from trellised plants than from staked ones or those allowed to lie on the ground. Tomato plants grown on trellises will bear heavily until frost, and according to some tests a single plant can produce as much as 62 pounds of tomatoes.

Basically, the "tomato ring" or corset method of trellising amounts to keeping each plant inside a wire cylinder which can be as wide and as tall as you want. We grow ours in half-barrels each about 2 1/2 feet across and the corset is 5 feet tall. Wire with a 6-inch mesh is best because it makes it easy to reach in and pick the fruit. Concrete reinforcing wire is ideal because it is rigid enough to be self supporting and it's readily available from lumber yards. If the wire is weak, a few stakes round the cylinders will keep them from being blown over.

To plant in the cylinder: After the soil has been loosened up, work in some organic matter (peat, compost, leafmold) and scatter some complete plant food such as 5-10-10 or 5-10-5, two pounds per 100 square feet. Or you can wait and feed your plants liquid plant food, such as 23-19-17, once every three or four weeks. Space plants three or four feet apart, and water them well. Apply a mulch of straw, sawdust, aluminum foil, plastic,

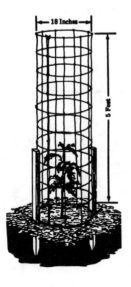

Growing tomato plants inside a wire "corset" is called the "Japanese' or "Chinese" method of training tomato vines. A corset this size will accommodate two plants.

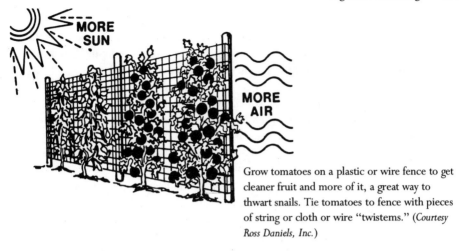

Grow tomatoes on a plastic or wire fence to get cleaner fruit and more of it, a great way to thwart snails. Tie tomatoes to fence with pieces of string or cloth or wire "twistems." (*Courtesy Ross Daniels, Inc.*)

or whatever is available. Place the wire cylinder around the plants soon after transplanting. As growth begins, keep all the branches inside the wire framework. The plants will eventually grow over the top of the cylinders and down the outside. Do not prune off any of the branches. From time to time you'll have to keep training the top if it gets out of control. Some gardeners tie the shoots onto the wire with soft cloth or old nylon stockings cut in pieces.

Some gardeners grow tomatoes on a fence stretched between two posts driven into the ground. Plastic netting or chicken wire fencing works well here. If you grow your tomatoes on a fence or straight trellis, train them just as you would in the corset.

TO HASTEN TOMATOES: If your tomatoes are slow to ripen, removing some foliage may hasten maturity by four or five days. Ripening and coloring of tomatoes depend upon fruit temperature, not light (putting green tomatoes in a bright window has little effect on coloring). Removing some of the foliage allows more direct sunshine to reach the fruit, raises the temperature, and thus hastens maturity. Tomatoes do not color up well at temperatures below 65 degrees F. or over 85 degrees F. Temperatures of 70 to 80 degrees F. are best for ripening tomatoes. Removing leaves has some advantages and some disadvantages. *Advantages*: Picking is easier and faster. Fruits and soil under the vines may dry off faster in mornings or after rains, thus reducing rots and molds. The amount of cracking may be reduced. *Disadvantages*: Exposed fruits may sunburn if a hot spell comes after you remove foliage. More fruits will be exposed to damage by early light frosts that normally would not harm fruits protected by leaves. Defoliation may cause an increase of anthracnose on fruits, or poor shoulder ripening of green-shouldered varieties.

TROUBLES: Tomatoes have several insect and disease problems but trellising and caging your tomatoes will eliminate many of them. Also, many varieties are disease-resistant—a good reason for checking your seed catalogues carefully before you buy.

Tomato hornworm. Large green caterpillar 2 1/2 to 3 inches long with diagonal white stripes on sides and a "horn" in the back. Blend so well with foliage that they are hard to spot. Chewed leaves and black droppings are telltale evidence. Hand picking is the best method of control. Since they later turn into the beautiful sphinx moth you may want to move them to a weedy area where they can feed on other vegetation.

Flea beetles. Tiny black beetles which cause small round holes in leaves resembling miniature buckshot holes. A light dusting of talcum powder is effective.

Blossom-end rot. Brown, leathery patch on the blossom end (bottom) of the tomato. *Control*: Use a mulch and give lots of water during hot summer days.

Leaf curl. Common on pruned and staked tomatoes on hot days and following heavy rains. No control.

Holes in fruit, due to snail (or slug) injury. Worse on mulched, unstaked plants. Stake or trellis tomatoes (see Chapter XIV for other controls).

Failure to ripen. Due to cloudy, wet weather, varieties. Have a few early varieties along with midseason and late ones.

Stunted or dwarfed plants. Check for walnut poisoning. Walnut roots exude a toxic material which stunts the plants. Plant tomatoes away from walnut trees. (See *Walnut Poisoning* in Chapter II.)

"Shoestring disease." Leaves narrow and deformed. Caused by a virus for which there's no control. Pull up and destroy affected plants.

Verticillium wilt. A fungus disease that causes leaves to wilt suddenly and turn brown. Verticillium is internal, hence no spraying is effective. Most home gardens are so small it's not practical to rotate crops, thus the disease builds up in the soil and remains for many years. *Control*: Plant disease-resistant types listed as such in seed catalogues as VF.

Fusarium. Another fungus disease that lives in the soil for many years. It enters the root system, plugs up the plant's plumbing. A sure method of diagnosis is to cut into a branch. If inside is brownish-black, you have fusarium wilt. Control consists of using wilt-resistant types. Seed catalogues indicate which ones are resistant. Because most garden soils harbor the fungus of the fusarium wilt for many years, rotation is of little value.

Poor fruit set. Why is it that tomato plants often will make nice growth but not produce heavy crops? The answer is temperatures, especially at night. When night temperatures remain above 75 degrees F. or drop below 59 degrees F. you get a poor fruit set. For some reason, flowers exposed to one or two nights of temperatures below 59 degrees F. will not be pollinated (or "fertilized") properly and about a week after the flowers have opened, the blossom will drop off, leaving a stub with no tomato. Spraying blooms with a blossom-set hormone will induce setting despite low night temperatures or a lack of natural pollination. Some varieties (such as Fireball, New Yorker, and Springset VF) seem to set at lower night temperatures, and that's one reason why they are fairly consistent early varieties. Cold Set is a variety which will set when temperatures at night drop below 55 degrees F. Spring Set is another one which sets when others won't.

HUSK TOMATO The Husk tomato is also called the strawberry tomato, dwarf cape gooseberry, or ground cherry. Botanically, the plant is *Physalis pruinosa*, and it has a yellow berry in a husk which is often used for preserves and pies. Two other species that are also used this way are *Physalis ixocarpa* (called tomatillo), with a purplish berry, somewhat sticky, and *P. peruviana* (also called cape gooseberry) with yellow berries. All of these are annuals, with the berry borne in a green to tan husk like that of the Japanese Lantern Plant, which is another species of Physalis. Do not eat any of the wild species, as they are poisonous if eaten in any quantity.

GREEN THUMB CARE: Start plants indoors and set out when weather is warm. They grow fine in full sun, and make a good tubbed plant.

TROUBLES: Lack of fruit, due to soil being too rich. Avoid heavy feedings of nitrogen.

TREE TOMATO The tree tomato is really not a tomato, it's *Cyphomandra betacea*, and we have yet to hear from a gardener who's had any luck growing this novelty. Fruit is dull red, the size and shape of an egg. Taste is similar to tomato. Plants grow ten feet tall, and have beautiful, broad leaves. They won't set blossoms or fruit until the second year (if you're lucky). You have to move them outdoors in summer and bring indoors in fall.

•Turnips

GREEN THUMB CARE: Turnips can be grown in early spring, but we suggest you wait until early fall to avoid maggot troubles. They like a moist soil. Sow in rows 12 inches apart, and thin to 3 or 4 inches. They mature quickly and if you want a real "quickie" grow Just Right, maturing in 35 to 40 days. This hybrid, small, tender, and mild, has clear white roots and should be for fall only, as it produces seed stalks if sown early. Excellent for greens as well as roots. Tokyo Market is good for spring planting as well as late summer, as are Tokyo Cross Hybrid and Purple Top White Globe.

TROUBLES: *Flea beetles on early crops.* Sprinkle with wood ashes or talcum powder.

Root maggot. Dust seeds in row with Sevin, ashes, or soak seeds for 15 minutes in kerosene before planting.

•Watermelons
Warm regions no longer have a monopoly on growing watermelons. You can grow sweet and tasty melons in the North if you select the right varieties. A black plastic mulch hastens maturity. Watermelons have the same culture as muskmelons (see). Sow in hills as for muskmelons, spacing hills six to ten feet apart, and use Hotcaps; or start in peat pots indoors three to four weeks before outdoor planting. Best varieties for the North or for gardeners who live in areas where seasons are short: Yellow Baby Hybrid (70 days), flesh bright yellow and juicy. Grows seven inches in diameter, ten to fifteen pounds. New Hampshire Midget (70 days), size of a cantaloupe, six to ten pounds; flesh is strawberry red, solid, and sweet. Sugar Baby (75 days), red flesh, not very seedy. Has a dark green, tough rind, weighs about eight pounds and is eight inches in diameter.

HOW TO TELL WHEN RIPE: If you enjoy guessing games, watermelons are a challenge. First, look for fruits that have about reached normal size for the variety. Next, check the "ground spot" to see if the portion that touches the ground is a dark yellowish color. A ringing sound on thumping indicates immaturity, whereas a ripe melon tends to sound hollow. Also, ripe fruits usually are slightly more rough or bumpy than immature ones.

A brown curl nearest the stem sometimes denotes a ripe watermelon, although many say it doesn't tell anything. When all of the above signs show positive on the earliest fruits, you can still wait a week before harvesting.

TROUBLES: Same as muskmelons (see).

Storing Your Vegetables and Fruit

It's heartbreaking to a gardener who raises a surplus of produce which could be used later when he has no good way to store it. Modern homes are too hot and dry to keep fruits and vegetables for any length of time, so gardeners have to do the best they can.

Home canning is still one of the best methods of preserving foods, but care must be taken to follow directions for proper processing time, especially for non-acid vegetables (underprocessing could result in botulism poisoning). The USDA and state colleges have bulletins with explicit canning instructions. For information on drying fruits and vegetables, see Chapter XII.

The key factor in ripening of fruits or vegetables is ethylene. All plant tissues produce this gas, and especially large amounts are produced by tomatoes, apples, pears, melons, and many other fruits, as well as vegetables. Ethylene speeds up the ripening process—it triggers the softening and the changes in flavor, aroma, and color associated with ripeness.

If you can keep the ethylene content of the atmosphere around your fruits and vegetables low, you can keep the produce from ripening so fast. Commercial growers use the "Controlled atmosphere" ("CA") method to keep fruit all winter. Home gardeners can reduce the effects of ethylene by storing high-ethylene producers away from "gas sensitive" crops such as root crops and leafy vegetables like cabbage.

Storage of vegetables in their natural state is the easiest and least expensive of all methods of food preservation. Roughly speaking, home garden vegetables have four different ideal storage conditions:

1. Cold and moist, 32 to 40 degrees F. and humidity 90 percent; carrots, beets, parsnips, salsify, rutabagas, turnips, celery.
2. Cold, moderately moist, 32 to 40 degrees F. and humidity 75 percent; potatoes, cabbage, cauliflower, Chinese cabbage.
3. Dry and very cool, 40 to 50 degrees F.; onions, beans, peas, and soybeans.
4. Dry and moderately cool, 50 to 55 degrees F.; pumpkins, squash.

Green (but mature) tomatoes can be kept for two months if picked before frost and stored at 55 degrees F. on shelves. They'll ripen over that period. You can wipe any dirt off with a dry cloth and then wrap individually in pieces of newspaper.

Some gardeners use a garbage can with a plastic liner for storing cabbage, carrots, turnips, potatoes, beets, pears, or apples. They put a layer of leaves in the bottom, then a layer of vegetables (don't let vegetables touch each other), then a layer of leaves, and so on until the can is nearly full. Put a thick layer (6 or 8 inches) of leaves on top last. Leaves should be slightly moistened or vegetables will dry out. You may need to add a few sprinkles of water from time to time. Do not seal the plastic liner, but fold it in under the cover. Folks tell us their vegetables keep in this manner in an unheated garage or breezeway all winter.

If your cellar lacks a good storage area, try sinking a clean garbage can in the garden (as described under *Apples* in Chapter XII) for storing crops. Heat from the ground will keep the fruit and vegetables in fine condition. Another trick is to use an old icebox or refrigerator buried backside down in the garden. Dig the hole deep enough so the door is a couple of inches below the ground level. Be sure to knock the lock off so no curious child could possibly lock himself in. Our neighbor's eight-cubic-foot refrigerator, stripped, holds five bushels of produce and has kept apples and vegetables from 20-below-zero weather, although he still covers it with straw for extra protection.

Some items, such as parsnips, turnips, salsify, carrots, and beets can be left in the ground if covered with a mulch of 12 to 18 inches of straw or leaves with boards over the top. Brussels sprouts and kale can be left in the garden until temperatures go down to 15 degrees F. Cauliflower, Brussels sprouts, as well as cabbage should be pulled rather than cut for storage and "replanted" in moist sand (they will keep better when their roots are in moist sand). You may not like the odor from cabbage kept in a basement, so keep it in a cellar entranceway, or the garage.

You may wonder why onions do not keep well. Some just are not good keepers, and either sprout or get soft. They like an attic or a very cool room with good air circulation (where it does not freeze). Dried peas, beans, and soybeans should be stored in closed containers (we use glass jugs) after they are thoroughly dry. Pumpkins and squash don't mind some warmth, but should not touch one another.

For added information on vegetables see our *Green Thumb Book of Fruit and Vegetable Gardening*.

The following guide to recommended spacing of plants per foot of row has been prepared to help those who have the space to plant a conventional garden. Some gardeners will get more yield than others. They may have more fertile soil, and they may use varieties that can be planted closer, such as the bush type of vine crops. Also by staking and trellising, more crops can be grown per square foot.

Under "Estimated Seed Needed," in some cases, we had to give number of seeds rather than packets, since packet sizes vary among seed companies. However, many do list, either on the envelope or in their catalogues, the number of seeds per packet or per ounce. Seed catalogues have a wealth of information and are worth studying before you plan your garden.

This chart has been compiled from information furnished by Cornell University, Michigan State University, Joseph Harris Seed Co., and our own test plots.

Vegetable	Row Length in Feet	Est. Yield	Est. Amt. Seed Needed	Days to Maturity	Depth to Plant in Inches	Number Seeds Per Ft.	Thinned or Transplanted Planted (Inches Apart)	No. Weeks to Sow Indoors Before Outdoor Planting
Asparagus	40	12 lbs	25 plants	3 to 4 years	6 to 8	plants	12 to 18	
Snap beans								
early	15	7 lbs	1/8 lb	50 to 55	1 to 2	6 to 8	do not	
midseason	15	7 lbs	1/8 lb	55 to 60	1 to 2	6 to 8	do not	
Late	15	7 lbs	1/8 lb	60 to 65	1 to 2	6 to 8	do not	
Pole beans	15	10 lbs	1/8 lb	65	1 to 2	2 to 3	do not	
Lima beans	50	4 lbs (shelled)	1/2 lb	65 to 85	1 to 2	3 to 4	do not	
Soy Beans	50	8 lbs (shelled)	1/4 lb	90 to 100	1 to 2	3 to 4	do not	
Beets								
early	10	10 lbs	1/8 oz	50 to 55	1/2 to 1	10	thin, 2 to 3	
late	15	15 lbs	1/8 oz.	55 to 75	1/2 to 1	10	thin, 2 to 3	
Broccoli	25	10 lbs	12 plants	60 to 80	plants		18 to 24	6 to 8
Brussels sprouts	25	7 lbs	12 plants	90 to 100	plants		18 to 24	6 to 8
Cabbage early and mid-season	12	6 heads	6 plants	60 to 75	plants		12 to 18	6 to 8
late	20	9 heads	10 plants	80 to 100	plants		12 to 18	4 to 6

Vegetable	Row Length in Feet	Est. Yield	Est. Amt. Seed Needed	Days to Maturity	Depth to Plant in Inches	Number Seeds Per Ft.	Thinned or Transplanted Planted (Inches Apart)	No. Weeks to Sow Indoors Before Outdoor Planting
Chinese Cabbage	15	12 heads	40 to 60 seeds	70	$1/2$	4 to 6	12 to 15	
Carrots	40	40	$1/6$ oz...	70 to 75	$1/4$	15 to 20	1 to 3	
Cauliflower								
early	5	3 heads	3 plants	55 to 65	plants		18 to 24	6 to 8
late	12	5 heads	6 plants	70 to 90	plants		18 to 24	6 to 8
Celeriac	10	6 lbs	30 seeds	120	$1/4$	4 to 6	12 to 14	10 to 12
Celery								
early	5	10 stalks	10 plants	85 to 90	plants		6 to 8	10 to 12
late	10	20 stalks	20 plants	95 to 125	plants		6 to 8	10 to 12
Chard (Swiss)	8	7 lbs	80 seeds	75 to 100	$1/2$	8 to 10	4 to 8	
Chicory	10	5 lbs	40 to 60 seeds	125 to 150	$1/2$	8 to 10	4 to 8	8
Chives	5	3 lbs	$1/2$ pkt	40 to 50	$1/4$	15 to 18	2 to 3	
Collards	25	20 lbs	75 seeds	80	$1/2$	8 to 10	4 to 8	
Corn Sweet								
early	100	85 ears	$1/8$ lb	65 to 75	2	1 to 2	9 to 1 2	
midseason	100	85 ears	$1/8$ lb	75 to 85	2	1 to 2	9 to 1 2	
late	100	80 ears	$1/8$ lb	85 to 95	2	1 to 2	9 to 1 2	
Cucumbers*	10	6 lbs	40 seeds	50 to 80	1	3 to 4	12 to 15 (hills 48" apart)	
Eggplants	6	12 fruits	3 plants	80 to 90	plants		18 to 24	6 to 8
Endive	6	10 heads	10 plants	90 to 120	$1/2$	4 to 6	9 to 12	
Kale	6	6 heads	6 plants	50 to 80	$1/2$	4 to 6	12 to 24	6 to 8
Kohlrabi	12	24 stems	100 seeds	60 to 80	1	6 to 8	2 to 4	6 to 8
Leeks	10	30 stalks	100 seeds	110	$1/2$	10 to 15	4 to 6	6 to 8

CAPSULE VEGETABLE PLANTING FOR CHART
CONVENTIONAL GARDENS (Continued)

Vegetable	Row Length in Feet	Est. Yield	Est. Amt. Seed Needed	Days to Maturity	Depth to Plant in Inches	Number Seeds Per Ft.	Thinned or Transplanted Planted (Inches Apart)	No. Weeks to Sow Indoors Before Outdoor Planting
Lettuce (leaf) 3 plantings	5	2 1/2 lbs	75 seeds	45 to 55	1/4 to 1/2	10 to 12	3 to 6	
Lettuce (semi-head) 3 plantings	15	15 heads	1/8 oz.	55 to 65	1/4 to 1/2	6 to 8	8 to 10	6 to 8 (optional)
Lettuce (head) 3 plantings	15	15 heads	1/8 oz.	70 to 85	1/4 to 1/2	4 to 6	12	6 to 8 (optional)
Muskmelon*	16	18 fruits	65 seeds	85 to 120	1/2	3 to 4	12 to 15 (hills 48" apart)	4 to 5
Mustard	10	6 lbs	50 seeds	45	1/4	10 to 15	4 to 6	
Okra	8	5 lbs	50 seeds	55 to 65	1/2	6 to 8	4	8 (optional)
Onions (plants)	30	25 lbs	120 plants	85 to 95	plants	12 to 15	2 to 5	8
Onions (seed)	30	25 lbs	360 seeds	100 to 120	1/2	10 to 12	2 to 4	6 to 8 (optional)
Onions (sets)	10	5 lbs	100 sets	85 to 90	1/2		2 to 4	
Parsley	3 plants		15 seeds	65 to 85	1/4 to 1/2	15	4 to 6	8
Parsnips	15	15 lbs	260 seeds	120 to 170	1/4	15 to 20	3 to 4	
Peas	100	28 lbs	1 lb	60 to 70	1	10 to 15	do not	
Peppers	10	10 lbs	10 plants	65 to 75	plants		12	8 to 10
Potatoes	50	2 to 4 bu.	30 tubers	90 to 120	6	1 tuber	per 18"	
Potatoes (sweet)	50	2 to 4 bu.	30 tubers	120	6	1 tuber	per 18"	
Pumpkins	3 hills	30 to 100 lbs	15 seeds	90 to 110	1/2	5 per hill	hills 72" apart	
Radishes (4 plantings)	12	8 lbs	140 seeds	30 to 65	1/2	10 to 15	1 to 2	
Rhubarb	8	8 lbs	3 plants	2 years	plants		24 to 36	
Rutabaga	15	15 lbs	90 seeds	80 to 100	1/2	4 to 6	6 to 10	

Vegetable	Row Length in Feet	Est. Yield	Est. Amt. Seed Needed	Days to Maturity	Depth to Plant in Inches	Number Seeds Per Ft.	Thinned or Transplanted Planted (Inches Apart)	No. Weeks to Sow Indoors Before Outdoor Planting
Salsify	15	15 lbs	225 seeds	140 to 150	$1/4$	15	1 to 3	
Spinach 2 plantings	10	5 lbs	$1/2$ oz.	45 to 50	$1/4$	15 to 20	2 to 4	
Squash, summer*	9 to 12	30 to 36 fruits	22 seeds	60 to 80	1	2 to 3	18 to 24 (hills 48" apart)	
Squash, winter*	12	5 to 10 fruits	25 seeds	90 to 120	1	2 to 3	24 (hills 48" apart)	
Tomatoes	40	2 bu.	10 plants	60 to 90	plants		24 to 48	6 to 8
Turnip	20	20 lbs	150 seeds	60 to 90	1	6 to 8	4 to 6	
Watermelon*	15	4 to 10 fruits	$1/8$ oz	70 to 130	1	2 to 3	18	4 to 5

*Compact vine types and bush varieties can be planted closer together.

CHAPTER XII

Home Fruit Culture

•

Landscape with Food Plants!

Many home owners fail to look into the merits of including fruits in their original landscaping plans, and find out too late that all fruit trees and many fruit bushes can do double duty producing food while adding beauty to the surroundings. This is especially true on small lots where each square foot is important. A home orchard can be planted on a plot a little larger than the average living room.

Apples, pears, peaches, plums, nectarines, apricots, sweet and sour cherries, Chinese chestnuts, black walnuts and many others all have delicate traceries of color and grace in spring when the blooms appear, provide bountiful shade in summer and bright leaves in the fall, and require little more care than trees that are purely ornamental.

If you've got a postage-stamp-size garden or yard, you can grow dwarf trees that give you full-size fruit and bear a lot sooner than the standard varieties. A mature dwarf tree only takes one third the space of a standard tree and can be harvested with a small step ladder.

Small bush fruits, such as currants, gooseberries, quince, and blueberries, may serve as a decorative planting in a sunny corner of the yard; grapes and raspberries (red, black, and purple) can do double duty as hedges on property lines if trained to grow on or between wires. Strawberries should not be attempted unless the planting can be moved every two or three years and a minimum of 100 square feet of garden space allotted to each 25 plants set out.

THE AGE OF BEARING Most standard apple trees rarely bear much before they are six or seven years old, the age of the tree being reckoned from the year of planting. Small fruits must have a year to settle in for fruit production. All other fruits you might be tempted to set out will bear sometime between these two extremes. The following list will give you an idea of when to expect fruit, as well as the relative planting distances and height for the trees, bushes, or plants.

General Care of Fruit and Nut Trees

Because of relative similarity in growth and habits, we will consider together the selection of planting stock, the planting, and the general culture of tree fruits and nuts. Specifics may be found in the discussions of the individual fruits which follow. For even more detailed information see our *Green Thumb Book of Fruit and Vegetable Gardening*.

Kind of Fruit	Bearing Age	Distance Apart	Height
Apples, standard	2 to 12 yrs.	35 × 35 ft.	25 ft.
Apples, dwarf	2 yrs.	15 × 15 ft.	15 ft.
Apricots	3 yrs.	20 × 20 ft.	15 ft.
Blackberries, Boysenberries, Dewberries, Loganberries	1 yr.	6 × 6 ft.	4 ft.
Blueberries	1 to 2 yrs.	3 × 6 ft.	4 ft.
Butternuts, Hickory Nuts, Walnuts, Black & English*	3 to 6 yrs.	35 × 35 ft.	40 ft.
Cherries, sour	2 to 3 yrs.	20 × 20 ft.	20 ft.
Cherries, sweet	3 to 4 yrs.	25 × 25 ft.	30 ft.
Chinese chestnuts	3 to 4 yrs.	35 × 35 ft.	40 ft.
Currants	2 yrs.	4 × 4 ft.	3 ft.
Gooseberries	2 to 3 yrs.	4 × 4 ft.	3 ft.
Grapes	2 yrs.	8 × 8 ft.	4 ft.
Peaches and Nectarines	2 to 3 yrs.	20 × 20 ft.	20 ft.
Pears, standard	3 to 4 yrs.	20 × 20 ft.	30 ft.
Pears, dwarf	2 yrs.	15 × 15 ft.	20 ft.
Plums	2 to 3 yrs.	20 × 20 ft.	20 ft.
Quinces	1 to 2 yrs.	15 × 15 ft.	15 ft.
Raspberries	1 to 2 yrs.	3 × 6 ft.	4 ft.
Strawberries	1 yr.	2 × 2 ft.	1 ft.

*See also Quick Reference Chart of Common Nut Trees later in this chapter.

BUYING FRUIT TREES Home gardeners are rightly intrigued by the new dwarf trees which number compactness, convenience, and high yield among their virtues. They can be planted 6 to 12 feet apart; their low-growing nature makes them easy to prune and spray as well as to harvest. They bear fruit two or three years after planting, as opposed to five to ten years for standard trees, and they are good producers: dwarf apples yield up to a bushel of fruit per tree as large or larger than fruit of standard varieties.

Previously, apples and pears were the only fruit trees that were dwarfed. The increased interest in small-property planting now finds dwarf peaches, nectarines, apricots, plums, and cherries available as well.

In deciding on dwarf fruit trees, give some consideration to the rootstocks that have been used to induce dwarfing. Your nurseryman will be glad to tell you the name of the dwarfing stock used in the trees that interest you. He will explain that trees dwarfed on Malling IX will grow no taller than a man, while trees dwarfed on Malling VII will attain the size of a small peach tree. Apple trees grown on the most dwarfing of all the rootstocks, Malling IX, require bracing or support because the root system is brittle and will break off easily. Apple trees (as well as dwarf peach and plum trees) grown on the semi-dwarfing Malling VII do not require support. Should you be especially interested in the tiny "man-sized" apple trees, do not be put off by the need to support the tree. All that is required is a strong stake driven into the ground near the tree, which is then firmly tied to the tree with a broad band of cloth or rubber hose. If you have several trees, you can support them as you would grapes by stringing two wires between two posts and securing the trees to the wires. Many gardeners still prefer standard size trees, and nurseries have plenty of varieties available in all kinds of fruits. Standards are usually less expensive than dwarf trees, and are useful as shade trees.

When buying fruit trees, consider their sex life. Many fruit trees need "rooster" trees for proper cross-pollination. A simple way to temporarily overcome the pollination problem is to borrow a bouquet of fresh fruit blooms from a neighbor and place it in water in a sunny spot where the insects like to work. Cut the bouquet when the most advanced blossoms are open, and the sooner you can get it in water, the better. Keep the blossoms fresh; wilted they are valueless. Of course, if you wish to pollinate apples, you must secure apple blossoms, pear blossoms for pears, etc. In the case of apples, Jonathan, Red Delicious, and Cortland are good "roosters." Your seed or nursery catalogue will list good pollinators.

A fruit tree novelty with attractive features for home planting is the so-called Five Fold or 5-in-1 (five varieties on one tree), producing in from three to eight years. Obvious advantages of the mutiple variety fruit tree are the readiness of cross-pollination between varieties and the ability to grow a variety of fruit in a small space. However, some apple varieties grow more vigorously than others; one disadvantage of 5-in-1 trees is that one variety will outgrow the others, and unless the tree is selectively pruned (being careful not to prune back too close to the graft union) the tree will eventually be mainly that one variety.

PLANTING FRUIT TREES Although fruit trees can be planted in spring or fall, early fall is the ideal time. The way you set them out spells the difference between success and failure. First, dig a hole large enough to spread the tree roots without twisting or crowding. Put the topsoil you dig up in one pile and the subsoil in another. Make the hole deep enough to set the tree 2 inches deeper than it grew in the nursery, with the bud or graft 2 inches below ground level. (Dwarfed trees are an exception to this rule, as the bud union must remain above ground level to prevent scion rooting and to permit the dwarfing root system to have its influence throughout the life of the tree.)

Now place 3 or 4 inches of topsoil in the hole you have prepared and prune the roots of your new tree lightly. The idea is to remove ragged tips and expose firm, lively root structure to the soil to encourage the sprouting of new fine roots. If you are planting in the fall, leave the top-trimming of the new tree for spring, except to remove branches that might rub together or limbs that grow from the trunk at a narrow angle.

Set your tree in the hole as straight as you can. Some small trees are crooked when dug from the nursery rows but will straighten considerably as they grow. Fill the hole two-thirds full of topsoil and tamp it firmly. Pour in a bucketful of water. After the water seeps away, fill the hole with the remaining soil, leaving a saucer-like depression to catch the rain. Be sure to remove the nursery tag from the little tree, as the wire will cut into the wood as new growth is made and will retard or possibly even kill the limb to which it has been attached. Dwarf trees are shallow-rooted, hence should be staked for the first two years.

PROTECTION AGAINST RODENTS It's a good idea to put tree guards around the trunk. One of the best we've seen is the Almor tree guard, made of coiled vinyl plastic. Wrapped around the tree, it keeps rabbits, mice and other rodents from chewing the bark, and protects against mechanical injury, winter sun, and wind scald. Other tree guards include aluminum foil, hardware cloth, and sisal wrap (sold by nurserymen).

PRUNING FRUIT TREES

SPRING PRUNING NEWLY PLANTED TREES If you are planting fruit trees in spring or have planted them the previous fall, you should prune out the tops. This should be done before buds swell and start to break. Bear in mind that over-pruning of a young tree will retard bearing and that the purpose of pruning is to shape the tree for both maximum attractiveness and fruit yield. Nut trees require little, if any, pruning except to remove dead or diseased branches. Peaches bear best if trained to an open center; that

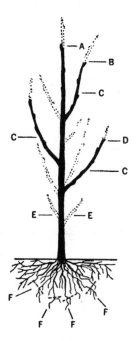

How to prune a young tree at planting time: (A) Shorten the tip or leader. (B) Shorten branches that might outgrow the leader. (C) Leave branches that are properly spaced. (D) Cut at a point where there is a bud pointing outward. (E) Remove branches that are too close to ground. (F) Remove broken or injured roots. Snip 1/2 inch off each so new feeder roots will form quickly. Note how branches are well spaced and narrow-angled crotches removed.

is, the main center branch is cut back radically to promote a bowl-shaped tree. Other fruit trees are trained to a modified "leader" pattern—the main center branch is allowed to grow upright until the tree reaches bearing age, and light is needed at the center of the tree.

Except for these differences, a newly planted fruit tree should be trimmed down to three to five husky side branches that are spaced 6 to 8 inches apart along the trunk of the tree. Branches with wide angles to the trunk are better than those with narrow angles. Wide-angled branches are stronger and will make up the "scaffold," or main branches, of the tree as it matures. In pruning, cut off the leader branch one-half to one-third of its length and cut back the side branches proportionately, remove all other small and spindly branches, and your first pruning job is done.

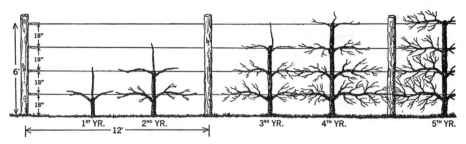

If you have limited space, apples can be trained to grow on fences or wire trellises. Set posts 12 feet apart with 4 wires strung 18 inches apart.

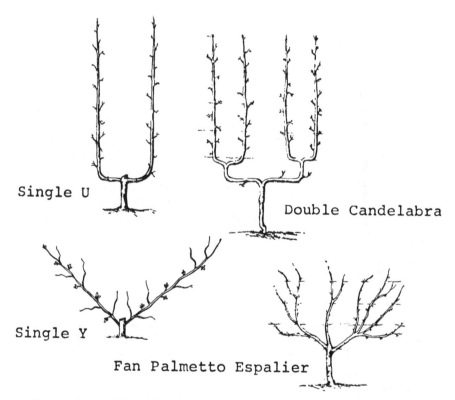

There are dozens of forms of espaliers, and you are limited only by your imagination as to shapes you can use. Here are a few of the basic types. (*Courtesy Stark Bros. Nursery*)

PRUNING AND TRAINING ESPALIER TREES This practice, limited more or less to dwarf pears and apples and stone fruits, is a combination of pruning and training the little trees to grow in a limited space, along a wall or trellis. The branches are started low and spread out and up as the tree grows, tying the stems to wire in the shape desired and limiting the growth of branches to fit the shape. Undesirable shoots are pinched out as they form. The result is unusually attractive, and fruit of exceptionally fine quality is produced.

PRUNING MATURE FRUIT TREES Why prune at all? You prune to get larger, finer fruit by opening up a tree so sunlight can get in to ripen fruit and sprays can get in to kill bugs. Cutting out dead and diseased limbs not only gives the tree relief from pests; it gives the tree a better shape and helps it to develop strong limbs which must carry heavy loads of fruit, sometimes in heavy winds and rain. You can overprune a tree and do much harm thereby, but with no pruning at all your pretty tree will soon become rough and scraggly-looking as well as unproductive.

On mature fruit trees, first remove limbs that are dead, broken, too high, or too low, or that rub or criss-cross one another. Skinny, weak limbs come out next along with those that crowd the center of the tree and keep out light and air. All of this can be done in winter after leaves have dropped, or in spring before the buds break out. On well established fruit trees, complete pruning should be done over a two- or three-year period, for cutting all the big branches out at once encourages an alternate menace: the growth of water sprouts and suckers around the trees.

Overpruning small young trees, as well as mature trees, causes them to overproduce new shoots which in turn reduces the production of fruiting wood and fruit itself. A "butcher-type" pruning program is both aimless and destructive, so confine your efforts at all times to a little pruning that you know is right; and when in doubt, prune lightly.

If you want to paint pruning wounds you can use powdered bordeaux mixed with raw linseed oil to the consistency of cream. Painting is seldom necessary after spring pruning, as wounds heal most readily over summer and are less likely than fall pruning wounds to suffer from winter injury.

The object of pruning any fruit tree is to open up the center to let sunlight in. Cut top back, thin out center and side branches, remove any branches that crisscross or rub against one another.

SOUTHWEST INJURY One common complaint we get is about tree trunks having the bark split, especially on the southwest side. This is called "southwest injury" and is due to changes in temperature (very cold nights followed by sunny days, see Chapter II).

FERTILIZING FRUIT TREES The greatest danger in fertilizing fruit trees is the promotion of winter injury due to overproduction of new growth in late fall. Time your feeding program to avoid such late growth; don't feed later than August 1. Then you can start to feed for the growing year ahead as early as December. One feeding in winter or early spring is usually sufficient. The best time to apply fertilizer is April or early May. This early feeding helps to set fruit, improves color, and encourages blooming.

A complete or balanced fertilizer is used on trees that are not yet bearing. For bearing-age trees, in general, you can use ammonium nitrate or nitrate of soda. You can also use a liquid foliage feeding spray that can be applied with insecticide. If available, you can apply manure around the base of the tree in winter. Never put fresh manure in a hole where it will come in contact with the roots of the tree; use rotted compost or leafmold instead. Here is a good general rule of thumb on the amount to use: For every year of the tree's growth use $1/4$ pound of 16 percent nitrate of soda. So, if the tree is 12 years old, it would take 3 pounds of nitrate of soda. All can be applied over a mulch in the spring.

For apples three to five years old, use $1/2$ pound of 10-10-10 or nitrate of soda, scattered around the base of the tree. Trees over five years old can get 1 to 2 pounds of ammonium nitrate or 3 to 6 pounds of 10-10-10. Pears one to five years old get $1/2$ pound of ammonium nitrate or 2 pounds of 10-10-10. Peaches and sour cherries five years old benefit from 3 or 4 pounds of 10-10-10 and prunes five to ten years of age, 1 to 2 pounds.

These materials are readily available in most garden supply stores, but if you cannot get them, you can feed your trees any kind of plant food. To feed with a substitute is better than not to feed at all. Scatter the food around the base of the tree, going as far out as the spread or the drip of the branches. Or you can punch holes in the ground to feed your trees (see illustration in Chapter II).

One fruit grower we know uses a liquid plant food (23-19-17) at the rate of about 1 pound per tree. One pound makes 30 gallons of food which he applies equally at three intervals: at the pre-pink or pink stage of blossom formation; in early full leaf; and once more in the summer. (You can combine and apply liquid plant food with pesticide sprays.) Liquid food may be applied over the whole tree, and what drips to the ground will be absorbed by the roots.

Insect and Disease Control

"ALL-PURPOSE" SPRAYING Commercial growers spray apples anywhere from seven to fourteen times (or more) a year to grow clean fruit, but you don't have to spray that often. A "home-made all-purpose" formula which will control most of your bugs and diseases has vastly simplified fruit growing for the home gardener. This formula can be used in all applications after the leaves have developed, and on all fruits and ornamental shrubs. For dormant sprays you can use lime sulfur, oils, and the dinitro or DN compounds. These will protect fruit trees from scale, mites, and others.

INGREDIENTS — "ALL-PURPOSE SPRAY"

Chemical	1 Gallon of Water	25 Gallons of Water
Malathion (25% Wettable Powder)	2 tbsps.	$1/2$ lb.
Methoxychlor (50% Wettable Powder)	3 tbsps.	$3/4$ lb.
Captan or Ferbam (50% Wettable Powder)	3 tbsps.	$3/4$ lb.
Sulfur	2 tbsps.	$1/2$ lb.

Methoxychlor controls plum curculio and other beetles; Malathion is for leafhoppers, codling moth, fruit moth, and other worms; Captan or Ferbam is included to prevent cedar rust and leaf spots, and sulfur to control apple scab, brown rot, and mildew.

To control psylla on pears, and aphids on all trees and shrubs, add nicotine sulfate at the rate of 2 teaspoonfuls per gallon. Nicotine is volatile and does not retain its strength in storage unless kept in a tightly sealed container. All of these materials are available at your local farm or garden store, or you can purchase prepared "all-purpose" formulas.

WHEN TO SPRAY: The timing of a spray for fruit pests is important. Try to spray at about the same time commercial growers spray, as shown in the chart below:

Time to Spray	Apples	Peaches Nectarinies, Apricots	Plums	Cherries	Pears
Dormant	X	X	X	X	X
"Green Tip"	X				
"Pre-Bloom"	X	X	X	X	X
"Bloom"	NO	NO	NO	NO	NO
"Petal Fall"	X	X	X	X	X
1st Cover	X	X	X	X	X
2nd Cover	X	X	X	X	X
3rd Cover	X			X	
4th Cover or more	X	X		X	

"Green Tip" (or "delayed dormant") means when flower buds have broken a little. "Pre-Bloom" means when flower buds begin to show color, but petals have barely begun to unfold. "Bloom" is when blossoms are open. *Never* spray then, because it will harm the bees doing the pollinating. "Petal Fall" is when the last petals have fallen from the blossoms. 1st Cover means ten days after "Petal Fall." 2nd through 4th Cover are best spaced at ten- to fourteen-day intervals after 1st Cover.

If you're discouraged with the effort involved in the spray program, remember that the most important sprays are "Pre-Bloom" and "Petal Fall" and you can combine some fertilizing right along with the control program.

An "all-purpose" formula applied throughout the growing season will check most major pests, and with four or five sprays properly timed, you should be able to eat your fruit in the dark with an easy mind!

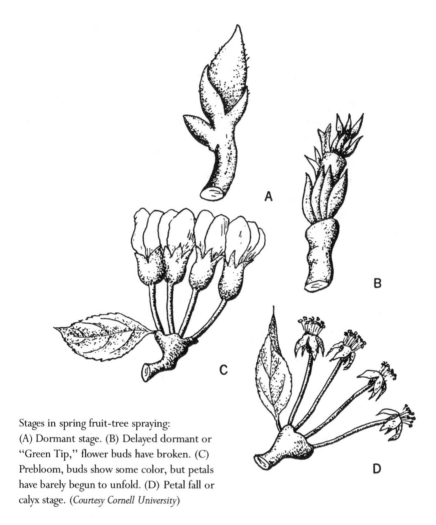

Stages in spring fruit-tree spraying:
(A) Dormant stage. (B) Delayed dormant or
"Green Tip," flower buds have broken. (C)
Prebloom, buds show some color, but petals
have barely begun to unfold. (D) Petal fall or
calyx stage. (*Courtesy Cornell University*)

FIGHT BUGS WITHOUT CHEMICALS Gardeners who do not like to use chemical pesticides often ask us for natural methods of control. We have devoted a separate chapter to organic, or natural, controls, so we will mention here *only* the ones most likely of use in fruit plantings and you will find more details in Chapter XIV. The organic gardener's all-purpose spray described in Chapter XIV is used for controlling white fly, aphids, spider mites, and other pests.

Here's another all-purpose spray for organic gardeners: Put through a grinder or blender 3 large onions, 1 whole garlic bulb (not just a clove), 1 hot pepper pod, and 2 tablespoons of cayenne pepper. Barely cover the mixture with water, and let it stand overnight. Put through a sieve in the morning. Then strain through a dish towel or nylon stocking. Put the liquid in a 1-gallon jug, fill the jug to the top with water, and it's ready to be used. Use a hand sprayer or one of the trombone types.

If spider mites are troublesome, the buttermilk spray described in Chapter XIV destroys a high percentage of mobile forms of mites and mite eggs as well.

OTHER ORGANIC PESTICIDES: These are also called "botanicals," since they are derived from various plant parts. One we have previously mentioned in this chapter, nicotine sulfate (Black Leaf 40), has been effective against aphids for years. It also kills other sap-sucking pests. Pyrethrum is the source of pyrethrins, which are made from the dried flower heads of various species of pyrethrums or "painted daisies" and it kills many chewing pests. Ryania, Derris, and rotenone are other well known "botanicals" discussed in Chapter XIV. We want to repeat the caution about rotenone: it is toxic to fish and nesting birds.

BIOLOGICAL INSECT CONTROL: An issue of the *North American Fruit Explorer* bulletin reports that farmers in Russia grow apples without using chemicals. It states: "Not a single gram of poison was used at a large orchard of the Belgorod Agricultural Experimental Station. A 3000-strong flock of starlings and titmice was used to control the pests. The result: the amount of injured fruit was 1/3 less in this 173-acre orchard than in the orchard using chemicals. The crop helped by the birds had the highest yield in the area. Young naturalists mounted 300 starling houses and 200 small titmouse houses, and almost every nest had young in the spring." So you can see it pays to encourage birds around your home (see Chapter II for a chart of plantings to encourage birds).

CONTROL INSECTS WITH INSECTS: Gardeners who grow wormy apples and other fruits will be interested in trichogramma, the microscopic natural enemy of the apple worm and all other members of the Lepidoptera order of insects (moths and butterflies). The trichogramma destroys the eggs which hatch into harmful worms.

The favorite foods of ladybird beetles or ladybugs are aphids or plant lice and mites; they eat a variety of other insects—fruit scales, mealybugs, bollworm, leaf worm, leafhoppers, and even the corn ear worm. Some of these destroy only eggs and larvae; the adults are too large for them to handle. Many people buy ladybugs in half-pint and gallon lots. One gallon contains about 75,000 ladybugs.

Another helpful insect you can buy is the praying mantis. This creature has an enormous appetite, eating aphids, flies, small caterpillars, and other soft-bodied pests. As it grows it eventually tackles such large insects as grasshoppers, beetles, and others.

See Chapter XIV for more detail on these and other insects that are natural enemies of the bugs that attack fruit crops.

SUGGESTIONS FROM AN ORGANIC GROWER: A friend, who had one of the largest organic fruit orchards in America, was asked how he grew blemish-free apples, and we are passing his ideas along to you:

1. Best control is to rake leaves from beneath trees and burn them, returning all ashes to under your trees.
2. Trees should be pruned in such a manner that sunlight can reach every leaf. This means pruning more than most people do. An infection known as "scab" is caused by spores released from dead apple leaves and old apples left on the ground. These spores are carried great distances by the wind and infect the leaves, twigs, green buds, and fruit. Bright sunlight deactivates them.
3. A tree planted on the west side of a building doesn't receive the early morning sun nor breezes which would dry the night dew, and therefore the disease problem is

increased. Always plant where trees will not be shaded and will have access to breezes which will dry the foliage.

4. Fungus diseases—cedar rust, white rot, and black rot—can be controlled by removing the gelatinous yellow spore masses from cedar trees (which spread them) and burning them. The period of infection is from the opening of apple tree buds until all the bloom petals have fallen.

5. Dead fruit limbs or branches should be removed and burned or sealed in plastic and discarded.

6. He applied a spray of kelp (seaweed) every two weeks from the first green bud stage until June 1 to kill aphids. He stopped insects crawling up the tree trunk by using a strip of Tanglefoot paper or a can of spray-on Tanglefoot.

7. Borers are destroyed or stopped by using a mixture of nine cups whitewash (hydrated lime—don't get any on your skin!) plus one cup bleaced flour, plus one can of red pepper. Mix with enough water to make it paint consistency. Pull the soil away one inch from the base of the trunk and apply with a coarse brush to the entire trunk up to where the lower limbs branch off. Keep cover on from March 1 to killing frost. This whitewash cure will also prevent "southwest injury."

8. He used miscible dormant oils (other non-toxic weapons available in garden supply stores) at the rate of 2 gallons per 100 gallons of water, applied in fall after leaves have fallen and again before young leaves show in the spring. These are called dormant sprays; the oils smother insect eggs, keeping them from hatching.

9. He suggested using plant extracts such as pyrethrins, rotenone, and ryania to aid in pest control. These materials adhere to the surface of the apple, but they can be easily washed off.

NO FLOWERS OR FRUIT? If you're wondering why your trees or bushes do not produce flowers or fruit, here are a few reasons:

1. Sex. Some plants are dioecious (pronounced "die-ee-shus"), meaning the male and female flower parts are found on separate plants. Only the female plant will fruit, and to do so it's necessary to have a male plant nearby. Nearly all fruit trees benefit from cross-pollination, and need a nearby rooster tree.

2. Rainy weather during the pollination season. Bad weather means no bees and incomplete pollination means a poor crop of fruit.

3. Dry weather. Causes fruit to drop prematurely. Applying a mulch of straw, peat, newspapers, etc., and watering during dry spells will help.

4. Poorly drained and infertile soils mean poor crops of fruits or berries.

5. Too much or too little pruning. Heavy pruning of shrubs whose buds have formed means you've cut off your source of berries and fruit. Too little pruning as well as overpruning may be the cause of too much vegetative growth and less fruiting.

6. Heavy feeding. Too rich a soil means a lot of bush and no fruits.

7. "Alternate bearing." Some plants will produce a heavy crop one year and the following year very little, mainly because the food reserves available to the tree have been used up.

8. Insects and disease. Both cause weakening which in turn prevents a crop.

9. Age. Some plants are simply too young to set fruit. Be patient. Dwarfs bear earlier, starting in their second or third year, but some standards will not bear until eight to fourteen years of age.

UNWANTED FRUIT You have a beautiful apple, plum, cherry, or nut tree but don't want the fruit crop. Unwanted fruit is especially annoying near swimming pools, fish ponds, drives and walks. Some nurserymen will spray your trees to prevent fruit formation, using low concentrations of growth hormones in combination with other chemicals. The Bartlett Tree Company recommends using Sevin (a common insecticide) in combination with naphthaleneacetic acid (the hormone spray fruit growers use). This combination gives a great reduction in fruit set if the timing is right, and it works better in some years than in others.

Note: Sevin is death on bees. Never spray during the blossoming period. Never spray during the day, when bees are active. Do it late in evening.

REWARDING FRUIT TREES, SHRUBS, AND PLANTS

•**Apples** (For information on Crabapples see Chapter II.) Today the USDA lists 7,000 varieties of apples, of which only 20 are considered valuable, and at this writing only 8 account for three-quarters of all commercial production. They are Red Delicious, McIntosh, Golden Delicious, Rome Beauty, Jonathan, Winesap, York, and Stayman. A good apple man can tell what part of the country you're from on the basis of the apple you ate as a child.

The varieties of apples you can grow in your garden make an endless list, but for simplification, choose at least one from among Red or Golden Delicious, Cortland, or Jonathan. They are all pollinators and necessary—at least one of them—to fruit production. Empire, developed at the New York State Experimental Station as a cross between Delicious and McIntosh, is an extremely high quality dessert apple, ripening two weeks after McIntosh. Jonagold, a cross between Golden Delicious and Jonathan, is an annual bearer, high in quality. Its fruit keeps until spring. Idared, another good long-keeping apple, ripens a month after McIntosh.

Our country is blessed with many good apple varieties that mature at different times. For late apples which store well, you can choose from among Jonagold, Northern Spy, and Red Jonathan. Red Duchess, Red Astrachan, Early McIntosh, Lodi, and Yellow Transparent are early summer apples. Study your nursery catalogue for varieties suited to your area.

HOT CLIMATE APPLES: Did you know it is possible to grow apples in hot climates such as Southern California and middle Florida? The variety called Beverly Hills was bred especially for growing in warm climates and does not require chilling to induce fruit bud formation. It's an early apple and of good eating quality. One of its parents is Early McIntosh.

OLD-FASHIONED VARIETIES: Do you have a hankering for the old apple varieties such as Summer Rambo, Pound Sweet, Maiden's Blush, Snow Apple (Fameuse), Pumpkin Sweet, or Golden Russet? Some nurseries are bringing back these oldies and they are now available in semi-dwarf forms.

The first settlers who came to this country found no apples growing here. Then settlers brought apple seeds with them, and as settlers moved south, west, and into Canada, they took seeds and seedlings with them. Before 1800, there were thousands of apple varieties in America; but many were suitable only for cider (hic!) or animal feed, and most were suitable only for home plantings.

As fruit growing became a highly specialized business, the antique varieties gradually gave way to modern varieties which have the following attributes: 1) productivity, 2) attractiveness, 3) uniformity, 4) ease of handling, 5) disease resistance, 6) good keeping qualities, and 7) dual usefulness, for dessert and processing.

During the Depression, a work project was set up to cut down neglected apple trees to control pests. Thousands of apple trees were cut down, and some old apple varieties were lost forever. Today, there's an effort being made to bring back and preserve old apple varieties, thanks to people like Miller Bros. Nursery, Canandaigua, New York, the Worcester County Horticultural Society, Old Sturbridge Village in Massachusetts, and others.

THINNING FRUIT: Too many sets on apple (or pear or peach) trees prevent flower bud formation for the next season. This results in alternate bearing, a heavy crop of small-sized fruit one year and no crop at all the next year. Crop thinning in the home garden is also an excellent idea to prevent an excess of "June drop," which litters the yard with small apples nature has dropped from the trees in her own attempt to thin the fruit that cannot be nourished by the tree.

There are both hormone and non-hormone sprays that can be used for this purpose. The hormone sprays contain naphthaleneacetic acid and may be applied successfully up to two weeks after the fruit has set. Follow the directions on the container, keeping in mind that this is a new and somewhat tricky process and can be overdone. Hand thinning is still the safest method, but time-consuming. If you decide to hand thin your apple trees, space the fruit you wish to leave on the tree about 4 to 6 inches apart, or one apple on every third or fourth spur. The result is handsome, large fruit and a tidy lawn. Good "gardenkeepers" consider the process well worth the effort.

STORAGE: Most homes today lack the dirt cellar floor or damp, cool basement of older homes where it was once possible to keep apples and potatoes all winter long. In today's home we have to make the best of what we've got. Don't pick apples too ripe if you're going to store them. The apple that's ready to eat when it comes off the tree is too ripe to keep well; on the other hand, the apple that's picked before it is truly mature (that is unripe) can shrivel, dry out, and turn brown. A cool spring will mean a later picking date; a warm spring will mean apples mature earlier. Apples picked at the proper time and stored as close to 32 degrees F. as possible will maintain high quality under storage for a long while.

A simple way to hold apples or pears firm and fresh into the following May is to set a new or very clean galvanized garbage can into a hole in a shady spot of your garden, deep enough so that the lip or rim of the can is just slightly above ground level, or you can use a discarded refrigerator such as we've described under *Storing Your Vegetables and Fruit* in Chapter XI. Place blemish- and disease-free apples in the can, replace the lid, and cover with a pile of straw or leaves to a depth of 12 to 18 inches. A board or stone

(12 to 18")

Fruits and vegetables keep well over the winter in a clean galvanized garbage can buried in the garden. Cover can with 12 to 18 inches of straw, leaves, or evergreen boughs.

may be placed over this covering to keep it from blowing off. Even though the ground around the can will be frozen during the winter, the apples will not freeze. It's a good idea to keep the apples in an unheated room or garage until the ground temperature gets cold, and also to keep them moist by spraying lightly with water before placing them in the winter storage can. (See also *Drying Fruits and Vegetables* at the end of this chapter.)

TROUBLES: A spray program such as we outlined earlier will control most of the major troubles you will encounter in your home apple orchard. If you want real satisfaction from your fruit tree efforts, make up your mind to spray before you visit the nursery for planting stock.

No fruit. Due to lack of pollination. In cloudy weather, or when temperature is below 65 degrees F., bees do little flying, hence cannot work the blossoms. Also cold spring or freezing weather kills the flower buds.

Small apples. Due to overproducing. Apples often produce more fruits than the tree can nurse, good reason for thinning them (see *Thinning*).

Wormy apples. Due to railroad worm, also called apple maggot (larvae of codling moth). Spray with all-purpose pesticide every two weeks starting about June 20 to check this No. 1 pest of apples.

Apple scab. Black scabs on skin. Use Captan in the all-purpose spray mixture.

Dying of apple trees. Borers in trunks. Look for sawdust or "frass" at the base of the tree, holes in the trunk. Use Borer Paste available at garden stores.

•Apricots One reason why apricots are disappointing in some areas is that the tree is an early bloomer, which means it's susceptible to spring frosts. If the blossoms escape frost, the young fruit is equally susceptible to cold temperature. This often means a crop one year, then none the next.

How can you do something about the temperature around an apricot tree? Plant an apricot tree next to a blacktop drive, or next to your house. Radiant heat from the blacktop or your house will often raise the temperature around the tree sufficiently to prevent blossom kill by the frost. The size of the tree, beauty of form, leaf, and fruit (plus blossoms) make the apricot ideal for planting near a flagstone or brick patio next to the home (bricks and stone hold heat). Two hardy varieties are Sungold and Moongold, both developed at the University of Minnesota. These will withstand temperatures of 25 degrees F. below zero. Both varieties are self-sterile, meaning you must plant one of each for good fruit set. Moorpark is self-fertile and needs no rooster tree. Nearly all apricots are self-fruitful and do not need two for cross-pollination.

Care of apricots is the same as for peaches.

●**Blackberries** If you're not lucky enough to have long blackberries growing wild in your vicinity, you might want to set out a few cultivated varieties such as Darrow, Bailey, and Hedrick if space permits to avail yourself of this tasty fruit. For a thornless variety there is one called Thornfree.

Blackberries grow canes one season, fruit the second, and then die down, only to be replaced by another set of canes. They like full sun and a well drained soil. Plant in fall or spring. In the wild, they're never pruned, yet bear profusely. You get larger fruit if you prune out weak and broken canes in spring, before growth starts. Thin out to eight or ten vigorous canes per row. Trim back the branches to twelve buds. In early June, when new shoots are about 3 feet high, pinch the tips off to force side buds into growth and produce squatty, well-branched canes. For maximum sweetness be sure to let berries become dead ripe before harvesting. After the crop is harvested, canes which produced fruit can be removed at any time.

TROUBLES: About the only trouble blackberries get is imperfect fruit, the work of the tarnished plant bug. Spray with Malathion just before the first flowers open.

●**Blueberries** Resistance to low temperatures, varieties that produce plump, juicy fruit in abundance, and handsome reddish-brown fall foliage are working their magic to increase the popularity of home grown blueberries. As a rule, blueberries need no spraying, thrive in sun or semi-shade, and produce fruit the year after planting. They are, however, soil-fussy and demand a humus-rich condition coupled with soil acidity.

You can have a soil test made to determine the acidity of your land—a subject we discuss in Chapter XIII—but for the small home garden, we like the method devised by Michigan State College for growing blueberries in tubs; you will want at least two, but probably no more than four to six blueberry plants of at least two varieties for cross-pollination. You can choose early, midseason, and late ones, and varieties we have found to be good are Jersey (late), Bluecrop (midseason), and Earliblue (early).

CULTURE: For tub culture, use clean oil drums cut in half with the bottoms and tops removed. Sink the tubs in the ground and fill with a mixture of $1/2$ bushel of sawdust or peat moss mixed with good garden soil. This mixture may then be acidified by adding from $1/4$ pound to 1 pound of ammonium sulfate or sulfur—the former for soils already acid, the latter for very alkaline or nearly neutral soils. Into these specially prepared "tubs" set out your blueberry plants early in spring, trimmed back to little more than half the size the nursery sends you. Trim off ragged root ends also and set the plants just a little deeper in the soil than they were in the nursery row (as indicated by the soil line on the plant).

Blueberries are great nitrogen feeders and might show yellow leaves if their nitrogen supply is not adequate. Ammonium sulfate is your remedy—as much as one handful around the base of each plant every three weeks until yellow leaves disappear, then cut the quantity to about 2 ounces per plant once or twice during the growing season. Do not use nitrate of soda for blueberries—the plants cannot convert or use the nitrogen in nitrate of soda.

Heavy pruning is important to good blueberry culture, as the plants have a tendency to overbear. A large number of fruit buds form on new shoot growth and if all these buds, each producing a cluster of from five to eight berries, are permitted to mature, your fruit will be small and inferior.

Prune your blueberries in early spring before the bushes bloom. A good rule of thumb is to allow one fruit bud for each 3 inches of new shoot growth, thereafter removing all sucker shoots and twiggy branches. The vigorous new shoots that remain should be about 6 inches in length and well spread.

TROUBLES: Blueberries have few troubles, but birds can get to the bush before you do. Try using a fiber-mesh netting (available in garden stores) over the bushes to salvage the major portion of the crop for the table. (See ANIMAL CONTROL).

•**Bush cherries and beach plums** Both these items are decorative shrubs as well as being grown for their fruit. Beach plums will grow in heavy or sandy soils, will tolerate salt spray, and can be trained into a small tree if desired. Bush cherries grow 4 to 5 feet tall, bear large, black, sweet fruit, and tolerate a wide range of soils.

Plant bush cherries and beach plums as you would plant any shrub. Make sure that the holes are large enough to accommodate all the roots without crowding. Plant to the same depth as the plants stood in the nursery row. Trim off about one-third of the tops of the plants before setting. No great amount of pruning is necessary, just enough to shape the plants and remove any dried, criss-crossing, or broken branches.

•**Boysenberry, dewberry, and loganberry** A lesser-known group of berries for the home gardener includes the Boysenberry, Dewberry, and Loganberry. For a tame fruit with a delicious wild taste, try these giant-fruited brambles if you have the space. All are not absolutely winter-hardy in the North, and the canes must be covered with straw 3 or 4 inches thick.

The loganberry is a hybrid originated in California, a cross between a western black dewberry and a red raspberry. The boysenberry is a cross between loganberry, raspberry, and blackberry. Its berries are tremendous—sometimes more than 2 inches long, on thorny canes. To confuse you further, there's the Youngberry, similar to the boysenberry, with or without spines. Also, there's the nectarberry, which is similar to the boysenberry, and there's even a thornless boysen. Those who've grown the thornless or "unarmed" sports find these do not produce as much as the thorny plants.

Among dewberries, Lucretia is a good one if you give it straw protection.

In general, all these brambles take the same care. Try not to grow them where tomatoes, eggplants, or peppers have grown recently, since these crops sometimes have a wilt disease which may carry over in the soil. Set plants 3 feet apart in rows, and if you grow them on a trellis, allow enough space between rows for your type of cultivator.

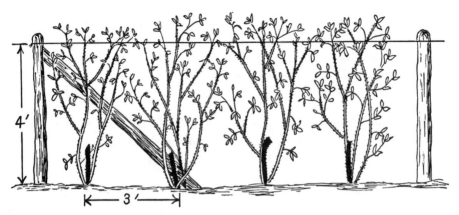

Training bramble fruits on a wire trellis. Plants can be spaced 3 to 6 feet apart.

In spring, cut back to one-half the previous year's growth and train the plants to a trellis 4 to 5 feet high. The new canes that grow up during the summer months should be trained back into the row to facilitate cultivation around the plants. After picking the fruit, the old canes which have borne the crop can be cut back close to the ground and the new canes can be trained to the trellis.

The boysenberry and its relatives are started by layering tips of new canes in fall. They root in spring and can be cut from the mother plant. Mulch the plants with sawdust, straw, or whatever is available to keep down weeds and conserve moisture. Feed same as raspberries (see).

•**Cherries** Both sweet and sour cherries live on a wide diversity of soils, provided they are well drained.

Sweet cherry varieties range from pink-fleshed, black-skinned Windsor and all pink and golden Royal Ann (called Napoleon in many catalogues) to the large, black, and temptingly juicy Black Tartarian and Schmidt's Bigarreau. Sweet cherries do not pollinate themselves, so figure on two different varieties for rooster effect, or your best efforts may come to naught.

Montmorency, the leading sour cherry variety, is self-fertile but may not be used to pollinate the sweet cherries which bloom earlier. An extremely hardy dwarf sour cherry is called North Star.

CULTURE: Cherries may be fall-planted, but also take happily to spring planting, following the general rules for fruit tree planting described under *General Culture of Fruit Trees*.

A wrinkle little known outside the trade in cherry growing is to spread the branches of the tree with notched boards when the tree is young and supple. This makes a broad and open tree and produces extra fruit. Apple growers do this on varieties which tend to grow straight up.

TROUBLES: The "all-purpose spray program" described at the beginning of this chapter will control most of the major insects and diseases you will encounter in growing cherries, with the possible exception of those years in which late frosts (against which there is no practical protection for the home gardener) "take" the blossoms. Should this happen, you will have to resign yourself to waiting for next year's crop. Birds are often a greater menace to sweet cherries than all the insects, diseases, and inclement weather combined. We have planted several mulberry trees, the fruit of which birds much prefer, hence they leave our cherries alone. (See sections on Animal Control and Insect and Disease Control).

•**Currants and gooseberries** Currants grow in any soil, even under shaded conditions, and do not winterkill. The culture of gooseberries is so similar that these two fruits will be discussed simultaneously. The Red Lake variety of currant—a large red berry—and Poormans gooseberry are generous yielders for the home garden. (Pixwell is the variety commonly found in catalogues but Poormans is superior.)

Some states prohibit the growing of currants and gooseberries because they serve as host to one stage of the pine blister rust. Before ordering plants from your nursery, be sure to consult the laws of your state.

CULTURE: Plant currants and gooseberries 3 inches deeper than they grew in the nursery, in either spring or fall. Tops should be cut back one half at planting time. After the plants are three years old prune out some of the older wood to stimulate growth and maintain fruit size. The plants are shallow-rooted, so it is necessary to mulch them well with sawdust, peat moss, or straw; and for feeding, a handful of nitrate of soda around each bush in early spring does nicely.

While gooseberries need little more pruning than the removal of dead, overgrown, and low-hanging branches, currants should have old canes removed. Ideally each currant bush should have three or four canes each of one-, two- and three-year-old growth after the bush has reached maturity. Currant pruning should be done in fall or late winter when the plants are completely dormant.

TROUBLES: These plants are quite free from troubles, except for mild infestation of aphids. Aphids cause warts or wrinkled leaves because they feed on the underside of the foliage, turning the leaves brown and reddish-brown on the upper side. Spray with nicotine sulfate, 2 teaspoons to a gallon of water, in early spring when the leaves are about $1/2$ inch in diameter. It is very important to cover the underside of the foliage where the aphids congregate. Early spraying is the secret of good control.

•**Elderberries** Elderberries thrive on most types of soil as long as it is well drained. Roots and tops should be pruned similarly to other shrubs at planting time and the plants set 2 inches deeper than they grew in the nursery row. Adams No. 1 and Johns are the varieties we recommend. While not handled by all nurseries, they are obtainable and far superior to the wild elderberry plants some gardeners dig up and transplant to their garden.

Elderberries will eventually reach 8 to 10 feet, and should be spaced 7 to 8 feet apart. They have attractive wheel-like white blossoms in June, and fruit in late August or September. We enjoy the blossoms dipped in pancake batter, deep fried to a golden brown, and dusted with confectioner's sugar. You'll relish them, too. Of course, there's nothing that beats elderberry pie or elderberry jam!

•**Figs** Home gardeners can grow figs outdoors or indoors. Figs like sun, well drained soil, and plenty of moisture. Many northern gardeners grow their figs in tubs, and move them indoors in fall (see Chapter VIII, CONTAINER GARDENING). Feed a liquid plant food in early spring.

CULTURE: Figs need very little pruning. Train to three or four branches, making sure they are as close to the ground as possible. Do pruning while the tree is young.

Figs pollinate themselves, so you don't have to worry about rooster trees. The fruit must ripen before you pick it. Wait until it starts turning a light purple. Some varieties, such as Brown Turkey, mature fruits earlier than others. If yours does not ripen before fall frost, cover with a blanket at night.

WINTER TREATMENT: 1) You can dig a hole alongside the tree, bend the tree over, place a rock or board over it. Cover with leaves, straw, hay, etc. and mound with a foot of soil. In spring, uncover tree, straighten it up and replace soil around roots. 2) You can put a snow fence around the tree, pack straw and leaves in between, then put tarpaper around the outside. 3) You can bring the tubbed plant indoors and keep it in a light, cool room for the winter.

TROUBLES: Figs have few troubles in northern areas, if properly cared for.

●Grapes No yard or garden should be without at least one or two grapevines. This vine gives you beauty, fruits to eat (or drink), leaves you can use for exotic dishes, and cool shade from a sizzling summer sun. Train your grapes on a trellis or arbor. If you want quality fruit, trim the vines (see grape pruning). If you're not interested in big fat bunches, and want screen effect, you can let the canes ramble.

When it comes to varieties, remember you can grow some type of grape in every section of America. Study your local nursery catalogues for the recommended varieties for your area. There are early, midseason, and late varieties. Late grapes are not suitable where frosts come early in fall. A good white seedless is Himrod, famous for its large, handsome clusters turning golden-yellow. Intertaken is a sister seedling, just as delicious.

There has recently been a revived interest in home making; it's difficult to beat the Concord or Niagara variety. French hybrids are popular. One that excels for both wine and dessert is Aurora Seibel No. 5279. Other Seibels include Seibel 1000, S. 5898, and S. 9549; Baco No. 1 is listed as Baco Noir, a good dark-blue grape. Be sure to study your nursery catalogue and order grapes for your own locality.

Grapes are not soil-fussy, but since they live and produce for as long as sixty to eighty years, you should do all you can to maintain high organic content of the soil in which you plant them. This can be done by adopting a biennial program of mulching around the plants with hay, sawdust, wood chips, compost, or peat moss.

START YOUR OWN GRAPES: One of the slickest ways to start your own grapes is to use a milk carton and vermiculite. Go to your friend who has grapes, get a cutting about 8 inches or so long, and try to have two good nodes (the spot where the buds are). Insert the cutting into the vermiculite, place in a sunny spot, and keep it moist. The woody stem will root within a month, with roots on both sets of nodes. March through May is the ideal time to try this, although you can root them in the summer in this manner. (The usual method for starting grapes from cuttings is to select them in the fall, store in moist sawdust in cellar until spring, then set them out in the garden where roots will form from the callus produced in fall and winter.) A slower method of starting grapes is by layering or making a tip cutting (see Plant Propagation).

PLANTING: Select one- or two-year-old grapevines for setting out and locate them away from frost pockets, in full sun, and considerably out from under the shade of trees to

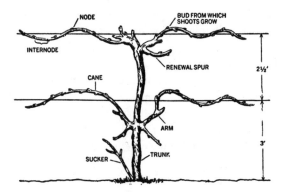

The average home gardener can avoid a lot of confusion by selecting 4 good canes and cutting out the rest. Try to prune your grape vine according to this diagram. Remove "sucker" growth in summer by yanking it off at the base. Regular pruning is done in late winter or early spring. (*Courtesy Michigan State University*)

prevent mildew of the vines. Where growing seasons are short, ripening can be hastened by planting on the south side of a building and training the vine against the wall. Heat from reflected sunlight on the wall will make the fruit ripen as much as a week earlier.

Usual spacing for grapes is 8 feet by 8 feet, but if space is limited you can set the plants on 7-foot centers. Holes should be dug 12 to 14 inches deep and 16 inches in diameter. We like to put some rotted compost in the bottom of the hole before planting the vine. Prune the top back so that you have two buds remaining. If you plant grapes in fall, hold the pruning over until spring; but in either season, trim off broken roots and any roots that are too long to fit without crowding into the hole.

Set the pruned vine into the hole so that the two buds are just above soil level, tamp soil firmly around the roots and into the hole, and water well. You can either mulch or cultivate the first year.

No trellis is needed the first year, since the vines can be trained on stakes placed next to the base of the plant. The second year, you will need support for the growing vines. We use metal posts about 8 feet long, driven 2 to 2 1/2 feet into the ground. On these posts, two wires should be strung, one 5 1/2 feet from the ground, and the second 2 feet below the top wire. This spacing will provide maximum exposure of leaf area to the sun and promote early fruit ripening.

PRUNING: No one thing is so completely disastrous to efforts to grow grapes as vines that have not been regularly and properly pruned. Better to be brave and hack away at your vines in good spirit than to say "I don't know how to do it" and neglect them entirely. The purpose of pruning is to limit the production of fruit and control cane growth so that cane and fruit are in balance at all times. For grapes grown in southern and far western regions check with your state agricultural experimental station for recommended pruning procedures.

In the main, the canes you want to save are last-year's canes about 5 to 8 feet long and about as thick as a lead pencil, or slightly thicker, and fairly short-jointed. Those buds near the center of the cane produce more than those at the base of the cane or near the tip. Thus, cut off the tips of the canes, leaving eight to twelve buds. Remove all unnecessary old wood as well as the less vigorous canes of last year's growth. That is the general idea of grape pruning.

Specifically, here is what you do:

1. At planting time, prune canes back, leaving only two buds.
2. Second year, prune off all growth except one strong cane, leaving three to five buds. Tie this cane to the first wire of the trellis for support.
3. Third year, leave two fruiting canes of six to eight buds each, tied to the first wire.
4. Fourth year, leave two longer fruiting canes of ten to twelve buds each, tying them to the bottom wire of the trellis.
5. Fifth year, leave three fruiting canes of ten to twelve buds each, tying the longest cane to the top wire of the trellis.

You will also want to leave a "spur" for each fruiting cane—a "spur" being simply a cane cut back to two buds. The reason for this is that the canes growing from this spur will be the fruiting canes to select from next year, and by following this program, fruiting canes are kept near the trunk of the vine.

Ordinarily, a total of four canes per vine is enough to leave on. A weak cane can support about forty buds and a thrifty vine about sixty. If your grapes are a giant mass of vines your total pruning motivation is to select four of the best canes per vine—cut all the rest out—and to select canes of last year's growth which have buds at reasonably close intervals. After you have finished a good pruning job, you should have a lot of "brush" to clear away, which is as it should be, and not a sign that you have just ruined your little vineyard.

FEEDING: Feeding grapes has a few tricks to it. On vines making exceptionally strong growth, use fertilizers sparingly or you'll get all "brush" and no fruit. Also, overfertilized vines won't harden off properly for winter and may kill back. Grape vines have long roots that extend as much as 8 feet from the base of the vine with most of the feeder roots 3 to 6 feet out from the base. Therefore, fertilizer applied to the base of the trunk will do almost no good at all. You must fertilize widely for grapes.

Grapes need potash and are fairly nitrogen-hungry at all times where yields are wanted. Provide the nitrogen needs of the vines by applying $1/3$ pound of nitrate of soda or $1/6$ pound of ammonium nitrate to each vine as soon as the buds start to swell in the spring. Potash should be supplied by the application of 2 pounds of potassium sulfate per vine.

CHECKING GRAPE PESTS: Most of the troubles in the backyard grape planting can be controlled by spraying early with bordeaux mixture to which has been added 2 ounces of Malathion, $1/4$ ounce of spreader, per $61/4$ gallons of bordeaux. Spray again with this mixture just before blossoming and a third time just after blossoming. For best results, spray grapevines when the leaves are dry. Many gardeners have good grapes and never bother to spray.

Do not blame bees, wasps, and hornets for damage you may find in your grapes. These insects do no damage to sound fruit, but are tempted to the vines by fruit that has popped open due to weather conditions. You will find this most often after a long drought followed by heavy rains late in the season. The grapes build up pressure under these conditions, causing the fruit to pop open and drop to the ground. See Animal control if squirrels or birds bother your grapes.

•**Nectarines** This "fuzzless peach" is so much like the peach in taste that many think it is a peach. It's probably a sport of the peach, with white or gold flesh. Nectarines and peaches will cross-pollinate. If you can grow peaches, you can grow nectarines, as they have about the same hardiness and same culture. The tree is self-fruitful, meaning you don't need a rooster tree. Two good varieties to grow are Surecrop and Garden State. (For culture see *Peaches*.)

•**Peaches** No garden fruit is more tempting, and where temperatures do not fall below −15 degrees F., peaches are easy to grow, provided they are given the right care at the right time. You can start with any type of soil, but be sure the drainage is good. Peaches will not stand wet feet, thus fertile, sandy loams are preferable, although heavier soils will do (see Chapter XIII for ways of improving soils).

Best varieties for the home garden are probably Golden Jubilee, Sun Haven, Red Haven, Hale Haven, or Elberta. While most peaches are self-fertile, all peaches will benefit from a cross-pollinator.

Can you start a peach tree from a pit? Sometimes it will produce a tree with good fruit, but usually it doesn't. Fruit from trees started from seed tends to be hard and lacks flavor. Peaches, apples, plums, and other fruits started from seed are referred to as common or "wild" and usually lack the quality of fruit trees purchased from a good nursery. Nurserymen bud a cultivated variety onto the seedling produced from seeds to produce good eating varieties.

PRUNING: Planted in spring or fall, peaches need very little pruning until they are three or four years old. Then you aim at having an open center tree with three, four, or five scaffold branches rising from the trunk, no higher than 36 inches from the ground. Most peach trees bear the third year after planting, and since the fruit is borne from side buds on one-year-old shoots, you'll need to do some pruning each year from then on to force out the new shoots. Old, neglected peach trees can be cut back to wood three years old or more and started out from there.

To start the open-center formation of your peach tree, the central leader or main branch of the tree should be kept low throughout the life of the tree, beginning the first year after planting. The scaffold branches are allowed to grow with less pruning, the lowest of which may be no more than a foot from the ground. Don't let branches lower than this remain on the tree. Remove the limbs that tend to fill up the center of the tree or make any part of the tree too dense. Head back any tall and ungainly limbs. The best time to prune peach trees is in March.

FEEDING: See *General Culture of Fruit Trees*.

THINNING: Peaches often set several times as many fruits as the tree can possibly develop. Thirty good leaves are needed to produce one peach, spaced 6 to 8 inches from its nearest neighbor. So think in terms of hand-thinning the crop right after "June drop" —the time that nature elects to thin the trees by letting many small peaches drop from trees that are loaded beyond capacity. At this time, you should look over the tree, limb by limb, and remove any peaches that are small, poorly shaped, damaged, or closer together than 6 to 8 inches.

PICKING: There is a trick to picking peaches that a lot of people don't know: Don't pick peaches too early! Leave the fruit on the trees at least until it has changed to a greenish-yellow color with up to 25 percent blush color. Delayed picking increases yield, too: One hundred bushels of unripe peaches today will make 109 bushels in two days more, 116 bushels five days from now, and 124 bushels next week! Besides an improvement in size and color, the flavor of tree-ripened fruit is far superior to the generally flat taste of peaches that have been picked too green.

TROUBLES: The worst attacks of insects and diseases on peach trees can be pretty well controlled by the "all-purpose spray program" outlined earlier. Peach-tree borers, leaf curl, and brown rot are the most common enemies of good peach production, and each is prevalent enough to make at least a minimum spray program necessary. Use Borer Paste on the trunks in November to check borer invasion, and Ferbam sprayed on branches during dormant season to prevent peach leaf curl. If it sounds like too much trouble, perhaps you would be better not to attempt peaches—but certainly plump, juicy, tree-ripened fruit is worth some effort.

● **Pears** Pears are among the easiest of tree fruits to grow in the home garden, almost as hardy as apples, and well acclimated to heavy clay or loam soils. Pears even tolerate a little wet feet, but a well drained soil produces better growth and a good soil will do wonders for your pear efforts. It is not generally known that the flavor, aroma, texture, and keeping qualities of pears are influenced more by the soil than anything else. Pears that are sour, dry, and bitter are usually the result of poor soil conditions. Also, give your pear trees good air drainage for prevention of disease and frost damage.

Bartlett, Bosc, Clapp's Favorite, and Seckel are excellent pear varieties, but if you choose to grow Bartlett and Seckel together (a favorite combination), do be sure to provide a pollinator, either in the form of a third pear variety, or by blossom bouquets of a compatible variety as explained under *Buying Fruit Trees* earlier in this chapter. Bartlett and Clapp's Favorite are very susceptible to fireblight, so if you plant these varieties, be prepared to watch for and deal with this disease.

Go easy with fertilizing pear trees—too much feeding encourages fast growth and makes the tree more susceptible to blight. Rather, put a screen around the base of the tree and use a mulch of sawdust, ashes, peat moss, etc., to keep weeds down and moisture in. Pears profit from thinning (see *Thinning* under *Apples*).

PICKING: It seems elementary to say anything about how and when to pick pears, but actually no other fruit requires as much care as this one. Just about every pear we know should be picked long before it is ready to eat. It is hard to say exactly when green pears should be picked for perfect flavor. A fair rule of thumb is to pick when the stem parts from the branch when the fruit is lifted. Some folks wait until the seeds are brown. You might watch the wormy pears, if you have any. When wormy fruit begins to turn yellow, that is the time to pick the green fruit, as injured fruit will ripen first. To ripen pears after they are picked, cover them with newspapers and keep them in a garage or on a cool porch. They ripen best at 65 degrees F. and 85 percent humidity or higher.

STORAGE: See *Apples*.

TROUBLES: Use the "all-purpose" spray and program for control of insects and diseases. Fireblight is recognizable by dead blossoms, leaves and twigs that turn black and remain on the trees. Cankers and mummified fruit may also be found. Inspect your trees and cut out infected wood. Fireblight spreads easily, so disinfect pruning tools after this chore by soaking them in a strong solution of household bleach.

Gritty or mealy fruit (or fruit that doesn't keep well). Picking too late (see *Picking*).

Pear psylla. Use Malathion.

●**Plums and prunes** The plum is well suited to most conditions in the North, where the tree is hardy. Plums are delicious home canned or made into plum butter and preserves. Prunes are a special class of plum which, because of their sugar content, may be successfully dried on the pit. Most popular for home growing in the Northeast are the Stanley, French, German, and Italian or Fellemberg prune which, incidentally, is not self-fruitful and must be grown with another plum tree nearby to pollinate it. For the rough-and-ready gardener, the Stanley is probably the best to try.

There are two Damson-type plums, French and Shropshire, which are blue with green flesh, and two Japanese-type plums, Burbank and Formosa, with red or red-yellow skins and yellow flesh, that are popular garden types. The Santa Rosa has a reddish-purple skin. Burbank and Formosa need "rooster" trees for pollination and should be grown with one of the other varieties mentioned for fruit production.

Don't be impatient for the fruit from plum trees. It will take anywhere from five to seven years after setting before they start to bear, and they cannot be pushed!

CULTURE: Planted in well drained soil, sprayed with the "all-purpose" spray plus the bordeaux mixture and fed about $1/8$ pound of ammonium nitrate per tree per year of age, plums will come along with little effort and yield delicious fruit for fresh eating, canning, or preserving for many years. Prune the branches only enough to remove those that are criss-crossing or crowding one another, and wait it out.

TROUBLES: *Black knot.* To prevent black knot and brown rot, keep the trees sprayed with Ferbam, bordeaux mixture or Captan at least every four weeks throughout the growing season regardless of whether they bear.

If you see a gummy, gelatinous material on plum fruit, you can be sure that your tree is under attack by the curculio insect. Be sure to gather and burn fallen fruit (or seal in plastic bag and discard) since the worm is inside the dropped fruit; otherwise worms will mature and come back to attack your fruit next year. *Control:* Spraying of Methoxychlor when fruit shucks begin to split, twice more at 10-day intervals.

●**Quince** There are two types of quince: the one grown for its handsome blooms (see *Flowering Shrubs — Chaenomeles*, in Chapter II), and the one grown for its fruit, *Cydonia*. The fruiting quince reaches 10 to 12 feet, and is quite hardy. Dwarf varieties are also available. The culture of both types of quinces is similar.

CULTURE: The quince bears very heavily, so to get large fruit you must remove the smallest ones a couple of weeks after the blossoms fade, while the stems are still soft enough to allow pinching them off. Quince fruit when ripe turns a beautiful golden-yellow.

Quinces are not edible out of hand but are popular for jelly, preserves, and quince honey. Many people also like to use the dried fruit for perfuming bedding and linens.

●**Raspberries** Raspberries probably give the home gardener as good a return in delicious fruit as he can get from any fruit plant. All raspberries do best in a well drained soil and are not particular as to whether it is clay or sandy loam. Even though they need quantities of water, they do not like wet feet. Drainage is the important factor.

Red raspberries have different growing habits than the black and purple raspberries, and require slightly different care and pruning. It is also well to remember that nothing can get out of hand faster than a neglected raspberry planting! You must be the boss in your raspberry patch or the plants will quickly take over, become diseased, and provide you with nothing but small, seedy fruit. You will regret that you ever set a plant.

While raspberries are producing fruit they are also struggling to perpetuate themselves, making, in the case of the red varieties, "suckers" or new shoots, and in blacks and purples, "tip-roots." These are the processes that must be watched carefully to keep things under control, which can be done by pruning, which we will get at in a moment.

Latham, Taylor, and Newburgh are good red raspberry varieties; Bristol is a recommended black and New Clyde a favorite purple. There are also fall-bearing red raspberries, one called September and a newer variety called Fall Red. Both bear two crops of fruit: one in early summer and one on the new canes in the fall. Many people harvest both crops, but some prefer to cut back the fruiting canes drastically in spring and concentrate on the fall crop. Fall-fruiting raspberries should be supported, as the berries are borne high on the cane tips which have a tendency to drag on the ground, bruising and dirtying the fruit.

A fine yellow variety now available is called Fall Gold and bears extra-large, delicious berries continuously from July to October. Heritage is a dandy new red.

PLANTING: We prefer that raspberries be planted as early in the spring as possible. They may be set in the fall (the latter part of October or the first two weeks in November) but spring planting is usually more successful. Space plants 3 feet apart in the row, setting them in shallow holes or an open furrow to a depth of 4 inches. Cover the roots with fine, loose soil and firm them with your hand or foot. Fill the rest of the hole loosely, leaving the top layer loose so that buds growing from the ground level can grow out easily. Water well, but do not place any fertilizer in contact with the roots when planting.

FEEDING: Feed 2 ounces of nitrate of soda or 1 ounce of ammonium nitrate per plant, spreading the fertilizer well out from the plants, since raspberries feed 3 to 4 feet from the canes. This feeding should be done in early spring, as feeding the plants in the fall might produce soft late growth that will be sure to winterkill. You can also use rotted manure or compost around the plants in spring.

PRUNING: The first thing to know about pruning raspberries is that the canes make growth one year, produce the fruit the next year, and then die. Once a raspberry cane has produced fruit, its function is over and it should be cut off at ground level, removed from the patch and burned or sealed in plastic and discarded. While not a total disease and insect control, destroying the old canes helps immeasurably.

All raspberries profit by a summer "tipping" or pruning the tops of the new shoots when the canes have reached a height of from 2 to 3 feet. Black and purple raspberries should be tipped at 2 feet before they make a long, spindly growth which arches over until the end touches the soil. It is at this point that the blacks and purples get out of hand, for the tip of the long cane will form a new plant and thus a whole new family of canes and arches and new plants. It takes only a couple of years to produce a massive bramble if summer tipping is neglected.

Red raspberries do not tip-root, but make suckers. These sucker plants should be thinned out every year, allowing the new canes to set no closer than 8 to 10 inches from one another. All raspberries need good air drainage and should not be allowed to grow too thickly.

Clean cultivation of the raspberry planting should be kept up until about the time the blossoms form. Then the plants may be mulched with straw or sawdust which does double duty, keeping down weeds and preserving soil moisture for the promotion of large fruit. After a harvest of red raspberries, mulch should be thinned to allow the new shoots to come up straight and true for the following year's crop.

TROUBLES: Raspberries fall heir to several insect pests; Malathion spray will check most of them. For raspberry fruit worm, apply when the first blossom buds appear, and repeat just before the blossom buds open. This treatment also checks raspberry sawfly, tarnished plant bug, and cane borers. If you're bothered by Japanese beetles, see section on Control of Insects and Diseases.

Diseases of raspberries are best controlled by providing good air circulation around the plants and segregating the reds from the purples and blacks as much as possible. In small plantings, either grow reds alone, or blacks and purples alone. If you must have all three, grow the blacks and purples at least 500 feet from the reds. This will help prevent possible mosaic infection in the blacks and purples from traveling to the reds.

•**Strawberries** Strawberries need well drained soil well supplied with humus. They need water, full sun, and protection from birds when in fruit; weeds must be kept down in the patch, plants should be spaced as they form, the bed should be mulched over winter, and some kind of protection against frost should be available when the blossoms are out. Plant food is needed, but care must be taken as to the time and the amount applied. In spite of all of this, many people grow strawberries with little or no effort, delighted with the fact that any strawberry picked and eaten ripe from one's own patch is a thing of great enjoyment. The persistent plants will give you some fruit no matter how neglectful you are of the things you should do for the best berries.

Strawberries come in three groups: early, midseason, and late. By using varieties from each of these groups, harvest can be extended from mid-May to late June. The list of varieties is great. For early production you can try Blakemore, New Empire, Earlidawn, Midland, Fairfax, Redglow, or Premier. For midseason fruit, try Surecrop, Guardian, Redchief, or Raritan. Useful late varieties include Ardmore, New Jersey Belle, and Sparkle. Gardeners who have room for only one variety probably should concentrate on a midseason type. See your nursery catalogue for a greater selection.

Everbearing strawberries set additional flower buds while the spring crop is being harvested, then they flower and fruit in late summer and fall, giving you two seasons of picking. Good everbearing varieties include Superfection, Ozark Beauty, and Ogallala. Of course, there are many other good ones. You should provide twenty-five plants for each member of your family for enough strawberries to eat at any one time. At the height of the season, you will have some extra for preserves or freezing out of this size planting. If space is limited you may want to grow the berries in "barrels," mounds, planter boxes, and hanging baskets (see Chapter VIII).

For best results, do not set strawberries where you have grown tomatoes, potatoes, peppers, or eggplant. Otherwise, you can include the rows in your vegetable garden rotation, as strawberries are seldom fruitful more than two or three years and new rows should be set at least every third year.

PLANTING: Very early spring is the best time to set out strawberries. Buy your plants from a good nursery, preferably a grower, where you can get freshly dug sets. If you must order through the mail, prune off the ends of roots before planting. If you cannot plant immediately, nip off the ends of the roots and heel in the plants, then plant in their permanent spot as soon as possible.

If you do not intend to spend a lot of time with your strawberry plants, allow 2 feet between each plant and 1 1/2 feet on each side of the plant row. All of this space will be well covered with plants by the end of the first growing season, and you will wonder in the next summer where you can put your feet when picking. Do not underestimate the ability of the strawberry to spread itself!

When setting strawberry plants, trim off ragged root ends. Make a slit in the soil and hold a plant with roots fanned out against one side of the slit, the "crown" or thick

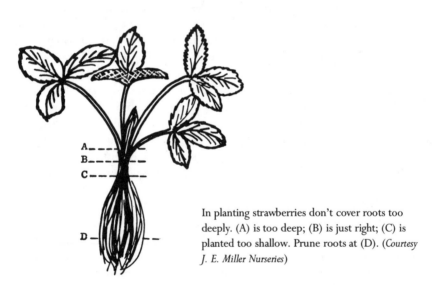

In planting strawberries don't cover roots too deeply. (A) is too deep; (B) is just right; (C) is planted too shallow. Prune roots at (D). (*Courtesy J. E. Miller Nurseries*)

part of the plant just even with the top of the slit. Now stamp the slit closed with your foot, firming the soil in around the roots and leaving no air space at the bottom of the slit. The crown of the plant should not be covered nor should the roots show above the ground.

After the plants show signs of new growth in the leaves you can commence a feeding program, using a complete formula fertilizer, applied in either liquid or dry form around the plants, about half a handful to a plant, hoed in lightly and then watered. This feeding may be continued at two-week intervals all through the first year.

Keep fertilizer away from the berry patch until the crop of fruit is off, as feeding at this time tends to make the berries soft and encourages rotting before they ripen. Do water the plants frequently all through the berry season, soaking the patch after you pick. This increases berry size wonderfully.

Blossoms on the newly set plants should be removed the first year to throw all possible strength into the plants for a good fruit crop the second year. Shortly after the blossoming season, "runners" will spring from the center of the plants, at the end of which, a few days later, a new plant will form and "set" in the ground. If you want highest possible yields of fine, big strawberries, no one plant should be allowed to make more than six of these new runner plants, which you space evenly around the plant in the row. All other runners should be removed as they form. Runner removal should be kept up all summer long. If you do not keep at it, your berry patch will end up as a matted row of plants which will produce a lot of berries the next year, but the fruit will be very small, difficult to pick, and not very nice to eat.

MULCHING: In late fall, just before very cold weather, cover the entire bed with a 2-inch blanket of straw or marsh hay. Leaves should be used as a last resort, as they tend to mat and may smother the plants. This mulching is necessary as strawberries not covered over winter tend to heave out of the ground as it alternately freezes and thaws, and this eventually breaks off the roots of the plants and kills them.

Early in spring of the following year, the mulch may be gradually removed. You can tell when to take the last of the mulch off by watching the color of the foliage. When it starts to turn a sickly green under the mulch, the plants should be fully exposed to the light. Keep the mulch you take off the plants right in the rows around the plants. This will serve to keep the fruit off the ground and keep it clean.

FROST CONTROL: Spring frosts are always a hazard to strawberry crops. Should a frost threaten when your strawberries are beginning to bloom, cover the rows overnight with newspapers or burlap bags. The blossoms are very sensitive to frost and a late frost can "take the crop" if the patch is not protected. Sprinkling the strawberry bed can also help protect against frost (and can mean the difference between an 80 percent and a 20 percent crop). Don't get alarmed if ice forms on the plants—just keep on sprinkling and the plants will usually come through in good shape. Leave the sprinkler on until all the ice has melted from the plants.

RENEWING THE BED: After the patch has produced its first crop, dig out small and unthrifty plants and fill the spaces with the new runners that will form again the second year. A winter mulch is again applied and removed in spring. After the second fruit harvest it is well to dig the plants under and work on a new patch. Diseases may take hold of an old patch about this time and the plants will be spindly. We used to think that two or three years was the maximum, but a strawberry patch can be made to fruit six years or longer. Many commercial growers fruit their fields eight years or longer.

Strawberry beds are usually abandoned because of weeds, overcrowding of the plants, winter injury, root diseases, or nematodes. Here are a few tips for renovating your patch for next year's crop:

1. Set a rotary lawn mower on high and mow all the leaves to a height of 1 to 3 inches—sounds brutal but new plants will come up from the mowed—off crowns.

2. If you have a rototiller remove a couple tines and run the machine down between the rows to a width of 15 inches or less.

3. Don't hesitate to space plants by removing the surplus until they are about 6 to 8 inches apart. Some people train the new plants so they resemble spokes in a wheel.

4. Feed your strawberry plants by using a liquid plant food. If you use a chemical or dry fertilizer such as 10-10-10, scatter it over the row when the foliage is *dry*.

5. Water the plants if rain doesn't come.

You should get a mass of new green leaves within a few days and they'll be husky by fall. It's better to grow a few, well managed plants, than a large, poorly managed planting.

HOW TO MAKE A STRAWBERRY BARREL: Use any wooden barrel you can move easily after it is filled with soil, since it must be moved into the garage for winter protection. Knock out the top and drill a 4-inch hole in the center of the bottom. Drill 1-inch holes at irregular intervals 9 inches apart all around the barrel.

Put a drainage core (4 inches in diameter) made of crinkled chicken wire, hardware cloth, or screening, from top to bottom in center of barrel. Hold core steady as you add 4 inches of crushed stone in the bottom of barrel, then fill gradually with 1 part each of sand, peat, loam, and compost. Insert strawberry plants in holes as you fill. Water thoroughly. Varieties of plants can be same as those you use in your garden. For winter protection, cover with straw and tie with twine, then move into garage.

If you can't locate a wooden barrel, you might try one of the metal strawberry pyramids sold by nurseries. Grown in the pyramid, the strawberries are easier to pick and easier to care for. Kits vary in size but a standard type holds 50 plants, has a 6 foot diameter base and is 3 terraces high. You can even buy pyramid-tailored bird netting.

TROUBLES: *Nubbins*. Hard, seedy fruit. Due to tarnished plant bug (see Chapter XIV).

Birds: See Chapter XVII.

Frost injury. See above.

Snails: See Chapter XIV.

Verticillium wilt. Use resistant varieties and rotate planting.

Cross-section of a strawberry barrel.

•**Nut culture** There's no reason why you can't grow edible nuts right in your own backyard. The trees are ornamental as well as productive, and they don't need spraying for a good crop.

Nearly all nut trees have the same cultural requirements, the two most important being a well-drained soil and the presence of a nearby "rooster" tree for cross-pollination. At planting time, dig holes 2 feet across and 2 or more feet deep, so roots will rest in a natural position. Fill around the roots with good topsoil and water well to drive out air pockets from the root area. Prune back the tree before planting to balance the loss of fine root hairs when trees were dug. (See *General Culture of Fruit Trees* in this chapter.) Most nut trees will bear from three to five years after planting. Walnuts usually take six years.

Here are some nuts to try: almonds, similar in culture to peaches; butternuts, chestnuts (Chinese); filberts (hazelnuts), and English walnuts, the Carpathian strain. Black walnuts are planted for high-quality lumber as well as nuts. There is a grafted black walnut called Thomas which bears large, thin-shelled nuts within two or three years after planting. Grafted hardy pecans are also offered by some nurseries. Most will start bearing within three to five years. Grafted trees are better than those started from seed. For more information on grafted nut trees, see our *Green Thumb Book of Fruit and Vegetable Gardening*. Also, you can write to the Northern Nut Growers Association, 4518 Holston Hills Road, Knoxville, Tennessee 37914.

STARTING NUT TREES: Your best bet is to buy trees from a reliable nursery, although with patience you can start your own from seed. Gather nuts in the fall and "stratify" them: pack the shucked nuts between alternate layers of sand in a box (covered with wire to keep out rodents) and sink the container in the ground or in a cold frame over the winter. In spring, plant the nuts in a well drained spot and watch them grow! They have to have this "cold winter" treatment before they'll germinate.

TROUBLES: "False" nuts or shrivelled kernels are usually due to lack of cross-pollination resulting from bad weather at flowering time. A safe practice is to plant at least two varieties together. Some gardeners practice "bouqueting": putting flowering twigs from another nut tree of the same species in a can of water close by your tree, just in case there's no rooster tree nearby. Anthracnose also may cause no meat in kernels and is worse in wet years. Thomas walnut is very susceptible to the disease, while Ohio is resistant to it.

No need to worry about the tiny maggot you see in the husks of walnuts or butternuts. This is the walnut husk maggot and in extreme cases may ruin the kernel, or cause the husks to stick to the shell. *Control*: In fall gather nuts as soon as they fall, and put them into buckets of water. This kills the maggots, leaving the husks, so they can't go into the soil for winter. Spraying is not practical for the home gardener.

Drying Fruits and Vegetables

It took a shortage of canning lids to induce gardeners to go back to the old-fashioned method of preserving fruits and vegetables, namely, drying. The proteins, carbohydrates, and minerals in fruits and vegetables are unchanged by the drying process. But in winter

QUICK REFERENCE CHART OF COMMON NUT TREES

Growing nuts in the backyard is a matter of selecting the right type for your climate and conditions. Nut trees can be grown in practically all parts of the U.S.

Kind of Nut	Mature Size	Planting Distance	Frost Damage	Soil	Life-Span
ALMOND *(Persica communus)*	Small (15 ft.)	20 ft.	Yes, blooms	Well-drained	Med. long
WALNUT and BUTTERNUT *(Juglans)*					
Black *(J. nigra)*	Very large	80 ft.	Rarely	Neutral	Very long
Butternut *(J. cinerea)*	Med. spreading	40 ft.	Very rarely	Neutral or slightly acid	Short
Japanese *(J. sieboldiana)*	Large spreading	60 ft.	Rarely	Neutral	Long
Heartnut *(J. sieboldiana cordiformis)*	Med. spreading	35 ft.	Rarely	Neutral	Long
Persian *(J. regia)*	Large, round head	50 ft.	Often	Slightly alkaline	Very long
HICKORY *(Carya)*					
Shagbark *(C. ovata)*	Large, upright	40 ft.	Rarely	Neutral	Med. long
Shellbark *(C. laciniosa)*	Large, upright	50 ft.	Rarely	Neutral	Med. long
Mockernut *(C. alba)*	Large, upright	50 ft.	Rarely	Neutral	Med. long
Hybrids	Large	50 ft.	Rarely	Neutral	Long
CHESTNUT *(Castanea)*					
Chinese *(C. molissima)*	Med. spreading	35 ft.	Very rarely	Acid	Med. long
Japanese *(C. crenata)*	Med. round head	40 ft.	Very rarely	Acid	Med. long
HAZELNUT OR FILBERT *(Corylus)*					
Filbert *(C. avellana)* hybrids	Bush or small tree to 15 ft.	20-25 ft.	Occasional	Neutral	Short, 20 yrs.
American *(C. americana)*	Bush to 8 ft.	10 ft.	Rarely	Neutral	Short, 20 yrs.
PECAN *(Carya illinoensis)*	Large, upright to 50 feet	50 ft.	Yes	Neutral	Med. long

This chart, prepared with the assistance of former professor of Pomology, Dr. L. H. MacDaniels of Cornell University, will help you select the tree for your backyard.

Disease Resistance	Insect Damage	Cross-Pollination	Varieties	Remarks
Good	None	Yes	New Hall's	Blooms early and often killed by frost in north
Good	Many pests	No	Sparrow, Elmer Myers, Thomas, Stambaugh	Varieties differ in hardiness and pest resistance
Poor	Fair	No	Craxezy, Buckley	Very hardy
Good	Fair	No	Seedlings only	Fast-growing, spreading, of tropical appearance
Good	Fair	No	Gettatly, Stranger, Wright, Walters	Nuts crack easily
Good	Husk maggots troublesome	Yes	Metcalfe, Hansen, Littlepage, Broadview	Carpathian strain hardy Some frost damage
Good	Usually not troublesome	Yes	Wilcox, Abscoda, Glober, Weschke	Difficult to transplant, needs extra care
Good	Some	Yes	Stanley	Nuts thick-shelled
Good	Some	Some varieties	Northern varieties: Major, Greenriver, Peruque	Hardy, but needs long growing season
Good	Some	Uncertain	Burton, Gerardi, Rockville	Attractive trees
Resists chestnut blight	Weevils	Yes	Nanking, Kuling, Abundance	Seedlings preferred in north
Resists blight	Weevils	Yes	Stein seedlings	Quality poor
Medium	None serious	Yes	Bixby, Buchanan, Reed, Potomac, Rush	Bud mites in some areas
Good	None serious	Yes	Winkler	Very hardy
Good	None	Yes	Elliott, Barton, Delight	Most not hardy in north but new "hardy" varieties promising

dried foods should be supplemented with fresh ones, nutritionists think, to assure a palatable and nutritious diet.

You don't need elaborate equipment for drying. Some people use the heat from the pilot light in a gas stove. Others use low heat from an electric stove.

However, there are directions for making more elaborate equipment if you feel you want to do a large amount of drying. Your state college will have ample information on drying fruits and vegetables. We have had good success drying small amounts on the lowest setting in our electric oven. Onions, chopped very fine and spread out on a clean fine mesh metal window screen, dry in about three to six hours. Apples and pears sliced $1/8$-inch thick dry in about the same length of time. Plum and peach halves take longer, from one to two days depending upon their moisture content. For grapes (seedless) to turn into raisins takes about the same length of time as peaches and plums halved. The best way to do corn is the way our mothers did it. Wood stoves and warming ovens made drying easy and inexpensive. Corn was especially delicious dried for two days in the "warming oven," then reconstituted during winter months. Boil corn for four or five minutes, until milk sets, then slice it off the ear. Spread it out on cookie sheets or wire mesh screen and dry. Soak the dried corn for two or three hours in water, then add milk, butter, salt and pepper and simmer on top of the stove or mix in a scalloped corn dish and bake in the oven. It has an almost caramel flavor.

Most fruit and vegetables should be dried in the temperature range of 120 degrees F. or so. The more rapid the drying, the better the product. Fruits are adequately dry when they are waxy or leathery in texture. Dried vegetables should be "bone dry," brittle so that they break with a snap.

Dried foods can be kept in air-tight jars and stored in a cool, dry place. Tightly closed screw-top peanut butter, jam, or mayonnaise jars are fine. You need good sealing to keep out weevils and other insects which thrive on dried fruits, vegetables, and grains. Dried fruits such as prunes, apricots, apples, raisins, etc. can be eaten without cooking. Onions and peppers which are easily dried into flakes or slices can be used in soups without soaking first.

To reconstitute dried fruits, soak in water for a couple of hours, then simmer in the same water until tender (do not overdo them). Fruits used for baking do not have to be soaked first.

Beans, peas, and corn need to be soaked for several hours before using.

If you are storing fresh fruits or vegetables, remember they are still living parts of plants. The cooler you can keep them the better. The rate of respiration (breathing), breakdown, and decay is just about doubled with each 18 degrees F. rise in temperature. If you can store fruits or vegetables immediately within 10 degrees F. above freezing (32 degrees F.), you can keep them almost "tree-fresh." For small amounts, your refrigerator hydrator space is an excellent storage.

Green Thumb Tips on Fruits and Nuts

*Fruit trees vary in their bearing age. Despite old wives tales, rusty nails in the soil won't help one bit! Beating the trunk of a nut tree does little or nothing to produce nuts.

*Failure to fruit may be due to early spring frost, too cold weather, or rain at blossoming time.

*All fruit and nut trees bear sooner or later, unless they lack a "rooster" tree.

*Bending the branches downward induces earlier bearing in fruit trees.

*Grafting will convert an undesirable tree into one with top quality fruit or nuts.

*Early fruit drop ("June drop") is nothing serious. It's nature's way of helping you have larger and better fruit.

*If space is limited, grow espalier trees. These are trained flat against a wall or trellis.

*Green apples will color up if placed on straw under a tree.

CHAPTER XIII

Soils & Fertilizers

•

The soil around your home is full of life! If you went out and scooped up a teaspoonful of it, you'd have as many as five billion living organisms in your hand. The top foot of your soil in 1,000 square feet contains about 20 pounds of bacteria, organisms so small that twenty trillion would weigh only an ounce. Some of these bacteria are "good," some are "bad." When temperature, moisture and food conditions are right, most bacteria reproduce simply by dividing in half every 20 minutes or so. If you took just one bacterium and let it divide in half, and all its descendants did likewise every 20 minutes for just a half a day, this single organism would be responsible for more than 85 billion bacteria!

Building Up the Home Garden Soil Bank

Building up the garden soil bank is a good investment for any gardener. If your soil seems heavy, drains poorly, bakes in summer, or seems just plain fagged out, or if your crops do poorly each year, then you need a soil improvement program of your own.

When no other factors are involved, such as shade or robber roots from nearby trees, insufficient drainage, or too much acidity, then organic matter is the heart of your soil improvement plan. To date, nothing has been discovered that is superior, on a cost basis. For building and conditioning soil fresh organic matter rots in the soil and slimy materials are formed by millions of soil microbes. These materials bind the soil particles together into loose crumbs, leaving pore space through which air and water can penetrate easily. Soils well supplied with organic matter remain in good condition to absorb rain throughout the season, and plant roots grow and breathe readily in such soils.

LOAM SOILS Most gardeners are familiar with the term "loam" but few know what it really is. A loam soil is one consisting of sand, silt, and clay particles, with sand predominating. (Roughly speaking, you could call the upper 8 inches of your garden soil a loam.)

Some loams are better than others. The secret is to build up a soil so that it is filled with nutrients and drains well. How does the home gardener get this organic matter which is to be added to the soil? There are three ways: you can save it, haul it in, or grow it.

1. Save all crop residues such as cornstalks, tomato and pea vines, etc., as well as leaves, lawn clippings, sawdust and wood shavings, and leafy garbage for use in a compost pile (see *How to Make a Compost Pile* in this chapter).

2. Obtain organic matter such as peat, manure, straw, sawdust, leaves, or similar materials and use as a mulch. This is described in detail under *Mulches*. Organic mulches slowly decompose, adding valuable humus and plant nutrients.

3. Grow organic matter in the form of a "cover crop" and let plant roots work on your soil. Later plow it under for humus. This will make the soil more friable, i.e., loose or easily crumbled.

Adding organic matter to your soil encourages earthworms to live there. These organisms are tremendously beneficial. They enrich the earth by passing more than 10 tons of dry earth through their bodies annually in one acre alone. They help build up topsoil, aerate soil, and enable rain water to seep down where it's helpful. Earthworms take organic matter down, and as part of their digestive process, mix it with subsoil. At the University of Georgia, it was found that a hundred worms could eat through 13 cubic feet of cow manure in three or four days, excreting a natural humus topsoil. Dead earthworms release about 40 to 50 pounds of nitrogen to an acre. Should you "plant" earthworms? In most cases they are already there. Add humus to the soil and they'll multiply. However, if your soil is in very poor shape and you want to upgrade it in a hurry, many concerns now commercially produce earthworms. For more on earthworms, see *Garbage Can Composting*.

CLAY SOILS Soils are either "heavy" or "light." A clay soil is heavy because it has finer particles which pack together more tightly than a sandy or light soil, which has larger particles. Both types of "problem soils" can be licked, although a clay soil can be most discouraging at times. If you have a clay soil, your job is to make it "breathe," because a soil not well aerated suffocates plants. Many tricks are used to loosen up a tight clay soil. One is to incorporate various homemade soil conditioners such as lawn clippings, corn cobs, leaves, garbage, compost, coal and wood ashes, sawdust, peat moss, wood chips, and any other form of organic matter. (See *Mulches*.) Humus opens the clay, encouraging earthworm is to be more active helpers. If you have a very bad drainage problem that involves your entire garden (or a large area) consult your state agricultural college for instruction in the use of clay tile (drainage tile) to correct it.

Adding sand to a clay-like soil may or may not loosen it. Sometimes the result is a concrete-like mixture harder than the original clay. Limestone (gypsum) has a loosening effect on a heavy clay soil, coagulating the fine particles into larger ones, allowing air and water to pass freely. There is little or no danger of applying too much lime to heavy soils because it breaks down slowly. The clay has a "buffer" effect, preventing the calcium in lime from making the soil alkaline, even when large quantities are used.

Another way to keep a clay soil in top condition is to avoid working it when it's wet. One day's work in a wet clay soil can harden the soil for the rest of the year. If you're one of those who likes to whip up a garden soil with a rotary power tiller before planting, you'll be surprised to know this working-over is bad for plants and makes a clay soil even worse. Fluffing up a soil breaks down the structure and plugs the soil pores, and as a result the earth turns to a sticky gumbo after the first rain. Millions of dollars are lost each year by farmers who try to make a pulverized bed out of their fields by overworking the soil.

Nature improves clay soils each time you have a drought. Drying destroys the water film that normally surrounds soil particles, causing them to form granules. This in turn gives soils larger pore spaces which means better aeration and a more workable and productive soil.

SANDY SOILS The sandier the soil, the easier to work, but the faster to dry out. You lose plant foods more quickly in sand than in clay soils. Fortunately, practices which help to loosen a heavy soil will also "tighten" a sandy soil. Apply organic matter in any form available. These materials act similarly to a blotter, holding moisture and nutrients. Sandy soils, unlike clay soils, may be worked early in spring, even while wet, without danger of "puddling" or caking.

Organic matter has some additional benefits that other "conditioners" can't duplicate. Moisture stored by the soil for plant use increases as the humus content goes up, and fertilizer elements are retained instead of being washed out by the first rains.

What Is a Cover Crop?

A cover crop is merely a temporary planting made to add organic matter to the soil and to assist in keeping it in good physical condition. The use of a commercial fertilizer to produce a heavier cover crop will usually benefit the garden crops which follow. If you have plenty of space, a good plan is to put a third or a half of your garden into a cover crop each year, then alternate or rotate the cover crop with your vegetable or flower planting. This method plus the addition of fertilizer and lime should produce a garden soil that's hard to beat. Cover crops are often called "green manure" crops, a good substitute for manure. Oats, buckwheat, and hardy domestic ryegrass are a few common cover crops. They hold nitrogen and other plant foods that might be leached away during the winter. Their tremendous root systems loosen heavy soils, and the added humus will help hold the particles of sandy soils together.

Oats, the fastest growing cover crop—ideal for slopes, level areas, and lawns—germinate quickly and form thick fibrous roots. Sow oats in spring, summer or early fall, using any variety that's available.

Buckwheat can be sown in July. It dies down in fall, and is plowed under in spring or fall. This fast-growing cover crop provides blooms from which bees make buckwheat honey.

Hardy domestic ryegrass makes a fine cover crop and soil builder because it develops heavy tops and large root systems that hold soil over winter and add many pounds of humus to the garden. Sow seed in among corn, tomatoes, or other crops at the rate of 3 pounds for about 10,500 square feet. Loosen the soil first with hoe or cultivator, then sow seed. We sow it at time of last cultivation, thus doing two jobs at once. *Do not cover the seed*: just sow it on freshly cultivated soil. It is a cool weather grass and makes most of its growth late in fall after other crops are harvested. Sown in July or August, domestic ryegrass does not go to seed that year and is plowed under before it seeds the following year. Hence, no danger of it becoming a weed.

If you want to plant sweet clover, first add about 50 pounds of limestone per 1,000 square feet unless the soil is already above the pH of 6.5 (see *Soil Acidity*). Sown in the spring, it will give you a green manure crop, roots and tops, which can be plowed under in fall or next spring.

Alfalfa, another legume, can also be used if the soil is sweet (has enough lime). The advantage of alfalfa over sweet clover is that you can make two or three cuttings during the growing season. This would allow you to mulch your early vegetables from your first cutting and use later cuttings on crops such as tomatoes and strawberries. Keep in mind that different kinds of roots do different kinds of jobs. Fine grass and clover roots are ideal for developing soil crumbs in the upper 6- to 12-inch layer. Alfalfa and sweet clover taproots extend deeper and, as they die and rot, leave channels for air and water movement.

Soot, Coal, and Wood Ashes

SOOT Coal soot is a limited source of nitrogen and some potash and phosphorus. It repels wireworms, maggots, cutworms, and snails. Do not use soot and lime together, or the nitrogen will be lost.

COAL ASHES Have very little or no plant food value, although in sufficient amounts they do improve the mechanical condition of a soil which packs hard. They can be used with manure without harm. Scatter over the garden and plow in.

They are dry and more or less antiseptic and discourage snails, snakes, and wireworms. Hence, screened coal ashes are good for greenhouse aisles, benches, and under potted plants, or you can work them into the soil of borders or beds to protect roses and other plants which do not like wet feet.

WOOD ASHES Unleached, contain all the minerals that were in the original wood. The most abundant elements are lime and potash. At one time wood ashes were the chief source of potash, the plant food that gives stiff stems and imparts increased vigor and disease resistance. Besides potash, wood contains about 2 percent phosphorus, the plant food that stimulates growth and root formation. Various woods differ greatly in value as plant foods. Twigs are richer than mature wood. Both hardwood ashes and softwood ashes are all right to use in the flower or vegetable garden. If you have a stubborn peony or iris bed, wood ashes scattered on them sometimes will force flowers into bloom.

Don't use wood ashes with manure unless the latter is well rotted. They can be added to the compost pile with leaves to hasten decomposition. Since wood ashes contain lime, don't use on soils for potatoes, and keep them away from acid-loving plants such as azaleas and rhododendrons.

Generally speaking, scattering ashes on the garden is a satisfactory method of getting rid of ashes, but a rather meager way of building up fertility. An 80-pound sack of lime, where needed, and one bag of 10-10-10 fertilizer will do more for the garden than several bushels of ashes. But if you've got them, use them. Keep in mind that if you add ashes year after year, the soil should be tested to make sure it's not overly sweet, or so saturated with ashes as to cause excessive drying of the soil.

Mulches

Tests at the Connecticut Agricultural Experimental Station show that some "waste" materials can help give you more flowers. Petunia plants with two thicknesses of newspapers as a mulch were not only larger, but produced from 50 to 80 percent more flowers than plants growing in unmulched plots. Plants that received a mulch of grass clippings, manila paper bags (with slits for water penetration), or salt hay, produced three times as many flowers as plants without any mulch. It was also noted that mulches of grass clippings, newspapers, and salt hay produced plants with fewer nematodes.

When you mulch you are borrowing a tip from nature, covering the soil to keep soil moisture in and temperatures from fluctuating. The purpose of a summer mulch is to save moisture and choke out weeds. A winter mulch is added after the ground is frozen (it's better for plants to freeze wet than dry). A winter mulch is not designed to keep out cold, but to prevent a phenomenon known as "heaving" which is due to alternate freezing and thawing, forcing plants upward and out of the ground. You might say that a summer and winter mulch act like a thermostat to the soil, maintaining a more constant temperature.

Flower and vegetable gardens, strawberry beds, grape vineyards, raspberry patches, newly planted trees, shrubs, and evergreens respond to a 4-inch mulch because it traps moisture in the soil, favoring the growth of roots. Generally speaking, a mulch of 2 to 3 inches is sufficient. There are many mulch materials available, and there's generally no danger in using too much of any one of them. However, excessive amounts of organic mulches, such as sawdust, wood chips, peat moss, and others used year after year may cause a temporary shortage of nitrogen (manifested by yellowing and stunting of plants). This can be overcome by adding nitrate of soda or any balanced fertilizer containing nitrogen (see discussion under *sawdust*). Here are some of the most commonly used mulches:

ALUMINUM MULCH Aluminum foil not only makes a good mulch but checks aphids and certain diseases spread by aphids. Some farmers put strips of aluminum foil in squash rows to keep out aphids, spreaders of the virus disease which stunts plants and causes yellowed, warted, unmarketable fruit. Farmers in New Jersey laid 4-inch strips of foil on five acres of squash as a test. Results: The squash yielded more than 600 half-bushel baskets per acre. They covered more than 40 acres with paper-backed aluminum and found that the foil saved $100 an acre in hoeing and cultivating, saved another $30 to $40 an acre in spraying expenses, and cut irrigation costs.

How does the foil actually work? No one knows for sure, but it is defintely established that aluminum repels aphids and prevents the spread of aphid-borne plant diseases.

BARK Waste material from the lumber and paper industries makes a fine mulch. It comes in various sizes, some so fine it can be used as a soil amendment, loosening the soil and improving its moisture-holding capacity. It is slightly acid, therefore particularly good for acid-loving plants. Apply 1 to 3 inches thick. As a mulch, and upon decomposition, it has a rich, dark appearance.

BUCKWHEAT HULLS These are light, clean, and do not mat or freeze. They may be dug into the soil, where they decay slowly, to build up humus. Apply 3 inches thick as an all-purpose mulch.

COCOA BEAN SHELLS This attractive mulch contains 3.2 percent nitrogen and 2 percent potash. It has a chocolate odor which disappears in a week and is ideal for new lawns, rose beds, in composts, and around trees and shrubs with little danger from fire.

On new lawns, use 150 pounds per 1,000 square feet. As a mulch, apply 1 to 3 inches thick in the flower borders, and around trees or shrubs.

COFFEE GROUNDS Valuable as soil conditioner and mulch, although low in nutrients (2 percent nitrogen, .4 percent phosphoric acid, and .5 percent potassium). Coffee grounds are acid, making them valuable around azaleas, rhododendrons, and other acid-lovers. As a mulch they can be 1 to 3 inches thick.

GROUND CORN COBS Excellent for rose beds, flower borders, vegetable gardens. Have your farmer neighbor grind some extra cobs for you. Can be applied 1 to 3 inches thick.

DUST MULCH Created by shallow surface cultivation, a layer of dust (pulverized earth) prevents upward movement of water and keeps it from evaporating. When the moisture hits the broken soil surface it stops, to be absorbed by plant roots.

EVERGREEN BOUGHS All kinds are suitable applied loosely around plants. Since they allow air to enter and prevent smothering, evergreens are ideal for perennials such as mums, foxgloves, and carnations over the winter. Needles are useful as summer mulch, although they may present a fire hazard. After Christmas holidays, many organizations invite you to bring your old Christmas tree to a recycling center, where the tree is ground up free of charge. Take advantage of such offers.

EXCELSIOR This finely shredded wood is free from weed seed, insects, and disease. It is more difficult to "fasten down" and keep from blowing away than most materials, but it lasts for years. If you have access to it, by all means use it. Three or four inches is good.

GLASS WOOL Makes a good mulch but tends to tear or blow away. It is the same as insulation materials (and itchy to handle). Use chicken wire to cover it.

GRAVEL MULCH, CRUSHED STONE, MARBLE CHIPS Come in various colors, sizes, and shapes, are easy to keep weed free and to maintain around trees or shrubs. They make a fine lawn substitute under shaded trees, and in spots where eaves drip and splash mud against the foundation. Our objection is that children like to scatter the stones around the house and lawn, a problem for lawn mowers.

LEAVES On most plants they make a poor mulch because they pack down and prevent the escape of moisture. Leaves should *not* be used to mulch roses or perennials. They are excellent on the compost heap, however, and a 2- to 3-inch layer can be useful around evergreens, trees, or shrubs. They can be shredded or not, but shredded is preferable. Oak leaves produce an acid mulch and are useful around azaleas and rhododendrons.

NEWSPAPERS A cheap, effective, readily available mulch. If left intact, place four or five thicknesses around the plants, or shred. Cover with peat moss to hide the papers. If you're unconcerned about appearance, place stones or soil along the edges. Paper ashes are alkaline and should not be used around acid lovers such as azaleas, rhododendrons, and holly.

In fall, you can rototill newspapers right into the soil. Don't worry about lead from newspapers being released into the soil and absorbed by plants. It won't be.

PEAT MOSS The common brown moss found in bales is called peat moss; the light-colored shredded or "stringy" moss which is less decomposed is called sphagnum. There are various size bales, but you can figure that 1 cubic foot of compressed baled peat will fluff out to 2 $1/2$ cubic feet, and about 5 cubic feet will equal 4 or more bushels. Most peats are acid, and are good around azaleas, rhododendrons, evergreens, and just about all other plants. Use a 3- or 4-inch thickness as a mulch. During dry weather peat moss tends to form a crust which is more or less waterproof. Stir up this crust from time to time so rainwater will enter more readily. Check soil underneath to make sure moisture is getting through. A bale of peat is compressed, sometimes gets lumpy, and is slow to take up moisture at first. Once you wet it, the material becomes soft, loose, and easy to spread.

PLASTIC MULCH Plastic film (polyethylene) makes a fine summer mulch for hastening maturity, conserving moisture, and controlling weeds. Best thickness is .0015 inch. Black plastic is preferred because it shuts out light, hence weeds cannot grow under it. During the day it absorbs the sun's heat more than do organic mulches, and that's why plastic-mulched plants are less liable to frost injury. It may be rolled or folded. Roll strips between rows to keep weeds out, or roll the mulch over moist soil, and with a knife, make slits and set plants in them. Water enters the slits and keeps soil moist even in dry spells. It's a good idea to give the soil one good soaking before laying the mulch. Ideal in strawberry patches, where it causes less rot (less than 50 percent) and makes picking easier. It's great for melons because they like the extra heat from the mulch. In fall, pick up and store. Plastic mulch can be used for about three seasons.

SALT MARSH HAY A clean, highly sought-after material because it does not contain grass and weed seeds, does not mat down or become soggy. It can be gathered up in the spring and used year after year. Salt marsh hay does not break down readily, hence it cannot be used as a cover crop or source of humus. It can be applied 3 to 6 inches thick.

SAWDUST Contrary to common belief, sawdust is not acid, nor is it toxic to plants or soils. Sawdust is organic matter, and is beneficial both as a mulch and a soil conditioner. Sawdust can be from hardwood or softwood, either weathered or unweathered. Used 3 inches thick, it's ideal for fruit trees, shrubs, perennials, around evergreens, and in border plantings. It has no value on lawns.

Sawdust sometimes turns plants yellow, as will manure, leafmold, and other carbonaceous materials. This is because the soil fungi and bacteria that decompose sawdust consume so much nitrogen that, temporarily, none is left for the plants, and leaves turn yellow, a hunger sign for the plants. This can be prevented and controlled by adding extra nitrogen, a cupful of nitrate of soda for each bushel of sawdust, or by watering the mulch with a balanced liquid plant food—a gallon of solution per bushel—once every four weeks.

SHREDDED BARK Milled bark is being used in soilless mixes for pot plants, as a substitute for peat moss. Used as a mulch or for pot plants, it promotes good growth among all plants (see *Bark*).

SNOW Called "poor man's manure," since it contains small amounts of ammonia, nitric acid, and other elements. It is also excellent winter protection for plants in cold regions.

STRAW Wheat, oats, or buckwheat straw is a good mulch, but has some disadvantages, especially as weed-seed carrier and as a fire hazard. Use 4 to 6 inches thick.

SUGAR CANE Shredded sugar cane waste (bagasse) commonly sold as chicken litter, is coarse textured, stays in place, remains loose and springy, admits passage of rain and melting snow, and thus makes a fine mulch. It has excellent insulation value. Apply 3 inches thick. It may cause a temporary shortage of nitrogen, as does sawdust (see *Sawdust*).

WOOD CHIPS Several manufacturers are putting out a portable wood chipper which chews up logs and limbs into chips. These chips may be used 3 inches thick, but be sure to add nitrogen as you would for sawdust. Ask your aborist or utility company for free woodchips.

How to Make a Compost Pile

THE GARBAGE MAKERS Every man, woman, and child contributes 5 to 7 pounds of rubbish to our earth daily. Isn't it a shame not to put these waste materials back into the earth so they can be reused?

The backbone of any soil is humus, the sponge-like substance derived from organic (plant and animal life) sources, such as leaves, lawn clippings, sawdust, evergreen needles, leafy garbage, coffee grounds, and dozens of similar materials. These materials should not be discarded but placed on the compost pile, which is like putting money in the bank.

HOW TO START A COMPOST PILE: As materials become available, start piling them in a spot away from the house, where it can be screened off by plants. Cement blocks laid end to end make a fine bin to hold your compost. Some gardeners use snow fence to make a circular enclosure for a compost pile. This helps to conceal the pile, and allows for good air circulation, hastening decomposition.

Cinderblock with air spaces

Good gardeners always have a compost pile, easily made from cinder blocks, chicken wire, or snow fence—even a garbage can or plastic bag. (*Courtesy Organic Gardening*)

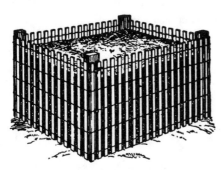

'Snowfence' bin

Add materials in such a way that the center is depressed to catch rainwater. From time to time add a layer of balanced fertilizer, 1 pound over a 6-inch layer where the compost is 10 feet long and 5 feet wide, or liquid plant food according to directions. This fortifies the compost and hastens decay. A liberal sprinkling of lime from time to time is helpful; it makes nutrients available to plants when the compost is put to use.

One of the best materials for the compost is leaves. A ton of them is equivalent to about 2 bags of balanced fertlizer in plant nutrients alone. People with sandy or clay soils should save all the leaves they can rake up, for leafmold has a miraculous ability to hold moisture. Subsoil can hold a mere 20 percent of its weight, good topsoil holds 60 percent, but leafmold can retain 300 to 500 percent of its weight in water. Leafmold from non-evergreens is richer in nutrients than that from conifers. All leaves are good property, so don't believe the story that leaves are too acid to be helpful to crops. Oak leaves, which are more acid and recommended for azaleas, rhododendrons, laurel, holly, and other acid-loving plants, can still be used for non-acid plants.

STIRRING THE PILE: Stirring "ripens the pile" (hastens decay) and aids in destroying insect pests, but it is not essential. A good idea is to cover the compost pile with polyethylene plastic. Make the compost in the regular manner, alternating leaves, clippings, sawdust, soil, table scraps, and other materials with a scattering of lime and fertilizer. Then water down the pile thoroughly and spread a sheet of black polyethylene over it. Use a piece large enough to allow about 18 to 20 inches of flap on each side. Cover the flaps with soil so the pile is completely enveloped and leave it alone for eight months. The beauty of plastic is that it hides the pile, and makes it break down quicker. The plastic hastens decay by trapping heat inside and preventing loss of moisture. No magic material can convert raw organic matter into humus overnight in a compost.

PLASTIC BAG COMPOSTING A large plastic bag (large garbage can liner size) makes a quick and easy composter. Fill bag with leaves, add a gallon of water, a shovelful of soil, and a pint of lawn fertilizer (don't use "weed and feed" types!) or liquid plant food. Store in garage over winter, and by spring you'll have a bag full of "black gold."

GARBAGE CAN COMPOSTING Since the average American family tosses out three-fourths of a ton of food a year, it should put the kitchen scraps in a garbage can and convert it to valuable humus for the garden. Garbage can composting is the answer for people in urban or suburban areas who wish to compost kitchen wastes, but have little room or cannot cover it properly to discourage insects and animals. The Environmental Education Committee of Rochester, New York, passes along the following suggestions for making your own compost in a garbage can.

1. Use a galvanized (or plastic) garbage can with a lid which fits well, and punch several small holes in the bottom.
2. Add 3 inches of good soil to the can.
3. Add some "angleworms" or "red worms" (sometimes referred to as manure worms or red wrigglers). *Note*: worms are optional, but it takes longer to break down the compost without them.
4. Set the can on two cement blocks with something beneath to catch any liquid draining out. This liquid is usually odorless and can be used on houseplants, tubbed plants, or garden plants.

5. Throw in kitchen wastes—potato peelings, lettuce leaves, coffee grounds, tea leaves—that ordinarily go into the garbage can.

6. Each addition of fresh garbage may be covered with a sprinkling of soil or shredded leaves, newspapers, grass clippings, sawdust, etc.

7. To fortify the mixture, sprinkle on a little liquid plant food from time to time.

Odor is usually lacking, but if coffee grounds are added they serve as a natural deodorant. If any odor should develop, shredded newspapers will take care of it almost immediately. Grease will be tolerated in moderate amounts, as will meat scraps. Chicken bones as well as egg shells can be added. They add calcium and even if they don't break down immediately, they will return into the soil as filler.

Watch out for onions and onion skins. Worms don't like them. Worms tolerate citrus skins in moderate amounts.

One regular-size garbage can will take care of a family of four if the children are small. Some families start one can in the fall, add another if this one fills up before spring, then dump and start over again. Others have two cans at the same time. A garage is a good place to keep the can. If your can contains worms, it must be stored in an area with above-freezing temperatures.

DISEASES AND INSECTS Because of danger of infecting the compost pile with plant diseases and insects, there are some materials to avoid. For example, iris leaves if borers have been a problem, peony tops if Botrytis blight blasted the buds, refuse from members of the cabbage family afflicted with black rot, corn stalks if borers or smut were present. If a compost is allowed to stand for two seasons with occasional forking over, it is doubtful that diseases and insects will persist any more than they do in the garden where plants have grown for years. A plastic sheet over the pile not only keeps out flies, but discourages stray dogs from digging in it.

HOW TO USE COMPOST SOIL You can tell when a compost pile is "done" simply by feeling it. Run it through your hands. If it's loose and fluffy, it's ready to grow. Use it in same proportion as you would peat moss. For example, in a potting mixture, use 1 part each of sand, rotted compost, and loam. In the garden or for a mulch, use it full strength.

For potting, screen through 1/2-inch mesh wire to remove coarse material, then mix with sand or garden loam or both. If used in the garden or as a mulch, no screening is necessary. Compost doesn't replace fertilizer. You still should fortify it with plant food and lime to achieve maximum use.

Chemical Tests Tell if Soil Is Sweet or Sour

Gardeners often come across the two-letter term, pH, before a number. If you've been baffled by the term, the explanation is that pH is a measure of soil reaction—whether it is "sweet" or "sour" (alkaline or acid). Let's say soil sweetness or sourness is measured by a pH yardstick. A pH of 7 in the yardstick means the soil is neutral: neither sour nor sweet.

A soil with a PH below 7 is acid or sour, and one with a pH above 7 is alkaline, or sweet. To test your soil to see if it is acid or alkaline, there are kits on the market which are simple to operate and fairly accurate. Just follow the directions that come with them.

This soil test alone doesn't solve all your garden or houseplant problems. Actually there are two useful soil tests: 1) Soil Acidity and 2) Major Elements. To us, the first is

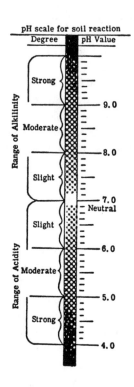

pH scale for soil reaction

Degree	pH Value

Range of Alkilinity

Strong
Moderate
Slight

9.0
8.0
7.0 Neutral

Range of Acidity

Slight
Moderate
Strong

6.0
5.0
4.0

This scale is a "yardstick" for measuring soil acidity. A pH reading of 7 is neutral; that is, neither acid nor alkaline. The smaller the number, the stronger the acidity.

the more important, but when your lawn or garden is producing well, you don't need a test. Carrots and beets are good indicators; if they grow well, you don't need lime.

The test for major elements is best made through your county agent or state college of agriculture testing service, but keep in mind that a soil test is no better than the soil sample you take. If the sample is not representative of the soil in the garden, the test results are meaningless. Here is an illustration: The plow layer of soil on each acre weighs about 2 million pounds. The average soil sample weighs about 1 pound. This means that if a sample is taken from five acres, that 1-pound sample sent for testing must represent some 10 million pounds of soil in the field! You just can't go out, scoop up a random can of soil, and send it in, and expect a comprehensive analysis.

HOW TO TAKE A SOIL SAMPLE Gather the soil in a clean container, using a garden spade or auger. If you use a spade, first dig a V-shaped hole 8 inches deep. Second, cut a $1/2$-inch thick slice of soil from the face of the hole. Third, trim away the soil from both sides of spade, leaving a 1-inch strip of soil down the middle of the spade. Fourth, place this in a clean pail. Take 15 samples from various sections in this manner, but avoid wet spots, lime piles, places where gasoline has been spilled, burned areas, or spots where fertilizer, etc., has been lying in piles. Mix in a pail, select 1 pint of the entire mixture, and throw the rest away.

Your store has soil-test cartons to use for mailing the sample to your state college. Or you can use a clean plastic bag. Send along as much information as possible, such as:

crops grown last year, plant foods used, and crop troubles. State colleges determine plant food deficiencies by chemical analysis of soils and plant tissue testing, and some use "quick" soil tests. If you plan to have a soil test made, talk to your county agent, or a successful neighboring farmer.

MAKING THE SOIL SWEETER Gardeners often use either too much lime or not enough. Cornell University analyzed several hundred home garden samples and found that one-third needed lime, one-third were just right, and one-third had too much. The common garden crops are happy with a slightly acid soil, so if your garden is in that condition, don't change matters. The majority of surface soils in the eastern United States are naturally acid, however, and require some liming for best production.

Here's what liming acid soil does: lowers soil acidity, supplies calcium and magnesium, and speeds the decay of organic matter and the liberation of nitrogen, promotes the growth of legumes such as clover, helps neutralize toxic iron and aluminum in soils, controls certain diseases like black leg of cabbage, improves physical condition of soils, and to a limited extent helps loosen up heavy clay soils. As mentioned earlier, wood ashes have the same effect on soils that lime does. Since more people are burning wood to cut down on the fuel bill, more ashes are available and should be used (see *Wood Ashes*).

LIME STRETCHES FERTLIZER: If home gardeners and farmers didn't use lime there would be a fertilizer shortage at least five times as bad as the one in 1974-75. Lime works as a team with plant foods to produce better plants. It increases the efficiency of fertilizer, "unlocking" certain nutrients, making them more available to plants.

The natural acidity of a soil is determined by the type of rocks from which the soil was originally derived. For example, quartz, granite, sandstone, and shale usually produce acid soils; marble and limestone produce sweet or alkaline soils. Often the subsoil is much less acid than the surface soil unless lime materials have been added.

Rainfall and removal of plant material from the soil tends to make surface soils more acid. Pollutants in the air are also making the soil more acid. Studies show that rain water, found to be alkaline in 1915, is now extremely acid in most parts of the world, some areas having a pH as low as 3. In areas where this acidic rainfall occurs, lakes and streams have become so acidified that fish die and tree growth slows markedly. On the other hand, soils around homes sometimes become alkaline or "sweet" because grading may have uncovered limey subsoils, or lime-rich fill may have been added. Continuous watering with water that is "hard' because of calcium and magnesium adds to the sweetness of a soil. These are factors to keep in mind, especially when acid-loving plants such as rhododendrons, azaleas, mountain laurel, blueberries, trailing arbutus, trilliums, and most lilies are to be grown. When planted on alkaline or neutral soils, these plants quickly become chlorotic (yellowed) and die. If you want to plant these in a limy soil, you will have to convert it to an acid condition by adding sulfur or aluminum sulfate as described later.

WHICH KIND OF LIME TO BUY: Four kinds of lime are commonly sold: burned lime, hydrated lime, ground limestone, and dolomitic limestone. 1) "Quicklime" is another term for burned lime (calcium oxide). In general, it should be avoided because of its caustic action on the skin. Never mark a children's playing field with it.

2) Hydrated lime is a fluffy white powder formed from burned lime and water. It is fast acting but expensive. 3) Ground limestone (calcium carbonate) is a grayish, gritty, very finely ground lime rock. This is the material most commonly used for counteracting acidity. It is slower to dissolve than hydrated lime and takes longer to work. Supply stores sometimes sell a mixture of hydrated lime and limestone combining benefits of both. Ground limestone is less expensive, keeps better, and is easy to apply. 4) Dolomitic lime has 20 to 30 percent magnesium, plus 30 to 50 percent calcium, and is available in both hydrated and ground stone types. Because magnesium is another element needed for plant growth, we recommend dolomitic limestone which is just about as inexpensive as the older forms. But you may not be able to get it from your dealer—if not, use one of the others.

Actually, any form of lime is useful, but keep in mind that the more concentrated forms such as the hydrated or burned lime forms should be used in lesser amounts. Roughly speaking, 100 pounds of ground limestone is equal in action to about 74 pounds of hydrated lime or 56 pounds of burned lime.

Gardeners who use the burned or staked lime should be careful not to allow it to sift inside their shoes, since the lime combined with moisture of perspiration is enough to blister tender skin. If it gets in your eyes, flush it out immediately.

HOW MUCH LIME TO USE AND WHEN: It's a fair rule of thumb that if no lime has been added during the past four years, then your garden (or lawn) probably needs it. An application of 50 pounds of lime per 1,000 square feet is a good rough-and-ready treatment. Then for regular applications, use 25 to 30 pounds per 1,000 square feet every three to four years thereafter. Apply either hydrated or ground limestone in fall or spring before plowing. We like fall application because it enables you to take advantage of the weather. Winter rain and snow help to carry the lime down into the soil where it can go to work quickly. In the spring, when this ground is plowed, the lime is turned under close to the subsoil and helps the roots to grow better.

If you have had your soil tested and the test shows a pH reading between 6 and 6.8, don't add lime. If pH is between 5.5 and 6, use 3 pounds of ground limestone to each 100 square feet on sandy soils, 5 pounds on heavier soils.

It pH reading is between 5 and 5.5, use double amounts. If pH is too high and crops do poorly, dust 1 pound of sulfur or add $1/2$ pound of manganese sulfate and about 1 ounce of borax to each 100 square feet of garden. These can be broadcast on the soil, or you can apply them to growing plants if dissolved in water and sprinkled on the foliage. Use 1 gallon of the solution for 100 square feet.

DANGERS OF OVERLIMING: Some minor but necessary elements such as boron, iron, manganese, and zinc become less available to plants when soils are heavily limed. Excessive liming may also result in chlorosis (yellowing of leaves) and poor growth. Correct this by acidifying (see below). Never put lime in contact with manure: it causes loss of nitrogen. Don't mix lime and fertilizer in a single application, as lime may cause loss of nitrogen and reduction in available phosphate. Apply three or four days apart.

MAKING SOILS MORE ACID As previously mentioned, soils may be too sweet for acid-loving plants such as azaleas, rhododendrons, laurel, lilies, blueberries, and others.

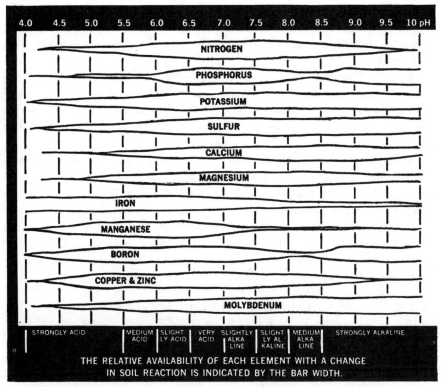

| 4.0 | 4.5 | 5.0 | 5.5 | 6.0 | 6.5 | 7.0 | 7.5 | 8.0 | 8.5 | 9.0 | 9.5 | 10 pH |

NITROGEN

PHOSPHORUS

POTASSIUM

SULFUR

CALCIUM

MAGNESIUM

IRON

MANGANESE

BORON

COPPER & ZINC

MOLYBDENUM

| STRONGLY ACID | MEDIUM ACID | SLIGHTLY ACID | VERY ACID | SLIGHTLY ALKALINE | SLIGHTLY ALKALINE | MEDIUM ALKALINE | STRONGLY ALKALINE |

THE RELATIVE AVAILABILITY OF EACH ELEMENT WITH A CHANGE
IN SOIL REACTION IS INDICATED BY THE BAR WIDTH.

The above chart shows how "soil reaction" (acidity or alkalinity) affects plants' ability to take up nutrients. The bands in the chart show the degree of availability of certain important plant nutrients under different soil conditions. For example, in a soil strongly or medium acid (pH 4.9 to 5.5), nitrogen, phosphorus, potassium, sulfur, calcium, magnesium, and molybdenum are less available to plants. In an alkaline soil (above pH 7.0) iron, manganese, boron, copper, zinc, and nitrogen can be "locked up."(*Courtesy Cornell University*)

Then the soil must be acidified with sulfur, ammonium sulfate, aluminum sulfate, or even iron sulfate (ferrous sulfate). Sulpfur is much the cheapest but also the slowest, whereas the sulfates have full action in the first season. Apply sulfur at the rate of 1 to 2 pounds per 100 square feet, depending on the acidity at the beginning. Use sulfates according to the following table:

Acidity of Soil at Start (as determined by pH test)	Ammonium or Aluminum Sulfate/Square Yard
Medium acid (pH 5 to 6)	$1/4$ lb.
Slightly acid (pH 6.5 to 7)	$1/2$ 1b.
Neutral to strongly alkaline (pH 7 to 8)	$3/4$ 1b.

Spread the sulfur or sulfates uniformly and mix thoroughly with the soil. "Acidified" soil does not always remain that way, because limy soil water is apt to rise from below. Also, angleworms are likely to mix the soil near the plants. On acidified soils, avoid use of all alkalizing materials, such as wood ashes, hard water, and compost made with lime.

Naturally high lime soils are almost impossible to acidify. If you must grow acid-loving plants, consider other methods, such as replacing soil in beds, or building raised beds with surface layers of acid soil or peat. Or, you may be able to overcome the high lime chlorosis in such plants with frequent iron chelate (pronounced "key-late") applications.

Adding iron chelate to the soil helps to avoid chlorosis on plants such as azaleas, gardenias, hydrangeas, roses, and many others. A plant with chlorosis has yellowed leaves with greenish veins and is a sick-looking specimen in general. This lack of iron in the plant is most common in alkaline soils.

For those iron-hungry plants, mix easily absorbed iron chelate (in powder form) with water and apply either to the leaves or soil. The amounts needed are unusually small. For example, greenhouse operators mix 1 ounce of iron chelate to 25 gallons of water and apply this solution to 100 square feet of bench crops.

Commercial Plant Foods

LIQUID PLANT FOODS Liquid fertilizers have come a long way in recent years. There are many advantages of liquid feeding, which is applied either on the foliage or at the base of plants. Foliar or foliage ("non-root") feeding was pioneered by nurseryman Thomas Reilly of Dansville, New York. He was one of the first to note that plant roots are not the only organs capable of plant nutrient absorption. Twigs, leaves, branches, buds, fruits, and even flowers have the ability to absorb nutrients. One advantage of foliar feeding is ease of application. Gardeners who use pesticide sprays can add liquid plant food to their solution and do two jobs in one, spraying and feeding. To foliage-feed, always buy a plant food made especially for the purpose.

STARTER SOLUTION: Liquid plant food makes ideal "starter" or "booster" solutions, helping young transplants to get off to a better start. Simply dip the roots in a weak fertilizer solution and plant while wet, or it may be applied around the plant as soon as it is set in the ground. A word of caution: if you make a home-made booster solution, try it first on a few plants because it may burn. You can make one from a common grade of fertilizer, such as 5-10-5, by dissolving 1 pound in 5 gallons of water. This liquid is applied in the row at the rate of 1 gallon to 20 feet of row either before planting or later. Many gardeners use a weak manure mixture for a starter solution. Rodale Farms at Emmaus, Pennsylvania, recommends the following formula: Fill a container one quarter full of fresh or dried manure (use only half as much if poultry manure is used). Add water until full. Stir several times during the next 24 hours. For use, dilute until the manure is a light amber—about the color of weak tea.

Liquid plant foods have many extra uses: 1) Soak bulbs in them one hour prior to planting. (Fresh manure should not be used on tulip and daffodil bulbs because of danger of Botrytis blight.) 2) Hastening decay of compost. 3) Coloring up evergreens. 4)

Feeding fruits and flowers. 5) Greenhouse feeding of benched and potted crops, applied with sprinkler or hose applicator. 6) Starting seeds in non-organic materials such as perlite, vermiculite, etc. 7) In soilless culture (hydroponics) to replace nutrients in the solution as they are used up. There is no known plant which does not respond to feedings of liquid plant foods.

WHAT DRY COMMERCIAL PLANT FOODS DO The most important plant foods in a commercially mixed fertilizer are nitrogen, phosphoric acid, and potash. Nitrogen gives dark green color to plants, promotes increased leaf, stem, and fruit growth, and improves the quality of leafy crops as well as hastening growth. Phosphorus stimulates early root formation and growth, gives a rapid and vigorous start to plants, hastens maturity, stimulates blooming, and aids in seed formation. Potash imparts increased vigor and disease resistance to plants, producing strong, stiff stalks. This reduces lodging (falling over) of plants.

WHAT'S IN THE FERTILIZER BAG? Are you confused by recommendations calling for "5-10-5," "5-10-10," or a similar analysis? Every mixed fertilizer sold has a guaranteed analysis, stating the proportions of nitrogen (N), phosphoric oxide (P), and potash (K), the "big three" elements required by law to be on the label. This analysis tells the buyer what he's getting in terms of "N-K-P." Thus a 5-10-10 fertilizer contains 5 percent nitrogen, 10 percent phosphorus, and 10 percent potash, or 25 pounds of the three primary nutrients in a 100-pound bag of fertilizer. The question you'll ask is: What constitutes the other 75 pounds of fertilizer you bought?

The 75 pounds remaining is inert material known as filler. It is necessary for manufacturers to add filler to dry fertilizers because pure forms of nitrogen, phosphorus, and potassium cannot be used as plant foods. Nitrogen is a gas, and phosphorus and potassium are two of the most active chemicals known and wouldn't be safe in pure form. Fertilizers must therefore contain their nutrients in diluted forms that are economical and safe to apply as well as easily assimilated by the plants (see *Liquid Fertilizers*).

Manure: Good or Bad?

Manure or dung has been used as a fertilizer for a long time: In Luke 13:8 of the Bible, a certain man had a fig tree that wouldn't bear. The gardener pleaded for delay in chopping it down, saying: "Let it alone this year till I shall dig about it and dung it."

For centuries good farmers around the world put manure back on the land because they knew it helped their crops. Then as chemical fertilizers became relatively cheap and convenient, manure was transformed from a rich asset into a bulky disposal problem. Manure was low in nutrients compared to the balanced chemical plant foods, and there were the additional drawbacks of possible weed seed content and plant disease transmission. It took a global fertilizer shortage to change thinking about manure. It takes the equivalent of 2 tons of diesel fuel to make a ton of nitrogen, so it's time we all reevaluated this "home grown" fertilizer. It's good stuff to have! While not especially high in nutrients, manure still boosts plants along. It is loaded with good organic matter, plus nitrogen, phosphorus, potash, and a wide spectrum of minor elements.

The big value of manure is its role as organic matter in building soil structure and improving the soil's moisture-holding capacity. Manure breaks down slowly in cool soils, faster as the soil warms up. Chicken, cow, horse, and rabbit manure are all great for your soils. See precaution listed under Hen Manure.

Manure is available today in forms which have largely overcome bulk, odor, and sanitation drawbacks. Garden stores handle all kinds of dehydrated and pasteurized manure: bird and bat (guano), human (heat-treated sewage), sheep, cow, and horse manure. No home gardener need be without a supply. If you cannot get barnyard manure, don't worry about it. With fertilizers you can use a wide variety of organic materials to make composted material which is disease- and weed seed-free, and which will do the same things manure will do.

MANURING THE GARDEN If you can get cheap manure, use it liberally on your vegetable garden. One ton of ordinary barnyard manure equals about 100 pounds of a 10-5-10 fertilizer. Since it is low in phosphorus, gardens should receive about 30 pounds of a 5-I0-I0 fertilizer for each 1,000 square feet of area *in addition* to the manure. Or, you could add superphosphate, about 100 pounds of the twenty percent grade to each ton of manure. Superphosphate and 5-10-10 are available at your feed and seed store.

Never put fresh, strawy manure on a garden that's ready to plow and seed. Broadcast fresh manure over the soil at least six to eight weeks before plowing. Then add a high-nitrogen fertilizer over the manure at the rate of 300 pounds per acre to help decompose the straw. Manure, like commercial plant foods, is gradually consumed and should be replenished.

Dried or dehydrated manure is available in most garden stores. Apply a light coating over the garden in spring. If you have a farmer friend who will give you all you want, then apply it one inch thick on your garden, and plow it in.

SOME MANURES AND ANIMAL BY-PRODUCTS GARDENERS ASK ABOUT

DOG MANURE: No reason why you can't use dog manure on the compost pile. It is rich in phosphorus—especially if the dogs have been fed their share of bones. Don't use it straight: mix it with leaves, grass clippings, garden and kitchen refuse, sawdust, and other plant wastes; then allow it to decompose at least a year. Dog manure may attract other dogs, so it's a good idea to arrange the compost heap so that a screen keeps them out.

KITTY LITTER: Is it okay to put spent kitty litter on the compost? Yes, if you scatter it around and it is left to decompose for one year. Either the alfalfa-based litter, which is green, or the granular clay litter is okay. Some doctors object to the use of cat manure for edible crops, saying there are disease organisms that can be transferred. We suggest you use it on ornamentals only. In any case, let it cure on the compost heap for a year.

HEN MANURE: Hen manure is higher in nitrogen, phosphorus, and potash than barnyard manure and should be used whenever possible. Fresh poultry manure can burn plants, but can be used safely if spread in the fall. It can be tilled under in fall or spring. About 2 tons of poultry manure can be applied to a 50′ × 100′ garden. Like other manures, this is unbalanced in plant food content and needs additional phosphate. This can be supplied by 100 pounds of 20 percent superphosphate to each ton of manure. Caution: Hen or chicken manure can cause scab on potatoes.

RABBIT MANURE: High in nitrogen and organic matter, you can mix it with peat moss or straw, or put it in compost. Leave it exposed for a month or so, then apply it to soil at the rate of 8 pounds per 100 square feet. Well rotted and mixed with peat, rabbit manure becomes a safe material. If fresh, apply as a light covering between the rows, but make sure it doesn't touch plants, as it is one of the strongest animal manures.

SHEEP AND COW MANURE: Are fairly quick acting organic fertilizers, good for houseplants if well rotted. Sheep manure has about 2 percent nitrogen, 1 percent phosphorus, and 2 percent potash. Cow manure has lower plant food content. Both are ideal for mixing with the soil to add humus. (See chart for rates of application.)

HORSE MANURE: Has roughly the same composition as cow manure, and gardeners who live near stables or race tracks should take advantage of it as a soil conditioner. (See chart for rate of application.)

BONE MEAL: Some still prefer bone meal as a fertilizer. Because it is so slow acting, there is no danger of its burning plants. It penetrates the soil at about an inch per season, so it's best to work it into the soil rather than sprinkle it on. Steamed bone meal, which contains about 1 to 2 percent nitrogen and about 22 to 30 percent phosphoric acid, is more quickly available to plants. Raw bone meal takes longer to break down so plants can absorb it. Bone meal is good for bulbs of all sorts, but an objection is that it often induces dogs to dig around in bulb plantings in search of phantom bones. Superphosphate is generally used instead of bone meal in today's garden practices, since the phosphorus in superphosphate is more readily available and the cost is less.

SEWAGE SLUDGE: Sludges make good soil improvers. They are equal to low analysis fertilizers containing from 1 to 3 percent nitrogen, phosphorus, and potash. The important things are that the nitrogen is in long-lasting organic form and the organic matter content is high enough to warrant use as a mulch or a manure substitute.

As for the sanitary status of sludge, there are widely differing opinions regarding its safety. If you use the heat-treated sludges, there is nothing to worry about from a sanitary standpoint. Such treatment is normally provided for material that is marketed. These sludges are useful as mulches around flowers, shrubs, and vegetables.

DIGESTED SLUDGE: Not heat-treated, should be used with some caution. One way is to incorporate it in the soil several months before vegetables to be eaten raw are grown. According to the United States Department of Agriculture, all danger is thought to be removed after the sludge has been in the soil for three months of a growing season. It's reasonable to assume that digested sludges are satisfactory for lawns, shrubs, flowers, and ornamentals.

Raw sewage sludge is not sterile and has undergone no process to kill any harmful organisms that might be in it, so for the home gardener we do not advise its use.

Our former teacher at Cornell University, Dr. L. H. McDaniels, a fine gardener, assisted us with this chart for feeding the garden.

RATE OF APPLICATION OF FERTILIZERS AND
SOIL AMENDMENTS FOR
THE FLOWER AND VEGETABLE GARDEN

Material	Form of Application	Rate of Application
Bonemeal	Dry	1-2 lbs. per 100 sq. ft. of soil
Leafmold	Wet or Dry	Same as for peat (see in chart)
Lime	Dry	Apply to correct acidity (See *Lime* in this chapter)
Liquid Plant Food	Solution only	Use as directed on label for foliage feeding or soil application
Manure (rotted; cow or horse)	As fertilizer	From 10 to 50 tons per acre or 4 bushels per 100 sq. ft. of soil As mulch 1″ deep on top of soil
Manure (rotted poultry, rabbit, or hog)	As fertilizer	5 tons per acre, or 1 bushel per 100 sq. ft. of soil
Mixed fertilizer (5-10-5; 5-10-10)	Dry	From 2 to 3 lbs. per 100 sq. ft. of soil, or 3″ pot to 3 bushels of soil, or 1 tsp. to a 5″ pot of soil
Mixed fertilizer (10-20-10; 15-30-15)	Dry	1 lb. or less per 100 sq. ft. of soil, or 2″ pot to 3 bushels of soil, or $1/2$ tsp. to a 5″ pot of soil
	Solution	1 oz. to 2 gals. of water
Muriate of Potash	Dry	300 lbs. per acre, or $1/2$ lb. per 100 sq. ft. of soil
	Solution	$1/2$ lb. in 10 gals. of water applied to 100 sq. ft. of soil; or $1/2$ cup of solution to 5″ pot of soil
Nitrate of Soda	Solution	Same as sulfate of ammonia
Peat or Compost	Incorporated in topsoil Mulch	5 bushels to 100 sq. ft. of soil for garden 1″ layer

Material	Form of Application	Rate of Application
Sulfate of ammonia	Dry Solution	1 lb. to 100 sq. ft. of soil 1 lb. in 30 gals. of water applied to 100 sq. ft., or 1 cup of solution to 5″ pot of soil
Sulfate of potash	Dry	Same as for muriate of potash
Superphosphate (16 or 20%)	Dry	1,000 lbs. per acre, 5 lbs. per 100 sq. ft., 3″ pot to a bushel of soil
Tankage or Sewage	Dry	4″ pot to 3 bushels of soil; 5 lbs. per 100 sq. ft.
Urea	Solution only	5 oz. to 35 gals. of water applied to 100 sq. ft. of soil or 1 cupful of solution to 5″ pot of soil

MORE ORGANIC MATERIALS
USED BY NATURAL GARDENERS

For home gardeners interested in other organic materials, we present the following chart showing the percentage of nitrogen, phosphorus, and potassium content.

Organic Concentrates	Nitrogen (% N)	Phosphorus ($\%P_2O_5$)	Potassium ($\%K_2O$)
Animal Tankage	9.0	10.0	1.5
Bat Guano	10.0	4.5	2.0
Bone Charcoal and Bone Black	1.5	32.0	.0
Bone Meal	4.0	23.0	.0
Castor Pomace	6.0	1.9	.5
Cocoa-shell Meal	2.5	1.5	2.5
Cottonseed Meal	6.0	2.5	1.5
Dried Bloodmeal	13.0	1.5	.8
Dried Cattle Manure	2.0	1.8	2.2
Dried Sheep and Goat Manure	1.4	1.0	3.0
Fish Meal	10.0	6.0	.0
Fish Scrap	5.0	3.0	.0
Garbage Tankage	2.5	1.5	1.5
Hoof and Horn Meal	12.0	2.0	.0
Sewage Sludge	3.0	2.5	0.4
Soybean Meal	7.0	1.2	1.5
Steamed Bone Meal	.8	30.0	.0

Organic Concentrates	Nitrogen (% N)	Phosphorus (%P$_2$O$_5$)	Potassium (%K$_2$O)
Tobacco Dust and Stems	1.5	.5	5.0
Wood Ashes	.0	2.0	6.0
Wool Wastes	7.5	.0	.0
Bulky Organic Materials			
Alfalfa Hay	2.50	.50	2.10
Alfalfa Straw	1.50	.30	1.50
Bean Straw	1.20	.25	1.25
Cattle Manure (fresh)	.55	.15	.45
Cotton Bolls	1.00	.15	4.00
Grain Straw	.60	.20	1.10
Hog Manure (fresh)	.50	.35	.45
Horse Manure (fresh)	.65	.25	.50
Olive Pomaces	1.20	.80	.50
Peanut Hulls	1.50	.12	.78
Peat and Muck	2.30	.40	.75
Poultry Manure (fresh)	1.00	.85	.45
Sawdust and Wood Shavings	.20	.10	.20
Seaweed (Kelp)	.60	.09	1.30
Sheep Manure (fresh)	1.05	.40	1.00
Timothy Hay	1.02	.20	1.50
Winery Pomaces	1.50	1.50	.80

Courtesy Brooklyn Botanic Garden

Green Thumb Tips on Soils and Fertilizers

*You can make a good flower or vegetable garden in almost any type of soil. Good soils are usually made, not born. You can tame the wildest soil into a productive one by following the tips in this chapter.

*Don't be discouraged if you have a heavy soil. It can be as productive as a sandy loam. Crops on sandy soils suffer more quickly from dry spells than do those on heavier soils.

*Never work a heavy soil when it's wet.

*When spading or plowing the garden soil, go to a depth of 8 inches. More than that brings up undesirable subsoil.

*Removing small stones from the garden each year is hardly worth the effort, as more keep coming to the surface.

*Don't be afraid to use lime, fertilizers, and compost to fortify your soils. Organic gardeners need not fear that plant foods are harmful to themselves or to their crops.

*High-potency fertilizer mixtures, soluble in water, do a lot to get young plants off to a fast start and increase the survival rate, but don't forget to fortify your soil with organic matter to keep them healthy.

CHAPTER XIV

Organic Gardening and IPM

•

The philosophy behind organic gardening is not new, but in recent years interest in it has grown markedly. People have joined the organic movement because they've rebelled against additives in foods, chemicals in the soil and water, pollutants in the air, and dangerous pesticides sprayed on fruits and vegetables. In fact, the balance of nature has been precariously disturbed because the number of good bugs, as well as bad, has been diminished. Many harmful insects have developed resistance to common pesticides, making it even more difficult to control them.

In a nutshell organic, or natural, gardening is 1) using natural methods of pest control versus chemical (synthetically produced) pesticides, and 2) raising plants without the use of chemical fertilizers. Strict organic gardeners use only fertilizers made from decayed organic matter (matter derived from once-living organisms), and such non-organic fertilizers found in the earth as limestone and rock phosphate.

There are varying degrees of adherence to the above definition. Some people who consider themselves organic gardeners incorporate some chemically produced fertilizers with strictly "organic" fertilizers. Such pesticides as nicotine sulfate, Pyrethrum, and rotenone are accepted by most because the bases of these materials are living plants.

At the present time, with today's population, it would be impossible to produce enough food by strict organic methods to feed the people of the United States, let alone the rest of the world. Often the best ideas of the two schools can be used with great success. The important thing is to cut down on the use of dangerous pesticides and to convert waste materials into good soil and fertilizer. This not only alleviates the garbage disposal problem but improves the quality of the environment.

We firmly believe that more time and money must be devoted to developing resistant varieties of fruits and vegetables. We want to move toward the use of natural pest controls as well as less toxic, biodegradable synthetic materials, and we're thankful that more research is directed toward this end. It has been proven beyond a doubt that such pesticides as DDT and Dieldrin (now banned) drastically upset the balance of nature and have left residual deadly poisons in our environment. Today, researchers at various state colleges are discovering natural control methods with exciting possibilities. Home gardeners who are readers of our columns frequently send us tips and formulas they have found useful. There is no reason why you shouldn't experiment and contribute your own ideas to this worthwhile cause.

For the home gardener, natural gardening is an ideal way to recycle refuse, get in tune with nature, and provide a balanced ecosystem right in one's own backyard. Every home gardener should recycle his own garbage whether he augments it with chemical fertilizers or not. Even city gardeners can make "no odor" compost in closed garbage cans or plastic bags. (See Chapter XIII, SOILS AND FERTILIZERS.)

One of the newest and most widely accepted methods for coping with tough insects and diseases involves a concept known as Integrated Pest Management, or IPM. Based on the idea that no *single* method is able to combat all pests, IPM marshalls all of the best chemical and non-chemical methods into a single program to fight pest population. IPM does not mean getting rid of all chemical or organic methods; rather it joins them with biological controls, genetic engineering, and anything else needed to fight stubborn insects and diseases.

Billions of dollars have been spent fighting pests, and yet, until the concept of IPM came into being, no one had devised a cooperative method for destroying them. This combination of natural controls and chemicals is the closest man has come to thwarting pests and we welcome the idea, even if parts if it appear to violate conventional thinking.

Natural Controls

Natural controls of insects and diseases involves at least seven different facets of organic gardening, each of which we will discuss: 1) Natural Enemies and Parasites, 2) Hand Picking, 3) Sanitation and Crop Rotation, 4) Resistant Varieties, 5) Repellents, 6) Attractants, 7) Companion Planting, and 8) Organic Pesticides (i.e., those made from something produced by nature as opposed to those synthetically produced).

Many methods of natural control came from our readers and listeners, many from the Rodale Press in Emmaus, Pennsylvania, the Brooklyn Botanic Garden, and Nichols Garden Nursery of Albany, Oregon. We have discovered many for ourselves, and are continually finding new ones. Don't hesitate to experiment in your own garden, as long as you use good common sense. You may find a solution to share with others.

NATURAL ENEMIES AND PARASITES With the banning of "hard" pesticides—those that have harmful residual effects—more effort is being applied to finding effective natural controls. Education is needed to shift a chemically and commercially oriented society to one in which the balance of nature is respected. A good place to start is in the classroom, where for years biology classes have cut up frogs in order to "study" them when plastic models might do just as well. Similarly destructive practices are depleting our supply of some of nature's best bug catchers. Children should be taught how beneficial frogs and toads are in our environment, as are birds, dragonflies, spiders, praying mantises, and ladybird beetles, to name a few. (See also Chapter XII.)

LADYBUGS: for example, will feed on almost any insect that's not too big for it to tackle. Aphids are their favorites, and in its lifetime one single ladybug will polish off between 500 to 1,000 aphids. There are about 370 species of ladybugs native to North America and most of them feed on other insects, so you can see how valuable they are.

BIRDS: Great bug catchers; encourage them around your home. They need plenty of food in winter, so you must provide snack bars around your property, keeping them

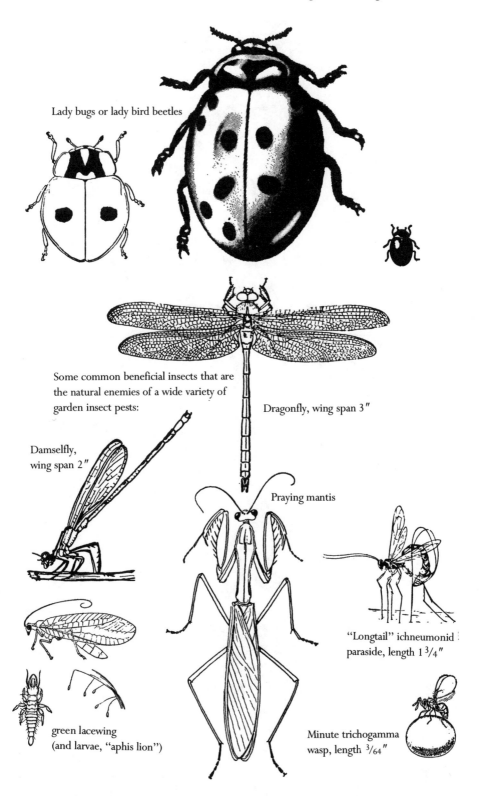

Lady bugs or lady bird beetles

Some common beneficial insects that are
the natural enemies of a wide variety of
garden insect pests:

Dragonfly, wing span 3″

Damselfly,
wing span 2″

Praying mantis

"Longtail" ichneumonid
paraside, length 1 3/4″

green lacewing
(and larvae, "aphis lion")

Minute trichogamma
wasp, length 3/64″

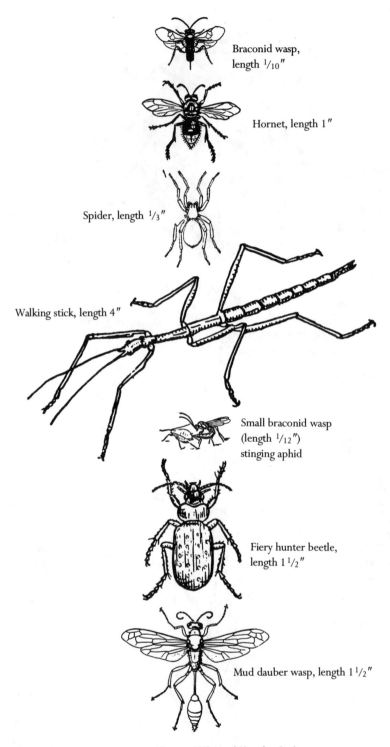

Braconid wasp, length ¹/₁₀"

Hornet, length 1"

Spider, length ¹/₃"

Walking stick, length 4"

Small braconid wasp (length ¹/₁₂") stinging aphid

Fiery hunter beetle, length 1 ¹/₂"

Mud dauber wasp, length 1 ¹/₂"

(Courtesy USDA and Hercules, Inc.)

filled at all times from late fall to spring. But they'll make up for it in summer. For the record: one yellow-billed cuckoo snacked upon 217 fall webworms in a sitting, while another lunched briefly on 250 tent caterpillars. Of a pair of flickers, one tossed off 5,000 ants in succession, while its less voracious spouse polished off a mere 3,000. Three nighthawks downed 60 grasshoppers, 500 mosquitoes, and 1,000 ants, while a redwinged blackbird made light work of 28 cutworms. Birds eat all day long and stoke their young besides, so encourage them to stay around. (See *Shrubs for Birds* in Chapter II.) *Note*: Once you start a bird feeder, birds depend upon it, so you must keep it filled at all times during the winter and early spring when food is scarce.

DRAGONFLIES, OR "DARNING NEEDLES": These insects as well as spiders, hornets and wasps, are all misunderstood creatures of great benefit to man. On late summer evenings we have watched swarms of dragonflies come into our yard just before sunset and snatch mosquitoes and other insects out of mid-air by the hundreds. Scientists tell us a single dragonfly can gather as many as 50 mosquitoes and crush and store them in its mouth before eating.

PRAYING MANTIS: These green, brown, or gray creatures with front legs bent as though in prayer are strictly carnivorous, so they will not eat plants. They eat enormous quantities of flies, small caterpillars, Japanese beetles, and soft-bodied insects, and they live in harmony with ladybugs. (Praying Mantises are often tame enough to become pets and eat raw meat or insects from your fingers.) These two natural predators are available to organic gardeners in quantity from reliable dealers. The mantises are supplied in the form of egg cases (approximately 200 eggs per case) which hatch on your own grounds, and the ladybugs (ladybird beetles) are packaged in lots of 100 or more.

ENCARSIA FORMOSA: These are tiny wasps which have been used in England and Canada for years to control white flies. Before the natural control movement caught on, it was difficult to find a source of Encarsia in this country. It was difficult to import them due to restrictions. Since chemical control has been spotty, the demand for Encarsia has jumped and now many supply catalogs offer it. (See sources at end of chapter. There are many other good sources not mentioned). We found they did a great job, but once the white flies are gone the encarsia disappears also, since the white fly is their only source of food. The adult is about one-fortieth of an inch long. All adults of encarsia except one or two in 1,000 are females and reproduce without mating. The female searches for white fly nymphs and pupae (immature stages) on the leaves. It lays eggs inside the nymph or egg, causing it to turn black.

Beneficial nematodes: There are beneficial nematodes which can destroy borers, grubs, and cutworms and still be harmless to humans, pets, birds, and bees.

LACEWING FLY: One of the eatingest of all creatures, eats plenty of aphids and other small insects. Larva stage is called aphid lion.

TRICHOGRAMMA WASPS: Attack only the butterfly and moth family, stinging the larvae of many fruit pests. Trichogramma can be purchased in vials from garden supply catalogues.

SPIDERS: If you can stand to have spiders around, they are very beneficial in the home, in greenhouses, and in the garden, catching flying and crawling insects in their webs.

SPIDER MITE KILLERS: Spider mites have their own predators—phytoseiulus persimilis, Amblyseius californicus and Phytoseiulus longipes, which are mites, also.

TOADS: Are good helpers. One can eat 3,000 insects per month. In a greenhouse keep a small pan of water under the bench, as they need water to survive.

CHAMELEONS: Small lizards available in pet stores eat any kind of pest that moves. In a greenhouse, or indoors, spray the foliage of some plant daily, as this is the way they get water. If they clean up the insects for you, then they must be fed meal worms until a new supply comes along.

MOLES AND SKUNKS: Both feed on quantities of insects. They are especially fond of grubs and beetles in lawns, sometimes rooting up whole areas—indicating infestation of grubs or beetles.

For a complete up-to-date guide to suppliers of beneficial organisms in North America, write to: Biological Control Services Program, California Department of Food and Agriculture, 3288 Meadowview Road, Sacramento, California 95932. It's a great bargain for anyone interested in biological control.

HAND PICKING

One of the best methods of controlling larger insects is hand picking. This may sound like a tedious process, but a few minutes regularly spent doing a careful inspection above and below the leaves and on the stems for such insects as tomato hornworm, Japanese beetles, potato beetles, and cabbage worms is a worthwhile project. Friends of ours knock insects off into cans of detergent water as they walk through their vegetable or flower garden. This method along with the help of birds, toads, and other natural predators keeps their gardens almost free of pests.

CONTROLLING PLANT DISEASES.

Coping with plant diseases is much easier than coping with insect pests. Today's technology concentrates on producing disease-resistant fruits and vegetables. That means you can plant many varieties that require no fungicides. As yet we have no insect-resistant varieties, but research is progressing.

In general, most ornamentals have diseases which can be fought with Captan, or bordeaux mixture (copper). For the home gardener, most fruit diseases can be checked with Captan alone. Most vegetable diseases likewise can be checked or prevented with Captan.

Manufacturers have made it easier for home gardeners to cope with diseases and insects by making all purpose formulas. These contain the least harmful ingredients with short residual life. There's no need to apply them until symptoms appear. You can build up plant vigor so they can resist both insects and diseases. Keep your soil well fortified with organic matter. Water well during droughts and your plants will have enough stamina to cope with almost anything.

SANITATION

A prerequisite to successful organic gardening is sanitation—in the garden, the greenhouse, and the plant room. We have eight easy rules for you to follow:

1. *Remove and destroy diseased plants*. Do not put them on the compost pile. Spores can blow around or be introduced back into the garden. Burn the plants or discard in a closed container.

2. *Keep weeds away from flowers and vegetables.* A number of weeds are infected with viruses that can be carried by insects which travel between weeds and cultivated plants. Similarly, keep grass mowed around flower beds and vegetable gardens. This allows good air circulation and reduces the area insects can hide in. Mowed areas are easily "debugged" by birds and other natural predators. *Note*: Don't eliminate natural nesting sites such as trees and shrubs in the vicinity.

3. *If you have space, practice crop rotation*—planting crops in different spots each year. This prevents diseases from building up in the soil.

4. *Keep trimmings and other trash picked up* so bugs cannot hide underneath and over the winter.

5. *Inspect plants you buy or get from friends* before putting them in your home or planting them in your garden. Cuttings from friends also should be "quarantined" for a week or two to see if any insects hatch from eggs which may be on the plants. Learn to recognize telltale evidence left by insects, such as a sticky substance on leaves which could indicate aphids or scale insect. A mottled yellowing could indicate tiny red spider mites, and distorted blooms could mean you have thrips.

6. *Instead of soil, use soilless materials (or sterilized media) for rooting cuttings and starting seeds.* Sterile materials such as peat moss, perlite, vermiculite, (washed) sand (obtainable from a lumber yard), and combinations of these are good insurance against damping-off disease and other soil-borne problems.

7. *Do not use soil in which plants have become diseased, unless you sterilize it* by baking it for a half hour at 180 degrees F. or pasteurize it by pouring boiling water over it until the temperature reaches 180 degrees F. You can fill a seed flat with soil, pour boiling water over the soil, cover with aluminum foil, and then poke a meat or candy thermometer through the foil to note the temperature. Let soil dry a day or so before you sow seeds.

The Ontario, Canada, Department of Agriculture and Foods has kindly given us a chart which shows the temperatures required to kill soil-borne pests by heat treatment of 30 minutes. (Bear in mind that temperatures above 180 degrees F. may destroy organic material and soil structure.)

The following pests can be controlled at these temperatures:

Nematodes	120 degs. F.
Damping-off and soil rot organisms	130 degs. F.
Most pathogenic bacteria and fungi	150 degs. F.
Soil insects and most plant viruses	160 degs. F.
Most weed seeds	175 degs. F.
Some resistant weeds and viruses	212 degs. F.

STERILIZING POTS Don't hesitate to reuse pots, but be sure to sterilize them first. Pots can be sterilized by boiling (clay pots) or treating with bleach solution (clay or plastic pots). See Chapter IX for instructions.

8. *Add acetic acid to control various fungi in the soil.* Acetic acid is the active agent in ordinary vinegar, and you can buy acetic acid crystals or liquid acetic acid in drug stores and mix your own solution. Mix 1 quart of acid crystals in 25 gallons of

water. If you buy liquid acetic acid note the percentage of acid and adjust your dilution accordingly. For example, a 56 percent solution of acetic acid should be diluted at the rate of 1 quart of solution to 12 gallons of water. Use 2 quarts of solution for each square foot of soil 4 inches deep. Do not apply to living plants. The acid in the soil lasts for only a short time and has no aftereffects, since it increases the acidity temporarily but the soil quickly returns to its original condition.

CONTROL OF POWDERY MILDEW: Powdery mildew is a fungal disease which can be severe late in the growing season when days are warm and nights are cool. That's one reason why it's important to select mildew-resistant varieties of ornamentals. Also, give your plants lots of room for good air circulation and water *before* noon. To prevent mildew on any plant, spray with a solution of 1 teaspoon of baking soda in a quart of water (see roses). Japanese researchers who discovered the effectiveness of this spray on cucumbers, eggplants and strawberries suspect that alkalinity acounts for its effectiveness in suppressing fungal diseases.

DAMPING-OFF: To prevent damping-off of seedlings, soak 1 teaspoon of dried chamomile flowers in a quart of water for 2 or 3 days. Strain and use the water on seedlings to prevent the disease. Also, use fan to circulate air.

RESISTANT VARIETIES

One solution to the problem of disease is to use resistant varieties of plants whenever possible. Plant breeders are constantly working toward this goal. For example, there are now available several varieties of tomatoes resistant to fusarium and verticillium wilts and several strawberry varieties resistant to Red Stele disease and other problems. When you read seed catalogues look for the letters F, N, or V beside each variety. These indicate a resistance to fusarium, nematodes, or verticillium. In the chapters on fruits, vegetables, and flowers, we have listed many of these resistant varieties.

REPELLENTS Nature was generous in giving us many plants and other materials which are obnoxious to insect pests, and organic gardeners have taken advantage of this fact. Most of these were discovered by accident and we can assume there are still more to be discovered. Here are some repellents used by organic gardeners.

APHIDS (plant lice): Place an aluminum foil mulch underneath plants. Reflection of light rays causes aphids to fly away or fall off. (See *Mulches* in Chapter XIII for detailed discussion of aluminum foil as a mulch.) Spray with garlic (see formula at end of chapter). Dust wood ashes on the plants.

CORN EAR WORM: Squirt mineral oil on silk near tips of corn ear, making sure you don't cover entire length of silk. Do this when tassels are shedding pollen.

MOSQUITOES: Repelled by apple cider vinegar. Rub it over your arms or other exposed parts of the body.

NEMATODES: Can be eliminated by planting marigolds alone for two or three years in infested soils. For beneficial nematodes, refer to natural controls.

ROOT MAGGOTS (on cabbage, cauliflower, broccoli, kohlrabi, turnips, rutabagas). Use tarpaper squares around crops to repel turnip maggots and wireworms. Cut a slit in the square and a hole in the middle and slip around plant, laying it flat on ground.

RADISH MAGGOTS: Soak seeds in kerosene for two or three minutes before sowing.

SNAILS AND SLUGS: Repel with wood ashes, lime, and cinders placed around plants. (see also *Small Animal Control* in Chapter XVII.)

CUT WORMS: A milk carton with top and bottom removed is one of the most effective ways of discouraging cutworm damage to newly set plants without using chemical controls. Just remove top and bottom of carton, slip it over the plant, and firm it in the ground. Aluminum foil collars or tin cans with bottoms removed serve the same purpose. Be sure the barriers are pushed 1 inch into the ground and extend 2 inches above the ground.

FLYING INSECTS: While not strictly a repellent, yellow electric light bulbs in outdoor living areas decrease the number of flying insects at night.

Pheromones and Other Traps and Barriers

A safe, modern method for coping with insects is the use of Pheromone ("Ferrow-Moan") traps. Pheromones are powerful chemical sex attractants emitted by female insects. They work on male insects like perfume works on men. These chemicals are detected by the males, assisting them in locating unfertilized females for mating. These natural pheromones have been identified and are synthetically produced in the laboratory to lure males to their death—an ideal trick for insect pest management.

Traps come in several designs and work for specific insects. The inner surface of the trap bottom is coated with a sticky substance and the pheromone-treated material is placed inside the trap. Attracted (and excited) males enter the trap through openings in the side but instead of getting stuck on a female, they get stuck on the bottom. The whole concept is new and the idea is to trap males so they can't mate with females. Also, commercial growers use the traps not only for controlling pests, but also for detecting the presence of a pest and if the pest population is increasing, peaking, or decreasing.

Several other nontoxic traps attracts bugs like magnets. Here are some we've been using:

Tangle-trap: A sticky substance is spread on a bright reflective surface to attract flying insects away from your plants. No insecticides are used. Controls aphids, whiteflies, leafhoppers, black flies, moths per style thus far and gnats. White surfaces are more attractive to tarnished plant bugs and flea beetles.

Yellow Sticky Trap: Contain wire loop holders, easy to push into the soil. Effective against whiteflies, aphids and fungus gnats.

Yellow Sticky Bar: Used outdoors to trap aphids, whiteflies, leafoppers, and many other insects.

Sticky Tube Trap: Yellow color lures aphids, whiteflies, leafhoppers, black flies, moths, and gnats away from plants. Captures them when they land. Uses no pesticides.

Insect Barrier: These are lightweight polypropylene row covers which keep out bean leaf beetles, cabbage worms, cabbage maggots, carrot weevils, Colorado potato beetle, cucumber beetles, leafhoppers, leafminers, squash bugs, squash vine borers, and other pests. Made of translucent polypropylene fabric which transmits 95% of sunlight and causes no heat build-up. You can leave covers on in summer without harming heat-sensitive plants. Comes in a variety of sizes and lasts for two seasons or longer.

Tanglefoot Pest Barrier: Wrapped around a tree trunk, it controls gypsy moth, tussock moth, forest tent caterpillar, Army worm and many others.

Floating Row Cover: Made of organic materials; provides frost protection down to 28 degrees F., letting in sun, water and air, and shielding plants from many insects. You can plant crops two weeks earlier than usual and extend late harvest of fall crops. Transmits 85% of sun, lasts 20 weeks before sun weakens its fibers.

Red Spheres apple sized trap: Coated with sticky Tangle-trap; controls apple maggot fly which can cause railroad tunnels. Females attracted by scented lures. Hang in apple trees.

Fly Trap: Contains special scent which attracts flies.

Japanese Beetle Trap: There are Japanese beetle traps to be found in garden center and garden catalogues which do a reasonable job of catching the pest. O. C. Barringer, garden writer for the *Raleigh News and Observer*, sent us this slick tip for controlling Japanese beetles: Open a can of fruit cocktail and let it sit in the sun for about a week so it will ferment well. Then suspend it with wires (strung through holes near the top of the can) across the top of a pail, or stand it on bricks or wood blocks in the pail. Fill the pail with water to the edge of the can. The beetles will fall in the pail by the hundreds and drown. A white enamel pail works best, a yellow plastic one next best.

Lights: While yellow lights repel insects, it has been found that blue lights attract insects. There are blue electrolized lights on the market, but they are not discriminating, and unfortunately attract useful insects as well as harmful ones. They may attract more insects to the area than they eliminate. Also, the sound emitted when an insect strikes the surface is disturbing to some people and to pets, especially dogs. Black light traps are available which attract European Chafers; their effectiveness is debatable.

Grapefruit and orange skin: Place cut side down in your garden. Slugs and snails are attracted to citrus and crawl into them so you can gather and destroy the pest. One gardener we know caught over 300 slugs in one evening.

COMPANION PLANTING

Organic gardeners have long used the idea of intercropping for insect and disease control. They call it "companion" planting and the basic principle behind it is that juices or odors of certain plants are offensive to certain insects. One theory is that the mixture of vapors emitted by a variety of plants growing close together confuses the insect population and keeps certain pests in check, or even repels them, thereby reducing their damage to the plants. Companion planting works in another way, too. A plant may be grown beside a vegetable so that the pest will be induced to feed upon *it*. Such would be the reason for planting mustard in among cabbage and related plants, since the cabbage butterfly prefers to lay its eggs on the mustard.

Although to date we have not had too much success with companion planting, many swear by this method and seem to have good luck with it. Following are some of the recommendations sent to us by our organic gardening friends

Shoofly plant (*Nicandra physaloides*) planted among tomatoes, peppers, and vine crops which are susceptible to white fly.

Cosmos, asters, marigolds, and chrysanthemums interspersed among beans for Mexican bean beetles.

Tomatoes planted near asparagus to repel asparagus beetles.

Sage and mint to repel cabbage butterflies on cabbage and related crops.

Nasturtiums, garlic, and savory for insects troubling lima beans.

Marigolds and savory for insects troubling pole beans.

Basil for insects eating eggplant.

Radishes and nasturtiums among melons.

Dill with tomatoes.

Many organic gardeners plant anise, artemisia, feverfew, hyssop, French lavender, tansy, tarragon, and yarrow among their flowers and vegetables and tell us they have excellent results in repelling insects. We have much to learn about to this facet of the plant world, but eventually balanced planting may be an important means of insect control.

Organic Pesticides

Scientists are discovering more and more plants that produce natural bactericides, fungicides, and insecticides. One very promising souce of natural plant products is the neem tree—*Azadirachta indica*. It produces Margosan O, which commerical growers now use to fight pests on beet Army worms, caterpillars, gypsy moth, leafminers, loopers, mealbugs, thrips and whiteflies. Margosan O is environmentally sound and should work into any program. Consult your state experiment station about it. Several household materials are also effective against insect pests. While many of these are inorganic, they are considered low-hazard, biodegradable substances. Liquid household detergents, for example, are manufactured from petroleum, an organic material.

We are inclined to feel there is a thin line between many newer synthetic pesticides (not acceptable to strict organic gardeners), household substances (often acceptable), and controls like rotenone, pyrethroids, or nicotine sulfate (acceptable). In fact, there is now a synthetic pyrethroid that has the same properties as those extracted from pyrethrum plants.

Here are some acceptable organic controls that gardeners find effective:

HOUSEHOLD DETERGENTS: There is a new generation of insecticides so safe you can mix it right in your kitchen sink. 1) Here's one from the USDA: Mix 1 teaspoon of liquid dishwashing detergent, with 1 cup of vegetable oil. Shake vigorously to emulsify and add to a quart of tap water. Use at 10 day intervals as an all-purpose spray for white flies, spider mites, aphids and various insects on carrots, celery, cucumbers, eggplants, peppers and others. We've used it on evergreens and other ornamentals. *Note:* Test on a single plant first, as it may cause tip burn. This is a contact insecticide, so in order to work, the mix must be sprayed directly on the pest. 2) LIQUID DETERGENT ALCOHOL SPRAY: Mix 1 teaspoon of liquid dish washing detergent plus 1 cup of rubbing alcohol (around 70%) in 1 qt. of water. Test on a few leaves first to make sure no harm is done to sensitive plants. Spray top and bottom sides of leaves, or if plant is small and potted, invert it in a large pan of solution (holding soil ball securely) and gently swish back and forth. Repeat in 7 days.. 3) LIQUID DETERGENT—HOT PEPPER SPRAY: Steep 3 tbs of dry, crushed hot pepper in $1/2$ cup hot water (covered) for half hour, strain out the particles of peppers and mix solution with the liquid detergent formula mentioned above. Good on a number of insects for both indoor and outdoor plants. NOTE: Apply on plants outdoors. Do NOT use on windy day. AVOID breathing fumes. Can be irritating to nose and eyes. You can substitute Hot Tabasco Sauce or Louisiana Hot Sauce for hot pepper. Some gardeners add the liquid from 3 cloves of garlic steeped for half an hour in $1/2$ cup of hot water.

PYRETHROIDS: Both the natural ones derived from the pyrethrum plant (*Chrysanthemum cinerariaefolium*) and the synthetic substitutes are highly effective against a wide range of insects. Each should be used according to manufacturers' directions.

ROTENONE: An old remedy that is very good for Mexican bean beetle. It is produced from derris, a plant found in Central and South America, and kills aphids, thrips, and chewing insects on contact. *Note*: Toxic to fish and nesting birds.

RYANIA: Made from ground stems and roots of a South American shrub. Controls European corn borer and various other worms. Use per directions on the container.

SABADILLA: Made from seeds of a South American lily. Used for squash bugs and stink bugs. Irritating to eyes and lungs if care is not taken. Use according to manufacturer's directions.

TALCUM POWDER: Found to be effective against flea beetles and corn ear worm. A light dusting on the surface of the leaves after every rain is all that is necessary.

TOMATO LEAVES, CRUSHED: If you prefer not to use a chemical spray, try crushed tomato leaves for leaf spot diseases. Grind 2 cups of leaves to a puree, add 5 pints of water and 1 ounce of cornstarch to make a black spot spray. This solution may be refrigerated until it is used up. Or grow tomatoes in with your rose bushes. As we mentioned in Chapter VII, tomato leaves fight black spot disease because they contain solanine, a chemical that has an inhibiting effect on black spot fungus.

NICOTINE SULFATE (Black Leaf 40): Derived from tobacco and great for aphids. Kills most soft-bodied sucking insects on contact. Do not inhale or spill on the skin. Use according to manufacturers' directions. *Note*: Nicotine concentrates are extremely poisonous.

Even though nicotine sulfate is an accepted organic spray, treat it with respect. It is lethal enough to combat nearly all the pests listed here. However, in certain cases other materials are preferred. For example, Bacillus sprays are ideal for Colorado potato Beetle, cabbage loopers, Mexican bean beetles, etc. Milky spore disease controls Japanese beetle larvae. Apple maggot fly, apple tree borers and Japanese beetle *adult stages* can be trapped with pheromone attractants.

TOBACCO WATER: Cigar and cigarette butts also will kill worms in the soil of houseplants. Mix a solution the color of brown tea to pour on the soil. Don't let anyone drink it by mistake. It kills fungus gnats, symphylids, centipedes, root lice, and other underground pests, and it could kill you. If you have aphids or other insects in your terrarium or dish garden, ask a friend who smokes to blow cigarette smoke into the glass jar, then seal the top. The smoke knocks plant lice for a loop.

SNUFF: For tiny flies or worms in the soil of houseplants, try sprinkling snuff on the surface. A gardener wrote us: "My husband uses snuff. I can't stop him but its better than smoking as I can't stand the smoke. We sprinkled some snuff around the soil of our houseplants and watered it in; it works great!"

Note: Do not use homemade tobacco remedies on tomatoes, peppers, eggplants, and other members of the Solanum family. It could spread tobacco virus to these plants.

HOT PEPPER: Cats, dogs, many insect pests, and snails can be discouraged by a dusting of powdered hot pepper or a spray of hot pepper sauce. You can also mix the pepper with the garlic and onion sprays mentioned elsewhere.

SALT: Use a salt shaker and sprinkle a tiny bit directly on slugs or snails to quickly eradicate them.

OIL AND SULFUR SPRAYS: Petroleum oils (of organic dervation) have been used successfully for killing insects for over 200 years and are still popular. The oil and sulfur sprays are applied only on "hard" or woody plants, and you have a choice of two types: 1) Dormant oil, which should be used *only* when plants are dormant, as in winter or early spring. 2) Summer oil, used during the growing season and restricted to woody plants. Some oil sprays can be applied in either summer or winter. The manufacturers' labels will tell you. Miscible oil sprays kill insects and eggs such as overwintering leafrollers and aphid and mite eggs. They also kill scale insects and adult mites. Dilute with water according to manufacturers' directions. The oils cause little or no harm to most beneficial insects, and resistance to sprays does not build up with oils.

LIME SULFUR: An old timer still used by both organic and non-organic gardeners. It is applied during the dormant period and kills most species of mites as well as mite eggs and those of many other insects. Lime sulfur also has fungicidal value and can be used on fruit trees as well as ornamentals. *Note*: Lime sulfur applied to plants near the house will stain the paint. Apply cautiously near buildings.

SOAPS AS INSECTICIDES: Soap suds will kill many soft-bodied insects such as aphids. The old-fashioned soaps were derived from plants (coconuts, olive, palm, cottonseed), or from animal fat such as whale oil, fish oil, or lard. Many home gardeners feel that vegetable- or plant-based soaps are more effective aphicides than those derived from petroleum.

GARLIC AND ONIONS: Raw onions or garlic ground up into a puree makes a good bug killer. This puree is soaked in warm water overnight, then strained. The liquid can be sprayed on roses, fruit trees, and flowers. It does a great job killing aphids and other pests, including apple borers. Scrape off any loose bark on the trunk and swab the liquid on. Many gardeners make a paste of onion water and wood ashes and paste this on tree trunks.

T. A. Tovstoles, a Russian biologist, experimented with a water solution of onion skins. Used as a spray three times daily at five day intervals, the solution gave an almost complete kill of Hemiptera, a parasite which attacks more than 100 different species of plants. Onion spray will also serve as a nontoxic fumigant.

ORGANIC GARDENER'S ALL-PURPOSE SPRAY: An all-purpose organic spray used for controlling white fly, aphids, woolly aphids, and red spider mites in a greenhouse and outdoors consists of 3 ounces of chopped garlic cloves (use a garlic press), soaked in 2 teaspoons of mineral oil for twenty-four hours. Slowly add 1 pint of water in which 1/4 ounce of oil-based (for example, coconut oil) soap or soap chips has been dissolved. Stir well, then strain and squeeze this liquid through fine gauze or an old nylon stocking. Store in a tightly sealed glass jar. When ready to use, dilute 1 part garlic mixture to 20 parts of water in the sprayer. The odor does not linger and there is no chance of burning or damaging the foliage. The spray will help control white fly, aphids, woolly aphids, and red spider mites.

GARLIC-RED PEPPER SPRAY: Grind up a large bulb of garlic—a *bulb*—not a clove (a large onion can be substituted, but garlic is preferred), add a tablespoon of ground cayenne pepper and 1 quart of water and let it steep for an hour. Strain what you need into a sprayer or watering can and store the remainder in a tightly covered jar in the refrigerator. It will remain potent for several weeks. Reported to be effective on all kinds of chewing and sucking insects.

RHUBARB LEAVES: A good aphid killer. Boil 1 lb of chopped leaves in 1 quart of water for 30 minutes. Strain and use liquid as a spray against aphids and other pest.

ORGANIC SPRAY WITH SPEARMINT LEAVES: Put into a blender 1 cup each of chopped spearmint leaves and green onion tops and $1/2$ cup of chopped hot red pepper, adding $1/2$ cup of water to assist in blending. Pour this solution into a gallon of water. Add $1/2$ cup of liquid detergent (preferably a lemon-scented one). Dilute this by adding $1/2$ cup of the mixture to a quart of plain tap water. If the plant is small you can dunk it in this solution, or you can strain it and spray it on. A window-cleaner sprayer works like a charm for applying this all-purpose spray. Effective on all chewing insects; some report good results on sucking insects.

BUTTERMILK SPRAY FOR SPIDER MITES: Mix $1/2$ cup of buttermilk and 4 cups of wheat flour with 5 gallons of water. Spray it on leaves, both top and bottom sides. Repeat in ten days to get any that hatch out. Has been found to be very effective.

BACTERIAL CONTROL is the use of bacteria to infect insect pests. *Bacillus thuringiensis*, a spore-type disease, is bacteria produced commercially and marketed to kill off the larvae of butterflies and moths that are enemies of vegetable crops such as broccoli, cauliflower, lettuce, potatoes, etc. Tests show the bacillus to be highly active and able to retain its capacity to control susceptible lepidoptera larvae for at least ten years.

BACILLUS: Since the discovery of the bacterium Bacillus thuringiensis (Bt) back in 1901, a lot has been done to expand its insect killing potential. Bt is effective against some of our toughest pests—members of the lepidoptera or butterfly family including European corn borers, cabbage looper and others. A new strain of Bt, San Diego, works on the Colorado potato beetle, one of the most destructive pests against not only potatoes but also tomatoes and even eggplants. The Colorado potato beetle has developed an immunity to some of our toughest chemical pesticides (including the banned Temik). The new bacterium Bt var. San Diego, discovered in 1985, is being used against the potato beetle.

Fungus gnats, the tiny flylike pest that buzzes around your head while you read, can be checked with a new biological strain of Bacillus thuringiensis called Bt H-14. Also Bt Israelensis kills mosquito larvae (wrigglers) in pools and ponds. Take care not to get in eyes.

MILKY SPORE DISEASE: For over a quarter of a century milky spore disease has been used to kill the grub stage of the Japanese beetle. Manufacturers collect grubs and inoculate them with the bacteria. They are made into a powder which is applied to the soil where the bacteria attack healthy grubs. Apply any time the ground is not frozen. Do not expect immediate results, as several years may elapse before the disease becomes fully effective. There is some evidence that today's crop of Japanese beetles is developing resistance to milky spore disease.

As a final note, completely eradicating insects or diseases on crops may not be altogether desirable. In some cases, plants damaged by insects or disease may actually grow better. According to the University of Idaho, prune trees infected with ringspot virus have yielded from one-half to seven times more fruit than non-infected trees. Also, the infected trees were stimulated in growth and were more resistant to cytospora canker.

Dr. P. Harris of the Agriculture Canada Research Station (Regina, Saskatchewan) noted that many shrubs grow more vigorously when "lightly browsed" by insects, and Dr. Harris found removal by insects of some flowers on cotton plants and leaves on potatoes increases the yields of these plants. Small mite infestations on cucumbers may make them yield better. Dr. Harris suggests two reasons for these effects: Light pruning by insects early in the season stimulates new growth. Secondly, growth hormones are produced either by the insects themselves or by the plant in response to the insect attack.

So, perhaps insects or disease may not be as bad as popular articles and advertising paint them to be. At any rate, the time will never come when plants and insects don't live side by side, so we'd better give up the idea of completely eradicating them and consider some symbiosis that is of mutual advantage to the garden, the plants, and even the insects.

Write for a copy of The Necessary Catalog, Box 305, New Castle, Virginia, 24127. The owners, Necessary Trading Co., specialize in organic growing techiques.

Gardens Alive! is a catalog loaded with environmentally-responsible products for growing. Address: Box 149, Sunman, Ind. 47041.

Ringer Corp, 9959 Valley View Rd., Minneapolis, MN 55344, has developed many growth products that work in harmony with the environment.

Note: There are many other reliable companies (and seed catalogs) which offer supplies for everyone, whether you are a "chemical" or "organic" gardener.

CHAPTER XV

Plant Propagation

•

One of the greatest joys of gardening is plant propagation, the science of increasing plants from existing ones. Plant propagation falls into two main categories: 1) Raising plants from seed or spores. Such plants are produced by sexual union, and the process is referred to as sexual propagation. 2) Raising plants "vegetatively," or without benefit of sexual union. This method, known as asexual propagation or vegetative reproduction, includes division, cuttings, grafting, and budding.

Sexual propagation by seed gives rise to many new strains valuable to horticulture, and without it we would not get most of our new varieties. Asexual increasing does not produce new strains, but is of importance to the home gardener because it is generally quicker and maintains the identical characteristics of the parent plant. For example, a red rose started by cuttings will produce plants with red flowers. However, seed from a red rose may not produce red-flowered plants.

Most of our common shrubs can be propagated from cuttings. Some root best from hardwood cuttings, others respond to the softwood cutting, while some can be started by both methods.

All methods of reproduction cannot be used on all plants. For example, single-stemmed plants cannot be divided, while shrubs, evergreens, and herbaceous plants which take a long time to grow are not usually started from seed, except to produce new varieties.

In the production of fruit trees, many varieties are grown by "grafting" buds of a selected tree on vigorous seedling rootstocks. The rootstock hastens growth of the tree, but the bud preserves the exact identity of the tree from which it was taken.

Seed or Sexual Propagation of Plants

It's fun to start your own plants from seed, but start with *good* seed! Seed is cheap, relatively speaking, so buy the best from a good seedhouse so you can be sure of good germination and trueness to name. If you do wish to save some seed select it from your best plants, those showing outstanding growth or yield.

SAVING YOUR OWN SEED FROM YOUR OWN PLANTS For seed purposes, make sure the plant and fruit are free from disease. The plant should be husky, well-shaped, and have a good growing habit. When the fruits are fully ripened, pick and remove the seeds, then spread them out to dry and store when thoroughly dry. Your seeds will produce "open-pollinated," or non-hybrid, plants which may or may not have the characteristics of the parent. Especially with hybrid plants, we feel it is not practical to save your own seed, since you are not sure what the results will be. Hybrid seed is more

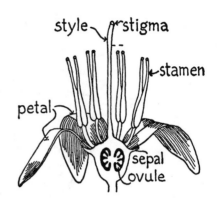

Parts of a simple flower. Note: Stigma is the female part that receives pollen; stamen or anthers, the male element that produces pollen.

expensive than the regular or open-pollinated varieties, but the plants have outstanding characteristics. For example, to produce hybrid petunia seed, seedsmen use two selected parents, which probably took anywhere from four to eight years to perfect. Cross-pollination is done with tiny brushes, a tedious and exacting job. The hand operations make hybrid seeds more expensive than when the job is done by bees and insects. So you're repaid for your investment several times by a bigger and better—and dependable—harvest. (Seed from hybrid plants themselves may revert to their grandparents or great-grandparents and be a conglomeration of colors and shapes.)

You might be interested in breeding a new plant. It takes a full book to tell how plants are hybridized, but in a nutshell, here's what you do: 1) Snip off the male elements of a flower before they have a chance to discharge pollen to an awaiting female element (pistil); 2) Gather pollen (male element) from another plant in same genus, and dust it on the female portion (remember, you took away her rooster element). The pollen you took from an outside plant will be responsible for something different in the offspring. The Burpee Seed Company tried unsuccessfully for 20 years to produce a white marigold. In 1975 the company paid a 67-year-old gardener $10,000 for a white marigold she produced in her own backyard, and she knew little if anything about hybridizing!

SOWING SEED INDOORS

THE PLANTING MEDIUM Seeds do not need rich soil to germinate. The main thing is to have a loose, well drained mixture. You can't just scoop up a box of garden soil and expect it will do for starting seed indoors. We prefer to use a sterile soilless mix (available at garden stores). However, if you insist on using your own soil you must sterilize it by one of the following four methods (see also *Soil Sterilization* in Chapter XIV, ORGANIC GARDENING):

BAKING: Get the soil mixture fairly moist and fill a roasting pan 3 or 4 inches deep. Level it off and cover the pan with heavy aluminum foil, sealing down the edges. Punch a small hole through the middle of the foil and insert the bulb of a meat thermometer into the center of the mixture. Bake at 180 degrees F. for thirty minutes. Avoid high oven temperatures, since they destroy organic matter and soil structure.

Sow seed in a tray filled with dampened soilless planting mix. Or use Jiffy pellets, root cubes, peat pots, or other seed starters. Fine seed should be merely scattered on top and pressed in lightly. Water again by setting seed box in a pan of water until top of mix is thoroughly wet. This self-watering process is called "subirrigation."

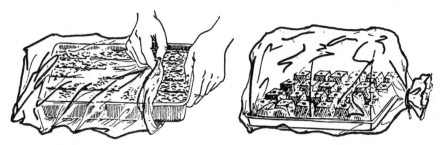

Cover tray and pan with plastic sheet or glass, or slip tray inside a clear plastic bag to conserve moisture and trap heat inside. Place in temperature of 72-75 degrees F (day and night) until germination starts. As soon as seed sprouts, remove from plastic bag and keep moist by subirrigation.

Seeds can also be germinated in pots enclosed in plastic bags. (*Courtesy Under Glass Magazine*)

After first true leaves appear, separate and transplant each seedling into pots or boxes. (*Courtesy Edward Gottlieb and Associates, Ortho Garden Products*)

HOT WATER: Insert a cooking thermometer into a box of soil and pour boiling water onto the soil until the temperature reaches 180 degrees F. Let soil dry a day before sowing seed.

PRESSURE COOKING: Place soil in pressure cooker and cook for fifteen minutes at 10 pounds pressure.

COMMERCIAL DISINFECTANTS: Patented products are available from garden supply stores. Follow the manufacturer's directions.

After sterilizing, you can mix this soil with one part peat and one part builders' sand. These materials are relatively sterile, hence won't harbor the damping-off disease which makes tiny seedlings flop over.

SOILLESS MIXES Instant soilless mixes are sterile, ready to use, and porous, so tiny roots penetrate them easily. You can make your own by mixing 1 part finely pulverized sphagnum peat moss, and 1 part vermiculite, 1 part perlite. Or, you can use any of the mixes on the market such as Jiffy-Mix, Pro-Mix, Redi-Earth, etc. Don't be fooled by "potting soil," which can be just plain muck. Get one of the products made up of sterile materials: peat, perlite, vermiculite, terralite, etc. Many "potting soils" are not sterilized and may contain insects, weed seeds, and diseases harmful to plants.

You use soilless mixes just as they come from the bag, and they are money savers because you can be more sure of good germination. Seedlings have balanced root and top growth, transplant easier, and produce husky plants faster due to the quick take-off of the young seedlings. Soilless mixes are also useful for growing pot plants and as a rooting medium for a wide range of plants, including mums, poinsettias, succulents, and foliage plants.

SOWING Sow thinly and do not cover fine seed such as petunias. Simply press the seed in lightly.

Some seed needs light for germination and therefore cannot be covered; others should be covered lightly, and some are not fussy. For the most part, all vegetables and most flower seeds need a bit of cover. With seeds which do not need light for germination, use a flour sifter and shake a very light coat of peat moss or one of the instant soil mixes over the seeds. For a chart of light and heat requirements of annual seeds see Chapter IV, ANNUALS.

If you sow too thick, you can get spindly plants. Plan to sow about ten to seven small seeds or four to seven large seeds per inch of row.

WATERING This step is most important. The secret is to *never* let the seed dry out any time during the germination period. One drying out can be fatal. Do not water from the top, since this favors damping-off disease. Instead, set the container in a pan of warm water so that water seeps up from below. We keep an inch of water in the pan all during the germinating period and place a pane of glass or piece of clear plastic over the box to keep moisture in. But be sure to remove the cover as soon as seeds sprout, as the seedlings need air.

HEAT The seed will germinate more quickly if the pan is placed on a radiator for bottom heat. If you have no convenient place to get bottom heat, you should probably invest in a small heating cable, available at garden stores (and inexpensive).

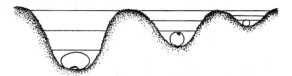

SOW SEED AT DEPTH 3 X DIAMETER OF SEED

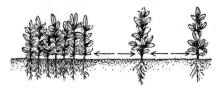

THIN OUT SEEDLINGS TO GIVE
PLANTS ROOM TO DEVELOP

SPACE LARGE SEEDS WHILE SOWING IN ROWS OR IN HILLS

(Courtesy Geo. J. Ball, Inc,)

Nearly all seeds like a constant day and night germination temperature of 70 to 75 degrees F. It's easy to maintain this during the day, but at night when you lower the temperature your seed flat gets colder than the room itself. If under 65 degrees F., the seed is apt to rot inside the seed coat. After seeds sprout, you can move them to a cool bright window because seedlings like it cooler. *Remember to remove glass or plastic cover as soon as the seedlings are up.*

A FOOLPROOF SEED SPROUTER If you "just can't get any seed to grow," we've got the answer: build yourself a simple seed-starting chamber. Put together a frame of 1-by-4-inch boards, 3 feet by 2 feet, or whatever size fits your space. Staple a plastic sheet over the top of the frame, lapping it over the sides so it doesn't pull off. Bury a heat cable one inch deep in sand or soil, and place a shallow pan over it. Fill your seed box with a good starting medium, sow the seed, place the box in the pan, and keep adding water to the pan until the soil mix is completely saturated. Cover with the plastic-covered wood frame and wait for the seeds to sprout. Keep about an inch of water in the pan. Heat and moisture are trapped inside the frame and sprout even the toughest ones. Best temperature is around 72 to 75 degrees F.

On hot days, be sure to ventilate your seed starter. All you do is raise one edge to let heat escape. Otherwise, heat will build up inside and cook tender seedlings or sprouting seed. Remove the box of seedlings as soon as they sprout.

There are a few seeds which require a cool germinating temperature (about 60 degrees F.) such as parsley, rosemary and verbena.

Note: Remember to use a good seed-starting material.

CARE OF SEEDLINGS When the seedlings are an inch or so tall and have two sets of true leaves, transplant to pots or boxes and grow in a well lighted spot. Now they need lots of air and a fairly loose soil, but they aren't ready for plant food until a week or so later, and always water new transplants. If you have no sunny windows, seedlings can be grown under fluorescent lights in the basement. While seed needs heat for germination, seedlings like it cool (55 to 60 degrees F.) for sturdy growth. Too high a temperature and lack of sunlight cause spindly soft growth.

Try making a self-watering plant box. All you need is a Fiberglass wick, a wooden box, and a slightly smaller pan. Drill a hole in the bottom of the box and draw a wick 8 inches long and 1 inch wide through it. Fray the top of the wick and imbed it in the soil; the bottom of the wick drops into the pan below. If you fill the pan once a week, the soil will keep moist and the seedlings will prosper.

TRANSPLANTING: Seedlings large enough to handle should be separated and transplanted to other boxes, flats, or pots for huskier growth. (Left together, the tiny plants will act like weeds among themselves in competition for water and nutrients.) Peat pots are excellent. Avoid breaking any roots in the transplanting process. The tiny plants need all the roots and leaves possible and win recover faster from transplanting if you leave them intact. For more information on care of seedlings and types of pots and containers, see Chapter VIII.

Put the transplanted seedlings in a hotbed if you have one or in a coldframe after danger of cold weather has completely passed to let them "harden" or adjust to outdoor conditions before planting in garden.

INSTANT PLANT POTS: Home gardeners have good luck using Jiffy-7 Pellets, "pot" and potting soil in one. The pellets are enclosed in nylon nets that let the roots grow right through the side. You set them out, directly in the ground as they are. The pellets, which are wafer-like before soaking, should be set close together in a pan, water added from above or below, and in minutes these highly compressed pellets absorb seven times their weight in water and expand to seven times their original size. They swell into a cylindrical plant container approximately $2'' \times 2''$, all ready for sowing seed, transplanting, or rooting cuttings.

Some gardeners have complained that roots have trouble penetrating the nylon netting which is wrapped around the peat pellet. That's why it's a good idea to take a razor blade and slit the sides of the netting at planting time. Or you can use a less expensive pellet, compressed but without nylon mesh (although some feel the netless pellets do not hold together long enough). They are useful for bedding vegetable plants, and ideal for rooting geraniums, poinsettias, azaleas, and other houseplants. There are two sizes: expanded cylinders $2'' \times 2\,1/8''$, and regular, $1\,1/4''$ by $1\,3/4''$. They both have flat bottoms making them harder to tip over. There are a number of cubes and wedges made from rockwool, Oasis, and other synthetic materials that are ideal for starting plants from seeds and cuttings.

Any type of pot that can be planted pot and all is handy, and could save your young plants "transplanting trauma." However, we have noticed with many of the fiber-growing pots that roots stay confined inside if the walls of the pot become dry. That's why it's a good idea to tease the sides of the pots apart (without disturbing the roots) at time of setting plants into the garden.

Note: When setting out potted plants growing in organic containers such as peat pots, never let part of the pot remain above ground. Why? The exposed edge acts like a wick, and when the hot sun (plus wind) hits it moisture is drawn up from the hidden remainder. This robs the roots of moisture and is one reason why individually potted spring plants really go to pot. Always water thoroughly after planting.

SOWING SEED OUTDOORS You don't need a greenhouse to start fast-growing seeds and seedlings such as zinnias and marigolds, radishes and lettuce. Mother Nature sows a lot of seeds directly into the ground, but when she does it dozens of seedlings are apt to come up in an inch of soil. Thus, if you sow seed outdoors, you should do it one of two different ways: 1) Sow seed rather thickly (say four to six per inch) and thin them out when they are ready for transplanting. Plant the "thinlings" wherever you want them and water well. 2) Sow a seed or two in the spot where you want the plant to grow. This saves you the job of thinning and transplanting. Some people think that transplanted seedlings do better than those never transplanted. There's probably no difference in growth between the two.

Sowing seeds outdoors is tougher because the young plants have to fight the elements. Don't cover too deeply. Press fine seeds into soil. Heavier seed can be lightly covered with peat or a mulch of some sort. A good general rule is to plant at a depth of three times the diameter of the seed; this maintains moisture and prevents damage from a blazing sun. Even with high-germinating seeds some gardeners like to sow more than is necessary. That's fine, because accidents of the weather are likely to destroy some plants and you'll need some to fill vacancies. The distance you space your plants depends to some extent upon varieties you grow, but don't crowd seeds, seedlings, or plants. Be sure to thin seedlings so that each plant has room to spread. (For information on thinning vegetables see chart at end of Chapter XI.) Keep seedlings misted on hot, sunny days.

KEEPING LEFTOVER SEED That seed you had left over from last year is still good if you kept it in a dry place (best storage temperature is around 40 degrees F.). When relative humidity is between 30 and 40 percent, seed can stand a below-freezing temperature, but if stored in a damp area, freezing temperatures might kill it. There may be a slight drop in germination of "held-over" seed. Left-over seed can be kept easily, using facial tissue and powdered milk: 1) Place the seed (or packets of seed) in glass jar. 2) Put a couple of tablespoons of powdered milk in facial tissue and roll it into a "cigar." Fasten with rubber bands. 3) Place the rolled tissue inside the glass jar with seed. The milk draws moisture away from the seed. 4) Screw top on tightly and store in refrigerator or a dark room at 40-50 degrees F.

TESTING YOUR SEED For a simple way to test seed before planting, place a known number on a piece of moist blotter or thick paper towel and keep them moist between two plates at room temperature. Check daily to be sure blotters are moist. The germination of most seeds can be checked in five to seven days, and it should be at least 80 percent. If you put out twenty seeds and only two of them sprout, that means 10 percent germination, which is very low.

Asexual or Vegetative Propagation of Plants

DIVISION

The simplest form of increasing plants asexually is known as division. Most perennials can be increased in this manner, as can most flowering shrubs. All you do is take an axe, a large knife, or a spade, and cut the clump or rootstock into convenient sizes for planting. Then lift the sections with a spade fork and replant where you want them. Multi-stemmed, fibrous-rooted houseplants such as African violets, begonias, and ferns, are also easily divided. Knock the plant from the pot (see illustration of the proper way to do this, under *Houseplants*), lay it on a solid surface and cut through the center of the root ball and stems. Repot the sections.

CUTTINGS

Propagation by cuttings involves the ability of the plant to send out roots from an injured or cut surface. Almost all plants can be grown from cuttings. The time it takes for a cutting to root may vary from one week (coleus) to several weeks (evergreens and certain woody shrubs).

ROOTING MATERIALS For years, coarse, clean sand (builder's sand available from any lumber yard) and peat moss have been standard rooting materials for cuttings. They are

Three simple steps in dividing a plant: 1. African violet needs repotting. 2. Plant is divided with a sharp knife thrust through the crown. 3. Section of divided plant, ready for repotting.

both excellent and some gardeners like to mix the two. Many use vermiculite, which is mica ore that has been put under high heat until the layers of mica pop or separate, resulting in a material that is spongy, water retentive, and free from disease. Vermiculite can be used alone or mixed with other media. We especially like perlite, a volcanic ash which also has been subjected to high heat. It too can be used alone or mixed. Both these materials are readily available at garden stores.

Of the different media, we lean a bit toward perlite. It is light, inexpensive, retains moisture, and is porous enough to allow air to flow through it.

Jiffy Peat Pellets (also called Jiffy-7, available at garden stores and in catalogues, described earlier in this chapter) are great for rooting cuttings. Merely insert the cutting in the expanded "pellet" and keep it moist until roots form. Pellet and all is then planted, but we recommend slitting the nylon net at time of transplanting. There are other propagating media made of a mixture of organic and inorganic materials. These are especially adapted for cuttings but can be used for seeds also.

ROOTING POWDERS: Gardeners who want to use plant hormone powders to stimulate rooting can do so, but we don't think you gain anything on cuttings easy to root. Sometimes they are advantageous on hard-to-root plant cuttings, and if you want to use a hormone the best way to apply it is in powder form.

You can buy small packets or cans, but for the home garden a packet is plenty, since a pound can will treat over 40,000 cuttings. Just dip the base end in the powder before inserting it in the rooting material. The most likely use for hormone powder is on hardwood cuttings. In the spring, these cuttings have a callus on the lower end and that's the time to dip them in plant hormone powder.

NATURAL ROOTING HORMONE: If you're looking for a natural way to stimulate rooting of woody cuttings, try using willow tea. Cut branch tips (new growth) from a willow tree of any species. Strip off the leaves, cut the shoots into 1 inch long pieces, cover with water, and let soak for 24 hours. Discard shoots and soak your cuttings in the willow extract. Use the extract soon after making it, and prepare another batch for your next cuttings.

You can root cuttings in a soil mixture of vermiculite, peatmoss and some earth-worm castings. Castings contain growth hormones that stimulate rooting. Use a tablespoon of castings (or more) per pot.

To see if a cutting is rooted, gently push a small stick (pencil) into the medium an inch or so away from the plant. Pry up carefully and observe.

SOFTWOOD CUTTINGS Softwood cuttings, or "tender tips," should be taken from shrubs during the summer months. Select only the tips (3 to 8 inches in length). Cut the stem at a node, and insert in sharp, coarse sand, perlite, or a mixture of sand and peat moss. About half the leaves should be removed from the lower end and the cutting then planted firmly in moist rooting medium to a depth equal to about one half its length. You can propagate roses, mums, hydrangeas, dogwood, and many perennials this way. Softwood cuttings of perennials such as mums can be taken in spring as well as summer.

Softwood cuttings are also used for propagating houseplants and plants such as geraniums and begonias. Often they are referred to as "slips." Just as with shrubs, the

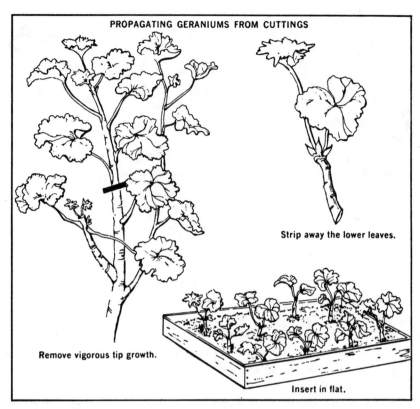

PROPAGATING GERANIUMS FROM CUTTINGS

Strip away the lower leaves.

Remove vigorous tip growth.

Insert in flat.

You can increase your geranium supply by taking tip cuttings and rooting them in a box of sand, perlite, or vermiculite. Keep rooting material moist.
(*Courtesy Under Glass Magazine*)

cutting is taken just below a node or leaf joint. In both cases it is helpful, after the cuttings are inserted in the rooting medium (especially if air is dry), to place a plastic covering over the cutting to conserve moisture. The whole pot or box may be enclosed in plastic.

Cuttings for houseplants can be taken anytime. Most houseplant cuttings can be rooted in plain water. This applies to leaves (in the case of African violets, begonias, etc.) as well as stem cuttings. A simple propagator (which can be used for softwood or hardwood cuttings) consists of a 6-inch clay pot with coarse sand or perlite standing in a tray of water. If air is dry, put a plastic cover over the cuttings.

SEMI-HARDWOOD CUTTINGS For many woody plants a semi-hardwood cutting method can be used. This is similar to softwood cuttings except that the wood is somewhat hardened or past the tender-tip stage.

Most semi-hardwood cuttings are made between the beginning of June and the middle of July from shrubs growing outdoors. These include roses, boxwood, oleander, weigela, dogwood, forsythia, privet, viburnum, and deutzia, to name a few.

A clay pot makes a fine home propagator for
starting your own house plants. Place a small pot
in center for watering. Sand, perlite, or
vermiculite is used for rooting. Rooting pot
enclosed with plastic bag to trap moisture and
heat.

Take 4- to 6-inch cuttings from the end or side shoots that are still growing or have
only recently stopped growing. Stick these in any moist rooting medium and keep
shaded for several days. After that, give them stronger light and keep the humidity high.
Always protect them from strong sun and excessive drying. After rooting takes place
(usually a couple of months) remove and pot up, or move to permanent spot in the
garden.

An inverted glass jar makes a fine miniature greenhouse for starting such plants as
roses, pivet, and evergreens directly in the ground. In fact, two simple propagators are: a
glass jar containing 3 or 4 inches of moist peat moss or perlite, covered with plastic and
sealed with a rubber band, and a plastic 1-quart freezer bag with either moist medium
inside, sealed with a twistem. These are useful for all hardwood or semi-hardwood
cuttings. Coarse vermiculite can be used also.

HARDWOOD CUTTINGS are a common method of making new plants of fruits, such
as blueberries, and a wide variety of woody ornamental plants such as spiraea, barberry,
butterfly bush, lilac, grapes, and others.

You start these by gathering cuttings in the fall, anytime after frosts have matured
the wood and leaves have fallen, or anytime during winter dormancy. The cuttings can
be from 6 to 10 inches long, and with most plants it's best to cut about $1/2$ inch below
the lowest bud and $1/2$ inch or more above the uppermost bud. Tie the cuttings in a
bundle (anywhere from ten to twenty-five, if you wish), with the basal ends (butt ends)
all in the same direction. Bury them horizontally in moist sand or sawdust in the cellar.

In the spring, set the cuttings, butt end down either in a cold frame or outside, in
rows about 18 inches apart, with the cuttings 2 to 4 inches from each other. The top
bud should be about even with or slightly above the ground level. Make sure the earth is
packed firmly about the lower end so the cuttings will not dry out. On hot summer days,
water the cuttings to hasten rooting. Some cuttings which are hard to root in plain

Three types of hardwood cuttings: terminal or tip cuttings ready to be inserted in rooting material; leaf-bud cutting; heel cutting with sliver of old wood attached.

garden loam often do better in a mixture of sand and granulated peat, equal parts by volume. Usually at the beginning of the second year the cuttings should be transplanted, and at the end of the second year they can be moved to a permanent position in a garden.

LEAF CUTTINGS Any houseplant of which the leaves or leaf stalks (petioles) are more or less fleshy can be propagated by leaf cuttings. This method is commonly used with begonias, Lifeplant (*Bryophyllum*), African violets, gloxinias, peperomias, and others. You can use a medium such as coarse sand, perlite, or vermiculite—or just plain water.

The water method is simple. We have good luck putting about an inch of water in a shallow dish—a soup dish or layer-cake pan is fine—and then putting large leaves around the edge so that their stem end is in the water. Large begonia leaves root well this way, so do African violet leaves. African violets and similar leaves also root well in a tumbler of water. We put a piece of foil over the tumbler, large enough so that we can bend the edges down over the sides, then poke holes in the foil just large enough to insert the leaf stem. A regular-size glass will hold about four or five leaves in this manner. Leaves root quickly supported in this way.

To root leaves in other media, you can use the simple propagator mentioned under *Softwood Cuttings*. Fill a clay pot with one of the mediums and set in the tray of water (keep about $1/4$ inch of water in it). Cut the leaf stem short and insert it up to the base of the leaf in the medium. With begonias and other heavily-veined leaves insert the whole leaf or cut it into wedge-shaped pieces, each having a part of a main vein running down through the center, terminating at the stem end. Place each wedge with about an inch of this stem end half an inch deep in moist medium.

You can also lay the whole leaf on the medium and make slits in the veins about 2 inches apart. Pin down with hairpins at the points of these slits. After rooting takes place you can cut the leaf in segments, with roots on each segment. New little plants will form where the roots are. All this is exciting, but we have better luck with the soup-dish method and the cut wedges.

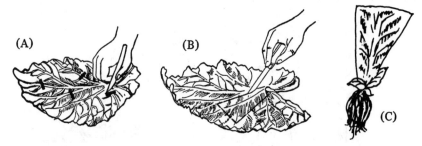

Large-leaved plants such as begonias can be rooted by: (A) Laying whole leaf on rooting medium and scoring leaf at the main veins. Little plantlets will form each place leaf is scored. (B) Cutting a section of the leaf so that the narrow point intersects at the midrib and stem. (C) Roots and a small plant will form where triangle is inserted in rooting medium.

TISSUE CULTURE A method of propagation that has become a real boon to commerical growers is called tissue culture. Thousands of plants can be produced in a single flask or container, using plant tissue and agar solution. For the home gardener, the process is a bit complicated, but you can write to your state college for information on this method of plant propagation. College and high school students are enthused about it and anyone can get instructions.

LAYERING Most woody ornamentals may be propagated by "layering," a system used by nurserymen and gardeners alike to increase plants of trees, vines, evergreens, or shrubs. Plants increased by layering always "come true," that is, have the same flowers, fruit, and leaf characteristics of the parent plant.

There are several forms of layering. Simple layering is done by making a trench 8 inches deep near the plant to be increased. Put 2 or 3 inches of loose soil back in the trench, then slit and bend a stem, placing the wounded area 3 or 4 inches deep in the prepared trench. The tip of the stem, with foliage intact, is left to protrude above ground and you firm the soil around the stem to hold it in place (or use a bent piece of coat hanger or a rock to hold it down). Roots form in the slit area in from one to six months.

Air layering is done by slitting the stem as you do with simple layering. Pack 3 or 4 handfuls of moist sphagnum moss around the wound and wrap the entire ball with plastic, tied tightly at each end. Rooting takes place in three months, more or less, depending upon the plant. Air layering is used to shorten tall woody-stemmed tropical plants which grow spindly or leggy. These include dracaenas, ficus, some philodendrons, dieffenbachias, croton, and many others.

Mound layering, or stool layering, starts in early spring. You cut a well established shrub back to 6 inches above soil level, then mound the base of the plant with soil so top of stub ends are buried. Shoots arise from the cut stems, and as they grow taller, the soil is gradually worked among them so that by fall the old cut ends are buried 4 or 5 inches below the surface. The following spring the mound of soil is gently forked away and the rooted stems are cut off and set out as young plants.

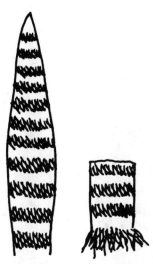

Narrow-leaved plants can be rooted by cutting segments of the leaves and inserting in rooting medium.

Root cuttings: Many plants can be rooted by inserting segments of roots in moist rooting medium.

In simple layering a branch is buried in a depression and pegged down with a piece of wire. Roots will form within 1 to 6 months. Rooting is faster with some plants than others.

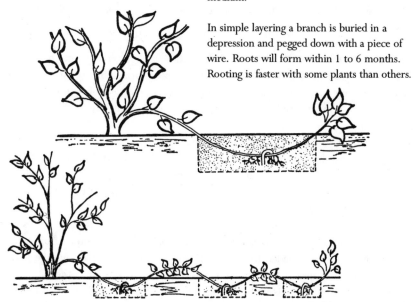

Multiple layering consists of bending and burying branches in several places.

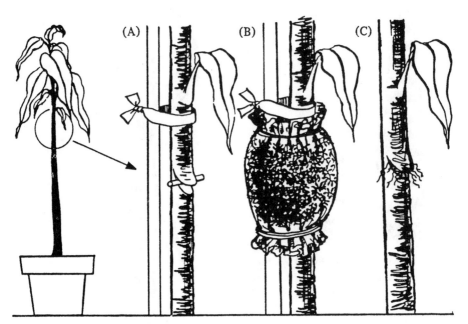

Select spot where you want to shorten plant. (A) Make a slit in bare stem and insert piece of toothpick. (B) Wrap wound with damp sphagnum moss held in place with a piece of plastic sheet tied securely at both ends. (C) After several months, roots are formed in the wound. Remove plastic sheet and sphagnum, cut the rooted section off below roots and pot up in a clay pot of loose soil mix. Remainder of plant will send out new shoots.

CARE OF LAYER-ROOTED PLANTS: When the young layered stems have rooted sufficiently they can be cut away from the parent plant preferably in early spring and planted where you want them. Water well during dry spells, especially during the first growing season. Watering and feeding each season will stimulate growth and produce stronger plants.

BUDDING This is the practice used to produce the three-in-one or five-in-one fruit trees that are so handy for gardeners with small space. Also, dwarf trees are produced by budding fruit varieties onto a dwarfing understock. Home gardeners can add other varieties to their established fruit trees by budding or they can convert a "wild" seedling into a good variety using the same technique.

Keep in mind that you must use related trees if you are going to have success with your budding project. For example, you cannot select a bud from a stone fruit (such as peach) and bud it onto a seeded fruit (such as apple). All apple trees could be budded on one another, or an apricot and a peach could be budded one on the other.

Best time to do budding is in August or the first part of September, when the sap is running and bark lifts easily from the wood. Sharpen your knife, select a good fruit tree, and look for some nice fat buds on this year's growth. You'll find the buds in the axils of the leaves, the place where leaves are joined to the branch. Buds taken from the central

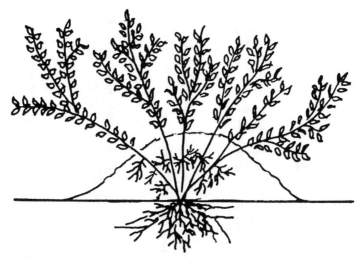

Mound layering is another simple way to increase plants. Mound soil over the base of the plant, after you scar or slit the stem bark. Roots form in the wounded area and the newly rooted plants are severed and set out.

Root trailing plants by placing pots in ground under runners and inserting vine in soil in the pots (a wire staple can be used to pin it down). After rooting, plant is cut from parent.

two-thirds of the growth are better than buds taken from the tip or bottom ends of the growth. The bud is cut off with the leaf, then part of the leaf stem is removed, leaving about a half inch as a handle for inserting the bud (see illustration).

Make a "T" slit in the young, green wood of this season's growth in the parent tree and insert the bud. Then, with a strip of rubber band, wrap the bud in the T-shaped slit you made in the twig. Keep in mind that buds "take" quicker and better if inserted in young, tender growth; the thicker the bark, the less likely the buds are to succeed. You can tell within a month if your bud has "taken." If it has turned brown and dried looking instead of retaining its "live tissue look" then it has not survived.

GRAFTING Grafting is nothing more than transferring a piece of twig (called scion) from one tree to a limb or branch (called stock) of another tree in such a way as to join the narrow cambium layer of growing cells of each at some point so that a union is secured. Growth takes place in this single layer of cells lying just between the inner bark and the wood. You must bring this layer of cells of scion and stock in contact with each other as perfectly as possible or they will not unite and grow.

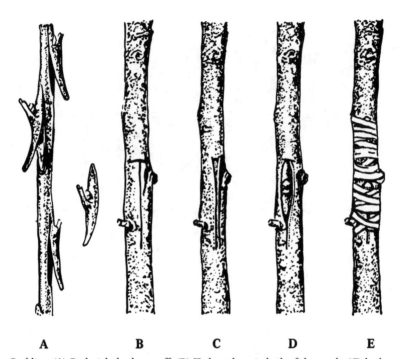

A   **B**   **C**   **D**   **E**

Budding: (A) Bud stick, buds cut off; (B) T-shaped cut in bark of the stock; (C) bark raised along both sides of the cut; (D) bud inserted in the T-slot; (E) completed bud graft wrapped with rubber band to prevent drying.

There are several types of grafting: cleft graft, side graft, inlay graft, etc. For more detailed instructions see our *Green Thumb Book on Fruit and Vegetable Gardening*.

Spring is the time to try your hand at grafting. Twigs that have made growth of from 1 to 2 feet the previous season usually provide the best scion wood. Buds should be plump and mature. The midportion of the one-year growth is usually best. Scion wood can also be collected during the dormant period in winter and kept wrapped in a cloth in a refrigerator hydrator. When it comes to budding and grafting, illustrations are worth a thousand words. Therefore we are including illustrations which can be studied before you try your hand.

Old timers still seal grafts with grafting wax but it's easier to use plastic tape to make the seal airtight. Petroleum jelly has also been found to make a good seal so the tissues will not dry out. A good grafting wax may be made by mixing 1 pound of rosin, 3 ounces of linseed oil, and 5 pounds of paraffin together. This may be applied with a brush.

RIDGE GRAFTING An emergency measure used for saving the life of a shrub or tree girdled by rodents or other causes is called bridge grafting. Immediately after the injury, small twigs of the same species or from the tree itself can be inserted in the wounded part so that the cambium layers (just below the bark) are joined at both ends. Use plenty of twigs and wax or tape in place. Water and food will then be transported through the twigs and enable scar tissue to heal the wound.

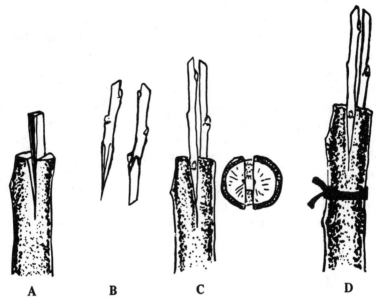

Cleft grafting: (A) Stock prepared for grafting; (B) two wedge-shaped scions prepared for each split stock; (C) scions inserted in stock so cambium layers touch; (D) cleft graft covered with plastic freezer bag to prevent drying.

Inlay grafting (1) cut scions ready for nailing; (2) back on stock removed; (3) scions nailed in place so that cambium layers touch; (4) cut surfaces thoroughly waxed. (*New York State College of Agriculture*)

Green Thumb Tips on Propagation

*When starting plants from seed, do as commercial growers do: Use a sterile soil substitute such as sand, vermiculite, perlite, or a sand-peat-vermiculite mix. Avoid soil, unless you sterilize and dilute it with one of the above.

*Seed may be started outdoors safely at the time when maples are coming into full leaf, or they may be started earlier indoors in a cold frame or hotbed.

*Wrapping your graft with pieces of plastic (drycleaning bags are fine) helps insure success. Plastic bags are also ideal for covering a box of germinating seeds.

*Plant breeding can produce a new and interesting flower for you. Try transferring pollen from one plant to another (make sure they're in the same family) and see what you get.

*Nature sometimes produces a new variety on an old plant. This sudden change is called "mutation" or "sport." Keep your eye open for mutations.

*Plantsmen are still on the prowl for new natural varieties—and may pay well for them.

CHAPTER XVI

Home Greenhouses, Hotbeds, & Cold Frames

•

A Greenhouse is Good for Your Health

Time was when only the idle rich, nurseries, and a few "plant freaks" had greenhouses, but not today. Greenhouses are popping up all over.

Hobby greenhouses are blooming for good reasons: 1) People want to "vacation" in their own backyards, stay off clogged highways, and get back to nature on their own grounds. In frustrating times when everyone is filled with tension, puttering under glass is great therapy. 2) With costs shooting up, many want to start their own vegetable and bedding plants, and grow the vegetables year round. 3) The indoor plant boom has brought a craving for more plant space (and "winter gardens") as well as increased interest in home propagation.

Today you can build a greenhouse of any size and at almost any cost. If you're handy you can build your own from scratch (even using scrap materials). Or buy one of the many (relatively inexpensive) prefabricated greenhouses that come ready to assemble. (Prefabricated greenhouses can also be assembled on your grounds by the company, but this gets out of the realm of the inexpensive.) It is recommended that you buy or build the largest greenhouse you can afford, because when you've discovered the joy of greenhouse gardening your family of growing plants will increase rapidly. A small investment in a greenhouse may be the best investment you ever made.

Advantages of ready-made greenhouses:

1. Usually neater than homemade types.
2. Parts are precision-made and they fit better.

Disadvantages of ready-made greenhouses:

1. Usually more expensive.
2. You may have to pay freight charges.
3. They don't always fit your own situation.

Advantages of homemade greenhouses:

1. Can be made from a wide range of materials.
2. Cheaper than factory-made types.
3. Can be made in off sizes.

Whether you want to make yours out of aluminum, wood, or other material will depend on your budget. The new rigid fiberglass materials allow plenty of light to enter and are as good as glass for growing plants. Study the advertisements in horticultural journals and write for literature before you decide to build.

Prefabricated (or "knock-down") greenhouses come with a complete set of plans and instructions from the manufacturer. For making your own "from the ground up," state agricultural colleges are a fine source of bulletins and pamphlets with practical designs and full instructions for construction, including recommended arrangement of benches and walks. Don't hesitate to "ask the man who owns one" (greenhouse) for information on how to build one or how to grow plants under glass.

The following pages give some green thumb guidelines; for greater detail you can consult one of the many books on greenhouse gardening. Our own book, *Organic Gardening Under Glass*, Rodale Press, Emmaus, Pennsylvania (how to raise fruits, vegetables, and flowers) has information based on our twenty-five years as commercial florists and greenhouse operators.

Which Material—Glass, Fiberglass, or Plastic?

Gardeners have a bewildering assortment of greenhouse coverings (called "skins"). Study catalogs from greenhouse manufacturers before you decide and be sure to subscribe to Hobby Greenhouse Association. They have a directory of greenhouse manufacturers that is kept current. Your greenhouse is a onetime lifetime investment. Look them over before you decide. Also, you may want to consult Ortho's "Greenhouse: Planning, Installing and Using."

GLASS It's more breakable, thus more dangerous and difficult to install. It lasts indefinitely, but becomes somewhat brittle with age. If glass cracks and shatters, the entire panel must be replaced. Still, for permanence (and appearance) we prefer glass.

FIBERGLASS Many new, good types are on the market. This material is strong and is not vulnerable to hail or stone damage, but some types get dirty, and do not let in as much light as glass. Many fiberglass panels are covered with a laminated film of polyvinyl fluoride ("Tedlar") which offers resistance to weather, sunlight, and acids.

Fiberglass is 4.4 times more efficient than glass in retaining heat, and 70.8 times as efficient as polyethylene film. Fiberglass panels mean fewer joints through which heat can escape. Corrugation in some types make very tight fit at lap joints, conserving heat.

After several years, fiberglass transmits less light. Another disadvantage is flammability. It will burn when exposed to open flame, but if you're careful with heating units etc. there's no need to worry about your fiberglass greenhouse burning.

PLASTIC FILM Inexpensive, but the least permanent (and least desirable) is flexible plastic film. Construction of a plastic greenhouse per square foot is initially one-sixth to one-tenth the cost of glass. It can be heated as efficiently as glass, but is temporary. Two layers of plastic are better than one, since the dead air spaces give insulation which cuts down on heat loss. This also reduces condensation of moisture on the inside of the plastic. Plastic film is usually stapled on, and replaced as it deteriorates and becomes unsightly. Estimated life of polyethylene is about three years. Newer types last longer. (Polyethylene breaks down due to ultraviolet rays of the sun.)

Thickness of plastic varies from 2 mils. (.002 inches) to 15 mils. (.015) inches. The thicker, the more expensive per square foot. Weatherable polyethylene plastic film, 4 mils. thick ($^1/_{250}$ inch) is the least expensive (and least satisfactory) covering material for hobby greenhouses. Plastic is available in many widths from 2 feet to 40 feet.

Sheet plastic is rolled on and stapled to the roof and sash bars. When the plastic has been applied, wood lath is tacked over the bars. If the plastic house is to be used during the winter months and a snow load is expected, roof bars should be no farther than 20 inches apart.

Greenhouse Types

Yours can be freestanding, which means completely separate from your home. Or, it can be a lean-to type, which is "half of a greenhouse." There are even window greenhouses which can be bought ready to assemble, or you can make your own. A fully freestanding greenhouse has about 50 percent more growing space than a lean-to, but costs more. It also costs more to heat in winter than a lean-to, and because it is separate from the house, involves the added expense of running electric wires and pipes to it. A big advantage to the greenhouse attached to the house is that you can walk from a warm house to your glass house without trudging through rain or snow. Also, it's cheaper to heat the lean-to because one wall is against the side of your house and gets some of its heat from your living area.

Of the large number of greenhouse designs, three major types are conventional, sash, and quonset. Others such as geodesic have been slow to catch on.

If you are going to use glass, fiberglass or plastic a simple design for do-it-yourselfers is.

THE SASH GREENHOUSE: The roof is made up of panels or sashes. The panels are constructed to slide in channels on the roof. Panels covered with sheet plastics are easy to handle. Ventilation is achieved by sliding the panels up and down or by means of ventilators at the roof top. The important and outstanding advantages of this house is that the panels can be removed and stored in a dark room when the greenhouse is not in use. This greatly increases the life of plastic.

You can have a free-standing (left) or lean-to greenhouse. (*Courtesy* Flower and Garden)

QUONSET GREENHOUSES: Patterned after the quonset huts of World War II and designed especially for plastics. The half-circle frames are made of either wood or metal (aluminum). They are covered with one piece of plastic. The greatest advantage is the ease of erection and covering with plastic. Ventilation is only by exhaust fans at the ends of the house.

The details of framing need not be elaborate but must be sufficient. A simple design using 2 × 4's and 2 × 2's can be erected without highly skilled labor.

Before you attempt to build a greenhouse write to a number of greenhouse manufacturers for their catalogues. Study the designs. You may decide it is less expensive to buy a ready-made one and put it together. If you have access to glass you can buy just the frame. Remember that greenhouse glass should be double thickness.

Location Is Important

Where you put your greenhouse makes a big difference between success and failure. Remember, a greenhouse is a sunhouse. Locate your glass house so it gets the maximum available light, especially during the short winter days (at least three hours of wintery sunlight daily). *Don't make the mistake of locating your greenhouse in a spot where your home (or trees) will shade it from the sun.* But keep it as close to the house as possible for convenience. For one thing, electric lines, water, and drainpipes are often handy for hooking into the the greenhouse, thus saving money.

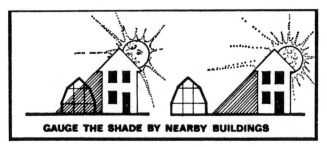

In locating a greenhouse, make sure nearby buildings do not cut off sun. (*Courtesy* Flower and Garden)

A well-placed deciduous tree can provide shade in summer and let sun enter in winter. (*Courtesy* Flower and Garden)

A greenhouse can run north and south, or east and west. It doesn't make much difference. Simply place your greenhouse where it will get the most November to February sunlight. A freestanding greenhouse can be faced in any direction. Usually, if the ends face east and west, the plants on the north side are apt to get some shade. If a greenhouse is attached to your home, give it a south, southeast, or southwest exposure, in that order. A western exposure provides adequate growing light, but needs shading in summer.

Some greenhouses are located on roof tops, ideal for city dwellers. These houses can be faced in any direction so long as they are not shaded by nearby buildings. Window greenhouses can be attached on the east, south, or west side of your home, but make sure they are not shaded by trees in winter.

Some greenhouses are built on a foundation, others (especially plastic types) are simply placed on the ground. For glass in the North, it's a good idea to dig a foundation at least three feet deep and pour a concrete footing. Where temperatures seldom go below freezing, the glass-to-ground greenhouse needs nothing more than a wooden sill of 2 × 6 boards or a 6-inch concrete footing. In the North, it is best to have the footing 3 feet deep, or more.

Be sure to lay your greenhouse water pipes before you lay the footing so you won't end up stumbling over water pipes (or digging up the aisle to install them underground later). Make sure your doors are hinged so that they swing away from the windy direction, instead of into it. Otherwise, you'll spend a lot of time repairing doors and hinges. A gust of wind can snap off a door quickly, especially if it opens into the wind.

HEATING Cost will vary, depending on size of greenhouse, fuel used, and severity or length of winter. You can install a hot-water system, no-vent gas heater, oil-fired warm air heater, or an electric heater. Compare fuel prices before deciding. Any fuel, with either a hot-water or warm-air system, will heat a greenhouse economically and efficiently. Consult greenhouse manufacturers for information on heaters, but don't skimp on heater output.

Open-flame heaters which use natural or bottled gas, kerosene or oil must be vented, using a masonry chimney, or a metal or transite stack. If you don't vent them, their fumes can scorch or burn tender foliage. By sure to check them on cold nights, since a draft can sometimes put out the flame. Greenhouses which are too airtight are apt to snuff out heater flames due to lack of oxygen. Allow tiny cracks in the bottom of doors to admit oxygen.

The so-called no-vent gas heater is one of the best for home greenhouses. The combustion chamber is entirely sealed off outside the greenhouse, and no combustion fumes can harm plants by consuming greenhouse air. No chimney is needed. Built-in blower fans provide even heat distribution. Most of them need no electricity for heat— just for the optional fan, so you would still have heat during a power outage in winter.

Probably the perfect answer for heating the small greenhouse is the electric heater. It is easy to install, completely automatic, and includes a built-in thermostat—with a temperature range anywhere from 50 to 95 degrees F. Many use the farmer's "milk house" heater (farm-supply stores have them) which is simply plugged into an outlet. Such heaters are equipped with a thermostat and a fan distributes the air.

SAVING FUEL: You owe the sun a debt of gratitude for heating your greenhouse during the day. At night, the heat comes from your pocketbook. Lowering greenhouse temperatures both saves on fuel and helps plants grow better. Lower temperatures slow down growth, adding to plants' overall vigor. During the day a good temperature range is 60 to 65 degrees F. A common fallacy is that you need the same amount of heat at night as during the day. Plants like it cool at night. Night temperatures can be as low as 45 to 50 degrees F., but probably the ideal night temperature is 50 to 55 degrees F.

Remember that since a low night temperature results in slower growth, plants take a longer time to flower. Commercial bedding plant growers know that petunias take eight more days from seed to flower if night temperature is dropped from 70 to 60 degrees F. If you sow and transplant later in the spring, you can save fuel and seedlings will still grow fast because of increased light intensity and duration and higher natural temperatures. All tropical plants (such as African violets, gloxinias, episcias) like a consistently warm temperature so keep these "heat-lovers" in the warmest part of your greenhouse.

For starting seeds you need more heat—at least 72 degrees F. both day and night. You can guarantee ample heat for seeds at night by using a heat cable on a small section of a bench. Make yourself a small "propagating house" inside your greenhouse (see Chapter XV).

Here are a few fuel-saving tips:

1. Make your greenhouse as airtight as possible, without shutting off the supply of air. A clear plastic sheet hung on the inside, separated by air space between it and the glass, forms an insulating blanket which can save between 30 and 40 percent on heat.
2. For extremely "loose" greenhouses, place a covering of polyethylene over the entire house.
3. Hang a sheet of heavy-gauge aluminum between the heat line and the outside wall. This reflects heat into the greenhouse where it can be used instead of being absorbed into the wall.
4. Add a double-door arrangement if possible. This forms an air space between the doors, saving heat. Opening the double door will take more time, but the saving in fuel is worth it.
5. Use drop cloth or plastic "skirts" around the base of propagation benches to help confine heat where needed.
6. Consider for heat-loving crops, especially some of the tropical foliage plants, a plastic enclosure over the benches.
7. A mulch under benches will help reduce heat loss to the soil. A couple of inches of coarse bark is fine.
8. Water with warmed water (65-70 degrees F.) for tropical foliage plants and some other warm-season plants grown during the cooler seasons. This means less heat units are taken up by cold water being warmed in the greenhouse.
9. Vent your electric clothes dryer into your greenhouse. This not only gives you extra heat, but extra humidity. The extra heat is usually welcome but on warm days greenhouse vents can be opened or dryer vent can be easily disconnected. A word of

caution: If your dryer is run by gas, there is a possibility of getting products of combustion which are fatal to some plants, particularly orchids. So, don't vent a gas dryer into your greenhouse.

10. Don't forget to lower your night temperature. If the outside temperature is 0 degrees F., by lowering the greenhouse temperature from 65 degrees F. to:

60 degrees F. you'll save 8 percent of your fuel
55 degrees F. you'll save 15 percent of your fuel
50 degrees F. you'll save 23 percent of your fuel
45 degrees F. you'll save 31 percent of your fuel
40 degrees F. you'll save 38 percent of your fuel

For more information on best temperatures for growing specific plants see *Growing Plants Under Lights* in this chapter, also Chapter IX. Temperatures for growing in the greenhouse would be comparable.

BENCHES A greenhouse bench, for your plants and soil or pots, should be at handy working height and at least 4 or 5 inches deep to keep soil from drying out. Less than 4 inches will not maintain good root growth. You will want to be able to level off soil so that it rests about an inch below the top board to prevent water run off.

No need for expensive material for benches. Any lumber is all right; however, hemlock, pecky cypress, and redwood are best because they last longer. You can add a preservative to these and other types of lumber to make them more resistant to rot, but be careful not to use preservatives which are harmful to plants. The only preservative we recommend for greenhouse benches is copper naphthenate.

Generally speaking, benches for the home greenhouse should not be over 2 1/2 or 3 feet wide. This makes it handy to reach plants from either side. Lumber which is 6 or 8 inches wide and 1 inch thick, planed on the "aisle side" is very satisfactory. One-quarter of an inch should be left between bottom boards for drainage. We use 2 × 4's for stringers and set them on cement blocks which are standing on end. If you want to use something even more durable than wood for benches, try Transite, which is made of asbestos and cement.

Some gardeners prefer to raise their crops in ground benches—benches set right on the ground and filled with soil. We prefer raised benches (about 3 feet off the ground) because we use the space underneath for starting bulbs and for growing shade-loving plants. Greenhouse space is usually in short supply.

POTS AND PLANT BOXES If you are using pots, clay or plastic are suitable. Used pots are as good as new ones, if sterilized by soaking in a tub of household bleach solution (see *Sterilizing Pots* in Chapter IX). The bleach is rapidly inactivated, so the solution should be reconstituted after each batch of pots has been sterilized. You can scrub both clay and plastic pots in hot soapy water before sterilizing. For large "flats" or boxes the sterilization process is rather cumbersome, so we merely set ours in full sun for several days after transplants have been removed in spring, then store in a dry, clean place until we're ready to use them again.

You can make your own plant boxes from wood or you can buy paper mâché or plastic. They can be any shape and size that fits the space available as long as they are at least 2 inches deep.

Some useful and space gaining Greenhouse items

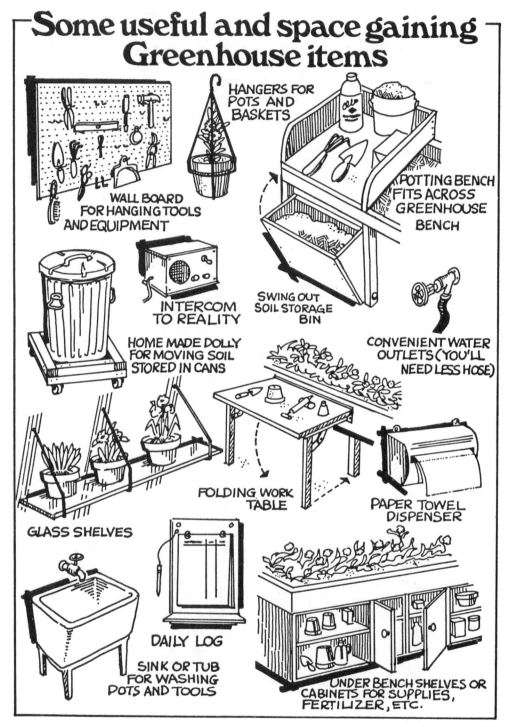

(*Courtesy Lord and Burnham*, Under Glass *Magazine*)

Maintaining Your Greenhouse

SOILS Soils for greenhouse pots and benches need not be a complicated mixture, and you don't need a lot of different mixes for different plants. A good all-purpose mix consists of one part each sand, peat, and ordinary garden loam (loam is the upper 8 inches of soil in your garden). Perlite or vermiculite can be added to loosen up heavy soils. Consistency is more important than fertility. Heavy mixtures mean poor drainage, while too loose a soil means water runs out too fast, and plants dry out quickly. Dehydrated cow or sheep manure can be used with your mixture, along with rotted compost, or leafmold. Some growers add 20 percent superphosphate to the soil mix at a rate of 4 ounces to the bushel. Or, you can use $1/4$ potful of 5-10-5, mixed with a bushel of soil. Later, you can feed your plants a liquid plant food applied with a hose applicator at time of watering (see *Watering* section). Mix your soil in a wheelbarrow (or a portable cement mixer, if available in the neighborhood).

WATERING For the hobbyist, nothing beats the hose for watering pots and benches. There is no need for installing complicated bench watering systems. Experience will teach you when to water, just by tooking at the soil and plants. One way to tell if a plant needs watering is to touch or press the soil with your fingers. Some growers use the listen test: they "tunk" the side of a pot with the nozzle end of a hose. A dull thud means soil is moist, but a hollow ring or a "tunk" means there's a need for water.

In the greenhouse or home, morning or early afternoon are the best times to water plants, since foliage has a chance to dry before evening, thus reducing the dangers of disease.

When you water a pot or the bench, give enough to soak the soil Don't tease your plants with a light sprinkling.

When watering, don't turn the faucet on full force but rather use a gentle stream. It does a better job of soaking the soil and also conserves water.

Have a hook near your faucet where you can hang the hose. It's good sanitation to keep the hose coiled up when not in use. Also watch those drips. They can cost you money and provide a breeding place for mosquitoes and other insects.

Remember that plants vary in their ability to tolerate either a dry or wet soil. Kalanchoes, sedums, crassulus, and other succulents as well as cacti do best in relatively dry soils, while hydrangeas, gardenias, geraniums, ferns, begonias, etc., do best with a constant supply of soil moisture. Most plants are not harmed by wetting the foliage, but there are exceptions. Mum plants may develop mildew or black spots on the foliage if moisture is left on overnight. Plants such as African violet, calceolaria, gloxinia, and others with thick, hairy foliage are injured if water is splashed on the foliage. On African violets, cold water (water lower than room temperature) will cause white or yellowish spots or rings on the leaves.

When a plant is repotted the soil should be watered immediately; water is needed to encourage root formation. Plants in small pots dry out faster than those in larger pots, so they may need watering a second time during the day.

To keep potted plants uniformly moist you can use moisture mats—foam rubber or fiberglass mats, even "indoor/outdoor carpet." Put the mat or carpeting on top of the soil or cinders or sawdust in a bench. Pots are placed on the mat and water is applied. Capillary attraction carries water from the mat to the pot automatically.

HUMIDITY The ideal humidity in a greenhouse is about 60 percent. Normal watering of plants in the enclosed space of a greenhouse releases moisture into the air and keeps plants happy. In summer, the air gets drier, and to correct this you can install a humidifier. Most humidifiers work on the aerosol principle; water in the reservoir is mechanically atomized into minute particles and discharged into the surrounding air, insuring rapid evaporation of the particles into humidity. Another type of greenhouse humidifier consists of a fan which circulates air through aspenwood pads, kept moist by a built-in pump. The simplest way to add moisture to the greenhouse air is to wash down the aisles each morning. It is not a good idea to syringe the plants to maintain humidity, unless you do it early in the morning so the foliage can dry off before nightfall.

VENTILATION Good ventilation is needed for three reasons: 1) To prevent diseases by removing moisture from leaves. 2) To help maintain the proper temperature. 3) To allow removal of air pollutants and the entry of fresh air. Mildew and other fungus diseases increase where air is stagnant in greenhouses. The simplest way to get fresh air into the greenhouse is to open vents or doors a crack. If your heater has no fan that can be operated independently, install an electric fan. You can use an exhaust fan at one end and open louvres at the other end, so that during mild weather the fan can draw air from outdoors right through the entire length of the house. It's a good idea to screen your doors and ventilators in summer, not only for air circulation but to keep bees and insects out. Bees will pollinate certain flowers such as snapdragons, causing the blossoms to drop.

If you're looking for a more elaborate ventilation system, you can try the fan-jet system which provides year-round air circulation plus power ventilation. Greenhouse catalogues list some good fan-jet systems. A unit is installed under a side bench, a few inches away from the end wall. A motorized shutter is installed through the masonry wall and a circular polyethylene tube is attached to the fan-jet collar, extending the full length of the greenhouse under the bench. The tube has exhaust holes punched at intervals and air is circulated through the perforated plastic duct.

Some gas heaters are equipped with a fan circulator. In warm weather, you turn off the heater but leave the fan on at times when the ventilators and doors are not wide open. *Note*: It's a good idea to keep fans going at *night* to prevent moisture from collecting on leaves. This prevents mildew from ruining your crops. On hot sunny days, summer or winter, you'll want to raise the vents to let heat escape and to get fresh air for plants. Close the vents at night to save heat. On hot, humid nights of spring and summer, leave the vents open to prevent condensation on foliage.

SHADING In winter, your greenhouse needs all the light it can get. In summer if you have a glass house you want to cut down on the sun to keep your greenhouse cooler. (Fiberglass doesn't need shading.) There are several ways to shade your greenhouse.

1. The simplest and cheapest is to mix white latex house paint (the cheapest grade available) with water and apply with a paint roller attached to a long handle. The proportion of paint to water would be one to eight, for example 1 cup of paint to 8 cups of water, one gallon of paint to eight gallons of water. (The shading can be applied inside or outside; we prefer outside where it will largely weather away by early fall.)

2. Shading paste, thinned with benzine or gasoline to a watery consistency. Apply twice a year on the outside of glass in mid-spring and early July. One gallon covers 600 square feet.

3. Some still use whitewash—hydrated lime mixed with water to form a milky solution. Apply with a roller. Disadvantage: Lime attacks aluminum.

4. Use aluminum roll-up shades for curved and straight eaves. Shades should run from glass to ground.

5. Use plastic roll shades made of woven Saran to reduce light, running up and down from ridge to sill.

6. Vinyl plastic shading in an attractive green color is available in rolls of various widths and thicknesses. Wash the glass with a wet sponge, then smooth the plastic onto the wet glass with a stiff wallpaper brush or squeegee.

TEMPERATURE ALARMS If you live in the North you should have an alarm system to alert you if the temperature drops. You can lose your entire collection of plants in one night due to a power or heater failure. Alarm systems are inexpensive and installation is simple. A high-low temperature alarm, operated by a battery, sets off a bell or buzzer in your home. It's a good investment.

Note: Be sure to use a battery for your source of power, and check it every fall to make sure it will carry your alarm system through the winter. Place the alarm bell or buzzer in your bedroom, if you're a heavy sleeper. If your alarm systems happen to fail you, and the temperature drops to freezing inside before you discover it, spray your plants with a mist of tap water. Strangely enough this warms up plants, even if ice crystals form on them momentarily. We saved a whole calla lilly crop by this method one frigid night.

As a safety precaution, it might be a good idea to have a stand-by oil or kerosene stove in case something happens to your main source of heat. Be sure these are vented.

Your Obedient Servants—Automation Controls

If you have to watch your pennies, automatic systems of watering, ventilating, shading, misting, and humidifying can be skipped in favor of doing these chores by hand. If money's no object then you can put automatic devices to work to be your hired hand. Don't attempt to go too automatic because half the fun of greenhouse gardening is working with your plants.

HEATING CONTROLS The one automatic control every greenhouse *should* have is a thermostat. Most heaters suitable for greenhouses have built-in thermostats. If you run heating pipes from the house you should add a "zone" with thermostat, and if you buy a heater without a thermostat, you should have one installed. The mercury types are very effective. Be sure to locate in a shaded spot (*not* full sun, or near a heater or boiler), where it doesn't get drafts. Clean your thermostat two or three times during the winter so spider webs don't prevent it from going on.

AUTOMATIC WATERING A master-control system of watering is fine, but since plants vary in their water needs you may not find it handy. A simple system for bench plants includes a length of plastic hose perforated the entire length with tiny openings. One end is attached to a faucet and the hose is placed on the soil between plants. If you really want a lazy man's way to water pot plants, buy a kit containing hollow plastic tubes attached to a molded rubber distributor. A lead weight on the end of each tube holds it in place and water is automatically funneled into the pot. This system can be obtained with an automatic time-clock control.

There are *humidistats* and *automatic misting* systems, but we would put these at the bottom of the priorities. If you are interested, you can get information from greenhouse manufacturers.

VENTILATION CONTROL Automatic ventilation is one of the "frills" we'd keep over all the others. You set the thermostat out of direct sun and draft, and an electric motor opens and closes roof vents automatically. Greenhouse temperatures are stabilized and controlled regardless of outside weather, even when you're not home. This keeps your plants from cooking when the sun comes out unexpectedly after a cool, cloudy period earlier in the day. The reverse is also true; when it turns cool without warning the vent closes automatically. The standard automatic system uses only 10 watts per motor. If there should be a power failure, roof sash closes instantly to keep heat in until service is restored.

Controlling Insects and Diseases under Glass

Since the warmth and humidity of a greenhouse are ideal for rapid growth of insects and diseases, you'll have to be on the alert to keep them out—and down.

1. Sanitation: The number-one means for controlling pests is sanitation. Prevention is easier than eradication. The most common way for insects and diseases to get into your greenhouse is from plants given to you by well-meaning friends. Spray gift plants carefully, check over the foliage for pests, and "quarantine" them for a couple of weeks before you bring them in.
2. Remove and destroy diseased plants and other refuse.
3. Sterilize used pots and flats using household bleach solution (see Chapter IX).
4. In watering, avoid wetting the foliage. Ventilate and circulate heat in the greenhouse to avoid stagnant air and condensation of moisture. Water early in the day so leaves can dry.
5. Don't crowd plants; they need air circulation.
6. Hang hose nozzle on hook to avoid picking up—and spreading—disease organisms.
7. Examine plants periodically. Get the bugs before they get a chance to get your plants.
8. Avoid overwatering and overfeeding, as they can encourage disease problems.
9. Be sure to provide good air circulation because blights are favored by poor circulation—especially at cool and high temperatures.
10. Pull up weeds that grow in and under benches and near the outside of the greenhouse.
11. Screens on doors and vents eliminate most large pests since adults cannot enter to lay eggs.

(See Chapter XIV and Chapter IX for additional information on preventing and controlling plant troubles indoors.)

CHEMICAL CONTROL Very likely, you'll have to contend with three types of insects: sucking, chewing, and rasping. Sucking pests include aphids, white flies, scale, and mealybugs. Chewing pests include ants, cutworms, leafroller, leaf tiers and a few others. Control by spraying with stomach poison such as Malathion. Rasping pests include thrips. Control these and aphids by spraying with a contact insecticide such as Pyrethrum or nicotine sulfate. Scale insects are difficult to control by spraying. Look over your plants and dislodge by scrubbing them with soft toothbrush and soapy water. Red spider mites are so small you can hardly see them with the naked eye. See section on Control of Insects and Diseases. Syringing foliage on hot days keeps them down. Smoke bombs available from greenhouse-supply firms kill most pests, but insects develop immunity to the bomb and you must switch to sprays. A good general purpose spray can be made using: 1 1/2 teaspoons of Malathion (50 percent EC); 2 tablespoons Captan (50 percent WP), 1 teaspoon of household detergent per gallon of tap water. Cover undersides of leaves, and spray once a week or so.

Snails and slugs feed at night. The best control is to go out at night and catch them at work. Hand pick and destroy. Also, keep area under benches clean so slugs cannot hide under debris. (For more information see Section on Control of Insects and Diseases.)

ORGANIC MEANS OF CONTROL Organic gardeners keep insect and disease population down without resorting to high-powered chemicals. Some botanical pesticides used in the greenhouse: nicotine sulfate (Black Leaf 40) is good for aphids and certain sucking pests. Pyrethrum kills thrips and white flies on contact. Ryania is good for certain leaf chewing insects. Rotenone kills aphids, thrips and other chewing insects. Sabadilla—good for stinkbugs and squash bugs. (For a description of these organic pesticides see Chapter XIV.) Garlic-red pepper spray is a home-made organic spray used by serious organic gardeners: spray plants as soon as you see infestation starting. White flies (also called "flying dandruff"), one of the toughest pests to lick, can be controlled by spraying with liquid household detergent as a contact insecticide, 1 tablespoon per gallon of water. Cover top and bottom of foliage.

Greenhouses are especially adaptable for natural control methods. Lacewing flies, ladybugs, praying mantis, and other natural predators which prey on harmful insects, as well as other biological control methods, are listed in detail in Chapter XIV.

Chameleons are interesting little creatures that make good bug catchers. They love the warm humid air of a greenhouse and will eat any tiny creature that moves. Since they take their moisture from drops of water on the leaves of plants the foliage of certain plants must be misted daily to insure ample water to survive. Some people grow a plant or two, such as a gardenia or camellia, which should be misted daily anyhow, especially for their "pet" chameleons. They feed upon insects and will sometimes completely eradicate them. Then their diet must be fortified by mealworms.

Another small animal that lives well in a greenhouse is the toad, if small pans of water are kept under the bench. One toad can eat three thousand insects per month. Like the chameleon, they will need to be fed mealworms if their insect diet diminishes.

Spiders are not liked by many people but we find they do a good job of keeping flying insects cleaned up under benches and in corners. When the supply of insects is gone they move on to other quarters.

Year 'Round Greenhouse Gardening Fun

Greenhouse gardening is a twelve-month operation, but some months are busier than others. The secret for a continuous show is to plan well in advance. For example, plant tulip, daffodil, and hyacinth bulbs in fall for winter and spring show. Then start seed of tomatoes, peppers, eggplants, herbs, melons, and other vegetables in spring for setting outdoors in warm weather; start seed of slow-growing annual flowers and even perennials for planting out later.

You can have a show every month of the year under glass—because the climate is controlled. The busiest time is spring, when you use your greenhouse for starting new plants from cuttings and seeds, for setting outdoors, plus starting some to grow in fall and early winter indoors.

Probably the slackest months are July, August, and September, although you can have blooms and edible crops growing even during these warm months.

Perhaps the best advice for your first year of indoor gardening is: don't overload yourself with more plants than you can comfortably handle. You might better get the feel of handling plants before you opt for a whole crowded houseful of them.

During the "doldrum" greenhouse days of summer, many plants like to be placed outdoors on the shady side of your home, or under a tree. Don't let them dry out completely. Also, spray them with Malathion once a week, and before you bring them indoors in fall, give them a careful checking over, plus another spray so you don't introduce pests into your greenhouse.

Greenhouse Projects You'll Enjoy

A big advantage of owning your own greenhouse is that you can start your own plants from seeds or cuttings—and do it anytime of the year. Homegrown plants are cheaper and you are sure of what you're getting.

STARTING FROM SEED The number-one reason hobbyists (and commercial growers) have poor luck starting seed is lack of heat. Moisture evaporating from the surface of a seed flat cools the soil by ten degrees or more. Another reason why seed flats are cooler than the surrounding air is that often water from the tap is as cold as 45 or 50 degrees F. Such cold water can lower the temperature considerably. Most seed needs temperatures of 70 to 72 degrees F., *day and night*. In a greenhouse it is easy to maintain 70 degrees F. just from the sun, but after the sun goes down so does the heat. The best way to handle this problem is to build a propagating chamber or a seed starter, using an electrical heating cable with thermostat. (See "A Foolproof Seed Sprouter" in Chapter XV.)

STARTING SEEDS: Study the vital information in seed catalogues and on the backs of seed packets. These may tell you if a seed needs light or darkness for germination (see chart in Chapter IV for this and other information on annual seed germination; see also *Starting Your Own Plants* in Chapter XI).

Use a light, porous mixture for starting seeds. It must also be sterile to avoid damping-off disease, the villain that makes seedlings topple over and wilt. We prefer to use one of the soilless mixes such as Jiffy-Mix, Pro-Mix, Redi-Earth, etc., which commercial plantgrowers use.

Do not sow seed thickly, and do not bury it, especially fine seed. Fine seed such as petunia, begonia, and impatiens have little pushing-up power and if covered it will rot. Broadcast or sow seed in rows, omitting a covering if seed is fine. Fine seed nestles down into the crevices and is firmly embedded, without your packing it down. Coarse seed (such as zinnia) can be covered lightly with a loose material such as milled sphagnum moss or Jiffy-Mix. A good rule of thumb is to sow seed at a depth three times the diameter of seed. *A note of caution*: Do not let germinating seeds dry out. Water seed box from below (see *Watering* [sub-irrigation] in Chapter XV) and keep a small amount of water in the pan at all times. After seeds have sprouted they can be moved to a spot on the bench.

SEED STARTERS: Seed can be started in Peat Pellets, Jiffy Pots, peat pots, pressed manure pots, paper cups with holes punched in bottom, fiber pots, plastic and clay pots, and some people even use egg shells. Jiffy Strips (peat pots hitched together) Oasis, Rockwool and other media are some of the useful inventions now available. Seeds and cuttings are inserted in the center. All you do is line the pellets, cubes or pots in a flat tray, plant and water well.

(For more information see Chapter XV, PLANT PROPAGATION.)

TIME OF SOWING If you live in an area where spring frosts threaten outdoor crops in May or June, better not start your plants too early. Gauge your seed-sowing date in the greenhouse according to the day you are safely able to transplant outdoors. For sowing dates of annual flower seeds see chart in Chapter IV.

For example, our traditional outdoor planting date is May 30. So we start such items as tomatoes about six weeks earlier, or about April 15. Peppers, eggplants, and other slower growing items can be started 8 weeks before or about the first of March. Seed catalogues and the back of seed packets give planting tips and usually tell how many weeks in advance to start seed indoors. See *Vegetable Chart*.

TRANSPLANTING When most seedlings are about 1 1/2 inches tall, they can be transplanted into pots or boxes. Use a soil mixture of 1 part each of sand, peat, and loam. In about a week give them a feeding of balanced plant food. They can be grown here for three or four weeks, then set out in a cold frame to toughen them up or "harden them off." Vegetable seedlings seldom if ever need pinching: if they're a bit leggy simply set a bit deeper when transplanting. If flower seedlings seem to be growing a bit tall, pinch the tips back to make them bushy. Pinching invariably makes stockier flower plants with more blooms per plant. Plants for your greenhouse bench also benefit from pinching.

STARTING PLANTS FROM CUTTINGS Your hobby greenhouse pays for itself in many ways, especially when it comes to rooting your own plants from cuttings. You don't need fancy gadgets to do root cuttings and there are some good materials for starting them available today. See Chapter XV for a discussion of these various rooting media. We often put cuttings directly in the bench, water well, then put glass jars over the top, just as you would with rose cuttings outdoors. However, rooting in the greenhouse is much faster.

Bottom heat is helpful in rooting; the heat cable you use for starting seed can also be used for starting houseplants and woody cuttings. If you want to root only a few, nothing beats a home-made plant propagator consisting of a large flower pot filled with sand. A small pot plunged into the center has a drainage hole in it. You fill the large pot with perlite, vermiculite, sand, etc. and insert the cuttings close together into the propagator. Pour water into the small pot.

Grafting and budding are other means of propagating plants in the greenhouse. For complete information on rooting cuttings, grafting, and budding, see Chapter XV, PLANT PROPAGATION.

GROWING BEAUTY UNDER GLASS While fruits, vegetables, and herbs are the big bonus for some hobbyists, others prefer to grow flowering plants and foliages. In the controlled climate of a greenhouse you can grow tropical plants even when the outside temperature is zero or colder. The choice is yours, and you can grow bulbous plants, orchids, violets, as well as many bench crops.

Easy to Grow Cut Flowers

Your hobby greenhouse enables you to enjoy fresh flowers in mid-winter when your spirits need perking up. No limit to the number of flowers you can grow indoors, or for outdoor use later on. Here are a few to try:

CARNATIONS: May be started from seed, or you can buy rooted cuttings. See your local greenhouse for a few rooted or uprooted cuttings. Grow them in pots or in the bench. Main troubles include aphids, whitefly, and red spider mites. (See section on Insect and Disease Control, Chapter XIV.)

CHRYSANTHEMUMS: No cut flower gives the long-lasting show per square foot of bench than mums. Buy rooted cuttings and grow in pots or benches. Mums need pinching for more blooms per plant. Use your greenhouse to get more mileage from outdoor mums. If they are apt to get caught in a fall freeze before bloom, dig them up and bring them into the greenhouse where they'll bloom.

SNAPDRAGONS: Perhaps the most versatile of greenhouse flowers. Be sure to use varieties bred for indoor culture since outdoor garden snaps will make a lot of grassy growth, but produce few or no flowers. Start plants from seed. Snaps are a good economy flower, preferring a cool night temperature, 48 to 50 degrees F., and a day temperature of 60 to 65 degrees F. The more you cut the blooms, the more blooms appear.

OTHER CUT FLOWERS TO TRY: Baby's Breath (gypsophila), feverfew, Forget-Me-Not, gerbera or Transvaal daisy, roses, scarlet plume (*euphorbia fulgens*), statice or sea lavender (*Limonium*): sweet peas, wall flower (*chieranthus*), stocks, asters, calendula—any that take your fancy.

Regardless of which you raise, you can get more mileage from cut flowers if you remember a few tricks florists use: The only food cut flowers have is the sugar that was stored in the leaves and stems during daylight hours. So cut flowers in early evening or late afternoon. After cutting, place them in very warm water (100 degrees F.) instead of cold water. A home-made preservative consists of 1 teaspoon of lime or lemon juice, 1 teaspoon of household bleach, and 1 teaspoon sugar to each quart of water.

ANNUALS For indoor, or to start in your greenhouse for outdoor show, try any of the following: African daisy (*Dimorphotheca*) as pot or bedding plant; ageratum, pot or bedding; alyssum, good in a window box, or pot or bedding; asters, ideal for cut flowers, pot, or bedding. Bachelor's Buttons, ideal for cut flowers, or bedding; balsam, pot or bedding; begonia (fibrous-rooted), excellent pot or bedding plant; Browallia, good in hanging baskets, pots, and urns. Calendula, cut flowers, pot, or bedding; annual carnation, cut flowers, pot plants; chrysanthemum (annual), pot plants and cut flowers; cockscomb (Celosia), dwarfs are good for pots or bedding; coleus, good for indoor pots and outdoor bedding; cosmos, cut flowers and border plant. Dahlias (annual), good pot plant or bedding; Dusty Miller, ideal for urns, boxes, pots, and tubs. Firebush (*Amaranthus*), background plant outdoors. Gazania, cut flowers, pot or bedding; geranium, grown from seed, ideal for pot or bedding; gerbera, one of the showiest flowers for cutting; gloriosa daisy, good indoor plant or for outdoor borders. Heliotrope, bedding plant or winter pot plant. Impatiens, ideal for hanging baskets, pots, tubs, or bedding. Lobelia, bedding plant or in hanging baskets, boxes, and urns. Marigolds, ideal as cut flowers, borders, bedding or background plants, or in pots or urns; Morning Glory, climbs up strings and trellises indoors and outdoors. Nasturtium, ideal as border plants, pots or hanging baskets; Nicotiana (sweet-scented tobacco), dwarfs good for pot or bedding. Periwinkle (Vinca), bedding or winter potting; petunia, pot, bedding, hanging baskets; phlox (annual) hanging baskets, boxes, borders; pinks (annual dianthus) hanging baskets, bedding, and cut flowers. Snapdragon, colorful cut flowers in pots or benches—be sure to grow greenhouse types indoors, outdoor types for transplanting outdoors; statice (annual) dry for winter bouquets or use fresh; stocks, (annual) use greenhouse varieties for indoor flowers, start outdoor stocks inside for outdoor show. Verbena, good border plant, hanging basket, or pot plant but likes a cool germinating temperature. Zinnia, ideal for indoor cut flowers, or outdoor show.

Bulbs under Glass for Year Round Pleasure

Your greenhouse is a great place to grow all kinds of tender bulbs. Tulips, daffodils, crocus, scilla, grape hyacinths are all forced early in the greenhouse. Pot them any time from October to December. Set daffodil and tulip bulbs $1/2$ inch apart with tips just showing above soil surface. Water the pots well and store in cool (about 50 degrees F.) completely dark place for ten to twelve weeks. After that, gradually bring into green-house for forcing. The paper-white narcissus can be forced to bloom without a cold-storage period. Just put bulb in a 4-inch pot or vase of pebbles, add water, and watch it grow. For amaryllis, pot the bulb in a 5-inch pot, so $1/3$ of bulb sticks out; place in cool spot in subdued light for a few weeks until growth begins, then place on bench and give ample water. Calla lily: pot bulb in 5-inch pot. Clivia or Kafir lily (a fleshy rooted plant): pot in 6-inch pot and keep it in same container year after year. Others to try include anemone, achimenes, agapanthus (Lily of the Nile), tuberous begonia, caladium, cannas (dwarf), freesia, haemanthus, iris (bulbous), oxalis, tuberose (*Polianthes*), ranunculus (florists), tigridia (Tiger or Shell flower).

(For more information see Chapter VI, BULBS, CORMS, AND TUBERS.)

Foliage Plants

Most foliage plants like a warm greenhouse, high humidity, rich humusy soil, good ventilation, and diffused light. For the light conditions most foliage plants prefer the greenhouse should be shaded winter and summer—but especially in summer. Here are a few to try: Achimenes, Airplane (or Spider) plant (Chlorophytum), Aluminum Plant (Pilea), Artillery Plant, aspidistra, Baby's Tears (Helxine), Bird of Paradise, boxwood, bromeliads, cactus, Century Plant, Chinese evergreen, coleus, cordyline, Croton, Dumb Cane, dracena, English Ivy, episcia, ferns (Boston and Asparagus), figs (Ficus), Rubber Plant, Fittonia, Jade Plant, Kalanchoe, Kangaroo Vine, Norfolk Island Pine, Palms (many genera), Parlor Maple, Pick-a-Back Plant, Prayer Plant, Rosary Vine, scindapsus (pothos), shamrock (oxalis), Snake Plant, Strawberry begonia (Saxifraga), syngonium, Velvet Plant (*Gynura*), Watermelon Plant (Peperomia), Wax Plant (*Hoya*).

There are hundreds of others worth growing in your greenhouse (see Chapter IX).

Growing Vegetables under Glass

The vegetable you'll grow most is the tomato, easily started from seed. A good greenhouse tomato is mighty tasty when there's 6 inches of snow outdoors, and has no resemblance to the tasteless ones found in the store. Many varieties are bred mainly for greenhouse forcing, although we've grown Moreton Hybrids, Supersonic, and Big Boy in our greenhouse. Commercial growers use Michigan Ohio Forcing Hybrid, or Tuckcross-533 Hybrid. A good pink is Ohio MR 12. If you like the small tomatoes, try Presto and Pixie Hybrid, the size of a half dollar; Tiny Tim (plants only 10 inches high); Patio Hybrid, fruit 2 inches in diameter. Small Fry is a prolific hybrid cherry tomato, plant growing about a foot high. Gardener's Delight is delicious, about the same size as Presto. Both should be trellised or staked. The husk or Strawberry tomato (also called ground cherry), is not a real tomato (see Chapter XI), makes a good potted plant for the greenhouse. Its fruit is tasty eaten out of hand or in pies.

Tomatoes in the greenhouse can be grown in pots, tubs, and hanging baskets. They take the same general culture as in the garden (see Chapter XI). If you don't have a fan in your greenhouse pollination will have to be done by hand (with a soft brush, transfer pollen by going from plant to plant and "tickling" the blossoms).

Other vegetables you may want to try include beans (bush, pole, and baby limas), beets, carrots, chard, corn (midget types), cress, cucumbers (Femland is good for the greenhouse or try one of the mini-cukes such as Cherokee), dandelions (seed of tame varieties available from many seed houses), eggplants (try Morden Midget and Early Dwarf), endive, onions, garlic, leeks.

Lettuce is one of the easiest to grow. Try Buttercrunch, Salad Bowl, and Tendergreen. A number of new varieties from England and Holland show great promise for greenhouse culture.

Mushrooms can be grown under the bench. Obtain spawn from a seed house (see Chapter XI).

Muskmelons of any kind can be trained to grow up a string or trellis; try Harper hybrid. Sugar Baby, Yellow Baby, and other "icebox" watermelons do well under glass. All members of the onion family can be greenhouse-grown. For peas, grow the edible-podded type. They are a cool-weather crop, so start in mid-winter in the greenhouse. Sweet potatoes grow up a wire or trellis. Let them climb up to take advantage of the space under the roof.

Radish grows fine in the greenhouse, except in mid-winter. You can harvest a crop three weeks after sowing seed. In mid-winter it takes about four to six weeks to harvest a crop due to day length and temperatures. In fall months, it's hard to get them to form bottoms.

Rhubarb should be left outdoors in fall until after a hard freeze, then brought indoors. Best way is to make a planting box full of loose soil. Bury the clumps in the soil in fall. Bring into the greenhouse in February for forcing.

Herbs Under Glass

Another benefit of owning your own greenhouse is fresh herbs all year round. Herbs require little care under glass. They'll need an occasional syringing to keep dust off and make them fresh-looking. If insects happen to bother them, spray with soap and water.

GROW IN CONTAINERS: Clay or plastic pots, tubs, boxes and even the bench can be used for growing herbs. Any kind of container is suitable. (See Chapter VIII for suggestions.) Baskets hanging from the roof take up little space. Place pots along the edges of benches so the herbs can hang over the sides.

HOW TO START: You can buy seed and start your own or buy started plants from the nursery, catalogue, or garden store. When the plants start to get twiggy or woody, snip them back to encourage new growth. It's also a good idea to replace old plants with new ones started from seed. See Chapter X for more detail on culture of individual herbs, including harvesting and storing.

The list is endless. but here are a few you can try:

Basil: 12 varieties. One plant takes 4 square inches of space.

Chives: A clump grows in 4-inch pot.

Dill: Grow in pot or bench, needs staking.

Fennel: Plant in bench 6 inches apart.

Lemon Balm: One or two plants grown in 8- to 10-inch space.

Lemon Verbena: One plant in 5-inch pot, or four square inches of space.

Sweet Marjoram: One plant per 5-inch pot.

Nasturtium: Grow in hanging basket from roof.

Parsley: One plant needs 4 square inches or grow in bench.

Peppergrass: Sow seed in box and grow under bench.

Peppermint: Plant root or seeds in 5-inch pot, keep watered under bench.

Rosemary: Grow one plant in 5-inch pot.

Sage: Allow one plant per 5-inch pot. Remove dead wood.

Savory: One plant 4 to 5 inches apart, or 1 in pot.

Shallots: Place 2 inches deep, 2 inches apart in bench.

Spearmint: Plant root or seeds in 5-inch pot, and grow under bench.

Tarragon: Put root cuttings in 8-inch pot, or allow one plant per 8 square inches.

Thyme: Sow seeds in pots, thin to one or two plants per 4-inch pot.

Watercress: Grow in boxes under bench, keep watered.

GROW YOUR OWN FRUITS UNDER GLASS

What a surprise you're in for when you find out what kinds of fruits you can grow under glass! We've raised blueberries, blackberries, strawberries, even gooseberries and currants in our greenhouse. Don't hesitate to try all kinds, and even if you harvest only enough for a meal, it's worth the effort to taste an exotic fruit or pick a berry in the winter months. Just one or two plants of each in tubs or boxes can give an endless amount of satisfaction.

•**Banana** Many species of banana plants are used for ornamental purposes. The fruit of some species must be cooked to be edible. The Dwarf Banana (*Musa nana cavendishii*) produces delicious fruit; likes a loose, humusy soil and uniform supply of moisture. Buy started plants from a reliable nursery.

•**Citrus** Family includes lemons, limes, oranges, grapefruit, and tangerines. Wonderful for foliage, flowers, and fruit. *C. aurantifolia* bears small, edible limes. C *Limonia ponderosa* (Ponderosa lemon) produces edible lemons weighing over 2 pounds. *C. mitis* (Calamondin or miniature orange) has fragrant white flowers, edible fruits 1 to $1^1/_2$ inches in diameter. *C nobilis deliciosa*, the Mandarin orange, is a fine citrus for the greenhouse.

CULTURE: All citrus like a loose, well drained soil, one part each of sand, peat, and loam fortified with $^1/_2$ cup of bone meal to each peck. A good soaking once a week is ample. Also syringe leaves to wash away dust and to keep insects down. Spring or early summer is a good time to give citrus a light pruning, cutting out any extra-long shoots for symmetry. Repot every three or four years. During the summer you can place the plants outdoors in a partially shaded spot, keep watered, and in fall, bring in before frost. Summer treatment ripens the wood and prepares fruit for fall and winter display. Citrus likes cool temperatures, 40 to 50 degrees F. at night, during winter. Also, give full sun and plenty of fresh air. Temperature and sunlight are important in bringing plants into flower and fruit.

In a greenhouse, hand pollination is needed for decorative fruit. All citrus need pollination indoors, and you can help this along by using a small paintbrush or tip of your finger to tickle each bloom, spreading pollen from one flower to another.

PROPAGATION: Seeds, cuttings, or purchased plants. For edible fruits your best bet is buying grafted or budded plants from the nursery.

TROUBLES: *Failure to flower*. Due to lack of summer ripening period (see *Culture*). Dropping of buds, flowers, and small fruits, due to lack of light, improper water (too much or too little), or high temperature.

Black coating on leaves. Sooty blotch, or mold gathering on secretions from aphids or scale. Wash off with detergent or soapy water. Spray with Malathion, 1 teaspoon to 2 quarts of water, to check pests.

Yellowing of leaves. Due to poor drainage, too much water, poor light, or pests in the soil.

•**Fig** In a small greenhouse, dwarf figs can be harvested over a long period. Buy started plants and grow in tubs which can be moved outdoors in summer and brought indoors in fall. (See Chapter XII.)

TROUBLES: Look for scales, aphids, red spider mites. See Section on Insect and Disease Control

Failure to bear: Due to lack of pollination, age of plant, or insufficient light.

•**Pineapple** Cut the top off a pineapple, with about an inch of fruit attached, lay it aside for a week to get a callus (leathery tissue forming over the cut). Place in a soup bowl with a small amount of water in bottom. Rooting takes place within a few weeks. After that, pot it up in a 6-inch pot of sand, peat, and loam. After several months a "red bud" (blossom cluster) may form. Or you can force it by placing a plastic bag over the mature plant, enclosing an apple inside the tent. Apples give off ethylene gas which will force the plant to flower and form fruit.

Other fruits such as mango, papaya, date, are also suitable for greenhouse growing. The avocado, sprouted from an avocado pit, develops into a green, luxuriant plant.

Hydroponics is merely the process of growing plants in a nutrient solution, rather than soil. It's simple—nutrient-rich water solution is washed or pumped through light gravel, sand or perlite which anchor the roots. The process is also called aquaculture, nutriculture, or just plain hydroculture. Anyone interested in pursuing hydroponics should write to the Hydroponic Society of America, Box 6067, Concord CA 94553.

How to Make Hotbeds and Cold Frames

Cold frames and hotbeds are similar in construction but serve different purposes. They differ primarily in their source (and degree) of heat and degree of insulation.

COLD FRAMES A cold frame utilizes the sun's heat, with no artificial heat supplied. The soil is warmed during the day, then gives off heat at night to keep the plants warm. The frame may be banked with insulating material like straw, sawdust, or leaves to insulate it from the cold outside air. Or mats of straw, paper, or cloth may be placed over the sash at night to conserve the heat.

Cold frames are used to "harden" plants which have been started in the greenhouse or hotbed before transplanting to the garden. The process of hardening matures succulent tissues, thereby reducing injury from sudden temperature drop and from conditions which favor rapid drying after transplanting. Cold frames can also be used for starting plants in spring or summer.

Early lettuce and radishes as well as bulbs and perennials can be forced in a cold frame a few weeks before normal season. Cold frames are also used for azaleas, heather, hydrangeas, and other tender plants. These plants may be set directly in the soil of a cold frame or in pots or flats. Chrysanthemum "mother" plants and biennials are also placed in a cold frame for winter protection. Cyclamen, azaleas, and some houseplants may be grown in a cold frame during the summer. Partial shade should be given to these plants in the summer by using lath sash or a roll of snow fence in place of the glass sash.

Since cold frames are movable, they can be erected or set over beds of pansies, violets, primroses, etc., in very early spring to bring these plants into bloom ahead of normal season. Just set the frame over the plants which are to be forced and bank the outside with leaves or straw to keep out the cold. Rhubarb can be forced a couple of weeks earlier in the same manner. All types of woody cuttings can be propagated during summer months.

Spring-flowering bulbs planted in flats or pots of soil can be placed in the cold frame in the fall, then removed after proper storage to the house or greenhouse for forcing. (Leave them in cold storage until the first week in January, then remove.) To do this, pot up the bulbs and place in the frame. Cover the pots with 6 to 8 inches of peat moss or sawdust for insulation. Additional protection is provided to keep the temperature from fluctuating by banking the sides and covering the glass as previously described.

HOTBEDS Hotbeds are cold frames which have artificial heat added plus extra insulation. Heated frames or hotbeds are used for bulbs, azaleas, hydrangeas, and chrysanthemums during winter and fall. They are ideal for starting vegetable and annual flowering plants from seed. Propagation of cuttings from woody plants and ground covers such as pachysandra can also be accomplished in a hotbed. Lettuce, radishes and onions can be grown in the hotbed in late winter and early spring. They are a good place to start perennials from seed in fall and winter.

CONSTRUCTION OF COLD FRAMES AND HOTBEDS Cold frames are built of wood 2 inches thick for rigidity, but wood only an inch thick may be substituted. Cypress, redwood, or hemlock are the best now available. Heartwood grades are best because they are most resistant to decay. However, there are corrosive effects from compounds contained in redwood. For this reason, it is suggested that aluminum or hot dipped galvanized nails, screws, or bolts be used to fasten the wood.

Wood-preserving materials that contain zinc or copper are best for treating wood to be used in frame construction. Wood that has been treated for decay resistance with pentachlorophenol, mercury, or creosote compounds must *not* be used in plant-growing structures. Toxic fumes from these compounds will injure or kill plants.

The standard sash for covering cold frames and hotbeds is 3 feet wide by 6 feet long with three rows of 10-inch glass lapped to allow rainwater to run lengthwise. (Some gardeners use old window or storm sash.) Construction can be made simpler by using plastics stapled to sash. The various materials available for glazing of sash if glass is used are discussed under *Greenhouses*. You can make a hotbed or cold frame any size you wish. It's a good way to use up scrap lumber. We have made many over the years and none cost more than a few dollars.

A hotbed or heated frame is similar in construction to a cold frame except for the addition of an 8-inch board below the ground. The walls are sometimes insulated and are usually higher than those of cold frames to permit tall-growing plants to be placed in them.

Artificial heat is supplied by electricity, i.e. light bulbs or electric cable, steam pipes, hot-water pipes (if connected to the house), even fresh horse manure.

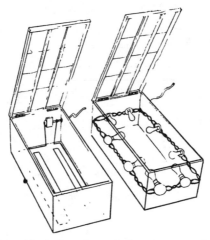

A small electrically heated hotbed may be made from scrap material around your home. You can buy heating cable from greenhouse supply companies, garden centers, or seed houses. Left: hotbed heated by cable. Right: light bulbs are used as a source of heat.

A plastic-covered electric cable is the most frequently used method of heating hotbeds. The covering is necessary to resist corrosion. A thermostat controls the heat in the cable automatically, assuring constant temperature.

Heating cables can be purchased in various lengths and used on a 110-volt power supply. Ask for cable especially made for hotbed use, since it is watertight with waterproof thermostats. Both the heating cable and thermostats can be purchased from garden supply houses.

To install the cable in a frame, put a 12-inch layer of fine gravel or cinders below the hotbed to provide both insulation and drainage. Next, add a 1-inch layer of sand or soil which acts as a bed for laying out the electric cable. Loop the cable back and forth across the bed, 3 inches from the sides and with the lines 6 inches apart. On top of the cable place hardware cloth, 1/4-inch mesh, to act as a heat conductor and help keep uniform temperatures. Soil or coarse sand is then placed on the hardware cloth to a depth of 4 to 6 inches.

For less expensive heating, use electric light bulbs. Use eight 25-watt bulbs for heating a 3'×6' frame mounted on a strip of wood spanning the bed just beneath the center of the sash. If fewer bulbs are used, they must be of higher wattage. A thermometer set in the soil of the frame (or simply laid on the soil surface) will help you tell if the heat will be sufficient for your purposes. Porcelain sockets and waterproof electric wire cable must be used for the installation.

Fresh horse manure is an inexpensive way to heat your hotbed. The horse population has never been greater, which means piles of horse manure available for the asking. Dig a hole under the frame 8 inches deep (see illustration), fill with fresh horse

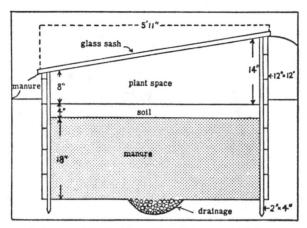

Cross-section of a homemade hotbed heated by manure, an old-fashioned method that's coming back in style.

manure then cover with loose soil to a depth of 3 or 4 inches. (The manure must be renewed every year.)

CARE OF COLD FRAMES AND HOTBEDS Seeds started in a cold frame or hotbed can be sown directly in the earth of the frame or in flats or pots. If the seed is to be sown directly, the soil is prepared by spading and raking to provide a finely-pulverized bed. A4-inch layer of peat moss added before spading is beneficial.

For sowing in pots or flats, 3 or 4 inches of the soil is removed and replaced with cinders. This provides drainage for the bed and prevents worms from entering the pots or flats.

Cuttings may be started in the frames during the summer months by substituting sand, sand and peat, or perlite for the soil.

Ventilation of the frames during the spring months is important. The temperature inside the frames should not rise above 70 degrees F. during periods of sunshine. Use wooden blocks to raise or lower the sash on the side opposite the direction of the wind, then close the sashes before sundown to conserve heat. If the night temperature is expected to fall below 40 degrees F., cover the sash with insulating mats.

Watering must be done in the morning so that the plants will dry off before the frame is closed for the night. Care must be taken to avoid getting the soil too wet during periods of low temperature and cloudy days. Such conditions favor damping-off fungus, which quickly kills young seedlings.

Gardening under Lights

All plants need light in order to grow. With insufficient light, they become spindly, unattractive, and unproductive. Many gardeners like to garden during winter when days are short but do not have windows which provide enough light. An inexpensive way to overcome this is to use lights.

Fluorescent lights for indoor plant growing are available under a wide variety of trade names and all can be used with a considerable degree of success.

Fluorescent tubes have been found to be quite adequate for plants that do not need full sun. They provide only blue and red light, without the far red found in sunlight. When plants which normally like full sun are grown only for transplanting into the garden, fluorescent alone is sufficient, but if they are to bloom well indoors, an incandescent bulb must be added to the light system to provide far red light. For most plants the proper ratio is 20 to 25 watts of incandescent light for each 20 watts of fluorescent light. Should some of your plants still not bloom, use a 40-watt incandescent bulb.

There are many plants which will bloom satisfactorily under fluorescent lights alone. African violets, begonias, gloxinias, impatiens and episcias are good examples. We have good luck combining winter light from a northeast window with a fluorescent fixture. The window itself does not provide enough light, nor would the fluorescent alone, but with the two, we have blooms from begonias, geraniums, and kalanchoes all winter long.

Incandescent light must almost never be used alone, however. Plants grown only under incandescent light tend to grow tall and spindly and bloom prematurely. Some flowering bulbs are an exception.

There are many excellent specially-made fixtures on the market for home gardeners. They come in all sizes and arrangements. You can purchase adjustable shelved plant stands with fluorescent lights underneath, or fixtures on adjustable legs which can be set on tables, benches, or stands. Many are decorative as well as utilitarian. Some are built into terrarium-like cases for humidity-loving plants such as orchids.

If you wish to make your own, you can start by using a 4-foot, 2- or 3-tube, 40-watt industrial fixture with a reflector. For convenience and efficiency a poultry-type clock switch which will turn lights on and off can be placed in the circuit. If the temperature is abnormally low, i.e., lower than 50 degrees F. at times, provision should also be made for a heating cable, probably with its own separate circuit, to provide bottom heat. Follow the instructions for installation of heating cable under *Hotbeds*.

You may prefer either the "pink light" tubes or daylight (cool white) fluorescent; many growers feel that plants respond better to a combination of the two.

The names manufacturers give to their fluorescent lamps are not to be taken literally. Trying to select lamps from a manufacturer's availability chart is an exercise in theory, not very helpful to the amateur. A "daylight" lamp does not really simulate daylight, a "natural white" lamp does not actually duplicate the sun's light, and a "cool white" lamp feels no different to the touch than a "warm white" lamp. Have your garden center clerk help you select the fluorescent lamp which best suits your pocketbook.

Intensity of the light is an important factor to be considered. Each plant has its own requirements, and in order to vary the intensity with maximum flexibility, the fixture should be hung on pulley arrangements. Raising the fixtures decreases light intensity at plant level: lowering the fixture increases it. For seedlings of vegetable and flower plants, it's advisable to lower the fixture to within 6 inches of the plants. Some spring-flowering bulbs can be forced at lower intensities, thus calling for a greater distance from the fixture. Tulips and daffodils can be 24 inches away—in fact they are one of the few types of plants that can be forced with incandescent lights only.

TEMPERATURE FOR SEEDLINGS For seedlings to grow well a temperature range of 60 to 65 degrees F. must be maintained at night, with a daytime temperature 5 degrees F. higher. This temperature range equals roughly what you may maintain in most rooms of your house. Annual plants also need at least a 10-degree drop at night: they simply cannot grow stocky and vigorous when the temperature is constantly in the 70- to 80-degree F. range. With this overstimulation, the plants become weak and spindly.

Plants for the garden may also be grown successfully at a day and night temperature range of 50 to 55 degrees F. A basement or porch can be used to good advantage here. Note that seeds requiring 65 to 75 degrees F. for germination should be germinated at that temperature. After the seedlings have come up, they may be kept at 50 to 55 degrees F. See charts in Chapter XV, PLANT PROPAGATION; Chapter IV, FLOWERING ANNUALS, and Chapter XI, VEGETABLE GARDENING.

LIGHTING OF SEEDLINGS When artificial light is used try to light plants fourteen to eighteen hours per day from time of sowing (except seeds requiring darkness for germination; see chart in Chapter IV) until garden size. The young plants would grow too slowly if lighted for fewer hours per day.

Some flowering plants and vegetables grow well at only nine hours per day. However, the plants will grow much faster if they are lighted eighteen hours per day. Allow four to twelve weeks growing time from seeding to planting size depending upon the specific vegetable or flower. For annual flowers see chart at end of Chapter IV. For vegetables see reference under each item in Chapter XI. The following is a chart showing time, temperature, and light intensity requirements for cuttings and seedlings of some commonly grown plants.

CUTTINGS AND SEEDLINGS*

Plant	Duration	Temperature (F.)	Height Above Plants
Alyssum	15 hours	65°-70°	6-8 inches
Chrysanthemum	15 hours	55°-65°	6-8 inches
Dahlia	15 hours	60°-70°	6-8 inches
Marigold	15 hours	60°-70°	6-8 inches
Petunia	15 hours	60°-70°	6-8 inches
Stock	15 hours	55°-65°	6-8 inches
Zinnia	15 hours	65°-70°	6-8 inches
Tomato	15 hours	65°-76°	6-8 inches
Peppers	15 hours	72°-75°	6-8 inches
Cabbage and related plants	14 hours	55°-65°	6-8 inches
Melons	15 hours	72°-75°	6-8 inches

*Based on information furnished by University of Wisconsin.

The George W. Park Seed Company has kindly given us their findings on growing annuals for winter bloom and bedding plants for the garden. The following plants need at least sixteen hours of light (6 to 8 inches above the plants) but not more than eighteen hours. The same light requirements apply for the first six weeks whether the plants are grown to bloom indoors or for bedding plants outdoors.

Aster	Gaillardia	Poppy	Snapdragon
Calliopsis	Gomphrena	Portulaca	Sunflower
Celosia	Marigold	Rudbeckia	Verbena
Cornflower	Morning Glory	*Salpiglossis*	Zinnias
Cosmos	Petunia	Salvia	
Dahlia	Phlox	Scabiosa	

ANNUALS FOR WINTER BLOOM These plants start blooming eight to twelve weeks from date of sowing if they are lighted as mentioned and kept at day and night temperatures of 70 to 75 degrees F. All will not bloom within the same length of time. Petunias will take twelve weeks or more whereas many varieties of marigolds will bloom in eight weeks. See "Seed Starting Chart" in Chapter IV.

The seedlings may be thinned to stand 2 inches apart or may be transplanted in 2 1/4-inch Jiffy Pots or other containers. The plants will not branch well, but bloom normally and quickly. Start seeds under fluorescent lights only; turn on incandescent bulbs after six weeks.

BEDDING PLANTS FOR THE GARDEN A young plant should first grow many side branches and then flowers. It needs a strong foundation on which it can build a dazzling display of flowers all summer long. A plant with only one stalk already in bloom will seldom grow to any appreciable size. Following the temperature and day-length schedules given above will produce compact, bushy plants which bloom soon after they are planted in the garden. Use fluorescent lights only. When side branches are showing and the leaves of neighboring plants touch each other, give the plants more space or the side branches will not develop properly.

VEGETABLE PLANTS Vegetable seeds may be started and seedlings grown under lights in the same manner as bedding plants for the garden. Cool season crops should be given the low temperature treatment, lighting all plants sixteen to eighteen hours per day from sowing until garden size.

Cool-temperature vegetables include cabbage, Brussels sprouts, broccoli, cauliflower, lettuce, collards, mustard, radishes, onions, parsley, and spinach. After seed is up, transplant when 1 inch tall and grow cool, 55 to 65 degrees F. Herbs may also be started under lights in the same manner as bedding plants and vegetables. See *Herbs*.

High-temperature vegetables are eggplant, tomato, pepper, squash, melons, and cucumbers. (See *Starting Your Own Plants* in Chapter XI.) Best germination temperature is 75 degrees F.

HOUSEPLANTS Most houseplants grown under fluorescent light, including seedlings, thrive on fourteen to sixteen hours of light out of every twenty-four in a temperature range of 62 to 70 degrees F., and 40 to 60 percent humidity. The usual routine is to turn on the fluorescent unit around 7:00 A.M. and off at about 10:00 P.M. Here's where it's handy to have an automatic timer so that the lights are turned on and off regularly. Add incandescent bulbs when flowers are desired and thereafter while the plants are flowering.

Some houseplants require separate lighting schedules for their two stages of development. In the first, vegetative stage, the plants grow branches and leaves. In the second stage, flowers are formed, and this is the most critical time. What actually triggers these plants to form buds is the number of hours of complete darkness. The critical "day length" of many popular flowers is discussed in this book under individual flower entries. When you switch off the lights, the room must be totally dark, with no light from windows or lamps in the room or any source, reaching the plants. This is easily done in a basement where there is likely to be no light at all. If light does reach your plants, cover them with a heavy opaque cloth extending to the floor, in order to shut out all light.

Remember that some plants are especially sensitive to day length and may not flower if given too long a light period such as the Christmas Cactus and Poinsettia (see in Chapter IX).

The following chart gives you an idea of the requirements of some common houseplants that can be grown under lights:

LIGHT AND TEMPERATURE CHART *

Plant	Duration	Temperature (F.)	Height Above Plants
African violets	12-18 hours	60°-65°	10-12 inches
Begonias	12 hours	60°-65°	8-10 inches
Calceolaria	9 hours	40°-50°	6-8 inches
Cineraria	15 hours	40°-50°	6-8 inches
Cyclamen	15 hours	50°-60°	6-8 inches
Geraniums	15 hours	55°-50°	6-8 inches
Gloxinia	15 hours	55°-60°	10-12 inches
Kalanchoe	9 hours	65°	8-10 inches
Most other houseplants	12-18 hours	60°-65°	12-24 inches

*University of Wisconsin

BULBS UNDER LIGHTS Spring-flowering bulbs need a cool treatment in fall (see *Tulips* section). After the cool period, they can be forced into bloom under lights. Light should be placed 12 to 15 inches above the leaves. They should be lighted twelve hours at 50 to 60 degrees F.

The following bulbs bloom under incandescent lights (100 watts is sufficient): daffodils, tulips, (for both choose early-flowering varieties), hyacinths, crocuses, chionodoxa, muscari, puschkinia, snowdrops, and scilla.

The following will bloom under fluorescent lights: allium, amaryllis, anemone, bletilla, calla, cyclamen, Dutch iris, epidendrum, freesia, fritillaria, ranunculus, tuberous begonias, gloxinias, and other bulbous gesneriads.

Of all the lilies, the Easter lily is one of the easiest to grow under fluorescent lights. Only two 20-watt tubes are needed. Plant the bulb in a 6-inch pot of well drained soil level with the surface and store in a dark place at a temperature of 55 to 60 degrees F. Water regularly while the roots are growing and in three to four weeks sprouts will appear. Now place the lily under the lights at a distance of 10 inches, giving nine hours of light a day, raising the tubes as the stem grows. Longer day length will reduce the number of flowers and make the plant too tall. A light intensity of 400 to 500 foot-candles is best. Most other spring bulbs need no fertilizer, but feed your lilies once a week with liquid fertilizer. The best growing temperature is 55 degrees F., although it may be as high as 70 degrees F.

For more detailed information on greenhouses, coldframes, and hot beds, see *Organic Gardening Under Glass*, Rodale Press. See also *Greenhouses; Planning, Installing, and Using*, Ortho Books. You can also join Hobby Greenhouse Association, a nonprofit organization dedicated to promoting greenhouse gardening as a hobby or vocation. It disseminates practical information in its quarterly magazine. Write to Hobby Greenhouse Association, 8 Glen Terrace, Bedford, MA 01730-2048.

CHAPTER XVII

Insect and Animal Control

•

Controlling Insects in and Around the Home

The best way to control insects (or diseases) in the home, greenhouse, or garden (for garden insects see *Other Common Garden Insect Pests*) is by practicing sanitation and prevention. Sanitation means picking off and destroying dead leaves, cleaning up debris, sterilizing pots, etc. Prevention means such things as avoiding overfeeding and overwatering, eradicating any plant that's heavily infested and spraying with a pesticide before troubles get out of hand. An ounce of prevention is still worth a pound of cure.

SPRAYERS: If you spray you might want to try a cordless electric (rechargeable) sprayer. We find them easy to operate and carry. They contain from $1/2$ to a gallon of spray and have an adjustable nozzle which enables spray materials to be directed to the undersides of leaves where insects are likely to congregate. Agitate sprayers frequently to keep solution mixed.

There are many compressed-air sprayers which hold between 1 and 3 gallons of spray. Types which attach to a garden hose are also popular. The jar attachment contains a concentrated solution which dilutes as it comes from the hose.

The "slide trombone" sprayer is one of the best for the home gardener. It's light and will reach tree tops 30 feet high. The nozzle adjusts from fine mist to full stream. Mix spray in a bucket and put the hose in and start spraying. You work it like a trombone.

Be sure to wash and clean all sprayers as soon as the job is done.

DUSTING: For dusting, get a good plunger-type duster, holding 1 to 3 pounds, with a spoon nozzle which allows the dust to be directed to the undersides of the leaves, where bugs and disease organisms congregate.

Personally, we prefer spraying to dusting, because sprays stick to the foliage longer than dusts and can be applied at any time during the day (but with less danger of plant injury if applied in early morning or late afternoon). Dusting is appealing to some gardeners, because dust is all ready to use. It sticks better if put on in early morning or late evening, when the foliage is moist. Apply a thin layer and repeat as often as necessary to keep new growth covered. Don't work on the theory that if a little does a lot of good, a lot will be even better. A heavy dose makes a plant unsightly and may be injurious.

There are nearly a million kinds of insects so you can see why it is impossible to list them all here. We have chosen for this chart those which most commonly trouble home gardeners and homemakers. For insect problems on specific plants, refer to the plant under the appropriate chapter. If you have trouble identifying a particular insect write to your state agricultural college for help.

Here are the insects we receive the most complaints about and tips for coping with them. Remember, only one tenth of one percent of all insects is bad.

Insect	Description	Damage	Natural Control	Chemical Control
ANT	1/8″ to 1/2″ brown, black or red. Live in colonies.	Live in mulches, lawns, and invade homes. Found in cupboards looking for sweet foods. Dry out plant roots, often build anthills on lawns. Nuisance in outdoor eating areas.	Pour boiling water on hill, or ammonia water.	Spray or dust with Nicotine solution.
APHIDS or "PLANT LICE"	Light green (white, black, pink, red, brown, lavender, yellow) plump, soft-bodied pests 1/12–1/8″ long, found in both wingless and winged forms on tips of shoots.	Suck plant juices, check growth, secrete sticky honeydew.	Ladybugs a natural predator. Use aluminum foil as a mulch.	Nicotine sulfate or Malathion, 1 tb. to 1 gallon.
BIRD LICE	Tiny (1/16″) specks in bird houses, on porches where birds gather or nest.	Nuisance to humans if nests near house. In great numbers can kill baby birds.	Provide sand for birds to take dust baths.	Early in spring, clean out old nest and destroy debris. Flush with detergent water solution.
CENTIPEDE	Flat, brownish, fast-moving insect, 1″–3″, many pairs of legs. Beneficial, as it feeds upon smaller insects.	Sting can be painful. Found in soils, basements, greenhouses, laundry rooms. Also in plant soils. Not harmful to plants.	Use vacuum sweeper on them. Also dust with hot pepper in area where found.	Spray with Malathion or Diazinon. Borax discourages them if dusted in area where found.

Insect	Description	Damage	Natural Control	Chemical Control
CLOVER MITES	Hordes of tiny ($1/30''$) mites, resemble crawling pepper specks on foundation and clapboards, harmless to humans and most plants.	Crawl over grasses and enter homes via foundation. Crawl on furniture, indoor walls & ceilings, but cause no damage to houseplants. Will stain if crushed.	None known.	Chemical control not easy. Try dust or spray of Malathion.
CLOTHES MOTH	Small whitish-gray moth $3/8''$ lays eggs in dark areas.	Larvae eat fabrics of woolen and synthetic fibers.	Line closets with cedar. Use Ced-o-Flora spray.	Napthalene flakes or balls.
COCKROACHES	Brownish cricket-like pest 1"- $1 1/2''$ long. Found along baseboard, food storage areas; come out at night. Breed rapidly in warm areas.	Spread filth, contaminate food.	Spiders. Keep all food tightly covered in storage. Keep crumbs cleaned up.	Boric acid powder applied with small hand duster in cabinet shelves, under sinks, etc. Poison baits and contact poisons used with care.
CUTWORM	$1 1/2''$ grayish "C"-shaped grub found in soil.	Cut young plants off at ground level.	Birds, ducks, geese. Wrap piece of wax paper, tarpaper, foil (or put milk carton) around base of plant for a barrier. Be sure barrier is pushed into soil so worm can't get under.	Dust with wood ashes around base of plant.
EARWIGS	$3/8''$ to $3/4''$ long, pair of pinchers on end. Brown.	A nuisance on plants and in homes. Will eat blossoms. Enter homes by newspapers, mop, laundry. Attack plants only.	Leave rags outdoors; each morning drop in boiling water. Hand pick and destroy. Bantam chickens clean them up.	None satisfactory.

485

Insect	Description	Damage	Natural Control	Chemical Control
FLIES *Blow fly* *House fly* *Horse fly* *Cluster fly* *Buckwheat fly* *Honey fly*	Winged pests, all similar in appearance, many generations per year. Housefly: gray-black, $1/3$″;Blow fly: blue-black, $1/2$″; Horse fly: black, 1″; Cluster fly: black, $1/3$″.	Housefly and Blow fly contaminate food. Horse fly bites animals and humans. The only harmless one is the Cluster or Buckwheat Fly which is only a nuisance. Buzz around lights. Not attracted to food. Blow fly larvae can kill baby birds.	Eaten by spiders, wasps, and hornets. Seal up cracks and chinks around clapboards, under windows. Fly paper, vacuum sweeper. See note below.	Various pyrethrins available in garden- and farm-supply stores are highly effective.
FRUIT FLY (*Vinegar fly*)	Tiny brown gnat-like fly. $1/16$″ long.	Attracted to rotting fruit or fermenting juice.	Remove fruit, seal juices in closed container.	None satisfactory.
FLEAS *Sand Fleas* *Cat Fleas* *Dog Fleas*	Brownish pests that will bite humans as well as animals. Worse in summer and fall. About $1/10$″ long, hardshelled, jump when touched.	Bite causes irritation. Brought in from outdoors by cats, dogs, and mice. Breed in rugs, furniture.	Dust animals with talc. Vacuum rugs, cat and dog beds, furniture daily. Shampoo rugs and furniture to get rid of heavy infestation.	Dust animals with flea powder, also their beds. Spray rugs and stuffed furniture with aerosol flea killers. Put flea collars on cats and dogs. Shampoo rugs and furniture. For bad infestations call exterminator.
GNATS (*Fungus gnats*)	Tiny $1/20$″ long flies, similar to vinegar fruit fly, only black and smaller.	Larvae feed on roots and and soft stems. Stunts plants.	(Same as for Symphylids)	(Same as for Symphylids)

Insect	Description	Damage	Natural Control	Chemical Control
INDIAN MEAL WORM	**Moth is dirty white, $^1/_2''$** long. Larvae $^1/_2''$, white and plump.	Larvae spin silken webs, feed on stored food, especially grains, cereals, crackers, dried fruits, nuts. Adult flies around at night.	Put cereals and dried fruits in tightly closed containers and sealed plastic bags and insert a couple of bay leaves in each. Use vacuum sweeper in cracks and corners of cupboards and pantries. Put bay leaves on shelf.	Remove all food and utensils from infested area. Vacuum and wash with soap and water. Spray or brush a solution of 5% Methoxychlor on shelves and corners, allow to dry, put down clean shelf paper. Replace contents to shelf.
LEAF TIERS (*Leaf rollers*)	Greenish larvae, $^8/_{10}''$.	Roll leaves and web them together. Worse on outdoor and greenhouse plants.	Crush with fingers, hand pick, and destroy. Put screens in greenhouse.	Spray with Malathion.
MEALYBUGS	White cottony puffs, $^2/_{10}'' - ^3/_{10}''$.	Suck juices, weaken plants. Secrete sticky honeydew which attracts sooty mold.	Touch each mass with cotton swab dipped in alcohol. Scrub with toothbrush and soapy water.	See alcohol-detergent formulas.
MIDGES	Tiny ($^1/_8'' - ^1/_{16}''$) long-legged flying insects. Larvae are small maggots, white.	Most feed on leaves, cause galls, or deform buds and flowers. Some bite humans. Net-winged midge is beneficial.	Cut out galls and destroy.	Spray with Methoxychlor.
MILLIPEDES	Cylindrical, light-brown to dark-brown. $1'' - 1^1/_2''$ long. Coil when at rest or when disturbed.	Can injure plant roots and sprouting seeds.	Tobacco stems soaked in laundry soap. Pour on base of plants. Hand pick.	Dust soil with Sevin.

Insect	Description	Damage	Natural Control	Chemical Control
MOSQUITOES	Universally recognized pest. Breed in moist spots.	Sting, suck blood, cause irritation, a general nuisance.	Oil of Citronella or vinegar rubbed on arms, face, exposed parts of body. Dragonfly and certain wasps. Bats.	Spray shrubs, wet spots and lawns with Malathion. Don't let water stand in containers or low spots.
NEMATODES *Eel worm*	Microscopic, but a big troublemaker. To test for nematode, plant pumpkin seeds in soil and allow to germinate. Pull up seedlings and check roots for small lumps or galls. If these are present, destroy plant, pot and all.	Attack roots, leaves, buds, stunt growth, weaken plants. Cause galls on roots.	Rotate crops in greenhouse, garden. Marigolds planted in bench or garden soil reduce nematode population. Don't splash water on plants while watering. They spread from leaf to leaf in film of water. Destroy badly infected plants. Use beneficial nematode preparation.	None that's practical for home gardener.
SCALE INSECTS	Hard and soft forms, sizes from $1/20$ – $3/10$″, circular, elliptical, or oyster shell-like. Covered with waxy coat of armor, Brown, black, or white.	Suck plant juices, secrete sooty mold. Weaken plants.	Hand pick and burn. Scrub with soap and water, using soft toothbrush. Mash with fingers.	See alchohol-detergent formulas, Chapter XIV.
SILVERFISH	Wingless grayish fast-moving pest, $1/4$ – $1/2$″ long. Found in books, shelves, and places where old papers are, Prefer damp spots.	Eat book bindings, paper, glue on bindings.	None.	Dust with Methoxychlor.

Insect	Description	Damage	Natural Control	Chemical Control
SKELETONIZING INSECTS, *Leaf-chewing insects*	Many kinds whose larvae (grubs, caterpillars, etc.) eat holes in leaves.	Green portion eaten out, leaving holes or lacework. Weakens plants.	Same as for tarnished plant bug. Bacillus thuringiensis, a bacterium which attacks larvae of moth and butterfly family. Commercially marketed; read label.	Malathion.
SLUGS AND SNAILS	Slug is a shell-less snail. (both are actually mollusks) Vary in size from 1/8″–8″. Leave slimy silver tracks. Night marauders, hide under damp boards, leafy trash, stones, in the daytime.	These pests have ravenous appetites; chew holes in leaves; may eat entire bedding plant, may even work in soil of house-plants.	Scatter sand, tobacco dust, sulfur, wood ashes, coal ashes, lime — anything dry— around plants. Carry a salt-shaker and sprinkle salt on them. Beer, alcohol, household bleach kept in shallow pans in area where slugs are attracted to them. Hand pick and destroy. Look for them at night, when they do their dirty work. Place citrus skins, hollow side down, around plants. After snails crawl in, drop skins in pail of boiling water. Or place boards in area where they hide during day, then scrape off and destroy.	Metaldehyde baits. (But very poisonous, use caution around children and pets.)

Insect	Description	Damage	Natural Control	Chemical Control
SOW BUGS & PILL BUGS	1/3" - 1/2". Related to crabs and crayfish. Found in damp soils. Pill bug rolls into ball when disturbed. Sow bug a close relative, does not ball up, but scuttles for cover.	May gnaw into stems and crowns of plants when population gets too thick. Ordinarily feeds on organic matter in soil.	Hand pick and destroy.	Nicotine Solution.
SPIDER MITES	Tiny, hard-to-see pests. 50 span an inch. Tan, greenish, white, or bright red.	Cause stippling or distortion of plants, yellowing of leaves, webbing of growing tips.	Dip plants in soap suds. Syringe foliage to discourage. Spray with buttermilk spray (see Chapter XIV). Ladybugs love mites.	Spray with a miticide.
SPIDERS	Black or brown, 1/4" - 1" long. *Black Widow* has red "hourglass" marking, but is rarely deadly. Highly beneficial but usually unwelcome guests.	Bite of some can be painful. Spin unsightly webs which catch dust, insects. Most house spiders are harmless.	Sweep down webs with vacuum sweeper.	None
SPRINGTAILS (*magnified*)	Small, whitish, six-legged insect, 1/5" long, often found in house-plant soil. Jumps when you water plants.	Usually they are harmless, feeding on algae, fungi, and humus. Feed on roots only when population increases to large numbers. Often blamed for damage caused by Symphylids.	Tobacco drench as for Garden Symphylids.	Malathion, as for Symphylids.

490

Insect	Description	Damage	Natural Control	Chemical Control
GARDEN SYMPHYLIDS (or SYMPHYLAN)	Fast-moving, whitish worm, 1/4" long, 12 prs. of legs.	Feed on roots, stunt and yellow plants.	Drench soil with soapy tobacco water. Naptha soap is great; make a thick soap suds and put 1/2 cup around base of plant.	Dust Sevin on soil surface and water in. Or use nicotine sulfate, 1 tsp. to 2 quarts of soapy water.
TARNISHED PLANT BUG	Adult is flat and oval, 1/4", grayish-brown.	Causes malformation of leaves, leaf buds, flower buds.	Spray buds with garlic-red pepper spray (see Chapter XIV).	Malathion.
TERMITES	Many ants are called termites. Workers and soldiers 1/2" to 1" long; wingless, whitish-brown. Flying form means colony nearby.	Damage wood structures with their tunnels as well as plants near their nest.	Find out where they enter. Dust red pepper in runways.	Use aerosol spray from pressure cans to kill entire nests. Call exterminator.
THRIPS	Tiny pest 1/50" long; whitish, pale yellow.	Causes stippling, mottling distortion of foliage, distortion of bud and blooms, can keep buds from opening.	Spray with garlic-hot pepper solution (see Chapter XIV).	Nicotine Solution.
WASPS & HORNETS	Some resemble bees or large flying ants. 1/2" to 1" long.	Highly beneficial, eating many insects and larvae. Unwelcome because of nests built in attics and porches. Sting can be painful.	Spiders eat them. Destroy only if they present a hazard.	Spray at night when all have returned. Use Sevin with care. Remove nest at night and destroy.

491

Insect	Description	Damage	Natural Control	Chemical Control
WEEVILS	Adults are beetles and moths. Vary in size from $1/16''$ to $1''$.	Some feed on flowers and leaves outdoors and in greenhouses. Others get into cereals, grains, flour, dried foods.	Put bay leaves in cupboard where pest is. Dump out infested grains and cereals. Try hot pepper solution (see Chapter XIV).	None
WHITE FLIES: *Flying Dandruff*	Snow white pest, $1/16''$ long, winged.	Worst pest of plants in home, greenhouse, and many outdoor plants. Suck juices, secrete honeydew which attracts sooty mold. Has four stages of development which makes it difficult to control.	Try vacuum cleaner on undersides of leaves. Try parasite *Encarsia formosa*; pyrethrum spray. Ced-o-Flora spray (found in garden stores). Lemon-scented, liquid detergent, 1 tablespoon per gallon of water on undersides of leaves. Try sticky substance on yellow cardboard, or flypaper. Pest is attracted by yellow and green, repelled by blue and violet. Try antitranspirants (sprays used to prevent wilt on trees and shrubs in winter.) Use at rate of 1 oz. to 10 oz. water. Be sure to cover undersides of leaves.	Malathion will kill the adult stage, but will not touch the egg stage. Spray every 3 or 4 days for 40 days for complete eradication. Be patient. This is tough one to control. (For more controls See page 429 under organic Pesticides.)

Note: To protect nestlings, Cornell Laboratory of Ornithology advises the following:
Fashion a raised bottom in your bird house by using a $4 \times 6''$ piece of $1/2''$ mesh hardware cloth. Bend down $1''$ on each end and insert in bottom of box. Birds will build on top of screen. Blow fly larvae will fall through the screen to the bottom of the box where they cannot harm baby birds.

Other Common Insect Pests

In the preceding section we listed some troublesome insects in and around the home. There are a few other insect pests which may bother your fruits, vegetables, or ornamentals (many of these have been discussed in individual "Troubles" entries). Unless otherwise indicated they can be controlled chemically with an all-purpose insecticide containing either Diazinon, Malathion, or Sevin. Remember that Sevin is harmful to bees, so do not use it on blossoms or at the time of day when bees are active. For non-chemical means of control see Chapter XIV.

Leafhopper: $^1/_8''$ to $^1/_4''$ long. Jump quickly when plants are touched. Suck juices from leaves.

Japanese beetle: $^1/_2''$. Oval, greenish-blue metallic. Feeds in daytime on any kind of plant.

Garden fleahopper: $^1/_{12}''$ Black adult and greenish nymph. Suck sap from many species of plants.

Army worm: 1-2" long. Greenish with dark stripes. Travel in armies, devouring all crops.

Stink bug: $^3/_8''$ to $^5/_8''$ long. Shield-shaped bugs which suck sap from plants. Leave a bitter taste on berries and fruits.

Garden webworm: 1" to 1$^1/_2''$. Greenish, hairy, covered with dark spots. Spin fine webs wherever they go. Attack all types of garden crops.

Lace bug: $^1/_{16}''$ to $^1/_8''$. A small insect occurring in large numbers on leaves of trees, shrubs, and certain vegetables; skeletonizes leaves.

Grasshopper: Vary in size from $^3/_4''$ to 2$^1/_2''$. Green, tan, brown or pink. Feed on stems and leaves of most plants.

Wireworm, and adult beetle: Larva 1$^1/_2''$. Hard, dark brown, smooth; feed on seeds and roots. Adult is called click beetle, $^1/_{10}''$ to $^3/_4''$ in length. Makes clicking noise.

Flea beetle: Several species, $1/16''$ to $1/10''$. Black, shiny, jumping insects. Riddle foliage with tiny shot holes, spread virus disease.

Cabbage moth and larvae: $1 1/2''$ wide. Also called cabbage butterfly. Sulfur yellow, with black spots. Green larvae (1$''$) feeds on leaves.

Mole cricket: $1 1/2''$ long. Live in ground during day, come out at night. Tunnels cut off roots of seedlings.

Carrot rust fly: $1/6''$ long. Shiny black adult. Maggot feeds on roots of carrots and similar plants.

White grub: $1/2''$ to $1 1/4''$. Catch-all term for many root-chewing larvae found in the soil, causing injury to roots of plants.

Mexican bean beetle: $1/3''$. Yellow to coppery brown. Adult and larvae feed on undersides of leaves.

European corn borer: 1$''$. Brownish, smooth larvae, bore in stalks and ears of corn.

Squash bug: $1/2''$. Dark brown, mottled gray, hard shell, some with yellow spots along the edge of abdomen. Feeds on undersides of squash and pumpkin leaves.

Tomato hornworm: 3$''$. Large greenish caterpillar. Red horn projecting at rear. Oblique white stripes on sides. Defoliate plants. To control hand pick.

Corn ear worm: $1 1/2''$ long. Yellowish, green or brownish. Bore into buds, seed pods, flower stalks and ears.

Cucumber beetles: $1/5''$ long. Greenish-yellow beetles marked with black stripes or spots. Make sieve-like holes in leaves; leaves turn brown and drop.

Squash vine borer: 1$''$ long. Wrinkled white caterpillar with brown head. Bore into stems of pumpkins, and related crops.

Colorado potato beetle: $3/8''$. Hard shelled, broad, yellow with 10 black lines. Feed on potato foliage.

Plum curculio: $1/4''$ long. Adults equipped with snout. Lay eggs in crescent-shaped slot of fruit, eggs hatch into worms that tunnel into flesh of fruit.

Asparagus beetle: $1/4''$. Small, blue-black metallic, 3 yellow squares on wing covers. Larvae feed on foliage and stems of asparagus.

Pear psylla: Adult $1/10''$. Reddish brown. Lay pear-shaped eggs around the buds. Larvae cause stone-like structures and de-formed fruit.

Rose chafer: $1/2''$. Adults, tan. Feed on roses and many other plants. Larvae feed on roots of plants.

Wooly apple aphid: Snow-white clusters found on fruit trees. Purple-brown lice inside white mass. Deform foliage, secrete honeydew, injure roots.

Saw fly: $1/4''$ to $1/2''$ long. Slender. Adults lay eggs in plant tissue. Larvae ($1/2''$) defoliate many species of plants.

Round-headed apple borer: Adults $1''$ long. Reddish-brown with 2 white stripes. Lay eggs in bark at base of trunk. Larvae cause galleries or tunnels.

Codling moth: $1/2''$ to $3/4''$. Moth, grayish brown. Larvae (commonly called apple worm) $1''$, pinkish-white, enter calyx (bottom) of apples and form tunnels.

Gypsy moth: $1 1/2''$ long. Male is brown, female white or buff colored. Larvae feed on any kind of tree, evergreen and decid-uous. Control: Bacillus thuringiensis.

Cherry fruit fly: $1/16''$ to $1/4''$. Adults suck sap and deposit eggs on young fruits, hatching into cherry worms.

Spruce bud worm: Adult is $7/8''$ long. Brown with yellow stripe. Feed on evergreen buds.

BIRD AND ANIMAL CONTROL AROUND
THE GARDEN

Home gardeners find it frustrating to have worked hard planting a garden only to have it destroyed by animals. Over the years our fellow gardeners have sent thousands of suggestions for control. We have incorporated many of these in the following:

•**Cats and dogs** Cats like to sharpen claws on trees and furniture and may injure young trees. Most cats like to chew on houseplants. Cats may think flower beds and freshly cultivated areas are their "kitty litter box," and they dig holes, uproot or smother seedlings, and "burn" plants. Dogs frequent evergreens and dig up bulbs in search of or to bury bones. Dog urine may injure evergreens and lawns.

CONTROLS To prevent claw sharpening, make a scratching post from scrap lumber, covered with an old piece of rug.

Because cats need "greens" in their diet, grow a few toughies for them to chew on such as spider plant (chlorophytum) and florist's spikes (dracaena). Plant grass, oats, or rye grass seed in aluminum foil pans and let cats feast on the green leaves. Grow fresh catnip or dry some catnip and hang it in a nylon stocking.

REPELLENTS

ORANGES: Orange peels in a flower bed or potted plant keep out cats. Hot pepper flakes also work well.

Creosote repels both cats and dogs. (See Deer).

PEPPER MIXTURE: To keep dogs and cats away from shrubs, try the following: 1 ounce of cayenne pepper, $1^1/_2$ ounces of powdered mustard, and $2^1/_2$ ounces of flour. Shake these together in a box or bag to mix and dust on plants. (Avoid inhaling the dust or getting it into your eyes!)

MOTH FLAKES: Mix moth flakes in a concentrated solution of mineral spirits. The solvent evaporates, leaving the crystals to give off vapors. Works well when sprayed on plants and lasts a long time.

AMMONIA: Dip cotton in ammonia and hang on evergreens twice a week; use rope repellents on the market.

FENCES: You can use a fence, but it must be far enough away from shrubs so dogs cannot void on them.

BARBERRY THORNS: Clippings from barberry or rose bushes are often used as a thorny repellent to discourage dogs. Place these in front of evergreens where dogs are apt to congregate.

MOTH BALLS: Scatter moth balls in among the beds, and push them down in the soil. Spray shrubs with nicotine sulfate. Avoid use of bone meal: bone meal attracts dogs; use superphosphate 18 percent grade instead.

TOBACCO STEMS AND DUST: You can buy these in garden stores. Dust them in areas where animals are troublesome.

TURPENTINE: Dip a rag in turpentine and place it in a tin can at the base of evergreens. Scatter a little peat moss on top to prevent evaporation. From time to time add a tablespoon or two of turpentine to the can.

CREOLIN DISINFECTANT: This is obtainable in most drug stores. Put 2 tablespoons in a sprinkling can, fill it half full of water, and sprinke it in areas where dogs and cats are meddlesome. Sprinkle again after rains.

AROMATIC PLANTS: You can grow certain aromatic plants near evergreens and other plants to keep out dogs. Calendula, ornamental basil, and sage give off strong odors which pets do not like. Peppermint and spearmint repel some cats and dogs. We've been told that minced garlic works well, too.

As a last resort, you might try mudballs. One gardener tells us he makes up a supply of mudballs and when a dog comes around he gives the mudball a heave, and shouts "Scram!" The noise and the shattering mudball gives the dogs a scare and works well with cats—without harming them!

●**Bats and birds** Bats, pigeons, and sparrows can be messy on porches or in attics. Seal all openings; enclose ledges with hardware cloth. Apply vaseline to roosting areas. Bats and birds are extremely beneficial in cutting down on insect population. Putting up bat houses keeps these creatures where you want them. Bird houses, berried shrubs and trees for feathered friends will provide you with the safest of pesticides.

●**Birds in fruit and corn** Plant mulberry trees so birds will be attracted to these instead of other fruit. We have a huge white mulberry tree and the birds never touch our cherries.

For keeping birds out of fruit, use open mesh paper netting; plastic mesh sheets can be used over blueberry bushes.

Scarecrows don't scare birds anymore; animal replicas, such as mounds of fur resembling cats, hose for snakes, papier mâché owls, and baloon predators with scary eyes, etc. are more efffective.

Put pinwheels on posts in garden (see *Raccoons*). String mobiles between trees, flashy streamers between rows of plants.

Some of our readers tell us that to keep birds from eating corn, cherries, peaches, and other fruits, they make a solution of powdered sulfur and season it with red pepper (1 tablespoon of each per gallon of water), then spray on foliage. (Also very useful for keeping dogs away from shrubs).

Covering ears of corn with socks outsmarts birds (see *Raccoons*).

●**Deer** Often chew bark on fruit trees and ornamentals in winter. May rub antlers on trees and injure them. May eat certain vegetables in summer. Soak heavy twine or rags in creosote and lay the twine in the area where deer are apt to come. These animals do not like the smell of creosote and will stay away. In summer, we lay strips of the twine along the edge of the garden, and also tie some to stakes. It also keeps dogs away. Human hair is used by some to repel deer. Simply put a wad of hair near the plants.

In one test, Big Game Repellent (contain 36% rotten whole eggs) was effective. Some use scented soap with its wrapper left on, hung on branches. In tests Lifebouy soap was highly effective. Odor repellent seems to be more effective than taste repellents, since they also inhibit antler rubbing.

Another deterrent is an electric fence, operated by two flashlight batteries. It kicks out 4,000 volts (no amps) and not only keeps out deer but woodchucks, cats, dogs, rabbits, and other larger creatures. There's a new electric fence, operated by 2 flashlight batteries, that generates 5,000 volts (no amps) and it is moderately priced. Works well for woodchucks and raccoons.

There is no *easy* way to control deer. Until new and better forms of control are available, the home gardener will have to make defensive planting part of their landscaping plan. In other words, there are plants which are not dear to deer. For example, if evergreens are wrapped with burlap in winter, it keeps deer out. Never use clear or black plastic, as it burns the plants on summer days.

Even the traditional method of controlling deer—hunting— is not practical in many urban areas and biologists must find new means of regulating deer numbers. You might write to: Cornell University Resource Center, 8 Business and Technology Park, Ithaca, N.Y. 14850, and request a copy of "The Guide to Deer-Resistant Ornamental Plants."

• **Mice and rats** Very destructive around fruit trees, bulb beds, and food-storage areas. Rats destroy or contaminate millions of dollars worth of food yearly. Fortunately, mice and rats are in the diet of snakes, weasels, cats, foxes, owls, and hawks. Use snapback mice traps. Bait and set traps in runways or areas where mice are. Peanut butter or bacon make good baits. Poison baits can be used, but animals may die in partitions, causing bad odors. Pour hot pepper solution, 1 tablespoon to 2 quarts of water, down a rat hole.

• **Moles** Are usually beneficial animals. Moles eat very little plant life, but often dislodge plants while they burrow for insects and grubs. Mice use mole runways and do the real damage on bulbs and plant roots. *Control*: Harpoon-type traps. Treat lawns with Bacillus, effective in killing grubs which moles are after. (Some folks use red pepper, moth balls, garlic, or fiberglass insulation in the tunnels.) Drop castor bean seed in runways. Also, grow castor bean plants among flowers and vegetables to repel moles. *Note*: Castor bean seed is poisonous and should be kept away from children. If you prefer, use castor oil. Mix 1 pint of the oil with equal parts of a liquid detergent. Add a little warm water and beat into a foam. Put 2 or 3 tablespoons into a watering can of warm water and stir. Then douse the soil where the moles are. Douse it again and again. The moles will disappear for a period of from three to six months.

• **Rabbits** Biggest injury comes from girdling fruit trees and shrubs in winter when snow is heavy. They also eat tips of tulips and may eat vegetables if no clover is available. *Control*: Wrap stems of trees and shrubs with aluminum foil, spiral tree guards, or mesh, or spray with rosin-alcohol mixture. Dissolve 7 pounds of rosin in 1 gallon of denatured alcohol and paint tree trunks. In the garden, spray vegetables with aluminum sulfate solution: 1 ounce in gallon of water to which is added 1 cup of hydrated lime. *Caution*: Wash vegetables before eating. Sprinkle moth flakes in tulip beds, or push moth balls into soil just so top shows.

The *North American Fruit Explorer's* magazine states that liver will discourage rabbits from raspberries and fruit trees. Put a chunk of liver in a bucket of hot water and let it set for a half hour. Then strain this into a sprayer and spray it on brambles and fruit tree trunks. Smells bad but works well.

•**Raccoons** Can be devastating in a corn patch. They can tell when corn is ripe and won't move in until that time so devices can be applied at that period. *Control*: Readers have sent many tips which we'll pass along. Some swear by lights. An electric extension cord can be run from house to garden with a timer set to turn light on at dusk and off at dawn. A 100-watt bulb is sufficient. Some gardeners light a candle in a hurricane lamp in the middle of the patch. Also, a kerosene lantern is effective—whether it's the smell or the light, it does save crops.

Some gardeners have good luck sprinkling talcum powder on the silk and ears. Or, you might tie small pieces of cloth dipped in paint thinner on stakes spaced 10 feet apart around the outside perimeter of the corn. About every three days squirt a little paint thinner on each cloth.

After sweet corn silk has been properly pollinated by tassels (after the silks start to dry up), use old socks or nylon stockings to protect the ears. Slip a sock over each ear, being careful not to break it off. This cheats not only raccoons, but blue jays, blackbirds, starlings, woodchucks, squirrels, and other pests.

Use creosote rope to keep out raccoons. Measure off a length of rope (about clothesline weight) large enough to surround your corn patch. Soak this rope in creosote wood preservative for two days. Use an old metal dishpan or other large pan for this. Remove rope from creosote and let it dry until all liquid is evaporated. Then put metal (or wooden) stakes about 18 inches high at intervals around your patch. String the creosote rope on each stake so it is 12 to 15 inches off the ground and all around the patch. A farmer told us this method and we've passed it on to others who swear it works for them, too!

As soon as ears are ready, spread an 18-inch-wide strip of hydrated lime all around your corn patch so the ground is white. Keep it off the corn, as it would burn roots and stalks. Animals won't walk through it. (Protect hands while spreading, as it can "burn.") Bunched up anti-bird netting on the ground around corn patches deters animals and birds because their feet get tangled in it.
Put pinwheels on each fence post. Set them in various positions so the breeze hits them at various times.

As a last resort, put up an electric fence with a wire 4 inches from the ground (so coons cannot get under or over without touching it). If you enjoy the antics of coons, place a platform feeder on a tree, away from the vegetable garden, and fill it with all kinds of goodies: raw fish scraps, stale toast spread with bacon grease, cold oatmeal, and anything sugary and "fragrant." We do this with stale bread at 11:00 P.M. and find it protects our vegetable crops.

•**Skunks** Skunks are very beneficial animals, eating tremendous quantities of mice, grubs, and insects. These animals work at night, sometimes digging up lawns in search of grubs. If natural food is scarce, they may bother garbage cans for fish and meat scraps, etc. *Control*: Use box traps such as "Hav-a-Heart" with hamburger bait. Release animals in country. Carefully drop a plastic or old cloth sheet over box before carrying it to avoid getting "perfumed."

•**Snakes** Most snakes are harmless, yet to most people they aren't pleasant to have crawling about the lawn or garden. They eat many harmful rodents and insects but large snakes also eat toads, frogs, and birds which are beneficial. *Control*: Remove boards, rocks, and trash piles where they hide. Keep area around garden mowed, spread ashes and hydrated lime around wood piles, keep fireplace wood stacked in neat cords. Keep area around wood piles mowed.

If a snake enters the home, it may be looking for hibernating quarters, or mice. You can trap a snake by putting damp cloths on the floor near where the snake is thought to be. Cover damp cloths with dry cloths or burlap bags. Snake will crawl under or between the cloths, making it easier to remove it. Turkeys make good alarm bells, gobbling noisily if a snake is around, while geese, ducks and chickens will kill and eat snakes they can manage. Some dogs and cats are good snake killers. Hogs are, too. If you find it necessary to destroy a snake, crush its head, because snakes often "play dead" if stunned.

•**Squirrels and chipmunks** Sometimes occupy attics and double walls. Eat tips of spruce trees, bulbs, and some seeds and vegetables. They may eat pears and grapes when nuts are scarce. *Control*: Use box traps and release animals a few miles away. To keep them away from fruit, and if you enjoy watching them, provide a squirrel feeder with peanuts and sunflower seeds. Recently introduced are wafers with a "Fox Scent" to scare off rabbits, squirrels and chipmunks. Each wafer is infused with fox "essence", is silver-dollar size and can be hung with a built-in hanger unaffected by weather or water. The scented "fence" concept is new, but the idea sounds promising.

•**Woodchucks** Woodchucks are born in April or May. Both young and adult woodchucks eat vegetables, dig holes in hedgerows, orchards, fields, even lawns. *Control*: Fence off your garden with creosote rope, electric wires, paint thinner, or hydrated lime (see *Raccoons*). If woodchuck population is unbearable, you can resort to gassing with woodchuck bombs (available in farm stores) or run a hose from your automobile exhaust down into their hole. Be sure other entrance hole is covered with soil first. We prefer Hav-a-Heart traps (see *Skunks*).

APPENDIX

Conversion Charts For The Home Gardener

•

Few things are more exasperating to the home gardener than to read pesticide recommendations calling for "100 gallons per acre" or a "1 to 1,000 dilution." Since most gardeners have only a few houseplants or a small patch in the backyard, they are not interested in gallons per acre. With this in mind, we have prepared these tables which help get amounts down to usable size.

(For more conversion charts, see Index.)

DRY INSECTICIDES

For 100 gallons of water	For 50 gallons of water	For 25 gallons of water	For 6¼ gallons of water	For 3⅛ gallons of water
1 pound	8 ounces	4 ounces	1 ounce	1 T.
2 pounds	1 pound	8 ounces	2 ounces	2 T.
4 pounds	2 pounds	1 pound	4 ounces	4 T.

If manufacturer's instructions call for 1 pint of liquid (abbreviated EC for Emulsion Concentrate) per 100 gallons of water, then use the following table to reduce the proportions to a workable amount (T = 1 level tablespoon).

LIQUID INSECTICIDES

For 100 gallons of water	For 50 gallons of water	For 25 gallons of water	For 6¼ gallons of water	For 3⅛ gallons of water
½ pint	¼ pint (4 fl. oz.)	4 T. (2 fl. oz.)	1 T. (½ fl. oz.)	½ T. (¼ fl. oz.)
1 pint	½ pint (8 fl. oz.)	¼ pint (4 fl. oz.)	2 T. (1 fl. oz.)	1 T. (½ fl. oz.)
1 quart	1 pint (16 fl. oz.)	½ pint (8 fl. oz.)	4 T. (2 fl. oz.)	2 T. (1 fl oz.)

WORKABLE CONVERSIONS FOR SOIL AREAS

1 oz. per sq. ft. equals 2,722.5 lbs. per acre.

1 oz. per sq. yard equals 302.5 lbs. per acre.

1 oz. per 100 sq. ft. equals 27.2 lbs. per acre.

1 lb. per 100 sq. ft. equals 435.6 lbs. per acre.

1 lb. per 1,000 sq. ft. equals 43.6 lbs. per acre.

1 lb. per acre equals $^1/_3$ oz. per 1,000 sq. ft.

5 gals. per acre equals 1 pint per 1,000 sq. ft.

100 gals. per acre equals 2.5 gals. per 1,000 sq. ft.

100 gals. per acre equals 1 quart per 100 sq. ft.

100 gals. per acre equals 2.5 lbs. per 1,000 sq. ft.

AMERICAN DRY MEASURES

3 level teaspoons equal 1 tablespoon.

16 level tablespoons equal 1 cup.

2 cups equal 1 pint.

2 pints equal 1 quart.

8 quarts equal 1 peck.

4 pecks equal 1 bushel.

(Note: A liquid pint is 28.875 cubic inches; a dry pint is 33.6 cubic inches but for all practical purposes in measuring fertilizers, don't worry about the difference.)

AMERICAN FLUID MEASURES

80 drops equal 1 teaspoon (tsp.).

3 teaspoons equal 1 tablespoon (tbs.).

2 tablespoons equal 1 fluid ounce (fl. oz.).

8 fluid ounces equal 1 cup.

2 cups equal 1 pint (pt.).

2 pints equal 1 quart (qt.)

4 quarts equal 1 gallon (gal.).

1 gal. equals 4 qts., or 8 pts., or 128 fl. oz., or 256 tbs., or 768 tsp., or 61,400 drops.

1 quart equals 2 pts., or 32 fl. oz., or 64 tbs., or 192 tsp., or 15,360 drops.

1 pint equals 16 fl. oz., or 32 tbs., or 96 tsp., or 7,680 drops.

1 tbs. equals 3 tsp.or 240 drops.

(Note: The apothecaries' measures have 60 drops, or 1 fluid dram (medicine teaspoon); 4 fluid drams equal 1 tablespoon; 2 tablespoons equal 1 fluid ounce. The standard teaspoon is $^1/_3$ larger than the fluid dram or medicine teaspoon.)

MISCELLANEOUS MEASURES

1 acre equals 43,560 sq. ft. or 4,840 sq. yds., or 160 sq. rods.

1 tablespoon equals 3 teaspoons.

1 fluid ounce equals 2 tablespoons.

1 cup equals 8 fl. oz. or 16 tablespoons.

1 pint equals 2 cups or 16 fluid ounces.

1 U.S. gal. equals 231 cu. in. or 8.34 lbs. of water.

1 Imperial gal. equals 277.4 cu. in or 10 lbs. of water.

EMULSIONS OR WETTABLE POWDERS

Emulsions may be substituted for wettable powders and they leave less visible residue.

2 lbs. of 50% wettable powders equal 2 qts. of 25% emulsifiable solution.

4 lbs. of 50% wettable powder equals 3 pints of 50% emulsifiable solution.

1 lb. 25% wettable powder equals 1 pint 25% emulsifiable solution.

2 lbs. 50% wettable powder equal 2 $1/2$ qts. 20% emulsifiable solution.

2 lbs. 15% wettable powder equal $1/2$ pint 50% emulsifiable solution.

1 lb. 15% wettable powder equals $1/2$ pint 25% emulsifiable solution.

CONVERTING LIQUID MEASURES

Here are some figures you might want to use to convert liquid measures:

1 gal. equals 4 qts. or 8 pints or 16 cups or 128 oz., or 256 tablespoons or 768 teaspoons or 3,840 grams. 30 grams equal 1 oz. or 6 teaspoons; 1 teaspoon equals 5 grams.

From any of these equivalents we can find out the "parts per million" (PPM) usually recommended by manufacturer—for instance:

10 ppm—4 grams per 100 gals. or $4/5$ tsp. per 100 gals. water.

20 ppm—8 grams per 100 gals. or 1 $3/5$ tsp. per 100 gals. water.

40 ppm— 16 grams per 100 gals. or 3 $1/5$ tsp. per 100 gals. water.

40 ppm also equals $1/4$ tsp. per 8 gals. water.

60 ppm—24 grams per 100 gals. or 5 tsp. per 100 gals, or $1/2$ tsp. per 10 gals.

80 ppm—32 grams per 100 gals. or 6 tsp. per 100 gals, or $3/5$ tsp. per 10 gals.

100 ppm—40 grams per 100 gals. or 8 tsp. per 100 gals. or $4/5$ tsp. per 10 gals.

200 ppm—80 grams per 100 gals. or 16 tsp. per 100 gals. or 1.6 tsp. per 10 gals.

Ever wonder how small ppm really is? In a distance of 16 miles, 1 ppm is about 1 inch. In 12 days' time, 1 ppm is about 1 second; and in 2 years' time, it is about 1 minute. A 1-gram needle is 1 ppm of a 1-ton haystack, a single penny is 1 ppm of $10,000. It takes 10,000 ppm to equal 1 percent. So if you happen to read that a 30-inch tall corn plant has 40 ppm of nitrogen, it may sound like a lot, but it is still only 0.00004 percent.

DILUTION TABLE

Here's a helpful table in mixing items that come in liquid form:

1 to 1,000 . . $1/4$ tablespoon per gal. water.
1 to 750 . . $1/3$ tablespoon per gal. water.
1 to 50. $1/2$ tablespoon per gal. water.
1 to 250 . . 1 tablespoon per gal. water.
1 to 200 . . 1 $1/4$ tablespoons per gal. water.
1 to 150 . . 1 $2/3$ tablespoons per gal. water.
1 to 100 (about 1%) 2 $1/2$ tablespoons per gal. water.
1 to 50 (about 2%) 5 tablespoons per gal. water.
1 to 33 (about 3%) 7 $1/2$ tablespoons per gal. water.
1 to 25 (about 4%) 10 tablespoons per gal. water.
1 to 20 (about 5%) 12 $1/2$ tablespoons or $3/4$ cupfuls per gal.
1 to 10 (about 10%) 25 tablespoons or 1 $1/2$ cupfuls per gal.

CLAY POTS ARE HANDY FOR MEASURING

2 in. clay pot equals $1/3$ cup.
2 $1/2$ in. clay pot equals $2/3$ cup.
3 in. clay pot equals 1 cup.
4 in. clay pot equals 2 $1/2$ cups.
5 in. clay pot equals 4 $1/2$ cups.
6 in. clay pot equals 8 cups or 2 qts.

MEASURE FOR FERTILIZER

Superphosphate (20%) 1 to 2 tablespoons to an 8-qt. pail.
Wood ashes (4% potash) 1 cup to 8-qt. pail.
Dried blood (12% nitrogen) 3 tablespoons to 8-qt. pail.
Bone meal (20% phosphorus) 2 tablespoons to 8-qt. pail.
Complete fertilizer (such as 5-10-5) 4 tablespoons to 8-qt. pail.
Ground limestone 4 tablespoons to 8-qt. pail.
Muriate of potash (50-60% potash) 1 teaspoon to 8-qt. pail.
Nitrate of soda 1 tablespoon to a gallon.

The Metrics are Coming

The United States is slowly joining the rest of the world, and American gardeners may soon be growing plants by the metric system. We present this metric conversion chart in hopes that it will help you as you adjust too the metric measure.

APPROXIMATE CONVERSIONS FROM METRIC MEASURES

Symbol	When You Know	Multiply by	To Find	Symbol
LENGTH				
mm	millimeters	0.04	inches	in
cm	centimeters	0.4	inches	in
m	meters	3.3	feet	ft
m	meters	1.1	yards	yd
km	kilometers	0.6	miles	mi
AREA				
cm^2	square centimeters	0.16	square inches	in^2
m^2	square meters	1.2	square yards	yd^2
km^2	square kilometers	0.4	square miles	mi^2
ha	hectares (10,000 M^2)	2.5	acres	
MASS (weight)				
g	grams	0.035	ounces	oz
kg	kilograms	2.2	pounds	lb
t	tonnes (1000 kg)	1.1	short tons	
VOLUME				
ml	milliliters	0.003	fluid ounces	fl oz
l	liters	2.1	pints	pt
l	liters	1.06	quarts	qt
l	liters	0.26	gallons	gal
m^3	cubic meters	35	cubic feet	ft^3
m^3	cubic meters	1.3	cubic yards	yd3
TEMPERATURE (exact)				
°C	Celsius temperature	$9/5$ (then add 32)	Fahrenheit temperature	°F
°F	Fahrenheit temperature	(F-32) times $5/9$	Celsius temperature	°C

Courtesy U.S. Bureau of Standards.

Index

•